Business Ethics

10th Edition

William H. Shaw
San Jose State University

Dale E. Miller
Old Dominion University

Cengage

Australia • Brazil • Canada • Mexico • Singapore • United Kingdom • United States

Business Ethics, 10th Edition
William H. Shaw and Dale E. Miller

SVP, Product: Cheryl Costantini

VP, Product: Thais Alencar

Portfolio Product Director: Laura Ross

Portfolio Product Manager: Vanessa Manter

Product Assistant: Vivian Graham

Content and Digital Project Manager:
Pradhiba Kannaiyan

Vendor Content Manager: Ramesh Singh,
Lumina Datamatics Ltd.

Product Marketing Manager: Neena Bali

Content Acquisition Analyst: Andrea White

Production Service: Lumina Datamatics Ltd.

Designer: Sarah Cole

Cover Image Source: 4FR/E+/Getty Images

Previous edition(s): © 2019, © 2017, © 2014

For product information and technology assistance, contact us at
Cengage Customer & Sales Support, 1-800-354-9706
or **support.cengage.com.**

For permission to use material from this text or product, submit all
requests online at **www.copyright.com**.

Library of Congress Control Number: 2024932283

ISBN: 978-0-357-94725-8

Cengage
5191 Natorp Boulevard
Mason, OH 45040
USA

Cengage is a leading provider of customized learning solutions. Our
employees reside in nearly 40 different countries and serve digital learners
in 165 countries around the world. Find your local representative at
www.cengage.com.

To learn more about Cengage platforms and services, register or access
your online learning solution, or purchase materials for your course, visit
www.cengage.com.

Notice to the Reader

Printed in the United States of America
Print Number: 01   Print Year: 2024

Contents

Chapter 7   The Environment   196

Part Four | The Organization and the People in It   226

Chapter 8   The Workplace (1): Basic Issues   226

Chapter 9   The Workplace (2): Today's Challenges   258

Chapter 10   Moral Choices Facing Employees   287

Chapter 11   Job Discrimination   317

Preface

It's difficult to imagine an area of study that has greater importance to society or greater relevance to students than business ethics. As this text enters its tenth edition, business ethics has become a well-established academic subject. Most colleges and universities offer courses in it, and scholarly interest continues to grow.

Yet some people still scoff at the idea of business ethics, jesting that the very concept is an oxymoron. To be sure, recent years have seen the newspapers filled with lurid stories of corporate misconduct and felonious behavior by individual businesspeople, and many suspect that what the media report represents only the proverbial tip of the iceberg. However, these scandals should prompt a reflective person not to make fun of business ethics but rather to think more deeply about the nature and purpose of business in our society and about the ethical choices individuals must inevitably make in their business and professional lives.

Business ethics has an interdisciplinary character. Questions of economic policy and business practice intertwine with issues in politics, sociology, and organizational theory. Indeed, courses in business ethics are taught both by philosophy departments and by business schools, and where the course is being offered may make a difference to how it's structured. In a business school, considerable attention will probably be given to existing rules that can't be violated without consequences: rules found in the law, in the codes of ethics of professional associations, or just in the minds of the public. This is undeniably important information for an aspiring businessperson to have.

When philosophers teach business ethics, in contrast, they may be more willing to call current expectations into question. In a business ethics course taught by a philosopher, many discussions will center on the question of whether a given practice is morally wrong. Whether the practice is presently illegal or whether an opinion poll conducted today would show that the public generally condemns the practice may not be important considerations in reaching an answer. Of course, nothing precludes instructors who aren't philosophers from raising this sort of question, and business ethics courses that aren't taught by philosophers may still critically examine the status quo. Frequently, though, which department offers the course will determine where the most emphasis is placed.

The authors of this textbook are philosophers, and their approach to business ethics remains anchored in philosophy. Nevertheless, abstract questions in normative ethics and political philosophy mingle with analysis of practical problems and concrete moral dilemmas. Moreover, philosophical debates about how the world should be must still start from an understanding of how it is now; as Chapter 1 explains, sound moral arguments have factual as well as moral premises. So, the book is not an exercise in armchair speculation divorced from facts and figures.

• • •

Goals, Organization, and Topics

Business Ethics has four goals: to expose students to the important moral issues that arise in various business contexts; to provide students with an understanding of the moral, social, and economic environments within which those problems occur; to introduce students to the ethical and other concepts that are relevant for resolving those problems; and to assist students in developing the necessary reasoning and analytical skills for doing so. Although the book's primary emphasis is on business, its scope extends to related moral issues in other organizational and professional contexts.

The book has four parts. Part One, "Moral Philosophy and Business," discusses the nature of morality and presents the main theories of normative ethics and the leading approaches to questions of economic justice. Part Two, "American Business and Its Basis," examines the institutional foundations of business, focusing on capitalism as an economic system and the nature and role of corporations in our society. Part Three, "Business and Society," concerns moral problems involving business, consumers, and the natural environment. Part Four, "The Organization and the People in It," identifies a variety of ethical issues and moral challenges that arise out of the interplay of employers and employees within an organization, including the problem of discrimination.

Case studies enhance the main text. These cases vary in kind and in length, but they are all designed to enable instructors and students to pursue further some of the issues discussed in the text and to analyze them in more specific contexts. The case studies should provide a lively springboard for classroom discussions and the application of ethical concepts.

Business Ethics covers a wide range of topics relevant to today's world. Four of these are worth particular attention.

Business and Globalization

The moral challenges facing business in today's globalized world economy are well represented in the book and seamlessly integrated into the chapters. For example, Chapter 1 discusses ethical relativism; Chapter 4, outsourcing and globalization; and Chapter 10, overseas bribery and the Foreign Corrupt Practices Act. There are international examples or comparisons throughout the book. Moreover, almost all the basic issues discussed in the book (such as corporate responsibility, the nature of moral reasoning, and the value of the natural world—to name just three) are as crucial to making moral decisions in an international business context as they are to making them at home. In addition, cases 1.1, 2.3, 4.1, 5.1, 5.2, 7.2, 7.4, 9.5, and 10.4 deal explicitly with moral issues arising in today's global economic system.

The Environment

Because of its ongoing relevance and heightened importance in today's world, an entire chapter, Chapter 7, is entirely devoted to this topic. In particular, the chapter highlights recent environmental disasters, the environmental dilemmas and challenges we face, and their social and business costs, as well as the changing attitude of business toward the environment and ecology. Chapter 7 includes four case studies, one of which—7.1, which deals with the increasing price of flood insurance—is new in this edition. Another new case study—2.1, which looks at our treatment of animals—is also relevant to environmental concerns.

Health and Health Care

Far from being a narrow academic pursuit, the study of business ethics is relevant to a wide range of important social issues—for example, to health and health care, which is currently the subject of much discussion and debate in the United States. Aspects of this topic are addressed in the text and developed via cases throughout the book: 2.3, 4.2, 5.2, 6.1, and 9.4.

Colleges and Universities

Most colleges and universities are not businesses in the narrow sense of for-profit enterprises (although some are). However, this textbook is concerned with ethical issues that arise in organizations of all sorts, and institutions of higher education are organizations that play an important role in the lives of students and their instructors. Moreover, even public or nonprofit schools resemble businesses in many ways. They employ workers, for instance, and there are people who pay for the services they provide—even if most faculty members wince to hear students called "customers." While there was some discussion of higher education in prior editions, newly added material now makes this a point of emphasis. Five case studies concern higher education in different ways: 3.2, a new case on rising tuition costs; 4.5, a case on paying college athletes that's been updated to take account of new "Name, Image, or Likeness" rules; 8.1, a new case on pay equity in a university setting; 10.2, a new case concerned with conflicts of interest in instructors' choices about which textbooks to use; and 11.2. Also new is a discussion in Chapter 8 of the compensation received by part-time "adjunct" faculty.

· · ·

Changes in This Edition

Instructors who have used the previous edition will find the organization, general content, and overall design of the book familiar. However, the text has been revised throughout. Examples and information have been extensively updated. In particular, a number of chapters describe ways in which the COVID-19 pandemic has changed work and commerce since the ninth edition was published. Language has become more inclusive. In addition, a new author (who had taught from previous editions of the text) was introduced, and in places the text will reflect his sensibilities. At all times the goal has been to provide a textbook that students will find clear, understandable, and engaging.

The main text is supplemented with forty-eight case studies. The five new cases are described above. Some case studies from prior editions have been replaced by these new additions, and a few were simply removed to create space for fuller explorations of topics in the bodies of chapters. The decisions about which case studies were removed or replaced were guided by feedback solicited from instructors who teach from the book; only case studies that this feedback described as the least essential were replaced or removed.

· · ·

Ways of Using the Book

A course in business ethics can be taught in a variety of ways. Instructors have different approaches to the subject, different intellectual and pedagogical goals, and different classroom styles. They emphasize different themes and start at different places. Some of them may prefer to treat the foundational questions of ethical theory thoroughly before moving on to particular moral problems; others reverse this priority. Still other instructors frame their courses around the question of economic justice, the analysis of capitalism, or the debate over corporate social responsibility. Some instructors stress individual moral decision making; for others, it's social and economic policy.

Business Ethics permits teachers great flexibility in how they organize their courses. A wide range of theoretical and applied issues are discussed; and the individual chapters, the major sections within them, and the case studies are to a surprising extent self-contained. Instructors can thus teach the book in whatever order they choose, and they can easily skip or touch lightly on some topics in order to concentrate on others without loss of coherence.

· · ·

Acknowledgments

William H. Shaw wishes to acknowledge his great debt to the many people whose ideas and writing have influenced him over the years. Philosophy is widely recognized to involve a process of ongoing dialogue. This is nowhere more evident than in the writing to textbooks, whose authors can rarely claim that the ideas being synthesized, organized, and presented are theirs alone. Without colleagues, without students, and without a larger philosophical community concerned with business and ethics, this book would not have been possible.

He particularly wants to acknowledge a debt to Vincent Barry. Readers familiar with their textbook and reader *Moral Issues in Business* will realize the extent to which this book draws on that book.[1] *Business Ethics* is, in effect, a revised and updated version of the textbook portion of that collaborative work.

Dale E. Miller seconds all this and adds an expression of his gratitude to Shaw for recommending him to take on the revision process, which was just the latest in a history of kindnesses. It was, to be frank, a much bigger project than it seemed at first. The book contains a wealth of factual information, including many economic statistics, and of course this information falls out of date. Miller therefore also adds an expression of thanks to Cengage and their production partners for their patience when deadlines were missed.

---

[1] William H. Shaw and Vincent Barry, *Moral Issues in Business*, 13th ed. (Boston: Cengage Learning, 2016).

Chapter 1

The Nature of Morality

Learning Objectives

After completing this chapter, you should be able to:

1. Explain the nature, scope, and purpose of the philosophical field of business ethics.
2. Distinguish morality from etiquette, law, and professional codes of conduct.
3. Explain why religious texts and doctrines cannot by themselves answer all our ethical questions.
4. Describe the doctrine of ethical relativism and its difficulties.
5. Explain what it means to have moral principles, the nature of conscience, and the relationship between morality and self-interest.
6. Describe the social and psychological factors that sometimes jeopardize an individual's integrity.
7. Produce examples of valid moral reasoning.
8. Argue against purported moral standards, for example, through giving counterexamples.

Introduction

Every Silicon Valley Tech Startup Wants To Be the Next Apple and all their CEOs want to be the next Steve Jobs. But perhaps no tech startup wore its Apple envy on its sleeve quite so blatantly as the blood testing company Theranos.

No one enjoys blood tests: the needles sting and it's eerie to see your own blood fill vial after vial. But what's a minor inconvenience for most of us, just one of several indignities that we suffer at our annual physical, can be torture for people who are seriously ill and need many tests. And if blood testing can be miserable for adults, the suffering is even greater when the patient is a child.

Theranos claimed to "disrupt" blood testing. Instead of vials of blood drawn via needles from the patient's veins, its tests would require only small quantities of blood taken from a finger prick. This sort of testing is familiar to people with diabetes, who use it to measure their blood sugar. Theranos, though, claimed to be able to perform a wide variety of tests this way.

The founder of Theranos was Elizabeth Holmes, who founded the company in 2003 when she was only 19 years old. Like Jobs, she was a college dropout, having left Stanford University after one year. That might be coincidence, but she modeled herself on Jobs in other ways that were very deliberate, of which her closet full of black turtlenecks was only the

> Rather than acknowledge their failures, Holmes and Theranos chose a different path: deception.

most obvious. Theranos's technology was very self-consciously modeled on Apple's, too. Its first blood-testing machine, the "Edison," had the contours of an iMac and a touch screen reminiscent of an iPod or iPhone.

Theranos raised nearly a billion dollars from venture capitalists and other investors and was once valued at close to $10 billion. It opened clinics in Walgreens pharmacies and signed an agreement to place more in Safeway grocery stores. Holmes frequently sat down with journalists for interviews and so was a familiar face to television viewers. In addition to her invariable turtleneck, she was known for her surprisingly deep voice. In her TED Talk, she held out the vision of "A world in which no one has to say 'If only I'd known sooner.' A world in which no one ever has to say good-bye too soon."

What Theranos claimed to have achieved was remarkable. Extracting information from the tiny amount of blood held by its "nanotainer" is incredibly difficult. It becomes more challenging still when the samples must be shipped to be analyzed, because if some blood dries en route then there's even less to work with. Testing blood drawn through a finger prick adds a further set of complexities. In our fingertips, blood flows through tiny capillaries. Piercing these can damage the blood cells themselves. The samples are also more likely to be contaminated with the interstitial fluid that surrounds our cells.

Elizabeth Holmes

It's probably fair to say that Theranos made a genuine effort to overcome these challenges, but they never managed to do so. Inside, the Edison was a less-sophisticated piece of equipment than its sleek exterior suggested. It was based on a machine made by another firm, one originally designed not to perform medical procedures but to dispense glue. A robot arm duplicated the steps that a human technician would perform in conducting tests. It malfunctioned frequently, and even when it didn't produce error messages its tests' results were often inconsistent and inaccurate.

Rather than acknowledge their failures, Holmes and Theranos chose a different path: deception. They ran few tests on their own equipment. Most tests were secretly run on conventional blood-testing equipment made by other companies. However, because Theranos was collecting smaller amounts of blood than these machines had been designed to test, the samples had to be significantly diluted. Although these machines were reliable when operated properly, in Theranos's hands the results they gave were frequently inaccurate. Sometimes, as with a test for potassium levels, they regularly gave results that were wildly wrong.

Theranos and Holmes deceived investors and board members about the reliability of the company's testing, sometimes faking results in demonstrations. They obtained their contracts with Walgreens and Safeway by putting the logos of pharmaceutical companies on reports written by Theranos itself, falsely representing that their equipment and procedures had been independently validated. More than this, though, they also reported test results that they knew to be untrustworthy to patients and their doctors to use in making medical decisions.

The deception could only be maintained so long. Current and former Theranos employees struggled with the need to lie or remain silent. Patients and doctors saw that their test results looked very different when they were performed by Theranos than when they were performed by other labs. The beginning of the end came on October 16, 2015, when *Wall Street Journal* reporter John Carreyrou published a story titled "Hot Startup Theranos Has Struggled With Its Blood-Test Technology."

Today, Elizabeth Holmes has been sentenced to more than eleven years in prison for four fraud convictions. Sunny Balwani, Theranos's former president and chief operating officer—as well as Holmes's former romantic partner—received an even longer sentence. It became apparent at her trial that even Holmes's deep voice had been a deception; she testified in a notably higher register.[1]

Stories of business corruption and of greed and wrongdoing in high places have always fascinated the popular press, and media interest in business ethics has never been higher. But one should not be misled by the headlines and news reports. Not all moral issues in business involve giant corporations, and few cases of business ethics are widely publicized. The vast majority of them involve the mundane, uncelebrated moral challenges that managers, workers, and consumers face daily.

Although the misconduct at Theranos was complicated, once the basic outline is sketched the wrongdoing is pretty easy to see: deception, dishonesty, fraud, disregarding one's professional responsibilities, and unfairly injuring others for one's own gain. But many of the moral questions that arise in business are complex and difficult to answer. For example:

How far must manufacturers go to ensure product safety? Must they reveal everything about a product, including any possible defects or shortcomings? At what point does acceptable exaggeration become lying about a product or a service? When does aggressive marketing become consumer manipulation? Is advertising useful and important or deceptive, misleading, and socially detrimental? When are prices unfair or exploitative?

Are corporations obliged to help combat social problems? What are the environmental responsibilities of business, and is it living up to them? Are pollution permits a good idea? Is factory farming morally justifiable?

May employers screen potential employees on the basis of lifestyle, physical appearance, or personality tests? What rights do employees have on the job? Under what conditions may they be disciplined or fired? What, if anything, must businesses do to improve work conditions? When are wages fair? Do unions promote the interests of workers or infringe their rights? When, if ever, is an employee morally required to blow the whistle?

May employees ever use their positions inside an organization to advance their own interests? Is insider trading or the use of privileged information immoral? How much loyalty do workers owe their companies? What say should a business have over the off-the-job activities of its employees? Do drug tests violate their right to privacy?

What constitutes job discrimination, and how far must business go to ensure equality of opportunity? Is affirmative action a matter of justice, or a poor idea? How should organizations respond to the problem of sexual harassment?

These questions typify business issues with moral significance. The answers we give to them are determined, in large part, by our moral standards—that is, by the moral principles and values we accept. What moral standards are, where they come from, and how they can be assessed are some of the concerns of this opening chapter.

...

Ethics

Ethics (or moral philosophy) is a broad field of inquiry that addresses a fundamental query that all of us, at least from time to time, inevitably think about—namely, how should I live my life? That question, of course, leads to others, such as: What sort of person should I strive to be? What values are important? What standards or principles should I live by? Exploring these issues immerses one in the study of right and wrong. Among other things, moral philosophers and others who think seriously about ethics want to understand the nature of morality, the meaning of its basic concepts, the characteristics of good moral reasoning, how moral judgments can be justified, and, of course, the principles or properties that distinguish right actions from wrong actions. Thus, ethics deals with individual character and with the moral rules that govern and limit our conduct. It investigates questions of right and wrong, fairness and unfairness, good and bad, duty and obligation, and justice and injustice, as well as moral responsibility and the values that should guide our actions.

You sometimes hear it said that there's a difference between a person's ethics and their morals. This can be confusing because what some people mean by saying that something is a matter of ethics (as opposed to morals) is often what other people mean by saying that it's a matter of morals (and not ethics). In fact, however, most people (and most philosophers) see no real distinction between a person's "morals" and a person's "ethics." And almost everyone uses "ethical" and "moral" interchangeably to describe people we consider good and actions we consider right, and "unethical" and "immoral" to designate bad people and wrong actions. This book follows that common usage.

Business and Organizational Ethics

The primary focus of this book is ethics as it applies to business. **Business ethics** is the study of what constitutes right and wrong, or good and bad, human conduct in a business context. For example, would it be right for a store manager to break a promise to a customer and sell some hard-to-find merchandise to someone else, whose need for it is greater? What, if anything, should a moral employee do when their superiors refuse to look into apparent wrongdoing in a branch office? If you innocently came across secret information about a competitor, would it be permissible for you to use it for your own advantage?

An appreciation of the importance of ethics for a healthy society and a concern, in particular, for what constitutes ethical conduct in business go back to ancient times. The Roman philosopher Cicero (106–43 BCE), for instance, discussed the example, much debated at the time, of an honest merchant from Alexandria who brings a large stock of wheat to Rhodes where there is a food shortage. On his way there, he learns that other traders are setting sail for Rhodes with substantial cargos of grain. Should he tell the people of Rhodes that more wheat is on the way or say nothing and sell at the best price he can? Some ancient ethicists argued that although the merchant must declare defects in his wares as required by law, as a vendor he is free—provided he tells no untruths—to sell his goods as profitably as he can. Others, including Cicero, argued to the contrary that all the facts must be revealed and that buyers must be as fully informed as sellers.[2]

While questions about what it means for businesspeople to behave ethically have a long history, we're continually reminded of their importance. We seldom go more than two or three years between major business scandals, episodes that receive extensive media coverage. These scandals often provoke calls for various ethics reforms, whether in the form of new laws, stricter codes of ethics, or more ethics training. The course that you're taking right now was very likely created in response to some prior scandal. The fact that scandals keep occurring does not show that these reforms are not worthwhile. It may only show that the temptations for businesspeople to behave badly are very strong.

"Business" and "businessperson" are broad terms. A "business" could be a food truck or a multinational corporation that operates in several countries. "Businessperson" could refer to a street vendor or a company president responsible for thousands of workers and millions

Summary
Ethics deals with individual character and the moral rules that govern and limit our conduct. It investigates questions of right and wrong, duty and obligation, and moral responsibility.

of shareholder dollars. Accordingly, the word **business** will be used here simply to mean any organization whose objective is to provide goods or services for profit. **Businesspeople** are those who participate in planning, organizing, or directing the work of business.

But this book takes a broader view as well because it's concerned with moral issues that arise wherever employers and employees come together. Thus, it addresses organizational ethics as well as business ethics. An *organization* is a group of people working together to achieve a common purpose. The purpose may be to offer a product or a service primarily for profit, as in business. But many organizations are public (i.e., part of the government) or are private "nonprofits." Of the roughly 4,000 colleges and universities in the United States, for example, around 40 percent are public, around 40 percent are private but not intended to make a profit, and around 20 percent are for-profit. Only the last of these are businesses, but they are all organizations. The cases and illustrations presented in this book deal with moral issues and dilemmas in both business and nonbusiness organizations.

People occasionally poke fun at the idea of business ethics, declaring that the term is a contradiction or that business has no ethics. Such people take themselves to be worldly and realistic. They think they have a down-to-earth idea of how things really work. In fact, despite its pretense of sophistication, their attitude shows little grasp of the nature of ethics and only a superficial understanding of the real world of business. Reading this book should help you comprehend how inaccurate and mistaken their view is.

Summary
Business ethics is the study of what constitutes right and wrong (or good and bad) human conduct in a business context. Closely related moral questions arise in other organizational contexts.

· · ·

Moral versus Nonmoral Standards

Moral questions differ from other kinds of questions. Whether the old computer in your office can copy a pirated DVD is a factual question. By contrast, whether you should copy the DVD is a moral question. When we answer a moral question or make a moral judgment, we appeal to moral standards. These standards differ from other kinds of standards.

Wearing shorts and a tank top to a formal dinner party is tacky. Writing an essay that is filled with double negatives or lacks subject–verb agreement violates the basic conventions of proper language usage. Photographing someone at night without the flash turned on is a poor photographic technique. In each case, a standard is violated—fashion, grammatical, technical— but the violation does not pose a serious threat to human well-being.

Moral standards are different because they concern behavior that is of serious consequence.[3] The conventional moral norms against lying, stealing, and killing deal with actions that can hurt people. And the moral principle that human beings should be treated with dignity and respect uplifts the human personality. Whether products are healthful or harmful, work conditions safe or dangerous, personnel procedures biased or fair, privacy respected or invaded—these are also matters that seriously affect human well-being. The standards that govern our conduct in these areas are moral standards. Nor should we take for granted that morality only concerns how we treat other people. There may be moral standards that govern our treatment of nonhuman animals or entire ecosystems.

A second characteristic follows from the first. Moral standards take priority over other standards, including self-interest. Something that morality condemns—for instance, the burglary of your neighbor's home—cannot be justified on the nonmoral grounds that it would be a thrill to do it or that it would pay off handsomely. We take moral standards to be more important than other considerations in guiding our actions.

A third characteristic of moral standards is that their soundness depends on the adequacy of the reasons that support or justify them. For the most part, fashion standards are set by clothing designers, merchandisers, and consumers; grammatical standards by grammarians and students of language; technical standards by practitioners and experts in the field. Legislators make laws, boards of directors make organizational policy, and licensing boards establish standards for professionals. In those cases, some authoritative body is the ultimate validating source of the standards and thus can change the standards if it wishes. Moral standards are not made by such bodies. Their validity depends not on official fiat but rather on the quality of the

Moral standards concern behavior that seriously affects human well-being.

Moral standards take priority over other standards.

The soundness of moral standards depends on the adequacy of the reasons that support them.

arguments or the reasoning that supports them. Exactly what constitutes adequate grounds or justification for a moral standard is a debated question, which, as we shall see in Chapter 2, underlies disagreement among philosophers over which specific moral principles are best.

Although these three characteristics set moral standards apart from other standards, it's useful to discuss more specifically how morality differs from three things with which it's sometimes confused: etiquette, law, and professional codes of ethics.

Summary
We appeal to moral standards when we answer a moral question or make a moral judgment. Three characteristics of moral standards distinguish them from other kinds of standards.

Morality and Etiquette

Etiquette refers to the norms of correct conduct in polite society or, more generally, to any special code of social behavior or courtesy. In our society, for example, it's considered bad etiquette to chew with your mouth open or to pick your nose when talking to someone; it's considered good etiquette to say "please" when requesting and "thank you" when receiving, and to hold a door open for someone entering immediately behind you. Good business etiquette typically calls for writing follow-up letters after meetings, returning phone calls, and dressing appropriately. It's commonplace to judge people's manners as "good" or "bad" and the conduct that reflects them as "right" or "wrong." "Good," "bad," "right," and "wrong" here simply mean socially appropriate or socially inappropriate. In these contexts, such words express judgments about manners, not about ethics.

The rules of etiquette are prescriptions for socially acceptable behavior. If you violate them, you're likely to be considered ill-mannered, impolite, or even uncivilized, but not necessarily immoral. If you want to fit in, get along with others, and be thought well of by them, you should observe the common rules of politeness or etiquette. However, what's considered correct or polite conduct—for example, when greeting an elderly person, when using your knife and fork, or when determining how close to stand to someone you're conversing with—can change over time and vary from society to society.

Although rules of etiquette are generally nonmoral in character, violations of those rules can have moral implications. For example, the male boss who refers to female subordinates as "honey" or "doll" shows bad manners, but since these terms diminish the worth of female employees or perpetuate sexism they also raise moral issues concerning equal treatment and denial of dignity to human beings. More generally, rude or impolite conduct may sometimes fail to show the respect for other persons that morality requires of us. For this reason, it's important to exercise care, in business situations and elsewhere, when dealing with unfamiliar customs or people from a different culture.

Scrupulous observance of rules of etiquette, however, does not make a person moral. In fact, it can sometimes camouflage ethical issues. Suppose that someone cracks a joke that pokes fun at someone not present because they have a disability. Good manners might require letting the matter pass or even offering a "polite laugh." Morality, though, might instead require you to speak up and object.

Morality and Law

Before distinguishing between morality and law, let's examine the term *law*. Basically, there are four kinds of law: constitutional law, statutes, regulations, and common law.

Constitutional law refers to the U.S. Constitution, state constitutions, and court rulings on their requirements. The U.S. Constitution is the "highest law" in the United States; all other laws must be consistent with it. The courts have far-reaching powers to rule on the constitutionality of laws and to declare them invalid if they conflict with the Constitution. In the United States, the Supreme Court has the greatest judiciary power and rules on an array of cases, some of which bear directly on the study of business ethics. State courts may also rule on the constitutionality of state laws under state constitutions.

Statutes are laws enacted by legislative bodies. For example, the law that defines and prohibits reckless driving on the highway is a statute. Congress and state legislatures enact statutes. (Laws enacted by local governing bodies such as city councils are usually termed *ordinances*.) Statutes make up a large part of the law and are what many of us mean when we speak of "laws."

Limited in their time and knowledge, legislatures often set up boards or agencies whose functions include issuing detailed regulations covering certain kinds of conduct—**administrative regulations**. For example, state legislatures establish licensing boards to formulate regulations for the licensing of physicians and nurses. As long as these regulations do not exceed the board's statutory powers and are constitutional, they are legally binding.

Common law refers to the body of judge-made law that first developed in the English-speaking world centuries ago when there were few statutes. Courts frequently wrote opinions explaining the bases of their decisions in specific cases, including the legal principles those decisions rested on. Each of these opinions became a precedent for later decisions in similar cases. The massive body of precedents and legal principles that accumulated over the years is collectively referred to as "common law." Like administrative regulations, common law is valid if it harmonizes with constitutional and statutory law. Common law is an important part of the American legal system (although this is least true in Louisiana, interestingly, since the state's historical ties to France and Spain place it in a different legal tradition where precedents matter less).

People sometimes confuse legality and morality, but they are different things. On one hand, breaking the law is not always or necessarily immoral. On the other hand, the legality of an action does not guarantee that it's morally right. Let's consider these points further.

> Legality should not be confused with morality. Breaking the law isn't always or necessarily immoral, and the legality of an action doesn't guarantee its morality.

1. **An action can be illegal but morally right.** For example, helping a Jewish family to hide from the Nazis was against German law in 1939, but it would have been a morally admirable thing to have done. Of course, the Nazi regime was vicious and evil. By contrast, in a democratic society with a basically just legal order, the fact that something is illegal may provide a moral consideration against doing it. For example, one moral reason for not burning trash in your backyard may be that it violates an ordinance that your community has voted in favor of. Some philosophers believe that sometimes the illegality of an action can make it morally wrong, even if the action would otherwise have been morally acceptable. But even if they are right about that, the fact that something is illegal does not trump all other moral considerations. Nonconformity to law is not always immoral, even in a democratic society. There can be circumstances where, all things considered, violating the law is morally permissible, perhaps even morally required.

   Probably no one in the modern era has expressed this point more forcefully than Dr. Martin Luther King, Jr. Confined in the Birmingham, Alabama, city jail on charges of parading without a permit, King penned his now famous "Letter from Birmingham Jail" to eight of his fellow clergymen who had published a statement attacking King's unauthorized protest of racial segregation as unwise and untimely. King replied to this statement by arguing that we should follow moral law in preference to any human-made law. Because the statutes that established segregation were contrary to this higher law, people should feel entitled—and even required—to disobey them. In fact, King went so far as to call the validity of these statutes into question. He quoted the assertion by St. Augustine, the early Christian theologian, that "An unjust law is no law at all."[4]

> **Summary**
> Morality must be distinguished from etiquette (rules for well-mannered behavior), from law (statutes, regulations, common law, and constitutional law), and from professional codes of ethics (the special rules governing the members of a profession).

2. **An action that is legal can be morally wrong.** For example, brokers are not legally required to act in their customers' best interests, even when they are advising them on their retirement money.[5] Yet it would be wrong of them to push their clients into investments that are bad for them in order to reap a commission. Likewise, it may have been perfectly legal for companies who received government loans from the Paycheck Protection Program, a program meant to keep small businesses afloat during the COVID-19 pandemic, to devote millions of dollars to paying dividends to investors and buying back their own stock.[6] Still, the morality of their doing so is open to debate.

   Or, to take another example, suppose that you're driving to work one day and see an accident victim sitting on the side of the road, clearly in shock and needing medical assistance. Because you know first aid and are in no great hurry to get to your destination, you could easily stop and assist the person. Legally speaking, though, you're not obligated to stop and render aid. Under common law, the prudent thing would be to drive on, because by stopping you could thus incur legal liability if you

You come upon this scene—the car is turned over, and it's clear that an accident just took place. In most states, you're not legally obligated to stop and offer help to the victims.

fail to exercise reasonable care and thereby injure the person. Many states have enacted so-called Good Samaritan laws to provide immunity from damages to those rendering aid (except for gross negligence or serious misconduct). But in most states, the law does not oblige people to give such aid or even to call an ambulance. Moral theorists would agree, however, that if you sped away without helping or even calling for help, your action might be perfectly legal but would be morally suspect. Regardless of the law, such conduct would almost certainly be wrong.

What then may we say about the relationship between law and morality? To a significant extent, law codifies a society's customs, ideals, norms, and moral values. Changes in law tend to reflect changes in what a society takes to be right and wrong, but sometimes changes in the law can alter people's ideas about the rightness or wrongness of conduct. However, even if a society's laws are sensible and morally sound, it's a mistake to see them as sufficient to establish the moral standards that should guide us. The law cannot cover all possible human conduct, and in many situations it's too blunt an instrument to provide adequate moral guidance. The law generally prohibits egregious affronts to a society's moral standards and in that sense is the "floor" of moral conduct, but breaches of moral conduct can slip through cracks in that floor.

Professional Codes

Somewhere between etiquette and law lie **professional codes of ethics**. These are the rules that are supposed to govern the conduct of members of a given profession. Adhering to these rules is a required part of membership in that profession. Violation of a professional code may result in the disapproval of one's professional peers and, in serious cases, loss of one's license to practice that profession. Sometimes these codes are unwritten and are part of the common understanding of members of a particular profession. In other instances, these codes or portions of them may be written down by an authoritative body so they may be better taught and more efficiently enforced.

These written rules are sometimes so vague and general as to be of little value, and often they amount to little more than self-promotion by the professional organization. In other cases—for example, with attorneys—professional codes can be very specific and detailed. It's difficult to generalize about the content of professional codes of ethics, however, because they frequently involve a mix of purely moral rules (for example, client confidentiality), of professional etiquette (for example, the billing of services to other professionals), and of restrictions intended to benefit the group's economic interests (for example, limitations on price competition).

Given their nature, professional codes of ethics are neither a complete nor a completely reliable guide to one's moral obligations. Not all the rules of a professional code are purely moral in character, and even when they are, the fact that a rule is officially enshrined as part of the code of a profession does not guarantee that it's a sound moral principle. As a professional, you must take seriously the injunctions of your profession, but you still have the responsibility to critically assess those rules for yourself.

Regarding those parts of the code that concern etiquette or financial matters, bear in mind that by joining a profession you're probably agreeing, explicitly or implicitly, to abide by those standards. Assuming that those rules don't require morally impermissible conduct, then consenting to them gives you some moral obligation to follow them. In addition, for many, living up to the standards of one's chosen profession is an important source of personal satisfaction. Still, you must be alert to situations in which professional standards or customary professional practice conflicts with ordinary ethical requirements. Adherence to a professional code does not exempt your conduct from scrutiny from the broader perspective of morality.

Many corporations and other organizations have their own codes of ethics, and all of the preceding points apply to them as well. Of course, it would be naïve to assume that corporations or their employees always adhere to these codes. Perhaps the first major business scandal of this century was the massive accounting fraud perpetrated by the energy corporation Enron. Prior to the scandal, Enron received positive attention for its comprehensive code of corporate ethics; when the fraud was revealed and the company collapsed, former employees sold their copies of this code online. As *The Harvard Law Review* observes, "The Enron debacle makes clear that a corporate code of behavior is only as good as the people charged with enforcing it and those who must demonstrate the importance of compliance by their example."[7]

Where Do Moral Standards Come From?

So far you have seen how moral standards are different from various nonmoral standards, but you probably wonder about the source of those moral standards. Most, if not all, people have certain moral principles or a moral code that they explicitly or implicitly accept. Because the moral principles of different people in the same society overlap, at least in part, we can also talk about the moral code of a society, meaning the moral standards shared by its members. How do we come to have certain moral principles and not others? Obviously, many things influence what moral principles we accept: our early upbringing, the behavior of those around us, the explicit and implicit standards of our culture, our own experiences, and our critical reflections on those experiences.

For philosophers, though, the central question is not how we came to have the particular principles we have. The philosophical issue is whether those principles can be justified. Do we simply take for granted the values of those around us? Or, like Martin Luther King, Jr., are we able to think independently about moral matters? By analogy, we pick up our nonmoral beliefs from all sorts of sources: books, conversations with friends, movies, various experiences we've had. What is important, however, is not how we acquired the beliefs we have, but whether or to what extent those beliefs—for example, that women are more emotional than men or that telekinesis is possible—can withstand critical scrutiny. Likewise, ethical theories attempt to justify moral standards and ethical beliefs. The next chapter examines some of the major theories of normative ethics. It looks at what some of the major thinkers in human history have argued are the best-justified standards of right and wrong.

But first we need to consider the relationship between morality and religion on the one hand and between morality and society on the other. Some people maintain that morality just boils down to religion. Others have argued for the doctrine of *ethical relativism*, which says that right and wrong are only a function of what a particular society takes to be right and wrong. Both of those views are mistaken.

> You should take seriously the code that governs your profession, but you still have a responsibility to assess its rules for yourself.

> For philosophers, the important issue is not where our moral principles came from, but whether they can be justified.

...

Religion and Morality

Any religion provides its believers with a worldview, part of which involves certain moral instructions, values, and commitments. The Jewish and Christian traditions, to name just two, offer a view of humans as unique products of a divine creation that has endowed them with consciousness and an ability to love. Both these traditions posit creatures who stand midway between nature and spirit. On one hand, we're finite and bound to earth, not only capable of wrongdoing but also born morally flawed (original sin). On the other, we can transcend nature and realize infinite possibilities.

Religion generally involves not only a formal system of worship but also prescriptions for social relationships. One example is the mandate "Do unto others as you would have them do unto you." Termed the "Golden Rule," this injunction represents one of humankind's highest moral ideals and can be found in essence in many religions:

> Good people proceed while considering that what is best for others is best for themselves. (*Hitopadesa*, Hinduism)

> Thou shalt love thy neighbor as thyself. (*Leviticus* 19:18, Judaism)

> Therefore all things whatsoever ye would that men should do to you, do ye even so to them. (*Matthew* 7:12, Christianity)

> Hurt not others with that which pains yourself. (*Udanavarga* 5:18, Buddhism)

> What you do not want done to yourself, do not do to others. (*Analects* 15:23, Confucianism)

> No one of you is a believer until he loves for his brother what he loves for himself. (*Traditions*, Islam)

Although inspiring, such religious ideals are very general and can be difficult to translate into precise policy injunctions. Religious bodies, nevertheless, occasionally articulate positions on more specific political, educational, economic, and medical issues, which help mold public opinion on matters as diverse as abortion, the environment, national defense, and the ethics of scientific research. Roman Catholicism, in particular, has a rich history of formally applying its core values to the moral aspects of industrial relations and economic life. Pope Francis's 2013 apostolic exhortation, "The Gospel of Joy," stands in that tradition. There and elsewhere, the Pope has rejected an "economy of exclusion" and criticized blind faith in a free market that perpetuates inequality—a message that some politicians in Washington, D.C., are starting to listen to.[8]

Morality Need Not Rest on Religion

Many people believe that morality must be based on religion, either in the sense that without religion people would have no incentive to be moral or in the sense that only religion can provide moral guidance. Others contend that morality is based on the commands of God. None of these claims is convincing.

First, although a desire to avoid hell and to go to heaven may prompt some of us to act morally, this is not the only reason or even the most common reason that people behave morally. Often, we act morally out of habit or just because that is the kind of person we are. It would simply not occur to most of us to swipe an elderly lady's purse, and if the idea did occur to us, we wouldn't do it because such an act simply doesn't fit with our personal standards or with our concept of ourselves. We're often motivated to do what is morally right out of concern for others or just because it's right. In addition, the approval of our peers, the need to appease our conscience, and the desire to avoid earthly punishment may all motivate us to act morally. Furthermore, atheists generally live lives as moral and upright as those of believers.

> The idea that morality must be based on religion can be interpreted in three different ways, none of which is very plausible.

Second, the moral instructions of the world's great religions are general and imprecise: They do not relieve us of the necessity of engaging in moral reasoning ourselves. For example, the Bible says, "Thou shall not kill." Yet Christians disagree among themselves over the morality of fighting in wars, of capital punishment, of killing in self-defense, of slaughtering animals, of abortion and euthanasia, and of allowing foreigners to die from famine because we have not provided them with as much food as we might have. The Bible does not provide unambiguous solutions to these moral problems, so even believers must engage in moral philosophy if they are to have intelligent answers. On the other hand, there are lots of reasons for believing that, say, a cold-blooded murder motivated by greed is immoral. You don't have to believe in a religion to figure that out.

In fact, foundational religious texts like the Christian Bible sometimes seem to reflect different moral viewpoints in different passages. Believers may therefore need to engage in moral reasoning to decide which passages are meant to be taken most literally and to receive the most emphasis. For example, *Matthew* 19:21, where Jesus says "If you want to be perfect, go, sell your possessions and give to the poor, and you will have treasure in heaven" and *Matthew* 26:11, where he says "The poor you will always have with you," may seem to suggest different viewpoints about our duties toward people in poverty. A believer's interpretation of these passages may be influenced by what view of these duties they find most attractive in its own right. In other words, they may read the text through the lens of moral convictions that they have arrived at in other ways. What is more, there may be no real alternative to interpreting the text in this way if we want to read it in the most favorable light. Similar examples could be given from other faith traditions and texts. It may therefore be as true that believers get their religion from their morality as that they get their morality from their religion.

Third, although some theologians have advocated the **divine command theory**—that if something is wrong (like killing an innocent person for fun), then the only reason it's wrong is that God commands us not to do it—many theologians and certainly most philosophers would reject this view. They would contend that if God commands human beings not to do something, such as commit theft, it's because God sees that theft is wrong, but it's not God's forbidding theft that makes it wrong. All believers, of course, believe that God is good and that God commands us to do what is right and forbids us to do what is wrong. But this doesn't mean, say critics of the divine command theory, that it's God's saying so that makes a thing wrong, any more than it's your mother's telling you not to steal that makes it wrong to steal.

Most believers think instead that God has moral reasons to give us particular moral instructions or rules. They think, in other words, that when God commands us not to do things this is because these things were "already" wrong for some other reason. If God had no such reasons, then instead of saying "Thou shalt not steal" God might just as easily have said "Thou *shalt* steal." In that case, the divine command theory would entail that theft is morally right. To believe this is to see both God's choices and morality itself as arbitrary. Notice that saying that there's a deeper reason why theft is wrong than the fact that God commanded us not to steal does not require us to deny that God is ultimately responsible for morality. This deeper reason might have to do with how beings like us must treat each other if we're to enjoy satisfying lives, and that might depend on a human nature that God created.

All this is simply to argue that morality is not necessarily based on religion in any of these three senses. That religion influences the moral standards and values of most of us is beyond doubt. But given that religions differ in their moral beliefs and that even members of the same faith often disagree on moral matters, you cannot justify a moral judgment simply by appealing to religion—for that will only persuade those who already agree with your particular interpretation of your particular religion. Besides, most religions hold that human reason is capable of understanding what is right and wrong, so it's human reason to which you will have to appeal in order to support your ethical principles and judgments.

Summary
Morality is not necessarily based on religion. Although we draw our moral beliefs from many sources, for philosophers the issue is whether those beliefs can be justified.

. . .

Ethical Relativism

Some people do not believe that morality boils down to religion but rather that it's merely a function of what a particular society happens to believe. This view is called **ethical relativism**, the theory that what is right is determined by what a culture or society says is right. What is right in one place may be wrong in another, because the only criterion for distinguishing right from wrong—and so the only ethical standard for judging an action—is the moral system of the society in which the act occurs.

The Aztecs, for example, practiced human sacrifice. That practice would be condemned today virtually everywhere in the world. According to the ethical relativist, then, human sacrifice was right for the Aztecs and wrong for us. The relativist is not saying merely that the Aztecs believed that human sacrifice was acceptable, even morally required, and that we believe the opposite; that is acknowledged by everyone. Rather, the ethical relativist contends that human sacrifice really was morally right in Mexico during the existence of the Aztec empire because the Aztecs believed it to be right, but that it really would be wrong in, say, 21st century America because Americans today believe it to be wrong. Thus, for the ethical relativist there is no absolute ethical standard independent of cultural context, no criterion of right and wrong by which to judge other than that of particular societies. In short, what morality requires is relative to society.

Those who endorse ethical relativism point to the apparent diversity of human values and the multiformity of moral codes to support their case. From our own cultural perspective, some seemingly immoral moralities have been adopted. Polygamy, sex with minors, stealing, slavery, infanticide, and cannibalism have all been tolerated or even encouraged by the moral system of one society or another. In light of this fact, the ethical relativist believes that there can be no non-ethnocentric standard by which to judge actions.

Some thinkers believe that the moral differences between societies are smaller and less significant than they appear. They contend that variations in moral standards reflect differing factual beliefs and differing circumstances rather than fundamental differences in values. Our difference with the Aztecs over human sacrifice may have less to do with our valuing human life more than with our failure to share their belief that sacrifice was demanded by the gods and necessary to prevent the end of the world. If these thinkers are right, then the moral disagreement between cultures that is often cited as evidence for relativism may turn out to be nonexistent or at least scarce.

> Ethical disagreement does not imply that all opinions are equally correct.

But suppose they are wrong. The relativist's conclusion still does not follow. A difference of opinion among societies about right and wrong no more proves that none of the conflicting beliefs is true or superior to the others than two students' reaching different answers to a math question would show that the rules of math are different for the two of them. In short, disagreement in ethical matters does not imply that all opinions are equally correct.

Moreover, ethical relativism has some unsatisfactory implications. *First*, it undermines any moral criticism of the practices of other societies as long as their actions conform to their own standards. We cannot say that slavery in the pre–Civil War American South was immoral and unjust as long as that society held it to be morally permissible.

Second, and closely related, is the fact that for the relativist there is no such thing as ethical progress. Although moralities may change, they cannot get better or worse. Thus, we cannot say that moral standards today are more enlightened than were moral standards in the Middle Ages.

Third, from the relativist's point of view, it makes no sense for people to criticize principles or practices accepted by their own society. People can be censured for not living up to their society's moral code, but that is all. The moral code itself cannot be criticized because whatever a society takes to be right really is right for it. Reformers who identify injustices in their society and campaign against them are only encouraging people to be immoral—that is, to depart from the moral standards of their society—unless or until the majority of the society agrees with the reformers. The minority can never be right in moral matters; to be right, it must become the majority.

The ethical relativist is correct to emphasize that in viewing other cultures we should keep an open mind and not simply dismiss alien social practices on the basis of our own cultural prejudices. But the relativist's theory of morality doesn't hold up. The more carefully we examine it, the less plausible it becomes. There is no good reason for saying that the majority view on moral issues is automatically right, and the belief that it's automatically right has unacceptable consequences.[9]

Relativism and the "Game" of Business

In his essay "Is Business Bluffing Ethical?" Albert Carr argues that business, as practiced by individuals as well as by corporations, has the impersonal character of a game—a game that demands both special strategy and an understanding of its special ethical standards.[10] Business has its own norms and rules that differ from those of the rest of society. Thus, according to Carr, a number of things that we normally think of as wrong are really permissible in a business context. His examples include conscious misstatement and concealment of pertinent facts in negotiation, lying about one's age on a résumé, deceptive packaging, automobile companies' neglect of car safety, and utility companies' manipulation of regulators and overcharging of electricity users. He draws an analogy with poker.

> Poker's own brand of ethics is different from the ethical ideals of civilized human relationships. The game calls for distrust of the other fellow. It ignores the claim of friendship. Cunning deception and concealment of one's strength and intentions, not kindness and openheartedness, are vital in poker. No one thinks any the worse of poker on that account. And no one should think any the worse of the game of business because its standards of right and wrong differ from the prevailing traditions of morality in our society.[11]

Summary
Ethical relativism is the theory that right and wrong are determined by what one's society says is right and wrong. There are many problems with this theory. Also dubious is the notion that business has its own morality, divorced from ordinary ideas of right and wrong.

What Carr is defending here is a kind of ethical relativism: Business has its own moral standards, and business actions should be evaluated only by those standards.

One can question whether Carr has accurately identified the implicit rules of the business world (for example, is misrepresentation on one's résumé really a permissible move in the business game?), but let's put that issue aside. The basic question is whether business is a separate world to which ordinary moral standards don't apply. Carr's thesis assumes that any special activity following its own rules is exempt from external moral evaluation, but as a general proposition this is unacceptable. The Mafia, for example, has an elaborate code of conduct, accepted by the members of the rival "families." For them, gunning down a competitor or terrorizing a local shopkeeper may be a strategic move in a competitive environment. Yet we rightly refuse to say that gangsters cannot be criticized for following their own standards. Normal business activity is very different from gangsterism, but the point still holds. Any specialized activity or practice will have its own distinctive rules and procedures, but the morality of those rules and procedures can still be evaluated.

Moreover, Carr's poker analogy is itself weak. For one thing, business activity can affect others—such as consumers—who have not consciously and freely chosen to play the "game." Business is indeed an activity involving distinctive rules and customary ways of doing things, but it's not really a game. It's the economic basis of our society, and we all have an interest in the goals of business (in productivity and consumer satisfaction, for instance) and in the rules business follows. Why should these be exempt from public evaluation and assessment? Later chapters return to the question of what these goals and rules should be. But to take one simple point, note that a business/economic system that permits, encourages, or tolerates deception will be less efficient (that is, work less well) than one in which the participants have fuller knowledge of the goods and services being exchanged.

By divorcing business from morality, Carr misrepresents both.

In sum, by divorcing business from morality, Carr misrepresents both. He incorrectly treats the standards and rules of everyday business activity as if they had nothing to do with the standards and rules of ordinary morality, and he treats morality as something that we give lip service to on Sundays but that otherwise has no influence on our lives.

...

Having Moral Principles

At some time in their lives, most people pause to reflect on their own moral principles and on the practical implications of those principles, and they sometimes think about what principles people should have or which moral standards can be best justified. (Moral philosophers themselves have defended different moral standards; Chapter 2 discusses these various theories.) When a person accepts a moral principle, when that principle is part of their personal moral code, then naturally the person believes the principle is important and well justified. But there is more to moral principles than that, as the philosopher Richard Brandt emphasized. When a principle is part of a person's moral code, that person is strongly motivated to act as the principle requires and to avoid acting in ways that conflict with the principle. The person will tend to feel guilty when their own conduct violates that principle and to disapprove of others whose behavior conflicts with it. Likewise, the person will tend to hold in esteem those whose conduct shows an abundance of the motivation required by the principle.[12]

Other philosophers have, in different ways, reinforced Brandt's point. To accept a moral principle is not a purely intellectual act, like accepting a scientific hypothesis or a mathematical theorem. Rather, it also involves a desire to follow that principle for its own sake, the likelihood of feeling guilty about not doing so, and a tendency to evaluate the conduct of others according to the principle in question. We would find it very strange, for example, if Sally claimed to be morally opposed to cruelty to animals yet abused her own pets and felt no inclination to protest when some ruffians down the street set a cat on fire.

> Accepting a moral principle is not a purely intellectual act, like accepting a scientific hypothesis or a mathematical theorem.

Conscience

People can, and unfortunately sometimes do, go against their moral principles, but we would doubt that they sincerely held the principle in question if violating it did not bother their conscience. We have all felt the pangs of conscience, but what exactly is **conscience** and how reliable a guide is it? Our conscience, of course, is not literally a little voice inside us. To oversimplify a complex piece of developmental psychology, our conscience evolved as we internalized the moral instructions of the parents or other authority figures who raised us as children.

When you were very young, you were probably told to tell the truth and to return something you filched to its proper owner. If you were caught lying or being dishonest, you were probably punished—scolded, spanked, sent to bed without dinner, or denied a privilege. In contrast, truth telling and kindness to your siblings were probably rewarded—with approval, praise, maybe even hugs or candy. Seeking reward and avoiding punishment motivate small children to do what is expected of them. Gradually, children come to internalize those parental commands. Thus, they feel vaguely that their parents know what they are doing even when the parents are not around. When children do something forbidden, they experience the same feelings as when scolded by their parents—the first stirrings of guilt. By the same token, even in the absence of explicit parental reward, children feel a sense of self-approval about having done what they were supposed to have done.

As we grow older, of course, our motivations are not so simple and our self-understanding is greater. We're able to reflect on and understand the moral lessons we were taught, as well as to refine and modify those principles. As adults, we're morally independent agents. Yet however much our conscience has evolved and however much our adult moral code differs from the moral perspective of our childhood, those pangs of guilt we occasionally feel still stem from that early internalization of parental demands.

The Limits of Conscience

How reliable a guide is conscience? People often say, "Follow your conscience" or "You should never go against your conscience." Such advice is not very helpful, however. Indeed, it can sometimes be bad advice. *First,* when we're genuinely perplexed about what we ought to do,

> Telling someone to "follow your conscience" is not very helpful, and sometimes it can be bad advice.

we're trying to figure out what our conscience ought to be saying to us. When it's not possible to do both, should we keep our promise to a colleague or come to the aid of an old friend? To be told that we should follow our conscience is no help at all.

Second, it may not always be good for us to follow our conscience. It all depends on what our conscience says. An individual's conscience is no more an infallible moral guide than is a society's laws. On the one hand, sometimes people's consciences do not bother them when they should—perhaps because they didn't think through the implications of what they were doing or perhaps because they failed to internalize strongly enough the appropriate moral principles. On the other hand, a person's conscience might disturb the person about something that is perfectly all right.

Consider an episode in Chapter 16 of Mark Twain's *The Adventures of Huckleberry Finn*. Huck has taken off down the Mississippi on a raft with his friend, the runaway slave Jim, but as they get nearer to the place where Jim will become legally free, Huck starts feeling guilty about helping him run away:

> It hadn't ever come home to me before, what this thing was that I was doing. But now it did; and it stayed with me, and scorched me more and more. I tried to make out to myself that I warn't to blame, because I didn't run Jim off from his rightful owner; but it warn't no use, conscience up and says, every time: "But you knowed he was running for his freedom, and you could a paddled ashore and told somebody." That was so—I couldn't get around that, no way. That was where it pinched.

Here, Huck is feeling guilty about doing what we would all agree is the morally right thing to do. According to the moral principles that he had internalized, he was abetting a theft by helping Jim "steal" himself. But Huck is only a boy, and his pangs of conscience reflect the deeply flawed principles that he has picked up uncritically from the slave-owning society around him. Unable to think independently about matters of right and wrong, Huck in the end decides to disregard his conscience. He follows his compassion instead and sticks by his friend Jim. Compassion is not an infallible moral guide either. Sometimes it can cause us to focus so much on helping specific people who have an especially sympathetic plight that we lose sight of the "big picture." This can result in our treating other people unfairly or providing a short-term solution that causes bigger problems in the future. In this case, though, compassion did steer Huck right.

The point here is not that you should ignore your conscience but that the voice of conscience is itself something that can be critically examined. A pang of conscience is like a warning. When you feel one, you should definitely stop and reflect on the rightness of what you're doing. But you cannot justify your actions simply by saying you were following your conscience. Terrible deeds have occasionally been committed in the name of conscience.

Moral Principles and Self-Interest

Sometimes doing what you believe would be morally right and doing what would best satisfy your own interests may be two different things. Imagine that you're in your car hurrying along a quiet road, trying hard to get to an important football game in time to see the kickoff. You pass an acquaintance who is having car trouble. He doesn't recognize you. As a dedicated fan, you would much prefer to keep on going than to stop and help him, thus missing at least part of the game. Although you might rationalize that someone else will eventually come along and help him out if you don't, deep down you know that you really ought to stop. **Self-interest**, however, seems to say, "Keep going."

Consider another example. You have applied for a new job, and if you land it, it will be an enormous break for you. It's exactly the kind of position you want and have been trying to get for some time. It pays well and will settle you into a desirable career for the rest of your life. The competition has come down to you and one other person, and you believe correctly that she has a slight edge on you. Now imagine that you could spread a nasty rumor about her that would guarantee that she wouldn't get the job, and that you could do this in a way that wouldn't come back to you. Circulating this lie would clearly be wrong, but doing so would clearly benefit you.

Summary
Accepting a moral principle involves a motivation to conform one's conduct to that principle. Violating the principle will bother one's conscience, but conscience is not a perfectly reliable guide to right and wrong.

Some people argue that moral action and self-interest can never really conflict. Although some philosophers have gone to great lengths to try to prove this, they are almost certainly mistaken. They maintain that if you do the wrong thing, then you will be caught, your conscience will bother you, or in some way "what goes around comes around," so that your misdeed will come back to haunt you. This is often correct. But unfortunate as it may be, sometimes—viewed just in terms of personal self-interest—it may pay off for you to do what you know to be wrong. People sometimes get away with their wrongdoings, and if their conscience bothers them at all, it may not bother them very much. To believe otherwise not only is wishful thinking but also shows a lack of understanding of morality.

This is not to say that we should never act out of self-interest. We often have the opportunity to choose between several morally acceptable options, and in those cases doing what is best for ourselves may be entirely appropriate. When people act out of self-interest in appropriate ways, like when they choose the health insurance plan that makes the most financial sense for themselves given the choices their employer offers, the premiums, and their needs, we compliment their prudence. But morality serves to restrain our purely self-interested desires so we can all live together. The moral standards of a society provide the basic guidelines for cooperative social existence and allow conflicts to be resolved by an appeal to shared principles of justification. If our interests never came into conflict—that is, if it were never advantageous for one person to deceive or cheat another—then there would be little need for morality. We would already be in heaven. Both a system of law that punishes people for hurting others and a system of morality that encourages people to refrain from pursuing their self-interest at great expense to others help make social existence possible.

> Morality restrains our self-interested desires. A society's moral standards allow conflicts to be resolved by an appeal to shared principles of justification.

Usually, following our moral principles is in our best interest. This idea is particularly worth noting in the business context. It's clear how defrauding customers, cheating suppliers, or mistreating employees could come back to haunt a business. But notice one thing. If you do the right thing only because you think you will profit from it, you're not really motivated by moral concerns. Having a moral principle involves having a desire to follow the principle for its own sake—simply because it's the right thing to do. If you do the right thing only because you believe it will pay off, you might just as easily not do it if it looks as if it's not going to pay off. In addition, there is no guarantee that moral behavior will always benefit a person in strictly selfish terms. As argued earlier, there will be exceptions.

Although it may be impossible to prove to selfish people that they should not do the thing that best advances their self-interest (because if they are selfish, then that is all they care about), there are considerations that suggest it's not in one's overall self-interest to be a selfish person. People who are exclusively concerned with their own interests tend to have less happy and less satisfying lives than those whose desires extend beyond themselves. This is usually called the **paradox of hedonism**, but it might equally well be dubbed the "paradox of selfishness." Individuals who care only about their own happiness will generally be less happy than those who care about others. Moreover, people often find greater satisfaction in a life lived according to moral principle, and in being the kind of person that entails, than in a life devoted solely to self-gratification. Thus, or so many philosophers have argued, people have self-interested reasons not to be so self-interested. How do selfish people make themselves less so? Not overnight, obviously, but by involving themselves in the concerns and cares of others, they can in time come to care sincerely about those persons.

Summary
Part of the point of morality is to make social existence possible by restraining self-interested behavior. Sometimes doing what is morally right can conflict with one's personal interests. In general, though, following your moral principles will enable you to live a more satisfying life.

• • •

Morality and Personal Values

It's helpful to distinguish between morality in a narrow sense and morality in a broad sense. In a narrow sense, morality is the moral code of an individual or a society (insofar as the moral codes of the individuals making up that society overlap). Although the principles that constitute our code may not be explicitly formulated, as laws are, they do guide us in our conduct. They function as internal monitors of our own behavior and as a basis for assessing the actions of others. **Morality in the narrow sense** concerns the principles that do or should regulate people's conduct and relations with others. There is ample room to debate just what principles we should embrace, and a large part of moral philosophy involves assessing rival moral principles. Nevertheless, if there were not already fairly widespread agreement about these principles, our social order would not be sustainable.

We can also talk about our **morality in the broad sense**, meaning not just the principles of conduct that we embrace but also the values, ideals, and aspirations that shape our lives. Many different ways of living our lives would meet our basic moral obligations. The type of life each of us seeks to live reflects our individual values—whether following a profession, devoting ourselves to community service, raising a family, seeking solitude, pursuing scientific truth, striving for athletic excellence, amassing political power, cultivating glamorous people as friends, or some combination of these and many other possible ways of living. The life that each of us forges and the way we understand that life are both part of our morality in the broad sense of the term.

It's important to bear this in mind throughout your study of business ethics. Although this book's main concern is with the principles that ought to govern conduct in certain business-type situations—for example, whether a hiring officer may take an applicant's race into account, whether insider trading is wrong, or whether corporate bribery is permissible in countries where people turn a blind eye to it—your choices in the business world will also reflect your other values and ideals or, in other words, the kind of person you're striving to be. What sort of ideal do you have of yourself as a businessperson? How much weight do you put on profitability, for instance, as against the quality of your product or the socially beneficial character of your service?

The decisions you make in your career and much of the way you shape your working life will depend not only on your moral code but also on the understanding you have of yourself in certain roles and relationships. Your morality—in the sense of your ideals, values, and aspirations—involves, among other things, your understanding of human nature, tradition, and society; of one's proper relationship to the natural environment; and of an individual's place in the cosmos. Professionals in various fields, for example, will invariably be guided not just by rules but also by their understanding of what being a professional involves, and a businessperson's conception of the ideal or model relationship to have with clients will greatly influence their day-to-day conduct.

Summary
Morality in the sense of the rules or principles that regulate one's conduct toward others can be distinguished from morality in the broader sense of the values, ideals, and aspirations that shape a person's life.

There is more to living a morally good life, of course, than being a good businessperson or being good at your job, as Aristotle (384–322 BCE) argued long ago. He underscored the necessity of our trying to achieve virtue or excellence, not just in some particular field of endeavor but also as human beings. Aristotle thought that things have functions. The function of a piano, for instance, is to make certain sounds, and a piano that performs this function well is a good or excellent piano. Likewise, we have an idea of what it is for a person to be an excellent athlete, an excellent manager, or an excellent professor—it is to do well the types of things that athletes, managers, or professors are supposed to do.

But Aristotle also thought that, just as there is an ideal of excellence for any particular craft or occupation, similarly there must be an excellence that we can achieve simply as human beings. He believed that we can live our lives as a whole in such a way that they can be judged not just as excellent in this respect or in that occupation but as excellent, period. Aristotle thought that only when we develop our truly human capacities sufficiently to achieve this human excellence will we have lives blessed with happiness. Philosophers since Aristotle's time have been skeptical of his apparent belief that this human excellence would come in just one form, but many would underscore the importance of developing our various potential capacities and striving to achieve a kind of excellence in our lives. How we understand this excellence is a function of our values, ideals, and worldview—our morality in a broad sense.

Aristotle also emphasized the importance of character and of being a person whose life displays the various virtues that human beings are capable of achieving. A virtue is a trait or settled disposition; for example, a courageous, generous, or kind person is one who habitually acts in ways that are courageous, generous, or kind. A generous person does not debate whether to act generously; for them, acting generously is second nature. How we act, however, shapes the character we come to have; that is, we become a generous person by acting in generous ways, whereas we come to be selfish or stingy by acting in stingy or selfish ways. For Aristotle, it was therefore important to model ourselves on those who are virtuous and to try to act as they act. As we shall see in the next section, though, different social environments can make it easier or harder to develop virtuous habits and to be the kind of person we want to be.

· · ·

Individual Integrity and Responsibility

Previous sections discussed what it is for a person to have a moral code, as well as the sometimes conflicting pulls of moral conscience and self-interest. In addition, we have seen that people have values and ideals above and beyond their moral principles, narrowly understood, that also influence the lives they lead. And we have seen the importance of reflecting critically on both moral principles and our ideals and values as we seek to live morally good and worthwhile lives. None of us, however, lives in a vacuum, and social pressures of various sorts always affect us. Sometimes these pressures make it difficult to stick with our principles and to be the kind of person we wish to be. Corporations are a particularly relevant example of an environment that can potentially damage individual integrity and responsibility.

Organizational Norms

One of the major characteristics of an organization—indeed, of any group—is the shared acceptance of **organizational norms** and rules by its members. Acceptance can take different forms; it can be conscious or unconscious, overt or implicit, but it's almost always present, because an organization can survive only if it holds its members together. Group cohesiveness requires that individual members "commit" themselves—that is, relinquish some of their personal freedom in order to further organizational goals. One's degree of commitment—the extent to which one accepts group norms and subordinates self to organizational goals—is a measure of one's loyalty to the "team."

The corporation's overarching goal is profit. To achieve this goal, top management sets specific targets for sales, market share, return on equity, and so forth. For the most part, the norms or rules that govern corporate existence are derived from these goals. But clearly there's nothing in either the norms or the goals that necessarily encourages moral behavior; indeed, they may discourage it.

In a series of in-depth interviews with recent graduates of the Harvard MBA program in the 1990s, researchers Joseph L. Badaracco, Jr., and Allen P. Webb found that these young managers frequently received explicit instructions or felt strong organizational pressure to do things they believed to be sleazy, unethical, or even illegal.[13] The young managers interviewed by Badaracco and Webb identified four powerful organizational "commandments" as responsible for the pressure they felt to compromise their integrity:

> First, performance is what really counts, so make your numbers. Second, be loyal and show us that you're a team player. Third, don't break the law. Fourth, don't overinvest in ethical behavior.[14]

There is little reason to believe that the situation is very different today. According to a recent survey by the Ethics and Compliance Initiative, many more American employees felt pressured to compromise their organization's ethical standards in 2020 than in 2017.[15] Overall, the portion of respondents who reported experiencing such pressure jumped from 16 percent to 30 percent. Interestingly, the increase was most dramatic for individuals in management roles; in 2020, 63 percent of middle managers and 51 percent of top managers reported experiencing pressure to behave unethically. The same survey also showed a very marked increase in the portion of American employees who said they had experienced retaliation after reporting misconduct. Overall, 79 percent of employees who reported misconduct claimed to have experienced retaliation. Again, that was a significant increase from the 2017 survey, where the figure was only 44 percent. In 2020, about 90 percent of top managers who reported misconduct claimed to have suffered retaliation, and the figure for middle managers was roughly the same.

Pressure to meet corporate objectives, to be a team player, and to conform to organizational norms can sometimes lead people to act unethically.

Although most corporate goals and norms are not objectionable when viewed by themselves, they frequently put the people who must implement them into a moral pressure cooker. In addition, people can overlook the ethical implications of their decisions just because they are busy working on organizational goals and not looking at things from a broader perspective. In these ways, the need to meet corporate objectives, to be a team player, and to conform to organizational norms can sometimes lead otherwise honorable individuals to engage in unethical conduct.

Conformity

It's no secret that organizations exert pressure on their members to conform to norms and goals. What may not be so widely known is how easily individuals can be induced to behave as those around them do. A dramatic example is provided in the early conformity studies by social psychologist Solomon Asch.[16]

In a classic experiment, Asch asked groups of seven to nine college students to say which of three lines on a card matched the length of a single line on another card:

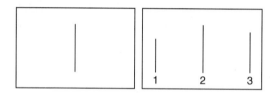

Only one of the subjects in each group was "naive," or unaware of the nature of the experiment. The others were shills or stooges of the experimenter, who had instructed them to make incorrect judgments in about two-thirds of the cases and in this way to pressure the naive subjects to alter their correct judgments.

The results were revealing. When the subjects were not exposed to pressure, they invariably judged correctly, but when the stooges all gave a false answer, the subjects changed their responses to conform with the unanimous majority judgments. When one shill differed from the majority and gave the correct answer, naive subjects maintained their position three-fourths of the time. However, when the honest shill switched to the majority view in later trials, the errors made by naive subjects rose to about the same level as that of subjects who stood alone against a unanimous majority.

Why did they yield? Some respondents said they didn't want to seem different, even though they continued to believe their judgments were correct. Others said that although their perceptions seemed correct, the majority couldn't be wrong. Still other subjects didn't even seem aware that they had caved in to group pressure. Even those who held their ground tended to be profoundly disturbed by being out of step with the majority and confessed to being sorely tempted to alter their judgments. Indeed, a subsequent study found that students who stood firm in their judgments suffered more anxiety than those who switched. One student with the strength of his correct convictions was literally dripping with perspiration by the end of the experiment.

In these experiments, which cumulatively included several hundred students, the subjects were not exposed to the authority symbols that people inside an organization face—bosses, boards of directors, professional peers—nor were they up against established policy and entrenched norms. Correct responses would not have had the serious career consequences that bucking the system can sometimes have for members of an organization: being transferred, dismissed, frozen in a position, or made an organizational pariah. And, of course, the students did not bring to these experiments the financial and personal investments that individuals bring to their jobs. Individuals within an organization are under greater pressure to conform than were the students in Asch's studies.

Groupthink

Almost all groups require some conformity from their members, but in extreme cases the demand for conformity can lead to what social psychologists call "groupthink." **Groupthink** happens when pressure for unanimity within a highly cohesive group overwhelms its members' desire or ability to appraise the situation realistically and consider alternative courses of action. The desire for the comfort and confidence that comes from mutual agreement and approval leads members of the group to close their eyes to negative information, to ignore warnings that the group may be mistaken, and to discount outside ideas that might contradict the thinking or the decisions of the group.

When under the sway of groupthink, group members may have the illusion that the group is invulnerable or that because the group is good or right, whatever it does is permissible. Individuals in the group tend to self-censor thoughts that go against the group's ideas and rationalize away conflicting evidence, and the group as a whole may implicitly or explicitly pressure potential dissenters to conform. Groupthink thus leads to irrational, sometimes disastrous decisions, and it has enormous potential for doing moral damage.

Diffusion of Responsibility

Pressure to conform to the group and to adhere to its norms and beliefs can lead to the surrender of individual moral autonomy. This tendency is enhanced by the fact that group actions frequently involve the participation of many people. As a result, responsibility for what an organization does can become fragmented or diffused throughout the group, with no single individual seeing himself or herself as responsible for what happens. Indeed, it may be difficult to say exactly who should be held accountable. This **diffusion of responsibility** inside an organization leads individuals to have a diluted or diminished sense of their own personal moral responsibilities. They tend to see themselves simply as small players in a process or as cogs in a machine over which they have no control and for which they are unaccountable. They rationalize to themselves contributing to actions, policies, or events that they would refuse to perform or to authorize if they thought the decision were entirely up to them. "It's not my fault," they think. "This would happen anyway, with or without me." Diffusion of responsibility encourages the moral myopia of thinking "I'm just doing my job," instead of taking a 20/20 look at the bigger picture.

Most social psychologists believe that an individual's sense of personal responsibility is inversely proportional to the number of people witnessing or involved in the episode. The more people who are observing an event, the less likely it is for any one of them to feel obliged to do something. In emergencies, we seem naturally to let the behavior of those around us dictate our response—a phenomenon often called **bystander apathy**. But the point is more general. In any large group or organization, diffusion of responsibility for its actions can lead individuals to feel anonymous and not accountable for what happens. Submerged in the group, the individual may not even question the morality of their actions.[17]

Pressure to conform to organizational norms and a diminished sense of personal responsibility for group behavior undermine individual integrity and moral autonomy. Business corporations are not necessarily worse than many other groups in this respect, but certainly the pressure in business to help the company make a profit or achieve its other goals, to do what is expected of you, and generally to be a loyal and cooperative team player can foster, or at least do nothing to inhibit, these group propensities. Beyond that, many corporations fail to institutionalize ethics. They don't articulate or communicate ethical standards to their members; they don't actively enforce them; and they retain structures and policies that thwart individual integrity. For example, when a Beech-Nut employee expressed concerns about the fact that the concentrate the company was producing for its "100% pure" apple juice contained nothing more than sugar, water, and chemicals, his annual performance review described his judgment as "colored by naïveté and impractical ideals."[18]

Employees frequently have to fight hard to maintain their moral integrity in a showdown with organizational priorities. In a dramatic example, on a June day in 2011, a US Airways captain with thirty years of experience stopped her flight from departing because she was worried that a backup power system was defective. The company pressured her to fly anyway, and when she refused to do so, security officials escorted her out of the airport and threatened to arrest her crew if they didn't cooperate. When other pilots backed her up and refused to fly the plane, US Airways finally had technicians service the plane. They confirmed that the component was faulty, and fixed it.[19]

Summary
Several aspects of corporate structure and function work to undermine individual moral responsibility. Organizational norms, pressure to conform (sometimes leading to groupthink), and diffusion of responsibility inside large organizations can all make the exercise of individual integrity difficult.

Diffusion of responsibility inside an organization can weaken people's sense of moral responsibility.

Business corporations are no worse than other groups, but many of them do little to protect individual integrity and moral autonomy.

Often, however, the problem facing people in business and other organization contexts is not that of doing what they believed to be right but rather of deciding what the right thing to do is. They can sometimes face difficult and puzzling moral questions, questions that need to be answered. How does one go about doing that? Is there some reliable procedure or method for answering moral questions? In science, the scientific method tells us what steps to take if we seek to answer a scientific question, but there is no comparable moral method for engaging ethical questions. There is, however, general agreement about what constitutes good moral reasoning.

• • •

Moral Reasoning

It's useful to view moral reasoning at first in the context of argument. An **argument** is a group of statements, one of which (called the **conclusion**) is claimed to follow from the others (called the **premises**). Here's an example of an argument:

Argument 1

If a person is a surgeon then they graduated from medical school.

Fran is a surgeon.

Therefore, Fran graduated from medical school.

The first two statements (the premises) of this argument happen to entail the third (the conclusion), which means that if I accept the first two as true, then rationally I must accept the third as also true. Not to accept the conclusion while accepting the premises would result in a contradiction—holding two beliefs that cannot both be true at the same time. In other words, if I believe that all surgeons graduated from medical school and that Fran is a surgeon (the premises), then I cannot deny that Fran is a medical school graduate (the conclusion) without contradicting myself. An argument like this one, whose premises logically entail its conclusion, is a **valid argument**.

An **invalid argument** is one whose premises do not entail its conclusion. In an invalid argument, I can accept the premises as true and reject the conclusion without any contradiction. Thus:

Argument 2

If a person is a surgeon then they graduated from medical school.

Fran graduated from medical school.

Therefore, Fran is a surgeon.

The conclusion of this argument does not necessarily follow from the true premises. I can believe that every surgeon is a medical school graduate and that Fran is a medical school graduate but deny that Fran is a surgeon without contradicting myself.

One way to show this is by means of a **counterexample**, an example that is consistent with the premises but is inconsistent with the conclusion. In this case, counterexamples are easy to find. Most graduates of medical school go into different specialties from surgery—cardiology, dermatology, etc.—and some decide to not practice medicine at all. These individuals are all counterexamples to this invalid argument. If an argument is valid (such as Argument 1), then no counterexamples are possible.

A valid argument can have untrue premises, as in the following:

Argument 3

If a person is a law school graduate, she must practice law.

Fran is a law school graduate.

Therefore, Fran must practice law.

Like Argument 1, this argument is valid. If I accept its premises as true, I must accept its conclusion as true; otherwise I will contradict myself. However, although Argument 3 is valid, it's unsound because one of its premises is false—namely, "If a person is a law school graduate, she must practice law." While most people who go to law school do practice law by working as attorneys, some pursue other careers. But notice why the argument is unsound—not because the type of reasoning it involves is invalid but because one of the premises is false. **Sound arguments**, such as Argument 1, have true premises and valid reasoning. **Unsound arguments** have at least one false premise, as in Argument 3, or invalid reasoning, as in Argument 2, or both.

Now let's consider some **moral arguments**, which can be defined simply as arguments whose conclusions are moral judgments. Here are some examples that deal with affirmative action for women and people of color in the workplace:

Argument 4

If an action violates the law, it is morally wrong.

Affirmative action on behalf of women and people of color in personnel matters violates the law.

Therefore, affirmative action on behalf of women and people of color in personnel matters is morally wrong.

Argument 5

If an action violates the will of the majority, it is morally wrong.

Affirmative action on behalf of women and people of color in personnel matters violates the will of the majority.

Therefore, affirmative action on behalf of women and people of color in personnel matters is morally wrong.

Argument 6

If an action redresses past injuries that have disadvantaged a group, it is morally permissible.

Affirmative action on behalf of women and people of color in personnel matters redresses injuries that have disadvantaged these groups.

Therefore, affirmative action on behalf of women and people of color in personnel matters is morally permissible.

Argument 7

If an action is the only practical way to remedy a social problem, then it is morally permissible.

Affirmative action on behalf of women and people of color in personnel matters is the only practical way to remedy the social problem of unequal employment opportunity.

Therefore, affirmative action on behalf of women and people of color in personnel matters is morally permissible.

The first premise in each of these arguments is a moral standard, the second an alleged fact, and the conclusion a moral judgment. *Moral reasoning* or argument typically moves from a moral standard, through one or more factual judgments about some person, action, or policy related to that standard, to a moral judgment about that person, action, or policy. Good moral reasoning will frequently be more complicated than these examples. Often it will involve an appeal to more than one standard as well as to various appropriate factual claims, and its argumentative structure may be more elaborate. Still, these examples illustrate its most basic form.

Moral judgments should be supported by moral standards and relevant facts.

Defensible Moral Judgments

If a moral judgment or conclusion is defensible, then it must be supportable by a defensible moral standard, together with relevant facts. A moral standard supports a moral judgment if the standard, taken together with the relevant facts, logically entails the moral judgment and if the moral standard itself is an acceptable standard. If someone argues that affirmative action for people of color and women is right (or wrong) but cannot produce a supporting principle when asked, then the person's position is considerably weakened. And if the person does not see any need to support the judgment by appealing to a moral standard, then they simply do not understand how moral concepts are used or are using moral words like "right" or "wrong" in unusual ways.

Keeping this in mind—that moral judgments must be supportable by moral standards and facts—will aid your understanding of moral discourse, which can be highly complex and sophisticated. It will also sharpen your own critical faculties and improve your moral reasoning and ability to formulate relevant moral arguments.

Patterns of Defense and Challenge

In assessing arguments, one must be careful to clarify the meanings of their key terms and phrases. Often premises can be understood in more than one way, and this ambiguity may lead people to accept (or reject) arguments that they shouldn't. For example, "affirmative action" seems to mean different things to different people (see Chapter 11 on job discrimination). Before we can profitably assess Arguments 4 through 7, we have to agree on how we understand "affirmative action." Similarly, Argument 5 relies on the idea of "violating the will of the majority," but this notion has to be clarified before we can evaluate either the moral principle that it is wrong to violate the will of the majority or the factual claim that affirmative action does violate the majority's will.

Assuming that the arguments are logically valid in their form (as Arguments 4 through 7 are) and that their terms have been clarified and possible ambiguities eliminated, then we must turn our attention to assessing the premises of the arguments. Should we accept or reject their premises? Remember that if an argument is valid and you accept the premises, you must accept the conclusion.

Let's look at some further aspects of this assessment process:

Summary
Moral reasoning and argument typically appeal both to moral standards and to relevant facts. Moral judgments should be entailed by the relevant moral standards and the facts, and they should not contradict our other beliefs. Both standards and facts must be assessed when moral arguments are being evaluated.

1. **Evaluating the factual claims.** If the parties to an ethical discussion are willing to accept the moral standard (or standards) in question, then they can concentrate on the factual claims. Thus, for example, in Argument 4 they will focus on whether affirmative action on behalf of women and people of color is in fact illegal. In Argument 7 they will need to determine whether affirmative action is really the only practical way to remedy the social problem of unequal employment opportunity. Analogous questions can be asked about the factual claims of Arguments 5 and 6. Answering them in the affirmative would require considerable supporting data.

2. **Challenging the moral standard.** Moral disagreements do not always turn on factual issues. The moral standard on which a given moral argument relies may be controversial. One party might challenge the standard, contending that it's implausible or that we should not accept it. The critic might do this in several different ways—for example, by showing that there are exceptions to the standard, that the standard leads to unacceptable consequences, or that it's inconsistent with the arguer's other moral beliefs.

    For example, suppose that Sam advocates for affirmative action in employment for women and people of color based on Argument 6 but that he opposes affirmative action for anyone else. Let us now imagine that Lynn challenges that argument by attempting to show that it has further implications that Sam does not accept. She points out that there are other groups in our history who have been and sometimes still are victims of discrimination, such as members of the Jewish or Catholic faiths and people of Irish or Italian descent. Affirmative action policies seemingly could be used to redress some of these past harms. Taking these factual claims together with the moral standard in Argument 6, "If an action redresses past injuries that have disadvantaged a group, it is morally permissible," we seem to be led to the conclusion that contrary to Sam's initial stance, workplace affirmative action favoring members of these further groups would be morally permissible.

At this point, Sam, or any rational person in a similar position, has three alternatives: abandon or modify the standard, alter his initial moral judgment and agree that affirmative action could be extended to benefit additional groups, or show how women and people of color fit the original principle even though the other groups do not.

3. **Defending the moral standard.** When the standard is criticized, then its advocate must defend it. Often this requires invoking an even more general principle. A defender of Argument 6, for example, might uphold the redress principle by appealing to some more general conception of social justice. Or they might try to show how the standard in question entails other moral judgments that both the critic and the defender accept, thereby enhancing the plausibility of the standard.

In the following exchange, Tina is defending the standard of Argument 5: "If an action violates the will of the majority, it is morally wrong":

Tina: Okay, do you think the government should impose a national religion on all Americans?

Jake: Of course not.

Tina: What about requiring people to register their handguns?

Jake: I'm all for it.

Tina: And using kids in pornography?

Jake: There rightly are laws against it.

Tina: But the principle you're objecting to—that an action violating the will of the majority is wrong—supports your moral stance on all these issues.

Of course, Tina's argument is by no means a conclusive defense for her moral standard. Other moral standards could just as easily entail the judgments she cites, as Jake is quick to point out:

Jake: Now wait a minute. I oppose a state religion on constitutional grounds, not because it violates majority will. As for gun control, I'm for it because I think it will reduce violent crimes. And using kids in pornography is wrong because it exploits and endangers children.

Although Tina's strategy for defending the standard about majority rule proved inconclusive, it does illustrate a common and often persuasive way of arguing for a moral principle.

4. **Revising and modifying the argument.** Arguments 4 through 7 are only illustrations, and all the moral principles they mention are very simple—too simple to accept without qualification. (The principle that it's immoral to break the law in all circumstances, for example, is implausible. Nazi Germany furnishes an obvious counterexample to it.) But once the standard has been effectively challenged, the defender of the argument, rather than abandoning the argument altogether, might try to reformulate it. For instance, the defender might replace the original, contested premise with a better and more plausible one that still supports the conclusion. For example, Premise 1 of Argument 4 might be replaced by: "If an action violates a law that is democratically decided and that is not morally unjust, then the action is immoral." Or the defender might revise the conclusion of their argument, perhaps by restricting its scope. A more modest, less-sweeping conclusion will often be easier to defend.

In this way, the discussion continues, the arguments on both sides of an issue improve, and we make progress in the analysis and resolution of ethical issues. In general, in philosophy we study logic and criticize arguments not to be able to score quick debating points but rather to be able to think more clearly and deeply about moral and other problems. Our goal as moral philosophers is not to "win" arguments but to arrive at the truth—or, put less grandly, to find the most reasonable answers to various ethical questions.

Summary
Philosophical discussion generally involves the revision and modification of arguments; in this way, progress is made in the analysis and resolution of moral and other issues.

Requirements for Moral Judgments

Moral discussion and the analysis of ethical issues can take different, often complicated, paths. Nevertheless, the preceding discussion implies that moral judgments should be (1) logical, (2) based on facts, and (3) based on defensible moral principles. A moral judgment that is weak on any of these grounds is open to criticism.

Moral Judgments Should Be Logical

To say that moral judgments should be logical implies several things. *First*, as indicated in the discussion of moral reasoning, our moral judgments should follow logically from their premises. The connection between (1) the standard, (2) the conduct or policy, and (3) the moral judgment should be such that 1 and 2 logically entail 3. Our goal is to be able to support our moral judgments with reasons and evidence, rather than basing them solely on emotion, sentiment, or social or personal preference.

Second, our moral judgments should be logically compatible with our other moral and nonmoral beliefs. We must avoid inconsistency. Almost all philosophers agree that if we make a moral judgment—for example, that it was wrong of Smith to alter the figures she gave to the outside auditors—then we must be willing to make the same judgment in any similar set of circumstances—that is, if our friend Brown, our spouse, or our father had altered the figures. In particular, we cannot make an exception for ourselves, judging something permissible for us to do while condemning others for doing the very same thing.

> Our moral judgments should follow logically from their premises.

> Our moral judgments should be logically compatible with our other beliefs.

Moral Judgments Should Be Based on Facts

Adequate moral judgments cannot be made in a vacuum. We must gather as much relevant information as possible before making them. For example, an intelligent assessment of the morality of insider trading would require an understanding of, among other things, the different circumstances in which it can occur and the effects it has on the market and on other traders. The information supporting a moral judgment, the facts, should be relevant—that is, the information should actually relate to the judgment; it should be complete or inclusive of all significant data; and it should, of course, be accurate or true.

Moral Judgments Should Be Based on Acceptable Moral Principles

We know that moral judgments are based on moral standards. At the highest level of moral reasoning, these standards embody and express very general moral principles. Reliable moral judgments must be based on sound moral principles—principles that are unambiguous and can withstand close scrutiny and rational criticism. What, precisely, makes a moral principle sound or acceptable is one of the most difficult questions that the study of ethics raises and is beyond the scope of this book. But one criterion is worth mentioning, namely, consistency with our **considered moral beliefs**.

Summary
Moral judgments should be logical and based on facts and acceptable moral principles. Conformity with our considered moral beliefs is an important consideration in evaluating moral principles.

These beliefs contrast with our gut responses, with beliefs based on ignorance or prejudice, and with beliefs we just happen to hold without having thought them through. As philosophy professor Tom Regan explains, our considered beliefs are those moral beliefs "we hold *after* we have made a conscientious effort . . . to think about our beliefs coolly, rationally, impartially, with conceptual clarity, and with as much relevant information as we can reasonably acquire."[20] We have grounds to doubt a moral principle when it clashes with such beliefs. Conversely, conformity with our considered moral beliefs is good reason for regarding it as provisionally established.

This does not imply that conformity with our considered beliefs is the sole or even basic test of a moral principle, any more than conformity with well-established beliefs is the exclusive or even fundamental test of a scientific hypothesis. (Copernicus's heliocentric hypothesis, for example, did not conform with what passed in the medieval world as a well-considered belief, the Ptolemaic view that the earth was the center of the universe.) But conformity with our considered beliefs seemingly must play some part in evaluating the many alternative moral principles that are explored in the next chapter.

Study Corner

Key Terms and Concepts

administrative regulations

argument

business

business ethics

businesspeople

bystander apathy

common law

conclusion

conscience

considered moral beliefs

constitutional law

counterexample

diffusion of responsibility

divine command theory

ethical relativism

ethics

etiquette

groupthink

invalid argument

moral arguments

moral standards

morality in the broad sense

morality in the narrow sense

organizational norms

paradox of hedonism

premises

professional codes of ethics

self-interest

sound arguments

statutes

unsound arguments

valid argument

Points to Review

- what happened at Theranos (pp. 1–2)

- three characteristics of moral standards (pp. 4–5)

- four types of law (pp. 5–6)

- what King's violation of the law shows (p. 6)

- the point of the example of not stopping to help an accident victim (pp. 6–7)

- shortcomings of professional codes as an ethical guide (pp. 7–8)

- where we get our moral standards (p. 8)

- three ways in which morality might be thought to be based on religion (pp. 9–10)

- three unsatisfactory implications of ethical relativism (p. 11)

- what's wrong with Carr's idea that business is a game with its own moral rules (p.12)

- what's involved in a person's accepting a moral principle (pp. 13–14)

- why telling someone "Follow your conscience" isn't very helpful advice (p. 14)

- the point of the Huckleberry Finn example (p. 14)

- what determines what a person will do when morality and self-interest collide (pp. 14–15)

- morality in the broad sense versus morality in the narrow sense (pp. 15–16)

- Aristotle and the ideal of achieving excellence (p. 16)

- what the experiments by Solomon Asch showed (p. 18)

- dangers of groupthink (p. 18)

- diffusion of responsibility (pp. 19–20)

- the difference between valid and invalid, sound and unsound, arguments (pp. 20–21)

- moral judgments as resting on moral standards and facts (p. 22)

- what it means to say moral judgments should be logical (p. 24)

- role of "considered moral beliefs" in the evaluation of moral principles (p. 24)

For Further Reflection

1. To what extent do our moral ideas reflect the society around us, and to what extent are we free to think for ourselves about moral matters?

2. Describe a situation in which you felt pressured to act against your moral principles or where you felt torn between conflicting moral values, rules, or principles. What did you do?

3. How do you explain the fact that in the business world, basically good people sometimes act immorally?

Case 1.1

Made in the U.S.A.—Dumped in Brazil, Africa, Iraq . . .

When It Comes to the Safety of Young Children, Fire is a Parent's nightmare. Just the thought of their young ones trapped in their cribs or beds by a raging nocturnal blaze is enough to make most mothers and fathers take every precaution to ensure their children's safety. Little wonder that when fire-retardant children's pajamas first hit the market, they proved an overnight success. Within a few short years more than 200 million pairs were sold, and the sales of millions more were all but guaranteed. For their manufacturers, the future could not have been brighter. Then, like a bolt from the blue, came word that the pajamas were killers. The U.S. Consumer Product Safety Commission (CPSC) moved quickly to ban their sale and recall millions of pairs. Reason: The pajamas contained the flame-retardant chemical Tris (2,3-dibromoprophyl), which had been found to cause kidney cancer in children.

Because of its toxicity, the sleepwear couldn't even be thrown away, let alone sold. Indeed, the CPSC left no doubt about how the pajamas were to be disposed of—buried or burned or used as industrial wiping cloths. Whereas just months earlier the manufacturers of the Tris-impregnated pajamas couldn't fill orders fast enough, suddenly they were worrying about how to get rid of the millions of pairs now sitting in warehouses.

Soon, however, ads began appearing in the classified pages of *Women's Wear Daily.* "Tris-Tris-Tris . . . We will buy any fabric containing Tris," read one. Another said, "Tris—we will purchase any large quantities of garments containing Tris." The ads had been placed by exporters, who began buying up the pajamas, usually at 10 to 30 percent of the normal wholesale price. Their intent was clear: to dump* the carcinogenic pajamas on overseas markets.[21]

Tris is not the only example of dumping. There were the 450,000 baby pacifiers, of the type known to have caused choking deaths, that were exported for sale overseas, and the 400 Iraqis who died and the 5,000 who were hospitalized after eating wheat and barley treated with a U.S.-banned organic mercury fungicide. Winstrol, a synthetic male hormone that had been found to stunt the growth of American children, was made available in Brazil as an appetite stimulant for children. DowElanco sold its weed killer Galant in Costa Rica, although the Environmental Protection Agency (EPA) forbade its sale to U.S. farmers because Galant may cause cancer. After the U.S. Food and Drug Administration (FDA) banned the painkiller dipyrone because it can cause a fatal blood disorder, Winthrop Products continued to sell dipyrone in Mexico City.

Manufacturers that dump products abroad clearly are motivated by profit, or at least by the hope of avoiding financial losses resulting from having to withdraw a product from the U.S. market. For government and health agencies that cooperate in the exporting of dangerous products, sometimes the motives are more complex.

For example, when researchers documented the dangers of the Dalkon Shield intrauterine device—among the adverse reactions were pelvic inflammation, blood poisoning, tubal pregnancies, and uterine perforations—its manufacturer, A. H. Robins Co., began losing its domestic market. As a result, the company worked out a deal with the Office of Population within the U.S. Agency for International Development (AID), whereby AID bought thousands of the devices at a reduced price for use in population-control programs in forty-two countries.

The agencies involved say their motives are humanitarian. Because the death rate in childbirth is relatively high in developing countries, almost any birth-control device is safer than pregnancy. Analogous arguments are used to defend the export of pesticides and other products judged too dangerous for use in the United States: Foreign countries should be free to decide for themselves whether the benefits of those products are worth their risks. In line with this, some developing government officials insist that denying their countries access to these products is tantamount to violating their countries' national sovereignty.

This reasoning has found a sympathetic ear in Washington, for it turns up in the "notification" system that regulates the export of banned or dangerous products overseas. Based on the principles of national sovereignty, self-determination, and free trade, the notification system requires that foreign governments be notified whenever a product is banned, deregulated, suspended, or canceled by a U.S. regulatory agency. The State Department, which implements the system, has a policy statement on the subject that reads in part: "No country should establish itself as the arbiter of others' health and safety standards. Individual governments are generally in the best position to establish standards of public health and safety."

Critics of the system claim that notifying foreign health officials is virtually useless. For one thing, governments in poor countries can rarely establish health standards or even control imports into their countries. Indeed, most of the developing countries where banned or dangerous products are dumped lack regulatory agencies, adequate testing facilities, and well-staffed customs departments.

Then there's the problem of getting the word out about hazardous products. In theory, when a government agency such as the EPA or the FDA finds a product hazardous, it's supposed to inform the State Department, which is to notify health officials in other nations. But agencies often fail to inform the State Department of the product they

---

* *Dumping* is a term apparently coined by *Mother Jones* magazine to refer to the practice of exporting to other countries products that have been banned or declared hazardous in the United States.

have banned or found harmful, and when it's notified, its communiqués typically go no further than U.S. embassies abroad. When foreign officials are notified by U.S. embassies, they sometimes find the communiqués vague or ambiguous or too technical to understand.

But even if communication procedures were improved or the export of dangerous products forbidden, there are ways that companies can circumvent these threats to their profits—for example, by simply changing the name of the product or by exporting the individual ingredients of a product to a plant in a foreign country. Once there, the ingredients can be reassembled and the product dumped. The United States does prohibit its pharmaceutical companies from exporting drugs banned in this country, but sidestepping the law is not difficult. "Unless the package bursts open on the dock," one drug company executive observes, "you have no chance of being caught."

Unfortunately for us, in the case of pesticides, the effects of overseas dumping are now coming home. In the United States, the EPA bans all crop uses of DDT and dieldrin, which kill fish, cause tumors in animals, and build up in the fatty tissue of humans. It also bans heptachlor, chlordane, leptophos, endrin, and many other pesticides, including 2,4,5-T (which contains the deadly poison dioxin, the active ingredient in Agent Orange, the notorious defoliant used in Vietnam) because they are dangerous to human beings. No law, however, prohibits the sale of DDT and these other U.S.-banned pesticides overseas, where thanks to corporate dumping they are routinely used in agriculture. In March 2023, the Center for Biological Diversity and the Center for International Environmental Law petitioned the EPA to create an administrative regulation that would have this effect.[22] In the petition, they note that the use of toxic pesticides in developing countries poses a particular risk to Indigenous people that may rise to the level of a violation of their human rights. They also write that "Often, pesticides that have been banned in the United States are used in developing nations, whose crops are then sold back in the United States." They describe this phenomenon as the "circle of poison."

Update

The Basel Convention is one of the most important international agreements regulating the transfer of waste from developed to developing nations, and recent amendments have further strengthened this treaty. The Ban Amendment entirely prohibits the transfer of many kinds of waste from developed into developing nations. While the United States signed the Basel Convention, it never formally ratified it into law. However, nearly all developing countries have ratified it, and the amendment prohibits them from accepting covered forms of waste from the U.S. The Ban Amendment was adopted in 1995 but was written so that it would go into effect only when three-fourths of the parties to the Convention ratified it. That happened only in 2019, when it was ratified by Croatia. In that same year another new amendment was adopted with immediate effect, one that bans the transfer of waste plastic in the same way as hazardous waste. Again, even though the United States is not a party to the Convention, it is still affected since now very few countries may legally receive its waste plastic. But there is no international police force responsible for enforcing the Basel Convention, and developing countries may not be able to prevent the arrival of materials that are covered by it.[23]

Friedrich Stark/Alamy Stock Photo

E-waste is routinely exported to developing countries, where there is little regulatory oversight of its processing despite potential health and environmental dangers.

Discussion Questions

1. Complete the following statements by filling in the blanks with either "moral" or "nonmoral" (e.g., factual, scientific, legal):

    a. Whether or not dumping should be permitted is a _____ question.

    b. "Are dangerous products of any use in the developing countries?" is a _____ question.

    c. "Is it proper for the U.S. government to sponsor the export of dangerous products overseas?" is a _____ question.

    d. Whether or not the notification system works as its supporters claim it works is a _____ question.

    e. "Is it legal to dump this product overseas?" is a _____ question.

2. Explain what dumping is, giving some examples. Does dumping raise any moral issues? What are they? What would an ethical relativist say about dumping?

3. Speculate on why dumpers dump. Do you think they believe that what they are doing is morally permissible? How would you look at the situation if you were one of the manufacturers of Tris-impregnated pajamas?

4. If no law is broken, is there anything wrong with dumping? If so, when is it wrong and why? Do any moral considerations support dumping products overseas when this violates U.S. law?

5. What moral difference, if any, does it make who is dumping, why they are doing it, where they are doing it, or what the product is?

6. Critically assess the present notification system. Is it the right approach, or is it fundamentally flawed? Should the United States move to ratify the Basel Convention?

7. Putting aside the question of legality, what moral arguments can be given *for* and *against* dumping? What is your position on dumping, and what principles and values do you base it on? Should we have laws prohibiting more types of dumping?

Case 1.2

Loose Money

Money Falling from an Armored Truck? That May Sound Pretty far-fetched, but it can and has happened. Take a recent six-month period. In August 2014, an armored truck left the Revel Casino Hotel in Atlantic City with a bag of money sitting on its roof. Video recordings show that it remained there unnoticed when the truck stopped at another casino. Sometime after that, however, the bag fell off, and the $21,000 it contained was never recovered. Two months later—on Halloween, to be precise—a bag of money worth an undisclosed sum spilled out of the rear door of an armored car after the door's lock malfunctioned. Numerous drivers on their morning commute along I-270 in Frederick County, Maryland, pulled over and hopped out of their cars to grab as much cash as they could. Then on Christmas Eve of the same year, nearly $2 million tumbled out of the back of an armored vehicle in a crowded business district of Hong Kong, creating havoc as pedestrians and motorists alike scrambled for the money. And, finally, back in New York a month later, the back door of an armored vehicle popped open on the Long Island Expressway—exactly why is uncertain—and a bag containing $178,000 fell out. When it hit the ground, it sent $20 and $100 bills flying through the air, which caused drivers to screech to a halt to chase the fluttering cash. When it was all over, only $40 was recovered.

After each of these accidents, local police appealed to people to return the scattered money to its rightful owners, saying that those who kept it might be guilty of theft. Whether anyone heeded their pleas has not been disclosed.

Discussion Questions

1. If you encountered a situation like those described, what would you do—turn the money into the authorities, grab what you can and keep it, or just ignore the whole thing? What factors would influence your decision? Is the decision a moral decision or some other kind of decision?

2. Is it dishonest to keep money that falls from an armored vehicle? Is it theft? In your opinion, what would be the right thing to do? Explain the values or moral principles that support your answer.

3. Some people think that if you take the money, you're hurting no one. Is that true? Would it make a difference if the money had fallen out of someone's purse or briefcase rather than out of an armored car? When and under what circumstances would you return property or money that you found to its rightful owner?

4. Do these cases pit morality against self-interest? Which of the following is true of you: "I am willing to do the right thing: (a) always, (b) only if the sacrifice is not too great, (c) only if doing so doesn't inconvenience me or cost me anything, or (d) only if doing so benefits me in some way"?

5. What factors explain why some people rush to take money that has fallen from a truck while others do not? In your view, to what extent is people's behavior in such situations influenced by what they see other people doing?

6. Does the principle "Finders Keepers" apply to cases like these?

Case 1.3
Just Drop off the Key, Lee

Hindsight, They Say, is 20/20. So, in Retrospect, It's Not So surprising that the boom in real estate prices of just a few years ago was followed by a painful collapse. Encouraged by low interest rates and a willingness of banks to lend money to almost anybody, many people had jumped into the housing market, sometimes buying expensive homes with mortgages they could barely afford, based on the belief, celebrated in televisions shows like *Flip This House*, that housing prices would continue to go up and up and up. But the law of gravity applies to housing prices, too, it seems. Inevitably, the housing market cooled down, and housing prices stopped rising; then they slowly reversed direction and began steadily declining. As a result, many people found themselves making mortgage payments on homes worth far less than what they had originally paid for them. Moreover, many of them had been talked into taking mortgages they didn't really understand, for example, mortgages with adjustable rates or with special "balloon" payments due after a few years, or that were too expensive for them to afford in the first place. The financial crisis of 2008 and the recession that followed only made things worse. Faced with monthly payments they could no longer sustain, these borrowers lost their homes through foreclosure. Widespread foreclosures, in turn, drove housing prices even lower, leaving more and more homeowners—by 2010 an estimated 5.4 million of them—"under water," that is, with mortgage balances at least 20 percent higher than the value of their homes.

Consider thirty-year-old software engineer, Derek Figg. He paid $340,000 for a home in the Phoenix suburbs. Two years later, its value had dropped to less than $230,000, but he still owed the bank $318,000. As a result, Figg decided to stop paying his mortgage, defaulted on his loan, and walked away from his home. Or consider Benjamin Koellmann. He paid $215,000 for an apartment in Miami Beach, which three years later was worth only $90,000. Although still paying his mortgage, he is thinking about following Figg's example.

What distinguishes Figg and Koellmann from many other homeowners whose homes are under water or who are in mortgage trouble is that both have good jobs and could afford to keep making their monthly payments—if they chose to. Moreover, they are smart guys and knew what they were doing, or thought they did, when they bought their homes. However, figuring that it would take years for their properties to regain their original value and that renting would be cheaper, they are among a growing number of homeowners who have either walked away from their mortgages or are considering it, not out of necessity but because doing so is in their financial interest. Experts call this "strategic default." Or, in the words of an old Paul Simon song, "Just drop off the key, Lee, and get yourself free."

As any financial advisor will tell you, there are lots of good reasons not to default on a mortgage. A foreclosure ruins a consumer's credit record for seven years, and with a low credit score, one must pay a higher interest rate on auto and other loans. Moreover, some states allow lenders to seize bank deposits and other assets of people who default on mortgages. Benjamin Koellmann also worries that skipping out on his mortgage might hurt him with a future employer or diminish his chance of being admitted to graduate school. Still, there's no denying that for some borrowers simply mailing in the keys and walking away can make sense. But that leaves one question unanswered: Do they have a moral responsibility to meet their financial commitments?

The standard mortgage-loan document that a borrower signs says, "I promise to pay" the borrowed amount. A promise is a promise, many people believe; they think you should keep making your mortgage payments even if doing so is inconvenient. In fact, 81 percent of Americans agree that it is immoral not to pay your mortgage when you can. George Brenkert, professor of business ethics at Georgetown University, is one of them. He maintains that if you were not deceived by the lender about the nature of the loan, then you have a duty to keep paying. If everybody walked away from such commitments, he reasons, the result would be disastrous. As Paola Sapienza, a finance professor at Northwestern University, points out, each strategic default emboldens others to take the same step, which he describes as a "cascade effect" with potentially damaging consequences for the whole economy. Economist David Rosenburg adds that these borrowers were not victims. They "signed contracts, and as adults should be held accountable."

Others disagree. Brent White, a law professor at the University of Arizona, says that homeowners should base the decision whether to keep paying or walk away entirely on their own interests "unclouded by unnecessary guilt or shame." They should take their lead from the lenders, who, he says, "ruthlessly seek to maximize profits or minimize loss irrespective of concerns of morality or social responsibility." People who think like Professor White also argue that the banks fueled the housing boom in the first place by loaning money, based on unrealistic appraisals of home values, to people who were unlikely to be able to keep up their payments in order to resell those loans to other investors. Others suspect a double standard. Homeowners are criticized for defaulting but businesses often declare bankruptcy even when they have money in the bank and could keep paying their bills. In fact, doing so is often thought to be a smart move because it trims their debt load and allows them to break their union contracts.

Benjamin Koellmann, for his part, remains conflicted. "People like me are beginning to feel like suckers. Why not let it go in default and rent a better place for less? . . . There is no financial sense in staying." Still, he struggles with the ethical side of the question: "I took a loan on an asset that I didn't see as overvalued," he says. "As much as I would like my bank to pay for that mistake, why should it?" John Gourson, chief executive of the Mortgage Bankers Association, concurs with this. In addition, he says, defaulting on your mortgage and letting your home go into foreclosure hurts the whole neighborhood by lowering property values. He adds: "What about the message they still send to their family and their kids and their friends?"

For his part, Derek Figg admits that defaulting was the "toughest decision I ever made." Still, he faced a "claustrophobic situation," he says, because if ever he lost or quit his job, he would have been unable to sell his house and move somewhere else. Moreover, he says, lenders "manipulated" the housing market during the boom by accepting dubious appraisals. "When I weighed everything," he says, "I was able to sleep at night."[24]

······································
Discussion Questions
······································

1. What would you do if you were in Figg's or Koellmann's situation? What factors would you consider?

2. Do people have a moral obligation to repay money that they borrow, as Professor Brenkert thinks, or is this simply a business decision based on self-interest alone, as Professor White thinks? Does it make a difference whether there is collateral that the lender receives if the borrower defaults, like a house?

3. "It is morally permissible for homeowners whose homes are under water to default on their mortgages even if they could continue to pay them." What arguments do you see in favor of this proposition? What arguments do you see against it?

4. When it comes to paying your debts, does it matter whether you borrow money from a bank or from an individual person? Explain why or why not.

5. Suppose your moral principles imply that you should keep on paying your mortgage, but financial self-interest counsels you to walk away. How are you to decide what to do?

6. Is defaulting on a mortgage morally any different than defaulting on a car loan and returning the car to the dealer? If so, in what way?

7. Are the banks responsible for the housing boom that enticed people to buy homes at inflated prices? If so, does this affect whether you have an obligation to repay your loan? What about Professor White's contention that the banks themselves care only about maximizing profit?

Case 1.4
The A7D Affair

Kermit Vandivier Could Not Have Predicted the Impact on His life of purchase order P-237138, issued by LTV Aerospace Corporation.[25] The order was for 202 brake assemblies for a new Air Force light attack plane, the A7D, and news of the LTV contract was cause for uncorking the champagne at the B. F. Goodrich plant in Troy, Ohio, where Vandivier worked. Although the LTV order was a small one, it signaled that Goodrich was back in LTV's good graces after living under a cloud of disrepute. Ten years earlier, Goodrich had built a brake for LTV that, to put it kindly, hadn't met expectations. As a result, LTV had written off Goodrich as a reliable source of brakes.

LTV's unexpected change of heart after ten years was easily explained. Goodrich made LTV an offer it couldn't refuse—a ridiculously low bid for making the four-disk brakes. Had Goodrich taken leave of its financial senses? Hardly. Because aircraft brakes are custom-made for a particular aircraft, only the brakes' manufacturer has replacement parts. Thus, even if it took a loss on the job, Goodrich figured it could more than make up for it in the sale of replacement parts. Of course, if Goodrich bungled the job, there wouldn't be a third chance.

John Warren, a seven-year veteran and one of Goodrich's most capable engineers, was made project engineer and lost no time in working up a preliminary design for the brake. Perhaps because the design was faultless or perhaps because Warren was given to temper tantrums when criticized, coworkers accepted the engineer's plan without question. So there was no reason to suspect that young Searle Lawson, one year out of college and six months with Goodrich, would come to think Warren's design was fundamentally flawed.

Lawson was assigned by Warren to create the final production design. He had to determine the best materials for brake linings and identify any needed adjustments in the brake design. This process called for extensive testing to meet military specifications. If the brakes passed the grueling tests, they would then be flight-tested by the Air Force. Lawson lost no time in getting down to work. What he particularly wanted to learn was whether the brake could withstand the extreme internal temperatures, in excess of 1,000 degrees F, when the aircraft landed.

When the brake linings disintegrated in the first test, Lawson thought the problem might be defective parts or an unsuitable lining. But after two more consecutive failures, he decided the problem lay in the design: The four-disk design was simply too small to stop the aircraft without generating so much heat that the brake linings melted. In Lawson's view, a larger, five-disk brake was needed.

Lawson knew well the implications of his conclusion. The four-disk brake assemblies that were arriving at the plant would have to be junked, and more tests would have to be conducted. The accompanying delays would preclude on-time delivery of the production brakes to LTV.

Lawson reported his findings and recommendations to John Warren. Going to a five-disk design was impossible, Warren told him. Officials at Goodrich, he said, were already boasting to LTV about how well the tests were going. Besides, Warren was confident that the problem lay not in the four-disk design but in the brake linings themselves.

Unconvinced, Lawson went to Robert Sink, who supervised engineers on projects. Sink was in a tight spot. If he agreed with Lawson, he would be indicting his own professional judgment: He was the man who had assigned Warren to the job. What's more, he had accepted Warren's design without reservation and had assured LTV more than once that there was little left to do but ship them the brakes. To recant now would mean explaining the reversal not only to LTV but also to the Goodrich hierarchy. In the end, Sink, who was not an engineer, deferred to the seasoned judgment of Warren and instructed Lawson to continue the tests.

His own professional judgment overridden, Lawson could do little but carry on. He built a production model of the brake with new linings and subjected it to the rigorous qualification tests. Thirteen more tests were conducted, and thirteen more failures resulted. It was at this point that data analyst and technical writer Kermit Vandivier entered the picture.

Vandivier was looking over the data of the latest A7D test when he noticed an irregularity: The instrument recording some of the stops had been deliberately miscalibrated to indicate that less pressure was required to stop the aircraft than actually was the case. Vandivier immediately showed the test logs to test lab supervisor Ralph Gretzinger. He learned from the technician who miscalibrated the instrument that Lawson had requested the miscalibration. Lawson later said he was simply following the orders of Sink and the manager of the design engineering section, who were intent on qualifying the brakes at whatever cost. For his part, Gretzinger vowed he would never permit deliberately falsified data or reports to leave his lab.

A month later, the brake was again tested, and again it failed. Nevertheless, Lawson asked Vandivier to start preparing the various graph and chart displays for qualification. Vandivier refused and told Gretzinger what he'd been asked to do. Gretzinger was livid. He again vowed that his lab would not be part of a conspiracy to defraud. Then, bent on getting to the bottom of the matter, Gretzinger rushed off to see Russell Line, manager of the Goodrich Technical Services Section.

An hour later, Gretzinger returned to his desk looking like a beaten man. He knew he had only two choices: defy his superiors or do their bidding.

"You know," he said to Vandivier, "I've been an engineer for a long time, and I've always believed that ethics and integrity were every bit as important as theorems and formulas, and never once has anything happened to change my beliefs. Now this. . . . Hell, I've got two sons I've got to put through school and I just . . ." When his voice trailed off,

it was clear that he would in fact knuckle under. He and Vandivier would prepare the qualifying data; then someone "upstairs" would actually write the report. Their part, Gretzinger rationalized, wasn't really so bad. "After all," he said, "we're just drawing some curves, and what happens to them after they leave here—well, we're not responsible for that." Vandivier knew Gretzinger didn't believe what he was saying about not being responsible. Both of them knew that they were about to become principal characters in a plot to defraud.

Unwilling to play his part, Vandivier decided that he, too, would confer with Line. Line was sympathetic; he said he understood what Vandivier was going through. But in the end, he said he would not refer the matter to chief engineer H. C. "Bud" Sunderman, as Vandivier had suggested. Why not? Vandivier wanted to know.

"Because it's none of my business, and it's none of yours," Line told him. "I learned a long time ago not to worry about things over which I had no control. I have no control over this."

Vandivier pressed the point. What about the test pilots who might get injured because of the faulty brakes? Didn't their uncertain fate prick Line's conscience?

"Look," said Line, growing impatient with Vandivier's moral needling, "I just told you I have no control over this thing. Why should my conscience bother me?" Then he added, "You're just getting all upset over this thing for nothing. I just do as I'm told, and I'd advise you to do the same."

Vandivier made his decision that night. He knew, of course, he was on the horns of a dilemma. If he wrote the report, he would save his job at the expense of his conscience. If he refused, he would honor his moral code and, he was convinced, lose his job—an ugly prospect for anyone, let alone a forty-two-year-old man with a wife and several children. The next day, Vandivier phoned Lawson and told him he was ready to begin on the qualification report.

Lawson shot over to Vandivier's office with all the speed of one who knows that, swallowed fast, a bitter pill doesn't taste so bad. Before they started on the report, though, Vandivier, still uneasy with his decision, asked Lawson if he fully understood what they were about to do.

"Yeah," Lawson said acidly, "we're going to screw LTV. And speaking of screwing," he continued, "I know now how a whore feels, because that's exactly what I've become, an engineering whore. I've sold myself. It's all I can do to look at myself in the mirror when I shave. I make me sick."

For someone like Vandivier, who had written dozens of them, the qualification report was a snap. It took about a month, during which time the brake failed still another final qualification test, and the two men talked almost exclusively about the enormity of what they were doing. In the Nuremberg trials they found a historical analogy to their own complicity and culpability in the A7D affair. More than once, Lawson opined that the brakes were downright dangerous, that anything could happen during the flight tests. His opinion proved prophetic.

When the report was finished, copies were sent to the Air Force and LTV. Within a week test flights were begun at Edwards Air Force Base in California. Goodrich dispatched Lawson to Edwards as its representative, but he wasn't there long. Several "unusual incidents" brought the flight tests literally to a screeching halt. Lawson returned to the Troy plant, full of talk about several near crashes caused by brake trouble during landings. That was enough to send Vandivier to his attorney, to whom he told the whole sorry tale.

Although the attorney didn't think Vandivier was guilty of fraud, he was convinced that the analyst/writer was guilty of participating in a conspiracy to defraud. Vandivier's only hope, the attorney counseled, was to make a clean breast of the matter to the Federal Bureau of Investigation. Vandivier did. At this point, both he and Lawson decided to resign from Goodrich. In his letter of resignation, addressed to Russell Line, Vandivier cited the A7D report and stated: "As you are aware, this report contains numerous deliberate and willful misrepresentations which . . . expose both myself and others to criminal charges of conspiracy to defraud."

Vandivier was soon summoned to the office of Bud Sunderman, who berated him mercilessly. Among other things, Sunderman accused Vandivier of making irresponsible charges and of arch disloyalty. It would be best, said Sunderman, if Vandivier cleared out immediately. Within minutes, Vandivier had cleaned out his desk and left the plant.

Two days later, Goodrich announced it was recalling the qualification report and replacing the old brake with a new five-disk brake at no cost to LTV.

Aftermath

- A year later, a congressional committee reviewed the A7D affair. Vandivier and Lawson testified as government witnesses, together with Air Force officers and a General Accounting Office team. All testified that the brake was dangerous.

- Robert Sink, representing the Troy plant, depicted Vandivier as a mere high school graduate with no technical training, who preferred to follow his own lights rather than organizational guidance. R. G. Jeter, vice president and general counsel of Goodrich, dismissed as ludicrous even the possibility that some thirty engineers at the Troy plant would stand idly by and see reports changed and falsified.

- The congressional committee adjourned after four hours with no real conclusion. The following day, the Department of Defense, citing the A7D episode, made major changes in its inspection, testing, and reporting procedures.

- The A7D eventually went into service with the Goodrich-made five-disk brake.

- Searle Lawson went to work as an engineer for LTV assigned to the A7D project.

- Russell Line was promoted to production superintendent.

- Robert Sink moved up into Line's old job.

- Kermit Vandivier became a newspaper reporter for the *Daily News* in Troy, Ohio.

Discussion Questions

1. Identify the main characters in this case, and explain what happened.

2. To what extent did Lawson, Vandivier, and Gretzinger consider the relevant moral issues before deciding to participate in the fraud? What was their reasoning? What would you have done if you were in their situation?

3. How did Sink and Line look at the matter? How would you evaluate their conduct?

4. Do you think Vandivier was wrong to work up the qualification report? Explain the moral principle or principles that underlie your judgment.

5. Was Vandivier right to "blow the whistle"? Was he morally required to so? Again, explain the moral principles on which your judgment is based.

6. Describe the different pressures to conform in this case and discuss the relevance of the concepts of groupthink and diffusion of responsibility. Do any of these factors excuse the conduct of particular individuals in this case? If so, who and why?

7. Should Goodrich be held morally responsible as a company for the A7D affair, or just the individuals involved?

8. What might Goodrich have done, and what steps should it take in the future, to ensure more moral behavior?

Chapter 2

Normative Theories of Ethics

Learning Objectives

After completing this chapter, you should be able to:

1. Summarize several important normative ethical theories: ethical egoism, act utilitarianism, Kant's ethics, Ross's "pluralistic" ethics, and rule utilitarianism.
2. Distinguish between consequentialist and nonconsequentialist approaches to ethics.
3. Apply different ethical theories to real-life situations to determine which courses of actions these theories would say are morally obligatory, morally forbidden, or morally permissible.
4. Evaluate different theories of ethics, identifying both arguments that might be made in their favor and objections that might be made to them.
5. Participate in a group of individuals with different ethical perspectives who must decide how an organization should behave.

Introduction

Head of a Premier Hedge Fund and Former President of the NASDAQ stock exchange, Bernard Madoff was a respected financier with a sterling reputation. So, when he stated in a speech that "in today's regulatory environment, it's virtually impossible [for fund managers] to violate the rules," his listeners were unlikely to have doubted what he was saying. They were even less likely to have foreseen how eerily prophetic his words would turn out to be when the Federal Bureau of Investigation arrested him a year later for perpetrating what may have been the greatest scam of all time.

Madoff's celebrated hedge fund, it turns out, was a total fraud—in essence, a gigantic Ponzi scheme. In a Ponzi scheme, a con artist takes in money from investors but keeps it for himself rather than investing it as promised. On paper, the profits of the investors continue to grow. If they want to redeem some of their fund shares for cash, the fraudster uses money from new investors to pay them. This keeps investors happy and content but clueless about what really happened to their money. It's only possible to keep a scam like this running as long as plenty of new people are "investing" their money and not too many are making withdrawals.

The fact that Madoff's phony hedge fund reported consistently strong returns in both good and bad markets, with never a down

> Madoff's celebrated hedge fund, it turns out, was a total fraud—in essence, a gigantic Ponzi scheme.

quarter, made a few financial analysts suspicious. However, the law doesn't require hedge funds to operate as transparently as it does mutual funds, and Madoff was notoriously secretive about his investment strategy. The Securities and Exchange Commission, which is charged with policing the financial marketplace, never noticed anything amiss, and most business observers and investment advisors simply thought that Madoff had the Midas touch. And so it seemed he did—until, that is, the financial crisis of 2008 when the meltdown on Wall Street led more and more of his investors to seek to redeem fund shares for cash. With new investors now few and far between, Madoff simply had no money to pay those investors who wanted to cash in some or all of their chips. Unable to keep the game up, he confessed to his sons that his fund was "one big lie." They promptly turned him in to the authorities.

Madoff's victims included insurance companies, pension and investment funds, banks in Europe and Asia, and a number of prominent individuals, such as Hall of Fame baseball pitcher Sandy Koufax, filmmaker Steven Spielberg, and actors Kevin Bacon and John Malkovich. Many of these people were bilked for millions and millions of dollars, in some cases losing nearly all their savings. Likewise, some of the charities that had invested with Madoff were completely ruined.

Having lost their assets, they were forced to shut down. A few investors, however, who had withdrawn money from their accounts on and off over the years, ended up in an ethical quandary. The money that they thought was in their Madoff accounts was, of course, gone, but over the years they had actually taken more money out of the fund, sometimes substantially more money, than they had initially put into it. But what they thought at the time to be legitimate profit was, they now realized, almost certainly money that Madoff had stolen from other clients. Should they keep quiet? Should they return the money to other investors, most of whom had ended up deep in the hole? Or should they insist that the money they received was legitimately theirs and push (along with all the other investors) to somehow get restitution of the balances that just a few weeks before they had assumed still remained in their Madoff accounts?

Under legal pressure, Boston philanthropist Carl Shapiro agreed to hand over to other victims the $625 million he had received from Madoff over the years. Irving Picard, the court-appointed trustee representing Madoff's victims, also sued Fred Wilpon and Saul Katz. He alleged that these successful investors, who then owned the New York Mets, should have known that the $300 million they had earned from their Madoff accounts were "fictitious profits." The suit was settled in 2012 for about half that sum (and the figure was lowered still further in 2016, to about $61 million, after more of the money that Madoff stole was recovered from other sources). As a general matter, though, the legal responsibilities of those Madoff investors who came out ahead are unclear; legal battles are still being waged. In 2021, a federal appeals court reinstated Picard's "clawback" lawsuit against Citigroup.

But it's not just factual or legal complexities that make the question difficult. There are competing moral considerations. If you yourself were scammed, it might seem that you have no moral obligation to help those whose losses were greater—after all, you were a victim, too. On the other hand, although Madoff was ostensibly paying you money that you were entitled to, you were, in fact, receiving embezzled funds. Do those later investors have a right to get their money back from you? Would you act wrongly in hanging on to what you were lucky enough to get from Madoff before his scheme crashed? Or are the Madoff investors morally required to pool their gains and try to equalize their losses?

You don't need to study moral philosophy to see that Madoff acted immorally. Only a complete scoundrel steals from charities, pension funds, and friends and acquaintances who have entrusted him with their life savings. In contrast, it isn't easy to know what an investor should do if they got more back from Madoff than other investors did—perhaps even more than their initial investment. Even if the person wants to do the right thing, what exactly does morality require, and how are we to determine what that is? On what basis are we to judge what is right or wrong?

Chapter 1 explained that defensible moral judgments must be underwritten by sound moral principles. That is because when we judge

In the 1920s, con artist Charles Ponzi told gullible investors that he could double their money in 90 days by buying postage reply coupons in other countries and redeeming them at the U.S. Post Office. In fact, he kept their money and paid early investors with money coming in from later investors.

Pictorial Parade/Archive Photos/Getty Images

something wrong, we are not judging simply that it is wrong but also that it is wrong for some reason or by virtue of some general characteristic.[1] Moral principles thus provide the basis for making moral judgments. The use of these principles, however, isn't a mechanical process by which one cranks in data and out pops an automatic moral judgment. Rather, the principles provide a conceptual framework that guides us in making moral decisions. Careful thought and open-minded reflection are always necessary to work from one's moral principles to a considered moral judgment.

But what are the appropriate principles to rely on when making moral judgments? The truth is that there is no consensus among people who have studied ethics and reflected on these matters. Different philosophical theories exist as to the proper standard of right and wrong. As the British philosopher Bernard Williams put it, we are heirs to a rich and complex ethical tradition, in which a variety of different moral principles and ethical considerations intertwine and sometimes compete.[2] This chapter will introduce several examples of such theories.

...

Philosophical Theories of Ethics

A note on how to think about these theories: Most people seem to employ different sorts of moral thinking in different circumstances, without really being able to explain why. In the classic "trolley problem," first formulated by Philippa Foot and later explored by Judith Jarvis Thomson (among many others), we are asked to imagine an out-of-control trolley or train speeding down a track where it is about to hit and kill five innocent people. By pulling a switch, you can send the trolley down a different track where it will only kill one person. Should you do it? Studies have shown that most people say that you should.

In the "footbridge" variation of the case, your choice is to push a person who is leaning over the edge a bridge onto the track to stop the trolley and save the five people. They will be killed in the process. (Assume that the person you could push is larger than you and that jumping onto the track yourself wouldn't stop the trolley. You know this because you're an expert on trolleys.) When presented with this version of the case, most people say that it's wrong to push the person—including many people who think it's right to pull the switch in the original case.

In the original trolley case, what seems to matter is that pulling the switch has a better outcome: one person dies rather than five. In the footbridge scenario, pushing the person also has a better outcome—again, one person dies rather than five—but that no longer seems to matter as much. Explaining why producing the best outcome is of paramount importance in one case but not the other is challenging. The most obvious difference between the cases is that in one we pull a switch and in the other we push a person with our own hands. But while this difference might be psychologically significant, it's not clear why it should matter morally.[3]

Most of the different moral or ethical theories that have been devised by philosophers are attempts to isolate and refine specific forms of moral thinking that people commonly use at least some of the time. Often, if not always, the philosophers who develop these theories are motivated by the thought that instead of going back and forth between several inconsistent ways of thinking about morality we should consistently use just one. These philosophers disagree, though, about which one this is. The theories that will be discussed here are just a sampling of the moral theories that philosophers have devised; the possibilities are much wider and more diverse than its possible to convey in one chapter.

Summary
Philosophical theories of ethics are often attempts to isolate and refine forms of moral thinking that people use every day.

...

Consequentialist and Nonconsequentialist Theories

In ethics, **normative theories** propose some principle or principles for distinguishing right actions from wrong actions. These theories can, for convenience, be divided into two kinds: consequentialist and nonconsequentialist.

According to **consequentialist theories**, the moral rightness of actions is determined solely by their results. Consequentialists (moral theorists who adopt this approach) determine what is right by weighing the ratio of good to bad that actions will produce.

One question that arises here is: Consequences for whom? Should one consider the consequences only for oneself? Or the consequences for everyone affected? The two most important consequentialist approaches, *ethical egoism* and *utilitarianism*, give different answers to this question. Egoism advocates individual self-interest as its guiding principle. Utilitarianism holds that one must take everyone into account. But both approaches agree that rightness and wrongness are solely a function of actions' results.

By contrast, **nonconsequentialist** (or *deontological*, from the Greek for "necessary") **theories** contend that right and wrong are determined by more than actions' likely consequences. Nonconsequentialists don't necessarily deny that consequences are morally significant, but they believe that other factors are also relevant to the moral assessment of an action. For example, a nonconsequentialist might hold that for Kevin to break his promise to

Summary
Consequentialist moral theories see the moral rightness or wrongness of actions as a function of their results. If the consequences are good, the action is right; if they are bad, the action is wrong. Nonconsequentialist theories see other factors as also relevant to the determination of right and wrong.

Cindy is wrong not simply because it has bad results (Cindy's hurt feelings, Kevin's damaged reputation, and so on) but because of the inherent character of the act itself. Even if more good than bad were to come from Kevin's breaking the promise, a nonconsequentialist might still view it as wrong. What matters is the nature of the act in question, not just its results. This idea will become clearer later in the chapter as we examine some specific nonconsequentialist principles and theories.

* * *

Ethical Egoism

A few years after Firestone first introduced its "500" steel-belted radial tires, it was discovered that their tread was prone to separate at high speeds, with a U.S. House subcommittee later concluding that the tires had led to thirty-four highway deaths. In response to the controversy, Firestone announced that it was discontinuing the "500." Newspapers at the time interpreted this to mean that Firestone would immediately remove the tires from the market. In fact, Firestone intended only a "rolling phaseout" (no pun intended) and continued to manufacture the tire. When a Firestone spokesperson was later asked why the company had not corrected the media's misinterpretation of its intent, the spokesperson said that Firestone's policy was to ask for corrections only when it was beneficial to the company to do so—in other words, only when it was in the company's self-interest.

The view that equates morality with self-interest is referred to as **ethical egoism**. It says that an act is morally right if and only if it best promotes the agent's own interests. (Here an "agent" is just whoever's action is being discussed. An agent can be a single person or, as in the Firestone example, an organization. The term isn't being used in the business sense of someone who acts on someone else's behalf.) Egoism makes personal advantage (in both the short and long run) the standard for measuring an action's rightness. If an action would produce more good for the agent than any alternative action would, then that action is morally right and anything else that they might do instead is morally wrong. One example of an ethical egoist is the author Ayn Rand, who promoted ethical egoism in novels like *Atlas Shrugged* and essays like "The Virtue of Selfishness."

Misconceptions about Egoism

There are some common misunderstandings about ethical egoism. One is that egoists do only what they like, that they believe in "eat, drink, and be merry." Not so. An egoist would be quite willing to undergo unpleasant, even painful experiences as long as this would be in their long-term best interest.

Another misconception is that all egoists endorse **hedonism**, the view that pleasure (or happiness) is the only thing that is good in itself, that it is the ultimate good, the one thing in life worth pursuing for its own sake. Although some egoists are hedonistic—as was the ancient Greek philosopher Epicurus (341–270 BCE)—other egoists have a broader view of what constitutes self-interest. Some of them identify a person's good with knowledge or power, others with what some modern psychologists call "self-actualization." Egoists may, in fact, hold any theory of what is good.

A final but very important misconception is that egoists cannot act honestly, be gracious and helpful, or otherwise promote other people's interests. Egoism, however, requires us to do whatever will best further our own interests, and this sometimes involves advancing the interests of others. Ethical egoism tells us to benefit others when we expect that our doing so will be reciprocated or when the act will bring us pleasure or in some way promote our own good. For example, egoism might discourage a shopkeeper from trying to cheat customers because it is likely to hurt business in the long run. Or egoism might recommend to the chair of the board that she hire her nephew as a vice president, who isn't the best candidate for the job but of whom she is very fond. Hiring the nephew might bring her more satisfaction than any other course of action, even if the nephew doesn't perform his job as well as someone else might. In short, ethical egoism doesn't preach that we should never assist others but rather that we have no basic moral duty to do so. The only basic moral obligation we have is to ourselves. Therefore, we are only required to act in the interests of others if that would be the best means to the end of promoting our own self-interest.

Psychological Egoism

Proponents of ethical egoism generally attempt to derive their basic moral principle from the alleged fact that human beings are by nature selfish creatures. According to this doctrine, **psychological egoism**, people are so constructed that they *must* behave selfishly. Psychological egoism asserts that all actions are selfishly motivated and that truly unselfish actions are therefore impossible. Even apparently self-sacrificial acts such as giving up one's own life to save the lives of one's children or blowing the whistle on organizational misdeeds at great personal expense are, according to psychological egoism, done to satisfy the person's own self-interested desires. For example, the parent may seek to perpetuate the family line or to avoid guilt, and the employee may be after fame or revenge.

According to egoism, we should assist others when doing so best promotes our own interests.

Criticisms of Ethical Egoism

Although egoism as an ethical doctrine has always had its adherents, the theory is open to several strong objections. It is safe to say that few, if any, philosophers today would advocate it as either a personal or an organizational morality. Consider these objections:

There are strong objections to egoism as an ethical doctrine.

1. **Psychological egoism isn't a plausible theory.** Self-interest motivates all of us to some extent, and we all know of situations in which someone pretended to be acting altruistically or morally but was really motivated only by self-interest. The theory of psychological egoism contends, however, that self-interest is the only thing that ever motivates anyone.

   This contention seems vulnerable to various counterexamples. Take the actual case of a man who pulled the driver out of the cab of a burning semi-tanker filled with gasoline and then simply drove away.[4] Or take a more mundane example. It's Saturday, and you feel like having a beer with a couple of pals and watching the ball game. On the other hand, you believe that you ought to take your children to the pool, as you earlier suggested to them you might. Of course, you love your children, and it will bring you some pleasure to go to the pool with them, but—let's face it—you'd prefer to watch the ball game. Nonetheless, you feel an obligation and so you go for a swim.

   These appear to be cases in which people are acting for reasons that are not self-interested. Of course, the reasons that lead you to take your children swimming—a sense of obligation, a desire to promote their happiness—are your reasons, but that by itself doesn't make them self-interested reasons. Still less does it show that you are selfish. Anything that you do is a result of your desires, but that fact doesn't establish what the believer in psychological egoism claims—namely, that the only desires you have, or the only desires that ultimately move you, are self-interested desires.

   Proponents of the theory of psychological egoism will claim that deep down, both the heroic man and the unheroic parent who took the children to the pool were really motivated by self-interest in some way or another. Adherents of psychological egoism can always claim that some yet-to-be-identified subconscious egoistic motivation is the main impulse behind any action. At this point, though, psychological egoism sounds a little far-fetched, and we may suspect its advocates of trying to make their theory true by definition.

2. **Psychological egoism doesn't really support ethical egoism, anyway.** The "law" of gravity is unbreakable. Humans are always subject to gravity unless they go so far into outer space that they're no longer attracted to the Earth—and even then, they aren't defying the law of gravity, since that law determines just how far from Earth you must go to become weightless. But the inevitability of our obeying the law of gravity doesn't do anything to show that we *should* obey it. What it shows, if anything, is that it's pointless to worry about whether we should. It's only worth making the point that people ought to do something if it's at least possible that they won't. According to psychological egoism, we'll always do what we think is in our own best interest. The theory says that self-interest's pull is as inescapable

as that of gravity. Even if this were plausible, it wouldn't by itself be enough to prove that ethical egoism is true. It would, though, be enough to make debating its truth pointless. If we're all going to act selfishly regardless of whether we believe that ethical egoism is true, then why should we worry about whether it's true? If psychological egoism were a plausible theory then this wouldn't give us a reason to believe ethical egoism but only a reason to ignore it. In fact, if psychological egoism actually were true then ethical egoism might be meaningless. We can understand ethical egoism as the view that we shouldn't act contrary to our own best interest. But it's not entirely clear what it means to say that we shouldn't do something that we're incapable of doing.

Summary
Ethical egoism is the consequentialist theory that an action is right if and only if it promotes the individual's best interests. Proponents of this theory base their view on the alleged fact that human beings are, by nature, selfish (the doctrine of psychological egoism). Critics of egoism argue that (1) psychological egoism is implausible, (2) psychological egoism doesn't support ethical egoism, (3) ethical egoism isn't really a moral principle, and (4) ethical egoism condones blatant wrongs.

3. **Ethical egoism isn't really a moral principle at all.** Many critics of egoism as an ethical standard contend that it misunderstands the nature and point of morality. As Chapter 1 explained, morality serves to restrain our purely self-interested desires so we can all live together. If our interests never came into conflict—that is, if it were never advantageous for one person to deceive or cheat another—then we would have no need for morality. The moral standards of a society provide the basic guidelines for cooperative social existence and allow us to resolve conflicts by appeal to shared principles of justification.

It is difficult to see how ethical egoism could perform this function. In a society of egoists, people might publicly agree to follow certain rules so their lives would run more smoothly. But it would be a very unstable situation, because people would not hesitate to break the rules if they thought they could get away with it. Nor can egoism provide a means for settling conflicts and disputes, because it simply tells each party to do whatever is necessary to promote effectively their interests.

4. **Ethical egoism condones blatant wrongs.** The most common objection to egoism as an ethical doctrine is that it sometimes condones actions that are blatantly immoral. Deception, theft, or even murder can be morally right according to the standard of egoism, if it advances the agent's self-interest (and the agent can get away with it).

In response, the defender of egoism might argue that this objection begs the question by assuming that such acts are immoral and then repudiating egoism on this basis. After all, their morality is the very issue that moral principles such as egoism are meant to resolve. Nevertheless, egoism fails to do justice to some of our basic ideas about right and wrong. A moral principle that permits murder, if it successfully advances one's self-interest, clashes with our firmest moral convictions. If anything is wrong, that is.

• • •

Utilitarianism: A First Look

Utilitarianism tells us to bring about the most happiness for everyone affected by our actions.

Jeremy Bentham and John Stuart Mill were important early utilitarians.

Utilitarianism is the moral doctrine that we should always act to produce the greatest possible balance of good over bad for everyone affected by our actions. By "good," utilitarians understand happiness or pleasure. Thus, the greatest happiness of all constitutes the standard that determines whether an action is right or wrong. Although the basic theme of utilitarianism is present in the writings of many earlier thinkers, Jeremy Bentham (1748–1832) and John Stuart Mill (1806–1873) were the first to develop the theory explicitly and in detail. Both Bentham and Mill were philosophers with a strong interest in legal and social reform. They used the utilitarian standard to evaluate and criticize the social and political institutions of their day—for example, the prison system and the disenfranchisement of women. As a result, utilitarianism has long been associated with social improvement.

Bentham viewed a community as no more than the individual persons who make it up. The interests of the community are simply the sum of the interests of its members. An action promotes the interests of an individual when it adds to the individual's pleasure or diminishes the person's pain. Correspondingly, an action adds to the happiness of a community only insofar as it increases the total amount of happiness that individuals enjoy. This is what Bentham had in mind when he argued for the utilitarian principle that actions are right if they promote the greatest human welfare, wrong if they don't.

For Bentham, pleasure and pain are merely types of sensations. He offered a "hedonic calculus" for evaluating pleasure and pain exclusively by their quantitative differences—in particular, by their intensity and duration. This calculus, he believed, makes possible an objective determination of the morality of anyone's conduct, individual or collective, on any occasion.

Bentham rejected any distinctions based on the type of pleasure except insofar as they might indicate differences in quantity. Thus, if equal amounts of pleasure are involved, throwing darts is as good as writing poetry and baking a cake as good as composing a symphony; watching Shakespeare's *Hamlet* has no more value than watching *The Bachelorette*. Although he himself was an intelligent, cultivated man, Bentham maintained that there is nothing intrinsically better about refined and intellectual pleasures than about crude or prosaic ones. The only issue is which yields the greater amount of enjoyment.

John Stuart Mill thought Bentham's concept of pleasure was too simple. He viewed human beings as having elevated faculties that allow them to pursue various higher kinds of pleasure. The pleasures of the intellect and imagination, in particular, have a higher value and do more to make us happy than those of mere physical sensation. Thus, for Mill the "utility" principle must take into consideration the relative quality of different pleasures and pains, not just their intensity and duration.[5] While this view leads Mill to think that humans are capable of more happiness than nonhuman animals, this is a matter of degree. Bentham and Mill agreed that the pleasure and pain of animals must be taken into account along with that of people; any animals capable of experiencing these sensations matter morally.

Although Bentham and Mill had different conceptions of pleasure, both men equated pleasure and happiness and considered pleasure the ultimate value. In this sense they were hedonists: Pleasure, in their view, is the one thing that is intrinsically good or worthwhile. Anything that is good is good only because it brings about pleasure (or happiness), directly or indirectly. Take education, for example. The learning process itself might be pleasurable to us; reflecting on or working with what we have learned might bring us satisfaction at some later time; or by making possible a career and life that we could not have had otherwise, education might bring us happiness indirectly. In contrast, critics of Bentham and Mill contend that things other than happiness are also valuable in and of themselves—for example, knowledge, friendship, and aesthetic satisfaction. The implication is that these things are valuable even if they don't lead to happiness.

> Bentham and Mill had different conceptions of pleasure, but they both equated it with happiness and believed that pleasure was the ultimate value.

Bentham and Mill cared about happiness because they implicitly identified it with well-being, that is, with what is good for people. In their view, our lives go well—we have well-being—just to the extent that our lives are pleasurable or happy. Some moral theorists have modified utilitarianism so that it aims at other consequences in addition to happiness. And some utilitarians, wary of trying to compare one person's happiness with another's, have interpreted their theory as requiring us not to maximize happiness but rather to maximize the satisfaction of people's desires or preferences. The focus here will be utilitarianism in its standard form, in which the good to be aimed at is human happiness or well-being, but what will be said about standard or classical utilitarianism applies, with the appropriate modifications, to other versions as well.

Utilitarianism in its most basic version, often called **act utilitarianism**, says that in any situation the right action for someone to perform is the one that would yield the most happiness. To do anything else would be wrong, that is, morally forbidden. Notice that this makes what it's right for a person to do depend on what alternative actions they have available. An action that would produce a great deal of happiness might still be wrong if it were possible to do something else instead that would produce even more. An action that would produce very little might be right if all the other options were even worse. Notice also that this means that in most situations there will only be one right or morally permissible action. Doing the very best we can is always morally required. The only exceptions are those rare situations where two (or more) actions "tie for first place" by producing equal amounts of happiness that are greater than the amounts produced by any alternatives. Then and only then does act utilitarianism allow that we may freely choose between our available options.

Act utilitarianism is the most straightforward way of taking utilitarian ideas that many people find attractive and incorporating them into a moral theory. In the original version of the trolley problem, most people intuitively reason like act utilitarians. The theory has been advocated by several important philosophers, including not only Bentham but also Peter Singer, who is arguably the most famous living philosopher in the English-speaking world. (Mill, in contrast, turns out to subscribe to a different version of utilitarianism, rule utilitarianism. We'll examine it later in the chapter.)

Six Points about Utilitarianism

Six important things to understand about utilitarianism.

Before evaluating utilitarianism, one should understand some points that might lead to confusion and misapplication. *First,* when deciding which action will produce the greatest happiness, we must consider unhappiness or pain as well as happiness. Suppose, for example, that an action would produce eight "units" of happiness and four units of unhappiness. Its net worth is four units of happiness. Suppose also that a second possible action would produce ten units of happiness and seven units of unhappiness; its net worth is three units. In this case, the act utilitarian would say that we should choose the first action over the second. If our circumstances are so unfortunate that any action that we might perform would lead not to happiness but to unhappiness, we should choose the one that brings fewer units of unhappiness.

Second, actions affect people to different degrees. Playing your radio loudly might enhance two persons' pleasure a little, cause significant discomfort to two others, and leave a fifth person indifferent. The utilitarian view isn't that each person votes on the basis of their pleasure or pain, with the majority ruling, but rather that we add up the various pleasures and pains, however large or small, and go with the action that brings about the greatest net amount of happiness. While utilitarians are often said to be concerned with the "greatest happiness of the greatest number," what they really want to maximize is simply the greatest happiness. Suppose that there are three people in a car. The two in the front seats are a little hungry and would like to get food. The one in the back has appendicitis and *really* wants to go to the hospital. There is little question that in this case the act utilitarian would favor disappointing the majority.

Third, because utilitarians evaluate actions according to their consequences and because actions produce different results in different circumstances, almost anything might, in principle, be morally right in some particular situation. For example, whereas breaking a promise generally produces unhappiness, there can be circumstances in which, on balance, more happiness would be produced by breaking a promise than by keeping it. In those cases, utilitarianism would require us to break the promise.

Fourth, utilitarians wish to maximize happiness not simply immediately but in the long run as well. All the indirect ramifications of an act have to be taken into account. Lying might seem a good way out of a tough situation, but if and when the people we deceive find out, not only will they be unhappy, but also our reputations and our relationships with them will be damaged. This is a serious risk that a utilitarian cannot ignore.

Fifth, utilitarians acknowledge that we often don't know with certainty what the future consequences of our actions will be. Accordingly, we must act so that the expected or likely happiness is as great as possible. If a doctor has a choice between leaving a patient's mild skin condition untreated or prescribing a drug that has a 1 percent chance of curing it and a 99 percent chance of killing the patient, then there's a possibility that writing the prescription will produce the best outcome. But the odds are definitely against it; the most likely result is that the patient dies. While there is some difference of opinion about this, many act utilitarians would say that writing the prescription would be wrong even if things worked out for the best and the patient were cured.

Sometimes it is difficult to determine the likely results of alternative actions, and no modern utilitarian really believes that we can assign precise units of happiness and unhappiness to people. But as Mill reminds us, we actually do have quite a lot of experience as to what typically makes people happy or unhappy. In any case, as utilitarians, our duty is to strive to maximize total happiness, even when it is difficult to know which action will produce the most good.

Summary
Act utilitarianism, another consequentialist theory, maintains that the morally right action is the one that provides the most happiness for all those affected. After assessing as best we can the likely results of each action, not just in the short term but in the long run as well, we are to choose the course of conduct that brings about the greatest net happiness.

Finally, when choosing among possible actions, utilitarianism doesn't require us to disregard our own pleasure. Nor should we give it added weight. Rather, our own pleasure and pain enter into the calculus equally with the pleasures and pains of others. In contrast with ethical egoism, therefore, utilitarianism embodies the notion that morality requires a sort of impartiality between ourselves and others. Even if we are sincere in our utilitarianism, we must guard against the possibility of being biased in our calculations when our own interests are at stake. For this reason, and because it would be time-consuming to do a utilitarian calculation before every action, utilitarians encourage us to rely on rules of thumb in ordinary moral circumstances. We can make it a rule of thumb, for example, to tell the truth and keep our promises, rather than to calculate possible pleasures and pains in every routine case, because we know that in general telling the truth and keeping promises result in more happiness than do lying and breaking promises.

Utilitarianism in an Organizational Context

Several features about utilitarianism make it appealing as a standard for moral decisions in business and nonbusiness organizations.

> Three features of utilitarianism make it appealing in an organizational context.

First, utilitarianism provides a clear and straightforward basis for formulating and testing policies. By utilitarian standards, an organizational policy, decision, or action is good if it promotes the general welfare more than any other alternative. A policy is considered wrong (or in need of modification) if it doesn't promote total happiness or utility as well as some alternative would. Utilitarians don't ask us to accept rules, policies, or principles blindly. Rather, they require us to test their worth against the standard of utility.

Second, utilitarianism provides an objective and attractive way of resolving conflicts of self-interest. This feature of utilitarianism dramatically contrasts with egoism, which seems incapable of resolving such conflicts. By proposing a standard outside self-interest, utilitarianism greatly minimizes and may actually eliminate such disputes. Thus, individuals within organizations make moral decisions and evaluate their actions by appealing to a uniform standard: the general good.

Third, utilitarianism provides a flexible, result-oriented approach to moral decision making. By recognizing no general kinds of actions as inherently right or wrong, utilitarianism encourages organizations to focus on the results of their actions and policies, and it allows them to tailor their decisions to suit the complexities of their situations. This facet of utilitarianism enables organizations to make realistic and workable moral decisions.

Critical Inquiries of Act Utilitarianism

Unsurprisingly, philosophers have asked several critical questions about act utilitarianism.

1. **Is act utilitarianism really workable?** Act utilitarianism instructs us to maximize happiness, but in difficult cases we may be very uncertain about the likely results of the alternative courses of action open to us. Furthermore, comparing your level of happiness or unhappiness with that of someone else is at best tricky, at worst impossible—and when many people are involved, the matter may get hopelessly complex. Even if we assume that it is possible to make comparisons and to identify the various possible results of each course of action that a person might take (and to determine the likelihood of each result), is it realistic to expect people to take the time to make those calculations and, if they do, to make them accurately? Some critics of act utilitarianism have contended that teaching people to follow the basic utilitarian principle would not, in fact, promote happiness because of the difficulties in applying utilitarianism accurately.

2. **Are some actions wrong, even if they produce good?** Like egoism, utilitarianism focuses on the results of an action, not on the character of the action itself. For utilitarians, no action is in itself objectionable. It is objectionable only when it results in less happiness than could otherwise have been brought about. Critics of utilitarianism, by contrast, contend that some actions can be immoral and thus are things we must not do, even if doing them would maximize happiness.

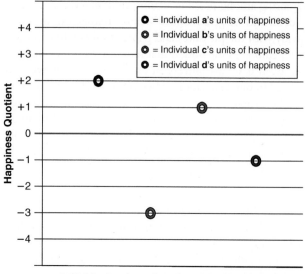

**Individuals whose happiness levels must be
measured and combined by the utilitarian.**

Can we estimate the effects of our actions well enough for
utilitarianism to work?

Summary

In an organizational
context, utilitarianism
provides an objective
way to resolve conflicts
of self-interest and
encourages a realistic
and result-oriented
approach to moral
decision making. But
critics contend that
(1) act utilitarianism
isn't really workable,
(2) some actions are
wrong even if they
produce good results,
and (3) act utilitarianism
incorrectly overlooks
considerations of justice
and the distribution of
happiness.

Suppose a dying woman has asked you to promise to send the $25,000 under her bed to her nephew in another part of the country. She dies without anyone else's knowing of the money or of the promise that you made. Now suppose, too, that you know the nephew is immature and irresponsible and, were the money delivered to him, it would be wasted in a week of outrageous partying. On the other hand, a very fine orphanage in your town needs such a sum to improve and expand its recreational facilities, something that would provide happiness to many children for years to come. It seems clear that on utilitarian grounds you should give the money to the orphanage, because this action would result in greater net happiness.

Many people would balk at this conclusion, contending that it would be wrong to break your promise, even if doing so would bring about a better outcome good than keeping it. Having made a promise, you have an obligation to keep it, and a deathbed promise is particularly serious. Furthermore, the deceased woman had a right to do with her money as she wished; it isn't for you to decide how to spend it. Likewise, having been bequeathed the money, the nephew has a right to it regardless of how wisely or foolishly he might spend it. Defenders of utilitarianism, however, would insist that promoting happiness is all that really matters and warn you not to be blinded by moral prejudice.

Critics of act utilitarianism respond that it's this theory that is morally blind because it not only permits but sometimes even requires us to perform immoral actions. Philosopher Richard Brandt states the case against act utilitarianism this way:

> Act-utilitarianism . . . implies that if you have employed a boy to mow your lawn and he has finished the job and asks for his pay, you should pay him what you promised only if you cannot find a better use for your money. . . . It implies that if your father is ill and has no prospect of good in his life, and maintaining him is a drain on the energy and enjoyments of others, then, if you can end his life without provoking any public scandal or setting a bad example, it is your positive duty to take matters into your own hands and bring his life to a close.[6]

Defenders of act utilitarianism would reply that these charges are exaggerated. Although it is theoretically possible, for example, that not paying the boy for his work might maximize happiness, this is extremely unlikely. Utilitarians contend that only in very unusual circumstances will pursuit of the good conflict with our ordinary ideas of right and wrong, and in those cases—like the deathbed promise—we should put aside those ordinary ideas. The anti-utilitarian replies that the theoretical possibility that utilitarianism may require such conduct shows it to be an unsatisfactory moral theory.

3. **Is act utilitarianism unjust?** Utilitarianism concerns itself with the sum total of happiness produced, not with how that happiness is distributed. If policy X brings two units of happiness to each of five people and policy Y brings nine units of happiness to one person, one unit each to two others, and none to the remaining two, then Y is to be preferred (eleven units of happiness versus ten), even though it distributes that happiness very unequally.

Worse still from the critic's point of view, utilitarianism may even require that some people's happiness be sacrificed to achieve the greatest overall amount of happiness. Sometimes the general happiness may be served only at the expense of a single individual or group. Fantasy writer Ursula Le Guin explores this worry in her short story "The Ones Who Walk Away from Omelas."[7] Omelas is an isolated community whose residents all live wonderfully happy lives—all except for one small child, who is kept locked up in a basement, alone, feeble minded, squatting naked in its own excrement, subsisting on "a half-bowl of corn meal and grease a day." Everyone in Omelas knows that, for reasons that are never explained, they can only be happy because of this child's misery. The ones who walk away from Omelas are those who decide that they cannot accept happiness on those terms and leave. If making one child miserable would bring happiness to a sufficiently large number of others, then the act utilitarian would have to approve of the arrangement, but it's impossible to read the story without believing (or hoping) that you would be among those who walk away.

Or consider the government's power of **eminent domain** (see Case 3.1). The government may appropriate private property for public use (after compensating the owner). Thus, the government may legally purchase your house from you to widen a highway—even if you don't want to sell the house at the price the government considers fair. The public interest is served at your private expense. Eminent domain is a familiar part of American law; it is even mentioned in the Fifth Amendment's "takings" clause. And it has a clear utilitarian rationale. But is it just?

The Interplay between Self-Interest and Utility

Both self-interest and utility play important roles in organizational decisions, and the views of many businesspeople blend these two theories. To the extent that each business pursues its own interests and each businessperson tries to maximize personal success, business practice can be called egoistic. But business practice is also utilitarian in that pursuing one's economic interests is thought to benefit society as a whole, and playing by the established rules of the competitive game is seen as advancing the social good. The classical capitalist economist Adam Smith (1723–1790) held such a view. He argued that leaving business and businesspeople free to pursue their self-interest will serve the good of society. Indeed, Smith believed that only through egoistic pursuits could the greatest economic benefit for the whole society be produced. The essence of Smith's position can be seen in the following passage from the *Wealth of Nations* (1776), in which Smith underscores the interplay between self-interest and the social good and between egoism and utilitarianism:

> Every individual is continually exerting himself to find out the most advantageous employment for whatever capital he can command. It is his own advantage, indeed, and not that of the society, which he has in view. But the study of his own advantage, naturally, or rather necessarily, leads him to prefer that employment which is most advantageous to the society. . . .
>
> As every individual, therefore, endeavours as much as he can . . . to employ his capital . . . [so] that its produce may be of the greatest value, every individual necessarily labors to render the annual revenue of the society as great as he can. He generally, indeed, neither intends to promote the public interest, nor knows how much he is promoting it. . . . He intends only his own security; and by directing that industry in such a manner as its product may be of the greatest value, he intends only his own gain, and he is in this, as in many other cases, led by an invisible hand to promote an end which was no part of his intention.[8]

Business practice is egoistic, but Adam Smith and others believe that it is also utilitarian because the pursuit of self-interest promotes the good of society.

Many today would agree with Smith* that the pursuit of self-interest is central to our economic system because it provides the motivating force that turns the wheels of commerce and industry. Although acknowledging that business is part of a social system and that certain ground rules are needed and should be followed, they would argue that society is best served by the active pursuit of self-interest within the established rules of business practice. Thus, what we might call **business egoism**—the view that it is morally acceptable (or even morally required) for individuals to pursue their economic interests when engaged in business—is defended on utilitarian grounds.

• • •

Kant's Ethics

Most of us find the ideal of promoting human happiness and well-being an attractive one. Despite the attractiveness of this ideal, many moral philosophers are critical of utilitarianism—particularly because, like egoism, it reduces all morality to a concern with consequences. Although nonconsequentialist normative theories vary significantly, adopting different approaches and stressing different themes, the writings of the preeminent German philosopher Immanuel Kant (1724–1804) provide an excellent example of a thoroughly nonconsequentialist approach to ethics. Perhaps few thinkers today would endorse Kant's theory on every point, but his work has greatly influenced subsequent philosophers and has helped shape our general moral culture.

Kant believed that moral reasoning isn't based on factual knowledge and that the results of our actions don't determine whether they are right or wrong.

Kant sought moral principles that don't rest on contingencies and that define actions as inherently right or wrong apart from any particular circumstances. He believed that moral rules can, in principle, be known as a result of reason alone and are not based on observation (as are, for example, scientific judgments). In contrast to utilitarianism and other consequentialist doctrines, Kant's ethical theory holds that we don't have to know anything about the likely results of, say, my telling a lie to my boss in order to know that it is immoral. "The basis of obligation," Kant wrote, "must not be sought in human nature, [nor] in the circumstances of the world." Rather it is *a priori*, by which he meant that moral reasoning isn't based on factual knowledge and that reason by itself can reveal the basic principles of morality.

Good Will

Chapter 1 mentioned Good Samaritan laws, which shield from lawsuits those rendering emergency aid. Such laws, in effect, give legal protection to the humanitarian impulse behind emergency interventions. They formally recognize that the interventionist's heart was in the right place—that the person's intention was irreproachable. And because the person acted from right intention, they should not be held liable for any inadvertent harm except in cases of extreme negligence. The widely observable human tendency to introduce a person's intentions in assigning blame or praise is a good springboard for engaging Kant's ethics.

Summary
Kant's theory is an important example of a purely nonconsequentialist approach to ethics. Kant held that only when we act from duty does our action have moral worth. Good will is the only thing that is good in itself.

Nothing, said Kant, is good in itself except **good will**. This doesn't mean that intelligence, courage, self-control, health, happiness, and other things are not good and desirable. But Kant believed that their goodness depends on the will that makes use of them. Intelligence, for instance, isn't good when exercised by an evil person.

By *will*, Kant meant the uniquely human capacity to act from principle. Contained in the notion of good will is the concept of duty: Only when we act from a sense of duty does our action have **moral worth**. When we act only out of feeling, inclination, or self-interest, our actions—although they may be otherwise identical with ones that spring from the sense of duty—have no true moral worth.

Suppose that you're the owner of a small convenience store. Late one night a customer pays for his five-dollar purchase with a twenty-dollar bill, which you mistake for a ten. Only after the customer leaves do you realize you short-changed him. You race out the front door and give him the ten dollars with your apologies, and he thanks you warmly.

---

*Chapter 4 examines Smith's position in more detail.

Can we say that you acted from good will? Not necessarily. You may have acted from a desire to promote future business or to cultivate a reputation for honesty. If so, you would have acted in accordance with, but not from, duty. Your apparently virtuous gesture just happened to coincide with what duty requires. According to Kant, if you don't will the action from a sense of your duty to be fair and honest, your action lacks moral worth. Actions have true moral worth only when they spring from a recognition of duty and a choice to discharge it.

What determines our duty? How do we know what morality requires of us? Kant answered these questions by formulating what he called the "categorical imperative." This extraordinarily significant moral concept is the linchpin of Kant's ethics.

The Categorical Imperative

We have seen that egoists and utilitarians allow factual circumstances or empirical data to determine moral judgments. In contrast, Kant believed that reason alone can establish the moral law. We need not rely on empirical evidence relating to consequences and to similar situations. Just as we know, seemingly through reason alone, such abstract truths as "Every change must have a cause," so we can arrive at absolute moral truth through nonempirical reasoning and thereby discover our duty. For Kant, the moral law must hold in all circumstances, free from any internal contradiction. If we can formulate this law or rule, he thought, everyone would be obliged to follow it without exception.

Kant believed that there is just one command (imperative) that is categorical and thus necessarily binding on all rational agents, regardless of any other considerations. From this one categorical imperative (that is, from this universal command), we can derive all the specific commands of duty. This is Kant's **categorical imperative**. While this can easily confuse someone who is encountering Kant for the first time, he believes both that there is only one categorical imperative and that it can be stated or formulated in very different ways. Kant insists that these different formulations are all equivalent in meaning and have precisely the same implications for which actions are right and which wrong.

Kant's initial statement of the categorical imperative, the **universal law** formula, says that we should always act in such a way that we can will the "maxim" of our action to be a universal law. By **maxim**, Kant meant the subjective principle of an action, the principle (or rule) that people in effect formulate in determining their conduct. For example, suppose building contractor Martin promises to install a sprinkler system in a project but is willing to break that promise to suit his purposes. His maxim can be expressed this way: "I'll make promises that I'll break whenever keeping them no longer suits my purposes." This is the subjective principle— the maxim—that directs his action.

Kant insisted that the morality of any maxim depends on whether we can will it to be a universal law governing everyone's conduct. Could Martin's maxim be universally acted on? That depends on whether the maxim as law would involve a contradiction. The maxim "I'll make promises that I'll break whenever keeping them no longer suits my purposes" could not be acted on universally. If everyone made promises without intending to keep them, the entire institution of promising would break down. People would not even bother trying to make promises, because everyone would know that no one could be relied upon to follow through. If someone tried to make you a promise, you would just walk away. In a world where everyone made promises that they didn't intend to keep, therefore, no one could make promises at all. The law would involve a contradiction.

Similarly, Kant reasoned, a law that allowed lying would involve a contradiction, because if everyone lied then people would not even bother listening to what anyone else had to say. And if people won't listen to one another then it is impossible to tell lies. Hence lying is always wrong. By contrast, there is no problem, Kant thinks, in willing promise keeping or truth telling to be universal laws.

Notice that, like utilitarianism, Kant's ethics incorporate the notion of impartiality. Utilitarianism does this by saying that one unit of happiness has the same value regardless of whether it is our own happiness or someone else's. Kant's ethics does this by saying that we cannot elevate ourselves above others by acting on maxims that we could not choose for everyone else to act on as well.

If you make a promise that you don't intend to keep, it is impossible to will the maxim governing your action as a universal law.

Summary

The universal law formula of Kant's categorical imperative states that an action is morally right if and only if we can will the maxim (or principle) represented by our action as a universal law. For example, a person making a promise with no intention of keeping it cannot universalize the maxim governing his action because if everyone followed this principle, promising would make no sense. Kant believed that the categorical imperative is binding on all rational creatures, regardless of their specific goals or desires and regardless of the consequences.

When Kant insists that a moral rule be consistently universalizable, he is saying that moral rules prescribe categorically, not hypothetically. A *hypothetical* prescription tells us what to do if we desire a particular outcome. Thus, "If I want people to like me, I should be nice to them" and "If you want to go to medical school, you must take biology" are **hypothetical imperatives**. They tell us what we must do on the assumption that we have some particular goal. If that is what we want, then this is what we must do; but if we don't want to go to medical school, then the command to take biology doesn't apply to us. In contrast, Kant's imperative is *categorical*: It commands unconditionally. It is necessarily binding on everyone, regardless of their specific goals or desires, regardless of consequences. A categorical imperative takes the form of "Do this" or "Don't do that"—no ifs, ands, or buts.

Universal Acceptability

There is another way of looking at the categorical imperative. Each person, through their own acts of will, legislates the moral law. The moral rules that we obey are not imposed on us from the outside. They are self-imposed and self-recognized, fully internalized principles. The sense of duty that we obey comes from within; it is an expression of our own higher selves.

Thus, moral beings give themselves the moral law and accept its demands on themselves. But that isn't to say we can prescribe anything we want, for we are constrained by reason and its requirements. Because reason is the same for all rational beings, we all give ourselves the same moral law. In other words, when you answer the question "What should I do?" you must consider what all rational beings should do. You can embrace something as a moral law only if all other rational beings could also embrace it. It must have **universal acceptability**.

To see whether a rule or principle is a moral law, we can thus ask if what the rule commands would be acceptable to all rational beings. In considering lying, theft, or murder, for example, you must consider the act not only from your own viewpoint but also from the perspective of the person lied to, robbed, or murdered. Presumably, rational beings don't want to be lied to, robbed, or murdered. The test of the morality of a rule, then, is whether all rational beings looking at the matter objectively and impartially could accept the rule regardless of whether the action in question was performed by them or done to them. This is an important moral insight, and most philosophers see it as implicit in Kant's discussion of the categorical imperative, even though Kant (whose writings are difficult to understand) did not make the point in this form.

The formula of universal acceptability has important applications. Suppose a man advocates a hiring policy that discriminates against women. For this rule to be universally acceptable, the man would have to be willing to accept it if he were a woman, something he would presumably be unwilling to do. Or suppose the manufacturer of a product decides to market it even though the manufacturer knows that the product is unsafe when used in a certain common way and that consumers are ignorant of this fact. Applying the universal-acceptability principle, the company's decision makers would have to be willing to advocate marketing the product even if they were themselves in the position of uninformed consumers. Presumably, they would be unwilling to do this. So the rule that would allow the product to be marketed would fail the test of universal acceptability.

Humanity as an End, Never as Merely a Means

In addition to the principle of universal acceptability, Kant explicitly offered another, very famous way of formulating the core idea of his categorical imperative. According to the **formula of humanity**, as rational creatures we should always treat other rational creatures as ends in themselves and never as only means to our own ends. This formulation underscores Kant's belief that every human being has an inherent worth resulting from the sheer possession of rationality. We must always act in a way that respects this humanity in others and in ourselves. When brokers at the Dallas office of Prudential Securities encouraged unnecessary buying and selling of stocks by their clients in order to reap a commission (a practice called "churning"), they failed to do this. They were treating their clients simply as a means to their own ends and not respecting them as persons, as ends in themselves.[9]

As rational beings, humans would act inconsistently if they did not treat everyone else the way they themselves feel entitled to be treated. Here we see shades of the Golden Rule. Indeed, Kant's moral philosophy can be viewed as a profound reconsideration of this basic nonconsequentialist principle. Because rational beings recognize their own inner worth, they would never wish to be used as if they were entities possessing value only as means to an end.

The universal law formula of the categorical imperative says that an action is morally right if and only if we could choose for its maxim to become a universal law of conduct. We now have two further ways of formulating his categorical imperative that may be easier to grasp and apply:

> *Universal acceptability formula:* An action is right if and only if its underlying principle is universally acceptable, that is, acceptable to all rational parties whether the action is done by them or to them.

> *Formula of humanity:* One must always act so as to treat other people as ends in themselves.

Again, Kant thinks that these different formulations of the categorical imperative are identical in meaning and have exactly the same implications in terms of what is right or wrong for us to do.

Two alternative formulations of the categorical imperative.

Kant in an Organizational Context

Like utilitarianism, Kant's moral theory has application for organizations.

First, the categorical imperative gives us firm rules to follow in moral decision making, rules that don't depend on circumstances or results and that don't permit individual exceptions. No matter what the consequences may be or who does it, some actions are always wrong. Lying is an example: No matter how much good might come from misrepresenting a product, such deliberate misrepresentation is always wrong. Similarly, it would be wrong to expose uninformed workers to some occupational health risk on the grounds that it advances medical knowledge.

Second, Kant introduces an important humanistic dimension into business decisions. One of the principal objections to egoism and utilitarianism is that they permit us to treat humans as means to ends. Kant's principles clearly forbid this. Many would say that respect for the inherent worth and dignity of human beings is much needed today in business, where encroaching technology and the pressure of globalization tend to dehumanize people under the guise of efficiency. Kant's theory puts the emphasis of organizational decision making where it belongs: on individuals. Organizations, after all, involve human beings working in concert to provide goods and services for other human beings. The primacy Kant gives the individual reflects this essential aspect of business.

Third, Kant stresses the importance of motivation and of acting on principle. According to Kant, it isn't enough just to do the right thing; an action has moral worth only if it's done from a sense of duty—that is, from a desire to do the right thing for its own sake. The importance of this point is too often forgotten. Sometimes when individuals and organizations believe that an action promotes the interests of everyone, they are actually rationalizing—doing what is best for themselves and only imagining that somehow it will also benefit others. Worse still, they may defend their actions as morally praiseworthy when, in fact, they are only behaving egoistically. They wouldn't do the morally justifiable thing if they didn't think it would pay off for them. By stressing the importance of motivation, a Kantian approach serves as a corrective to this. Even an action that helps others has moral value for Kant only if the person doing it is morally motivated—that is, acting on principle or out of moral conviction.

Summary
There are two additional formulations of the categorical imperative. The first says that the action must be acceptable to all rational parties whether it is done by them or done to them. The second says that one must always treat other people as ends, never merely as means.

Critical Questions about Kant's Ethics

As with ethical egoism and act utilitarianism, philosophers have raised several critical questions about Kantianism.

1. **What has moral worth?** According to Kant, the convenience store owner who returns the ten dollars to the customer is doing the right thing. But if his action is motivated by self-interest (perhaps he wants to get a reputation for honesty), then it doesn't have moral worth. That seems plausible. But Kant also held that if the owner does the right thing out of instinct,

habit, or sympathy for the other person, then the act still doesn't have moral worth. Only if it is done out of a sense of duty does the action have moral value. Many moral theorists have felt that Kant was too severe on this point. Do we really want to say that giving money to famine relief has no moral worth if one is emotionally moved to do so by pictures of starving children rather than by a sense of duty? We might, to the contrary, find a person with strong human sympathies no less worthy or admirable than the person who gives solely out of an abstract sense of duty. (Think of the example of Huck Finn in the last chapter.)

Summary

Kant's ethics gives us firm standards that don't depend on results; it injects a humanistic element into moral decision making and stresses the importance of acting on principle and from a sense of duty. Critics, however, worry that (1) Kant's view of moral worth is too restrictive, (2) the categorical imperative isn't a sufficient test of right and wrong, and (3) distinguishing between treating people as means and respecting them as ends in themselves may be difficult in practice.

2. **Is the categorical imperative an adequate test of right?** Kant said that a moral rule must function without exception. Critics wonder why the prohibition against actions such as lying or promise breaking must be exceptionless. They say that Kant failed to distinguish between saying that a person should not exempt himself or herself from a rule and that the rule itself cannot specify exceptions.

Consider an example that Kant himself discussed.[10] Imagine that a murderer comes to your door, wanting to know where your friend is so that he can kill her. Your friend is in fact hiding in your bedroom closet. Most people would agree that your obligation to your friend overrides your general obligation to tell the truth and that the right thing to do would be to lie to the murderer to throw him off your friend's trail. Kant disagreed. He maintained that you must always tell the truth—that is, in all circumstances and without exception. For him, telling the truth is an absolute or categorical obligation. Most people find the notion that the moral prohibition on lying is so absolute implausible.

In addition to worrying about whether Kant's categorical imperative is excessively rigid, we might also worry about whether it can account for all our moral obligations. One reason for starting with the examples of promise breaking and lying is that it is comparatively easy to explain how trying to make the maxims of these actions into universal laws would lead to contradictions. However, even in the other illustrations of the categorical imperative given by Kant himself, this is much harder to do. For instance, Kant suggests that we could not choose for the maxim that we will never help others to become a universal law, because sometimes we need help. From this, he concludes that we have some obligation to help others, even if how much and when is left indeterminate. However, we might question whether it's actually impossible for us to choose for this maxim to be a universal law, as opposed to our just being glad that it's not.

Is the categorical imperative an adequate test of right? A moral rule must function without exception, according to Kant. How applicable is that tenet to torture?

3. **What does it mean to treat people merely as means?** Kant's mandate that individuals must always be considered as ends in themselves and never merely as means expresses our sense of the intrinsic value of the human spirit and has profound moral appeal. Yet it isn't always obvious when people are being treated as ends and when merely as means. Slavery is a crystal-clear example of treating human beings merely as means, since it involves treating a fully rational human as if they were nothing more than a tool. The **formula of humanity** offers a compelling explanation of what makes slavery wrong. But if you have a job, your employer presumably only hired you as a means of advancing their own ends. Does that mean that you're being treated as a mere means? Does it matter that you agreed to do the job? Does it matter how many alternative jobs were available? Does it matter how well you're being paid? Remember that what the categorical imperative forbids is treating people as nothing more than means, not as using them as means to our ends while also treating them as having worth in their own right. Also, notice that Kant's ethics prohibits us from treating other persons merely as means, but not nonhuman animals. In contrast with utilitarians, Kantians have a hard time explaining how we can have any moral obligations at all to animals.

• • •

Other Nonconsequentialist Perspectives

For Kant, the categorical imperative provided the basic test of right and wrong, and he was resolutely nonconsequentialist in his application of it. You know now what he would say about the case of the deathbed promise: The maxim permitting you to break your promise cannot be universalized, and hence it would be immoral of you to give the money to the orphanage, despite its bringing about more happiness. But nonconsequentialists are not necessarily Kantians.

Ross's Pluralism and Prima Facie Obligations

Some nonconsequentialists are willing to recognize that we have a moral obligation to promote happiness and the general welfare, but they deny that all of morality can be reduced to this one obligation. In fact, they deny that any single principle can be the foundation of the entirety of morality. One influential philosopher who argued this way was the British scholar W. D. Ross (1877–1971).[11] Ross rejected both act utilitarianism and Kantianism as too simple and as untrue to the way we ordinarily think about morality and about our moral obligations. We see ourselves, Ross and like-minded thinkers contend, as being under diverse moral duties that cannot be reduced to a single obligation to maximize happiness or avoid other people merely as means. Often, these obligations grow out of special relationships into which we enter or out of determinate roles that we undertake. Our lives are intertwined with other people's in particular ways, and we have, as a result, certain specific moral obligations.

> Ross believed that we have various moral duties that cannot be captured by any one moral principle.

For example, as a professor, Dr. Rodriguez is obligated to assist her students in the learning process and to evaluate their work in a fair and educationally productive way—obligations to the specific people in her classroom that she doesn't have to other people. As a spouse, she must maintain a certain emotional and sexual fidelity to her partner. As a parent, she must provide for the individual human beings who are her children. As a friend to Smith, she may have a moral responsibility to help him out in a time of crisis. Having borrowed money from Chang, Rodriguez is morally obligated to pay it back. Thus, different relationships and different circumstances generate a variety of specific moral obligations.

In addition, we have moral duties that don't arise from our unique interactions and relationships with other people. For example, we ought to treat all people fairly, do what we can to remedy injustices, and make an effort to promote human welfare generally. The latter obligation is important, but for a nonconsequentialist like Ross, it is only one among various obligations that people have.

At any given time, we are likely to be under more than one obligation, and sometimes these obligations can conflict—that is, we may have an obligation to do *A* and an obligation to do *B*, where it isn't possible for us to do both *A* and *B*. For example, I promise to meet a friend on an urgent matter, and now, as I am hurrying there, I pass an injured person who is obviously in need of help. Stopping to aid the person will make it impossible for me to fulfill my promise. What should I do? For moral philosophers like Ross, there is no single answer for all cases. What I ought to do will depend on the circumstances and relative importance of the conflicting obligations. I have an obligation to keep my promise, and I have an obligation to assist someone in distress. What I must decide is which of these obligations is, in the given circumstance, the more important. I must weigh the moral significance of the promise against the comparative moral urgency of assisting the injured person.

Ross and many contemporary philosophers believe that all (or at least most) of our moral obligations are prima facie ones. A **prima facie obligation** is an obligation that can be overridden by a more important obligation. For instance, we take the keeping of promises seriously, but almost everyone would agree that in some circumstances—for example, when a life is at stake—it would be not only morally permissible, but morally required, to break a promise. Our obligation to keep a promise is a real one, and if there is no conflicting obligation, then we must keep the promise. But that obligation isn't absolute or categorical; it could in principle be outweighed by a more stringent moral obligation.

The idea of prima facie obligations gives us an attractive way to think about the case of the "inquiring murderer" that created problems for Kant's ethics, for example. Your obligation to tell the truth might be real but prima facie, and it might be outweighed by your obligation to protect your friend. The idea that our obligations are prima facie is foreign to Kant's way of looking at things.

Ross thought that our various prima facie obligations could be divided into seven basic types: duties of fidelity (that is, to respect explicit and implicit promises), duties of reparation (for previous wrongful acts), duties of gratitude, duties of justice, duties of beneficence (that is, to promote the general welfare), duties of self-improvement, and duties not to injure others.[12] Unlike utilitarianism and Kantianism, Ross's ethical perspective is pluralistic in recognizing a variety of genuine obligations. But contrary to Kant, Ross doesn't see these obligations as absolute and exceptionless. On both points, Ross contended that his view of morality more closely fits with our actual moral experience and the way we view our moral obligations.

Ross also saw himself as siding with commonsense morality in maintaining that our prima facie obligations are obvious. He believed that the basic principles of duty are as self-evident as the simplest rules of arithmetic and that any person who has reached the age of reason can discern that it is wrong to lie, to break promises, and to injure people needlessly. However, what we should do, all things considered, when two or more prima facie obligations conflict is often difficult to judge. Ross is an exception to the earlier observation that most philosophers who devise moral theories do so by isolating one form of moral thinking that we sometimes employ and saying that we should instead employ it in every situation. Instead of doing this, Ross's theory much more closely mirrors our "ordinary morality" without trying to eliminate any of its "messiness." On the one hand, this lets Ross avoid a problem that many other moral theorists face, which is that implications of their theories don't always match our considered moral beliefs. On the other, though, it means that Ross's theory doesn't help us much in deciding what to do, since it doesn't tell us how to resolve conflicts between prima facie obligations. Ross only tells us that we must exercise practical wisdom and hope we get it right. In deciding what to do in any concrete situation, he thought, we are always "taking a moral risk."[13]

How Much Does Morality Demand from Us?

Nonconsequentialists generally believe that utilitarianism presents too simple a picture of our moral world. In addition, they worry that act utilitarianism is excessively demanding. Stop and think about it: Isn't there something that you could be doing—for instance, volunteering at the local hospital or orphanage, collecting money for third-world development, helping the homeless—that would do more for the general good than what you are doing now or are planning to do tonight or tomorrow? Sure, working with the homeless might not bring you quite as much pleasure as what you would otherwise be doing, but if it would nonetheless

Ross's pluralistic ethical perspective differs from utilitarianism. Ross also rejected Kant's belief that our moral obligations are absolute and exceptionless.

maximize total happiness, then you are morally required to do it. However, by following this reasoning, you could end up working around the clock, sacrificing yourself for the greater good. This notion seems mistaken.

Most nonutilitarian philosophers, like Ross, believe that we have some obligation to promote the general welfare, but they typically view this obligation as less stringent than, for example, the obligation not to injure people. They see us as having a much stronger obligation to refrain from violating people's rights than to promote their happiness or well-being. From this perspective, a manufacturing company's obligation not to violate the Occupational Safety and Health Administration's (OSHA) regulations and thereby endanger the safety of its employees is stronger than its obligation to open up day-care facilities for their children, even though the cost of the two is the same. The company, in other words, has a stronger duty to respect its legal and contractual employment-related obligations than to promote its employees' happiness in other ways. Likewise, for a company to violate people's rights by despoiling the environment through the discharge of pollutants would be morally worse than for it to decide not to expand a job training program in the inner city, even if expanding the program would bring about more total good.

Different nonutilitarian philosophers may weigh these particular obligations differently, depending on their particular moral theory. But they typically believe that we have a stronger duty not to injure other people or to violate their rights in some other way than we do to assist people or otherwise promote their well-being. A utilitarian, concerned solely with what will maximize happiness, is less inclined to draw such a distinction.

Many moral philosophers draw a related distinction between actions that are morally required and charitable or **supererogatory actions**—that is, actions that would be good to do but not immoral not to do. Act utilitarianism doesn't make this distinction. Although we admire Mother Teresa and Albert Schweitzer for devoting their lives to doing good works among the poor, we see them as acting above and beyond the call of duty; we don't expect so much from ordinary people. Yet people who are not moral heroes or who fall short of sainthood may nonetheless be living morally satisfactory lives.

Nonutilitarian theorists see the distinction between morally obligatory actions and supererogatory actions not so much as a realistic concession to human weakness but as a necessary demarcation if we are to avoid becoming enslaved to the maximization of the general welfare. The idea here is that each of us should have a sphere in which we are free to pursue our own plans and goals, to carve out a distinctive life plan. These plans and goals are limited by various moral obligations, in particular by other people's rights, but the demands of morality are not all-encompassing.

Moral Rights

What, then, are rights, and what rights do people have? Broadly defined, a *right* is an entitlement to act or have others act in a certain way. The connection between rights and duties is that, generally speaking, if you have a right to do something, then someone else has a correlative duty to act in a certain way. For example, if you claim a "right" to drive, you mean that you are entitled to drive or that others should—that is, have a duty to—permit you to drive. Your right to drive under certain conditions is derived from our legal system and is thus considered a **legal right**.

In addition to rights that are derived from some specific legal system, we also have **moral rights**. Some of these moral rights derive from special relationships, roles, or circumstances in which we happen to be. For example, if Tom has an obligation to return Bob's car to him on Saturday morning, then Bob has a right to have Tom return his car. If I have agreed to water your plants while you are on vacation, you have a right to expect me to look after them in your absence. As a student, you have a right to be graded fairly, and so on.

Even more important are rights that don't rest on special relationships, roles, or situations. For example, the rights to life, free speech, and unhampered religious affiliation are widely accepted, not just as the entitlements of some specific political or legal system but as fundamental moral rights. More controversial, but often championed as moral rights, are the rights to medical care, decent housing, education, and work. Moral rights that are not the result

Nonutilitarian philosophers believe that we have a stronger obligation to respect people's rights and avoid injuring them than we do to promote their happiness.

Summary
Nonconsequentialists needn't be Kantians. W. D. Ross, for instance, rejects both Kantianism and utilitarianism, arguing that we are under a variety of distinct moral obligations. These are prima facie, meaning that any one of them may be outweighed in some circumstances by other, more important moral considerations. Nonconsequentialists believe that a duty to assist others and to promote total happiness is only one of a number of duties incumbent on us.

Human rights have four
important characteristics.

of particular roles, special relationships, or specific circumstances are called **human rights**. They have several important characteristics.

First, human rights are universal. For instance, if the right to life is a human right, as most of us believe it is, then everyone, everywhere and at all times, has that right. By contrast, there is nothing universal about your right that I keep my promise to help you move or about my right to drive 65 miles per hour on certain roads.

Second, and closely related, human rights are equal rights. If the right to free speech is a human right, then everyone has this right equally. No one has a greater right to free speech than anyone else. In contrast, your daughter has a greater right than do the daughters of other people to your emotional and financial support.

Third, human rights are not transferable, nor can they be relinquished. If we have a fundamental human right, we cannot give, lend, or sell it to someone else. We cannot waive it, and no one can take it from us. That is what is meant in the Declaration of Independence when certain rights—namely, life, liberty, and the pursuit of happiness—are described as "unalienable." By comparison, legal rights can be renounced or transferred, as when one party sells another a house or a business.

Fourth, human rights are natural rights, not in the sense that they can be derived from a study of human nature, but in the sense that they don't depend on human institutions the way legal rights do. If people have human rights, they have these rights simply because they are human beings. They don't have them because they live under a certain legal system. The law may attempt to protect human rights, to make them explicit and safe through codification, but the law isn't their source.

Philosophers distinguish
negative rights from positive
rights.

Rights, and in particular human rights, can be divided into two broad categories: negative rights and positive rights. **Negative rights** reflect the vital interests that human beings have in being free from outside interference. The rights guaranteed in the Bill of Rights—freedom of speech, assembly, religion, and so on—mostly fall within this category, as do the rights to freedom from injury and to privacy. Correlating with these are duties that we all have not to interfere with others' pursuit of these interests and activities. **Positive rights** reflect the vital interests that human beings have in receiving certain benefits. They are rights to have others provide us with certain goods, services, or opportunities. Today, positive rights often are taken to include the rights to education, medical care, equal job opportunity, comparable pay, and so on. Correlating with these are positive duties for appropriate parties to assist individuals in their pursuit of these interests.

Thus, a child's right to education implies not only that no one should interfere with the child's education but also that the necessary resources for that education ought to be provided. In the case of some positive rights—for example, the right to a decent standard of living, as proclaimed by the United Nations' 1948 Human Rights Charter—who exactly has the duty to provide the goods and services required to fulfill those rights is unclear. Also, interpreting a right as negative or positive is sometimes controversial. For example, is my right to liberty simply the right not to be interfered with as I live my own life, or does it also imply a duty on the part of others to provide me with the means to make the exercise of that liberty meaningful?

Moral rights provide grounds for making moral judgments that differ radically from act utilitarianism's grounds. For example, if workers have a moral right to be informed about potentially dangerous working conditions and to decide for themselves whether to undertake the work in question, then it would be wrong to violate this right—even if doing so would somehow promote the common good. Again, if employees have a right to compensation equal to what others receive for doing comparable work, then they cannot be paid less on the grounds that doing so would be economically efficient or in some other way result in greater overall utility.

Act utilitarianism, in effect, treats all such entitlements as subordinate to the general welfare. Thus, individuals are entitled to act in a certain way and entitled to have others allow or aid them to so act only insofar as acknowledging this right or entitlement achieves the greatest good. The assertion of moral rights, therefore, decisively sets nonconsequentialists apart from act utilitarians.

....

Summary
Nonconsequentialists typically emphasize moral rights— entitlements to act in a certain way or to have others act in a certain way. These rights can rest on special relationships and roles, or they can be general human rights. Rights can be negative, protecting us from outside interference, or they can be positive, requiring others to provide us with certain benefits or opportunities.

....

Nonconsequentialism in an Organizational Context

We have already looked at Kant's ethics in an organizational context, but, as we have seen, many nonconsequentialists (like Ross) are not Kantians, and their ideas also have important implications for moral decision making in business and nonbusiness organizations.

First, in its non-Kantian forms nonconsequentialism stresses that moral decision making involves the weighing of different moral factors and considerations. Unlike utilitarianism, nonconsequentialism doesn't reduce morality solely to the calculation of consequences; rather, it recognizes that an organization must usually take into account other equally important moral concerns. Theorists like Ross emphasize that, contrary to what Kant believed, there can often be rival and even conflicting moral demands on an organization. For example, obligations to employees, stockholders, and consumers may pull a corporation in different directions, and determining the organization's proper moral course may not be easy.

Second, nonconsequentialism acknowledges that the organization has its own legitimate goals to pursue. There are limits to the demands of morality, and an organization that fulfills its moral obligations and respects the relevant rights of individuals is morally free to advance whatever (morally permissible) ends it has—public service, profit, government administration, and so on. Contrary to utilitarianism, organizations and the people in them need not see themselves as under an overarching obligation to seek continually to enhance the general welfare.

Third, nonconsequentialism stresses the importance of moral rights. Moral rights, and in particular human rights, are a crucial factor in most moral deliberations, including those of organizations. Before it acts, any morally responsible business or nonbusiness organization must consider carefully how its actions will impinge on the rights of individuals—not just the rights of its members, such as stockholders and employees, but also the rights of others, such as consumers. Moral rights place distinct and firm constraints on what sorts of things an organization can do to fulfill its own ends.

Critical Inquiries of Nonconsequentialism

1. **How well justified are these nonconsequentialist principles and moral rights?** Ross maintained that we have immediate intuitive knowledge of the basic prima facie moral principles, and indeed it would seem absurd to try to deny that it is wrong to cause needless suffering or that making a promise imposes some obligation to keep it. Only someone the moral equivalent of colorblind could fail to see the truth of these statements; to reject them would seem as preposterous as denying some obvious fact of arithmetic—for example, that $12 + 4 = 16$. Likewise, it appears obvious—indeed, as Thomas Jefferson wrote, "self-evident"—that human beings have certain basic and inalienable rights.

    Yet we must be careful. What seems obvious, even self-evident, to one culture or at one time in human history may turn out to be not only not self-evident but actually false. That the Earth is flat and that heavier objects fall faster than lighter ones were two "truths" taken as obvious in former centuries. Likewise, the inferiority of women and of people of color was long taken for granted; this supposed fact was so obvious that it was hardly even commented on. The idea that people have a right to practice a religion that the majority "knows" to be false—or, indeed, to practice no religion whatsoever—would have seemed morally scandalous to many of our forebearers and is still not embraced in all countries around the world. Today many vegetarians eschew meat eating on moral grounds and contend that future generations will consider our treatment of animals, factory farming in particular, to be as morally benighted as slavery. So, what seems obvious, self-evident, or simple common sense may not be the most reliable guide to morally sound principles.

2. **Can nonconsequentialists satisfactorily handle conflicting rights and principles?** People today disagree among themselves about the correctness of certain moral principles. Claims of right, as we have seen, are often controversial. For example, do employees have a moral right to their jobs—an entitlement to be fired only with just cause? To some of us, it may seem obvious that they do; to others, perhaps not. And how are we to settle various conflicting claims of right? Jones, for instance, claims a right to her property, which she has

Summary
In an organizational context, nonconsequentialism (in its non-Kantian forms) stresses the plurality of moral considerations to be weighed. While emphasizing the importance of respecting moral rights, it acknowledges that morality has limits and that organizations have legitimate goals to pursue. Critics question whether (1) nonconsequentialist principles are adequately justified and whether (2) nonconsequentialism can satisfactorily handle conflicting rights and principles.

acquired honestly through her labors—that is, she claims a right to do with it as she wishes. Smith is ill and claims adequate medical care as a human right. Because he cannot afford the care himself, acknowledging his right will probably involve taxing people like Jones and thus limiting their property rights.

To sum up these two points: *First*, even moral principles that seem obvious or a matter of common sense have to be examined critically; and *second*, nonconsequentialists should not rest content until they find a way of resolving disputes among conflicting prima facie principles or rights. This isn't to suggest that nonconsequentialists cannot find deeper and theoretically more satisfactory ways of grounding moral claims and of handling disputes between them. The point to be underscored here is simply the necessity of doing so.

• • •

Utilitarianism Once More

Until now, our discussion of utilitarianism has focused on the classic and most straightforward version of it, namely, act utilitarianism. According to act utilitarianism, we have one and only one moral obligation, the maximization of happiness for everyone concerned, and every action is to be judged by this standard. But a different utilitarian approach, called rule utilitarianism, is relevant to the discussion of the moral concerns characteristic of nonconsequentialism—in particular, relevant to the nonconsequentialist's criticisms of act utilitarianism. The rule utilitarian would, in fact, agree with many of these criticisms. (Rule utilitarianism has been formulated in different ways, but this discussion follows the version defended by Richard Brandt.)

Rule utilitarianism maintains that the utilitarian standard should be applied not to individual actions but to moral codes as a whole. The rule utilitarian asks what moral code (that is, what set of moral rules) a society should adopt to maximize happiness. The principles that make up that code would then be the basis for distinguishing right actions from wrong actions. As Brandt explains:

> A rule-utilitarian thinks that right actions are the kind permitted by the moral code optimal for the society of which the agent is a member. An optimal code is one designed to maximize welfare or what is good (thus, utility). This leaves open the possibility that a particular right act by itself may not maximize benefit. . . . On the rule-utilitarian view, then, to find what is morally right or wrong we need to find which actions would be permitted by a moral system that is "optimal" for the agent's society.[14]

The "optimal" moral code doesn't refer to the set of rules that would do the most good if everyone conformed to them all the time. The meaning is more complex. The **optimal moral code** must take into account what rules can reasonably be taught and obeyed, as well as the costs of inculcating those rules in people. Recall from Chapter 1 that if a principle or rule is part of a person's moral code, then it will influence the person's behavior. The person will tend to follow that principle, to feel guilty when he or she doesn't live up to it, and to disapprove of others who fail to conform to it. Rule utilitarians must consider not just the benefits of having people motivated to act in certain ways but also the costs of instilling those motivations in them. As Brandt writes:

> The more intense and widespread an aversion to a certain sort of behavior, the less frequent the behavior is apt to be. But the more intense and widespread, the greater the cost of teaching the rule and keeping it alive, the greater the burden on the individual, and so on.[15]

Thus, the "optimality" of a moral code encompasses both the benefits of getting people to act in certain ways and the costs of bringing that about. Perfect compliance isn't a realistic goal. "Like the law," Brandt continues, "the optimal moral code normally will not produce 100 percent compliance with all its rules; that would be too costly."[16]

Some utilitarian thinkers in earlier centuries adopted or came close to adopting rule utilitarianism (although they did not use that term). For example, the 19th-century legal theorist John Austin wrote: "Utility [should] be the test of our conduct, ultimately, but not

The notion of an optimal moral code takes into account the difficulty of getting people to follow a given set of rules.

immediately. . . . Our rules [should] be fashioned on utility; our conduct, on our rules."[17] This accords well with the rule-utilitarian idea that we should apply the utilitarian standard only to the assessment of alternative moral codes; we should not try to apply it to individual actions. We should seek to determine the specific set of principles that would in fact best promote total happiness for society. Those are the rules we should promulgate, instill in ourselves, and teach to the next generation.

What Will the Optimal Code Look Like?

Rule utilitarians such as Brandt argue strenuously that the ideal or optimal moral code for a society will not be the single act-utilitarian command to maximize happiness. They contend that teaching people that their only obligation is to maximize happiness would not in fact maximize happiness.

First, people will make mistakes if, before they act, they try to calculate the consequences of each and every thing they might possibly do. *Second*, if all of us were act utilitarians, practices such as keeping promises and telling the truth would be rather shaky, because we could expect others to keep promises or tell the truth only when they believed that doing so would maximize happiness. *Third*, the act-utilitarian principle is too demanding, because it seems to imply that each person should continually be striving to promote total well-being.

Some of the principles of the optimal code would presumably be prima facie in Ross's sense—that is, capable of being overridden by other principles. Different principles would also have different moral weights. It would make sense, for example, to instill in people an aversion to killing that is stronger and deeper than the aversion to telling white lies. In addition, the ideal code would acknowledge moral rights. Teaching people to respect moral rights maximizes human welfare in the long run.

Many of the rules of the optimal code provide the sole basis for determining right and wrong. An action isn't necessarily wrong if it fails to maximize happiness; it's wrong only if it conflicts with the ideal moral code. Rule utilitarianism thus gets around many of the problems that plague act utilitarianism. At the same time, it provides a plausible basis for deciding which moral principles and rights we should acknowledge and how much weight we should attach to them. We try to determine those principles and rights that, generally adhered to, would best promote human happiness.

Still, rule utilitarianism has its critics. There are two common objections. *First*, act utilitarians maintain that a utilitarian who cares about happiness should be willing to violate rules in order to maximize happiness. Why make a fetish out of the rules?

Second, nonconsequentialists, while presumably viewing rule utilitarianism more favorably than act utilitarianism, still balk at seeing moral principles determined by their consequences. They contend, in particular, that rule utilitarians ultimately subordinate rights to utilitarian calculation and therefore fail to treat rights as fundamental and independent moral factors.

Rule utilitarians believe that the optimal moral code will not consist of just one rule—to maximize happiness.

Summary
Rule utilitarianism is a hybrid theory. It maintains that the correct principles of right and wrong are those that would maximize happiness if society adopted them. Rule utilitarianism applies the utilitarian standard not directly to individual actions but rather to the choice of the moral principles that are to guide individual action. Rule utilitarianism avoids many of the standard criticisms of act utilitarianism.

Critics of rule utilitarianism raise two objections.

• • •

Making Moral Decisions Together: A Practical Approach

Theoretical controversies permeate the subject of ethics, and as we have seen, philosophers have proposed rival ways of understanding right and wrong. These philosophical differences of perspective, emphasis, and theory are significant and can have profound practical consequences. This chapter has surveyed some of these issues, but obviously it cannot settle all of the questions that divide moral philosophers. Fortunately, however, many problems of business and organizational ethics can be intelligently discussed and even resolved by people whose fundamental moral theories differ (or who have not yet worked out their own moral ideas in some systematic way). This section discusses some important points to keep in mind when analyzing and discussing business ethics and offers, as a kind of model, one possible procedure for making moral decisions collaboratively.

Recall that moral judgments should be logical and based on facts and sound moral principles.

In the abstract, it might seem impossible for people to reach agreement on controversial ethical issues, given that ethical theories differ so much and that people themselves place moral value on different things. Yet, in practice, moral problems are rarely so intractable that open-minded and thoughtful people cannot, by discussing matters calmly, rationally, and thoroughly, make significant progress toward resolving them. Chapter 1 stressed that moral judgments should be logical, should be based on facts, and should appeal to sound moral principles. Bearing this in mind can often help, especially when various people are discussing an issue and proposing rival answers.

First, in any moral discussion, make sure that the participants agree about the relevant facts. Often, moral disputes hinge not on matters of moral principle but on differing assessments of what the facts of the situation are, what alternatives are open, or what the probable results of different courses of action will be. For instance, the directors of an international firm might acrimoniously dispute the moral permissibility of a new overseas investment. The conflict might appear to involve some fundamental clash of moral principles and perspectives when, in fact, it is the result of some underlying disagreement about the likely effects of the proposed investment on the lives of the local population. Until this factual disagreement is acknowledged and dealt with, little is apt to be resolved.

Second, once there is general agreement on factual matters, try to spell out the moral principles to which different people are, at least implicitly, appealing. Seeking to determine these principles will often help people clarify their own thinking enough to reach a solution. Sometimes they will agree on what moral principles are relevant and yet disagree over how to balance them. Identifying this discrepancy can be helpful. Bear in mind, too, that skepticism is in order when someone's moral stance on an issue appears to rest simply on a hunch or an intuition and cannot be related to some more general moral principle. As moral decision makers, we are seeking not only an answer to a moral issue but an answer that can be publicly defended, and the public defense of a moral judgment usually requires an appeal to general principle. By analogy, judges don't hand down judgments based simply on what strikes them as fair in a particular case. They must relate their decisions to general legal principles or statutes.

A reluctance to defend our moral decisions in public is almost always a warning sign. If we are unwilling to account for our actions publicly, chances are that we are doing something we cannot really justify morally. In addition, Kant's point that we must be willing to universalize our moral judgments is relevant here. We cannot sincerely endorse a principle if we are not willing to see it applied generally. Unfortunately, we occasionally do make judgments— for example, that Alfred's being late to work is a satisfactory reason for firing him—that rest on a principle we would be unwilling to apply to our own situations; hence the moral relevance of the familiar question: "How would you like it if . . . ?" Looking at an issue from the other person's point of view can cure moral myopia.

Obligations, Effects, Ideals

As a practical basis for discussing moral issues in organizations, it is useful to try to approach those issues in a way that is acceptable to individuals with differing moral viewpoints. We want to avoid presupposing the truth of one particular theoretical perspective. By emphasizing factors that are relevant to various theories, both consequentialist and nonconsequentialist, we can find some common ground on which moral decision making can proceed. Moral dialogue can thus take place in an objective and analytical way, even if the participants don't fully agree on all philosophical issues.

What factors or considerations, then, seem important from most ethical perspectives? Following Professor V. R. Ruggiero, we can identify three shared concerns.[18] The first is with *obligations*, that is, with the specific duties or moral responsibilities that we have in a given situation. Every significant human action—personal and professional—arises in the context of human relationships. These relationships, the roles we have assumed, and the expectations

Summary
Despite disagreements on controversial theoretical issues, people can make significant progress in resolving practical moral problems through open-minded and reflective discussion. One useful approach is to identify the (possibly conflicting) obligations, ideals, and effects in a given situation and then to determine where the emphasis should lie among these different considerations.

created by our previous actions can be the source of particular duties and rights. In addition, we are obligated to respect people's human rights. Obligations bind us. In their presence, morality requires us, at least prima facie, to do certain things and to avoid doing others. Even utilitarians can agree with this.

A second concern common to most ethical systems is with the *effects* of our actions. When reflecting on a possible course of action, one needs to take into account its likely results. Although nonconsequentialists maintain that things other than consequences or results can affect the rightness or wrongness of actions, few if any of them would ignore consequences entirely. Almost all nonconsequentialist theories place some moral weight on the results of our actions. Practically speaking, this means that in making a moral decision, we must identify all the interested parties and how they would be affected by the different courses of action open to us.

The third consideration relevant to most ethical perspectives is the impact of our actions on important *ideals*. An **ideal** is some morally significant goal, virtue, or notion of excellence worth striving for. Clearly, different cultures impart different ideals and, equally important, different ways of pursuing them. Our culture respects virtues such as generosity, courage, compassion, and loyalty, as well as more abstract ideals such as peace, justice, and equality. In addition to these moral ideals, there are institutional or organizational ideals: efficiency, product quality, customer service, and so forth. Does a particular act serve or violate these ideals? Both consequentialists and nonconsequentialists can agree that this is an important consideration in determining the moral quality of actions.

In isolating these three concerns common to almost all ethical systems—obligations, effects, and ideals—Ruggiero provided a kind of practical synthesis of consequentialist and nonconsequentialist thought that seems appropriate for our purposes. A useful approach to moral questions in an organizational context will therefore reflect these considerations: the obligations that derive from organizational relationships or are affected by organizational conduct, the ideals at stake, and the effects or consequences of alternative courses of action. Any action that honors obligations while respecting ideals and benefiting people can be presumed to be moral. An action that does not pass scrutiny in these respects will be morally suspect.

This view leads to what is essentially a two-step procedure for evaluating actions and making moral choices. The *first step* is to identify the important considerations involved: obligations, effects, and ideals. Accordingly, we should ask if any basic obligations are involved. If so, what are they and who has them? Who is affected by the action and how? How do these effects compare with those of the alternatives open to us? What ideals does the action respect or promote? What ideals does it neglect or thwart? The *second step* is to decide which of these considerations deserves emphasis. Sometimes the issue may be largely a matter of obligations; other times, some ideal may predominate; still other times, consideration of effects may be the overriding concern.

> A two-step approach to moral decision making is to identify the relevant obligations, ideals, and effects and then decide which consideration deserves the most emphasis.

If two or more obligations conflict, it is obvious that we should choose the stronger one, and when two or more ideals conflict, or when ideals conflict with obligations, we should obviously honor the more important one. Similarly, when rival actions have different results, we should prefer the action that produces the greater good or the lesser harm. But in real-world situations, deciding these matters is often difficult, and there is no easy way of balancing obligations, effects, and ideals when these considerations pull in different directions. The fact is that we have no sure procedure for making such comparative determinations, which involve assessing worth and assigning relative priorities to our assessments. In large part, the chapters that follow attempt to sort out the values and principles embedded in the tangled web of frequently subtle, ill-defined problems we meet in business and organizational life. It is hoped that examining these issues will help you (1) identify the obligations, effects, and ideals involved in specific moral issues and (2) decide where the emphasis should lie among the competing considerations.

Study Corner

Key Terms and Concepts

act utilitarianism

business egoism

categorical imperative

consequentialist theories

eminent domain

ethical egoism

formula of humanity

good will

hedonism

human rights

hypothetical imperative

ideal

legal rights

maxim

moral rights

moral worth

negative rights

nonconsequentialist theories

normative theories

optimal moral code

positive rights

prima facie obligations

psychological egoism

rule utilitarianism

supererogatory actions

universal acceptability

universal law

utilitarianism

....

Points to Review

- consequentialist versus nonconsequentialist normative theories (pp. 35–36)

- the difference between egoism as an ethical theory and egoism as a psychological theory (pp. 36–37)

- four problems with egoism (pp. 37–38)

- Bentham's and Mill's differing views of pleasure (p. 39)

- six points about utilitarianism (pp. 40–41)

- three features of utilitarianism in an organizational context (p. 41)

- three critical inquiries of utilitarianism (pp. 41–43)

- the deathbed-promise example (pp. 42–43)

- business as combining self-interest and social good (or egoism and utilitarianism) (pp. 43–44)

- the convenience store owner and acting from a sense of duty (p. 44)

- Martin's promise as an illustration of the categorical imperative (p. 45)

- hypothetical imperatives versus the categorical imperative (p. 46)

- two further formulations of the categorical imperative (pp. 47–48)

- three features of Kant's ethics in an organizational context (p. 47)

- three critical inquiries of Kant's ethics (pp. 47–49)

- how Ross's theory differs from utilitarianism and from Kant's categorical imperative (pp. 49–50)

- four important characteristics of human rights (p. 52)

- the difference between negative and positive rights (p. 52)

- how rule utilitarianism differs from act utilitarianism (pp. 54–55)

- what rules are included in the optimal moral code (p. 55)

- two objections to rule utilitarianism (p. 55)

- two points drawn from Chapter 1 that can help moral discussions (p. 56)

- two-step procedure for morally evaluating actions and choices (p. 57)

....

For Further Reflection

1. What value, if any, do you see in business students studying the basics of ethical theory?

2. Which normative theory or general approach to ethics do you find the most plausible or attractive, and why?

3. Can people who disagree about normative ethical theory still reach agreement on practical ethical questions in the business world? If so, how?

Case 2.1
A Day at the Zoo

A Trip to the Zoo Is Often the Highlight of a Child's Summer Vacation. And if the zoo visit is a class field trip, a chance to climb on a yellow bus and escape the classroom for a day, that's better still. Many adults enjoy zoos, too, and it's by no means unusual to see them there without children in tow.

However, hard questions have been asked about the morality of keeping wild animals in captivity for our enjoyment. In his essay "Against Zoos," philosopher Dale Jamieson starts with a simple premise, namely, that there is a presumption against caging wild animals. "If we are justified in keeping animals in zoos," Jamieson writes, "it must be because there are some important benefits that can be obtained only by doing so."[19] In other words, we should assume that zoos are guilty of moral wrongdoing unless they can prove themselves innocent through showing that the end—the good they do in the world—justifies the means—locking animals in cages.

The premise seems to be a plausible one. After all, animals have evolved in live in specific environments. They have instinctive ways of behaving that are adapted to those environments, which for some animals includes roaming over wide areas. Elephants, who are among the most popular zoo exhibits, may travel up to 30 miles per day in the wild. Many animals show signs of stress in captivity, like tigers who pace their cages incessantly, and it's reasonable to assume that this is connected to their not being able to act on their instincts. We might also find the idea of animals not being able to lead lives that reflect their "true natures" morally troubling, even apart from any concerns about whether the animals themselves are content.

Zoos' defenders would reply that they do much good. For example, zoos claim to conserve species that might otherwise go extinct. One of the biggest successes in this area is the Arabian oryx, an antelope native to the Middle East. The wild oryx was hunted to extinction in the 1970s. However, American zoos had bred the oryx in captivity, and modest numbers have now been reintroduced into their native habitat.

Zoos also provide educational programming, which is the reason that schools can justify class trips. They conduct and support scientific research, both in the zoos themselves and in animals' native habitats. And, of course, many people greatly enjoy them.

Zoos' defenders might observe that life in the wild is often not very pleasant or safe. For instance, many animals die from predation, which is a polite way of saying that they're eaten by other animals. There is a reason that the poet Alfred, Lord Tennyson described nature as "red in tooth and claw." (There is a reason to write Tennyson's name in this odd-looking way, too, which is that he was made a baron.) Animals may starve to death or die of thirst, especially as climate change alters their habitats. And when wild animals are sick or injured there is usually no veterinarian to tend them.

Given this, zoos' defenders might add, the lives of many zoo animals are definitely safer and are probably more comfortable than those of their wild cousins. At a modern, well-funded zoo, animals' enclosures are designed to resemble their natural habitats and to offer them considerable space. Animals receive state of the art medical care. They are protected against zoogoers who might try to torment them by, for example, throwing things at them. (In 2007, a tiger at the San Francisco Zoo escaped its enclosure and mauled three young men who had been seen harassing her, killing one.)

Unfortunately, not all zoos are modern or well funded. Most are not even accredited. To be accredited, zoos (like colleges and universities) must show that they operate in accordance with best practices. The Association of Zoos and Aquariums (AZA) is the major accrediting body for zoos and aquariums in the United States. However, only about 10 percent of zoos or wild animal exhibitors licensed by the U.S. Dept. of Agriculture are AZA-accredited. Many of these are for-profit, whereas 89 percent of accredited zoos are public or nonprofit.[20] Some of these unaccredited zoos offer visitors the chance to hold and have their picture taken with wild animals. Experts say that this is usually a miserable experience for the animals themselves. The Greater Wynnewood Exotic Animal Park, familiar to fans of the Netflix series *Tiger King*, was an example of an unaccredited facility.

Jamieson remains skeptical that zoos produce great enough benefits to overcome the presumption against keeping animals in captivity. He casts doubt on how valuable the educational programming or research that zoos perform is, noting research that shows that people who spend time in nature themselves are much more knowledgeable about animals than those who go to zoos. He also argues that the conservation work done by zoos is hampered by the fact that many of their animals are genetically inbred, making them less than ideal candidates for release into the wild.

Zoos nevertheless retain their popularity. The AZA reports that the facilities it accredits have 183 million visitors a year in the United States alone, more than attend MLB, NFL, NBA, and NHL games combined.[21] They also promote the fact that 79 percent of visitors "feel better about companies that support wildlife conservation at zoos and aquariums" and that 66 percent "are more likely to buy products and services from those companies."

....
Discussion Questions
....

1. How do we trade off the pleasure that many of us take in watching wild animals up close against their displeasure at a life spent in captivity? Does their displeasure matter at all, morally speaking? Does an animal's pain or suffering matter less than an equal amount of pain or suffering experienced by a human?

2. How would utilitarians approach the question of whether zoos ought to be permitted? How might nonconsequentialists, for example Kant or Ross, approach it differently?

3. Given that zoos do exist, how would an act utilitarian think through whether it's morally acceptable to visit? How would a rule utilitarian approach this question differently? Would their conclusion be the same?

4. How do zoos differ from the situation described in "The Ones Who Walk Away from Omelas"? How are they similar?

5. Is it wrong to treat nonhuman animals merely as means? Does it matter what sort of animal it is (e.g., an oyster versus a cow)?

6. Should we think of nonhuman animals as having negative or positive rights? If the pleasure that we would get from eating an animal adds up to ten units, say, and the pain that this would cause the animal is only three units, then are we justified in eating it? Or could the animal have a right not to be eaten that "trumps" this utilitarian calculation? Again, does it matter what sort of animal it is?

7. Should zoos that cannot meet the animal welfare standards of groups like the AZA be closed, even though this will greatly reduce people's opportunities to see wild animals?

Case 2.2
The Ford Pinto

There Was a Time When the "Made in Japan" Label Brought a predictable smirk of superiority to the face of most Americans. The quality of most Japanese products usually was as low as their price. In fact, few imports could match their domestic counterparts, the proud products of Yankee know-how. But by the late 1960s, an invasion of foreign-made goods chiseled a few worry lines into the countenance of U.S. industry. In Detroit, worry was fast fading to panic as the Japanese, not to mention the Germans, began to gobble up more and more of the subcompact auto market.

Never one to take a backseat to the competition, Ford Motor Company decided to meet the threat from abroad head-on. In 1968, Ford executives decided to produce the Pinto. Known inside the company as "Lee's car," after Ford president Lee Iacocca, the Pinto was to weigh no more than 2,000 pounds and cost no more than $2,000.[22]

Eager to have its subcompact ready for the 1971 model year, Ford decided to compress the normal drafting-board-to-showroom time of about three-and-a-half years into two. The compressed schedule meant that any design changes typically made before production-line tooling would have to be made during it.

Before producing the Pinto, Ford crash-tested various prototypes, in part to learn whether they met a safety standard proposed by the National Highway Traffic Safety Administration (NHTSA) to reduce fires from traffic collisions. This standard would have required that by 1972 all new autos would be able to withstand a rear-end impact of 20 miles per hour without fuel loss and that by 1973 they be able to withstand an impact of 30 miles per hour. The prototypes all failed the 20-miles-per-hour test.

In 1970, Ford crash-tested the Pinto itself, and the result was the same: ruptured gas tanks and dangerous leaks. In collisions, the neck of the tank, which is where gas is put in, could easily break off. At the same time, the tank itself would be driven onto various mounting bolts, which could poke through it. The only Pintos to pass the test had been modified in some way—for example, with a rubber bladder in the gas tank or a piece of steel between the tank and the rear bumper.

Thus, Ford knew that the Pinto represented a serious fire hazard when struck from the rear, even in low-speed collisions. Ford officials faced a decision. Should they go ahead with the existing design, thereby meeting the production timetable but possibly jeopardizing consumer safety? Or should they delay production of the Pinto by redesigning the gas tank to make it safer and thus concede another year of subcompact dominance to foreign companies? Ford not only pushed ahead with the original design but also stuck to it for the next six years.

What explains Ford's decision? The evidence suggests that Ford relied, at least in part, on cost–benefit reasoning, which is an analysis in monetary terms of the expected costs and benefits of doing something. There were various ways of making the Pinto's gas tank safer. Although the estimated price of these safety improvements ranged from only $5 to $8 per vehicle, Ford evidently reasoned that the increased cost outweighed the benefits of a new tank design.

How exactly did Ford reach that conclusion? We don't know for sure, but an internal report, "Fatalities Associated with Crash-Induced Fuel Leakage and Fires," reveals the cost–benefit reasoning that the company used in cases like this. This report was not written with the

Pinto in mind; rather, it concerns fuel leakage in rollover accidents (not rear-end collisions), and its computations applied to all Ford vehicles, not just the Pinto. Nevertheless, it illustrates the type of reasoning that was probably used in the Pinto case.

In the "Fatalities" report, Ford engineers estimated the cost of technical improvements that would prevent gas tanks from leaking in rollover accidents to be $11 per vehicle. The authors go on to discuss various estimates of the number of people killed by fires from car rollovers before settling on the relatively low figure of 180 deaths per year. But given that number, how can the value of those individuals' lives be gauged? Can a dollars-and-cents figure be assigned to a human being? NHTSA thought so. In 1972, it estimated that society loses $200,725 every time a person is killed in an auto accident (adjusted for inflation, today's figure would, of course, be considerably higher). It broke down the costs as follows:

Future productivity losses	
Direct	$132,000
Indirect	41,300
Medical costs	
Hospital	700
Other	425
Property damage	1,500
Insurance administration	4,700
Legal and court expenses	3,000
Employer losses	1,000
Victim's pain and suffering	10,000
Funeral	900
Assets (lost consumption)	5,000
Miscellaneous accident costs	200
Total per fatality	$200,725

Putting the NHTSA figures together with other statistical studies, the Ford report arrived at the following overall assessment of costs and benefits:

Benefits

Savings: 180 burn deaths, 180 serious burn injuries, 2,100 burned vehicles

Unit cost: $200,000 per death, $67,000 per injury, $700 per vehicle

Total benefit: (180 × $200,000) + (180 × $67,000) + (2,100 × $700) = $49.5 million

Costs

Sales: 11 million cars, 1.5 million light trucks

Unit cost: $11 per car, $11 per truck

Total cost: 12.5 million × $11 = $137.5 million

Thus, the costs of the suggested safety improvements outweighed their benefits, and the "Fatalities" report accordingly recommended against any improvements—a recommendation that Ford followed.

Likewise, in the Pinto case, Ford's management, whatever its exact reasoning, decided to stick with the original design and not upgrade the Pinto's fuel tank, despite the test results reported by its engineers. Here is the aftermath of Ford's decision:

- Between 1971 and 1978, the Pinto was responsible for a number of fire-related deaths. Ford puts the figure at 23; its critics say the figure is closer to 500. According to the sworn testimony of Ford engineers, 95 percent of the fatalities would have survived if Ford had located the fuel tank over the axle (as it had done on its Capri automobiles).

- NHTSA finally adopted a 30-miles-per-hour collision standard in 1976. The Pinto then acquired a rupture-proof fuel tank. In 1978, Ford was obliged to recall all 1971–1976 Pintos for fuel-tank modifications.

- Between 1971 and 1978, approximately fifty lawsuits were brought against Ford in connection with rear-end accidents in the Pinto. In the Richard Grimshaw case, in addition to awarding over $3 million in compensatory damages to the victims of a Pinto crash, the jury awarded a landmark $125 million in punitive damages against Ford (later reduced by the judge to $3.5 million).

- On August 10, 1978, the 1973 Ford Pinto that eighteen-year-old Judy Ulrich, her sixteen-year-old sister Lynn, and their eighteen-year-old cousin Donna were riding in was struck from the rear by a van near Elkhart, Indiana. The gas tank of the Pinto exploded on impact. In the fire that resulted, the three teenagers were burned to death. Ford was charged with criminal homicide. The judge in the case advised jurors that Ford should be convicted if it had clearly disregarded the harm that might result from its actions, and that disregard represented a substantial deviation from acceptable standards of conduct. On March 13, 1980, the jury found Ford not guilty of criminal homicide.

For its part, Ford has always denied that the Pinto is unsafe compared with other cars of its type and era. The company also points out that in every model year, the Pinto met or surpassed the government's own standards. But what the company doesn't say is that successful lobbying by it and its industry associates was responsible for delaying for seven years the adoption of any NHTSA crash standard. Furthermore, Ford's critics claim that there were more than forty European and Japanese models in the Pinto price and weight range with safer gas-tank position. "Ford made an extremely irresponsible decision," concludes auto safety expert Byron Bloch, "when they placed such a weak tank in such a ridiculous location in such a soft rear end."

Has the automobile industry learned a lesson from Ford's experience with the Pinto? Many people would probably answer, yes, carmakers are more concerned about safety these days. That's one reason it shocked the nation to learn in 2014 that General Motors had known for years that defective ignition switches on some of its models prevent their airbags from deploying in crashes. (The bags need to draw on the car's power system.) And yet—for reasons that are still unclear—the company did nothing about the problem, ignoring possible fixes proposed by its engineers and telling customers and accident victims that there was no evidence of a flaw. According to GM, the faulty switches have led to thirteen deaths, but an independent review of federal crash data puts the number of fatalities at 303.

··
Discussion Questions
··

1. What moral issues does the Pinto case raise?

2. Suppose Ford officials were asked to justify their decision. What moral principles do you think they would invoke? Assess Ford's handling of the Pinto from the perspective of each of the moral theories discussed in this chapter.

3. Utilitarians would say that jeopardizing motorists doesn't by itself make Ford's action morally objectionable. The only morally relevant matter is whether Ford gave equal consideration to the interests of each affected party. Do you think Ford did this?

4. Is cost–benefit analysis a legitimate tool? What role, if any, should it play in moral deliberation? Critically assess the example of cost–benefit analysis given in the case study. Is there anything unsatisfactory about it? Could it have been improved upon in some way?

5. Speculate about Kant's response to the idea of placing a monetary value on a human life. Is doing so ever morally legitimate?

6. What responsibilities to its customers do you think Ford had? What are the most important moral rights, if any, operating in the Pinto case?

7. Would it have made a moral difference if the savings resulting from not improving the Pinto gas tank had been passed on to Ford's customers? Could a rational customer have chosen to save a few dollars and risk having the more dangerous gas tank? What if Ford had told potential customers about its decision?

8. The maxim of Ford's action might be stated thus: "When the cost of a safety improvement would hurt the bottom line, it's all

Some consumers knew their Pintos were dangerous.

right not to make it." Can this maxim be universalized? Does it treat humans as ends in themselves? Would manufacturers be willing to abide by it if the positions were reversed and they were in the role of consumers?

9. Should Ford have been found guilty of criminal homicide in the Ulrich case?

10. Are carmakers these days concerned enough about safety? Why do you think GM failed to address the ignition switch problem?

11. Is it wrong for business to sell a product that isn't as safe as it could be, given current technology? Is it wrong to sell a vehicle that is less safe than competing products on the market? Are there limits to how far automakers must go in the name of safety?

Case 2.3
Blood for Sale

Sol Levin Was a Successful Stockbroker in Tampa, Florida, When He recognized the potentially profitable market for safe and uncontaminated blood and, with some colleagues, founded Plasma International. Not everybody is willing to make money by selling their own blood, and in the beginning Plasma International bought blood from people addicted to drugs and alcohol. Although innovative marketing increased Plasma International's sales dramatically, several cases of hepatitis were reported in recipients. The company then began looking for new sources of blood.[23]

Plasma International searched worldwide and, with the advice of a qualified team of medical consultants, did extensive testing. Eventually, they found that the blood profiles of several rural West African tribes made them ideal prospective donors. After negotiations with the local government, Plasma International signed an agreement with several tribal chieftains to purchase blood.

Business went smoothly and profitably for Plasma International until a Tampa paper charged that Plasma was purchasing blood for as little as fifteen cents a pint and then reselling it to hospitals in the United States and South America for $25 per pint. After one recent disaster, the newspaper alleged, Plasma International had sold 10,000 pints, netting nearly a quarter of a million dollars.

The newspaper story stirred up controversy in Tampa, but the existence of commercialized blood marketing systems in the United States is nothing new. Approximately half the blood and plasma obtained in the United States is bought and sold like any other commodity. By contrast, the National Health Service in Great Britain relies entirely on a voluntary system of blood donation. Blood is neither bought nor sold. It is available to anyone who needs it without charge or obligation, and donors gain no preference over nondonors.

In an important study, economist Richard Titmuss showed that the British system works better than the American system in terms of economic and administrative efficiency, price, and blood quality. The commercialized blood market, Titmuss argued, is wasteful of blood and plagued by shortages. In the United States, bureaucratization, paperwork, and administrative overhead result in a cost per unit of blood that is five to fifteen times higher than it is in Great Britain. Hemophiliacs, in particular, are disadvantaged by the U.S. system and have enormous bills to pay. In addition, commercial markets are much more likely to distribute contaminated blood.

Titmuss also argued that the existence of a commercialized system discourages voluntary donors. People are less apt to give blood if they know that others are selling it. Psychologists have found similar conflicts between financial incentives and moral or altruistic conduct in other areas.[24] Philosopher Peter Singer has elaborated on this point in the case of blood:

> If blood is a commodity with a price, to give blood means merely to save someone money. Blood has a cash value of a certain number of dollars, and the importance of the gift will vary with the wealth of the recipient. If blood cannot be bought, however, the gift's value depends upon the need of the recipient. Often, it will be worth life itself. Under these circumstances blood becomes a very special kind of gift, and giving it means providing for strangers, without hope of reward, something they cannot buy and without which they may die. The gift relates strangers in a manner that is not possible when blood is a commodity.
>
> This may sound like a philosopher's abstraction, far removed from the thoughts of ordinary people. On the contrary, it is an idea spontaneously expressed by British donors in response to Titmuss's questionnaire. As one woman, a machine operator, wrote in reply to the question why she first decided to become a blood donor: "You can't get blood from supermarkets and chain stores. People themselves must come forward; sick people can't get out of bed to ask you for a pint to save their life, so I came forward in hopes to help somebody who needs blood."
>
> The implication of this answer, and others like it, is that even if the formal right to give blood can coexist with commercialized blood banks, the respondent's action would have lost much of its significance to her, and the blood would probably not have been given at all. When blood is a commodity, and can be purchased if it is not given, altruism becomes unnecessary, and so loosens the bonds that can otherwise exist between strangers in a community. The existence of a market in blood does not threaten the formal right to give blood, but it does away with the right to give blood which cannot be bought, has no cash value, and must be given freely if it is to be obtained at all. If there is such a right, it is incompatible with the right to sell blood, and we cannot avoid violating one of these rights when we grant the other.[25]

Both Titmuss and Singer believe that the weakening of the spirit of altruism in this sphere has important repercussions. It marks, they think, the increasing commercialization of our lives and makes similar changes in attitude, motive, and relationships more likely in other fields. And,

indeed, the introduction of money often changes relationships. Day-care centers, for example, sometimes have a problem with parents showing up late to collect their children, forcing teachers to stay after closing time. To solve the problem, economists recommend charging parents a fee for being tardy. However, when this solution was tested at ten day-care centers in Israel, the result was that the number of late pick-ups doubled.[26] Whereas before the parents had viewed themselves as having a responsibility to the hard-working staff to pick up their children on time and felt guilty about failing to do so, now they saw the matter in purely commercial terms, a service to be purchased for a fee.

Update

Dr. Arthur Matas, a prominent kidney-transplant surgeon, is pushing for one change that it's doubtful either Titmuss or Singer would like. Lately, he's been traveling the United States making the case for lifting the legal ban on kidney sales. That ban was imposed in 1984 by an outraged Congress after a Virginia physician had proposed buying kidneys from poor people and selling them to the highest bidder. By contrast, Dr. Matas isn't trying to make money. He would like the government to handle kidney sales, and the kidneys to go to whoever is at the top of the current waiting list, whether the patient is rich or poor. And that list grows longer every year as the gap continues to widen—it's now nearly five to one—between patients in need and the number of kidneys available from either living or deceased donors.

With eligible patients often waiting for five or six years, more and more people are taking Dr. Matas seriously, but many experts still balk at the idea of organ sales. One of them is Dr. Francis Delmonico, a professor at Harvard University and president of the network that runs the nation's organ-distribution system. He worries that Dr. Matas's plan would exploit the poor and vulnerable, that it would cause altruistic kidney donations to wither, and that wealthy patients would manage to find a way around a regulated market to get a kidney faster.[27]

Yet Matas is not alone. Another proponent of allowing kidney donors to sell their organs is the philosopher James Stacey Taylor, in his book *Stakes and Kidneys: Why Markets in Human Body Parts Are Morally Imperative.*[28] Among other points, he notes that making it impossible for people to sell organs doesn't necessarily mean that there will be more altruistic behavior, since some people who would have sold their organs if this were possible would have used the money they gained altruistically. He also observes that most voluntary kidney organ donors are White and that it is easier for a donor to match with a recipient of the same race. A system that relies purely on voluntary donations may therefore have the inadvertent consequence that fewer organs are available for people of color.

While Dr. Delmonico's worries about a market for organs should be taken seriously, it's worth noting that the wealthy have an easier time getting organs even under the current system. The late Apple CEO Steve Jobs, who was a resident of California, received a liver transplant (for which he was arguably a poor candidate) in Tennessee. Only someone with considerable wealth would be able to satisfy the requirements for getting a transplant from across the country, like being able to arrive there within just a few hours.[29] And while it's likely true that it's mostly people living in hardship who would choose to sell a kidney, whether making this illegal would make them better off is at least debatable. Advocates of a market-based approach like Taylor would be quick to point out that if we take an opportunity for making money away from people in need while doing nothing else to help them then we may only be leaving them worse off.

Discussion Questions

1. Is Sol Levin running a business "just like any other business," or is his company open to moral criticism? Defend your answer by appeal to moral principle.

2. Did Plasma International strike a fair bargain with the West Africans who supplied their blood to the company? Or is Plasma guilty of exploiting them in some way? Explain your answer.

3. What are the contrasting ideals of the British and U.S. blood systems? Which system, in your opinion, better promotes human freedom and respect for people? Which system better promotes the supply of blood?

4. Examine the pros and cons of commercial transactions in blood from the egoistic, the utilitarian, and the Kantian perspectives.

5. Are Titmuss and Singer correct to suggest that the buying and selling of blood reduces altruism? Does knowing that you can sell your blood (and that others are selling theirs) make you less inclined to donate your blood?

6. Singer suggests that although the right to sell blood doesn't threaten the formal right to give blood, it is incompatible with "the right to give blood, which cannot be bought, which has no cash value, and must be given freely if it is to be obtained at all." Assess that idea. Is there such a right?

7. Many believe that commercialization is increasing in all areas of modern life. If so, is it something to be applauded or condemned? Is it wrong to treat certain things—such as human organs—as commodities?

8. Do you believe that we have a moral duty to donate blood? If so, why and under what circumstances? If not, why not?

9. Do bans on selling blood or organs violate our right to control our own bodies?

Chapter 3

Justice and Economic Distribution

Learning Objectives

After completing this chapter, you should be able to:

1. Explain how different thinkers have taken the concept of justice to be related to fairness, equality, rights, and desert.
2. Present and evaluate arguments for and criticisms of utilitarian, libertarian, and Rawlsian approaches to thinking about distributive justice.
3. Apply these different theories of distributive justice to different challenges that societies face in order to say how their proponents would address these challenges.

Introduction

It's Good To Be a CEO. According to the Economic Policy Institute, compensation for CEOs at the largest 350 U.S. corporations averaged $27.8 million in 2021, an 11.1 percent increase over 2020. (This includes compensation in both cash and stocks.) Adjusted for inflation, this represents an increase of over 1,460% since 1978. By their calculation, the average CEO in this group made 399 times as much as a typical worker in 2021, a new high.[1]

We know that there's a wide gulf between the earnings of the Americans with the highest and lowest incomes. But is there too much economic inequality? Most Americans—61 percent, in fact—say yes, according to a 2020 poll by the Pew Research Center.[2] How people answered this question correlated with their partisan identity: 78 percent of those who call themselves Democrats or "lean" toward that party said that there is too much inequality in the United States. Only 41 percent of those who belong to or lean toward the Republican party said the same.

If inequality is a problem, it's growing larger. According to the U.S. Census Bureau, inequality in American household incomes increased by 1.2 percent from 2020 to 2021.[3] This statement raises an interesting question: how can we quantify inequality?

Economists measure inequality using a number known as the **Gini coefficient** (or Gini index), which is named after the Italian statistician Corrado Gini (1884–1965). The easiest way to explain how this number is derived is to start with a story and then move to a picture.

> The average CEO at one of America's 350 largest corporations made 399 times as much as a typical worker in 2021, a new high.

Imagine that you're facing a group of ten people standing side by side. They're standing in order based on the size of their incomes, with whoever has the lowest income on your left and whoever has the highest income on your right. You know how much each one makes. Suppose that you also know that taken together their incomes add up to $1 million per year.

Now imagine that you're standing directly in front of the first of these people, the one farthest to your left and so the one whose income is lowest. If it happened that everyone in the group had the same income, which would mean that what order they were in didn't matter, then this individual would make $100,000. They all would. But suppose that's not the case. Rather, the first person's income is only $10,000. This means that the 10 percent of the population with the lowest incomes earned only 1 percent of the $1 million total. Now suppose that you move to the right and stand in front of the second person, who makes $20,000. When you add this to the $10,000 made by the first individual, you learn that the lowest-earning 20 percent of the group makes $30,000, 3 percent of the group's total income. You might keep moving down the line, computing a new cumulative total each time that you stand in front of a new person. This would tell you how much of the group's total $1 million income goes to the lowest-earning 30 percent, 40 percent, 50 percent, and so on. Imagine now that the last person in the group makes $500,000 per year. That means that when you're in front of the ninth person you'll calculate that the lowest-earning 90 percent of the population accounts for $500,000—only 50 percent of the total.

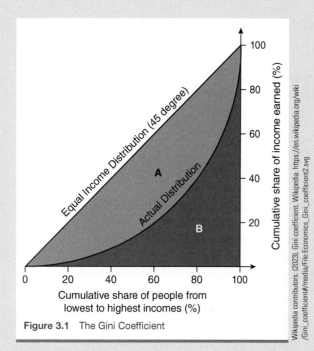

Figure 3.1 The Gini Coefficient

Figure 3.1 depicts exactly this sort of procedure, carried out at the level of an entire society. The horizontal axis represents the population, from whoever has the lowest income to whoever has the highest. Imagine moving along that axis in small increments—1/100th of the total distance at a time. At the first stop, you determine how much of the society's total income goes to the lowest-earning 1 percent. Say that the answer is .1 percent of the total—1/1000th. So, you make a dot 1/100th of the way along the horizontal axis and 1/1000th of the way up the vertical axis. Then you move another tiny step to the right and do the same again. Each dot will be higher than the one before, since a cumulative total is always growing larger, but how much higher depends on the society's level of income equality. If the members of this society have roughly equal incomes, then each new dot will be almost as far above the one before it as it is to the right. If there's significant inequality, with just a few people having incomes much higher than everyone else's, then there won't be much vertical change in the dots until you get very close to the right end of the horizontal axis, when they will suddenly shoot up rapidly. The curve will then look like a hockey stick. (The last dot will necessarily be at the top of the vertical axis, since by definition the cumulative sum of each individual's income must equal the society's total.)

Figure 3.1 pictures the outcome of this operation, with the curve that separates regions A and B simply the product of "connecting the dots." The curve will look different for every society. In a society where people's incomes are more equal than they are in the one pictured, the curve will come closer to the 45 percent degree line that represents a perfectly equal income distribution. In a less equal society, the curve will stay closer to the horizontal axis until the end and then rise rapidly. If we did this figure for a more equal society, therefore, region A would be smaller

than pictured here. For a society with greater inequality, region A would be larger. This suggests that we can represent the level of inequality in a society by asking what portion of the area of the triangle that's formed by regions A and B together is occupied by region A. And this is how we calculate the Gini coefficient:

Area A/(Area A + Area B)

The Gini coefficient will be smaller for societies where the income distribution is more equal, larger for societies with higher levels of inequality. (Sometimes the Gini coefficient is given as a number between 0 and 1, where 0 would indicate complete equality, and sometimes it's multiplied by 100 and given as a percentage.)

What the Census Bureau found is that from 2020 to 2021 the Gini coefficient in the United States rose from 0.488 to 0.494. But without context, those are just numbers. So, let's look at how those values position the United States relative to other countries. According to the World Bank, a Gini coefficient of 0.494 puts the United States in proximity to countries like Zimbabwe (0.503 in 2019) and Costa Rica (0.487 in 2021).[4] The highest Gini number in the World Bank database is South Africa's (0.630 in 2014). The lowest is the Slovak Republic's (0.232 in 2019). If you organize the Gini indices of all the countries in the world from highest to lowest, the United States falls roughly in the middle. However, we do have more income inequality than most of the countries that we usually think of as being most similar to the United States, namely highly developed democracies. A coefficient of 0.494 is considerably higher than Canada's 0.325 (2018), the United Kingdom's 0.326 (2020), Japan's 0.329 (2013), or Australia's 0.343 (2019)—not to mention Sweden's 0.289 (2020) or Norway's 0.277 (2019)!

To be fair, some of these comparisons may be misleading. A country's Gini co-efficient will vary a little depending on exactly how it's calculated—for example, whether the income figures are for individuals or households, whether the incomes used include transfer payments from government programs like Temporary Assistance for Needy Families (TANF) or the Supplemental Nutrition Assistance Program (SNAP, formerly known as food stamps), and whether pre- or post-tax income is used. The Congressional Budget Office (CBO) calculates Gini coefficients using several different approaches. In their most recent report, which covers 2019, the Gini coefficients that they offered for the United States ranged from almost 0.600, when pre-tax earnings from sources other than government transfer programs were included, to just over 0.400 for income after transfer payments and taxes.[5] Still, this shows that the United States has significantly more income inequality than other highly developed democracies regardless of which precise calculation we use.

The same CBO report also provides additional 2019 data that helps to illustrate both how transfer payments and taxes serve to reduce income inequality and how much still remains even after they're taken into account.

Average Incomes of Americans Before and After Transfer Payments and Income Taxes (2019)

	Average Income Before Transfer Payments and Income Taxes	Average Income After Transfer Payments and Income Taxes
Bottom 20%	$23,800	$38,900
Middle 20%	$81,800	$74,800
Top 20%	$332,100	$252,100
Top 1%	$2 million	$1.4 million
Top 0.01%	$43 million	$30 million

If we had figures for the top 0.001 percent, then no doubt their average incomes would be far above $30 million even after income taxes were taken into account. Similarly, if we had figures for the bottom 1 percent, let alone the bottom 0.01 percent, their average incomes would be much lower than $38,900.

It might be obvious that government transfer payments boost the incomes of those on the bottom rungs of the economic ladder, but it's worth pausing for a moment to think about how income taxes affect income inequality. Economists describe taxes as proportional when people pay the same portion of their income in tax regardless of their income. Taxes are regressive when they consume a higher portion of the income of people who make less. Taxes are progressive when people with higher incomes pay a higher percentage of their incomes.

The sales taxes that most states employ are regressive, because people who make less need to spend most of their incomes, whereas those who make more can save and invest a portion of theirs. In contrast, the federal income tax is progressive. For 2022, a single filer pays 10 percent on the first $10,275 of their taxable income, 12 percent on the next $31,500 (up to $41,755), and so on through several more tax "brackets." Those fortunate enough to have incomes that place them in the top bracket pay 37 percent on earnings that exceed $539,000. (Note that they only pay 37 percent on earnings over $539,000, not their entire income. They still pay 10 percent on the first $10,275, 12 percent on the next $31,500, and so on through several more brackets. These percentages are referred to as **marginal tax rates**, which is an economist's way of saying that they apply to income above a certain threshold.)

When we compare the pre- and post-tax incomes of the highest-earning 20 percent, let alone the highest-earning 0.01 percent, we can see that this progressive approach to taxation does do something to moderate income inequality. Yet it would do still more if the tax rate for those in the highest-income bracket were even higher. Since the federal income tax was created following the ratification of the Sixteenth Amendment in 1913, the highest marginal rate has changed numerous times. At different points in history, it has been much higher and somewhat lower than it is today. Sometimes these changes have reflected the government's need to raise more money in the face of national emergency, like when the top rate rose from 81 percent to 88 percent in 1942 as the country entered World War II. Other changes have reflected the different economic philosophies of the politicians and parties in power. From 1951 through 1963, the top rate was above 90 percent, until President Lyndon B. Johnson and a Democratic-controlled Congress brought it down to 77 percent in 1964. It was 70 percent when President Ronald Reagan entered the White House in 1980 and 28 percent when he left in 1988. To be clear, though, looking at the highest marginal rate alone doesn't give you the full picture of how the income tax has changed over the years, since other changes have happened as well. The number of brackets has varied over the years, as have the income levels associated with them. What income counts as taxable has also changed over time.

Another limitation of focusing too much on the published tax rates is that these don't entirely reflect the **effective tax rates**, the rates that people actually pay. One way in which these differ is that money received from the sale of assets like stock and real estate doesn't generally fall under the normal income tax. Instead, people who receive income from these sources pay a lower **capital gains** tax. The highest tax rate on capital gains is currently 20 percent. People with larger incomes have more money to invest in assets that will eventually produce capital gains. Income tax rates also don't reflect federal payroll taxes that fund programs like Social Security and Medicare. These eat up a significant amount of a worker's paycheck—at present, 6.2 percent—but you only pay Social Security taxes on the first $160,200 that you earn each year. That means that these taxes consume a larger percentage of the earnings of someone who makes $50,000 a year than someone who makes $500,000: 6.2 percent versus 1.99 percent. They are, to that extent, regressive. And this is not even to mention the various tax shelters and tax avoidance strategies available to wealthy individuals and their accountants. In 2012, investor Warren Buffet—then the second-richest person in America, now the seventh-richest—made headlines when he announced that his secretary paid a higher overall federal tax rate than he did: 35.8 percent versus 17.4 percent.[6] Buffet is perhaps a rare example of someone who has championed reform to the tax system even though it works in his favor.

So far, we have considered income inequality in America. It is important to distinguish between income—the flow of money into your pocket or bank account—and wealth—the things of value that you own (minus your debts). If you own a house, then that's part of your accumulated wealth, although it will only be a source of income if you rent it to someone else. According to Pew, "The wealth gap among upper-income families and middle- and lower-income families is sharper than the income gap and is growing more rapidly."[7] In principle, you could calculate a Gini coefficient for a country's distribution of wealth in much the same manner as for its distribution of income. In practice, the necessary data might be harder to come. In the United States, note, we're required to report our incomes for tax purposes but not our wealth. However, the same Pew report adds that,

> the wealth gap between America's richest and poorer families more than doubled from 1989 to 2016. In 1989, the richest 5% of families had 114 times as much wealth as families in the second quintile [one tier above the poorest 20%], $2.3 million compared with $20,300. By 2016, this ratio had increased to 248, a much sharper rise than the widening gap in income.

In a major book titled *Capital in the Twenty-First Century*, the French economist Thomas Piketty argues that the return on investments of accumulated wealth generally tends to grow more quickly than income from labor.[8] Moreover, people who are already very wealthy will generally get a higher return on their investments than those who have less. Other things equal, therefore, the rich tend to get richer more quickly than anyone else. And since wealth tends to be retained within families via inheritance, large fortunes can accumulate over generations. A case in point: one small family, the heirs of Walmart founder Sam Walton, have a combined fortune of over $240 billion.[9]

Some Americans may see the economic inequality in our society as a natural consequence of a system in which people are held accountable for their choices, being allowed to sink if they don't work hard but also being able to move to a more favorable socioeconomic status than they were born into if they make the right choices. Of course, the fact that some inherit great wealth doesn't entirely harmonize with this self-image of a country where we rise or fall based on our own work ethic. Moreover, many countries with significantly less inequality than the United States have more social mobility, especially the "Nordic" countries like Denmark and Norway.[10]

· · ·

The Nature of Justice

Justice is an old concept with a rich history, a concept that is fundamental to any discussion of how society ought to be organized. Philosophical concern with justice goes back at least to ancient Greece. For Plato and some of his contemporaries, justice seems to have been the paramount virtue or, more precisely, the sum of virtue with regard to our relations with others. Philosophers today, however, generally distinguish justice from the whole of morality. The complaint that something is unjust is more specific than that it's bad or immoral. What, then, makes an act, policy, or institution unjust? Unfortunately, the terms *just* and *unjust* are vague, and different people use them in different ways. Still, talk of justice or injustice typically focuses on at least one of several related ideas: fairness, equality, desert, and rights.

Questions of justice typically focus on fairness, equality, desert, or rights.

First, **justice** is often used to mean *fairness*. Justice frequently concerns the fair treatment of members of groups of people or else looks backward to the fair compensation of prior injuries. Exactly what fairness requires is difficult to say, and different standards may be pertinent in different cases. If corporate manager Smith commits bribery, he is justly punished under our laws. If other managers commit equally serious crimes but are allowed to escape punishment, then Smith suffers a comparative injustice because he was unfairly singled out. But Smith and other white-collar criminals are treated unfairly and thus unjustly, although this time for the opposite reason, if stiffer sentences are meted out to common criminals for less grave offenses.

One way that unfairness creates injustice occurs when like cases are not treated in the same fashion. Following Aristotle, most philosophers believe that we are required, as a formal principle of justice, to treat similar cases alike except where there is some relevant difference. This principle emphasizes the role of impartiality and consistency in justice, but it's a purely formal principle because it's silent about which differences are relevant and which are not. Furthermore, satisfying this formal requirement doesn't guarantee that justice is done. For example, a judge who treats similar cases alike can succeed in administering fairly and nonarbitrarily a law that is itself unjust (like a statute requiring racial segregation).

Related to Aristotle's fairness requirement is a second idea commonly bound up with the concept of justice: *equality*. Justice is frequently held to require that our treatment of people reflect their fundamental moral equality. While Aristotle's formal principle of justice doesn't say whether we are to assume equality of treatment until some difference between cases is shown or to assume the opposite until some relevant similarities are demonstrated, a claim of injustice based on equality is meant to place the burden of proof on those who would endorse unequal treatment. Still, the premise that all persons are equal doesn't establish a direct relationship between justice and economic distribution. We all believe that some differences in the treatment of persons are consistent with equality (punishment, for example), and neither respect for equality nor a commitment to equal treatment necessarily implies an equal distribution of economic goods.

Despite equality, then, individual circumstances—in particular, what a person has done—make a difference. We think it's unjust, for example, when a guilty person goes free or an innocent person is punished, regardless of how others have been treated. This suggests that in addition to equal or impartial treatment, justice has a third aspect, the idea of *desert*. Justice requires that people get what they deserve or, as a number of ancient moralists put it, that each receives their due.

This is closely related to a fourth and final idea—namely, that one is treated unjustly when one's moral *rights* are violated. John Stuart Mill, in fact, made this the defining characteristic of injustice. In his view, what distinguishes injustice from other types of wrongful behavior is that it involves a violation of the rights of some identifiable person:

> Whether the injustice consists in depriving a person of a possession, or in breaking faith with him, or in treating him worse than he deserves, or worse than other people who have no greater claims—in each case the supposition implies two things: a wrong done, and some assignable person who is wronged. . . . It seems to me that this feature in the case—a right in some person, correlative to the moral obligation—constitutes the specific difference between justice and generosity or beneficence. Justice implies something which it is not only right to do, and wrong not to do, but which some individual person can claim from us as a moral right.[11]

Rival Principles of Distribution

Justice, then, is an important subclass of morality in general, a subclass that generally involves appeals to the overlapping notions of fairness, equality, desert, and rights. Turning to the topic of **distributive justice**—that is, to the proper distribution of social benefits and burdens (in particular, economic benefits and burdens)—we see that a number of rival principles have been proposed. Among the principles most frequently recommended as a basis of distribution are these: to each an equal share, to each according to individual need, to each according to personal effort, to each according to social contribution, and to each according to merit. Each one of these principles has its advocates, and each seems plausible in some circumstances, but only in some. There are problems with each. For example, if equality of income was guaranteed, then the lazy would receive as much as the industrious; however, effort is hard to measure and compare, and what one is able to contribute to society may depend on one's luck in being at the right place at the right time. And so on. No single principle seems to work in enough circumstances to be defended successfully as the sole principle of justice in distribution.

It often seems that we simply employ different principles of distributive justice in different circumstances. For example, corporations in certain industries may be granted tax breaks because of their social contribution, whereas welfare payments generally rest on need, and business firms typically base promotions on meritorious performance. Moreover, multiple principles may often be relevant to a single situation. Sometimes they may pull in the same direction, as when wealthy professionals such as doctors defend their high incomes simultaneously on grounds of superior effort, merit, social contribution, and even (because of the high cost of malpractice insurance) need. Or the principles may pull in different directions, as when a teacher must balance effort against performance in assigning grades to pupils. Some philosophers are content to leave the situation here. As they see it, there are various equally valid, prima facie principles of just distribution—equality, need, effort, and so on—and one must try to find the principle that best applies in the given circumstances. If several principles seem to apply, then one must simply weigh them the best one can.

Summary
Justice is one important aspect of morality. Talk of justice and injustice generally involves appeals to the related notions of fairness, equality, desert, and rights. Economic or distributive justice concerns the principles appropriate for assessing society's distribution of social benefits and burdens, particularly wealth, income, status, and power.

Some philosophers believe that there are a number of equally valid principles of just distribution. We must determine which one best applies in a given situation.

The Alderson Federal Prison Camp in West Virginia housed domestic guru Martha Stewart. Similar to this detention center, Butner Federal Correctional Institution, where convicted Ponzi-schemer Bernie Madoff served his sentence, is the type of institution that has come to be known as a "country-club prison." How is this sort of description likely to affect some people's notion of just desert and equality of justice?

Summary
Economic distribution might be based on pure equality, need, effort, social contribution, or merit. Each of these principles is plausible in some circumstances but not in others. In some situations, the principles pull us in different directions. Dissatisfied with a pluralistic approach, moral philosophers have sometimes sought to develop more general theories of justice.

Other philosophers seek a general theory of economic justice. The utilitarian, libertarian, and Rawlsian theories are important examples.

In his book *Spheres of Justice*, Michael Walzer pursues a more sophisticated version of this pluralistic approach.[12] Skeptical of the assumption that justice requires us to implement (in different contexts) some basic principle or set of principles, Walzer argues

> that different goods ought to be distributed for different reasons, in accordance with different procedures, by different agents; and that all these differences derive from different understandings of the social goods themselves—the inevitable product of historical and cultural particularism.[13]

Different norms and principles govern different distributive spheres, and these norms and principles are shaped by the implicit social meanings of the goods in question. He continues:

> Every social good or set of goods constitutes, as it were, a distributive sphere within which only certain criteria and arrangements are appropriate. [For example], money is inappropriate in the sphere of ecclesiastical office. . . . There is no single standard [against which all distributions are to be measured]. But there are standards (roughly knowable even when they are also controversial) for every social good and every distributive sphere in every particular society.[14]

As Walzer sees it, distributive criteria are determined by the particular historically shaped social meanings of the goods in question. The philosophical task is to tease out the inner logic of each type of good, thus revealing the tacit, socially shared values that govern (or should govern) its distribution.

Walzer's historically informed discussion of topics such as medical care or dirty and degrading work are rich and intriguing, but his view implies that when it comes to issues of distributive justice, the best philosophers can do is to try to unravel the implicit, socially specific norms that govern the distribution of different goods in a particular society. Many contemporary philosophers disagree. They believe that we should step further back than Walzer does from existing norms and social arrangements and seek some general theory of justice in economic distribution, on the basis of which we can assess current social practices. Three such theories are the utilitarian, the libertarian, and the Rawlsian (egalitarian).

• • •
The Utilitarian View

For utilitarians, as Chapter 2 explained, happiness is the overarching value. Whether one assesses the rightness and wrongness of actions in terms of how much happiness they produce, as an act utilitarian does, or uses happiness as the standard for deciding what moral principles a society should accept as the basis for determining right and wrong, as a rule utilitarian does, happiness is the only thing that is good in and of itself. On that, utilitarians are agreed.

Earlier, we considered John Stuart Mill's idea that injustice involves the violation of the rights of some identifiable person. This is what distinguishes it from other types of immoral behavior. As a rule utilitarian, Mill has an easier time explaining the existence of rights than an act utilitarian would. According to Mill, to have a right to something is to have a valid claim on society to enforce a rule that protects me in the possession of that thing, either by the force of law or through education and opinion. And I have that valid claim in the first place because society's protection of my possession of that thing is warranted on utilitarian grounds. "To have a right, then, is . . . to have something which society ought to defend me in the possession of. If the objector goes on to ask why it ought, I can give him no other reason than general utility."[15] What utilitarianism identifies as rights are certain moral rules, the observance of which is of the utmost importance for the long-run, overall maximization of happiness.

Accordingly, Mill summed up his view of justice as follows:

> Justice is a name for certain classes of moral rules which concern the essentials of human well-being more nearly, and are therefore of more absolute obligation, than any other rules for the guidance of life; and the notion which we have found to be of the essence of the idea of justice—that of a right residing in an individual—implies and testifies to this more binding obligation.
>
> The moral rules which forbid mankind to hurt one another (in which we must never forget to include wrongful interference with each other's freedom) are more vital to human well-being than any maxims, however important, which only point out the best mode of managing some department of human affairs.[16]

Although justice for Mill was ultimately a matter of promoting social well-being, not every issue of social utility was a matter of justice. The concept of justice identifies certain important social utilities—that is, certain rules or rights, the upholding of which is crucial for social well-being.

For utilitarians, then, justice is not an independent moral standard distinct from their general principle. Rather, the maximization of happiness ultimately determines what is just and unjust. Critics of utilitarianism contend that knowing what will promote happiness is always difficult. People are bound to estimate consequences differently, thus making the standard of utility an inexact and unreliable principle for determining what is just. Mill, however, did not see much merit in this criticism. For one thing, it presupposes that we all agree about what the principles of justice are and how to apply them. This is far from the case, Mill argued. Indeed, without utilitarianism to provide a determinate standard of justice, one is always left with a plethora of competing principles, all of which seem to have some plausibility but are mutually incompatible.

As an example, Mill pointed to the conflict between two principles of justice that occurs in the realm of economic distribution. Is it just or not, he asked, that more talented workers should receive a greater remuneration? There are two possible answers to this question:

> On the negative side of the question it is argued that whoever does the best he can deserves equally well, and ought not in justice to be put in a position of inferiority for no fault of his own; that superior abilities have already advantages more than enough . . . without adding to these a superior share of the world's goods; and that society is bound in justice rather to make compensation to the less favoured for this unmerited inequality of advantages than to aggravate it.[17]

> Mill believed that justice concerns certain rules or rights that are vitally important for human well-being.

Summary
Utilitarianism holds that the maximization of happiness ultimately determines what is just and unjust. Mill contended, more specifically, that the concept of justice identifies certain rules or rights—the upholding of which is crucial for promoting well-being—and that injustice always involves violating the rights of some identifiable individual.

This argument sounds plausible, but then so does the alternative answer:

> On the contrary side it is contended that society receives more from the more efficient labourer; that, his services being more useful, society owes him a larger return for them; that a greater share of the joint result is actually his work, and not to allow his claim to it is a kind of robbery; that, if he is only to receive as much as others, he can only be justly required to produce as much.[18]

Here we have two conflicting principles of justice. How are we to decide between them? The problem, Mill said, is that both principles seem plausible:

> Justice has in this case two sides to it, which it is impossible to bring into harmony, and the two disputants have chosen opposite sides; the one looks to what it is just that the individual should receive, the other to what it is just that the community should give.[19]

Each disputant is, from their own point of view, unanswerable. "Any choice between them, on grounds of justice," Mill continued, "must be perfectly arbitrary." What, then, is the solution? For Mill, the utilitarian, it was straightforward: "Social utility alone can decide the preference."[20] The utilitarian standard must be the ultimate court of appeal in such cases. Only the utilitarian standard can provide an intelligent and satisfactory way of handling controversial questions of justice and of resolving conflicts between competing principles of justice.

One consequence of Mill's utilitarian approach is that he believes that the principles of justice can evolve over time, in response to changes in the "facts on the ground." For instance, Mill is optimistic that over generations people will move slowly in the direction of being less selfish and more concerned about the well-being of other people. When enough progress has been made in this direction, the utilitarian calculus may arrive at a different answer about which principles of justice we'd do best to adopt. In fact, Mill concludes that the principles of justice best suited for his time would allow more talented workers to earn more, since alternatives like paying everyone equally or according to their need would encourage selfish workers to do little or no work. Yet he adds that if a day comes when people have attained "a much higher moral condition of human nature" then this may no longer be the case.[21] In a world where people could be counted on to work to the best of their ability even without being materially rewarded for doing do, the optimal principles of justice might require paying everyone the same.

Utilitarianism and Economic Distribution

Utilitarianism doesn't tell us which economic system will produce the most happiness. That question hangs on the social, economic, and political facts.

The utilitarian theory of justice ties the question of economic distribution to the promotion of social well-being or happiness. Utilitarians favor whichever economic system will bring the most good for society as a whole. But what system is that? Utilitarianism itself, as a normative theory, provides no answer. The answer depends on the relevant social, economic, and political facts. The facts in question aren't merely simple, relatively easy to determine matters, like what the unemployment rate is right now. They include much more complicated and controversial matters about what the consequences of adopting different laws and policies would be, and perhaps ultimately facts about human nature, for example, just how strong self-interest is relative to our other sources of motivation. Two people who are both committed utilitarians, but who disagree about these facts—which may involve their subscribing to different theories in economics and political science—will probably reach very different conclusions about what justice requires.

A utilitarian must understand the various possibilities, determine their consequences, and assess the available options. Obviously, this is not a simple task. Deciding what sort of economic arrangements would best promote human happiness requires the utilitarian to consider many things, including (1) the type of economic ownership (private, public, or mixed); (2) the way of organizing production and distribution in general (pure laissez faire, markets with government planning and regulation, or fully centralized planning); (3) the type of authority arrangements within the units of production (worker control versus managerial prerogative); (4) the range and character of material incentives; and (5) the nature and extent of the social welfare safety net.

Utilitarians must balance various countervailing considerations (i.e., factors that point in different directions). On the one hand, for instance, from a utilitarian perspective there's a clear sense in which it's desirable for individuals to act in ways that contribute to making society richer—so that there's more wealth to be used to add to people's pleasure—and to eliminate waste and inefficiency. At first glance, at least, this might seem to favor a heavy reliance on a free-market economic system, one with minimal regulation or redistribution of wealth via taxation and government welfare programs, where individuals and businesses are rewarded for productivity and penalized for idleness and inefficiency.

On the other hand, though, this kind of economic system can result in considerable economic inequality, which for utilitarians is problematic. One reason it's problematic is that inequality appears to be correlated with various social ills. More equal societies, such as Sweden and Finland, with a relatively narrow gap separating their richest and poorest citizens score higher on various indices of social well-being. In terms of infant mortality, life expectancy, malnutrition, obesity, teenage pregnancy, economic insecurity, personal anxiety, and other measures, they fare better than do societies like the United States that have greater inequality.[22]

Another reason utilitarians tend to favor greater inequality of income goes back to what economists call the **declining marginal utility of money**. This phrase simply means that successive additions to one's income produce, on average, less happiness or welfare than did earlier additions.

The declining utility of money follows from the fact, as Richard Brandt explains it, that the outcomes we want are preferentially ordered, some being more strongly wanted than others:

> So a person, when deciding how to spend his resources, picks a basket of groceries which is at least as appealing as any other he can purchase with the money he has. The things he doesn't buy are omitted because other things are wanted more. If we double a person's income, he will spend the extra money on items he wants less (some special cases aside), and which will give less enjoyment than will the original income. The more one's income, the fewer preferred items one buys and the more preferred items one already has. On the whole, then, when the necessities of life have been purchased and the individual is spending on luxury items, he is buying items which will give less enjoyment. . . . This conclusion corresponds well with commonsense reflection and practice.[23]

In sum, if you must choose between giving $10 to someone who's penniless and someone who's a millionaire, it seems likely that it's the person who's destitute who will benefit most from it. For them, the money might represent the difference between eating and going hungry, whereas the millionaire can already easily afford all of life's necessities and many, many luxuries. If they can find any use for an extra $10, it will only be to buy something that's very low on their list of priorities.

From a utilitarian perspective, the ideal economic distribution would seem to be one where everyone receives an equal slice of a really large pie, where the pie represents the economy's total output of goods and services—the gross national product. But the decisions that determine how large the pie will be aren't independent from the decisions that determine how similar in size each individual's slice is; the same policies that would make the slices more equal might make the overall pie smaller. In this case, utilitarians may differ about what balance between economic growth and economic equality will maximize overall happiness. They may also differ over the extent to which we're really forced to choose between these goals.

Mill's Views on Economics

Utilitarians differ widely over what sort of economic arrangement will maximize happiness. Since we've already introduced Mill as an important historical utilitarian, it may be worthwhile to present some of his views as an illustration of how a utilitarian might balance different countervailing considerations Yet, it's important to remember that people who share his utilitarianism might reach entirely different conclusions.

One of the most distinctive aspects of Mill's views on what used to be called "political economy" is his emphasis on **worker participation**. In his *Principles of Political Economy*, originally published in 1848, Mill argued for the desirability of breaking down the sharp and

Summary
Utilitarians must examine various factual issues to determine which economic system and principles will best promote social well-being or happiness. This requires them to balance countervailing considerations.

hostile division between the producers, or workers, on the one hand, and the capitalists, or owners, on the other. Not only would this be desirable, it was also, he thought, something that the advance of civilization was tending naturally to bring about: "The relation of masters and workpeople will be gradually superseded by partnership, in one or two forms: in some cases, association of the labourers with the capitalist; in others, and perhaps finally in all, association of labourers among themselves."[24] These developments would not only enhance productivity but also—and more importantly—promote the fuller development and well-being of the people involved. The aim, Mill thought, should be to enable people "to work with or for one another in relations not involving dependence."[25]

By the association of labor and capital, Mill had in mind different schemes of profit sharing. For example, "in the American ships trading to China, it has long been the custom for every sailor to have an interest in the profits of the voyage; and to this has been ascribed the general good conduct of those seamen." This sort of association, however, would eventually give way to a more complete system of worker cooperatives:

> The form of association, however, which if mankind continue to improve, must be expected in the end to predominate, is not that which can exist between a capitalist as chief, and workpeople without a voice in the management, but the association of the labourers themselves on terms of equality, collectively owning the capital with which they carry on their operations, and working under managers elected and removable by themselves.[26]

What that transformation implied for Mill was nothing less than "the nearest approach to social justice, and the most beneficial ordering of industrial affairs for the universal good, which it's possible at present to foresee."[27]

Mill's vision of workers owning their own firms may seem very "anti-capitalistic." In fact, Mill himself described it as "socialism." Yet he sees the government as playing almost no role in the transformation that he describes. He anticipates that workers will buy firms from capitalists, not take them by force through the government or revolution. He is also a firm believer in the value of economic competition. In sum, Mill doesn't fit neatly within our usual ways of categorizing people's economic beliefs. (If the terms "capitalism" and "socialism" aren't familiar, they're defined in the next chapter, but be aware that Mill uses "socialism" much more broadly than it's typically used today.)

Criticism of the Utilitarian Approach

> The same criticisms that have been raised against utilitarianism as a moral theory can be raised against it as an account of distributive justice.

There's not much need to elaborate on criticisms of the utilitarian approach to thinking about distributive justice, because several objections to utilitarianism were introduced in the previous chapter. If those objections persuaded you to reject utilitarianism as an account of morality in general, then you're unlikely to think that it offers an adequate account of that specific part of morality concerned with distributive justice.

• • •

The Libertarian Approach

> Libertarians refuse to restrict individual liberty even if doing so would increase overall happiness.

Whereas utilitarians associate justice with social utility, philosophers who endorse what is called **libertarianism** identify justice with an ideal of liberty. For them, liberty is the prime value, and justice consists in permitting each person to live as they please, free from the interference of others. Accordingly, one libertarian asserts, libertarianism is "a philosophy of personal liberty—the liberty of each person to live according to his own choices, provided he doesn't attempt to coerce others and thus prevent them from living according to their choices."[28] Such views show clearly the libertarian's association of justice with liberty and of liberty itself with the absence of interference by other persons.

Libertarians firmly reject utilitarianism's concern for total social well-being. Utilitarians are willing to restrict the liberty of some, to interfere with their choices, if doing so will promote greater net happiness than not doing so. Libertarians cannot stomach that approach. As long as you are not doing something that interferes with anyone else's liberty, then no person, group, or government should disturb you in living the life you choose—not even if its doing so would maximize social happiness. Although some utilitarians come close to libertarians in their enthusiasm for the free market, true libertarians are nonconsequentialists.

Although individual liberty is something that all of us value, it may not be the only thing we value. For the libertarian, however, liberty takes priority over other moral concerns. In particular, justice consists solely of respect for individual liberty. A libertarian world, with a complete commitment to individual liberty, would be a very different world from the one we now live in. Consider the following: The government registers young men for military service and can, if it chooses, draft them; laws require adults to wear seatbelts in cars and helmets on motorcycles, while forbidding them from ingesting substances that the legislature deems harmful or immoral (such as cannabis in many states and cocaine in all of them); and the state imposes taxes on our income to—among many other things—support needy citizens, provide loans to college students, and fund various projects for the common good. From a libertarian perspective, none of these policies is just.

Given the assumption that *liberty* means "noninterference," libertarians generally agree that liberty allows only a minimal or "night-watchman" state. Such a state is limited to the narrow functions of protecting its citizens against force, theft, and fraud; enforcing contracts; and performing other such basic maintenance functions. In this view, a more extensive state— in particular, one that taxes its better-off citizens to support the less-fortunate ones—violates the liberty of individuals by forcing them to support projects, policies, or persons they have not freely chosen to support.

Nozick's Theory of Justice

Although libertarians differ in how they formulate their theory, the late Harvard professor Robert Nozick (1938–2002) offers a very influential statement of the libertarian case in his 1974 book *Anarchy, State, and Utopia*.[29] Nozick's challenging and powerful advocacy of libertarianism has stimulated much debate, obliging philosophers of all political persuasions to take the libertarian theory seriously. His views are thus worth presenting in detail.

Nozick begins from the premise that people have certain basic moral rights, which he calls **Lockean rights**. By alluding to the political philosophy of John Locke (1632–1704), Nozick wishes to underscore that these rights are both negative and natural. They are negative because they require only that people forbear from acting in certain ways—in particular, that we refrain from interfering with others. Beyond this, we are not obliged to do anything positive for anyone else, nor is anyone required to do anything positive for us. We have no right, for example, to be provided with satisfying work or with any material goods that we might need. These negative rights, according to Nozick, are natural in the sense that we possess them independently of any social or political institutions.

These individual rights impose firm, nearly absolute restrictions (or, in Nozick's phrase, "side constraints") on how we may act. We cannot morally infringe on someone's rights for any purpose. Not only are we forbidden to interfere with a person's liberty in order to promote the general good, we're prohibited from doing so even if violating that individual's rights would somehow prevent other individuals' rights from being violated. Each individual is autonomous and responsible and should be left to fashion their own life free from the interference of others—as long as doing so is compatible with the rights of others to do the same. Only an acknowledgment of this almost absolute right to be free from coercion, Nozick argues, fully respects the distinctiveness of individuals, each with a unique life to lead.

A belief in these rights shapes Nozick's theory of economic justice, which he calls the **entitlement theory**. Essentially, Nozick maintains that people are entitled to their holdings (that is, goods, money, and property) as long as they have acquired them fairly. Stated another way, if you have obtained your possessions without violating other people's Lockean rights, then you are entitled to them and may dispose of them as you choose. No one else has a legitimate claim on them. If you have secured a vast fortune without injuring other people, defrauding them, or otherwise violating their rights, then you are morally permitted to do with your fortune whatever you wish—bequeath it to a relative, endow a university, or squander it in riotous living. Even though other people may be going hungry, justice imposes no obligation on you to help them.

Summary
The libertarian theory identifies justice with liberty, which libertarians understand as living according to our own choices, free from the interference of others. They reject utilitarianism's concern for total social well-being.

According to Nozick's theory, you're entitled to your holdings if you have acquired them without violating other people's rights.

The *first principle of Nozick's entitlement theory* concerns the original acquisition of holdings—that is, the appropriation of unheld goods or the creation of new goods. If a person acquires a holding in accordance with this principle, then they are entitled to it. If, for example, you discover and remove minerals from the wilderness or make something out of materials you already legitimately possess, then you have justly acquired this new holding. Nozick doesn't spell out this principle or specify fully what constitutes a just original acquisition, but the basic idea is clear and reflects the thinking of John Locke.

Property is a moral right, said Locke, because individuals are morally entitled to the products of their labor. When they mix their labor with the natural world, they are entitled to the resulting product. Thus, if a man works the land, he is entitled to the land and its products because through his labor he has put something of himself into them. This investment of self through labor is the moral basis of ownership, Locke wrote, but he acknowledged limits to this right:

> In the beginning . . . men had a right to appropriate, by their labour, each one of himself, as much of the things of nature, as he could use. . . . Whatsoever he tilled and reaped, laid up and made use of, before it spoiled, that was his peculiar right; whatsoever he enclosed, and could feed, and make use of, the cattle and product was also his. But if either the grass of his inclosure rotted on the ground, or the fruit of his planting perished without gathering, and laying up, this part of the earth . . . was still to be looked on as waste, and might be the possession of any other.[30]

In this early **state of nature** (the phrase is Locke's) prior to the formation of government, property rights were limited not only by the requirement that one not waste what one claimed, but also by the restriction that "enough and as good" be left for others—that is, that one's appropriation not make others worse off. Later, however, with the introduction of money, Locke thought that both these restrictions were overcome. You can pile up money beyond your needs without its spoiling; and if your property is used productively and the proceeds are offered for sale, then your appropriation leaves others no worse off than before.

Nozick's second principle concerns transfers of already-owned goods from one person to another: how people may legitimately transfer holdings to others and how they may legitimately get holdings from others. If a person possesses a holding because of a legitimate transfer, then they are entitled to it. Again, Nozick doesn't work out the details, but it's clear that acquiring something by purchase, as a gift, or through exchange would constitute a legitimate acquisition. Gaining something through theft, force, or fraud would violate the principle of justice in transfer.

Nozick's third and final principle states that one can justly acquire a holding only in accord with the two principles previously discussed. If you come by a holding in some other way, you are not entitled to it.

Nozick sums up his theory this way:

1. A person who acquires a holding in accordance with the principle of justice in acquisition is entitled to that holding.

2. A person who acquires a holding in accordance with the principle of justice in transfer, from someone else entitled to the holding, is entitled to the holding.

3. No one is entitled to a holding except by (repeated) applications of principles 1 and 2.

In short, the distribution of goods in a society is just if and only if all are entitled to the holdings they possess. Nozick calls his entitlement theory "historical" because what matters is how people come to have what they have. If people are entitled to their possessions, then the distribution of economic holdings is just, regardless of what the actual distribution happens to look like (for instance, how far people are above or below the average income) or what its consequences are. The contrast here is with "ahistorical" theories, which would allow to judge that some distributions of holdings are unjust regardless of how they came about. A simple ahistorical theory might say that any distribution of wealth is unjust if its Gini coefficient is above a certain value, for instance, regardless of how people came to have what they do.

Summary

The libertarian philosopher Robert Nozick defends the entitlement theory. This theory holds that the distribution of goods, money, and property is just if people are entitled to what they have—that is, if they have acquired their possessions without violating the rights of anyone else.

All that matters for Nozick is how people came to have what they have, not the pattern or results of the distribution of goods.

Nozick's Wilt Chamberlain Example

Nozick argues that respect for liberty inescapably leads one to repudiate other conceptions of economic justice in favor of his entitlement approach. One of his most ingenious examples features Wilt Chamberlain, the late basketball star.

Suppose, Nozick says, that things are distributed according to your favorite non-entitlement theory, whatever it is. (He calls this distribution D_1.) Again, you might think about this in terms of a distribution that has a specific Gini coefficient. Now imagine that Wilt Chamberlain signs a contract with a team that guarantees him $5 from the price of each ticket. Whenever people buy a ticket to a game, they drop $5 into a special box with Chamberlain's name on it. To them, seeing him play is worth $5. Imagine then that in the course of a season, 1 million people attend his games, and Chamberlain ends up with far more than the average income—far more, indeed, than anyone else in the society earns. This result (D_2) upsets the initial distributional pattern (D_1). Can the proponent of D_1 complain? Nozick thinks not:

> Is [Chamberlain] entitled to this income? Is this new distribution, D_2, unjust? If so, why? There is *no* question about whether each of the people was entitled to the control over the resources they held in D_1; because that was the distribution (your favorite) that (for the purposes of the argument) we assumed was acceptable. Each of these persons *chose* to give [$5] of their money to Chamberlain. . . . If D_1 was a just distribution, and people voluntarily moved from it to D_2, transferring parts of their shares they were given under D_1 . . . isn't D_2 also just? If the people were entitled to dispose of the resources to which they were entitled (under D_1), didn't this include their being entitled to give it to, or exchange it with, Wilt Chamberlain? Can anyone else complain on grounds of justice?[31]

Having defended the legitimacy of Chamberlain's new wealth, Nozick pushes his case further, arguing that any effort to maintain some initial distributional arrangement like D_1 will interfere with people's liberty to use their resources as they wish. To preserve this original distribution, he writes, society would have to "forbid capitalist acts between consenting adults":

> The general point illustrated by the Wilt Chamberlain example . . . is that no [non-entitlement] principle of justice can be continuously realized without continuous interference with people's lives. Any favored pattern would be transformed into one unfavored by the principle, by people choosing to act in various ways; for example, by people exchanging goods and services with other people, or giving things to other people. . . . To maintain a pattern one must either continually interfere to stop people from transferring resources as they wish to, or continually (or periodically) interfere to take from some persons resources that others for some reason chose to transfer to them.[32]

Summary
In the Wilt Chamberlain example, Nozick argues that other theories of economic justice inevitably fail to respect people's liberty.

Action Plus Sports Images/Alamy Stock Photo

Wilt Chamberlain was the greatest basketball player of his era and one of the greatest of any era.

The Libertarian View of Liberty

Libertarianism clearly involves a commitment to leaving market relations—buying, selling, and other exchanges—totally unrestricted. (Chapter 4 examines the nature of market economies in general and capitalism in particular.) Force and fraud are forbidden, of course, but there should be no meddling with the uncoerced exchanges of consenting individuals. Not only is the market morally legitimate, but any attempt to interfere with voluntary and nonfraudulent transactions between adults will be unacceptable, even unjust. Thus, libertarians are for economic laissez faire and against any governmental economic activity that interferes with the marketplace, even if the point of the interference is to enhance the performance of the economy.

It's important to emphasize that libertarianism's enthusiasm for the market rests on this nonconsequentialist commitment to liberty. By contrast, utilitarians who defend an unregulated market do so on the ground that it works better than either a planned, socialist economy or the sort of regulated capitalism with some welfare benefits that we in fact have in the United States. If a utilitarian defends laissez faire, they do so because of its consequences. If we convinced a utilitarian that some other form of economic organization would better promote human well-being, the utilitarian would advocate that instead. With libertarians, this is definitely not the case. As a matter of fact, libertarians typically believe that unregulated capitalist behavior best promotes everyone's interests. But even if, hypothetically, someone like Nozick were convinced that some sort of socialism or welfare capitalism would outperform laissez-faire capitalism economically—leading, say, to greater productivity, a shorter workday, and a higher standard of living—they would still reject this alternative as morally unacceptable. To tinker with the market, however beneficial it might be, would involve violating someone's liberty. If a laissez faire system really does work better than the alternatives, in addition to respecting people's rights, then that's just the proverbial cherry on top.

Libertarians say that their commitment to an unrestricted **free market** reflects the priority of liberty over other values. However, libertarians don't value liberty in the mundane sense of people's freedom to do what they want to do. Rather, libertarians understand freedom in terms of their theory of rights, thus building a commitment to private property into their concept of liberty. According to them, being able to do what you want doesn't automatically represent an increase in your liberty. It does so only if you remain within the boundaries set by the Lockean rights of others. Likewise, one is unfree or coerced only when one's rights are infringed.

> Libertarians build a commitment to private property into their concept of liberty.

Imagine, for example, that having purchased the forest in which I occasionally stroll, the new owner bars my access to it. It would seem that my freedom has been reduced because I can no longer ramble where I wish. But libertarians deny that this is a restriction of my liberty. My liberty is restricted if and only if someone violates my Lockean rights, which no one has done. Suppose that I go for a hike in the forest anyway. If the sheriff's deputies arrest me, they prevent me from doing what I want to do. But according to libertarianism, they don't restrict my liberty, nor do they coerce me. Why not? Because my hiking in the forest violates the landowner's rights.

Here, libertarians seem driven to an unusual use of familiar terminology, but they have no choice. They cannot admit that abridging the landowner's freedom to do as he wants with his property would expand my freedom. If they did, then their theory would be in jeopardy. They would have to acknowledge that restricting the liberty or property rights of some could enhance the liberty of others. In other words, if their theory committed them simply to promoting as much as possible the goal of people doing what they want to do, then libertarians would be in the position of balancing the freedom of some against the freedom of others. But this sort of balancing and trading off is exactly what libertarians dislike about utilitarianism.

If liberty means being free to do what you want, it's not true that libertarians value it above everything else. What they value are Lockean property rights, which then set the parameters of liberty. Libertarians frequently contend that (1) private property is necessary for freedom and (2) any society that doesn't respect private property rights is coercive. But libertarianism makes point (1) true by definition, and (2) is incomplete. Any system of property (whether Lockean, socialist, or something in between) necessarily puts restrictions on people's conduct; its rules are coercive. What one system of property permits, another forbids. Society X prevents me from hiking in your woods, whereas society Y prevents you from stopping me. Both systems of rules are coercive. Both grant some freedoms and withhold others.

Markets and Free Exchange

Libertarians defend market relations, then, as necessary to respect human liberty (as their theory understands liberty). However, in doing so, libertarians don't assert that, morally speaking, people *deserve* what they receive from others through gift or exchange, only that they are *entitled* to whatever they receive. The market tends generally, libertarians believe, to reward people for skill, diligence, and successful performance. Yet luck plays a role, too. Jack makes a fortune from having been in the right place at the right time with jeggings, while Jill loses her investment because the market for bottled water collapses. The libertarian position is not that Jack deserves to be wealthy and Jill doesn't; rather, it's that Jack is entitled to his holdings if he has acquired them in accordance with the principles of justice.

The same point comes up with regard to gifts and inheritance. Inheritance strikes many people as patently unfair. How can it be just, they ask, that one child inherits a vast fortune; the best schooling; and social, political, and business connections that will ensure their future, while another child inherits indigence, inferior schooling, and connections with crime? At birth, neither youngster deserves anything—a fact suggesting, perhaps, that an equal division of holdings and opportunities would be the only fair allocation. For his part, Nozick contends that deserving has no bearing on the justice of inherited wealth; people are simply entitled to it as long as it's not ill-gotten. Or looking at it the other way, if one is entitled to one's holdings, then one has a right to do with them as one wishes, including using them to benefit one's children.

According to libertarians, a totally free market is necessary for people to exercise their fundamental rights. Sometimes, however, unregulated market transactions can lead to disastrous results. Unfortunately, this is more than just a theoretical possibility. Amartya Sen, the Nobel Prize–winning economist, has shown how in certain circumstances changing market entitlements have led to mass starvation. Although the average person thinks of famine as caused simply by a shortage of food, Sen and other experts have established that famines are frequently accompanied by no shortfall of food in absolute terms. Indeed, even more food may be available during a famine than in nonfamine years—if one has the money to buy it. Famine occurs because large numbers of people lack the financial wherewithal to obtain the necessary food.[33]

For example, drought may cause food output in one area to decline and the peasants in that area to starve because they lack the means to buy food from elsewhere, even though there is no dearth of food in the country as a whole (Ethiopia in 1973). Or famine may result when the purchasing power of one occupational group shoots up, ruining the chances of other groups, whose nominal incomes have not changed, to buy food (Bengal in 1943). A reduction of food output because of potato blight triggered the great Irish famine of the 1840s, which killed a higher proportion of the population than any other famine in recorded history. But if one looks at the United Kingdom as a whole, there was no shortage of food. Food could certainly have moved from Britain to Ireland if the Irish could have afforded to purchase it. As it was, at the height of the famine, food was exported from Ireland to England because the prosperous English could pay a higher price for it.[34] (A relevant background factor here is that much of the agricultural land was on large estates owned by landlords who did not live in Ireland.)

Libertarians would find it immoral and unjust to force people to aid the starving or to tax the affluent in order to set up programs to relieve hunger or prevent famines in the first place. Nor does justice require that a wealthy merchant assist the hungry children in his community to stay alive. And it would certainly violate the merchant's property rights for the children to help themselves to his excess food. Nevertheless, although justice doesn't require that one assist those in need, libertarians would generally acknowledge that we have some humanitarian obligations toward others. Accordingly, they would not only permit but also presumably encourage people to voluntarily assist others. Justice doesn't require the merchant to donate, and it forbids us from forcing him to do so, but charity on his part would be a good thing. This reflects the libertarian's firm commitment to **property rights**: What you have legitimately acquired is yours to do with as you will.

Libertarians don't contend that people morally deserve what they get in a free market, but only that they are entitled to it.

Unregulated market transactions can sometimes lead to disastrous results, as Amartya Sen has shown.

Summary
Libertarians operate with a distinctive concept of liberty, defend free exchange and laissez-faire markets without regard to results, put a priority on freedom over all other values, and see property rights as existing prior to any social arrangements. Critics contest each of these features of libertarianism.

According to the libertarian theory of justice, people of means have no obligation to help the homeless. Assuming that they didn't acquire their wealth by force or fraud, it's theirs to dispose of entirely as they wish.

Property Rights

Nozick's theory makes property rights nearly sacrosanct. From the perspective of libertarianism, property rights grow out of one's basic moral rights, reflecting one's initial creation or appropriation of the product, some sort of exchange or transfer between consenting persons, or a combination of these. Property rights exist prior to any social arrangements and are morally antecedent to any legislative decisions that a society might make. However, Nozick's critics argue that it's a mistake to think of property as a simple, pre-social relation between a person and a physical thing.

> Nozick's critics argue that it's a mistake to think of property as a simple pre-social relation between a person and a thing.

First, property is not restricted to material objects like cars, watches, or houses. In developed societies, it may include abstract goods, interests, and claims. For instance, property may include the right to pay debts with the balance in a bank account, the right to dividends from a corporate investment, and the right to collect from a pension plan one has joined. In fact, the courts have counted as property a wide range of items such as new life forms, an original idea, pension payments, the news, or a place on the welfare rolls.[35]

Second, property ownership involves a bundle of different rights governing one's ability to possess, use, manage, dispose of, or restrict others' access to something in certain specified ways. The nature of this bundle differs among societies, as do the types of things that can be owned. In any society, property ownership is structured by the various implicit or explicit rules and regulations governing the legitimate acquisition and transfer of various types of goods, interests, and claims. Not only do property rights differ between societies, but the nature of ownership can also change over time in any given society. As a general trend, the social restrictions on property ownership in the United States have increased dramatically during our history (much to the displeasure of libertarians).

> Most nonlibertarian theorists believe that property rights are determined by social institutions.

For these reasons, most nonlibertarian social and political theorists view property rights as a function of the particular institutions of a given society. This is not to say that a society's property arrangements cannot be criticized. On the contrary, their morality can be assessed just as the morality of any other institution can.

Criticism of the Libertarian Approach

Perhaps the main criticism that has been made of the libertarian approach is that there's no widely accepted argument for why we should accept the so-called Lockean theory of rights. Nozick, for instance, essentially takes the existence of Lockean rights for granted. When we turn to Locke himself, what we find is that at points he can sound very much like a consequentialist.

This is significant, because it means that he may not have seen property rights as being quite so absolute as later libertarians who invoke his name. Locke reasons that property rights are necessary to ensure humanity's continued survival. But then we might wonder whether this means that we can deprive people of their property under dire circumstances where this is necessary to save the lives of others. While Nozick's answer to this question would pretty clearly be "no," Locke himself seems to think that if one person is in severe need and another has more than enough wealth, then the first has a right to some of the second's excess:

> God, the Lord and Father of all, has given no one of his children such a property in his peculiar portion of the things of this world, but that he has given his needy brother a right to the surplusage of his goods; so that it cannot justly be denied him, when his pressing wants call for it: and therefore no man could ever have a just power over the life of another by right of property in land or possessions; since it would always be a sin, in any man of estate, to let his brother perish for want of affording him relief out of his plenty.[36]

Perhaps the main criticism that has been made of the libertarian approach is that there's no widely accepted argument for why we should accept the Lockean theory of rights.

* * *

Rawls's Theory of Justice

A Theory of Justice by John Rawls (1921–2002) is generally thought to be the most influential work of the post–World War II period in social and political philosophy, at least in the English language.[37] Even those who are not persuaded by Rawls find themselves obliged to come to terms with his thinking. Although Rawls's basic approach is not difficult to follow, *A Theory of Justice* elaborates his ideas with such painstaking care and philosophical thoroughness that even vigorous critics of the book pay sincere tribute to its many virtues. (This includes his Harvard colleague Robert Nozick, despite the fact that Nozick's *Anarchy, State, and Utopia* was written as a rebuttal to *A Theory of Justice*.)

By his own account, Rawls presents his theory as a modern alternative to utilitarianism, one that he hopes will be compatible with the belief that justice must be associated with fairness and the moral equality of persons. Rawls firmly wishes to avoid reducing justice to a matter of social utility. At the same time, his approach differs fundamentally from Nozick's. Rawls conceives of society as a cooperative venture among its members, and he elaborates a conception of justice that is thoroughly social. He doesn't base his theory, as Nozick does, on the postulate that individuals possess certain natural rights prior to any political or social organization.

Rawls's strategy is to ask what principles people would choose to govern their society if they were in the "original position."

Two features of Rawls's theory are particularly important: his hypothetical contract approach and the principles of justice that he derives from it. Rawls's strategy is to ask what we would choose as the fundamental principles to govern society if, hypothetically, we were to meet for this purpose in what he calls the **original position**. He then elaborates the nature of this original position, the constraints on the choice facing us, and the reasoning that he thinks people in the original position would follow. In this way, Rawls offers a modern variant of social contract theory, in the tradition of Hobbes, Locke, Rousseau, and other earlier philosophers. Rawls argues that people in the original position would agree on two principles as the basic governing principles of their society and that these principles are, accordingly, the principles of justice. The first is a guarantee of certain familiar and fundamental liberties to each person. The second—more controversial—holds in part that social and economic inequalities are justified only if those inequalities benefit the least-advantaged members of society. These principles are examined at some length later in this chapter.

The Original Position

Various principles of economic justice have been proposed, but an important question for philosophers is whether, and how, any such principles can be justified. Thinking of possible principles of economic distribution is not very difficult, but proving the soundness of such a principle, or at least showing it to be more plausible than its rivals, is a challenging task. After all, people seem to differ in their intuitions about what is just and unjust, and their sentiments are bound to be influenced by their social position. Nozick's entitlement theory, for example, with its priority on property rights, is bound to seem more plausible to a corporate executive than to a migrant farmworker. The justice of a world in which some children are born into wealth while other children struggle to get by on welfare is unlikely to seem as obvious to the poor as it may to the well-to-do.

The strategy Rawls employs to identify and justify the basic principles of justice is to imagine that people come together for the purpose of deciding on the ground rules for their society, in particular on the rules governing economic distribution. Although in the past, groups of people have written down constitutions and similar political documents, never have the members of a society decided from scratch on the basic principles of justice that should govern them. Nor is it even remotely likely that people will do this in the future. What Rawls imagines is a thought experiment. The question is hypothetical: What principles would people choose in this sort of original position? If we can identify these principles, Rawls contends, then we will have identified the principles of justice precisely because they are the principles that we would all have agreed to.

The Nature of the Choice

On what basis are we to choose these principles? The most obvious answer is that we should select principles that strike us as just. But this won't work. Even if we all agreed about what is just and unjust, we would be relying on our already existing ideas about justice as a basis for choosing the principles to govern our society. Philosophically, this approach doesn't accomplish anything. We would simply be going in a circle, using our existing conception of justice to prove the principles of justice.

Rawls suggests instead that we imagine people in the original position choosing solely on the basis of self-interest: Each individual chooses the set of principles for governing society that will be best for himself or herself (and loved ones). We don't have to imagine that people are antagonistic or that outside of the original position they are selfish; we simply imagine that they hope to get the group to choose those principles that will, more than any other possible principles, benefit them. If people in the original position can agree on some governing principles on the basis of mutual self-interest, then these principles will be, Rawls thinks, the principles of justice. Why? Because the principles are agreed to under conditions of equality and free choice. By analogy, if we make up a game and all agree ahead of time, freely and equally, on how the game is to be played, nobody can later complain that the rules are unfair.

The Veil of Ignorance

If people in the original position are supposed to choose principles on the basis of self-interest, agreement seems unlikely. If Carolyn has vast real estate holdings, she will certainly want rules that guarantee her extensive property rights, whereas her tenants are likely to support rules that permit rent control. Likewise, the wealthy will tend to advocate rules rather like Nozick's entitlement theory, whereas the poor will, on the basis of their self-interest, desire a redistribution of property. Conflicts of self-interest seem bound to create totally irreconcilable demands. For instance, artists may contend that they should be rewarded more than professional people, men that they should earn more than women, and laborers that they merit more than people with desk jobs.

Given that some rules would benefit one group while other rules would benefit another, it seems improbable that people in the original position would concur. As a way around this problem, Rawls asks us to imagine that people in the original position don't know what social position or status they hold in society. They don't know whether they are rich or poor, nor do they know their personal talents and characteristics—whether, for example, they are athletic or sedentary, artistic or tone deaf, intelligent or not very bright, or physically sound or handicapped in some way. They don't know their race or their gender. Behind what Rawls calls the **veil of ignorance**, people in the original position know nothing about themselves personally or about what their individual situation will be once the rules are chosen and the veil is lifted. They do, however, have a general knowledge of history, sociology, and psychology—although no specific information about the society they will be in once the veil is lifted.

Under the veil of ignorance, the people in Rawls's original position have no knowledge about themselves or their situation that would lead them to argue from a partial or biased point of view. No individual is likely to argue that some particular group—such as White men, property owners, star athletes, or philosophers—should receive special social and economic privileges when, for all that individual knows, they will be a woman of color, propertyless, unathletic, and bored by philosophy when the veil is lifted. Because individuals in the original position are all equally ignorant of their personal predicaments and they are all trying to advance their self-interest, agreement is possible. The reasoning of any one person will be the same as the reasoning of each of the others, for each is in identical circumstances and each has the same motivation. As a result, no actual group has to perform Rawls's thought experiment. People who read Rawls's book can imagine that they are in the original position and then decide whether they would choose the principles Rawls thinks they would.

The veil of ignorance, in effect, forces people in the original position to be objective and impartial and makes agreement possible. Also, according to Rawls, the fact that people have no special knowledge that would allow them to argue in a biased way accords with our sense of fairness. The circumstances of the original position are genuinely equal and fair, and because of this, the principles agreed to under these conditions have a good claim to be considered the principles of justice.

Rawls's approach is connected to ideas that we encountered in the last chapter. Rawls is a nonconsequentialist, obviously enough, and though he isn't a strict Kantian he is deeply influenced by Kant's ideas. The original position can be understood as Rawls's interpretation of the Kantian notion that for something to be morally justified it must be universally acceptable. According to Rawls, principles of justice must be universally acceptable to people who are willing to be reasonable and not try to gain any special advantage for themselves. The veil of ignorance is a device for ensuring reasonability.

> The veil of ignorance eliminates bias and makes the original position a fair way of choosing principles.

Choosing the Principles

Although people in the original position are ignorant of their individual circumstances, they know that whatever their particular goals, interests, and talents turn out to be, they will want more, rather than less, of what Rawls calls **primary social goods**. These include not only income and wealth but also rights, liberties, opportunities, status, and self-respect. Of course, once the veil of ignorance is lifted, people will have more specific ideas about what is good for them. For example, they may choose a life built around religion, one spent in commerce and industry, or one devoted to academic study. But whatever these particular individual goals, interests, and plans turn out to be, they will almost certainly be furthered, and definitely never limited, by the fact that people in the original position secured for themselves more rather than less in the way of primary goods.

How, then, will people in the original position choose their principles? *A Theory of Justice* explores in depth the reasoning that Rawls thinks would guide their choice. At the heart of Rawls's argument is the contention that people in the original position will be conservative, not in the political sense of that word but in the sense of playing it safe: they won't wish to gamble with their futures. In setting up the ground rules for their society, they are determining their own fates and those of their children. This exercise is not something to be taken lightly, a game to be played and replayed. Rather, with so much at stake, people will reason cautiously.

Consider, for example, the possibility that people in the original position will set up a feudal society: 10 percent of the population will be nobles, living lives of incredible wealth, privilege, and leisure; the other 90 percent will be serfs, toiling away long hours to support the extravagant lifestyles of the aristocracy. Perhaps some people would consider the joy of being a pampered noble so great that they would vote for such an arrangement behind the veil of ignorance, but they would be banking on a long shot. When the veil of ignorance is lifted, the odds are nine to one that they will be poor and miserable serfs, not lords. Rawls thinks that people in the original position will not, in fact, gamble with their futures. They will not agree to rules that make it overwhelmingly likely that they will have to face a grim life of hardship.

Summary
John Rawls's theory of justice lies within the social-contract tradition. He asks us to imagine people meeting in the original position to choose the basic principles that are to govern their society. Although in this original position people choose on the basis of self-interest, we are to imagine that they are behind a veil of ignorance, with no personal information about themselves. Rawls contends that any principles agreed to under these circumstances have a strong claim to be considered the principles of justice.

What people in the original position would actually do, Rawls believes, is follow what game strategists call the **maximin rule** for making decisions. According to this rule, you should select the alternative under which the worst that could happen to you is better than the worst that could happen to you under any other alternative—that is, you should try to *maxi*mize the *min*imum that you could receive. This rule makes sense when you care much more about avoiding an unacceptable or disastrous result (such as being a serf) than about getting the best possible result (being a noble) and when you have no real idea what odds you are facing. It's a conservative decision principle, but Rawls thinks that people in the original position will find it a rational and appropriate guideline for their deliberations.

What this means is that even if the odds were reversed in the example above—if it were possible to have a society where 90 percent of the people could be lords and 10 percent serfs—parties in the original position still would not choose it. The high probability of ending up as a lord would not be enough to persuade them to run the risk of ending up as a serf. Even if they were given the choice of a society like Omelas, which was described in the last chapter, they would opt against it. They would assume that when they came out from behind the veil of ignorance they would be the child locked in the basement. Rawls argues that for similar reasons, people in the original position will not adopt the utilitarian standard to govern their society, because the utilitarian principle might sacrifice the well-being of some to enhance society's total happiness. People in the original position, Rawls argues, will not be willing to risk sacrificing their own happiness, once the veil of ignorance is lifted, for the greater good.

Rawls's Two Principles

Rawls believes that people in the original position would endorse his two principles.

Rawls argues that after considering various alternatives, people in the original position will eventually endorse the following two principles as the fundamental governing principles of their society:

1. Each person is to have an equal right to the most extensive total system of equal basic liberties compatible with a similar system of liberty for all.[38]

2. Social and economic inequalities are to satisfy two conditions: First, they are to be attached to positions and offices open to all under conditions of fair equality of opportunity; and second, they are to be to the greatest expected benefit of the least-advantaged members of society.[39]

These are the principles of justice because they would be agreed to in an initial situation of equality and fairness.

These principles, because they are agreed to in an initial situation of equality and fairness, will be the principles of justice. Once these two principles of justice have been endorsed, people in the original position can gradually be given more information about their specific society. They can then go on to design their basic social and political institutions in more detail.

According to Rawls, the first principle takes priority over the second, at least for societies that have attained a moderate level of affluence. The liberties Rawls has in mind are the traditional democratic ones of freedom of thought, conscience, and religious worship, as well as freedom of the person and political liberty. Explicitly absent are "the right to own certain kinds of property (e.g., means of production), and freedom of contract as understood by the doctrine of laissez-faire." The first principle guarantees not only equal liberty to individuals but also as much liberty to individuals as possible, compatible with others having the same amount of liberty. There is no reason why people in the original position would settle for anything less.

All regulations could be seen as infringing on personal liberty, because they limit what a person may do. The law that requires you to drive on the right-hand side of the road denies you the freedom to drive on either side whenever you wish. Some would argue that justice requires only an equal liberty. For example, as long as every motorist is required to drive on the right-hand side of the road, justice is being served; or if everyone in a theocratic society is forbidden to criticize the dominant religion, then all are equal in their liberty. But Rawls argues that if more extensive liberty is possible, without inhibiting the liberty of others, then it would be irrational to settle for a lesser degree of liberty. In the case of driving, permitting me to drive on either side of the road would only interfere with the liberty of others to drive efficiently to their various destinations. In the theocracy example, in contrast, free speech could be more extensive without limiting anyone's liberty.

The second principle concerns social and economic inequalities. Regarding inequalities, Rawls writes:

> It is best to understand not *any* differences between offices and positions, but differences in the benefits and burdens attached to them either directly or indirectly, such as prestige and wealth, or liability to taxation and compulsory services. Players in a game do not protest against there being different positions, such as batter, pitcher, catcher, and the like, nor to there being various privileges and powers as specified by the rules; nor do the citizens of a country object to there being the different offices of government such as president, senator, governor, judge, and so on, each with their special rights and duties.[40]

Rather, at issue are differences in wealth and power, honors and rewards, and privileges and salaries that attach to different roles in society.

Rawls's second principle states that insofar as inequalities are permitted—that is, insofar as it's compatible with justice for some jobs or positions to bring greater rewards than others—these positions must be open to all. In other words, there must be meaningful equality of opportunity in the competition among individuals for those positions in society that bring greater economic and social rewards. This, of course, is a familiar ideal, but what exactly a society must do to achieve not just legal but full and fair equality of opportunity will be a matter of debate.

The other part of the second principle is less familiar and more controversial. Called the **difference principle**, it's the distinctive core of Rawls's theory. It states that inequalities are justified only if they work to the benefit of the least-advantaged members of society. By "least-advantaged," Rawls simply means those who are least well-off. But what does it mean to require that inequalities work to the benefit of this group?

Imagine that we are back in the original position. We wish to make sure that under the principles we choose, the worst that can happen to us once the veil of ignorance is lifted is still better than the worst that might have happened under some other arrangement. We might, therefore, choose strict social and economic equality. With an equal division of goods, there's no risk of doing worse than anyone else and no danger of being sacrificed to increase the total happiness of society. In the case of liberty, people in the original position do insist on full equality, but with social and economic inequality, the matter is a little different.

Suppose, for instance, that as a result of dividing things up equally, people lack an incentive to undertake some of the more difficult work that society needs done. It might then be the case that allowing certain inequalities—for example, paying people more for being particularly productive or for undertaking the necessary training to perform some socially useful task—would work to everyone's benefit, including those who would be earning less. If so, then why not permit those inequalities?

Compare these two diagrams:

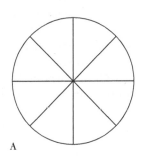

A

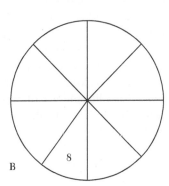

B

Summary
Rawls argues that people in the original position would follow the maximin rule for making decisions. They would choose principles guaranteeing that the worst that could happen to them is better than the worst that could happen to them under any rival principles. Rawls argues that they would agree on two principles: (1) Each person has a right to the most extensive scheme of liberties compatible with others having the same amount of liberty. (2) To be justified, any inequalities must be to the greatest expected benefit of the least advantaged and open to all under conditions of fair equality of opportunity.

Each pie represents a possible social and economic distribution among eight basic groups in society (the number eight is arbitrary). In Figure A, things are divided equally; in Figure B, unequally. Suppose, then, that because a society permits inequalities as an incentive to get people to work harder or to do work that they otherwise wouldn't have wanted to do, the overall amount to be distributed among society's members increases—that is, the economic pie grows in size from A to B, and the people with the thinnest slice of B are better off than they would have been with an equal slice of A.

Which society will people in the original position prefer? Obviously, the one represented by Figure B, because the least they could receive in B (the skinny slice labeled 8) is bigger than any of the eight equal slices in A. People in the original position don't care about equality of distribution as a value in and of itself; they want the social and economic arrangement that will provide them with the highest minimum. One useful way to think about the choice in the original position is to say that the parties there assume that however the pie is divided, once they step out from behind the veil of ignorance they'll turn out to be the person with the smallest slice. So they'll prefer the way of organizing society whose smallest slice is still bigger than the smallest slice of any of the alternatives.

Rawls is not trying to prove that the benefits received by the better-off will always, or even usually, trickle down to the least advantaged (although, of course, some people believe that). Rather, his point is simply that people in the original position wouldn't insist on social and economic equality at all costs. If permitting some people to be better-off than the average resulted in the least-well-off segment of society being better-off than it would have been under a strictly equal division, then this is what people in the original position will want. Rawls's difference principle is intended to capture this idea. Rawls's principles permit economic inequalities only if they do in fact benefit the least advantaged.

For example, imagine a society that embraced a sort of perfect communism where everyone was paid exactly the same whatever form of work they did. In that society, it might be very hard to motivate people to do difficult, demanding jobs that take many years of training, like working as surgeons. But everyone is better off in a society that has enough surgeons. Allowing some people make more money than others as a way to encourage them to take on these roles would therefore seem entirely warranted from the standpoint of parties in the original position.

Consider the recurrent proposal to lower further the income tax on capital gains (that is, on personal income from the sale of assets like stocks, bonds, and real estate). Proponents claim that reducing the tax will spur trading in financial assets, which in turn will lead to growth in tax revenues, and that the cut will trigger more long-term investment, helping revitalize the economy. Critics of the proposal contest both claims. Still, everyone agrees that the tax break would certainly increase the income of those who are already very rich because the wealthiest 0.1 percent of the nation receives half of all capital gains income. Will lowering taxes on the rich benefit the least-advantaged members of society more in the long run than any alternative tax policy?

This question illustrates the application of Rawls's difference principle in a practical context, but we must remember that Rawls intends his principles to be used not as a direct guide to day-to-day policy decisions but rather as the basis for determining what form society's primary social, political, and economic institutions should take in the first place. What will these institutions look like? More specifically, what sort of economic system will best satisfy Rawls's difference principle? Rawls doesn't answer this question. He sees it as primarily a question for economists and other social scientists, whereas the task of philosophers like himself is the preliminary one of working out a satisfactory conception of justice. Rawls does appear to believe, however, that a liberal form of capitalism, with sufficient welfare provisions, would satisfy his principles, but he doesn't rule out the possibility that a democratic socialist system could do so as well.

People in the original position don't want equality at all costs. They will permit inequality if it improves the lot of the least advantaged.

Fairness and the Basic Structure

Rawls intends his theory as a fundamental alternative to utilitarianism, which he rejects on the grounds that maximizing the total well-being of society could permit an unfair distribution of burdens and benefits. Utilitarianism, in Rawls's view, treats people's pleasures and pains as completely interchangeable: A decrease of happiness here is justified by greater happiness there. Within a person's own life, such trade-offs are sensible. An increase of pain now (as the dentist fills a cavity in my tooth) is justified in terms of greater happiness later (no painful, rotted tooth). But between individuals, as when Jack's happiness is decreased to provide Jill with a more-than-compensating gain, such trade-offs are morally problematic.

Thus, Rawls stresses that, in his view,

> each person possesses an inviolability founded on justice that even the welfare of society as a whole cannot override. . . . Therefore . . . the rights secured by justice are not subject to political bargaining or to the calculus of social interests.[41]

And he emphasizes that the difference principle

> excludes, therefore, the justification of inequalities on the grounds that the disadvantages of those in one position are outweighed by the greater advantages of those in another position. This rather simple restriction is the main modification I wish to make in the utilitarian principle as usually understood.[42]

Rawls, however, is equally unsympathetic to the libertarian approach adopted by Nozick. While they are both nonconsequentialists, their thinking still differs in fundamental ways. One difference concerns the relation they take to exist between the rights of individuals and what Rawls calls a society's "**basic structure**, the fundamental social institutions and their arrangement into one scheme."[43] Nozick starts with a Lockean view about what rights we as individuals have. He treats these rights as part of the "fabric of the universe," we might say. He then says that to be just, a society's basic structure must respect these rights. Rawls, in contrast, takes the idea of a just basic structure to be more fundamental than any theory of rights. According to Rawls, we can't know what rights individuals possess until we've decided what a just basic structure would look like. We have the rights that a society with a just basic structure would respect.

Benefits and Burdens

One theme that is central to Rawls's theory deserves particular attention. Inevitably, there will be natural differences among human beings—in physical prowess, mental agility, and so on—but there is nothing natural or inevitable about the weight attached by society to those differences. For Rawls, a desirable feature of any account of justice is that it strives to minimize the social consequences of purely arbitrary differences that are due to sheer luck. He stresses that no one deserves their particular natural characteristics. We cannot say that fashion models deserve to be attractive or that Harvard professors deserve to be blessed with excellent minds any more than we can say that Fred merits his shortness or Pamela her nearsightedness. Their attributes are simply the result of a genetic lottery. But Rawls goes beyond this to argue that even personal characteristics like diligence and perseverance reflect the environment in which one was raised. Think about how different your character and personality might be if you had been born into a different environment and subject to different influences: different parents, different siblings, different teachers. Rawls would say that the fact that you happen to have received the upbringing you did is the product of undeserved luck.

> We do not deserve our place in the distribution of native endowments, any more than we deserve our initial starting place in society. That we deserve the superior character that enables us to make the effort to cultivate our abilities is also problematic; for such character depends in good part upon fortunate family and social circumstances in early life for which we can claim no credit. The notion of desert does not apply here.[44]

Rawls rejects utilitarianism because it could permit an unfair distribution of benefits and burdens.

Contrary to Nozick, Rawls believes that social justice concerns the basic structure of society, not transactions between individuals.

Summary
Rawls rejects utilitarianism because it might permit an unfair distribution of burdens and benefits. Contrary to the entitlement theory, he argues that the primary focus of justice should be the basic social structure, not transactions between individuals. He contends that society is a cooperative project for mutual benefit and that justice requires us to reduce the social and economic consequences of arbitrary natural differences among people.

For Rawls, a desirable feature of any account of justice is that it strives to minimize the social consequences of purely arbitrary differences that are due to sheer luck. He denies that people deserve the attributes they were born with or that reflect their environment and upbringing; all these qualities are ultimately the result of luck.

Accordingly, Rawls thinks we cannot really claim moral credit for our special talents or even our virtuous character. In Rawls's view, then, if our personal characteristics are not something that we deserve, we have no strong claim to the economic rewards they might bring. On the contrary, justice requires that the social and economic consequences of these arbitrarily distributed assets be minimized:

> Those who have been favored by nature, whoever they are, may gain from their good fortune only on terms that improve the situation of those who have lost out. The naturally advantaged are not to gain merely because they are more gifted, but only to cover the costs of training and education and for using their endowments in ways that help the less fortunate as well. No one deserves his greater natural capacity nor merits a more favorable starting place in society. But, of course, this is no reason to ignore, much less to eliminate these distinctions. Instead, the basic structure can be arranged so that these contingencies work for the good of the least fortunate. Thus we are led to the difference principle if we wish to set up the social system so that no one gains or loses from his arbitrary place in the distribution of natural assets or his initial position in society without giving or receiving compensating advantages in return.[45]

This important passage from *A Theory of Justice* reflects well Rawls's vision of society as a cooperative project for mutual benefit.

Criticism of Rawls's Theory

As a result of its being so influential, Rawls's theory has also been the subject of many criticisms. Of course, if you're a committed libertarian then you'll reject Rawls's theory because it doesn't adequately respect Lockean rights. But other criticisms of the theory are also possible.

Objections to Rawls's theory include the claims that parties in the original position are excessively risk-averse and that the theory turns a blind idea to historical injustices.

One familiar line of criticism is that parties in the original position would be less risk-averse than Rawls supposes and more willing to take into account the probability that they'll end up in different social positions when they step out from behind the veil. Suppose that a given way of organizing society would result in the vast majority of people being very well off, with just a few being not very well off at all. According to Rawls, people in the original position would pessimistically assume that they were going to be in the last group, ignoring the fact that statistically this is very unlikely. If they took the unlikelihood of this outcome into account, they might be more willing to gamble on this way of organizing society. If the parties in the original position took probabilities into account in this way, the result of their choice would be something very similar to utilitarianism instead of Rawls's two principles. In fact, before Rawls ever wrote about the original position the basic idea had been developed by a utilitarian, the Hungarian-American economist John Harsanyi (1920–2000).

Both Nozick and Rawls are sometimes criticized for their focus on what a perfectly just society would look like, one that had been just from the start, without taking into account the history of injustice in our society: slavery, Jim Crow, Native Americans' being driven off their land, and so forth. They are not blind to this history. Both, though, think that the most productive approach for philosophers is to start by developing an "ideal theory" that explains how things should have happened and then working out what corrective actions are needed to account for departures from this perfectly just trajectory. (Nozick even suggests that in a society with a pervasive history of injustice, something like Rawls's theory might be more just in practice than his own entitlement theory, since the difference principle would do something to rectify the many instances in which the entitlement theory has been violated.)[46] Whether this is the right approach is of course open to debate; the philosopher of race Charles Mills (1951–2021) was among the foremost critics of the strategy of prioritizing ideal theory.[47]

Study Corner

Key Terms and Concepts

basic structure

capital gains

declining marginal utility of money

difference principle

distributive justice

effective tax rate

entitlement theory

free market

Gini coefficient

justice

libertarianism

Lockean rights

marginal tax rates

maximin rule

original position

primary social goods

property rights

state of nature

veil of ignorance

worker participation

....

Points to Review

- distribution of income and wealth in the United States (pp. 65–68)

- distinction between income and wealth (pp. 67–68)

- difference between progressive, regressive, and neutral taxation (p. 67)

- four related ideas bound up with the concept of justice (pp. 68–69)

- Aristotle's formal principle of justice (p. 68)

- John Stuart Mill's definition of injustice (p. 69)

- some different principles often used as a basis of distribution (p. 69)

- Walzer's pluralistic approach to distributive justice (pp. 70–71)

- how a utilitarian like Mill looks at justice (p. 71)

- Mill's discussion of whether more-talented workers should receive greater pay (pp. 71–72)

- utilitarianism and the declining marginal utility of money (p. 73)

- Mill's view of worker participation (pp. 73–74)

- three principles of Nozick's entitlement theory (pp. 75–76)

- Locke's account of property rights (p. 76)

- the point of the Wilt Chamberlain example (p. 77)

- how libertarians understand freedom in terms of rights (pp. 78–79)

- Amartya Sen's analysis of famines (p. 79)

- how libertarians and nonlibertarians differ in their view of property rights (p. 80)

- the nature of the choice and the reasoning people would use in the original position (pp. 81–82)

- Rawls's two principles of justice (p. 84)

- the point illustrated by the "two pies" diagram (p. 85)

- how Rawls's theory differs from utilitarianism and libertarianism (pp. 87–88)

- why Rawls thinks we should minimize the social consequences of natural differences (p. 88)

....

For Further Reflection

1. What does the concept of justice mean to you?
2. Which theory of distributive justice do you find most convincing?
3. Is the United States an economically just society?

Case 3.1

Eminent Domain

Susette Kelo's Nondescript, Pink Clapboard House Sits Above the Thames River in the Fort Trumbull area of New London, Connecticut. It's surrounded by vacant lots, where neighbors once lived. One by one, these neighbors have left, and their homes have been razed. Their property has been taken over by the City of New London, which has used its power of eminent domain to clear the land where dozens of homes once stood in order to prepare the way for new development.[48]

Eminent domain is the ancient right of government to take property from an individual without consent for the common good—for example, to build a highway, an airport, a dam, or a hospital. The U.S. Constitution recognizes that right, permitting private property to be taken for "public use" as long as "just compensation" is paid. In this case, however, New London is taking land from one private party and giving it to another. By tearing down Susette Kelo's old neighborhood, the city hopes to attract new development, which in turn will help revitalize the community and bring in more tax revenue. "This isn't for the public good," says Kelo, a nurse who works three jobs. "The public good is a firehouse or a school, not a hotel and a sports club."

Connecticut officially designates New London a blighted area. When the Navy moved its Undersea Warfare Center away from New London, taking 1,400 jobs with it, the city's already high rate of unemployment only got worse. Much of its housing stock is old and second-rate. The Fort Trumbull area, in particular, is—or was, anyway—a rather gritty neighborhood, where earlier generations of immigrants struggled to get a start. But New London saw a chance to turn things around when the pharmaceutical company Pfizer built a $350 million research center along the river below historic Fort Trumbull. Since then, city and state governments have created a park around the fort, cleaned up the Navy's old asbestos-laden site, and opened the riverfront to public access. Now the city wants to build a hotel, office buildings, and new homes to fill the riverfront blocks around Fort Trumbull. And it's not talking about new homes for people like Susette Kelo.

"We need to get housing at the upper end, for people like the Pfizer employees," says Ed O'Connell, the lawyer for the New London Development Corporation, which is in charge of the city's redevelopment efforts. "They are the professionals, they are the ones with the expertise and the leadership qualities to remake the city—the young urban professionals who will invest in New London, put their kids in school, and think of this as a place to stay for 20 or 30 years." And housing developers want open space to work with; they don't want to build around a few old properties like Ms. Kelo's and that of her neighbors, Wilhelmina and Charles Dery.

Age 87 and 85, respectively, the Dery's live in the house Wilhelmina was born in. The city is willing to pay a fair price for their home, but it's not an issue of money. "We get this all the time," says their son Matt. "'How much did they offer? What will it take?' My parents don't want to wake up rich tomorrow. They just want to wake up in their own home."

Unfortunately for the Derys, in 2005 the U.S. Supreme Court upheld the city's condemnation rights. In a close, 5-to-4 decision, it ruled that compulsory purchase to foster economic development falls under "public use" and is thus constitutionally permissible. "Promoting economic development is a traditional and long accepted function of government," Justice John Paul Stevens wrote for the majority. Intended to increase jobs and tax revenues, New London's plan "unquestionably serves a public purpose." In her dissenting opinion, however, Justice Sandra Day O'Connor objected: "Under the banner of economic development, all private property is now vulnerable to being taken and transferred to another private owner, so long as it might be upgraded. . . . Nothing is to prevent the state from replacing any Motel 6 with a Ritz-Carlton, any home with a shopping mall, or any farm with a factory."

The Supreme Court's decision pushes the debate over eminent domain back to the states and local communities. Although many cities have successfully used eminent domain to rebuild decayed urban areas or spark economic growth,[49] resistance to it has intensified, with political and legal battles being fought far beyond Susette Kelo's home in New London. For example, in Highland Park, New Jersey, the owners of a photography studio worry that a plan to redevelop their street will force them out of the location they've occupied for twenty-five years. In Port Chester, New York, a state development agency wants the site of a small furniture plant for a parking lot for Home Depot, and its owners are resisting. And in Salina, New York, twenty-nine little businesses—with names like Butch's Automotive and Transmission, Syracuse Crank and Machine, Gianelli's Sausage, and Petersen Plumbing—are battling local government's use of eminent domain to pave the way for DestiNY's proposed 325-acre, $2.67 billion research-and-development park.

Like New London, Salina desperately needs big ideas and big development, and it may not get another chance soon. But is tearing down these businesses fair? "We're here," says Philip Jakes-Johnson, who owns Solvents & Petroleum Service, one of the twenty-nine businesses in question. "We pay our taxes. We build companies and run them without tax breaks." Brian Osborne, another owner, adds: "Everything I and my family have worked for over the past 25 years is at stake because of the way eminent domain is being used in this state and across the country."

Update

In 2009, Pfizer announced that, as a cost-cutting measure, it was closing its New London facility and transferring its 1,400 employees to a campus the company owns in Groton, Connecticut. Nothing was built on the Fort Trumbull site.

Susette Kelo challenged the city of New London's use of eminent domain.

a minimum to limit its effect by declaring that the prevention of possible future blight is not a sufficient reason for property to be seized. However, when a case is appealed to the Court it will be heard only if four justices vote in favor, a process known as "granting certiorari." Only three justices voted in favor of hearing Eychaner's case—Justices Thomas, Kavanaugh, and Gorsuch—so the ruling of the Appellate Court of Illinois in favor of the seizure's constitutionality stands.[50]

··
Discussion Questions
··

1. Did New London treat Susette Kelo and her neighbors fairly? Assuming that the proposed development would help to revitalize New London, is it just for the city to appropriate private property around Fort Trumbull?

2. Are towns such as New London and Salina pursuing wise, beneficial, and progressive social policies, or are their actions socially harmful and biased against ordinary working people and small-business owners?

3. Do you believe that eminent domain is a morally legitimate right of government? Explain why or why not.

4. "If 'just compensation' is paid, then by definition those who lose their property cannot claim that they have been treated unjustly." Assess this argument. Can compensation be just even if one of the parties is unwilling to accept it?

5. Is it fair to the community if an individual refuses payment and blocks a socially useful project? Putting legal issues aside, are there situations in which it would be morally permissible for government to seize private property for the public good with less than full compensation or even with no compensation at all?

6. Assess the concept of eminent domain, in general, and the plight of Susette Kelo and her neighbors, in particular, from the point of view of the different theories of justice discussed in this chapter. Is it possible to square the government's exercise of eminent domain with a libertarian approach to justice?

7. Should the Supreme Court have taken Eychaner's case and overturned or limited *Kelo*?

In 2005, the City of Chicago used its power of eminent domain to seize a vacant lot owned by Fred Eychaner. The property was turned over to the Blommer Chocolate Company as part of a development plan. In contrast with the land taken in New London, this part of Chicago was not blighted. However, the city argued that it was seizing the land in part to prevent blight from developing in the future. The city acted only after Eychaner had refused Blommer's offer to buy the land for $824,980. When Eychaner sued, the court upheld the seizure, but the jury awarded him $2.5 million. In a subsequent trial this amount was increased to $7.1 million. However, Eychaner sought to have the case heard before the U.S. Supreme Court. Some thought that the Court might use the case to overturn *Kelo*, or at

Case 3.2
A College Education: Who Should Pay?

While a Recent Spurt of Inflation Has Caused the Prices of Most of the things that Americans buy to increase, the price of one of the largest purchases that individuals and families make has been climbing for years: a college education. According to the College Board, in 1979–80 the average advertised price of tuition, fees, room, and board at a public four-year university was $9,420. In 2022–23, it was $23,250. That is a 147% increase. And these prices have been adjusted for inflation, with the price for 1979–80 being given in "2022 dollars," which means that the cost of college increased by 147% *on top* of the general rise in prices over this period.[51] Private non-profit four-year universities charged $20,250 in 1979–80 (again, in 2002 dollars), $53,430 in 2022–23. That is an increase of 164%. The price of public community colleges also went up by 164%, rising from $1,460 to $3,860.

The steady rise of the increase in the price tag of a college diploma was briefly interrupted by the COVID-19 pandemic, which may have been a response to the fact that many colleges and universities faced a choice between encouraging students to return to campus under uncertain conditions or moving classes online.[52] However, with the worst of the pandemic over and the inflation rate soaring, schools are looking at raising prices yet again. The *Washington Post* warns that "Colleges and universities across the country, squeezed by sharply rising labor and supply costs, are taking steps to fortify their revenue and resume their pre-pandemic patterns of annual tuition increases."[53] Federal financial aid is available to help students who qualify. In 2022–23, though, the maximum Pell grant that a student could receive was capped at $6,895. Only about a third of undergraduates receive Pell grants, moreover, and the average award was considerably less than the maximum: $4,166.[54]

Rising tuition makes a difference to who chooses to go to college and where they go. The National College Attainment Network calculates that only 24 percent of public four-year schools and 40 percent of public community colleges were genuinely affordable for students who qualified for Pell grants.[55] Moreover, a recent study by Drew Allen and Gregory C. Wolniak found that at both community colleges and less-selective public four-year universities tuition increases result in fewer students of color attending.[56]

There is no simple explanation for why college has become so expensive. Various factors have been cited as causes, and each may be a part of the larger story. One factor is that many four-year schools have invested heavily in amenities to offer students an experience that goes far beyond an education: fancy dining halls, climbing walls, "lazy rivers," and so on.[57] Another is that some schools pursue expensive strategies to move up in rankings like the ones compiled by *U.S. News and World Report*: inefficiently small class sizes, faculty salaries above the market rate, and an excessive emphasis on reputation-building faculty research.[58] A third is that universities employ an increasingly high percentage of people in non-faculty roles; this is the so-called "administrative bloat" problem.[59] Finally, in some cases, schools (especially private universities) may be advertising higher prices than they expect most students to pay, with students from the most affluent families paying the full "sticker" price and the rest receiving a discount.[60] This last point means that at certain schools, the rising prices may be more apparent than real.

But another factor also contributes to the rising cost of higher education, which is that state governments spend considerably less on their public college and university systems than they did in the past. As a result, these schools must rely more heavily on their other major source of funding: students. According to a 2019 report from the Center on Budget and Policy Priorities, "In 1988, students—through tuition—provided about a quarter of public colleges and universities' revenue, while state and local governments provided the remaining three-quarters. Today, that split is much closer to 50-50."[61] This split is likely even closer to 50-50 today, because state budgets were slashed starting in 2020 as the COVID-19 pandemic slowed economic activity and cut deeply into tax revenues. According to the National Education Association, state-level funding for higher education dropped $3.6 billion from 2020–21 to 2021–22.[62]

It might be tempting to think that this drop in state funding is not a major reason that tuition has gone up, since it has climbed even more sharply at private than at public universities. However, it would be a mistake to overlook the ways in which the different factors that have been listed are connected. Public colleges and universities charge students who reside in the same state lower tuition, to reflect the fact that they and their families have already provided support through their tax dollars. As state spending on higher education has declined, many universities have worked harder to attract out-of-state and international students who pay a higher rate. This is at least part of the reason that public schools have been spending more on amenities and on trying to move up in rankings. But private schools are competing for students with the "publics," so they must also spend more to keep up—and of course they pass these costs on to students. (Related government policy changes may explain some of the administrative bloat at public colleges and universities. Schools are under much more scrutiny than previously to make sure that money is not being wasted and that students are learning. Completing the forms and producing the reports needed to satisfy the state and accreditors on these points requires thousands of extra hours per year of administrative work.)

One way to look at this shift toward requiring students to pay more of their cost of attendance at public colleges and universities is as a simple policy question about how much states can afford to spend. But there's another way to look at it, too, which is as a shift from viewing higher education as a "public good" to a "private good."

On the one hand, you might believe that everyone benefits from living in a society where a higher portion of the population has a university degree, whether because this promotes prosperity across the economy or because college graduates are better-informed voters and citizens. A rising tide, as they say, floats all boats. In this case, you might think that it makes sense for the public to make significant collective investments in public colleges and universities.

On the other hand, you might believe that the benefits of higher education are enjoyed first and foremost by the college graduates themselves, primarily in the form of higher paychecks. In that case, you might think that it makes sense that they should be the ones to pay, since they're the ones who reap the rewards. After all, you might reason, there's some analogy between what a college education does for a person's mind and what physical exercise does for their body. While there may be some indirect benefits to society as a whole when people exercise more, we're each the primary beneficiary of our own workouts. And, for this very reason, the government doesn't subsidize gym memberships.

Discussion Questions

1. Should states assume more of the burden of paying for public colleges and universities? Should the federal government offer more and larger Pell grants? Or should students and their families be primarily responsible for paying for higher education?

2. How would a utilitarian answer the questions above? What different factors would enter their calculation?

3. How would a libertarian like Nozick answer? What solutions might a libertarian offer to the problem of talented students who can't afford to pay for higher education on their own?

4. How would Rawls answer these questions? How do the different parts of his second principle of justice bear on them?

5. How would a utilitarian, a libertarian, and a Rawlsian each approach the question of whether the government should forgive student loan debt?

6. How much truth is there in the claim that even people without a college education benefit from living in a society in which many other people do?

7. If you're attending a public college or university, how would you explain to someone who has never attended college or university or someone who is attending a private school why it is just for them to taxed to subsidize the cost of your education? If you're at a private college or university, then does it seem unjust that you're being taxed to subsidize the cost of the public higher education system?

Case 3.3

Poverty in America

The Number of Americans Officially Classified as Living in Poverty has declined, although it is still quite large. The U.S. Census Bureau reports that in 2021, 37.9 million people were below the poverty line. That's actually down significantly from ten years ago, when as a result of the economic crisis and recession of 2008–09—the most serious economic meltdown since the Great Depression of the 1930s—the figure was close to 50 million.[63] Nevertheless, nearly 60 years after President Lyndon B. Johnson declared "war on poverty," about 11.6 percent on the population are still in its grasp.

It's worth adding, however, that the official poverty numbers are only a rough guide to how many Americans face severe economic deprivation. An individual or family is said to be in poverty if their pre-tax income falls below a certain threshold. These threshold amounts were determined in the early 1960s by taking the cost of a very basic diet and multiplying it by three. They have since been adjusted for inflation. In 2021, these thresholds were $14,097 for a single adult (under age sixty-five) and $27,949 for a family of four. The Census Bureau has developed an updated supplemental poverty measure that is meant to be reflect life in twenty-first century America. It factors in the actual costs of expenditures like medical care and Internet access, as well as regional differences in housing costs; it also considers benefits from government programs that the official measure ignores. In 2021, 7.8 percent of the population was in poverty according to this supplemental measure. While that's lower than the official poverty rate, two points are worth bearing in mind. First, in 2021, people received relief payments from the federal government due to the COVID-19 pandemic, and those benefits were temporary. Second, this means that tens of millions of people were still in poverty even after government relief payments were considered.

Poverty is particularly hard on children. Among other things, it mars their brain development. This is not just a result of poor nutrition or exposure to environmental toxins, as one might expect. Rather, according to Dr. Lauren Fasig Caldwell, director of American Psychological Association's Children, Youth and Families Office, children in poverty "may experience toxic stress" that can "disrupt development of brain architecture and physiological systems," leading to "impairment of cognitive, social and emotional development."[64] This in turn may impact "an individual's physical and mental health throughout adulthood." According to the Joseph Rowntree Foundation, people who grow up in poverty are more likely to make decisions based on short-term considerations as opposed to long-term goals.[65] Obviously, this might have implications for the ability of people who grew up in poverty to escape it.

Furthermore, millions of Americans endure hunger. According to the U.S. Department of Agriculture, 10.2 percent of U.S. households lacked "food security" in 2021, which means that they "were uncertain of having or unable to acquire enough food to meet the needs of all their members because they had insufficient money or other resources for food,"[66] and 3.8 percent had very low food security, which effectively means that they experienced hunger. Five million children lived in households where both children and adults were food insecure. As much as parents try to shield their children, over 500,000 children lived in households where even children were very food insecure.

In addition, in most cities a visitor is likely to see people roaming the streets in tattered clothing, picking their food out of garbage cans and sleeping in doorways or in makeshift shacks and abandoned cars. Contrary to the popular perception that the homeless consist mostly of young men with drug, alcohol, or mental-health problems, the majority are simply jobless individuals or families who cannot afford housing. The U.S. Interagency Council on Homelessness reported in 2022 that half a million Americans were sleeping without proper shelter each night and that over the course of a year more than a million families and individuals would do so.[67]

People in different walks of life and in different circumstances experience poverty. In the United States today, the "working poor"—members of the labor force who don't earn enough to pull themselves and their families out of poverty—number 6.3 million.[68] The federal minimum wage was set at $7.25 per hour in 2009 and has not been raised since. (Some states and cities have higher minimums.) Adjusted for inflation, it is lower today than it has been since the 1940s.[69] Someone working 40 hours a week, every week, for that wage cannot raise their family out of poverty.

Many poor people are unable to work and depend on outside assistance, but living decently on welfare has always been difficult, if not impossible. The old system of AFDC (Aid to Families with Dependent Children) was popular when it was created in 1935 and most AFDC recipients were widows. Public support for the program ebbed as many Americans came to believe that AFDC discouraged its recipients from marrying and from working. As a result, benefits grew even stingier. By the time AFDC came to an end in 1996, welfare benefits had fallen, in real terms, to 51 percent of what they had been in 1971.[70] With annual cash allowances for a family on AFDC ranging from $1,416 in Mississippi to $6,780 in New York, even in the most generous states stipends were never enough to allow a family to escape from poverty.[71]

In 1996, Congress replaced AFDC with TANF (Temporary Assistance to Needy Families). Under the new system, the entitlement of poor people to support has been replaced by block grants to the states to run their own welfare programs. The grants are limited to a certain amount of money; if they run out, the states are not required to make additional expenditures. The size of the grants has not increased since the program's creation; according to the Center on Budget Policies and Priorities, this has resulted in their losing almost 40 percent of their value to inflation.[72] The Center further observes that "in 2020, for every 100 families in poverty nationwide, only 21 received TANF cash assistance," and that "TANF's history of racism means that it fails to reach many families in states where Black children are likelier to live."

Welfare recipients are required to work for pay or to enroll in training programs, and financial support is limited to a lifetime maximum of five years. This shift in policy has been controversial. Since the TANF system began, the number of people receiving welfare benefits has declined, but experts disagree about the reasons: Is it a growing economy offering more opportunities, the success of the new approach in encouraging welfare recipients to make themselves employable, or simply people who are not able to take care of themselves being denied support?

Some people assert that those described as "poor" in the United States are pretty well-off by world standards. Probably many of us have driven through depressed neighborhoods and seen cars in driveways and TVs playing through windows. It is a very different image than the pictures that we see of people in the most dire need in the developing world. But the United States is the richest country in the world. To whom should we be comparing ourselves? In 2016, the National Poverty Center conducted an analysis of how poverty in America compares to global standards. They looked at four measures of quality of life: life expectancy, infant mortality, risk of homicide, and risk of incarceration. Based on these measures, they concluded, "In all four domains, America's poor rank far lower than what is seen in the most affluent countries, and instead find themselves in the company of countries with just a fraction of the GDP [gross domestic product, a measure of economic productivity]

of the United States."[73] Using 2019 data, Mark R. Rank, the Herbert S. Hadley Professor of Social Welfare at Washington University in St. Louis and creator of the *Confronting Poverty* website, similarly concludes that in comparison to 25 other nations with highly developed economies "the U.S. rates of poverty are substantially higher and more extreme."[74]

While there is widespread agreement among experts that America has a poverty problem, there is no consensus about what to do about it. In 2015, the (generally conservative) American Enterprise Institute and the (generally liberal or progressive) Brookings Institution assembled a politically diverse working group of policy experts—conservatives and Republicans, progressives and Democrats, and centrists and non-partisans—to discuss what measures the country should take.[75] The group's members observed that while there is a broad consensus on three foundational values that pertain to poverty, conservatives and progressives frequently disagree about how to weigh these values against each other. They also disagree about how to act on them, and specifically on the role that government should play in combating poverty. Nevertheless, one takeaway from the working group was how much these different groups can agree upon.

The first of these values was *opportunity*:

> Of course, in a free society with a free market, some families will end up far wealthier than others, and some parents will be more inclined or more able than others to prepare their children to grasp the opportunities that will come their way. Children don't begin life or education at the same starting line, and the question of how much the government should do to narrow the gaps in opportunity is a difficult one. Progressives generally believe that government should be more active and can be more effective than do conservatives. But this difference shouldn't obscure the fact that nearly all Americans would prefer to live in a society in which opportunities for self-advancement are more widely available, especially to those at the bottom of the income distribution, than is now the case.

The second value that this group discussed was *responsibility*:

> Conservatives tend to believe that a society's high expectations of personal responsibility and upright behavior encourage the best in its citizenry. They argue further that it is proper to hold individuals accountable and that even when doing so seems unfair, failing to demand accountability risks the spread of irresponsibility. Progressives tend to believe that unpredictable labor markets, the stresses and pressures of modern life, enduring discrimination, and broader social influences often block people from supporting themselves, and so there are limits to how much accountability we can rightfully demand. Nevertheless, both sides accept that illness (both physical and mental), economic dislocations and recessions, and just plain bad luck will always leave some people in need of help.

The third and final value was *security*:

> Today, progressives and conservatives disagree on just how comprehensive social insurance should be, and on whether government is the best way to provide it. Progressives often look to Canada and Northern Europe and admire their more extensive social protection, but conservatives often want to reduce the major social welfare programs, or privatize some of their functions. The left tends to believe that a

wealthy society can afford to offer wider and more generous forms of support, but the right is concerned that efforts to guarantee security often undermine people's sense of personal responsibility, lead to greater dependency, and make it more difficult for people to reach their full potential. But both sides agree that people need some source of security against the vicissitudes of life. Both sides realize that there will always be some individuals who can't care for themselves, for reasons beyond their control.

Despite their political differences, the working group was able to reach agreement on twelve different recommendations for addressing poverty. They concluded that the United States should, among other things, "Promote a new cultural norm surrounding parenthood and marriage," "Promote delayed, responsible childbearing," "Make work pay more for the less educated," and "Close resource gaps to reduce education gaps."

Discussion Questions

1. Does the existence of poverty imply that our socioeconomic system is unjust? Does the concentration of poverty in certain groups make it more unjust than it would be otherwise?

2. What are the causes of poverty? Are they structural or individual? How is one's answer to this question likely to affect one's view of the justice or injustice of poverty?

3. What moral obligation, if any, do we have individually and as a society to reduce poverty? What steps could be taken? What role should business play? The government?

4. How would a utilitarian view the facts about poverty? What are the implications for our society of the concept of the declining utility of money?

5. How would a libertarian like Nozick view poverty in the United States? How plausible do you find the libertarian's preference for private charity over public assistance?

6. How would our economy be assessed from the point of view of Rawls's difference principle? Can it be plausibly maintained that, despite poverty, our system works to "the greatest expected benefit of the least advantaged"? Is this an appropriate standard?

7. Which of the values of opportunity, responsibility, and security is the most important? Least? How should we seek to balance them? For instance, how much economic security should we be willing to give up in order to increase economic opportunities or to hold people more accountable for their choices?

Chapter 4

American and Global Capitalism

Learning Objectives

After completing this chapter, you should be able to:

1. Recount the definition of capitalism, capitalism's major historical stages, and some of its key features.
2. Present and assess two classical moral justifications of capitalism—one based on the right to property and the other on Adam Smith's concept of the "invisible hand."
3. Explain and evaluate several familiar criticisms of capitalism—in particular, the persistence of inequality and poverty, capitalism's implicit view of human nature, the rise of economic oligarchies, the shortcomings of competition, and employees' experience of alienation and exploitation on the job.
4. Analyze some of the problems facing capitalism in the United States today—in particular, the decline of manufacturing, along with job outsourcing and the trade deficit; an excessive focus on the short term; and changing attitudes toward work.

Introduction

October Is Often Said To Be a Bad Month for Stocks. This Was certainly true in 2008. On Friday, October 10, 2008, the Dow Jones Industrial Average capped the worst week in its 112-year history with its most volatile day ever as the index swung 1,019 points in one trading session. In the weeks that followed, the gyrating stock market calmed down. As the dust settled, however, stockholders and mutual fund investors—many of them employees diligently saving for retirement—were forced to come to terms with the cold reality that their portfolios were worth only about half of what they had been a year before. And what was true of Wall Street was also true of Hong Kong, Mumbai, Tokyo, Johannesburg, Frankfurt, and London as stock markets around the world bottomed out. Capitalism is a worldwide system, and what happens on Wall Street reverberates around the globe, and vice versa, because the economies of all capitalist nations are intricately interconnected and their markets tightly intertwined.

In this case, it was the United States that pushed the world economic system into crisis. The collapse of the U.S. subprime mortgage market, following the bursting of the real estate bubble, had been causing financial jitters since early in 2008. But only that autumn

> ....
>
> The Collapse of the
> U.S. subprime mortgage
> market, following
> the bursting of the real
> estate bubble, had been
> causing financial jitters
> since early in 2008.
>
> ....

did it become clear that a number of once wealthy and haughty U.S. financial institutions were floating perilously on an ocean of debt. In an effort to maximize profit, they had underwritten loans that left them with potential liabilities thirty to forty times greater than their underlying assets. With that kind of exposure, it doesn't take much to bring the whole house of cards down. And that's what began happening.

When AIG, the world's biggest insurer, began tottering, the U.S. government rushed to its assistance, fearing that its collapse would wreak havoc throughout the financial system. The government had already facilitated the sales of Bear Stearns, the investment bank and brokerage firm, and Washington Mutual Bank to JPMorgan Chase; both institutions were about to go under. It had also effectively nationalized the mortgage giants Fannie Mae and Freddie Mac, to keep them afloat. Now, after rescuing AIG, the U.S. Treasury Department and Federal Reserve Board were worried that they were sending the wrong message to the business world, namely, that they were prepared to rescue any financial firm that needed help. So, a few days after bailing out AIG, they decided to let Lehman Brothers, a global financial services firm that was in deep trouble, go bust. The rapid demise of Lehman Brothers and the government's willingness to let it happen, however, immediately caused credit markets to panic, the movement of capital to freeze, investors to flee, the stock market to plunge—and the world economy to begin sliding inexorably into recession.

Governments around the world moved quickly to try to stabilize financial markets and free-up credit by lowering interest rates and propping up their banks and other financial institutions. The United States pumped money into its financial system on an unprecedented scale—taking over bad assets, guaranteeing debts, and pouring new capital into private capitalist firms. Anyone predicting even a few months earlier that liberals and conservatives in Congress would rapidly unite to approve a bank bailout of over $700 billion—that's more than $2,000 for every person in the country—would have been dismissed as a lunatic. But that's what happened. Moreover, a few months later the government bailed out General Motors and Chrysler, which were both floundering, and oversaw their restructuring.

Although these emergency operations could not stave off the worst economic slump that most Americans had ever seen, they probably prevented the financial meltdown of 2008 from turning into a 1930s-style depression. After the crisis, as most of the loans it had made were repaid with interest and the assets it had acquired were sold, the government eventually made a modest profit on the money it had dispensed. But its unprecedented economic intervention may have changed the face of capitalism forever.

But what exactly is the nature of the economic system called capitalism? What are its underlying values, principles, and economic philosophy? What has it accomplished, and what are its prospects for the future? This chapter examines these and related questions.

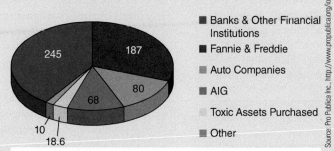

TARP Outflows (in Billions of Dollars)

- Banks & Other Financial Institutions
- Fannie & Freddie
- Auto Companies
- AIG
- Toxic Assets Purchased
- Other

Source: Pro Publica Inc., http://www.propublica.org/ion/bailout

President George W. Bush signed into law the Troubled Asset Relief Program (TARP) to address the financial meltdown resulting, primarily, from the subprime mortgage crisis. Under his administration and that of President Obama, TARP funds were used to bail out a number of American banks and other companies, thus helping to stabilize the economy.

Looking back in history, one must credit capitalism with helping break the constraints of medieval feudalism, which had severely limited individual possibilities for improvement. In place of a stifling economic system, capitalism offered opportunities for those blessed with imagination, an ability to plan, and a willingness to work. Capitalism must also be credited with enhancing the abundance and diversity of consumer goods beyond Adam Smith's wildest dreams. It has increased material wealth and the standard of living and has converted cities from modest bazaars into treasure troves of dazzling merchandise. In light of such accomplishments and the acculturation process that tends to glorify them, it's important to take a balanced approach to considering capitalism's virtues and vices.

...

Capitalism

Capitalism can be defined as an economic system that operates on the basis of profit and market exchange and in which the major means of production and distribution are in private hands. The United States, which has the world's largest national economy, is a fundamentally capitalist country. All manufacturing firms are privately owned, including those that produce military hardware for the government. Almost all other businesses—small, medium, and large—are also privately owned, including banks, insurance firms, power companies, and transportation companies. Although the government itself expends money on many things, no central governing body dictates to these private owners what or how much of anything will be produced. For example, officials at Apple, Caterpillar, or Ford Motor Company design their products and set their own production goals in anticipation of consumer demand.

The private ownership and market aspects of capitalism contrast with its polar opposite, socialism. **Socialism** is an economic system characterized by public ownership of property and a planned economy. Under socialism, a society's productive equipment is owned not by individuals (capitalists) but by public bodies. Socialism depends primarily on centralized planning rather than on a market system for both its overall allocation of resources and its distribution of income; crucial economic decisions are made not by individuals but by

Summary
Capitalism is an
economic system
in which production
and distribution are in
private hands, operating
on the basis of profit
and market exchange.
Socialism is an economic
system characterized
by public ownership of
property and a planned
economy. Worker control
socialism is a hybrid,
market-oriented form of
socialism.

government. In the former Soviet Union, for example, government agencies decided the number of automobiles—including models, styles, and colors—to be produced each year. Top levels of the Soviet government formulated production and cost objectives, which were then converted to specific production quotas and budgets that individual plant managers had to follow.

A hybrid economic system advocated by some socialists (and once approximated by the former Yugoslavia) is **worker control socialism**. Individual firms respond to a market when deciding what to produce and acquiring the necessary factors of production. However, the workforce of each enterprise controls the enterprise (although it may elect or hire managers to oversee day-to-day operations), and profits accrue to the workers as a group to divide in whatever manner they agree on. Although the workers manage their factories, the capital assets of each enterprise are owned by society as a whole and not by private individuals.

It's important to remember that while America is fundamentally a capitalist country, it's not a "pure" capitalism. Its government is far from the "nightwatchman state" described in the last chapter. Instead, the American government plays a very active role in the economy, by regulating and subsidizing businesses and by providing a social safety net, albeit—as again, we saw in the last chapter—less of a safety net than many other developed democracies provide.

Also worth remembering is that as "capitalism" has been defined here, these other developed countries are also fundamentally capitalistic, even the Nordic countries like Sweden, Norway, and Denmark. Admittedly, the word "socialism" is today sometimes used very broadly to include countries that have extensive social welfare policies, even if they retain private ownership of the means of production. This broader use of the term probably started with conservative critics of social welfare programs who wanted to link these programs in people's minds with repressive countries like the Soviet Union. Now some supporters of a Nordic-style welfare state, like Senator Bernie Sanders, have started to describe themselves as socialists. However, in a 2015 speech at Harvard, Danish Prime Minister Lars Løkke Rasmussen said:

> I know that some people in the US associate the Nordic model with some sort of socialism. Therefore, I would like to make one thing clear. Denmark is far from a socialist planned economy. Denmark is a market economy. … The Nordic model is an expanded welfare state which provides a high level of security to its citizens, but it is also a successful market economy with much freedom to pursue your dreams and live your life as you wish.[1]

Historical Background of Capitalism

What we know as "capitalism" did not fully emerge until the Renaissance in Europe during the 15th and 16th centuries. Before the Renaissance, business exchanges in medieval Europe were organized through guilds, which were associations of individuals involved in the same trade.

Today, if you want a pair of shoes you head for a shoe store, where you find an array of shoes. If nothing strikes your fancy, you set out for another shop, and perhaps another, until at last you find what you want. Or, more likely, you sit down at your computer and order a pair online. You certainly wouldn't ask the clerk to have someone make you a pair of shoes. Under the guild organization, shoemakers were also shoe sellers and made shoes only to fill orders. If they had no orders, they made no shoes. The shoemaker's sole economic function was to make shoes for people when they wanted them. His labor allowed him to maintain himself, not advance his station in life. When the shoemaker died, his business went with him—unless he had a son to inherit and carry on the enterprise. As for shoe quality and cost, the medieval shopper could generally count on getting a good pair of shoes at a fair price because the cobblers' guild strictly controlled quality and price.

Weaving was another big medieval trade. In fact, in the 14th century, weaving was the leading industry in the German town of Augsburg. Little wonder, then, that an enterprising young man named Hans Fugger became a weaver when he settled there in 1357. But young Hans had ambitions that stretched far beyond the limits of the weaving trade and the handicraft guild system. And they were grandly realized, for within three short generations, a family of simple weavers was transformed into a great German banking dynasty.[2]

Not content with being a weaver, Hans Fugger began collecting and selling the products of other weavers. Soon he was directly employing the other weavers, paying them for their labor, and selling their products as his own. His sons continued the business and expanded it in new directions, as did his grandsons, especially Jacob Fugger, the foremost capitalist of the Renaissance. Among other things, Jacob Fugger lent large sums of money to the Hapsburg emperors to finance their wars. In return, he obtained monopoly rights on silver and copper ores, which he then traded. When Fugger bought the mines themselves, he acquired all the components necessary to erect an extraordinary financial dynasty and to make himself one of the richest people of all time.

Like latter-day titans of American industry, Fugger employed thousands of workers and paid them wages, controlled all his products from raw material to final market, set his own quality standards, and charged whatever the traffic would bear. In one brief century, what was once a handicraft inseparable from the craftsperson had become a company that existed outside any family members. What had once motivated Hans Fugger—namely, maintenance of his station in life—had given way to gain for gain's sake, the so-called profit motive. Under Jacob Fugger, the company amassed profits—a novel concept—that well exceeded the needs of the Fugger family. And the profits were measured not in goods or land but in money.

Capitalism has undergone changes since then. The kind of capitalism that emerged in the Fuggers' time is often termed **mercantile capitalism**, which is capitalism that is based on mutual dependence between state and commercial interests. Central to mercantile capitalism is the belief that the economic health of a nation is determined by the bullion (precious metals, gold, and silver) it possesses and that therefore government should regulate production and trade with the goal of encouraging exports while keeping out imports, thus building up the nation's bullion reserves. A prudent nation should strive to be economically self-sufficient while using sea power, if it can, to control foreign markets and establish colonies for the benefit of the mother country.

During the 18th and 19th centuries, however, new economic ideas spread. These emphasized the importance of competition and open markets and of freeing trade and production from government oversight. Trade between nations was now seen as mutually beneficial, and national wealth and prosperity were no longer identified with bullion. With the Industrial Revolution, industrialists replaced merchants as the dominant power in a capitalist economy, and the period of **industrial capitalism** emerged, which is associated with large-scale industry. In the United States, the confluence of many factors after the Civil War—including a sound financial base, the technology for mass production, expanding markets for cheaply manufactured goods, and a large and willing labor force—produced industrial expansion. Exploiting these fortuitous conditions was a group of hard-driving, visionary entrepreneurs, called "robber barons" by their critics and "captains of industry" by their supporters: Cornelius Vanderbilt, Cyrus McCormick, Andrew Carnegie, John D. Rockefeller, Jay Gould, and others.

As industrialization increased, so did the size and power of business. The private fortunes of a few individuals could no longer underwrite the accelerated growth of business activity. The large sums of capital necessary could be raised only through a corporate form of business, in which risk and potential profit were distributed among numerous investors. The success—indeed, survival—of a business enterprise came to depend on its having the financial wherewithal to reduce prices while expanding production and either eliminating or absorbing competition. As various industries strove to strengthen their financing and shore up their assets, what is called **financial capitalism** emerged, characterized by pools, trusts, holding companies, and the interpenetration of banking, insurance, and industrial interests. Hand in hand with this development, the trend continued toward larger and larger corporations, controlling more and more of the country's economic capacity.

The economic and political challenges of the Great Depression of the 1930s helped usher in still another phase of capitalism, often called **state welfare capitalism**, in which government plays an active role in the economy, attempting to smooth out the boom-and-bust pattern of the business cycle through its fiscal and monetary policies. In addition, government programs like Social Security and unemployment insurance seek to enhance the welfare of the workforce, and legislation legitimizes the existence of trade unions. Conservative politicians sometimes advocate less government control of business, but in reality the governments of all capitalist countries are deeply involved in the management of their economies.

Summary
Capitalism has gone through several stages: mercantile, industrial, financial, and state welfare. Many believe we are now at a new stage, globalized capitalism.

These days, the increasingly worldwide scale of capitalism leads many contemporary commentators to see **globalized capitalism** as a new stage or level of capitalist development. Capitalism has always involved international trade, but today—thanks to the computer, the Internet, satellites, cell phones, and other technological advances—the economies of most countries are becoming more and more integrated, a process labeled *globalization*. Although the world is still far from constituting a single global economy, investment capital is more mobile than ever, and the currencies, stock exchanges, and economic fortunes of all capitalist countries are bound together in a single financial system. The business operations of a growing number of companies take place on a world stage. Capitalist enterprises are more likely than ever before to utilize foreign components and draw on foreign labor or services, to export products or provide services abroad, and to acquire or start foreign subsidiaries or engage in joint ventures with overseas companies. Many apparently national companies produce one component in one country and another component in a different country, assemble them in a third country, and market them throughout the world.

> Although capitalism will continue to evolve, it has four characteristic features.

Although the study of capitalism's evolution is best left to economic historians, it is important to keep in mind capitalism's dynamic nature. There is nothing fixed and immutable about this or any other economic system; it is as susceptible to the forces of change as any other institution. Nevertheless, the capitalism we know today does have some prominent features that were evident in the earliest capitalistic businesses.

• • •

Key Features of Capitalism

Complete coverage of capitalism's central features and defining characteristics has filled many a book. Four features of particular significance—the existence of companies, profit motive, competition, and private property—will be discussed here.

Companies

Chapter 2 mentioned the Firestone case, in which a media misrepresentation was left uncorrected. When asked why Firestone officials had not corrected the error, a Firestone spokesperson said that Firestone's policy was to ask for corrections only when it was beneficial to the company to do so. Expressions like "Firestone's policy" and "beneficial to the company" reflect one key feature of capitalism: the existence of companies or business firms separate from the human beings who work for and within them.

"It's not in the company's interests," "The company thinks that," "From the company's viewpoint," "As far as the company is concerned"—all of us have heard, perhaps even used, expressions like these that treat a business organization like a person or at least like a separate and distinct entity. This way of speaking reflects a basic characteristic of capitalism: Capitalism permits the creation of companies or business organizations that exist separately from the people associated with them. We take the existence of companies for granted, but some experts believe that it is not church or state but the company that is "the most important organization in the world."[3]

Today, the big companies we're familiar with—General Electric, Microsoft, Verizon, Procter & Gamble—are, in fact, incorporated businesses, or corporations. Chapter 5 discusses the nature of the modern corporation, including its historical evolution and its social responsibilities. Here, it's enough to observe that, in the 19th century, Chief Justice John Marshall defined a *corporation* as "an artificial being, invisible, intangible, and existing only in the contemplation of law." Although a corporation is not something that can be seen or touched, it does have prescribed rights and legal obligations within the community. Like you or me, a corporation may enter into contracts and may sue or be sued in courts of law. It may even do things that the corporation's members disapprove of. The corporations that loom large on our economic landscape hark back to a feature of capitalism evident as early as the Fugger dynasty: the existence of the company.

Profit Motive

A second characteristic of capitalism lies in the motive of the company: to make profit. As dollar-directed and gain-motivated as our society is, most of us take for granted that human beings are by nature acquisitive creatures who, left to their own devices, will pursue profit with all the instinctual vigor of a cat chasing a mouse. However, as economist Robert Heilbroner points out, the "profit motive, as we understand it, is a very recent phenomenon. It was foreign to the lower and middle classes of Egyptian, Greek, Roman, and medieval cultures, only scattered throughout the Renaissance times, and largely absent in most Eastern civilizations." The medieval church taught that no Christian ought to be a merchant. "Even to our Pilgrim forefathers," Heilbroner writes, "the idea that gain ought to be a tolerable—even a useful—goal in life would have appeared as nothing short of a doctrine of the devil."[4]

Profit in the form of money is the lifeblood of the capitalist system. Companies and capitalists alike are motivated by a robust appetite for monetary gain. Indeed, the **profit motive** implies and reflects a critical assumption about human nature: that human beings are basically economic creatures who recognize and are motivated by their own economic interests.

> The profit motive is central to capitalism. It assumes that economic self-interest motivates human beings.

Competition

If self-interest and an appetite for profit drive individuals and companies, then what stops them from bleeding society dry? What stops capitalists from ripping off the rest of society?

Adam Smith provided an answer in his famous treatise on political economy, *An Inquiry into the Nature and Causes of the Wealth of Nations* (1776). Free **competition**, said Smith, is the regulator that keeps a community activated only by self-interest from degenerating into a mob of ruthless profiteers. When traditional restraints are removed from the sale of goods and from wages and when all individuals have equal access to raw materials and markets (the doctrine of **laissez faire**, a French phrase meaning "to let [people] do [as they choose]"), we are all free to pursue our own interests. In pursuing our own interests, however, we come smack up against others similarly motivated. If any of us allow blind self-interest to dictate our actions—for example, by price gouging or employee exploitation—we will quickly find ourselves beaten out by competitors who charge less or pay better wages. Competition thus regulates individual economic activity.

To sample the flavor of Smith's argument, imagine an acquisitive young woman in a faraway place who wants to pile up as much wealth as possible. She looks about her and sees that people need and want strong twilled cotton trousers, so she takes her investment capital and sets up a jeans factory. She charges $45 for a pair of jeans and soon realizes handsome profits. The woman's success is not lost on other business minds, especially manufacturers of formal slacks and dresses, who observe a sharp decline in those markets. Wanting a piece of the jeans action, numerous enterprises start up jeans factories. Many of these start selling jeans for $40 a pair. No longer alone in the market, our hypothetical businesswoman must check her appetite for profit by lowering her price or risk folding. As the number of jeans on the market increases, their supply eventually overtakes demand, and the price of jeans declines further and further. Inefficient manufacturers begin to lose money and go out of business. As the competition thins out, the demand for jeans slowly balances with the supply, and the price regulates itself. Ultimately, an equilibrium is reached between supply and demand, and the price of jeans stabilizes, yielding a normal profit to the efficient producer.

In much this way, Adam Smith tried to explain how economic competition steers the individual pursuit of self-interest in a socially beneficial direction. By appealing to their self-interest, society can induce producers to provide it with what it wants—just as manufacturers of formal slacks and dresses were enticed into jeans production. But competition keeps prices for desired goods from escalating; high prices are self-correcting because they call forth an increased supply.

> Competition makes individual pursuit of self-interest socially beneficial.

Private Property

In its discussion of the libertarian theory of justice, Chapter 3 emphasized that property should not be identified only with physical objects like houses, bicycles, and smartphones because one can own things, such as stock options, that are not physical things at all. Nor should ownership be thought of as a simple relationship between the owner and the thing owned. Rather, property ownership involves a complex bundle of rights and rules governing how, under what circumstances, and in what ways both the owner and others can use, possess, dispose of, and have access to the thing in question.

Capitalism requires private ownership of the means of production.

Private property is central to capitalism. To put it another way, capitalism as a socioeconomic system is a specific form of private property. What matters for capitalism is not private property simply in the sense of personal possessions, because a socialist society can permit people to own cars, television sets, and running shoes. Rather, capitalism requires private ownership of the major *means of production* and distribution. The means of production and distribution include factories, warehouses, offices, machines, computer systems, trucking fleets, agricultural land, and whatever else makes up the economic resources of a nation. Under capitalism, private hands control these basic economic assets and productive resources. Thus, the major economic decisions are made by individuals or groups acting on their own in pursuit of profit. These decisions are not directly coordinated with those of other producers, nor are they the result of some overall plan. Any profits (or losses) that result from these decisions about production are those of the owners.

Summary
Four key features of capitalism are the existence of companies, profit motive, competition, and private property.

Capital, as an economic concept, is closely related to private property. Putting it simply, capital is money that is invested for the purpose of making more money. Individuals or corporations purchase various means of production or other related assets and use them to produce goods or provide services, which are then sold. They do this not for the purpose of being nice or of helping people out but rather to make money—more money, they hope, than they spent to make the goods or provide the services in the first place. Using money to make money is at the heart of the definition of capitalism.

• • •

Two Arguments for Capitalism

People tend to take for granted the desirability and moral legitimacy of the political and economic system they live in. Americans are no exception. America is a society that encourages individual competition, praises capitalism, promotes the acquisition of material goods, and worships economic wealth. Newspapers, television, movies, and other forms of popular culture celebrate these values, and rarely are we presented with fundamental criticisms of or possible alternatives to the American socioeconomic order. It is not surprising, then, that many people blithely assume, without ever bothering to question, that the capitalist economic system is a morally justifiable one.

Yet as thinking people and moral agents, we need to reflect on the nature and justifiability of our social institutions. The proposition that capitalism is a morally acceptable system is open to debate. Whether we decide that capitalism is morally justified will depend, at least in part, on which general theory of justice turns out to be the soundest. Chapter 3 explored in detail the utilitarian approach, the libertarian alternative, and the theory of John Rawls. Now, against that background, this chapter looks at two basic ways defenders of capitalism have sought to justify their system: (1) the argument that the moral right to property guarantees the legitimacy of capitalism and (2) the utilitarian-based economic argument of Adam Smith. The chapter then considers some criticisms of capitalism.

The Natural Right to Property

Americans live in a socioeconomic system that guarantees certain property rights. Although people are no longer permitted to own other people, they are certainly free to own a variety of other things, from livestock to stock certificates and from private homes to whole blocks of apartment buildings. A common defense of capitalism is the argument that people have a fundamental, **natural right to property** and that the capitalist system is simply the outcome of this right.

One argument for capitalism is that it reflects people's natural right to property.

This sort of argument will be familiar from the discussion of libertarianism in the previous chapter. As we saw there, Locke attempted to base the right to property in human labor. According to Locke, when individuals mix their labor with the natural world, they are entitled to the results. This idea seems plausible in many cases. For example, if Carl diligently harvests coconuts on the island he shares with Adam, while Adam himself idles away his days, then most of us would agree that Carl has an entitlement to those coconuts that Adam lacks. But property ownership as it actually exists in the real world today is a complex, socially shaped phenomenon. This is especially true in the case of sophisticated forms of corporate and financial property—for example, bonds and stock options.

One could, of course, reject the whole idea of a natural right to property as a fiction, as, for example, utilitarians do. In their view, although various property systems are possible, there is no natural right that things be owned privately, or collectively, or in any particular way whatsoever. The moral task, according to utilitarians, is to determine which property system, which way of organizing production and distribution, has the greatest utility.

Even if one believes that there is a natural right to property at least under some circumstances, one need not believe that this right leads to capitalism or that there is a right to have a system of property rules and regulations exactly like the one we now have in the United States. In other words, even if Carl has a natural right to his coconuts, there may still be moral limits on how many coconuts he can rightfully amass and what he can use them for. When he takes his coconuts to the coconut bank and receives more coconuts as interest, his newly acquired coconuts are not the result of any new labor on his part. When we look at capitalistic property—that is, at socioeconomic environments in which people profit from ownership alone—then we have left Locke's world far behind.

A defender of capitalism may reply, "Certainly, there's nothing unfair about Carl's accruing these extra coconuts through his investment; after all, he could have eaten his original coconuts instead." And, indeed, within our system this reasoning seems perfectly correct. It is the way things work in our society. But this fact doesn't prove that Carl has some natural right to use his coconuts to earn more coconuts—that is, that it would be unfair or unjust to set up a different economic system (for example, one in which he had a right to consume coconuts but no right to use them to accrue more coconuts). The argument here is simply that the issue is not an all-or-nothing one. We may have a fundamental right to property, without that right being unlimited or guaranteeing capitalism as we know it.

Summary
One basic defense of capitalism rests on a supposed natural moral right to property. Utilitarians deny the existence of such rights; other critics doubt that this right entitles one to have a system of property rules and regulations identical to the one we now have in the United States.

Adam Smith's Concept of the Invisible Hand

Relying on the idea of a natural right to property is not the only way and probably not the best way to defend capitalism. Another, very important argument defends capitalism in terms of the many economic benefits the system brings, claiming that the free and unrestrained market system that exists under capitalism is more efficient and more productive than any other possible system and is thus to be preferred on moral grounds. Essentially, this is a utilitarian argument, and again it's an argument that we discussed in the last chapter. One doesn't have to be a thoroughgoing utilitarian to take it seriously, however. As we saw in Chapter 2, almost every normative theory puts some moral weight on the consequences of actions. Thus, if capitalism does indeed work better than other ways of organizing economic life, then this outcome will be a relevant moral fact—one that will be important, for instance, for Rawlsians.

This section sketches Adam Smith's economic case for capitalism, as presented in *The Wealth of Nations*. Smith argues that when people are left to pursue their own interests, they will, without intending it, produce the greatest good for all. Each person's individual and private pursuit of wealth results—as if guided (in Smith's famous words) by an **invisible hand**—in the most beneficial overall organization and distribution of economic resources. Although the academic study of economics has developed greatly since Smith's times, his classic arguments remain extraordinarily influential.

Smith took it for granted that human beings are, by nature, acquisitive. Self-interest and personal advantage, specifically in an economic sense, may not be all that motivate people, but they do seem to motivate most people much of the time. At any rate, they are powerful enough forces that any successful economic system must strive to harness them. We are, Smith thought, strongly inclined to act so as to acquire more and more wealth.

A second argument for capitalism is that it is the most efficient and productive economic system. This is basically a utilitarian consideration.

In addition, humans have a natural propensity for trading—"to truck, barter, and exchange." Unlike other species, we have an almost constant need for the assistance of others. Yet because people are creatures of self-interest, it is folly for us to expect others to act altruistically toward us. We can secure what we need from others only by offering them something they need from us:

> Whoever offers to another a bargain of any kind, proposes to do this. Give me that which I want, and you shall have this which you want, is the meaning of every such offer; and it is in this manner that we obtain from one another the far greater part of those good offices which we stand in need of. It is not from the benevolence of the butcher, the brewer, or the baker that we expect our dinner, but from their regard to their own interest. We address ourselves, not to their humanity but to their self love, and never talk to them of our own necessities but of their advantages.[5]

This disposition to trade, said Smith, leads to the division of labor—dividing the labor and production process into areas of specialization, which is the prime means of increasing economic productivity.

Thus, Smith reasoned that the greatest utility will result from unfettered pursuit of self-interest. Individuals should be allowed unrestricted access to raw materials, markets, and labor. Government interference in private enterprise should be eliminated, free competition encouraged, and economic self-interest made the rule of the day. Because human beings are materialistic, acquisitive creatures, we will, if left free, engage in labor and exchange goods in a way that results in the greatest benefit to society. In our efforts to advance our own economic interests, we inevitably act to promote the economic well-being of society generally:

> Every individual is continually exerting himself to find the most advantageous employment for whatever capital he can command. It is his own advantage, indeed, and not that of the society, which he has in view. . . . [But] by directing that industry in such a manner as its produce may be of the greatest value, he [is] . . . led by an invisible hand to promote an end that was no part of his intention. . . . By pursuing his own interest he frequently promotes that of society more effectually than when he really intends to promote it.[6]

To explain why pursuit of self-interest necessarily leads to the greatest social benefit, Smith invoked the law of supply and demand, which was alluded to in our discussion of competition. The law of supply and demand tempers the pursuit of self-interest exactly as competition keeps the enterprising capitalist from becoming a ruthless profiteer. The law of supply and demand similarly solves the problems of adequate goods and fair prices.

Summary
The utilitarian defense of capitalism is associated with the classical economic arguments of Adam Smith. Smith believed that human beings are acquisitive and that they have a natural propensity for trading, and he insisted that when people are left free to pursue their own economic interests, they will, without intending it, produce the greatest good for all.

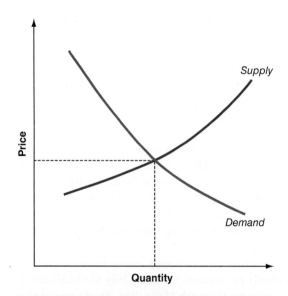

A traditional supply–demand curve. The point at which supply and demand meet is called the "equilibrium" and determines the price.

Some think the law of supply and demand even solves the problem of fair wages, for labor is another commodity up for sale like shoes or jeans. Just as the price of a new product at first is high, like the jeans in our earlier hypothetical example, so, too, are the wages of labor in a new field. But as labor becomes more plentiful, wages decline. Eventually they fall to a point at which inefficient laborers are eliminated and forced to seek other work, just as the inefficient manufacturers of jeans were forced out of that business and into others. And like the price of jeans, the price of labor then stabilizes at a fair level. As for the inefficient laborers, they find work and a living wage elsewhere. In seeking new fields of labor, they help maximize the majority's opportunities to enjoy the necessities, conveniences, and trifles of human life.

Some modern defenders of capitalism claim that it operates as Smith envisioned and can be justified on the same utilitarian grounds. But not everyone agrees.

· · ·

Criticisms of Capitalism

These two arguments for capitalism have not persuaded everyone that it is a morally justifiable system, and there are both theoretical and operational objections to it that need to be considered. *Theoretical* criticisms challenge capitalism's fundamental values, basic assumptions, or inherent economic tendencies. *Operational* criticisms focus more on capitalism's alleged deficiencies in actual practice (as opposed to theory)—in particular, on its failure to live up to its own economic ideals.

The following criticisms are a mix of both theoretical and operational concerns. They raise political, economic, and philosophical issues that cannot be fully assessed here. The debate over capitalism is a large and important one; the presentation that follows should be viewed as a stimulus to further discussion and not as the last word on the pros and cons of capitalism.

Inequality

Chapter 3 and Case 3.3 documented the profound economic inequality that exists in our capitalist society. The disparity in personal incomes is enormous; a tiny minority of the population owns the vast majority of the country's productive assets; and our society continues to face poverty and homelessness. With divisions of social and economic class comes inequality of opportunity. A child born to a working-class family, let alone to a teenager in an economically depressed inner-city neighborhood, has life opportunities and possibilities unequal to those of children born to wealthy, college-educated, stock-owning families. This reality challenges capitalism's claim of fairness, and the persistence of poverty and economic misfortune provides the basis for a utilitarian objection to it.

Few doubt that poverty and extreme inequality are bad things, but defenders of capitalism make several responses to those who criticize it on these grounds:

1. A few extreme supporters of capitalism simply deny that it is responsible for poverty and inequality. Rather, they say, government interference with the market causes these problems. Left to itself, the market would eliminate unemployment and poverty while ultimately lessening inequality. The Great Depression that struck the U.S. economy in 1929 is sometimes blamed on the government's passing a major tariff, or tax on imports, even though this tariff was not put into place until 1930.[7] But neither theoretical economics nor the study of history supports this reply. Most economists and social theorists would agree that in the past eighty years or so activist government policies have done much, in all the Western capitalist countries, to reduce poverty and, to a lesser extent, inequality.

2. More moderate defenders of capitalism concede that in its pure laissez-faire form, capitalism does nothing to prevent and may even foster inequality and poverty. However, they argue that the system can be modified or its inherent tendencies corrected by political action, so that inequality and poverty are reduced or even eliminated. Critics of capitalism

Critics argue that poverty and extreme inequality challenge the fairness of capitalism and its claim to advance the interests of all. Defenders of capitalism respond to this in different ways.

Summary
Critics question the basic assumptions of capitalism (theoretical challenges) and whether it has delivered on its promises (operational challenges). One criticism is that capitalism produces severe inequality and is unable to eliminate poverty. Another is that capitalism wrongly assumes that human beings are rational economic maximizers and that well-being comes from ever greater material consumption. It is also alleged that capitalism offers us no higher sense of human purpose.

reply that the policies necessary to seriously reduce inequality and poverty are either impossible within a basically capitalist economic framework or unlikely to be carried out in any political system based on capitalism. As we have seen, the Nordic countries like Sweden, Denmark, and Norway seem to have gone further in combatting inequality and poverty than any other countries with economic systems that count as capitalistic by the definition given here. So what one thinks about this moderate defense of capitalism may depend on whether you think that they have reduced these social ills to acceptable levels.

3. Finally, defenders of capitalism argue that the benefits of the system outweigh this weak point. According to this argument, inequality is not so important if living standards are rising and if even the people with the lowest incomes have better lives than they did in previous times. This contention rests on an implicit comparison with what things would be like if society were organized differently and is, accordingly, difficult to assess. Naturally, it seems more plausible to those who are relatively favored by, and content with, the present economic system than it does to those who feel disadvantaged by it.

Human Nature and Capitalism

The theory of capitalism rests on a view of human beings as rational economic creatures, individuals who recognize and are motivated largely by their own economic self-interest. Adam Smith's defense of capitalism, for instance, assumes that consumers have full knowledge of the diverse choices available to them in the marketplace. They are supposed to know the price structures of similar products, to be fully aware of product differences, and to be able to make the optimal choice regarding price and quality.

But the key choices facing today's consumers are rarely simple. From foods to drugs, automobiles to appliances, fertilizers to computers, the modern marketplace is a cornucopia of products whose nature and nuances require a high level of consumer literacy. Even with government agencies and public interest groups to aid them, today's consumers are rarely an equal match for powerful industries that can influence prices, control product quality, and create and shape markets. The effectiveness of advertising, in particular, is difficult to reconcile with the picture of consumers as the autonomous, rational, and perfectly informed economic maximizers that economics textbooks presuppose when they attempt to demonstrate the benefits of capitalism. Consumers frequently fall short of perfect rationality and often seem under the sway of social and psychological forces they are unaware of. (Advertising and consumer rationality are discussed in more depth in Chapter 6.)

According to some critics of capitalism, however, what is objectionable about capitalism's view of human beings as essentially economic creatures is not this gap between theory and reality but rather the fact that it presents little in the way of an ideal to which either individuals or societies may aspire. As Hungarian-American businessman George Soros puts it, "Humans are capable of transcending the pursuit of narrow self-interest. Indeed, they cannot live without some sense of morality. It is market fundamentalism, which holds that the social good is best served by allowing people to pursue their self-interest without any thought for the social good . . . that is a perversion of human nature."[8] Not only does capitalism rest on the premise that people are basically acquisitive, individualistic, and materialistic, but in practice capitalism strongly reinforces those human tendencies. Capitalism, its critics charge, presents no higher sense of human mission or purpose, whereas other views of society and human nature do.

Critics charge that capitalism reinforces materialism and offers no higher sense of human purpose.

Christianity, for example, has long aspired to the ideal of a truly religious community united in *agape*, selfless love. And socialism, because it views human nature as malleable, hopes to see people transformed from the "competitive, acquisitive beings that they are (and that they are *encouraged* to be) under all property-dominated, market-oriented systems." In the more "benign environment of a propertyless, nonmarket social system," socialists believe that more cooperative and less selfish human beings will emerge.[9] Such positive ideals and aspirations are lacking in capitalism—or so its critics maintain.

Capitalism operates on the debatable assumption that human beings find increased well-being through ever greater material consumption.

Finally, an implicit assumption of capitalism is that human beings find increased well-being through ever greater material consumption. That's why the avid pursuit of economic gain, as mediated through the invisible hand of the market, is supposed to make us all better off.

Moreover, contemporary capitalism needs people to keep on buying and consuming goods for the system to continue running. Consumer demand makes the economic wheels turn. And that, in turn, requires people in general to choose working more so they can consume more rather than working less, having more leisure, and buying fewer things. However, this bias in favor of material consumption runs up against the fact, according to social psychologists, that people today—in America, Europe, and Japan—are no more pleased with their lives than people were in the 1950s, despite the very substantial increase in standard of living that all these societies have enjoyed.[10]

How might a defender of capitalism respond to these objections? One possible reply might be that the picture of human nature described here is in fact accurate, whether we like it or not. Another reply might be that, strictly speaking, capitalism doesn't presuppose that that people are single-mindedly motivated by the desire to buy things for themselves, but rather only that they're strongly motivated by the desire to make money so that they can ensure that it's spent on the things that matter to them. What matters to them might be satisfying their own materialistic desires, but it might also be benefiting others—giving money to their church or, if they're wealthy enough, endowing universities, hospitals, and museums. From a theoretical standpoint, therefore, capitalism may be compatible with the recognition that most of us do have broader concerns than ourselves or our families. Adam Smith shared this recognition, and explored this aspect of human nature in his "other" great book, *The Theory of Moral Sentiments*.[11]

Competition Might Not Be What it's Cracked Up to Be

As we have seen, one of the key features of capitalism is competition. Unfettered competition supposedly serves the collective interest while offering rich opportunities for the individual. But competition is one of the targets of capitalism's critics. They contend that capitalism breeds oligopolies that eliminate competition and concentrate economic power, that a system of corporate welfare protects many businesses from true marketplace competition, and finally that competition is neither generally beneficial nor desirable in itself.

> Critics contend that capitalism's supposed commitment to competition is belied by oligopoly and corporate welfare. Some also challenge the belief that competition is desirable and beneficial.

Capitalism Breeds Oligopolies

As early as the middle of the 19th century, the German philosopher and political economist Karl Marx (1818–1883) argued that capitalism leads to **oligopolies**—a concentration of property and resources, and thus economic power, in the hands of a few. The most extreme version of an oligopoly is a **monopoly**, where one firm has a market entirely to itself. When one or a few firms control the supply of some good or service they can restrict supply, which allows them to command a higher price and make more profit. (Take another look at the supply and demand curves pictured a few pages ago. Imagine that the supply curve shifted to the left, which would indicate that suppliers were not willing to offer as many units. Where would this new supply curve intersect the demand curve? What would this mean for the equilibrium price?) High costs, complex and expensive machinery, intense competition, and the advantages of large-scale production all work against the survival of small firms, said Marx. Many see proof of Marx's argument in today's economy.

Before the Industrial Revolution, capitalism was characterized by comparatively free and open competition among a large number of small firms. As late as 1832, for instance, hardly any private firms in the United States had ten or more employees.[12] Since then, the economy has come to be dominated by a relatively small number of enormous companies that, to a distressing extent, can conspire to set prices, eliminate competition, and monopolize an industry. For example, the four biggest airlines control over two-thirds of domestic air travel, and ten brewing companies sell over two-thirds of the entire world's beer.[13] Today, the 500 largest U.S. firms constitute almost two-thirds of the American economy, with combined revenues of over $16 trillion.[14]

Antitrust laws have sometimes fostered competition by breaking up monopolies, as happened with Standard Oil and AT&T. In 2001, the government went after Microsoft for "exclusionary and predatory" businesses practices; currently, it's trying to block the same corporation's acquisition of game manufacturer Activision.[15] On the whole, however, such actions have proved ineffectual in halting the concentration of economic power. And despite calls to break up or restrict the operations of those banks and other financial institutions that are so large that the government cannot allow them to fail without endangering the whole economy (as happened in 2008), financial reform legislation passed by Congress in 2010 and intended to prevent future crises did not address this problem at all.

Because of their sway over the market and their political clout, the gigantic corporations that we know today have so altered the face of capitalism that Adam Smith would have trouble recognizing it. As a result, in terms of competition, our present-day economic system differs significantly from the textbook model of capitalism. One expert puts it this way:

> In surveying the American business system it is obvious that competition still exists; however, it is not a perfect competition. Often it is not price competition at all. With the possible exception of some farm markets where there are still large numbers of producers of similar and undifferentiated products (wheat, for instance), virtually every producer of goods and services has some control over price. The degree of control varies from industry to industry and between firms within an industry. Nevertheless, it does exist, and it amounts to an important modification in our model of a free-enterprise economy.[16]

These days, in fact, some of the most vigorous corporate competition occurs not in the marketplace but in Washington, D.C., where companies jockey for competitive advantage by getting Congress to pass laws that help them and hold back their rivals. In 2015, American corporations spent over $2.5 billion on lobbying.[17] That's $34 for every $1 that labor unions and public interest groups spent on lobbying.

A defender of capitalism might respond here that even if firms will try to grow large enough to exercise oligopoly or even monopoly power, new competitors can always emerge. They might point to Amazon's challenge to Walmart in the retail arena, for instance, or Tesla's "disruption" of the automotive industry. They might also point out that it's only because the government plays such a large role in regulating the economy that corporations find it profitable to invest in lobbying. If government had less power, there would be less to gain by winning its favor.

Corporate Welfare Programs Protect Businesses

When the United States slapped a 25 percent tariff of many imported steel products in 2018, it was continuing a nearly fifty-year tradition of cosseting the steel industry with various subsidies and protections that have cost the country a small fortune.[18] Similarly, U.S. quotas on sugar imports in recent years have resulted in the domestic price of sugar being three and a half times the world market price. As a result, to survive, American candy makers have been forced to move production to countries where sugar is cheaper at the cost of thousands of U.S. jobs.[19] In 2020, 39 percent of net farm income came from government subsidies rather than crop sales.[20] The federal government also inflates the price that farmers receive for growing at least one crop, corn, by requiring the petroleum industry to sell billions of gallons of ethanol fuel every year.[21] Forty percent of the nation's corn crops goes to the production of ethanol.

Subsidies and protections for steel, sugar, food, and ethanol are only the most blatant examples of the way **corporate welfare** assists business and protects it from competition. Thanks to duties, fees, and restrictions on imported products, American consumers pay far more for goods than they otherwise would. And that, of course, is in addition to what corporate subsidies cost consumers as taxpayers.

Every year the federal government doles out billions of dollars to private business in direct subsidy programs. For example, the 2022 CHIPS and Science Act includes $39 billion in subsidies to incentivize the manufacture of semiconductors in the United States.[22] Earlier, the 2009 American Recovery and Reinvestment Act made available tens of billions of dollars in loans and loan guarantees for alternative energy production. The program was much criticized at the time for having loaned $535 million to failed solar energy company Solyndra (although, on the whole, the program has been profitable for the U.S. government).[23]

In addition, there are the tax breaks that corporations receive. A recent U.S. government report revealed that between 2014–2018, an average of 44 percent of large corporations owed no federal income tax in a given year. More remarkably, perhaps, an average of 25 percent of *profitable* large corporations had no federal income tax liability.[24] In 2021, AT&T had earnings of $29.6 billion (after paying state and local taxes). Instead of paying federal income tax, it received a $1.2 billion refund.[25]

State governments also pamper business with subsidies and protectionist restrictions on competition. For example, cities and states frequently provide tax breaks to corporations to lure them to, or prevent them from leaving, the local area. These subsidies cost taxpayers upwards of $100,000 in tax revenue for every job that the locality is hoping that the companies will bring to the area. Frequently, if not invariably, the broader economic benefits that the tax incentives were meant to produce never materialize.[26]

Corporate welfare was taken to a whole new level in 2008 by the federal government's $700 billion Troubled Assets Relief Program. As was noted previously, TARP was put together in response to the financial meltdown. It enabled the government to purchase non-liquid, difficult-to-value assets from banks and other financial institutions, in particular so-called collateralized debt obligations, which had been hit hard by foreclosures caused by the real estate slump. The theory was that by authorizing the Treasury Department to buy these "troubled assets"—assets, that is, that the banks couldn't sell on the open market for the simple reason that no one was willing to buy them—TARP would increase the banks' liquidity and improve their balance sheets, thus stabilizing the financial system. In addition to "cash for trash," TARP provided funds for the government to purchase loans from and make direct equity investments in the banks themselves, and the Treasury Department was creative in finding ways to assist the banks outside the TARP framework at a potential cost to tax payers that was greater than TARP itself. Given the crisis that the nation was facing, few doubt the necessity of something like TARP or of the Treasury Department's taking bold measures. And in the end, the government came out ahead as the loans it had made were repaid with interest and the assets it had purchased were sold at a profit. Nevertheless, with few strings attached, and with most banks choosing to shore up their bottom line by sitting on the money (or using it for executive bonuses) rather than to help stimulate the economy by lending it out, the bailout represents an unprecedented commitment of taxpayer money to save what had been some of the largest and wealthiest firms in the country, and their well-heeled managers, from the consequences of their own greed, recklessness, and mismanagement.

Those who defend a purer, more laissez-faire form of capitalism are among the most vociferous critics of corporate welfare. Those who favor a more moderate capitalism, one in which government plays a larger role, might reply to these criticisms by saying that while many corporate welfare initiatives do not serve the public good, subsidies and tax breaks can be socially beneficial when employed judiciously. Sometimes these programs do make a profit for the government, as already noted. And sometimes they produce other benefits, or at least address other worries.

Take the CHIPS and Science Act, for instance. The U.S. government has reason to encourage domestic production of computer chips over and above job creation. Currently, much of the production of advanced microchips occurs in Asia, especially in Taiwan. A war in Asia, and in particular an invasion of Taiwan by the People's Republic of China, would cut off the supply of these chips. Moreover, in weighing the use of tariffs to protect U.S. companies from foreign competition, it's important to note that in at least some cases other countries are offering subsidies to their own firms. While this makes their goods cheaper for U.S. consumers, if U.S. companies aren't provided with subsidies of their own or protected by tariffs then they may not be competing with foreign countries on a level playing field. (Of course, in many cases other countries can point to U.S. subsidies to justify their own tariffs and subsidies.)[27]

Competition Is Not a Good

Because the profit motive governs capitalism, it should not be surprising that even those companies that preach the doctrine of free competition are willing to shelve it when collusion with other firms, or government tariffs and subsidies, make higher profits possible. How else to explain the fact that the United States forbids foreign companies from owning airlines in America and prevents foreign airlines from flying routes that pick up passengers at more than one American city? In these ways, capitalism fails to live up to its own ideal. This was something

Summary
Critics of capitalism also charge that competition is not what it's cracked up to be because (1) capitalism breeds oligopolies, (2) corporate welfare often shelters business from competition, and (3) competition is not a good thing.

that worried Adam Smith, who once wrote, "People of the same trade seldom meet together, even for merriment or diversion, but the conversation ends in a conspiracy against the public, or in some contrivance to raise prices."[28]

Unlike Adam Smith, however, some critics of capitalism repudiate competition as an ideal, arguing that it is neither beneficial in general nor desirable in itself. They point to empirical studies establishing that in business there is frequently a negative correlation between performance and individual competitiveness. In other words, it is often cooperation, rather than competitiveness, that best enhances both individual and group achievement. According to Alfie Kohn, the reason is simple: "Trying to do well and trying to beat others are two different things."[29] Competition is an extrinsic motivator; not only does it not produce the kinds of results that flow from enjoying the activity itself, but also the use of extrinsic motivators can undermine intrinsic motivation and thus adversely affect performance in the long run. The unpleasantness of competition can also diminish people's performance.

The critics also contend that competition often precludes the more efficient use of resources that cooperation allows. When people work together, coordination of effort and an efficient division of labor are possible. By contrast, competition can inhibit economic coordination, cause needless duplication of services, retard the exchange of information, foster copious litigation, and lead to socially detrimental or counterproductive results such as business failures, mediocre products, unsafe working conditions, and environmental neglect. When presented with examples of the beneficial results of competition, the critics argue that on closer inspection the supposed advantages turn out to be short-lived, illusory, or isolated instances.

Former British Prime Minister Winston Churchill (1874–1965) once said that democracy is the worst system of government except for all the others. Defenders of competition might say something similar about it as a way of organizing the economy. They might point out, for instance, that the planned economies of countries like the former Soviet Union were not very successful at offering their citizens a high standard of living. There one could spend hours in line to buy basic items like groceries or toilet paper.[30] A major purchase, like an appliance or an automobile, might involve spending years on a waiting list for a product that was far inferior to what was available in the West.[31]

Exploitation and Alienation

Karl Marx argued that as the means of production become concentrated in the hands of the few, the balance of power between capitalists (bourgeoisie) and laborers (proletariat) tips further in favor of the bourgeoisie. Because workers have nothing to sell but their labor, said Marx, the bourgeoisie is able to exploit them by paying them less than the true value created by their labor. In fact, Marx thought, it is only through such **exploitation** that capitalists are able to make a profit and increase their capital. And the more capital they accumulate, the more they can exploit workers. Marx predicted that eventually workers would revolt. Unwilling to be exploited further, they would rise and overthrow their oppressors and set up an economic system that would truly benefit all.

The development of capitalist systems since Marx's time belies his forecast. Legal, political, and economic changes have tempered many of the greedy, exploitative dispositions of early capitalism. The 20th century witnessed legislation curbing egregious worker abuse, guaranteeing a minimum wage, and ensuring a safer and more healthful work environment. The emergence of labor unions and their subsequent victories significantly enlarged the worker's share of the economic pie. Indeed, many of the specific measures proposed by Marx and his collaborator Friedrich Engels in the *Communist Manifesto* (1848) have been implemented in capitalist countries: a program of graduated income tax, free education for all children in public schools, investiture of significant economic control in the state, and so on.

Still, many would say that although democratic institutions may have curbed the excesses of capitalism, they can do nothing to prevent the alienation of workers that results from having to do unfulfilling work. Again, because of the unequal positions of capitalist and worker, laborers must work for someone else—they must do work imposed on them as a means of satisfying the needs of others. As a result, they inevitably come to feel exploited and debased. And this is true, critics of capitalism claim, not just of manual laborers but also of white-collar workers.

But what about workers who are paid handsomely for their efforts? They, too, said Marx, remain alienated, for as the fruits of their labor are enjoyed by someone else, their work ultimately proves meaningless to them. The following selection from Marx's "Economic and Philosophic Manuscripts" (1844) summarizes his notion of **alienation** as the separation of individuals from the objects they create, which in turn results in one's separation from other people, from oneself, and ultimately from one's human nature:

> The worker is related to the *product of his labor* as to an *alien* object. For it is clear . . . that the more the worker expends himself in work the more powerful becomes the world of objects which he creates in face of himself, the poorer he becomes in his inner life, and the less he belongs to himself. . . . The worker puts his life into the object, and his life then belongs no longer to himself but to the object. . . . What is embodied in the product of his labor is no longer his own. The greater this product is, therefore, the more he is diminished. The *alienation* of the worker in his product means not only that his labor becomes an object, assumes an *external* existence, but that it exists independently, *outside himself*, and alien to him, and that it stands opposed to him as an autonomous power. . . .
>
> What constitutes the alienation of labor? First, that the work is *external* to the worker, that it is not part of his nature; and that, consequently, he does not fulfill himself in his work but denies himself. . . . His work is not voluntary but imposed, *forced labor*. It is not the satisfaction of a need, but only a *means* for satisfying other needs. Its alien character is clearly shown by the fact that as soon as there is no physical or other compulsion it is avoided like the plague. External labor, labor in which man alienates himself, is a labor of self-sacrifice. . . . Finally, the external character of work for the worker is shown by the fact that it is not his own work but work for someone else, that in work he does not belong to himself but to another person. . . .
>
> We have now considered the act of alienation of practical human activity, labor, from two aspects: (1) the relationship of the worker to the *product of labor* as an alien object which dominates him . . . [and] (2) the relationship of labor to the *act of production within labor*. This is the relationship of the worker to his own activity as something alien and not belonging to him. . . . This is *self-alienation* as against the above-mentioned alienation of the *thing*.[32]

In Marx's view, when workers are alienated they cannot be truly free. They may have the political and social freedoms of speech, religion, and governance, but even with these rights, individuals still are not fully free. Freedom from government interference and persecution does not necessarily guarantee freedom from economic exploitation and alienation, and it is for this kind of freedom that Marx and Engels felt such passion.

Some would say that one need not wade through Marxist philosophy to get a feel for what Marx and others mean by worker alienation. Just talk to workers themselves, as writer Studs Terkel did. In different ways, the hundreds of workers from diverse occupations whom Terkel interviewed speak of the same thing: dehumanization.

> Mike Fitzgerald . . . is a laborer in a steel mill. "I feel like the guys who built the pyramids. Somebody built 'em. Somebody built the Empire State Building, too. There's hard work behind it. I would like to see a building, say the Empire State, with a foot-wide strip from top to bottom and the name of every bricklayer on it, the name of every electrician. So when a guy walked by, he could take his son and say, 'See, that's me over there on the 45th floor. I put that steel beam in.' . . . Everybody should have something to point to."
>
> Sharon Atkins is 24 years old. She's been to college and acidly observes, "The first myth that blew up in my face is that a college education will get you a worthwhile job." For the last two years she's been a receptionist at an advertising agency. "I didn't look at myself as 'just a dumb broad' at the front desk, who took phone calls and messages. I thought I was something else. The office taught me differently."
>
> . . . Harry Stallings, 27, is a spot welder on the assembly line at an auto plant. "They'll give better care to that machine than they will to you. If it breaks down, there's somebody out there to fix it right away. If I break down, I'm just pushed over to the other side till another man takes my place. The only thing the company has in mind is to keep that machine running. A man would be more eager to do a better job if he were given proper respect and the time to do it."[33]

Marx argued that under capitalism workers are alienated in several different ways.

Summary
Karl Marx was an important 19th-century critic of capitalism. He argued that workers are exploited by capitalism and inevitably experience alienation.

One possible rebuttal to the objection that capitalism is alienating comes from philosopher Robert Nozick, whose ideas were discussed in the previous chapter. Nozick points out that under capitalism, companies compete for workers just like workers compete for jobs. Firms wanting to hire better workers therefore have a choice: either offer jobs that are less alienating or pay workers more so that they will tolerate the alienation.[34] If workers choose more alienating but better-paying jobs over less alienating but lower-paying ones, then Nozick might conclude that they aren't as distressed by alienation as Marx thinks they should be. Needless to say, a critic of capitalism might not find this response realistic.

• • •

Today's Economic Challenges

Capitalism faces a number of important critical questions, both theoretical and operational. These criticisms are a powerful challenge, especially to capitalism in its pure laissez-faire form. But, as we have seen, today's capitalism is a long way from the laissez-faire model. Corporate behemoths able to control markets and sway governments have replaced the small-scale entrepreneurs and free-wheeling competition of an earlier day. And governments in all capitalist countries actively intervene in the economic realm; they endeavor to assist or modify the so-called invisible hand; and over the years they have reformed or supplemented capitalism with programs intended to enhance the security of the workforce and increase the welfare of their citizens.

This reality complicates the debate over capitalism. Its defenders may be advocating either the pure laissez-faire ideal or some version of the modified state welfare capitalism that we in fact have. Likewise, those who attack the laissez-faire ideal may do so on behalf of a modified, welfarist capitalism, or they may criticize both forms of capitalism and defend some kind of socialism, in which private property and the pursuit of profit are no longer governing economic principles. We thus have a three-way debate over the respective strengths and weaknesses of laissez-faire capitalism, state welfare capitalism, and socialism.

The rest of this chapter leaves this fundamental debate behind. Instead of looking at criticisms of capitalism in general and at issues relevant to any capitalist society, it examines some of the more specific socioeconomic challenges facing the United States today. These include (1) the decline of American manufacturing and the related problems posed by the outsourcing of jobs and the growing U.S. trade deficit; (2) business's obsession with short-term results; (3) and changing attitudes toward work.

The Decline of American Manufacturing

Manufacturing has declined in the United States as American companies have conceded manufacturing dominance to foreign competitors.

Historically, capitalists have made money by producing goods. Manufacturing was the backbone of the American economy and the basis of its prosperity. In industry after industry, however, U.S. companies have conceded manufacturing dominance to foreign competitors. Today, for example, one can't buy a television made in the United States. Whereas manufacturing accounted for 27 percent of GDP in the mid-1960s, since then it has fallen to half that, and today manufacturing employs less than 10 percent of the American workforce.[35]

Since the 1980s, many U.S. manufacturers have been closing up shop or curtailing their operations and becoming marketing organizations for other producers, usually foreign. The result is the evolution of a new kind of company: manufacturers that do little or no manufacturing. They may perform a host of profit-making functions—from design to distribution—but they lack their own production base. Instead, they **outsource**, buying parts or whole products from other producers, both at home and abroad. The traditional vertical structure of manufacturing, in which the manufacturer makes nearly all crucial parts, is thereby replaced by a network of small operators. Companies that in years past were identified with making goods of all sorts now are likely to produce only the package and the label. In contrast to traditional manufacturers, they have become, in current business jargon, **hollow corporations**.

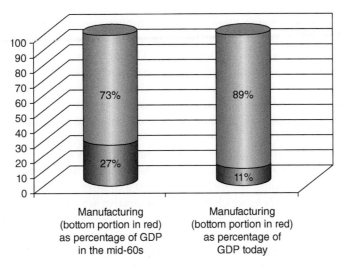

As a percentage of gross domestic product, manufacturing in the United States has declined by more than 50 percent since the 1960s.

Proponents of the new system describe it as flexible and efficient, a logical outcome of the drive to lower the costs of doing business. But critics worry whether the United States can prosper without a strong manufacturing base. As Tsutomu Ohshima, a senior manufacturing director of Toyota Motor Corporation, puts it: "You can't survive with just a service industry."[36] In wages, productivity, and innovation, the service sector fails to compare with basic industry. Manufacturing jobs generate "employment multipliers," creating significantly more jobs in other fields than do service jobs.[37] Because the rate of technical change is higher in manufacturing than in other sectors, it's hard to imagine the United States sustaining its technological leadership with a withered manufacturing sector.[38]

The COVID-19 pandemic revealed another reason to be concerned with the outsourcing of manufacturing, which is that the global supply chain is more fragile than we might once have thought. When the pandemic struck, a number of countries that produce medical supplies like gloves and masks kept them for their own use instead of exporting them.[39] Moreover, China's government responded to the pandemic with a "zero-COVID" policy that kept many of their factories and ports idle, which had global implications for the availability of many goods.[40] Prior to the pandemic there were some signs that some American companies were "reshoring" jobs to the United States, and the pandemic may have accelerated this movement. More money was spent on factory construction in the United States in 2022 than ever before.[41]

Outsourcing Jobs

As America's manufacturing base dwindles and U.S. firms outsource more and more of their operations, millions of jobs have moved abroad. But it's no longer just blue-collar jobs that are disappearing. White-collar jobs have also been outsourced. While so far this has not happened to the extent that some analysts expected, there are signs that employers may be renewing their efforts to move many jobs that were done by telework during the pandemic entirely out of the country.[42] Because skilled, highly educated people in other countries work for far less than do their American counterparts, outsourcing these jobs overseas makes U.S. firms leaner and more profitable. But can America lose these jobs and still prosper, especially if outsourcing also exerts downward pressure on the salaries of the jobs that remain? That's the question that is worrying more and more people.

Most mainstream economists are upbeat. They believe that outsourcing jobs increases shareholder wealth and benefits consumers by keeping prices down and that as old jobs move overseas, the economy will create new ones at home—higher-level jobs that add greater product value than the lost jobs did. Although they can't predict the new industries and occupations that will emerge to replace the old ones, these economists are confident that it will happen. Even in

Summary
Our capitalist socioeconomic system is facing a number of challenges. These include the decline of American manufacturing and the related problems of job outsourcing and a growing trade deficit. Economists disagree about whether outsourcing benefits America overall and about the risks posed by our indebtedness to foreign countries.

this optimistic scenario, however, there are genuine human costs. Sometimes economists refer to this downside as "short-term friction," but of course that's not how it feels to those workers whose relatively high-paying jobs are outsourced. They still have bills and mortgages to pay. And there's no reason to suppose that they will be the ones who eventually fill the "replacement" positions that the economy will supposedly create. Moreover, if they remain unemployed, settle for lower-paid work, or retire early, their lowered incomes affect their families, communities, and local businesses. In this way, then, the welfare of some is being sacrificed for the greater good of society.

A minority of economists, however, are challenging the rosy assumption that, despite the costs, outsourcing benefits America overall. Going back to the 19th-century economist David Ricardo, conventional economic theory has taught that a country should focus on producing for the world market those goods in which it has a **comparative advantage**—the goods that it can produce at a lower opportunity cost than other countries can. These are the goods that it can produce more cheaply relative to other goods than is the case in other countries. *Comparative* advantage does not mean *absolute* advantage. Two countries can benefit from trade even if one is better—or more efficient—than the other at producing everything. Suppose that one country is both much more efficient at producing computers than another and slightly more efficient at producing clothing. What Ricardo showed is that the first country will be better served to invest its resources in computer factories and leave sewing clothing to the second. By trading computers for clothing at the market exchange rate, the countries will each be getting what the other produces more cheaply than they would if they produced it themselves: the first country will give up fewer computers for a given quantity of clothing, and the second country will give up less clothing for a given number of computers.

If countries sell what they are comparatively better at producing and buy from other countries what those countries are comparatively better at producing, then in theory free trade benefits everyone. But the situation changes, or so some economists are now arguing, if a country's competitive edge comes solely from cheaper labor, especially in a world in which advanced telecommunication makes it possible for brainpower to zip around the world. In this case, there's no identifiable point at which the outsourcing process should stop: Even the so-called replacement jobs will move overseas. In theory, of course, wages in countries such as China and India should eventually rise to the point where outsourcing provides no benefit to American firms. But it will be decades and decades before that happens, if it ever does, and in the meantime white-collar wages in the United States have a long way to fall. In addition, if cheaper white-collar labor slashes the prices of those exports in which the United States has a comparative advantage, that could hurt the economy overall. For these reasons, even Paul Samuelson, the dean of American economists, has acknowledged that "comparative advantage cannot be counted on to create . . . net gains greater than net losses from trade."[43]

The U.S. Trade Deficit

As the United States continues to run an enormous trade deficit, its foreign borrowing keeps increasing—with risky consequences, according to some economists.

For roughly fifty years, the United States has been steadily losing its share of both foreign and domestic markets. The nation's huge balance-of-trade deficit is the most visible sign of this. After decades and decades of trade surpluses, the United States has posted a trade deficit every year since 1975. The trade deficit is the gap between the value of the goods and services that the United States imports from other countries and the value of the goods and services that it exports to them. In 2022, the trade deficit was over $948 billion.[44] The nation's imports totaled about $3,958 billion and its exports totaled about $3,010 billion. On balance, the United States actually exports considerably more services than it imports. This means that the trade deficit would be much larger if we confined our attention to goods (e.g., "physical stuff"): about $1.2 trillion.

The trade deficit is distinct from the budget deficit that the government accumulates when government spending exceeds tax revenues. Nevertheless, these two deficits are connected. The economics here are too complicated to describe in detail. However, the short version is that the reason that Americans can afford to buy more from other countries than they sell to these countries is that some of these countries are willing to lend America money, and in no small part they do this by lending the American government money through buying government bonds—an "export" that's not reflected in export figures. (A slightly longer version: Americans pay dollars to manufacturers in other countries. In some of these countries, especially China, governments buy these dollars from manufacturers, paying them in their own currency. That gives these foreign governments large holdings of U.S. dollars, which they then invest by buying U.S. Treasury bonds.)

Some economists believe that it is irrelevant that the United States buys more than it sells. Although we are now the world's largest debtor nation, they reason, we are still the world's largest and most important economy, so foreigners don't mind lending us money. Other economists, however, are worried by the country's consumption-happy ways. They fear that the United States is creating unsustainable global imbalances.[45] In their view, unless both domestic savings and the production of tradable goods increase dramatically, these imbalances will go on causing economic pain at home and serious dislocations abroad. Some people also worry that its growing trade deficit makes the United States vulnerable to economic extortion. What happens, they ask, if overseas lenders choose to stop financing our debt or even "dump" their Treasury bonds? (The mainstream economic view is that even China could cause only mild economic pain this way.)[46]

Opposition to the trade deficit was especially prominent in the administration of President Donald Trump, who campaigned on the urgency of reducing the trade deficit with China.[47] But there are also critics of the trade deficit within the Democratic Party, such as Senator Bernie Sanders.[48]

Exclusive Focus on the Short Term

Observers of the business scene have long charged that U.S. companies are preoccupied with short-term performance at the expense of long-term strategies. According to the critics, this **short-term focus** tends to make U.S. corporations unimaginative, inflexible, and ultimately uncompetitive. These business strategists urge U.S. companies to become more visionary—to define long-term goals and to be willing to stick to them even at the expense of short-term profit. Some businesspeople have accepted that advice, as evidenced by the willingness of Amazon and other dot-com companies to lose money for years as they attempt to build market share. Yet many American companies appear less willing than foreign rivals to gamble on long-term research and development or to sacrifice current profits for benefits ten or fifteen years into the future. By comparison with countries such as Germany and Japan, established U.S. corporations continue to be obsessed with their stock market performance and to govern themselves far more by short-term indicators such as share value and quarterly profits. As a result, they often sacrifice capital improvements or fail to make strategic investments.[49] Some worry that America may lose its technological edge because of this.[50]

An exclusive focus on the short term can also encourage dubious business practices. As management consultants Adrian Slywotsky and Richard Wise write, "Many [American] companies with apparently strong growth records in recent years have achieved them through relatively short-term, unsustainable tactics—acquisitions, international expansion, price increases, or accounting gimmicks."[51] Indeed, many theorists blame the financial meltdown of 2008–2009 on a short-term focus on profits that ignored long-term risks.[52]

Moreover, there's no question that corporate America's obsession with short-term performance—when coupled with what former Federal Reserve Chairman Alan Greenspan famously called "infectious greed"[53]—has created a high-pressure economic environment conducive to fraudulent behavior. Since the exposure of criminal conduct at Enron in late 2001, a long list of companies—including Adelphia Communications, Computer Associates, Dynegy, Global Crossing, Qwest, Rite Aid, Tyco International, WorldCom, Xerox, and Fannie Mae, to name the best-known cases—have been found to have manipulated financial data or committed outright fraud so as to appear to meet their short-term financial goals. These and other revelations of unethical conduct, in turn, have weakened the trust necessary for the efficient functioning of our economic system. That is why President George W. Bush once stated that "America's greatest economic need is higher ethical standards." Although it's true, as he also said, that "in the long run, there's no capitalism without conscience; there is no wealth without character," Bush may have

Many observers believe that American corporations are too focused on short-term performance.

An obsession with short-term performance can lead to fraudulent behavior.

neglected the extent to which a relentless emphasis on short-term results pressures some of the nation's most prominent business leaders to do things they normally wouldn't do. [54] As one business ethicist writes:

> Managing a corporation with the single measure of share price is like flying a 747 for maximum speed. You can shake the thing apart in the process. It's like a farmer forcing more and more of a crop to grow, until the soil is depleted and nothing will grow. Or like an athlete using steroids to develop muscle mass, until the body's health is damaged.
>
> Enron's problem was not a lack of focus on shareholder value. The problem was a lack of accountability to anything except share value. This contributed to a mania, a detachment from reality. And it led to a culture of getting the numbers by any means necessary. [55]

Changing Attitudes Toward Work

People's attitudes about work are changing, and some worry that the famous American work ethic is disappearing.

Some commentators believe that the socioeconomic problems facing America today include not only a shrunken manufacturing sector, outsourced jobs, a trade deficit, and a short-term performance mentality but also the challenge of coming to grips with people's changing attitudes toward government, social institutions, business, and work. And with regard to work in particular, there's little question that, in recent decades, people's ideas about its value and the role it should play in their lives have been evolving. The fabled American work ethic seems to be fading away. Or is it?

At first glance, the answer would seem to be no. After all, Americans work a lot, more than workers in any other highly industrialized country. To take the most extreme contrast, the average American worker puts in over 400 hours more per year than their German counterpart—the equivalent of more than ten 40-hour weeks. [56] But appearances can be deceptive.

The so-called **work ethic** values work for its own sake, seeing it as something necessary for every person. It also emphasizes the belief that hard work pays off in the end and is thus part and parcel of the American Dream. "If you work hard enough," the expression goes, "you'll make it." Today, however, fewer people believe this than before. Long before the COVID-19 pandemic, economic uncertainty and pessimism had led to an increasing number of Americans starting to question the traditional American work ethic. "I see more of a 'me-first' attitude," observed management professor Abigail Hubbard in 1995. [57]

The pandemic exacerbated this skepticism toward the idea that we ought to expect to spend more than a third of our waking hours in our workplaces (and even more on the commute). During the pandemic, many "essential" workers—especially those in health care, but also those working retail jobs—worked even longer hours in fraught and dangerous conditions. At the same time, many others began working from home, for instance, college professors who found themselves teaching online midway through the spring 2020 semester. In the first group, "burnout" may be contributing to an unwillingness to continue to make work the center of their lives. In the second, having experienced freedom from the need to report to the workplace each day may leave many workers unwilling to go back to the old ways of working.

One consequence of the pandemic is that more workers are now trying to negotiate to continue to work remotely. One recent survey found that 48 percent of workers planned to pursue a remote position when they were ready for a new job.[58] But it also means that more people are leaving the workforce altogether, a phenomenon that's been called "The Great Resignation" (although the number of people leaving their jobs had been climbing even before the pandemic).[59]

Summary
An exclusive focus on short-term performance can prevent business from pursuing long-term goals and strategies, and it can encourage dubious, even fraudulent, business practices. People's changing attitudes toward work represent another challenge facing our socioeconomic system, according to some experts.

According to University of Iowa history professor Benjamin Hunnicutt, the pandemic has led many American workers to question the nation's quasi-religious devotion to work. "The experience of being away from work has awakened people. There are other things to do—there are walks to take in the park, there's life beyond work that [people] had not thought about before." Duke University professor of Women's Studies Kathi Weeks observes that "People are saying that they are systematically underpaid, they get a ridiculously low share of the value that they produce over the course of the day. They're doing most of the work, and yet they're treated badly and receive wages that they cannot live on. The pandemic was the straw that broke the camel's back." [60] Research and consulting firm Gartner finds that "65% of employees say the pandemic has made them rethink the place work should have in their lives, and 52% of employees say it made them question the purpose of their day-to-day jobs."[61]

Companies are responding to these changes in various ways. According to *Forbes*, "Many employers appear to be trying almost anything they can think of to encourage workers to stay—including providing free food and gym memberships, gift cards and letting them bring their dogs to work."[62] In some instances, employers are offering more pay. (See Case 4.3 for two major examples.) More companies are also offering employees more flexible schedules, remote working options, and shorter workweeks.[63] So many are doing so, in fact, that business-district restaurants and bars that served office workers are struggling, especially on Mondays and Fridays.[64]

Study Corner

Key Terms and Concepts

alienation	globalized capitalism	oligopolies
capital	hollow corporations	outsource
capitalism	industrial capitalism	profit motive
comparative advantage	invisible hand	short-term focus
competition	laissez faire	socialism
corporate welfare	mercantile capitalism	state welfare capitalism
exploitation	monopoly	work ethic
financial capitalism	natural right to property	worker control socialism

Points to Review

- how capitalism, socialism, and worker control socialism differ (pp. 97–98)

- the story of the Fugger dynasty (pp. 99–100)

- five historical stages of capitalism and their characteristics (pp. 99–100)

- four key features of capitalism (pp. 100–102)

- criticisms of the natural-right-to-property argument for capitalism (p. 103)

- how the invisible hand guides self-interest in a socially beneficial direction (pp. 103–105)

- responses to criticisms of capitalism because of inequality and poverty (pp. 105–106)

- capitalism's assumptions about human nature (pp. 106–107)

- oligopolies and corporate welfare under capitalism (pp. 107–109)

- why some critics reject competition as an ideal (pp. 109–110)

- different ways workers are alienated, according to Marx (pp. 110–111)

- the decline of American manufacturing, its manifestations and implications (pp. 112–113)

- conflicting views of outsourcing (pp. 113–114)

- why the trade deficit causes some economists to worry (pp. 114–115)

- negative consequences of an exclusive focus on the short term (p. 115)

- changes in the work ethic (pp. 116–117)

For Further Reflection

1. What do you see as the strongest moral consideration in favor of capitalism? What do you see as the strongest objection to it?

2. How capitalist is our economic system today?

3. What do you see as the major economic challenges facing our society today and, in particular, your generation?

Case 4.1
Catastrophe in Bangladesh

Rana Plaza Was a Nondescript Eight-Story Building in a Modest suburb of Dhaka, Bangladesh. Owned by Sohel Rana, a politically well-connected figure, it housed a bank and a few shops on its lower floors, but most of Rana Plaza was given over to five garment factories. They employed around 5,000 people making clothes for companies in North America and Europe. In April 2013, cracks appeared in the building's structure. Building inspectors ordered Rana Plaza to be evacuated, after which the bank and the shops immediately closed—but not the garment factories. They ordered their employees to return to work the following day. On that fateful day—April 24, 2013—at around 9:00 A.M., Rana Plaza collapsed: 1,129 garment workers were killed, and around 2,500 were injured. It was the deadliest garment factory disaster ever, and probably the most lethal accidental collapse of a building in modern history.[65]

In the aftermath, Sohel Rana and the owners of the five garment factories were arrested along with an engineer who was accused of having helped Rana to add three illegal stories to the building. The Bangladesh High Court ordered the property seized and the assets of the factory owners frozen to ensure that the workers' salaries were paid. The Bangladesh government suspended the local mayor and several inspectors who were accused of negligence in renewing the licenses of the garment factories. Families of the victims received some short-term assistance from the government, but workers who are too seriously injured to work are desperate, and in many families, children have had to go to work because their mothers are dead.

Since the disaster, there has been some soul searching in the West. Documents and remnants of apparel link the Rana Plaza factories to twenty-five European and American clothing brands or clothing retailers, including Walmart. That's not too surprising. Almost all the clothing that Americans and Europeans wear is manufactured in developing countries like Bangladesh. And no wonder. Although the minimum wage for garment workers in Bangladesh was raised substantially after the Rana Plaza disaster, it is still only $68 per month. As a result, since 1998 clothing costs for American consumers have dropped 7 to 8 percent, and corporate profits have been high. In this world of globalized capitalism, many people are asking, what are the responsibilities of companies and consumers to workers in faraway countries?

One monitoring group estimates that Bangladesh's 5,000 factories could be elevated to Western safety standards for, on average, $600,000. That would add up to $3 billion. However, if that were spread over five years, it would add only about 10 cents to the factory price of each of the 7 billion garments that Bangladesh sells every year to Western brands. Meanwhile, several prominent retailers and labor groups have joined forces to create a $40 million compensation fund to aid the victims of the Rana Plaza collapse. Among the retailers who have contributed to the fund are Bon Marché, El Corte Inglés, Primark, and Loblaw, a Canadian company. "Following the collapse," says Robert Chant, a senior vice president at Loblaw, "we came very quickly to the conclusion that compensation was not only a necessity for the survivors, but a responsibility for the many retailers sourcing from Rana Plaza."

No American companies, however, have agreed to join the compensation effort, which has raised less than half of its target. Walmart, for example, denies that it has any responsibility, saying that the garments it sold were produced there without its knowledge by a Canadian contractor. And it is true that Western companies do not own garment factories in developing countries like those in Rana Plaza, and they do not directly employ the workers who make the apparel they sell. Those workers work for companies that work for other companies that provide the garments to Western clothing companies and retailers.

Some experts believe that American companies are worried about possible legal liability or are afraid that they will appear hypocritical after denying that they were knowingly involved with the factories at Rana Plaza. Dan Rees of the International Labor Organization believes that contributing to the fund would not lead to liability. "At the moment, this effort needs support," he says. "It needs the backing of companies that were in Rana Plaza when it collapsed, that were there in the recent past before it collapsed, and that weren't there at all and want to show solidarity with the industry."

While they may be dragging their feet on compensation, Western retailers have reacted to public outrage over Rana Plaza by launching a major push to improve safety at the Bangladeshi factories they do business with. Instead of joining forces, though, they have divided into two, sometimes feuding, camps. The largest—the Bangladesh Accord for Fire and Building Safety—has more than 150 members. The Accord includes fourteen American companies, but most of its members are European. The other organization—the Alliance for Bangladesh Worker Safety—comprises twenty-six companies, all of them American or Canadian. Both organizations are off to a good start, hiring inspectors and investigating factories in Bangladesh, but they argue about who is doing a better job. Fifteen American universities have sided with the Accord because it requires greater legal and financial commitments from its members, telling the licensees who produce the sweatshirts and other clothing bearing their logos to join it rather than the Alliance. Some observers are bothered by the division of safety efforts, but Professor Dara O'Rouke, an expert on workplace monitoring at the University of California, Berkeley, believes that the Accord-Alliance competition has an upside. "It's pushing both sides to raise the bar on what they are doing to improve safety," she says.

The word "sweatshop" conjures up visions of workers toiling in cramped and dingy factories for paltry wages. But if you lived in a developing nation and had no other opportunity but a low-wage sweatshop job, you might well be happy to take it. Critics contend that such "opportunities" still amount to exploitation.

Update

The Alliance for Bangladesh Worker Safety ceased operations in 2018. The Bangladesh Accord for Fire and Building Safety is still in existence and has been extended beyond Bangladesh to neighboring Pakistan. However, the Bangladeshi government aims to take over responsibility for ensuring worker safety through its Bangladesh Remediation and Coordination Cell. In 2023, a report by the Center for Business and Human Rights at New York University found that "there is no doubt that overall, the industry in Bangladesh is safer today than in 2013."[66] It added, though, that "some buyers are taking advantage of their Bangladeshi business partners. Not only are they seeking to extract the greatest volume of products from suppliers at the lowest possible price, they are also looking to suppliers to offset their losses at a time of global economic instability."

Discussion Questions

1. Are workers in overseas garment factories exploited? What are the moral pros and cons of outsourcing garment manufacturing to countries where workers are paid so little?

2. Is outsourcing an inevitable feature of globalized capitalism? Are sweatshops? Do Americans gain more from sweatshops (in terms of cheaper products) than they lose (in terms of jobs)?

3. American Apparel is a clothing manufacturer, distributor, and retailer that does not outsource. It pays its workers, on average, over $12 an hour. Could other U.S. clothing companies do the same thing?

4. Do companies have a responsibility to monitor the conduct of the companies that they do business with either directly (suppliers, contractors) or indirectly (subcontractors)? Do clothing companies have a responsibility to see that the people who ultimately make their clothes do so in safe working conditions? Do they have a responsibility to see that those people are paid a decent wage?

5. Do companies whose clothing was being made in Rana Plaza have an obligation to help the victims or their families? What about companies who have had clothing made there in the past, but not at the time of the collapse? Dan Rees suggests that even garment companies with no association with Rana Plaza should contribute out of solidarity with the industry. Explain why you agree or disagree with this.

6. In your view, are Western companies sincere about trying to improve factory safety, or is it just a public-relations effort?

7. Do American consumers who wear clothing produced in countries like Bangladesh bear some responsibility for the wages and conditions of workers there? Do they bear some responsibility for the Rana Plaza collapse? Many consumers know or at least suspect that the clothes they wear are made by workers in developing nations. Does this affect their moral responsibilities?

8. Many American consumers say that they don't like having their clothes made by overseas workers who live in poverty, are paid low wages, and experience unhealthy or oppressive conditions. Would you pay more for clothing that is made in factories that meet American safety standards? If so, how much more?

9. What, if anything, should consumers do to make foreign factories safer? Can consumer pressure get American companies to improve the pay and working conditions of foreign factory workers?

Case 4.2
Licensing and Laissez Faire

The United States Is a Capitalist Country, and the System of medical care is, to a significant extent, organized for profit. True, many hospitals are nonprofit, but the same cannot be said of doctors, who, judged as a whole, form an extremely affluent and privileged occupational group.

Sometimes physicians themselves seem a little uncomfortable about the business aspect of their professional lives or worry that outsiders will misinterpret their attention to economic matters. For example, the professional journal *Medical Economics*, which discusses pocketbook issues such as malpractice insurance, taxes, fees, and money management ("Are You Overpaying Your Staff?" is a typical cover story), works hard at not being available to the general public. When a subscriber left his copy on a commercial airliner, another reader found it and sent the mailing label to the magazine; the magazine's editor sent a cautionary note to the subscriber. The editor advises readers to "do your part by restricting access to your personal copies of the magazine. Don't put them in the waiting room, don't leave them lying about in the examination rooms, and don't abandon them in public places."[67]

Medical Economics probably suspects that even in our capitalist society many people, including probably most doctors, would not like to think of physicians simply as medical entrepreneurs who are in it for the money. And, indeed, many people in the United States and many more in other countries criticize the American medical system for being profit oriented. They think medical care should be based on need, and that ability to pay should not affect the quality of medical treatment one receives. Interestingly, though, some people criticize medical practice in the United States as being insufficiently market oriented; prominent among them was the late Milton Friedman, a Nobel Prize–winning economist at the University of Chicago.

Friedman was a long-standing critic of occupational licensure in all fields. His reasoning is straightforward: Licensure—the requirement that one obtain a license from a recognized authority in order to engage in an occupation—restricts entry into the field. Licensure thus permits the occupational or professional group to enjoy a monopoly in the provision of services. In Friedman's view, this contravenes the principles of a free market to the disadvantage of us all.

Friedman had no objection to certification—that is, to public or private agencies certifying that an individual has certain skills. But he rejected the policy of preventing people who do not have such a certificate from practicing the occupation of their choice. Such a policy restricts freedom and keeps the price of the services in question artificially high. When one reads the long lists of occupations for which some states require a license—librarians, tree surgeons, pest controllers, well diggers, barbers, carpet installers, movie projectionists, florists, upholsterers,

makeup artists, even potato growers, among many others[68]—Friedman's case gains plausibility. But Friedman pushed his argument to include all occupations and professions.

Does this mean we should let incompetent physicians practice? Friedman would say yes.[69] In his view, the American Medical Association (AMA) is simply a trade union, though probably the strongest one in the United States. It keeps the wages of its members high by restricting the number of those who can practice medicine.

The AMA does this not only through licensure but also, even more effectively, through controlling the number of medical schools and the number of students admitted to them. Today, for instance, over 42,000 applicants vie every year for roughly 18,000 medical school vacancies. The medical profession, Friedman charged, limits entry into the field both by turning down applicants to medical school and by making standards for admission and licensure so difficult as to discourage many young people from ever trying to gain admission. And, in fact, fewer students apply to medical school these days than in the 1990s.

Viewed as a trade union, the AMA has been singularly effective. As recently as the 1920s, physicians were far down the list of professionals in terms of income; the average doctor made less than the average accountant. Today, physicians constitute the profession that arguably has the highest status and the best pay in the country. The median income for primary-care physicians is $185,000. For general surgeons it is $306,000. And in certain specialties, it is a great deal higher. Cardiologists, pain specialists, radiologists, hand surgeons, and others often earn over half a million dollars a year.[70] American doctors earn far more than their foreign counterparts do, even in countries where average wages are similar to those in the United States. Still, the medical establishment remains worried. It believes that there are too many doctors in the United States, and that "this surplus breeds inefficiency and drives up costs."[71]

The economic logic behind this proposition is murky. An increase in the supply of barbers, plumbers, or taxi drivers does not drive up the cost of getting a haircut, having your pipes fixed, or taking a cab. Why should it be different with doctors? Critics of the medical profession believe that its real worry is the prospect of stabilizing or even declining incomes. In any case, the doctors have written two prescriptions.

The first is to reduce the number of medical students by closing some medical schools; the second is to make it more difficult for foreign doctors to practice in the United States. Although the medical establishment has often expressed concern about the quality of foreign medical training, today the worry is strictly a matter of quantity. "We've got to stop the pipeline of foreign medical graduates," says Dr. Ed O'Neil of the Center for the Health Professions at the University of California,

San Francisco. "They are a big chunk of physician oversupply. . . . We're just trying to be rational."[72] As for homegrown doctors, Congress followed medical advice. To stem the supposed glut, it decided a few years ago to pay hospitals around the country hundreds of millions of dollars to decrease the number of physicians they train. It now turns out, however, that the United States (which already has fewer doctors per 1,000 people than do almost all European countries)[73] is predicted to have a physician shortage of at least 125,000 by 2025.[74]

Medical licensure restricts the freedom of people to practice medicine and prevents the public from buying the medical care it wants. Nonetheless, most people would probably defend the principle of licensure on the grounds that it raises the standards of competence and the quality of care. Friedman would contest this. By reducing the amount of care available, he contended, licensure also reduces the average quality of care people receive. (By analogy, suppose that automobile manufacturers were forbidden to sell any car that did not have the quality of a Mercedes-Benz. As a result, people who owned cars would have cars of higher average quality than they do now. But because fewer people could afford cars and more of them would, therefore, have to walk or ride bicycles, such a regulation would not raise the quality of transportation enjoyed by the average person.) Friedman charged, furthermore, that the monopoly created by the licensing of physicians has reduced the incentive for research, development, and experimentation, both in medicine and in the organization and provision of services.

Since Friedman initially presented his argument, some of the alternatives to traditional practice that he proposed have come to pass; prepaid services have emerged, and group- and clinic-based practices are on the increase. But what about his main contention that instead of licensure we should allow the marketplace to sort out the competent from the incompetent providers of medical services?

Friedman's critics contend that even if the licensing of professionals "involves violating a moral rule" against restricting individuals' "freedom of opportunity," it is still immoral to allow an unqualified person to engage in potentially harmful activities without having subjected the person to adequate tests of competence.[75] Despite the appeal of Friedman's arguments on behalf of free choice, the danger still remains, they say, that people will be victimized by the incompetent.

Consider, for example, the dietary supplements and bogus medications—things like "healing gels" or "ionic silver"—offered as preventions or cures for the H1N1 (swine flu) virus.[76] Or the quack remedies and treatments peddled to patients with AIDS here and abroad. Bottles of processed pond scum and concoctions of herbs, injections of hydrogen peroxide or of cells from the glands of unborn calves, the eating of bee pollen and garlic, $800 pills containing substances from mice inoculated with the AIDS virus, and even whacking the thymus gland of patients to stimulate the body's immune system—all these are among the treatments that have been offered to desperate people by the unscrupulous and eccentric. Deregulation of the medical field seems most unlikely to diminish such exploitation.

Update

The role of states in licensing physicians has become more contentious due to the COVID-19 pandemic. Some medical professionals prescribed and promoted treatments for COVID-19 that have been shown to be ineffective (e.g., ivermectin—an anti-parasitic medication used, among other things, to deworm horses). Several states have pursued revoking the licenses of these doctors and physician's assistants on the grounds that they harmed patients.[77] Other states, though, have passed legislation preventing state medical boards from using this as a reason to revoke doctors' licenses.[78] What some see as a means of quality control necessary to protect patients against dangerous and possibly politically motivated misinformation, others see as a way to impose an orthodoxy on doctors rather than letting them exercise their independent medical judgment. Those in the latter camp would remind us that the "medical establishment" is not always correct. In the first stages of the pandemic, the guidance from public health officials was that the general public should not be wearing masks. As more was learned, their guidance shifted in the opposite direction.

Discussion Questions

1. What explains the fact that licenses are required for so many occupations? What do you see as the pros and cons of occupational licensure in general? Does it have benefits that Friedman overlooked?

2. Do you believe that licensure in medicine or any other field is desirable? If so, in which fields and under what circumstances? What guidelines would you use to determine where licensure is needed?

3. Is occupational licensure consistent with the basic principles and values of capitalism? Is it a violation of the free-market ideal? How would you respond to the argument that licensure illegitimately restricts individual freedom to pursue a career or a trade?

4. Does licensure make the market work more or less effectively? Would you agree that as long as consumers are provided with accurate information, they should be permitted to make their own choices with regard to the services and products they purchase— even when it comes to medical care? Or is licensing necessary to protect them from making incorrect choices?

5. Friedman and others view the AMA as a trade union, and they believe that the high incomes of doctors are due more to artificial restrictions on the free market than to the inherent value of their services. Is this an accurate or fair picture of the medical profession?

6. Is licensing an all-or-nothing issue? Or is it possible that although only licensed professionals should be permitted to perform certain services, paraprofessionals and laypersons could perform less expensively but equally competently other services now monopolized by licensed professionals?

7. Should physicians who prescribed ineffective COVID-19 treatments like ivermectin lose their licenses?

Case 4.3
One Nation under Walmart

The Huge Corporations That Produce Our Cars, Appliances, computers, and other products—many of them household names like Nike, Coca-Cola, and Johnson & Johnson—are a familiar feature of contemporary capitalism.

But Walmart represents something new on the economic landscape. Now the world's largest company (by revenue), Walmart has achieved its corporate preeminence not in production but in retail. No other retailer, at any time or in any place, has ever come close to being as large and influential as Walmart has become. After years of nonstop growth, there are now more than 10,500 Walmart stores worldwide (including Sam's Clubs), and over 230 million shoppers visit its stores each week. And the company is opening more stores all the time as it moves beyond its stronghold in the rural South and Midwest and into urban America. As a result, the company's marketplace clout is enormous. In just the first quarter of 2023, its total earnings were over $140 billion.

The good news for consumers is that Walmart has risen to retail supremacy through the bargain prices it offers them. The retail giant can afford its low prices because of the cost efficiencies it has achieved and the pressure it puts on suppliers to lower their prices. And the larger the store gets, the more market clout it has and the further it can push down prices for its customers.

Everyone, of course, loves low prices, but not everyone, it seems, loves Walmart. Why not? Here are some of the charges that critics level against the retail behemoth:

- Walmart's buying power and cost-saving efficiencies force local rivals out of business, thus costing jobs, disrupting local communities, and injuring established business districts. One Walmart worker replaces approximately 1.4 other local retail workers, and typically within five years after a Walmart supercenter opens, two other supermarkets close. Further, Walmart often insists on tax breaks when it moves into a community, so its presence does little or nothing to increase local tax revenues.

- Walmart is staunchly anti-union and has traditionally paid low wages. The government effectively subsidized this low pay: in 2020, a government report found that large numbers of Walmart employees were enrolled in the Supplemental Nutrition Assistance Program and Medicaid.[79] However, in March of 2023 Walmart did raise its minimum wage for store employees to $14/hour.

First Lady Michelle Obama teamed up with Walmart on an initiative that will result in the company offering a larger selection of healthy foods at more affordable prices. What does such an alliance suggest about the relationship between business and society and between business and politics?

For these reasons, Walmart's expansion is frequently meeting determined local resistance, as concerned residents try to preserve their communities and their local stores and downtown shopping areas from disruption by Walmart through petitions, political pressure, and zoning restrictions. As one economist remarks, for Walmart "the biggest barrier to growth" is not competition from rivals such as Target or Winn-Dixie stores but "opposition at the local level." As a result, Walmart has begun responding to the criticism that it is a poor corporate citizen and miserly employer by improving employee health insurance coverage and adopting greener business practices. And even its usual critics applauded when the company responded rapidly to Hurricane Katrina, sending truckloads of water and food, much of it reaching residents before federal supplies did.

When it comes to Walmart, Professor John E. Hoopes of Babson College encourages people to take a long-term view: "The history of the last 150 years in retailing would say that if you don't like Walmart, be patient. There will be new models eventually that will do Walmart in, and Walmart won't see it coming." And, indeed, in recent years the company's sales growth has slipped as the Internet has changed people's shopping habits and as other discounters have done a better job of attracting affluent consumers and providing higher quality and better service.

In the meantime, where you stand on Walmart probably depends on where you sit, as Jeffrey Useem writes in *Fortune* magazine: "If you're a consumer, Walmart is good for you. If you're a wage-earner, there's a good chance it's bad for you. If you're a Walmart shareholder, you want the company to grow. If you're a citizen, you probably don't want it growing in your backyard. So, which one are you?"

Update

Professor Hoopes was right. There is a new retail model, namely ecommerce. And while Walmart is a major ecommerce player, they take second place to Amazon—the world's second-largest corporation by revenue. Critics of Amazon have charged it with many of the same failings that have been attributed to Walmart: a destructive effect on local businesses,[80] low pay,[81] and mistreatment of its workers.[82] (Amazon has a $15 minimum hourly wage. In October 2022, it implemented a $16 minimum wage for warehouse employees and drivers.)[83]

Discussion Questions

1. Do you like Walmart? Do you shop there? If so, how frequently? If not, why not?
2. Is there a Walmart store in your area? If so, has it had any impact on your community or on the behavior of local consumers? If there's no store in your area, would you be in favor of Walmart opening one? Explain why or why not.
3. Is Walmart's rapid rise to retail dominance a positive or a negative development for our society? What does it tell us about capitalism, globalization, and the plight of workers?
4. Can a retailer ever become too large and too powerful?
5. Is opposition to Walmart's expansion a legitimate part of the political process or is it unfair interference with our market system and a violation of the company's rights? Do opponents of Walmart have any valid concerns?
6. Why do you think Walmart raised its minimum wage, and what impact do you think it will have?
7. Are there any significant ethical differences between Walmart and Amazon? You might think here about their effects on communities, their effects on the environment, their treatment of employees, and their treatment of customers.

Case 4.4
A New Work Ethic?

You Would Think That Employees Would Do Something if They discovered that a customer had died on the premises.

But that's not necessarily so, according to the Associated Press, which reported that police discovered the body of a trucker in a tractor trailer rig that had sat—with its engine running—in the parking lot of a fast-food restaurant for nine days. Employees swept the parking lot around the truck but ignored the situation for over a week until the stench got so bad that someone finally called the police.

That lack of response doesn't surprise James Sheehy, a human resources manager in Houston, who spent his summer vacation working undercover at a fast-food restaurant owned by a relative.[84] Introduced to coworkers as a management trainee from another franchise location who was being brought in to learn the ropes, Sheehy was initially viewed with some suspicion, but by the third day the group had accepted him as just another employee. Sheehy started out as a maintenance person and gradually rotated through various cooking and cleaning assignments before ending up as a cashier behind the front counter.

Most of Sheehy's fellow employees were teenagers and college students who were home for the summer and earning additional spending money. Almost half came from upper-income families and the rest from middle-income neighborhoods. More than half were women, and a third were underrepresented groups. What Sheehy reports is a whole generation of workers with a frightening new work ethic: contempt for customers, indifference to quality and service, unrealistic expectations about the world of work, and a get-away-with-what-you-can attitude.

Research shows that over 25% of theft from businesses is by employees.[85] Sheehy's experience was in line with this. He writes that the basic work ethic at his place of employment was a type of gamesmanship that focused on milking the place dry. Theft was rampant, and younger employees were subject to peer pressure to steal as a way of becoming part of the group. "It don't mean nothing," he says, was the basic rationale for dishonesty. "Getting on with getting mine" was another common phrase, as coworkers carefully avoided hard work or dragged out tasks like sweeping to avoid additional assignments.

All that customer service meant was getting rid of people as fast as possible and with the least possible effort. Sometimes, however, service was deliberately slowed or drive-through orders intentionally switched in order to cause customers to demand to see a manager. This was called "baiting the man," or purposely trying to provoke a response from management. In fact, the general attitude toward managers was one of disdain and contempt. In the eyes of the employees, supervisors were only paper-pushing functionaries who got in the way.

Sheehy's coworkers rejected the very idea of hard work and long hours. "Scamming" was their ideal. Treated as a kind of art form and as an accepted way of doing business, scamming meant taking shortcuts or getting something done without much effort, usually by having someone else do it. "You only put in the time and effort for the big score" is how one fellow worker characterized the work ethic he shared with his peers. "You got to just cruise through the job stuff and wait to make the big score," said another. "Then you can hustle. The office stuff is for buying time or paying for the groceries."

By contrast, they looked forward to working "at a real job where you don't have to put up with hassles." "Get out of school and you can leave this to the real dummies." "Get an office and a computer and a secretary and you can scam your way through anything." On the other hand, these young employees believed that most jobs were like the fast-food industry: automated, boring, undemanding and unsatisfying, and dominated by difficult people. Still, they dreamed of an action-packed business world, an image shaped by a culture of video games and action movies. The college students in particular,

reports Sheehy, believed that a no-holds-barred, trample-over-anybody, get-what-you-want approach is the necessary and glamorous road to success.

Update

In addition to the "Great Resignation," another change in the workplace post-pandemic is the increased attention given to what's been described as "quiet quitting." Quiet quitting doesn't mean resigning without giving notice. Instead, it has been described as "people rejecting explicit and implicit requests to go above and beyond at work: no more 40-plus hour work weeks, responding to emails on the weekends or performing tasks outside written and agreed-upon assignments."[86] It reflects a more "transactional" attitude toward work, providing just the level of performance that one is being paid for and declining to do more without additional compensation. "Calibrated contributing" has been suggested as a less-loaded alternative term.[87] (While the term "quiet quitting" is new, there is some debate about whether the phenomenon is really more prevalent now than it was prior to COVID-19.)[88] Some management experts and business commentators see quiet quitting as a problem for companies to solve; others suggest that that it's entirely legitimate for employees to choose not to do more than they agreed to do when they were hired and to try to maintain a healthy work-life balance.

Discussion Questions

1. How typical are the attitudes that Sheehy reports? Does his description of a new work ethic tally with your own experiences?

2. What are the implications for the future of American business of the work ethic Sheehy describes?

3. Some might discount Sheehy's experiences either as being the product of one particular industry or as simply reflecting the immaturity of young employees. Would you agree?

4. Is it reasonable to expect workers, especially in a capitalist society, to be more devoted to their jobs, more concerned with quality and customer service, than Sheehy's coworkers were? What explains employee theft?

5. In what ways does the culture of our capitalist society encourage attitudes like those Sheehy describes?

6. Are workers who engage in "quiet quitting" at work and choose not to do more than the minimum doing anything objectionable?

Case 4.5
Paying College Athletes

Cam Newton Was Once the Star Quarterback of the Carolina Panthers. In his last year at Auburn University, he won the Heisman trophy, led his team to a national championship, and was the highest NFL draft pick. Although that degree of success couldn't have been predicted when Newton graduated from high school, that he had enormous talent and potential was obvious to college coaches around the country. Allegedly, his father offered to have Newton sign with Mississippi State University for a $180,000 under-the-table payment, a charge he denies. But what would be wrong with a system, some people are now asking, which permitted universities to bid for the services of players like Newton and to do so above board?[89]

College football is big business. With the introduction of a playoff system for the national championship, the television and other revenues that go to college football programs and to the NCAA promise to double or even triple. Right now, that money subsidizes the escalating salaries of coaches and athletic directors, who at the top football schools often make millions of dollars a year—in thirty-nine out of fifty states a college coach is the highest paid state official—as well as underwriting the construction of new and better football facilities. None of it goes to the players, who make the system possible. That strikes some people as unfair. After all, for players at Division 1 schools, football is a full-time, year-round job. Shouldn't they be compensated for doing it? Why should coaches get big salaries and players nothing?

Flush with money from television rights and maybe feeling a little guilty about sharing none of it with college athletes, the five largest football conferences—the SEC, ACC, Pac-12, Big 12, Big Ten—agree. They are pushing the NCAA to allow colleges to pay players a modest stipend, perhaps a few thousand dollars a year, and to permit college athletes to sign advertising endorsements. Various salary cap plans are also being tossed around that would limit the total amount that any college can spend on players. Critics of these ideas argue that players are already compensated. They receive tuition, room and board, and an education as well as a package of professional coaching and strength and fitness training that would, if purchased on the open market, be very expensive. In addition, they get exposure to scouts from the NFL. Critics also point to the fact that the vast majority of football programs—maybe nine out of ten—make no money. Some of them would be hard-pressed to pay their players much.

On the other hand, there are those who think that set stipends and salary caps are, at best, a halfway measure. They want a completely free market, in which colleges would bid for the services of high school recruits and those recruits would be free to negotiate contracts with the universities who want them. On this scenario, in the future a football powerhouse might

pay $180,000 for a player with Cam Newton's potential. But then player salaries might not go that high if it turns out that very few universities could afford to offer anywhere near that much. Still, the biggest and wealthiest athletic departments would almost certainly buy up the best college athletes, disrupting any semblance of competitive balance. Free-market advocates see no problem with this. They contend, in response, that the wealthiest programs—those with the big-name coaches, top-of-the-line athletic facilities, and super-duper dormitories for athletes—already get the lion's share of the top college players.

Still, this free-market, capitalistic approach runs up against the older ideal of college athletes as student amateurs. The National Labor Relations Board, however, has decisively rejected that ideal as a kind of myth. In March 2014, it ruled that football players on scholarship at Northwestern University have a right to form a union and bargain collectively over such things as how much time they devote to football, the control exerted by coaches, and the scholarships they receive, which the Board deemed a contract for compensation. The NLRB notes that Northwestern recruited players for their athletic skill, not their academic ability, and that it reported $235 million in revenue from football between 2003 and 2012. It also noted that players spend "many more hours" on football than on their studies—fifty to sixty hours per week during a one-month training camp and forty to fifty hours per week during the football season. The NLRB ruling sets a precedent that would clearly extend to other private universities. (State law regulates collective bargaining at public universities.)

For its part, the NCAA rejects the notion that student-athletes are employees. After all, if college football players are no longer amateurs, then why insist that they be students and go to classes? ("Why should we have to go to class if we came here to play FOOTBALL, we ain't come to play SCHOOL, classes are POINTLESS" is how Ohio State quarterback Cardale Jones, whose team won the college championship in January 2015, put it in a Twitter message.) Players would still represent the college they worked for on the football field, but they would be university employees, not students. That would make college football, in the most competitive conferences, a minor league of the NFL, but it would at least have the advantage of ending the recurrent scandals associated with efforts to keep athletes academic eligible.

Update

As with so many other topics discussed in this chapter, there has been significant change in the last few years. In this instance, though, the impetus for change was not the pandemic. Rather, it was the unanimous Supreme

Court ruling in *Alston v. NCAA*.[90] In this case, the Court ruled on the basis of the Sherman Antitrust Act that certain NCAA restrictions on the benefits that universities could provide athletes were illegal. The Court's ruling only applied to education-related benefits. However, in the aftermath of the ruling the NCAA liberalized its restrictions on college athletes' ability to participate in paid endorsements. Subject to various restrictions, college athletes may now be paid by companies (but not by their own universities) for the use of their "name, image, or likeness" (NIL). How much student-athletes can make via NIL deals will of course depend on their sport, their ability, and the national prominence of their university and team. It will also depend on their social media savvy and perhaps their appearance. Some college athletes, like Alabama quarterback Bryce Young and Louisiana State University gymnast Olivia Dunne, have apparently earned over $1 million.[91] (Young now plays for Newton's former team, the Panthers.)

Discussion Questions

1. What would be the likely results of letting universities bid financially for college athletes? Would allowing college players to negotiate the best contract they can be good or bad for college athletics? Would such a system be fair to schools that have less money to spend on athletes?

2. Is playing Division 1 college football a job? Should it bring monetary compensation? Are college athletes exploited workers? Are they being treated unfairly by not being allowed to share directly in the revenue that college football generates?

3. Should college players have the right to unionize? Is it a matter of fairness? How would unionization affect college athletics?

4. Is the ideal of the amateur student athlete representing their university already obsolete, or is it worth striving to preserve?

5. Suppose that instead of schools' having sports teams, all professional sports leagues had lower-tiered levels of competition (like the minor leagues in baseball) where younger athletes could be paid for playing while developing their abilities. Would this be a better system than currently exists?

6. If college athletics becomes completely professional, is there any reason to continue to require that athletes also be students?

7. Do collegiate athletics make important contributions to the diversity of the student bodies at some colleges and universities?

8. Will the NCAA's new NIL system help or harm college athletics? Does it solve any problems associated with student athletes not being directly paid? Is it fair to those student athletes in less-popular sports or at less-prominent schools?

Chapter 5

··

Corporations

···

Learning Objectives

···

After completing this chapter, you should be able to:

1. Explain what is distinctive about corporations, as opposed to sole proprietorships or partnerships, and the economic and ethical significance of the differences.

2. Distinguish between the two major theories of corporate social responsibility and assess the arguments for and against each.

3. Analyze the importance of institutionalizing ethics within corporations and mechanisms for doing this.

Introduction

In 1959, The Vice President of Ford Motor Company Described the modern business corporation as the dominant institution of American society. Today, few observers would disagree. As one of them puts it, "The modern corporation is *the* central institution of contemporary society."[1] As an aggregate, corporations wield awesome economic clout, but the dominant role of corporations in our society extends well beyond that. Not only do corporations produce almost all the goods and services we buy, but also they and their ethos permeate everything from politics and communications to athletics and religion. And their influence is growing relentlessly around the world.

By any measure, the biggest corporations are colossi that dominate the earth. Many of them employ tens of thousands of people, and the largest have hundreds of thousands in their ranks. Amazon has about 1.5 million employees worldwide, Home Depot over 470,000, and FedEx almost 465,000—not to mention the 2.1 million people who work for Walmart, the world's largest private-sector employer.[2] And their revenues are dazzling. For example, Dell Computer takes in more than $600 billion a year, Amazon more than $500 billion, and ExxonMobil more than $400 billion. Alliance Resource Partnerships brings in more than $2 billion per year, and this only puts it at the bottom of the list of the 1,000 American corporations with the highest revenues. Some corporations also generate astronomical profits. At present, the most profitable are in the technology sector, including Apple (almost $100 billion), Microsoft (nearly $75 billion), and Google/Alphabet (just under $60 billion). These are all American corporations, but of course there are enormous corporations headquartered around the world. To mention just one example outside of the United States, the German carmaker Volkswagen brings in almost $300 billion, has almost 675,000 employees, and makes a profit of over $18 billion—more than Walmart.

A modern corporation is a three-part organization, made up of (1) **stockholders**, who provide the capital, own the corporation, and enjoy liability limited to the amount of their investments; (2) managers, who run the business operations; and (3) employees, who produce the goods and services. However, many corporate giants are, to quote business analyst Anthony J. Parisi, less like a single company and more like "a fabulously wealthy investment club with a limited portfolio." Such companies invest in subsidiaries, whose heads "oversee their territories like provincial governors, sovereigns in their own lands but with an authority stemming from the power center. . . . The management committee exacts its tribute (the affiliate's profits from current operations) and issues doles (the money needed to sustain and

> ····················
>
> **By any measure, the biggest corporations are colossi that dominate the earth.**
>
> ····················

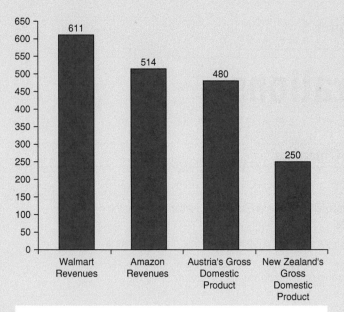

Comparison of the two top American corporations' revenues with the gross domestic product of two nations. Values are in billions of 2022 dollars.

expand those operations)."[3] In the best-run organizations, the management system is highly structured and impersonal. It provides the corporation's overall framework, the formal chain of command, which ensures that the company's profit objectives are pursued.

The emergence of corporate behemoths is one of the more intriguing chapters in the evolution of capitalism. Certainly, neither John Locke nor Adam Smith ever imagined the huge capitalist enterprises that emerged in the 19th century—in their day, hardly any private firms had more than a handful of employees—and that today dominate America's and, indeed, the world's economic, political, and social life. This book isn't the place to analyze why a people committed to an individualistic social philosophy and a free-competition market economy allowed vast oligopolistic economic entities to develop. Rather, the concern here is with the problem of applying moral standards to corporate organizations and with understanding their social responsibilities.

· · ·

The Limited-Liability Company

If you ask a lawyer for a definition of **corporation**, you will probably hear something like the following: A corporation is a thing that can endure beyond the natural lives of its members and that has incorporators who may sue and be sued as a unit and who are able to consign part of their property to the corporation for ventures of limited liability. **Limited liability** is a key feature of the modern corporation. The members of the corporation—unlike the members of a partnership or the proprietors of a business—are financially liable for the debts of the organization only up to the extent of their investments.

In addition to the limited liability of their members, corporations differ from partnerships in two ways.

Corporations differ from sole proprietorships, partnerships, and other forms of business association in two other ways as well. *First*, a corporation is not formed simply by an agreement entered into among its first members. An organization becomes incorporated by being publicly registered or in some other way having its existence officially acknowledged by the law. *Second*, unlike a partner, who is automatically entitled to his or her share of the profits of a partnership as soon as they are ascertained, the shareholder in a corporation is entitled to a dividend from the company's profits only when it has been "declared." Under U.S. law, dividends are usually declared by the directors of a corporation.

When we think of corporations, we naturally think of giants such as General Motors, ExxonMobil, Microsoft, or Walmart, which exert enormous influence over our economy and society. But the local independently owned convenience store may also be a corporation. (While some small businesses are legally incorporated, many others are "limited liability companies" [LLCs]. While there are some technical legal differences between LLCs and true corporations, both offer owners the protection of limited liability, and we can ignore the differences here.) Historically, the concept of a corporation has been broad enough to encompass churches, trade guilds, and local governments. Corporations may be either *for-profit* or *nonprofit* organizations. Princeton University, for example, is a nonprofit corporation. By contrast, Safeway, Lockheed Martin, McDonald's, and many other familiar companies aim to make money for shareholders. Corporations may be privately owned or owned (wholly or in part) by the government. Almost all U.S. corporations are privately owned; but Renault of France, for example, was once a publicly owned, for-profit corporation. (The U.S. Treasury did temporarily own some General Motors and Chrysler stock as part of the Troubled Asset Relief Program.) A small group of investors may own all the outstanding shares of a privately owned, profit-making corporation (a **privately held company**). Mars, Bechtel, Chrysler, and Enterprise Rent-A-Car are examples. Or stock may be traded among the general public (a **publicly held company**). All companies whose stocks are listed on the New York and other stock exchanges are publicly held corporations.

In 1911, Nicholas Murray Butler, president of Columbia University, declared that "the limited liability corporation is the single greatest discovery of modern times. . . . Even steam and electricity are far less important . . . and . . . would be reduced to comparative impotence without it."[4] Many business theorists and historians still agree with that assessment. The economic and ethical significance of limited liability shouldn't be overlooked. Consider three points.

First, when you purchase corporate stock there is a limit to how much you can lose but no limit to how much you can gain. Had you purchased $1,000 in Apple stock in 1985, your investment would be worth over $2 million today. But even if Apple had made different choices and failed, $1,000 is the most that you could have lost. No wonder, then, that so many people invest in the stock market and that corporations can amass huge stocks of capital.

Second, limited liability means that if a corporation goes bankrupt, then people to whom it owes money may not receive everything they are due, even if the owners of the corporation remain quite wealthy. Think here not only of people who chose to do business with the corporation but also people who didn't. If a corporation with assets of $10 million is successfully sued for $100 million, perhaps because it harmed people who lived in the vicinity of one of its facilities, the plaintiffs will not receive all the compensation that the courts have ruled they are due. While the corporation will pay the $10 million it has, the stockowners' houses and bank accounts will not be touched.

Third, we have seen that libertarian defenders of laissez-faire capitalism depict government interference with the economy as a violation of our so-called Lockean rights to own and control property. However, while people could exercise their Lockean rights by voluntarily joining together and forming a partnership, they couldn't create a company that offered them the protection of limited liability just by agreeing amongst themselves to do so. People might mutually agree not to sue each other for damages beyond a certain amount, but as the example in the previous paragraph illustrates, limited liability limits how much people outside the corporation, and so not party to any agreement, receive in compensation when they're damaged. A legal system that empowers people to create companies whose owners enjoy the safety of limited liability is doing more than merely protecting individuals' Lockean rights. It's therefore not clear that limited liability could exist in a purely laissez-faire society, like one governed by Nozick's entitlement theory.

Several stages mark the evolution of the corporation. The corporate form itself developed during the early Middle Ages, and the first corporations were towns, universities, and ecclesiastical orders. They were chartered by government and regulated by public statute. As corporate bodies, they existed independently of the particular individuals who constituted their membership at any given time. By the 15th century, the courts of England had evolved the principle of limited liability—thus setting limits, for example, on how much an alderman of the Liverpool Corporation might be required to pay if the city went bankrupt. During the medieval period, however, the law did not grant corporate status to purely profit-making associations. In those days, something besides economic self-interest had to be seen as uniting the members of the corporation: religion, a trade, shared political responsibilities.

This state of affairs changed during the Elizabethan era, as the incorporation of business enterprises began. European entrepreneurs were busy organizing trading voyages to the East and to North America. The East India Company, which epitomizes the great trading companies of this period, was formed in 1600, when Queen Elizabeth I granted to a group of merchants the right to be "one body corporate" and bestowed on it a trading monopoly to the East Indies.

Summary
Corporations are legal entities, with legal rights and responsibilities similar but not identical to those enjoyed by individuals. Business corporations are limited-liability companies—that is, their owners or stockholders are liable for corporate debts only up to the extent of their investments.

In the following decades, numerous other incorporated firms were granted trading monopolies and colonial charters. Much of North America's settlement, in fact, was initially underwritten as a business venture.

Although the earliest corporations typically held special trading rights from the government, their members did not pool capital. Rather, they individually financed voyages using the corporate name and absorbed the loss individually if a vessel sank or was robbed by pirates. But as ships became larger and more expensive, no single buyer could afford to purchase and outfit one, and the loss of a ship would have been ruinous to any one individual. The solution was to pool capital and share liability. Thus emerged the prototype of today's corporations.[5]

In the 19th century, government loosened restrictions on corporate charters.

The first instance of the corporate organization of a manufacturing enterprise in the United States occurred in 1813, but only after the Civil War did the movement toward the corporate organization of business gain steam.[6] The loosening of government restrictions on corporate chartering procedures in the 19th century marks this final stage of corporate evolution. Until the mid-1800s, prospective corporations had to apply for charters—in England to the Crown, and in the United States to state government. Charters were custom-crafted; each one was an individual act of legislation. Charters were often burdened with precise terms or limited to specific business objectives, all in the name of promoting the public good. (For example, a corporation might be chartered for the sole purpose of shipping freight between two cities, or a charter might designate where the new corporation could begin and end its proposed railroad line.) Critics of the incorporation system charged that it fostered favoritism, corruption, and unfair monopolies. Gradually, the old system of incorporation was replaced by the system we know today, in which corporate status is granted essentially to any organization that fills out the forms and pays the fees.

Two ideas were behind this change.

Lurking behind this change were two important theoretical shifts. *First*, underlying the old system was the mercantilist idea that a corporation's activities should advance some specific public purpose. But Adam Smith and, following him, Alexander Hamilton, the first U.S. secretary of the treasury, challenged the desirability of a direct tie between business enterprise and public policy. They believed that businesspeople should be encouraged to explore their own avenues of enterprise and that the "invisible hand" of the market would direct their activities in a socially beneficial direction more effectively than any public official could.

Second, when 19th-century reformers argued for changes in incorporation procedures, they talked not only about government favoritism and the advantages of a laissez-faire approach but also about the principle of a corporation's right to exist.[7] Any petitioning body with the minimal qualifications, they asserted, has the right to receive a corporate charter. By contrast, the early Crown-chartered corporations were clearly creations of the state, in accordance with the legal-political doctrine that corporate status was a privilege bestowed by the government as it saw fit. The reformers, however, argued that incorporation is a by-product of the people's right of association, not a gift from the state.

Summary
What we know as the modern business corporation has evolved over several centuries, and incorporation is no longer the special privilege it once was.

Even though the right of association supports relaxed incorporation procedures, the state must still incorporate companies and guarantee their legal status. Corporations must be recognized by the law as a single agent in order to enjoy their rights and privileges. To a large extent, then, the corporation remains, as Chief Justice John Marshall put it in 1819, "an artificial being, invisible, intangible, and existing only in the contemplation of the law."[8]

Corporations are clearly legal agents. They can enter into contracts, own property, and sue and be sued. But are they also moral agents? Corporations have definite legal responsibilities, but what, if any, social and moral responsibilities do they have?

· · ·

Corporate Moral Agency

In 2010, the Supreme Court dropped a political bombshell. In reviewing a case that most observers thought would revolve on the technicalities of campaign finance law, the Court, in a broad and unexpected ruling in *Citizens United v. Federal Election Commission*, struck down those provisions of the McCain-Feingold Act that had prohibited corporations from making "electioneering communications" before a presidential primary or a general election. In a split 5-to-4 decision, it held that corporations have a basic First Amendment right to participate in the political process and that the government may not prevent them from spending money to support the candidates they favor. Writing for the majority, Justice Anthony M. Kennedy argued that the Constitution prohibits "restrictions distinguishing among different speakers, allowing speech by some but not others." Although McCain-Feingold had allowed corporations to set up political action committees to advocate for their causes, this exception was not enough, Kennedy wrote, because it still "does not allow corporations to speak."

In a long and vigorous dissent, Justice John Paul Stevens criticized the decision for the damage it would do to our democracy and for "the conceit that corporations must be treated identically to natural persons in the political sphere." But *Citizens United* was not entirely without precedent. Over the years, the Court has granted corporations certain First Amendment protections and extended them other constitutional rights as well—for example, to due process (Fourteenth Amendment), against unreasonable searches and seizures (Fourth Amendment), to a jury trial (Seventh Amendment), to freedom from double jeopardy (Fifth Amendment), and to compensation for government takings (Fifth Amendment). In holding that the First Amendment gives corporations basically the same political rights as individual citizens, the Court further blurred the distinction between real persons and artificial or legal persons. However, in doing so, it has provided a basis for claiming that if corporations enjoy the same moral and political rights as citizens, then they bear the same responsibilities that individual human beings do. In other words, if corporations have the same rights that moral agents have, then, like individuals, they can and should be held morally responsible for their actions.

> Cases like *Citizens United* have blurred the distinction between individuals and corporations.

The problem, of course, is that corporations are *not* human beings. Or, to quote Lord Thurlow, an 18th-century lawyer, how can you "expect a corporation to have a conscience, when it has no soul to be damned and no body to be kicked?"[9] But although corporations are not people, they are collective entities that in some sense really exist, and they have an identity above and beyond the people whom they comprise at any given time. And the law recognizes them as "persons." Do they have moral obligations just as individual human beings do? Can they be held morally responsible, not just legally liable, for the things they do? The answer to these questions hangs on another question, namely: Does it make sense to view corporations as moral agents—that is, as entities capable of making moral decisions? If so, then corporations can be held morally responsible for their actions. They—and not just the individual human beings who make them up—can be seen as having moral obligations and as being blameworthy for failing to meet those obligations. They can, accordingly, be praised or blamed, even punished, for the decisions they make and the actions and policies they undertake.

> If corporations are moral agents, then they can be seen as having obligations and as being morally responsible for their actions, just as individuals are.

The task of determining whether corporations can make moral decisions is anything but simple. Immediately, we must ponder whether it makes sense to say that any entity other than an individual person can make decisions in the first place, moral or otherwise.

Can Corporations Make Moral Decisions?

Corporate internal decision (CID) structures amount to established procedures for accomplishing specific goals. For example, consider ExxonMobil's system, as depicted by Anthony J. Parisi:

> All through the Exxon system, checks and balances are built in. Each fall, the presidents of the 13 affiliates take their plan for the coming year and beyond to New York for review at a meeting with the management committee and the staff vice presidents. The goal is to get a perfect corporate fit. Some imaginary examples: The committee might decide that Exxon is becoming too concentrated in Australia and recommend that Esso Eastern move more slowly on that continent. Or it might conclude that if the affiliates were to build all the refineries they are proposing, they would create more capacity than the company could profitably use. One of the affiliates would be asked to hold off, even though, from its particular point of view, a new refinery was needed to serve its market.[10]

The implication here is that any decisions coming out of ExxonMobil's annual sessions are formed and shaped to effect corporate goals, "to get a perfect corporate fit." Metaphorically, all data pass through the filter of established corporate procedures, objectives, and decision-making guidelines. The remaining distillation constitutes the decision. Certainly, the participants actively engage in decision making. But in addition to individual persons, the other major component of corporate decision making consists of the framework in which policies and activities are determined.

The CID structure lays out lines of authority and stipulates under what conditions personal actions become official corporate actions. Some philosophers have compared the corporation to a machine or have argued that because of its structure it is bound to pursue its profit goals single-mindedly. As a result, they claim, it is a mistake to see a corporation as being morally responsible or to expect it to display such moral characteristics as honesty, considerateness, and sympathy. Only the individuals within a corporation can act morally or immorally; only they can be held responsible for what it does.

Others have argued in support of **corporate moral agency**. The CID structure, like an individual person, collects data about the impact of its actions. It monitors work conditions, employee efficiency and productivity, and environmental impacts. Professors Kenneth E. Goodpaster and John B. Matthews argue that as a result, there is no reason a corporation cannot show the same kind of rationality and respect for persons that individual human beings can. By analogy, they contend, it makes just as much sense to speak of corporate moral responsibility as it does to speak of individual moral responsibility.[11] Thomas Donaldson agrees. He argues that a corporation can be a moral agent if moral reasons enter into its decision making and if its decision-making process controls not only the company's actions but also its structure of policies and rules.[12]

Philosopher Peter French arrives at the same conclusion in a slightly different way.[13] The CID structure, says French, in effect absorbs the intentions and acts of individual persons into a "corporate decision." Perhaps no corporate official intended the course or objective charted by the CID structure, but, French contends, the corporation did. And he believes that these corporate intentions are enough to make corporate acts "intentional" and thus make corporations "morally responsible." Professor of philosophy Manuel Velasquez demurs. An act is intentional, says Velasquez, only if the entity that formed the intention brings about the act through its bodily movements. But it is only the people who make up the corporation who carry out the acts attributed to it. Velasquez concludes that only corporate members, not the corporation itself, can be held morally responsible.[14] A different route to the same conclusion might make reference to the moral emotions—in particular, guilt. One way to understand what it means for someone to be morally responsible for their actions is in terms of its being appropriate for them to feel guilty if they choose to act wrongly. If this is the correct understanding of moral responsibility, then an entity like a corporation that's incapable of feeling guilty is incapable of being morally responsible for what it does.

Corporate Punishment

The debate over corporate moral agency bears on the question of **corporate punishment**. Whether or not corporations are moral actors, the law can fine them, monitor and regulate their activities, and require the people who run them to do one thing or another. But one can talk in a literal sense about "punishing" corporations only if they are entities or "persons" capable of making moral decisions. And even if they are, not all the usual goals and methods of punishment make sense when applied to corporations. If corporations are moral agents, then the law can deter them with the threat of punishment, and it can force them to make restitution. Punishment can, perhaps, even rehabilitate a corporation, viewed as a moral agent. Retribution, as a goal of punishment, however, seems to have little application to corporations. And obviously, corporations cannot be jailed for breaking the law. Even imposing fines on them can be problematic. Financial penalties stiff enough to have an impact can easily injure innocent parties, for example, if they lead to layoffs, plant closures, or higher prices for consumers.

Summary
The question of corporate moral agency is whether a corporation is the kind of entity that can make moral decisions and bear moral responsibility for its actions. Philosophers disagree about whether CID structures make it reasonable to see corporations as morally responsible agents.

For this reason, economics professor Edwin T. Burton opposes prosecuting corporations. "A company can't commit a crime," he says. Referring to the criminal charges brought against SAC Capital, which in 2013 was fined $1.2 billion for insider trading, he says, "They should only go after the people doing the things wrong. There are innocent bystanders, a lot of them, who get hurt [by prosecuting the company]." Former federal prosecutor Preet Bharara disagrees, arguing that there are lots of different ways to punish wrongdoing and deter criminal behavior. Sometimes you charge individuals and send them to jail, and "sometimes you try to make the world understand that an entire institution deserves to be held blameworthy." Law professor Lawrence M. Friedman concurs. He points to the "expressive value" of punishing corporations. Treating what the corporation did as a criminal matter, he says, "makes an important statement about the seriousness of the wrongness."[15]

Vanishing Individual Responsibility

Some might argue that regardless of whether corporations as artificial entities can properly be held morally responsible, the nature and structure of a modern corporate organization allow nearly everyone in it to share moral accountability for what it does. In practice, however, this **diffusion of responsibility** can mean that no particular person or persons are held morally responsible. For example, does responsibility for an injury caused by a defective product fall on the shoulders of the worker who last handled the product, the foreman overseeing the running of the assembly line, the factory supervisor, the quality control team, the engineers who designed and tested the equipment, the regional managers who decided to produce the item, or the company's CEO, whose office is in another city? Indeed, each of these individuals may have been only following established procedures and decision-making guidelines. Inside a corporation, it may often be difficult, even impossible, to assign responsibility for a particular outcome to any single individual because so many different people, acting within a given CID framework, contributed to it in small ways.

Assigning individual responsibility for corporate outcomes is difficult.

This masking of moral accountability may not seem so surprising. After all, in situations that don't involve corporations, praising and blaming can also be problematic. But it raises the troubling possibility that the size and impersonal bureaucratic structure of the corporation may so envelop its members that it becomes vacuous to speak of individual moral agency. This, in turn, raises the specter of actions without actors in any moral sense—of defective products, broken laws, or flouted contracts, without any morally responsible parties.

This raises the possibility of actions for which no one is responsible. There are two ways to escape this conclusion.

There are two ways to escape this uncomfortable conclusion. *One* is to attribute moral agency to corporations just as we do to individual persons. *The other*, not necessarily incompatible with the first, is to realize that these days too many people are willing, even eager, to duck personal responsibility—"it's not my job," "there's nothing I can do about it," "I was just following procedure"—by submerging it in the CID structures of the modern corporation. Perhaps until CID structures are reconstituted to deal explicitly with noneconomic matters, we can expect more of the same evasion of personal responsibility.

The issue of corporate moral agency undoubtedly will continue to exercise scholars. Meanwhile, the inescapable fact is that corporations are increasingly being accorded the status of biological persons, with all the rights and responsibilities implied by that status. Before it was gobbled up by another corporation, Continental Oil Company expressed in an in-house booklet the public perception and its implications as follows:

> No one can deny that in the public's mind a corporation can break the law and be guilty of unethical and amoral conduct. Events . . . such as corporate violation of federal laws and failure of full disclosure [have] confirmed that both our government and our citizenry expect *corporations* to act lawfully, ethically, and responsibly.
>
> Perhaps it is then appropriate in today's context to think of Conoco as a living corporation; a sentient being whose conduct and personality are the collective effort and responsibility of its employees, officers, directors, and shareholders.[16]

Today, many companies and many of the people inside them accept without hesitation the idea that corporations are moral agents with genuinely moral, not just legal, responsibilities.

Summary
Individual responsibility can tend to vanish inside large, impersonal corporations. One response is to attribute moral agency to the corporation itself. Another is to refuse to let individuals duck their personal responsibility.

This point was illustrated when Colonial Pipeline of Atlanta published full-page advertisements in several newspapers headlined "We Apologize." The company used the ads to take responsibility for having spilled oil into the Reedy River of South Carolina three years before. True, the ads were part of a plea agreement with the U.S. Justice Department for having violated the Clean Water Act (the company also agreed to pay a $7 million fine). Yet the company's words had ethical overtones. As Laura Nash of Harvard Divinity School comments, they put "moral emotion into what is essentially a legal statement" because "the word 'apologize' . . . admits a sense of shame and humility."[17] Shame and humility were evident, too, when a few years later the world saw photographs of Charles Prince, the chief executive of Citigroup, and Douglas Petersen, Citibank Japan CEO, bowing their heads at a press conference in Tokyo in a public act of contrition for Citigroup's illegal actions in Japan.

Assuming it makes sense to talk of the moral responsibilities of corporations, what are they?

If, then, it makes sense to talk about the social and moral responsibilities of corporations, either in a literal sense or as a shorthand way of referring to the obligations of the individuals that make up the corporation, what are these responsibilities?

Summary

Despite continuing controversy over the concept of corporate moral agency, the courts, the general public, and many companies find the notion of corporate responsibility useful and intelligible—either in a literal sense or as shorthand for the moral obligations of individuals in the corporation.

· · ·
Rival Views of Corporate Responsibility

Tennessee Iron & Steel, a subsidiary of United States Steel, was by far the largest employer, purchaser, and taxpayer in Birmingham, Alabama in 1963. In the same city at the same time, racial tensions exploded with the bombing of an African American church that killed four Black children. The ugly incident led some to blame U.S. Steel for not doing more to improve race relations, but Roger Blough, chairman of U.S. Steel, defended his company:

> I do not either believe that it would be a wise thing for United States Steel to be other than a good citizen in a community, or to attempt to have its ideas of what is right for the community enforced upon the community by some sort of economic means. . . .
>
> When we as individuals are citizens in a community we can exercise what small influence we may have as citizens, but for a corporation to attempt to exert any kind of economic compulsion to achieve a particular end in the racial area seems to me quite beyond what a corporation can do.[18]

Not long afterward, Sol M. Linowitz, chairman of the board of Xerox Corporation, declared in an address to the National Industrial Conference Board: "To realize its full promise in the world of tomorrow, American business and industry—or, at least, the vast portion of it—will have to make social goals as central to its decisions as economic goals; and leadership in our corporations will increasingly recognize this responsibility and accept it."[19] Thus, the issue of business's corporate responsibility was joined. Just what responsibilities does a corporation have? Is its responsibility to be construed narrowly as merely profit making? Or more broadly to include refraining from harming society and even contributing actively and directly to the public good?

Summary

The debate over corporate responsibility is whether it should be construed narrowly to cover only profit maximization or more broadly to include acting morally, refraining from socially undesirable behavior, and contributing actively and directly to the public good.

The Narrow View: Profit Maximization

As it happened, the year preceding the Birmingham incident had seen the publication of *Capitalism and Freedom*, in which economist Milton Friedman (1912–2006) forcefully advocated the **narrow view of corporate responsibility**, that business has no social responsibilities other than to maximize profits:

> The view has been gaining widespread acceptance that corporate officials . . . have a social responsibility that goes beyond serving the interest of their stockholders. . . . This view shows a fundamental misconception of the character and nature of a free economy. In such an economy, there is one and only one social responsibility of business—to use its resources and engage in activities designed to increase its profits so long as it stays within the rules of the game, which is to say, engages in open and free competition, without deception or fraud. . . . Few trends could so thoroughly undermine the very foundations of our free society as the acceptance by corporate officials of a social responsibility other than to make as much money for their stockholders as possible.[20]

Although from Friedman's perspective the only responsibility of business is to make money for its owners, obviously a business may not do literally anything whatsoever to increase its profits. Gangsters pursue profit maximization when they ruthlessly rub out their rivals, but such activity falls outside what Friedman referred to as "the rules of the game." Harvard professor Theodore Levitt echoed this point when he wrote, "In the end business has only two responsibilities—to obey the elementary canons of face-to-face civility (honesty, good faith, and so on) and to seek material gain."[21]

What, then, are the rules of the game? Obviously, elementary morality rules out deception, force, and fraud, and the rules of the game are intended to promote open and free competition. Even proponents of the narrow view would not condone a corporation's sabotaging its competitor's factory. The system of rules in which business is to pursue profit is, in Friedman's view, one that is conducive to the laissez-faire operation of Adam Smith's "invisible hand" (discussed in Chapter 4). Friedman, a conservative economist, believed that if the market is allowed to operate with only the minimal restrictions necessary to prevent fraud and force, society will maximize its overall economic well-being. Pursuit of profit, he insisted, is what makes our system go. Anything that dampens this incentive or inhibits its operation will weaken the ability of the "invisible hand" to deliver the economic goods. As one recent writer puts it, "Corporations that simply do everything they can to boost profits will end up increasing social welfare."[22]

Because the function of a business organization is to make money, the owners of corporations employ executives to accomplish that goal, thereby obligating these managers always to act in the interests of the owners. According to Friedman, to say that executives have *social* responsibilities beyond the pursuit of profit means that they must sometimes subordinate owner interests to some social objective, such as controlling pollution or fighting inflation. They are then spending stockholder money for general social interests—in effect, taxing the owners and spending those taxes on social causes. But taxation is a function of government, not private enterprise; executives are not public employees but employees of private enterprise. The doctrine that corporations have social responsibilities beyond profit making thus transforms executives into civil servants and business corporations into government agencies, thereby diverting business from its proper function in the social system.

Friedman was critical of those who would impose on business any duty other than that of making money, and he was particularly harsh with business leaders who take a broader view of their social responsibilities: They may believe that they are defending the free-enterprise system when they give speeches proclaiming that profit isn't the only goal of business or affirming that business has a social conscience and takes seriously its responsibility to provide employment, refrain from polluting, eliminate discrimination, and so on. But these business leaders are shortsighted; they are helping to undermine capitalism by implicitly reinforcing the view that the pursuit of profit is wicked and must be regulated by external forces.[23]

Friedman acknowledged that corporate activities are often described as an exercise of "social responsibility" when, in fact, they are intended simply to advance the company's self-interest. For example, it might be in the long-term self-interest of a corporation that is a major employer in a small town to spend money to enhance the local community by helping to improve its schools, parks, roads, or social services, thereby attracting good employees to the area, reducing the company's wage bill, or improving worker morale and productivity. By portraying its actions as dictated by a sense of social responsibility, the corporation can generate goodwill as a by-product of expenditures that are entirely justified by self-interest. Friedman had no problem with a company pursuing its self-interest by these means, but he rued the fact that "the attitudes of the public make it in the self-interest [of corporations] to cloak their actions in this way."[24] Friedman's bottom line was that the bottom line is all that counts, and he firmly rejected any notion of corporate *social* responsibility that would hinder a corporation's profit maximization.

The Broader View: Corporate Social Responsibility

The rival position to that of Friedman and Levitt is simply that business has obligations in addition to pursuing profits. The phrase "in addition to" is important. Advocates of the **broader view of corporate responsibility** do not believe there is anything wrong with corporate profit.

Summary
Proponents of the narrow view, such as Milton Friedman, contend that diverting corporations from the pursuit of profit makes our economic system less efficient. Business's only social responsibility is to make money within the rules of the game. Private enterprise should not take on social goals or public responsibilities; these should be left to government.

Critics of the narrow view believe that businesses have other obligations besides making a profit.

They maintain, rather, that corporations have other responsibilities as well—to consumers, to employees, to suppliers and contractors, to the surrounding community, and to society at large. They see the modern corporation as a social institution that should consider the interests of all the groups it has an impact on. Sometimes called the **social entity model** or the **stakeholder model**, this broader view maintains that a corporation has obligations not only to its stockholders but also to other constituencies that affect or are affected by its behavior—that is, to all parties that have a legitimate interest (a "stake") in what the corporation does or doesn't do. Years ago, the chairman of Standard Oil of New Jersey expressed the basic idea this way: "The job of management is to maintain an equitable and working balance among the claims of the various directly affected interest groups . . . stockholders, employees, customers, and the public at large."[25]

If the adherents of the broader view share one belief, it is that corporations have responsibilities beyond simply enhancing their profits because, as a matter of fact, they wield such great social and economic power in our society and with that power must come social responsibility. As professor of business administration Keith Davis put it:

> One basic proposition is that *social responsibility arises from social power.* Modern business has immense social power in such areas as minority employment and environmental pollution. If business has the power, then a just relationship demands that business also bear responsibility for its actions in these areas. Social responsibility arises from concern about the consequences of business's acts as they affect the interests of others. Business decisions do have social consequences. Businessmen cannot make decisions that are solely economic decisions, because they are interrelated with the whole social system. This situation requires that businessmen's thinking be broadened beyond the company gate to the whole social system. Systems thinking is required.
>
> Social responsibility implies that a business decision maker in the process of serving his own business interests is obliged to take actions that also protect and enhance society's interests. The net effect is to improve the quality of life in the broadest possible way, however quality of life is defined by society. In this manner, harmony is achieved between business's actions and the larger social system. The businessman becomes concerned with social as well as economic outputs and with the total effect of his institutional actions on society.[26]

Proponents of the broader view, such as Davis, stress that modern business is intimately integrated with the rest of society. Business is not some self-enclosed world, like a private poker party. Rather, business activities have profound ramifications throughout society, and their influence on our lives is hard to escape. Business writer John Kay makes this point with reference to General Electric: "The company's activities are so extensive that you necessarily encounter them daily, often without knowing you are doing so. GE's business is our business even if we do not want it to be."[27]

On this view, then, although society permits and expects corporations to pursue their economic interests, they have other responsibilities as well. As the Mark Bertolini, the CEO of Aetna puts it, "companies are not just money-making machines."[28] Thus, for example, it is wrong for corporations to raid the pension funds of their employees, as many have done, or to evade taxes through creative accounting or by re-incorporating in tax havens such as Bermuda, even if doing so is legal and enhances the bottom line.[29] "We reasonably expect that GE should care that its engines are safe," writes John Kay, "not just that they comply with FAA procedures; that if there is a problem with its medical equipment the company will try to put it right, not cover it up; that GE financial statements are true and fair and not just compliant with accounting standards."[30]

Melvin Anshen has cast the case for the broader view of corporate responsibility in a historical perspective.[31] He maintains that there is always a kind of "social contract" between business and society. This contract is, of course, only implicit, but it represents a tacit understanding within society about the proper goals and responsibilities of business. In effect, in Anshen's view, society always structures the guidelines within which business is permitted to operate in order to derive certain benefits from business activity. For instance, in the 19th century, society's prime interest was rapid economic growth, which was viewed as the source of all progress, and the engine of

Summary
Defenders of the broader view maintain that corporations have responsibilities that go beyond making money because of their great social and economic power. Business is governed by an implicit social contract that requires it to operate in ways that benefit society. In particular, corporations must take responsibility for the unintended side effects of their business transactions (externalities) and weigh the full social costs of their activities.

economic growth was identified as the drive for profits by unfettered, competitive, private enterprise. That attitude was reflected in the then-existing social contract. Today, however, society has concerns and interests other than rapid economic growth—in particular, a concern for the quality of life and for the preservation of the environment. Accordingly, the social contract is in the process of being modified. In particular, Anshen writes, "it will no longer be acceptable for corporations to manage their affairs solely in terms of the traditional internal costs of doing business, while thrusting external costs on the public."[32]

In recent years we have grown more aware of the possible deleterious side effects of business activity, or what economists call **externalities**: the unintended negative (or in some cases positive) consequences that an economic transaction between two parties can have on some third party. Industrial pollution provides the clearest illustration. Suppose a factory makes widgets and sells them to your firm. A by-product of this economic transaction is the waste that the rains wash from the factory yard into the local river, waste that damages recreational and commercial fishing interests downstream. This damage to third parties is an unintended side effect of the economic transaction between the seller and the buyer of widgets.

Defenders of the new social contract, like Anshen, maintain that externalities should no longer be overlooked. In the jargon of economists, externalities must be "internalized"—that is, the factory should be made to absorb the cost of its pollution, either by disposing of its waste in an environmentally safe (and presumably more expensive) way or by paying for the damage the waste does downstream. On the one hand, basic fairness requires that the factory's waste no longer be dumped onto third parties. On the other hand, from the economic point of view, requiring the factory to internalize the externalities makes sense, for only when it does so will the price of the widgets it sells reflect their true social cost. The real production cost of the widgets includes not only labor, raw materials, machinery, and so on but also the damage done to the fisheries downstream. Unless the price of widgets is raised sufficiently to reimburse the fisheries for their losses or to dispose of the waste in some other way, the buyer of widgets is paying less than their true cost. Part of the cost is being paid by the fishing interests downstream.

Advocates of the broader view go beyond requiring business to internalize its externalities in a narrow economic sense. Keith Davis, for example, maintains that in addition to considering potential profitability, a business must weigh the long-range social costs of its activities as well. Only if the overall benefit to society is positive should business act:

> The expectation of the social responsibility model is that a detailed cost/benefit analysis will be made prior to determining whether to proceed with an activity and that social costs will be given significant weight in the decision-making process. Almost any business action will entail some social costs. The basic question is whether the benefits outweigh the costs so that there is a net social benefit. Many questions of judgment arise, and there are no precise mathematical measures in the social field, but rational and wise judgments can be made if the issues are first thoroughly explored.[33]
>
> While this new social contract might sound radical, when applied to corporations it's really a return to the original conception of corporations as entities that were created only to serve some larger public need than making a profit. Proponents of this view might argue that society is entitled to ask for something in return for offering corporate investors the protection of limited liability. Anyone who wanted to start a company focused more narrowly on profitability would still have the option of forgoing this protection and creating a sole proprietorship or partnership.

Advocates of the broader view believe that business must internalize its externalities and consider the social costs of its activities.

Stockholders and the Corporation

In one recent survey of Americans, only 2.2 percent of respondents described generating returns for shareholders as the most important requirement that a corporation must satisfy to operate justly.[34] (In contrast, just over 20 percent said that it is paying workers fairly, and just over 10 percent said that it is creating jobs in the United States.) In fact, even a majority of managers reject a profit-only philosophy of corporate management.[35] Advocates of the narrow view, however, believe that those attitudes reflect a misunderstanding of the proper relationship between management and stockholders. Stockholders own the company. They entrust management with their funds, and in return management undertakes to make as much money for them as it can. As a result, according to proponents of the narrow view, management has a **fiduciary duty** to maximize shareholder wealth, a duty that is inconsistent with any social responsibility other than the relentless pursuit of profit.

The narrow view holds that management's fiduciary duty to maximize shareholder wealth outweighs any other obligations.

> [A] fiduciary duty is a duty of a person in a position of trust to act in the interest of another person without gaining any material benefit, except with the knowledge and consent of that other person. . . . Although it is primarily a legal term, fiduciary duty can also be used to describe the purely ethical duty of a person in a position of trust.[36]

The managers of a corporation do indeed have a fiduciary responsibility to look after the interests of shareholders, a duty that is clearly violated by corporate executives who take advantage of their position to enrich themselves at company expense with extravagant bonuses, stock options, and retirement packages or to waste corporate money on jets, apartments, private parties, and various personal services that lack any plausible business rationale. But it doesn't follow from this, as proponents of the narrow view maintain, that the corporation should be run for the exclusive benefit of stockholders or that their interests always take priority over the interests of everyone else. To the contrary, argue critics of the narrow view, management has fiduciary responsibilities to other constituencies as well—for example, to employees, bondholders, and consumers. Hence, there's yet another name that has been applied to the broader view of corporate social responsibility; it's sometimes called the **multifiduciary view**. The duty to make money for shareholders is real, on this view, but it doesn't trump all of a company's other responsibilities. It is, to use some terminology that was offered in Chapter 2, a prima facie obligation that must be balanced against and may sometimes be outweighed by prima facie obligations to other corporate stakeholders. Indeed, it's debatable whether most shareholders believe that the duty to make money is as weighty as proponents of the narrow view think. Many of them may want the company they "own" to act in a morally responsible manner—say, by reducing its carbon footprint or by treating employees with respect—even if that means less profit.

Summary
Advocates of the narrow view stress that management's fiduciary duty to the owners (stockholders) of a corporation takes priority over any other responsibilities and obligates management to focus on profit maximization alone. Critics challenge this argument. They also point out that the assumption that stockholders own or control the corporation is dubious.

Against that point of view, however, Milton Friedman argued, "The whole justification for permitting the corporate executives to be selected by the shareholders is that the executive is an agent serving the interests of his principal."[37] This justification disappears, he believed, when executives expend corporate resources in ways that don't necessarily enhance the bottom line. They are then acting more like public servants than like employees of a private enterprise. But even if one agrees with Friedman that stockholders select corporate managers to act as their agents and advance their interests, this doesn't prove that those executives are bound to act solely to increase shareholder wealth, ignoring all other moral considerations. Undertaking to look after other people's interests or promising to try to make money for them creates a genuine obligation, but that obligation is not absolute. It doesn't eliminate all other moral responsibilities. By analogy, promising to meet someone at a certain time and place for lunch creates an obligation, but that obligation doesn't override one's duty to assist someone having a heart attack. And something that it would be immoral for you to do (such as making a dangerous product) doesn't become right just because you're acting on behalf of someone else or promised them that you would do it.

Friedman believed that if executives "impose taxes on stockholders and spend the proceeds for 'social' purposes, they become 'civil servants,' and thus should be selected through a political process."[38] He considered such a proposal absurd or, at best, socialistic. Yet others contend that corporations are too focused on profits, and they fear the damage to society when firms are willing to sacrifice all other values on the altar of the bottom line. They don't think it absurd at all that corporations should take a broader view of their social role and responsibilities. They see nothing in the management–stockholder relationship that would morally forbid corporations from doing so.

In fact, there is a new type of corporation, the so-called "**benefit corporation**," that's required to focus on more than the stockowners' returns. A majority of American states now allow firms to incorporate as benefit corporations. A benefit corporation is a for-profit corporation, not a nonprofit or charity; it is expected to make money for stockholders. However, it is also expected to produce a benefit for the larger public, and its managers are required to consider how their decisions would affect other stakeholders.[39] (Some details of the operation of benefit corporations, such as whether they need to have "benefit corporation" in their legal names, vary by state.) The reasoning behind the creation of benefit corporations is that if the officers and directors of a standard corporation were making business decisions that resulted in smaller returns for shareholders, then in principle the shareholders could sue—even if these decisions could be justified in terms of some social benefit other than profit. A lawsuit like this, based on the officers and directors' fiduciary duty, would not be easy to win. Still, the possibility is there. With a benefit corporation, investors are on notice that the people running the corporation will be balancing the fiduciary obligation to them against responsibilities to other stakeholders and to the public. This would make it far harder still for a stockowner to sue on the grounds of insufficient returns.

Who Controls the Corporation?

According to the narrow view of corporate responsibility, stockholders own the corporation and select managers to run it for them. That model may make sense for some small firms or when venture capitalists invest in a start-up company, but it doesn't accurately reflect modern corporate reality. To begin with, most stockholders purchase shares in a company from current stockholders, who acquired their shares the same way. Very few investors put their money directly into a corporation; rather, they buy secondhand shares that were initially issued years before. They pick companies that look profitable or seem likely to grow or whose products or policies appeal to them, or they may simply be following the advice of their broker. And they are generally prepared to resell their shares, perhaps even the same day they bought them, if it is profitable to do so. Stockholders have no legal obligation to the company. They are a far-flung, diverse, and ever-changing group. They come and go and rarely, if ever, have direct contact with the managers of the company or even know or care who they are.

From a legal perspective, strictly speaking, stockholders do not own the corporation. Rather, as law professor Lynn Stout writes, "corporations are independent entities that own themselves, just as human beings own themselves." Stockholders, of course, own a share of the company's stock, but that is "simply a contract between the shareholder and the corporation, a contract that gives the shareholder limited rights under limited circumstances." In this respect, stockholders are like bondholders, employees, and suppliers, all of whom have contractual relations with the corporate entity. "None 'owns' the company itself."[40]

Few economists or business theorists believe that stockholders are really in charge of the companies whose shares they hold or that they select the managers who run them. As long ago as 1932, Adolf Berle and Gardiner Means showed that because stock ownership in large corporations is so dispersed, actual control of the corporation has passed to management.[41] Today, as most business observers acknowledge, management handpicks the board of directors, thus controlling the body that is supposed to police it. "The CEO puts up the candidates; no one runs against them, and management counts the votes," says Nell Minow of Corporate Library, a corporate watchdog website. "We wouldn't deign to call this an election in a third-world country."[42] Even in those rare cases when shareholders put up their own candidates, such proxy fights are expensive and the incumbent management has the corporate coffers at its disposal to fight them.

As a result, the board of directors typically rubber-stamps the policies and recommendations of management. That's why it's not too surprising that the directors of Enron ignored shareholder interests and approved paying out $750 million in executive compensation—$140 million of it to its chairman—in a year when the company's entire net income was only $975 million. The Enron example is extreme, but the CEOs of major corporations are extraordinarily well compensated by any measure.

It's not always easy to say exactly how much compensation a CEO is receiving, because frequently a significant portion of their compensation comes in the form of "**stock options**"—the opportunity to buy shares of the corporation's stock at a preset price that may be well under its market price. These options can be very valuable, yet their value fluctuates with the value of the corporation's stock, at least until they're exercised. When the CEO exercises the options and buys the stock, then the difference between the price they paid and the market price at that time gives us the "realized" value of the option. As Tesla CEO, Elon Musk receives no salary and

Stockholders do not really own or control the companies whose shares they hold.

is paid entirely in stock options. In 2022, he was given the option to buy over 8 million shares at a price of just over $70 each. At the time, Tesla's stock was trading at $977 per share, so by exercising the options Musk could pay "only" $1.8 billion for nearly $25 billion worth of stock, giving the options a prospective value of about $23 billion. (Musk's compensation deal does require him to hold stocks for five years after buying them.) According to the Economic Policy Institute, "From 1978 to 2021, CEO pay based on realized compensation grew by 1,460%, far outstripping S&P stock market growth (1,063%) and top 0.1% earnings growth (which was 385% between 1978 and 2020, according to the latest data available). In contrast, compensation of the typical worker grew by just 18.1% from 1978 to 2021."[43]

Top CEOs often receive many perks on top of their salaries and stock options, like large payouts when their companies are acquired by other corporations (so-called "golden parachutes") and generous retirement packages. True, in the past couple of decades, institutional investors like pension funds and large mutual funds have endeavored to increase their sway over corporate policies, and in 2011 the Securities and Exchange Commission (SEC) gave shareholders the right to a nonbinding vote on corporate compensation plans once every three years—a "say to pay" vote. This is required by a law called the Dodd-Frank Act. But it's still exceedingly difficult for shareholders to change policies they don't like, because the voting rules favor management. For instance, management's ability to see preliminary votes coming in lets them make extra efforts to encourage stock owners who are likely to support its position to participate.[44] Executives can also exercise their stock options before a close vote, which gives them more votes of their own. The upshot is simple, according to Michael Jensen, professor emeritus at Harvard Business School: "The CEO has no boss." That, he says, is "the major thing wrong with large public corporations in the United States."[45]

• • •

Debating Corporate Responsibility

We can pursue the debate over corporate responsibility further by examining three arguments in support of the narrow view: the invisible-hand argument, the let-government-do-it argument, and the business-can't-handle-it argument. Advocates of the broader view of corporate responsibility reject all three.

The Invisible-Hand Argument

Adam Smith claimed that when each of us acts in a free-market environment to promote our own economic interests, we are led by an invisible hand to promote the general good. Like-minded contemporary thinkers such as Friedman advance the same **invisible-hand argument**. They point out that corporations, in fact, were chartered by states precisely with utility in mind. If businesses are permitted to seek self-interest, their activities will inevitably yield the greatest good for society as a whole. To invite corporations to base their policies and activities on anything other than profit making is to politicize business's unique economic function and to hamper its ability to satisfy our material needs. As Roberto C. Goizueta, former CEO of Coca-Cola, argues, "businesses are created to meet economic needs." When they "try to become all things to all people, they fail. . . . We have one job: to generate a fair return for our owners."[46] Accordingly, corporations should not be invited to fight against prejudice, to combat global warming, to contribute to the local community, or to improve working conditions or enhance the lives of employees, except insofar as these activities increase profits.

Yet this argument allows that corporations may still be held accountable for their actions. To the degree that they fulfill or fail to fulfill their economic role, they can be praised or blamed. And they can rightly be criticized for breaking the law or violating the rules of the game—for example, by shady accounting practices that mislead investors about company assets. But corporations should not be held morally responsible for noneconomic matters; to do so would distort the economic mission of business in society and undermine the foundations of the free-enterprise system.

The invisible-hand argument, however, runs up against the fact that modern corporations bear about as much resemblance to Smith's self-sufficient farmers and craftspeople as today's military bears to the Continental militia. Given the sway they have over our economy and society and the enormous impact they have on our lives, our communities, and our environment, today's gigantic corporations are more like public enterprises than private ones. They constitute powerful economic fiefdoms, far removed from the small, competitive producers of classical economics. Perhaps within a restricted area of economic activity, when the parties to the exchange are roughly equal, then each pursuing self-interest can result in the greatest net good. But in the real world of large corporations, the concept of an invisible hand orchestrating the common good often stretches credulity. For example, California deregulated its electricity market to promote competition and give the invisible hand room to operate. But the result was a disaster. Instead of cheaper energy, the state got power blackouts and soaring prices as energy companies adroitly and greedily manipulated the market. Each time the state tried to make the market work better, energy sellers devised new ways to exploit the system. The state government only stanched the crisis by a costly intervention that has basically put it in the power business.[47] More recently, energy deregulation in Texas contributed to blackouts and massive bills for consumers when unusually cold weather hit in the winter of 2021.[48]

The invisible-hand argument in favor of the narrow view of corporate responsibility is thus open to criticism as theoretically unsound and economically unrealistic. Moreover, in practice, the argument is complicated by the fact that corporations today find themselves in a social and political environment in which they are pressured by public opinion, politicians, the media, and various activist groups to act—or at least be perceived to be acting—as responsible corporate citizens, as socially conscious enterprises that acknowledge other values besides profit and that seek to make a positive contribution to our society. Few, if any, corporations can afford to be seen as exploiters of foreign labor, as polluters of the environment, or as indifferent to consumer welfare or the prosperity of our communities. Companies today religiously guard their name and their brands against the slander that they care only about profits. And the larger the corporation, the more susceptible it is to the demand that it behave with a developed sense of moral responsibility, and the more it needs to guard its image and to take steps to assure the public that it is striving to make the world a better place.

> The invisible-hand argument seems economically unrealistic. In addition, corporations today find it in their interest to acknowledge values other than profit.

This explains why in 2010–2011 Chevron rolled out a dramatic new advertising campaign in the *Wall Street Journal, New York Times*, and other newspapers. Each full-page ad featured a slogan, such as, "Oil companies should support the communities they're part of," "Oil companies should put their profits to good use," "It's time for oil companies to get behind renewable energy," or "Big Oil should support small business." Stamped in red after each statement were the words, "We agree." The company also ran a series of television ads in the same vein. Likewise, Rio-Tinto Alcan, the world's largest aluminum company, proclaims that it is committed to "maximizing value for all our stakeholders, especially by making a significant contribution . . . to the economic, social and environmental well-being of the communities in which we operate."[49] And Hewlett-Packard states that "a company has a responsibility beyond making a profit for its investors, including a commitment to enrich the business, lives and communities of its customers, partners and employees."[50]

Admittedly, some of this is merely public relations posturing, but it's also true that business success in today's world requires companies to respond to society's demand that they act as morally responsible agents. For purely self-interested reasons, even corporations that take a very narrow view of their responsibilities may have to behave as if they held a broader view. For example, in a world in which 88 percent of young people believe that companies have a responsibility to support social causes and 86 percent of them say that they switch brands based on social issues, a world in which 72 percent of job seekers prefer to work for a company that supports social causes,[51] corporate philanthropy promotes the bottom line. Moreover, almost all studies indicate that socially responsible corporate behavior is positively correlated with financial success and that the most profitable companies treat their consumers, employees, and business partners ethically.[52] Ironically, then, this gives companies a self-interested reason not merely to pretend to have a broad sense of social responsibility but, rather, to become the kind of company that really does want to make a positive mark in the world. Of course, whether we are talking about individuals or about corporations, there's no guarantee that acting morally will always pay off, and indeed if that is one's only motivation for doing the right thing, then one can hardly be said to be acting morally. Even so, there's little reason for either individuals or companies to believe that acting selfishly or sacrificing moral values to profits will pay off for them in the long run.

The Let-Government-Do-It Argument

According to the narrow view of corporate responsibility, business's role is purely economic, and corporations should not be considered moral agents. Some adherents of this view, however, such as economist and social critic John Kenneth Galbraith (1908–2006), reject the assumption that Smith's invisible hand will solve all social and economic problems or that market forces will moralize corporate activities. Left to their own self-serving devices, Galbraith and others warn, modern corporations will enrich themselves while impoverishing society. If they can get away with it, they will pollute, exploit workers, deceive customers, and strive to eliminate competition and keep prices high through oligopolistic practices. They will do those things, the argument continues, because as economic institutions they are naturally and quite properly profit motivated.

What is profitable for corporations, however, is not necessarily useful or desirable for society. How is the corporation's natural and insatiable appetite for profit to be controlled? Through government regulation, answer proponents of the **let-government-do-it argument**. They believe that the strong hand of government, through a system of laws and incentives, can and should bring corporations to heel. "I believe in corporations," Teddy Roosevelt once proclaimed. "They are indispensable instruments of our modern civilization; but I believe that they should be so supervised and so regulated that they shall act for the interests of the community as a whole."[53]

"Do not blame corporations and their top executives" for things like layoffs or urge them to acknowledge obligations beyond the bottom line, writes the economist Robert Reich, secretary of labor under President Clinton. "They are behaving exactly as they are organized to behave." He pooh-poohs moral appeals and rejects the idea that CEOs should seek to balance the interests of shareholders against those of employees and their communities. Rather, Reich says, "if we want corporations to take more responsibility" for the economic well-being of Americans, then government "will have to provide the proper incentives."[54]

The let-government-do-it argument rejects broadening corporate responsibility just as much as the invisible-hand argument does.

This advice sounds realistic and is intended to be practical, but the let-government-do-it argument rejects the notion of broadening corporate responsibility just as firmly as the invisible-hand argument does. The latter puts the focus on the market. Galbraith's and Reich's arguments put it on the *visible* hand of government. The two positions agree, however, in thinking that it is misguided to expect or demand that business firms do anything other than pursue profit.

Critics of the let-government-do-it argument contend that it is a blueprint for big, intrusive government. Moreover, they doubt that government can control any but the most egregious corporate immorality. They fear that many questionable activities will be overlooked, safely hidden within the labyrinth of the corporate structure. Lacking intimate knowledge of the goals and sub-goals of specific corporations, as well as of their daily operations, government simply can't anticipate a specific corporation's moral challenges. Rather, it can prescribe behavior only for broad, cross-sectional issues, such as bribery, price fixing, and unfair competition.

Legislation can certainly address egregious corporate wrongdoing, but it cannot provide corporations with much specific guidance about how to act in socially beneficial ways. Consider, for example, PepsiCo's decision to buy directly from small corn farmers in Mexico (rather than through middle men) and to guarantee, before they plant their crops, the price it will pay them. This program has changed the farmers' lives (they no longer have to trek to the United States to work odd jobs to make ends meet), increased their incomes, and strengthened their communities.[55] No government legislation could have brought this about.

Finally, is government a credible custodian of morality? If recent experience has taught anything, it is that government officials are not always paragons of virtue. Looked at simply as another organization, government manifests many of the same structural characteristics that test moral behavior inside the corporation. Furthermore, given the awesome clout of corporate lobbyists, one wonders whether, as moral police, government officials will do anything more than impose the values and interests of their most generous financiers. Can we seriously expect politicians to bite the hand that feeds them?

The Business-Can't-Handle-It Argument

In support of the narrow view of corporate responsibility, some maintain that it is misguided to encourage corporations to address nonbusiness matters. According to the **business-can't-handle-it argument**, corporations are the wrong group to be entrusted with broad responsibility for promoting the well-being of society. They are not up to the job for two reasons: (1) they lack the necessary expertise and (2) in addressing noneconomic matters, they inevitably impose their own materialistic values on the rest of society.

Some argue that business is the wrong group on which to place broad social responsibilities for two reasons.

Corporations Lack the Expertise

Those who develop the first point contend that business can't handle the job—that it is the wrong group to rely on to promote the well-being of society—because corporate executives lack the moral and social expertise to make other-than-economic decisions. To assign them non-economic responsibilities would be to put social welfare in the hands of inept custodians. For example, Robert Reich argues that corporate executives lack the moral authority to "balance profits against the public good" or "undertake any ethical balancing." They have no "expertise in making such moral calculations."[56] In his view, corporate leaders lack the moral insight or social know-how that a broader view of corporate responsibility would seem to require of them.

Against that, however, one can argue that we don't normally restrict the moral responsibilities of individuals, professional bodies, or other organizations to matters that fall within the narrow confines of their business or other expertise. We see nothing wrong, for example, with physicians advocating AIDS awareness or trying to promote the use of seat belts in automobiles, or with a teachers' union involving itself in a campaign to combat the use of illegal drugs. And ordinary citizens may sometimes have a duty to educate themselves about, and do what they can to address, social issues that fall outside their usual sphere of knowledge and activity. What, if anything, asks the critic, makes the social role of the corporation unique, so that its responsibilities and those of its employees should be confined solely to profit making?

The argument that corporations aren't up to addressing social issues because they lack the necessary expertise runs up against the fact that, often, it is only business that has the know-how, talent, experience, and organizational resources to tackle certain problems. If society, for example, wants to eradicate malaria in Africa or increase longevity at home, to reduce diesel engine emissions or retard global warming, to improve agricultural productivity while lowering the risks from pesticides, or to see that inner-city youth learn entrepreneurship or that community groups have the business skills necessary for success, then society will need the assistance of business. To take a specific illustration, Citibank supports microfinance programs in Mexico and India intended to give poor rural women the tiny loans they need, say, to buy a sewing machine and start their own business. True, as a Citigroup executive says, "there is not going to be a huge short-term profit" for the company.[57] But who is better able to help these women than a company like Citigroup?

Corporations Will Impose Their Values on Us

Others argue that corporations are the wrong group to address social issues, that business can't handle the assignment, for a different reason. They fear that if permitted to stray from strictly economic matters, corporate officials will impose their materialistic values on all of society. Broadening corporate responsibility will thus "materialize" society instead of "moralizing" corporate activity. More than fifty years ago, Harvard professor Theodore Levitt expressed this concern:

> The danger is that all these things [resulting from having business pursue social goals other than profit making] will turn the corporation into a twentieth-century equivalent of the medieval church. . . . For while the corporation also transforms itself in the process, at bottom its outlook will always remain materialistic. What we have then is the frightening spectacle of a powerful economic functional group whose future and perception are shaped in a tight materialistic context of money and things but which imposes its narrow ideas about a broad spectrum of unrelated noneconomic subjects on the mass of man and society. Even if its outlook were the purest kind of good will, that would not recommend the corporation as an arbiter of our lives.[58]

....

Summary
Three arguments in
favor of the narrow
view are the invisible-
hand argument, the
let-government-do-it
argument, and the
business-can't-handle-it
argument. Finding
flaws in each of these
arguments, critics
maintain there is no
solid basis for restricting
corporate responsibility
to profit making.

....

This argument seems to assume that corporations do not already exercise enormous discretionary power over us. But as Keith Davis points out, business already has immense social power. "Society has entrusted to business large amounts of society's resources," says Davis, "and business is expected to manage these resources as a wise trustee for society. In addition to the traditional role of economic entrepreneurship, business now has a new social role of trusteeship. As trustee for society's resources, it serves the interests of all claimants on the organization, rather than only those of owners, or consumers, or labor."[59]

As Paul Camenisch notes, business is already using its privileged position to propagate, consciously or unconsciously, a view of humanity and the good life.[60] Implicit in the barrage of advertisements to which we are subjected daily are assumptions about happiness, success, and human fulfillment. In addition, corporations or industry groups sometimes speak out in unvarnished terms about social and economic issues. For example, ExxonMobil disputes the notion that fossil fuels are the main cause of global warming and lobbies against capping global-warming emissions, while drug companies such as Eli Lilly, Procter & Gamble, and Bristol-Myers Squibb contribute to conservative think tanks that seek to reduce the regulatory powers of the U.S. Food and Drug Administration.

The point here is that business already promotes consumerism and materialistic values. It doesn't hesitate to use its resources to express its views and influence our political system on issues that affect its economic interests. If corporations take a broader view of their responsibilities, are they really likely to have a more materialistic effect on society, as Levitt suggests, than they do now? It's hard to believe they could. Levitt's view implies that there is some threat to society's values when corporations engage in philanthropy or use their economic and political muscle for other than purely self-interested ends. But society's values are not endangered when Sara Lee donates 2 percent of its pretax profits to charitable causes, mostly cultural institutions and organizations serving disadvantaged people,[61] or when General Mills gives away 3 percent of its domestic pretax earnings to community organizations, donates food to people in need, and helps inner-city companies to get up and running.[62] And where is the "materialization of society" if, instead of advertising on a silly situation comedy that reaches a large audience, a corporation spends the same amount underwriting a science program with fewer viewers solely out of a sense of social responsibility?

• • •

Institutionalizing Ethics Within Corporations

The criticisms of these three arguments in support of the narrow view of corporate responsibility have led many people inside and outside business to adopt the broader view—that the obligations of the modern business corporation extend beyond simply making money for itself. Society grants corporations the right to exist and gives them legal status as separate entities. It does this not to indulge the profit appetites of owners and managers but, as Camenisch says, as a way of securing the necessary "goods and services to sustain and enhance human existence."[63] In return for its sufferance of corporations, society has the right to expect corporations not to cause harm, to take into account the external effects of their activities, and whenever possible to act for the betterment of society.

Society permits corporations
to exist and, in turn, expects
them to act in a socially
responsible way.

The list of corporate responsibilities goes beyond such negative injunctions as "Don't pollute," "Don't misrepresent products," and "Don't bribe." Included also are affirmative duties such as "See that your product or service makes a positive contribution to society," "Improve the skills of your employees," "Seek to hire the disabled or other disadvantaged persons," "Contribute to the betterment of your community," "Be as green as possible," and "Enrich working conditions." The responsibilities of corporations are not necessarily limited to activities that are intrinsically related to their business operations but may reflect social responsibilities that each of us, whether individuals or institutions, has simply by virtue of our being members of society. Precisely how far each of us must go to meet these responsibilities depends largely on our capacity to fulfill them, which, of course, varies from person to person, institution to institution. But given their considerable power and resources, large corporations seem better able to promote the common good than most individuals or small businesses. Fans of the Spider-Man comics and movies will recognize the line "With great power comes great responsibility."

How corporations are to promote the common good cannot be answered very specifically; this will depend on the type of firm and its particular circumstances. Proponents of broadening corporate responsibility would agree, though, that the first step is for corporations to expand their moral horizons and make ethical conduct a priority. How to do this? At least four actions seem called for. Corporations should:

1. Acknowledge the importance, even necessity, of conducting business morally. Their commitment to ethical behavior should be unequivocal and highly visible, from top management down.

2. Make a real effort to encourage their members to take moral responsibilities seriously. This commitment would mean ending all forms of retaliation against those who buck the system and rewarding employees for evaluating corporate decisions in their broader social and moral contexts.

3. Avoid defensiveness in the face of public discussion and criticism. Instead, they should actively solicit the views of stockholders, managers, employees, suppliers, customers, local communities, and even society as a whole. Corporations should invite outside opinions and conduct a candid ethical audit of their organizational policies, priorities, and practices.

4. Recognize the pluralistic nature of the social system of which they are a part. Society consists of diverse, interlinked individuals and groups, all vying to maintain their autonomy and advance their interests. The actions of any one group invariably affect the interests of others. As part of society, corporations affect many groups, and these groups and the individuals they comprise affect corporations. Failing to realize this, corporations can lose sight of the social framework that governs their relationship with the external environment.

Undoubtedly, other general directives could be added to this list. Still, if corporate responsibility is to be expanded, then something like the preceding approach seems basic.

Limits to What the Law Can Do

Critics of the let-government-do-it argument question Galbraith's and Reich's view that society should not expect business to behave morally but rather should simply use government to direct business's pursuit of profit in socially acceptable directions. This issue is worth returning to in the present context. All defenders of the broader view of corporate responsibility believe that more than laissez faire is necessary to ensure that business behavior is socially and morally acceptable. Yet there is a tendency to believe that law is a fully adequate vehicle for this purpose.

Law professor Christopher Stone has argued, however, that there are limits on what the law can be expected to achieve.[64] Three of his points are particularly important. *First*, many laws, such as controls on the disposal of toxic waste, are passed only after there is general awareness of the problem; in the meantime, damage has already been done. The proverbial barn door has been shut only after the horse has left.

Second, formulating appropriate laws and designing effective regulations are difficult. It is hard to achieve consensus on the relevant facts, to determine what remedies will work, and to decide how to weigh conflicting values. In addition, our political system gives corporations and their lobbyists significant input into the writing of laws. Not only that, but the specific working regulations and day-to-day interpretation of the law require the continual input of industry experts. This is not a conspiracy but a fact of life. Government bureaus generally have limited time, staffing, and expertise, so they must rely on the cooperation and assistance of those they regulate.

Third, enforcing the law is often cumbersome. Legal actions against corporations are expensive and can drag on for years, and the judicial process is often too blunt an instrument to use as a way of managing complex social and business issues. In fact, recourse to the courts can be counterproductive, and Stone argues that sometimes the benefits of doing so may not be worth the costs. Legal action may simply make corporations more furtive, breeding distrust, destruction of documents, and an attitude that "I won't do anything more than I am absolutely required to do."

What conclusion should be drawn? Stone is not arguing that regulation of business is hopeless. Rather, what he wants to stress is that the law cannot do it alone. We do not want a system in which businesspeople believe that their only obligation is to obey the law and that it is morally permissible for them to do anything not (yet) illegal. With that attitude, disaster is just around the corner. More socially responsible business behavior requires, instead, that corporations and the people within them not simply respond to the requirements of the law but also hold high moral standards—and that they themselves monitor their own behavior.

People in business need to acknowledge that obeying the law is not their only obligation because the law alone cannot guarantee responsible business behavior.

Summary
Corporations and the people who make them up must have high moral standards and monitor their own conduct because there are limits to what the law can do to ensure that business behavior is socially and morally acceptable.

Ethics and efficiency aren't necessarily in opposition. Normal business activity requires some degree of ethics, and focusing only on profit maximization is socially inefficient in two situations.

Summary
All settled economic life requires trust and confidence. The adoption of realistic and workable codes of ethics in the business world can actually enhance business efficiency. This is particularly true when there is an imbalance of knowledge between the buyer and the seller.

Ethical Codes and Economic Efficiency

It is, therefore, important that corporations examine their own implicit and explicit codes of conduct and the moral standards that are being propagated to their employees. As mentioned earlier in this chapter and in Chapter 1, there is no necessary trade-off between profitability and ethical corporate behavior. Indeed, the contrary appears to be true: The most morally responsible companies are consistently among the most profitable companies. Yet ethical behavior in the business world is often assumed to come at the expense of economic efficiency. Defenders of the broader view, such as Anshen, as well as defenders of the narrow view, such as Friedman, seem to make this assumption. Anshen believes that other values should take priority over economic efficiency, whereas Friedman contends business should concern itself only with profit and, in this way, maximize economic well-being. In his important essay "Social Responsibility and Economic Efficiency," Nobel Prize–winning economist Kenneth Arrow has challenged this assumption.[65]

To begin with, says Arrow, any kind of settled economic life requires a certain degree of ethical behavior, some element of trust and confidence. Much business, for instance, is conducted on the basis of oral agreements. In addition, Arrow points out, "there are two types of situation in which the simple rule of maximizing profits is socially inefficient: the case in which costs are not paid for, as in pollution, and the case in which the seller has considerably more knowledge about his product than the buyer."

The first type of situation relates to the demand that corporations "internalize their externalities," discussed earlier in this chapter. In the second situation, in which the buyer lacks the expertise and knowledge of the seller, an effective code of ethics, either requiring full disclosure or setting minimal standards of performance (for example, the braking ability of a new automobile), enhances rather than diminishes economic efficiency. Without such a code, buyers may purchase products or services they don't need. Or because they don't trust the seller, they may refrain from purchasing products and services they do need. Either way, from the economist's point of view the situation is inefficient.

An effective professional or business code of ethics—as well as the public's awareness of this code—is good for business. Most of us, for example, have little medical knowledge and are thus at the mercy of doctors. Over hundreds of years, however, a firm code of ethical conduct has developed in the medical profession. As a result, people generally take for granted that their physician will perform with their welfare in mind. They rarely worry that their doctor might be taking advantage of them or exploiting them with unnecessary treatment. By contrast, used-car dealers have historically suffered from a lack of public trust.

For a code to be effective it must be realistic, Arrow argues, in the sense of connecting with the collective self-interest of business. And it must become part of the corporate culture, "accepted by the significant operating institutions and transmitted from one generation of executives to the next through standard operating procedures [and] through education in business schools."

For both Arrow and Stone, then, the development of feasible and effective business and professional codes of ethics must be a central focus of any effort to enhance or expand corporate responsibility. The question is how to create a corporate atmosphere conducive to moral decision making.

Corporate Codes of Ethics

What can be done to improve organizational climate so that individuals can reasonably be expected to act ethically? If those inside the corporation are to behave morally, they need clearly stated and communicated ethical standards that are equitable and enforced. This development seems possible only if the standards of expected behavior are institutionalized—that is, only if they become a fixture in the corporate organization. To institutionalize ethics within corporations, Professor Milton Snoeyenbos suggests that top management should (1) articulate the firm's values and goals, (2) adopt a code of ethics applicable to all members of the company, (3) set up a high-ranking ethics committee to oversee, develop, and enforce the code, and (4) incorporate ethics training into all employee-development programs.[66]

There are several steps companies should take to institutionalize ethics.

The company's code of ethics should not be window dressing or so general as to be useless. A **corporate code of ethics** should set reasonable goals and subgoals, with an eye on blunting unethical pressures on subordinates. In formulating the code, the top-level ethics committee should solicit the views of corporate members at all levels regarding goals and subgoals, so that the final product articulates "a fine-grained ethical code that addresses ethical issues likely to arise at the level of subgoals."[67] Moreover, the committee should have full authority and responsibility to communicate the code and decisions based on it to all corporate members, clarify and interpret the code when the need arises, facilitate the code's use, investigate grievances and violations of the code, discipline violators, and reward compliance; and review, update, and upgrade the code.

To help employees in ethically difficult situations, a good corporate ethics program must be user friendly. It should provide a support system with a variety of entry points, one that employees feel confident about using.[68] In addition, part of all employee-training programs should be devoted to ethics. At a minimum, this should include study of the code, review of the company's procedures for handling ethical problems, and discussion of employer and employee responsibilities and expectations. Snoeyenbos and others believe that institutionalizing ethics within the corporation in these ways, when supplemented by the development of industry-wide codes of ethics to address issues beyond a particular firm, will go far toward establishing a corporate climate conducive to individual moral decision making. Recall that, as was mentioned in Chapter 1, a corporate code of ethics is only as good as the leaders charged with enforcing it and with setting an example through their own compliance.

Corporate Culture

During the past two decades, organizational theorists and writers on business management have increasingly emphasized "corporate culture" as the factor that makes one company succeed while another languishes. Although intangible in comparison with things like sales revenue and profit margin, corporate culture is often the key to a firm's success. According to one study, 30 percent of the difference in performance between companies can be attributed to differences in culture, but only 5 percent to differences in strategy.[69]

What is **corporate culture**? A cover story in the *Harvard Business Review* defines it this way: "Culture is the tacit social order of an organization: It shapes attitudes and behaviors in wide-ranging and durable ways. Cultural norms define what is encouraged, discouraged, accepted, or rejected within a group. When properly aligned with personal values, drives, and needs, culture can unleash tremendous amounts of energy toward a shared purpose and foster an organization's capacity to thrive."[70] Corporate culture may be both overt and implicit. The formal culture of a corporation, as expressed in idealized statements of principles and values,

Summary
To improve organizational climate so that we can reasonably expect individuals to act morally, corporations need to institutionalize ethics. Among other things, this involves articulating their values and goals, adopting a code of ethics, setting up an ethics committee, and including ethics training in their employee-development programs. Attention to corporate culture is also crucial to the successful institutionalization of ethics inside an organization.

should also be distinguished from the informal culture that shapes the beliefs and behavior of individuals in the organization. In addition, there may be multiple and overlapping cultures within an organization because employees have different backgrounds, work in different divisions of the organization and even in different countries, and may be subject to different systems of rewards and sanctions.

Organizational theorists emphasize the importance of monitoring and managing corporate culture—beginning with an attempt to understand each corporation's distinctive culture—to prevent dysfunctional behavior and processes. As one consultant puts it, "A corporation's culture is what determines how people behave when they are not being watched."[71] If management does not make explicit the values and behavior it desires, the culture will typically develop its own norms, usually based on the types of behavior that lead to success within the organization. Thus, the desired values must be communicated and transmitted throughout the organization. Conduct congruent with them must be rewarded and conduct inconsistent with them sanctioned. Overlooking behavior that contradicts the desired norms can have the effect of encouraging and even rewarding it.

William Donaldson, former chairman of the U.S. Securities and Exchange Commission, emphasizes the importance of ethical leadership, of the example set by upper management. "The tone is set at the top," he says. "You must have an internal code that goes beyond the letter of the law to encompass the spirit of the company. Does that concept exist in all companies? No. All you have to do is look at executive compensation to recognize that we still have a long way to go."[72]

These points are crucial when it comes to corporate social responsibility. Management needs to understand the real dynamics of its own organization. At Sears, for example, new minimum work quotas and productivity incentives at its auto centers created a high-pressure environment that led employees to mislead customers and sell them unnecessary parts and services, from brake jobs to front-end alignments.[73] At Fannie Mae, an "earnings-at-any-cost culture" led to accounting fraud.[74] Goldman Sachs's formal culture proclaims that customers come first, but in fact, says one insider, employees refer to them as "Muppets."[75] Thus, it is necessary for socially responsible executives to ask: How do people get ahead in the company? What conduct is actually rewarded, what values are really being instilled in employees? Andrew C. Sigler, chairman of Champion International, stresses this point: "Sitting up here in Stamford, there's no way I can affect what an employee is doing today in Texas, Montana, or Maine. Making speeches and sending letters just doesn't do it. You need a culture and peer pressure that spells out what is acceptable and isn't and why. It involves training, education, and follow-up."[76]

Internal or external corporate responsibility audits can help close the gap between stated values, goals, and mission, on the one hand, and reality on the other.[77] Another aspect of follow-up is strict enforcement. For example, Chemical Bank terminates employees for violating the company's code of ethics even if they do nothing illegal, and Xerox dismisses people for minor manipulation of records and the padding of expense accounts. (By contrast, some of the nation's most prestigious stock brokerage firms have employed salespeople with long records of violating securities laws.)[78] In a recent but typical year, General Electric investigated 1,338 cases in which concerns had been raised internally about employee integrity. It dismissed 125 employees and took disciplinary action against 243 others for legal or ethical violations.[79] Executives at both Xerox and General Mills also emphasize that civic involvement is a crucial part of corporate ethics. As one General Mills executive puts it: "It's hard to imagine that a person who reads to the blind at night would cheat. . . ."[80]

Johnson & Johnson is widely seen as a model of corporate responsibility, especially because of its decisive handling of the Tylenol crisis of 1982, when seven people in the Chicago area died from cyanide-laced Extra-Strength Tylenol capsules. The company immediately recalled 31 million bottles of Tylenol from store shelves across the nation and notified 500,000 doctors and hospitals about the contaminated capsules. A toll-free consumer hotline was set up the first week of the crisis, and consumers were offered the opportunity to replace Tylenol capsules with a free bottle of Tylenol tablets. Johnson & Johnson was also open with the public instead of

Management must pay attention to the values and behavior reinforced by its corporate culture.

Maurice Hank Greenberg was the CEO of American International Group (AIG), a long-prosperous and respected insurance company, when it suddenly collapsed. AIG was said to have fostered a corporate culture that accepted excessive risk. But is corporate culture alone capable of bringing down a company like AIG?

being defensive about the deaths. Accurate information was promptly released, and domestic employees and retirees were kept updated on developments. The chairman of the company appeared on the talk show *Donahue* and on *60 Minutes* to answer questions about the crisis, and other executives were interviewed by *Fortune* and the *Wall Street Journal*. Note that all the evidence suggests that the capsules were tampered with only after they had reached stores; the bottles containing poisoned capsules were produced in different states. Arguably, at least, Johnson & Johnson was not really to blame.

Despite the setback—the recall alone cost Johnson & Johnson $50 million after taxes—Tylenol rebounded within a year, in large part because the public never lost faith in Johnson & Johnson. Yet many companies fail to emulate Johnson & Johnson's example. A case in point is the RC2 Corporation, which makes wooden Thomas the Tank Engine and other toy trains. In 2007, the public learned that many of the company's trains were made with lead paint, which can cause brain damage if a child ingests it. RC2, however, declined to issue refunds to unhappy parents but asked them to return the affected toys—at their own expense—in order to receive replacement trains and a free bonus gift. Unbelievable as it may seem, one of the toy cars that RC2 mailed out as a gift (a gray boxcar called Toad) was also made with lead paint. Even worse, RC2 executives hid from public view throughout this whole sorry episode, never explaining why their safety checks had failed or why they deserved to be trusted in the future.[81]

In the case of Johnson & Johnson, the company credits its seventy-year-old, one-page statement of values, known as the Credo, with enabling it to build the employee trust necessary for maintaining a firm corporate value system. The Credo acknowledges the company's need to make a sound profit while addressing its obligations to provide a quality product, to treat its employees fairly and with respect, and to be a good corporate citizen, supporting the community of which it is a member. The Credo is "the most important thing we have in this company," says chairman Ralph Larsen.

Creating and maintaining a morally sound corporate culture is an ongoing task, and even Johnson & Johnson hasn't always been able to live up to its own values. For instance, the company had to pay $7.5 million in fines and costs after admitting that wayward employees had shredded papers to hinder a federal probe into the marketing of an acne cream. "There was no excuse," admits Larsen. "But it is a huge undertaking to spread our values around the world."[82]

Study Corner

Key Terms and Concepts

benefit corporation

broader view of corporate
   responsibility

business-can't-handle-it argument

Corporate internal decision
   (CID) structures

corporate code of ethics

corporate culture

corporate moral agency

corporate punishment

corporation

diffusion of responsibility

externalities

fiduciary duty

invisible-hand argument

let-government-do-it
   argument

limited liability

multifiduciary view (of corporate
   responsibility)

narrow view of corporate
   responsibility

privately held company

publicly held company

social entity (stakeholder) model

stockholders (also known as stockowners)

stock options

Points to Review

- three ways corporations differ from partnerships (p. 128)
- privately held versus publicly held companies (p. 129)
- historical evolution of the corporation (pp. 129–130)
- two theoretical shifts that led to the relaxing of incorporation procedures (p. 130)
- significance of the Supreme Court's *Citizens United* decision (pp. 130–131)
- whether the CID structure is compatible with, or rules out, corporate moral responsibility (pp. 131–132)
- the concept of corporate punishment (pp. 132–133)
- problem of vanishing individual responsibility and two responses to it (p. 133)
- Milton Friedman's view of corporate responsibility (pp. 134–135)
- Melvin Anshen's idea of a social contract between business and society (pp. 136–137)

- how both fairness and economics support the internalizing of externalities (p. 137)
- whether shareholders control the corporation (p. 139)
- criticisms of the invisible-hand argument (pp. 140–142)
- difference between the let-government-do-it and the invisible-hand arguments (p. 142)
- two versions of the business-can't-handle-it argument (pp. 143–144)
- four things companies can do to become more socially responsible (p. 145)
- three limits to what we can expect the law to do (pp. 145–146)
- two situations in which the rule of maximizing profits is socially inefficient (p. 146)
- what top management should do to institutionalize ethics inside the company (p. 147)
- the importance of creating a morally oriented corporate culture (pp. 147–149)

For Further Reflection

1. Are corporations moral agents? Do they have moral responsibilities? Or, in your view, do only human beings have moral agency and moral obligations?

2. Which view of corporate social responsibility—the narrow or the broad—do you favor, and why?

3. When society extends the owners of a company the protection of limited liability, what can it ask for in return?

4. What do you think companies should do to make themselves more moral organizations? How can they promote a healthy moral climate inside the company?

Case 5.1
Yahoo in China

Shi Tao is a Thirty-Seven-Year-Old Chinese Journalist and Democracy advocate. Arrested for leaking state secrets in 2005, he was sentenced to ten years in prison. His crime? Mr. Shi had disclosed that the Communist Party's propaganda department had ordered tight controls for handling the anniversary of the infamous June 4, 1989, crackdown on demonstrators in Beijing's Tiananmen Square. A sad story, for sure, but it's an all too familiar one, given China's notoriously poor record on human rights. What makes Mr. Shi's case stand out, however, is the fact that he was arrested and convicted only because the American company Yahoo revealed his identity to Chinese authorities.[83]

You see, Mr. Shi had posted his information anonymously on a Chinese-language website called Democracy Forum, which is based in New York. Chinese journalists say that Shi's information, which revealed only routine instructions on how officials were to dampen possible protests, was already widely circulated. Still, the Chinese government's elite State Security Bureau wanted to put its hands on the culprit behind the anonymous posting. And for that it needed Yahoo's help in tracking down the Internet address from which huoyan1989@yahoo.com.cn had accessed his e-mail. This turned out to be a computer in Mr. Shi's workplace, Contemporary Business News in Changsha, China.

A few months after Shi's conviction, the watchdog group Reporters Without Borders revealed the story of Yahoo's involvement and embroiled the company in a squall of controversy. After initially declining to comment on the allegation, Yahoo eventually admitted that it had helped Chinese authorities catch Mr. Shi and that it had supplied information on other customers as well. But the company claimed that it had no choice, that the information was provided as part of a "legal process," and that the company is obliged to obey the laws of any country in which it operates. Yahoo co-founder, Jerry Yang, said: "I do not like the outcome of what happens with these things . . . but we have to comply with the law. That's what you need to do in business."

Some critics immediately spied a technical flaw in that argument: The information on Mr. Shi was provided by Yahoo's subsidiary in Hong Kong, which has an independent judiciary and a legal process separate from that of mainland China. Hong Kong legislation does not spell out what e-mail service providers must do when presented with a court order by mainland authorities. Commentators pointed out, however, that even if Yahoo was legally obliged to reveal the information, there was a deeper question of principle involved. As the *Financial Times* put it in an editorial: "As a general principle, companies choosing to operate in a country should be prepared to obey its laws. When those laws are so reprehensible that conforming to them would be unethical, they should be ready to withdraw from that market." Congressional representative Christopher H. Smith, a New Jersey Republican and chair of a House subcommittee on human

rights, was even blunter: "This is about accommodating a dictatorship. It's outrageous to be complicit in cracking down on dissenters." And in an open letter to Jerry Yang, the Chinese dissident Liu Xiabo, who has himself suffered censorship, imprisonment, and other indignities, wrote: "I must tell you that my indignation at and contempt for you and your company are not a bit less than my indignation and contempt for the Communist regime. . . . Profit makes you dull in morality. Did it ever occur to you that it is a shame for you to be considered a traitor to your customer Shi Tao?"

Whether profit is dulling their morality is an issue that must be confronted not just by Yahoo but also by other Internet-related companies doing business in China. Microsoft, for example, recently shut down the MSN Spaces website of a popular Beijing blogger whose postings had run afoul of censors. Google agreed to apply the Chinese censors' filter to its new Chinese search engine. And a congressional investigative committee has accused Google, Yahoo, and Cisco of helping to maintain in China "the most sophisticated Internet control system in the world." In their defense, the companies ask what good it would do for them to pull out of the Chinese market. They contend that if they resist the Chinese government and their operations are closed down or if they choose to leave the country for moral reasons, they would only deny to ordinary Chinese whatever fresh air the Internet, even filtered and censored, can provide in a closed society. It's more important for them to stay there, play ball with the government, and do what they can to push for Internet freedom. As Yahoo chairman Terry S. Semel puts it: "Part of our role in any form of media is to get whatever we can into those countries and to show and to enable people, slowly, to see the Western way and what our culture is like, and to learn." But critics wonder what these companies, when they are complicit in political repression, are teaching the Chinese about American values.

Some tech companies are turning to the U.S. government for help. Bill Gates, for example, thinks that legislation making it illegal for American companies to assist in the violation of human rights overseas would help. A carefully crafted American anti-repression law would give Yahoo an answer the next time Chinese officials demand evidence against cyber-dissidents. We want to obey your laws, Yahoo officials could say, but our hands are tied; we can't break American law. The assumption is that China would have no choice but to accept this because it does not want to forgo the advantages of having U.S. tech companies operating there.

Still, this doesn't answer the underlying moral questions. At a November 2007 congressional hearing, however, a number of lawmakers made their own moral views perfectly clear. They lambasted Yahoo, describing the company as "spineless and irresponsible" and "moral pygmies." In response, Jerry Yang apologized to the mother of Shi Tao, who attended the hearing. Still, Yahoo has its defenders. Robert Reich, for instance, argues that "Yahoo! is not a moral entity" and "its executives have only one responsibility . . . to make money for their shareholders and, along the way, satisfy their consumers." And in this case, he thinks, the key "consumer" is the Chinese government.

Update

How to deal with China continues to confound American Internet companies, and Western companies in general. In 2010, upset by the hacking of its servers by the Chinese government, which was trying to gain information about dissidents, and uneasy about continuing its complicity in Internet censorship, Google closed its mainland-based search engine, automatically redirecting searches to its Hong Kong affiliate. Hong Kong has an independent legal system, although its independence is being eroded. In June of 2023, Hong Kong's government was trying to stamp out online circulation of a song protesting against Chinese control of the city, and this at least raised the specter of Google's leaving Hong Kong as well.[84] Google had previously been developing a search engine designed specifically for the Chinese market, one that would comply with Chinese censorship laws, although it abandoned "Project Dragonfly" by 2019 in the face of public criticism.[85] Twitter doesn't operate in China, and ordinary Chinese citizens are blocked from using it, but new CEO Elon Musk dropped the previous practice of keeping posts by the Chinese (and Russian) governments out of users' feeds unless they specifically subscribed to them.[86] Critics allege that this facilitates the spread of pro-government propaganda. Musk's role as CEO of several major corporations may make it more challenging for him to resist Chinese demands, because while Twitter doesn't operate in China, Tesla wants to build and sell cars there. Meanwhile, Delta, American, and United airlines all bowed to Chinese pressure and revised their websites so that they no longer referred to Taiwan as a country.[87] In 2018, clothing retailer Gap apologized for selling a t-shirt featuring a map of China that did not include Taiwan, Tibet, or other territories to which China makes disputed claims.[88] (The shirt was not for sale in China.)

Discussion Questions

1. What moral issues does this controversy raise? What obligations should Yahoo have weighed in this situation? Was the company a "traitor" to its customer, as Liu Xiabo says?

2. In your view, was Yahoo right or wrong to assist Chinese authorities? What would you have done if you were in charge of Yahoo?

3. Is Jerry Yang correct that the company had "no choice"? Assuming that Yahoo was legally required to do what it did, does that justify its conduct morally?

4. Assess the actions of Yahoo and of Microsoft, Google, and Cisco from the point of view of both the narrow and the broader views of corporate responsibility. What view of corporate responsibility do you think these companies hold? Do you think they see themselves as acting in a morally legitimate and socially responsible way?

5. In light of this case, do you think it makes sense to talk of a corporation like Yahoo as a moral agent, or is it only the people in it who can be properly described as having moral responsibility?

6. Would American companies do more good by refusing to cooperate with Chinese authorities (and risk not being able to do business in China) or by cooperating and working gradually to spread Internet freedom? In general, under what circumstances is it permissible for a company to operate in a repressive country or do business with a dictatorial regime?

7. Assess the pros and cons of a law forbidding American high-tech companies from assisting repressive foreign governments.

Case 5.2

Drug Dilemmas

Everyone Knows How High the Cost of Prescription Medicines can be. While the vast array of different insurance plans and assistance programs offered by drugmakers means that many people will not pay the "sticker price" for their prescriptions, individuals may still be hit with an out-of-pocket price of $1,000 or more for individual medications. Those high prices are at least part of the reason that "pharma" is one of the most profitable sectors of our economy. However, many people are also inclined to accept high prices as the cost we must bear for drug research and the development of new medicines. But, in fact, the prices drug companies charge bear little relationship to the cost of making or developing them, and those prices could be cut dramatically without coming close to threatening their research and development (R&D) budgets. Between 1999 and 2018, less than 20 percent of the sales revenue of the large pharmaceutical companies went into R&D, about two-thirds of what they spent on marketing and administration.[89]

Moreover, the pharmaceutical industry is nowhere near as innovative as most people think. According to Marcia Angell, former editor in chief of the *New England Journal of Medicine*, only a handful of important drugs have been brought to the market in recent years, and they were based mostly on taxpayer-funded research. She writes, "The great majority of 'new drugs' are not new at all but merely variations on older drugs already on the market. These are called 'me-too' drugs. The idea is to grab a share of an established, lucrative market by producing something very similar to a top-selling drug." This is made possible by the fact that the Food and Drug Administration (FDA) will generally approve a drug if it is better than a placebo. "It needn't be better than an older drug," Angell says. "In fact it may be worse. There is no way of knowing, since companies do not test their drugs against older ones for the same conditions at equivalent doses." According to one analysis, fewer than half of the new drugs approved by the FDA between 2011–2021 contained new active ingredients ("new molecular entities").[90]

What is more, when drug companies do develop a new, superior treatment, they may withhold it from the market? Gilead has recently been accused of delaying until 2015 the sale of a new, safer treatment for HIV that could have been marketed as early as 2004.[91] The drug was an "upgrade" on one that Gilead already had under patent. By waiting to sell the new drug until the patent on the original was about to expire, Gilead could maximize the length of time that it held a patent on the best medication available. This would allow it to charge a higher price since it would not face competition from generic versions of the same drug. Gilead denies that the reason for the delay was to increase profits, claiming instead that in 2004 it didn't appear that the new version would be a significant improvement.

When it comes to research and innovation, the record of the big, profitable pharmaceutical corporations contrasts poorly with that of the small biotechnology companies that are responsible for most of today's medical advances. CV Therapeutics of Palo Alto, California, is one such company. Founded by cardiologist Louis G. Lange, it has developed a new drug, ranolazine, which promises to be the first new treatment for angina in over twenty-five years. The *Journal of the American Medical Association* has praised ranolazine as helping patients for whom standard therapies have failed. But this medical breakthrough has brought an ethical dilemma with it. Patients in Russia and Eastern Europe constituted 60 percent of the 1,000 or so test subjects involved in the studies that enabled CV Therapeutics to develop the drug. Now that the drug is ready, does the company have a moral obligation to make its drug available to them?

Other drug companies today are struggling with the same dilemma. They frequently test experimental drugs overseas, where there is less red tape and both doctors and patients are keen to participate in the tests. In Russia, for example, doctors are eager for the money they can get as study monitors, traveling to medical offices to make sure protocols are being followed. They also receive medical equipment such as treadmills for exercise testing. For their part, patients see it as a chance to get medications that they cannot afford to buy and that their government doesn't pay for. Moreover, says Richard Leach, the American business manager of a company called Russian Clinical Trials, "Eastern European and Russian people tend to be very compliant. . . . They will follow the trial and they will do whatever is asked. If they have to keep a diary, they do it. If they have to make office visits, they do it." (When the Russian invasion of Ukraine disrupted drug trials in some Eastern European countries, Georgia—the country, not the state—was touted as an alternative.[92] This was partly due to the fact that trials could be started there in as little as two months, versus the four to six months needed in Poland or Romania.)

With much drug testing now done in non-Western countries, and some taking place in the developing world, critics worry that drug companies are exploiting their human subjects. In the United States and other well-to-do countries, experimental subjects must be given full information about the nature of the research, and they have a right to refuse to participate without penalty or consequence for their usual health care. Not so in Africa and many poor regions, where doctors profit from enrolling their patients, and local officials sometimes encourage whole villages or provinces to enroll in research programs. Conducting research overseas not only saves drug companies money, but it also circumvents FDA restrictions, which require companies to gain its approval before human testing in the United States can begin. The FDA obliges companies to describe their proposed research in detail and to file plans for guaranteeing informed consent and for monitoring the progress of the study. They must set up a review board to monitor each clinical trial and to ensure that risks to human subjects are "reasonable in relation to anticipated benefits, if any, to subjects, and the importance of the knowledge that may reasonably be expected to result." In addition, all risk must be "minimized."

Requirements for foreign research are much looser, and there is very little oversight. "Companies can conduct preliminary studies of drugs in poorer countries before formal testing even begins," writes Marcia Angell. "Quite literally, the participants are used as guinea pigs, subjects of research that really should be done on experimental animals." And when it comes to formal testing, the FDA may not learn about it until the company applies for final approval of its new drug.

These moral issues, however, are not the concern of companies like Russian Clinical Trials. Nor do they see it as their business to ask what happens when the studies end. Dr. Alan Wood, general manager of Covance, another American firm that conducts medical trials in Eastern Europe, says quite plainly, "What our clients do is not our affair."

But what about the drug companies themselves? What, if anything, do they owe overseas test subjects when their new drugs pan out? Some companies never even sell their drugs in the poor countries where they were developed. Others do, but often there are few patients who can afford them. "This is something that the biotech industry, as it develops more and more drugs, will have to come to grips with," says Carl B. Feldbaum, president of the Biotechnology Industry Organization. "It's not that we are lacking compassion, but the economics are tough."

"Do we have an obligation to everyone in the trial or to everyone in the community, the province, the nation, the region, or the world?" asks Dr. Ruth Faden, director of the Berman Bioethics Institute at Johns Hopkins University. "We really haven't figured this out." She acknowledges, though, that "many physician investigators feel uncomfortable with the idea of using patients in studies and then not being able to continue to help them when the trial ends." We seem "to have hit a wall of moral unease," she says. "I'm not sure exactly where we ought to end up."

Dr. Lawrence O. Goskin, director of the Center for Law and the Public's Health at Georgetown and Johns Hopkins Universities, is also troubled. Drug companies, he says, should not be seen as "the deep pocket that helps everyone," yet there is something disturbing about "parachute research," in which a company drops into a country, conducts its drug research, and then leaves. "It raises the question of what ethical obligation, if any, there might be to give back and make sure there is access to the drug after the trials are over."

Drug companies are businesses, of course, and they have to decide whether they can earn enough money in a foreign country to justify applying for approval to market a new drug there, then setting up a business office, and hiring a sales force. Even if they decide to provide the drug to patients free of charge—so-called compassionate use—things are not so simple. They still have to set up a distribution system, train doctors to administer the drug, and monitor the patients who take it. In the case of life-saving drugs, such as those for combating AIDS, many companies do, in fact, provide them for free or at low cost in poor countries, especially to patients who were involved in their development. But with a drug like ranolazine, it's more complicated. Angina can cause terrible, crushing chest pains, and it can make the lives of chronic suffers miserable. Ranolazine can cut in half the number of angina attacks a patient suffers, but it's not a life-saving drug. It improves the quality of patients' lives, but it doesn't extend them.

Dr. Lange, meanwhile, is torn. His company is not a charity, and because CV Therapeutics is small, it can't afford to market ranolazine in countries where few people have enough money to buy it or to set up the distribution systems necessary to give it away. "We're not Merck," he says. "But we're concerned."

Discussion Questions

1. What explains the high price of prescription medicines in the United States? What if anything should be done about it? Do you believe that in the United States drug prices reflect the operation of a fair and competitive market?

2. Given the nature of their product, do pharmaceutical companies have ethical responsibilities that other corporations don't have? In your view, are the large U.S. drug companies good corporate citizens?

3. Are the large drug companies guilty of price gouging or of charging an unfair or exploitative price for their products? Should Americans be permitted to import drugs from Canada or other countries?

4. Assess the motivations of drug companies that do their testing overseas. Do you think test subjects are being exploited or taken advantage of? Under what circumstances, if any, are companies morally justified in testing overseas?

5. Do drug companies have an obligation to make new drugs available to patients who were involved in their development, either here or overseas? Does the size of the company make a difference? What would you do if you were Dr. Lange? What obligations, ideals, and consequences should he take into account?

6. Is it ethical for companies to decline to sell a useful drug like ranolazine in a poor country because they can make more money marketing it elsewhere?

7. When it comes to life-saving drugs, do pharmaceutical companies have a moral obligation to make them available in poor countries at little or no cost? Explain why or why not. What about effective but non-life-saving drugs like ranolazine?

Case 5.3
Free Speech or False Advertising?

With Annual Sales of Over $19 Billion and Annual Profits of around $1.9 billion, Nike is one of the giants in the sports apparel business, and its trademark "Swoosh" logo is recognized around the world. However, for a company of its size, Nike directly employs surprisingly few workers—only about 22,000. That is because overseas contractors manufacture all Nike's products. These independent contractors employ approximately 600,000 workers at 910 factories, mostly in China, Indonesia, Vietnam, and Thailand.

Like many other firms, Nike outsources its manufacturing to take advantage of cheap overseas labor. But the price of doing so began getting higher for Nike in the late 1990s, when anti-sweatshop activists started campaigning against the company, charging that the third-world workers making its products were exploited and abused. Activists on many college campuses, for instance, encouraged their peers to boycott Nike shoes and clothing and tried to pressure their universities' athletic departments not to sign deals with Nike for team sports apparel.

Instead of ducking the issue, as other companies might have, Nike responded vigorously to the criticisms. At the University of North Carolina, for example, Nike ran full-page ads in the student newspaper, asserting that it was a good corporate citizen and upheld humane labor standards. It sent representatives to meet with student activists, and company CEO Philip Knight took the unusual step of showing up at an undergraduate seminar on corporate globalization to defend his company. Nike issued press releases and sent letters to many college presidents and athletic departments, asserting, among other things, that Nike paid "on average, double the minimum wage as defined in countries where its products are produced" and that its workers "are protected from physical and sexual abuse."

Enter Marc Kasky, a fifty-nine-year-old San Francisco activist. He thought Nike's campaign was misleading the public about working conditions inside its factories, so he sued the company for false advertising under California's consumer protection law. In Kasky's view, the case was simply a matter of protecting consumers from corporate deceit. In response, Nike argued that the statements in question were protected by the First Amendment because they were made in news releases, letters to the editor, and op-ed essays and because they related to the company's labor practices—which are a matter of public concern—and not the products it sold. Two lower courts agreed with Nike, but then the California Supreme Court overturned their verdict, ruling in a 4–3 decision that the company's campaign was essentially commercial speech (which generally receives less First Amendment protection than political or personal speech) even though Nike was not specifically talking about shoes. In the court's view, Nike's speech was directed at customers and dealt with its business operations; the form in which the information was released was irrelevant. The judges, however, didn't determine whether Nike really did abuse workers or mislead consumers; it left those factual questions for a trial court to decide.

Nike then appealed the case to the U.S. Supreme Court. California Attorney General Bill Lockyer filed a brief in support of Kasky, which seventeen other states joined. The brief contended that the case was not about free speech but rather about "Nike's ability to exploit false facts to promote commercial ends." Harvard law professor Laurence Tribe, however, defended the company, arguing that treating Nike's letters and press releases as equivalent to advertising would undercut the ability of companies to speak out on political issues. He urged that the California decision would have a "chilling effect on freedom of speech." To this, however, the chief author of the California brief, deputy attorney general Roland Reiter, responded: "I believe the concerns expressed are really overblown. We have a company talking about itself. It's difficult to see why holding them to the truth would cause any kind of calamity." USC law professor Erwin Chemerinsky agreed. He argued that it didn't matter whether Nike issued the information in the form of a press release: "If a company makes false statements about its product or practices with the intent of increasing profits, that's commercial speech."

After having heard the case, however, the Supreme Court declined to decide the substantive legal issues at stake. Instead, it dismissed the case on a technicality and sent it back to California for trial. Before the trial began, however, Nike settled out of court with Kasky. As part of the deal, Nike agreed to donate $1.5 million to the Fair Labor Association, a sweatshop-monitoring group, and in a joint statement, Kasky and Nike "mutually agreed that investments designed to strengthen workplace monitoring and factory worker programs are more desirable than prolonged litigation." A happy ending? Not in everyone's eyes. Friends of Nike argued that because the Supreme Court did not act forthrightly to protect corporate speech, companies will be reluctant to discuss public issues involving their products. Those on the other side, however, responded that when disclosing information about wages and working conditions, companies should be held to the same standards of truth and accuracy as when they disclose financial data.[93]

Discussion Questions

1. In this case, was Nike engaged in commercial speech, or were its statements political or social speech? What determines whether speech is commercial or not?

2. Was the out-of-court settlement a reasonable resolution of this case? What would have been the good or bad consequences of the Supreme Court's deciding in Nike's favor? Of its deciding in Kasky's favor?

3. Should commercial speech receive less First Amendment protection than other types of speech, or does this violate the rights of corporations? Explain your answer.

4. Do corporations have the same moral rights as individual human beings? Should they have the same political rights? Is it morally permissible to limit the speech of corporations in ways that would be wrong if applied to the speech of individual citizens? If it is permissible, is it good public policy?

5. Does Nike have a social responsibility to address matters of public concern such as the working conditions in its overseas operations? If it chooses to do so, does it have an obligation to make its statements as truthful and accurate as it can? Under what circumstances should corporations be held liable for the truth of their public statements?

Case 5.4

Corporations and Religious Faith

In 2012, The Supreme Court Upheld Most of the Affordable Care Act, President Obama's signature health-care reform law. That law requires that employer-sponsored health care policies include contraceptive coverage. This is in line with a 2002 EEOC ruling that companies that provide prescription benefits to their employees but not birth control violate Title VII of the 1964 Civil Rights Act, which forbids discrimination on grounds of sex. Although the Obama administration has exempted religiously affiliated nonprofit employers, such as Catholic charities, from financing contraceptive coverage, for-profit companies remain bound by the requirement.

Two for-profit companies, however, challenged the rule—Hobby Lobby Stores, an arts-and-crafts chain, and Conestoga Wood Specialties, which makes kitchen cabinet doors. Based on their Christian religious beliefs, the owners of the companies oppose certain forms of contraception, such as the morning-after pill and various intrauterine devices (IUDs). That's because they believe that life begins when the sperm fertilizes the egg and that these forms of contraception violate the right to life of the fertilized egg by preventing it from attaching to the lining of the uterus, thus making them equivalent to abortion.

In June 2013, the U.S. Court of Appeals, Tenth Circuit, upheld Hobby Lobby's position. It ruled that a corporation, as a form of association, has a right to espouse its religious beliefs regardless of its profit-seeking status. The Green family, who own the company, formed it with the "intent to provide goods and services while adhering to Christian standards as they see them, and they have made business decisions according to those standards." The Court continued:

> Would an incorporated kosher butcher really have no claim to challenge a regulation mandating non-kosher butchering practices? . . . A religious individual may enter the for-profit realm intending to demonstrate to the marketplace that a corporation can succeed financially while adhering to religious values. As a court, we do not see how we can distinguish this form of evangelism from any other.

As the Court sees it, the owners of a company do not lose their right to follow their religious beliefs by incorporating, and it rejects the "notion that Free Exercise rights turn on Congress's definition of 'non-profit.'"

A month later, however, a different appellate court—the Third Circuit of the U.S. Court of Appeals—ruled against the Hahn family, who own Conestoga Wood Specialties, holding that "secular, for-profit corporations cannot engage in religious exercise." Although the owners may have a sincere religious objection to contraceptives that act on the fertilized egg, the Court reasoned, the owners are not identical with the corporation; it is a distinct legal entity. The Affordable Care Act does not require the Hahns to do anything. The responsibility for complying with the act falls on the corporation.

> "The fact that one person owns all of the stock does not make him and the corporation one and the same person, nor does he thereby become the owner of all the property of the corporation." . . . The Hahn family chose to incorporate and conduct business through Conestoga, thereby obtaining both the advantages and disadvantages of the corporate form. . . . The free exercise claims of a company's owners cannot "pass through" to the corporation.

The Court also rejected the contention that the Supreme Court's 2010 ruling in *Citizens United* extended not just political rights but also religious rights to corporations.

In both cases, the courts were concerned not only with the First Amendment but also with the federal Religious Freedom Restoration Act (RFRA) of 1993. That law sought to nullify a high court ruling that the state of Oregon could deny unemployment benefits to people for using illegal drugs even if the drug in question (peyote) was being used as part of a Native American religious ceremony. The RFRA provides, as a general rule, that "Government shall not substantially burden a person's exercise of religion." It can restrict a person's exercise of religion only if it has a compelling interest in doing so and if there is no less restrictive means of furthering that interest.

With the two appellate courts in disagreement, the Supreme Court was forced to weigh in. It did so in July 2014, ruling 5-to-4 that requiring the two family-owned corporations to pay for insurance coverage for contraception violated the RFRA. The court held that for-profit corporations are "persons" within the meaning of the RFRA, that requiring the companies in question either to provide contraceptive coverage or to pay substantial fines constitutes a substantial burden on their religious liberty, and that there were other "less restrictive" ways that the government could ensure access to contraceptive care.

For their part, the four dissenting judges were worried about the broad implications of the decision, with Justice Ruth Bader Ginsburg arguing that "its logic extends to corporations of any size, public or private," potentially allowing them to object on religious grounds not only to any kind of contraception but also to "health coverage of vaccines, or paying the minimum wage, or according women equal pay for substantially similar work." Ginsburg's dissent further raised a fundamental philosophical question: If the entire point of incorporation is to draw a distinction between the corporation and its owners, so that (because of limited liability) the owners refuse to take personal responsibility for the corporation's actions, then isn't letting the owners impose their personal religious outlook on the corporation letting them have it both ways?

In a sole proprietorship, the business and its owner are one and the same. By incorporating a business, however, an individual separates themself from the entity and escapes personal responsibility for the entity's obligations. One might ask why the separation should hold only when it serves the interest of those who control the corporation.

Discussion Questions

1. Although corporations are not human beings, they have a number of legal and political rights. Do they also have a First Amendment right that "Congress shall make no law . . . prohibiting the free exercise" of their religion? If so, was that right violated in this case?

2. Is it possible for corporations to have religious beliefs, or can only human beings have such beliefs? If corporations can be said to have religious beliefs, are those beliefs the same as the beliefs of the owners? What if there is not a single owner, but a number of different stockholders? What about the religious beliefs of the managers or employees—are they relevant to determining what the corporation believes?

3. The Hahns have a right to exercise their religion. Does this right transfer to any corporations they own?

4. Are corporations "persons"? Do you think that Congress intended the RFRA to apply to corporations?

5. Does the requirement that their health care policies include contraception impose a "substantial burden" on these companies' exercise of religion? Explain why or why not.

6. Both companies are privately held, meaning that their shares do not trade on the stock market. Does this fact affect the issue? If so, how?

Case 5.5
Corporate Taxation

In The United States, The Rate at Which Corporations are Taxed is 21 percent. (This flat rate went into effect in 2018; previously the rate had been variable, like the personal income tax, and the highest bracket went up to 35 percent.) But 21 percent is only the nominal rate; few if any corporations actually pay that much. You may recall some of the information about this given in Chapter 4, for example, that in 2021 AT&T had revenues of nearly $30 billion and rather than paying taxes it received a $1.2 billion refund. For many companies, tax avoidance is a sophisticated game—almost an art form. That's one of the main reasons why these days corporations pay a smaller share of the nation's taxes than they used to. In the 1950s, the revenue from corporate taxation amounted to about a third of total federal tax revenue. Today, this figure is down to about 6 percent.[94]

Historically, two of the biggest corporate tax breaks are accelerated depreciation of machinery and equipment and deferral of income from foreign sources.[95] In 2013, it came out that Apple, the nation's most profitable technology company, was also one of its most successful tax avoiders, thanks to a complex web of international subsidiaries the company has created. Many of those subsidiaries are incorporated in Ireland, where Apple negotiated a special tax rate of only 2 percent, although in

fact they are run from Cupertino, California. Furthermore, even though they are incorporated in Ireland, some of these offshore entities have no stated country of tax residence and thus pay no taxes at all, even though they hold tens of billions of dollars.

Other companies, such as Microsoft and Google, engage in "transfer pricing." This shifts profits generated in the United States to offshore tax havens where the IRS can't get at them. Companies accomplish this trick by transferring intellectual property rights to specially created foreign subsidiaries, which then charge the parent company stiff licensing fees for using its own intellectual property. These complex arrangements may involve subsidiaries in multiple countries, exploiting differences in their tax laws; they have names like "Double Irish with a Dutch Sandwich." But even low-tech companies can be good at shell games like this. Caterpillar cut its tax bill by $300 million a year simply by putting the name of a Swiss subsidiary on the invoices for parts it sent from the United States to customers around the world. Even Starbucks figured out how to play the game. It told shareholders that it was making large profits in Britain but filed U.K. tax forms showing losses, resulting in its paying no British taxes at all for three years in a row, despite billions of dollars in sales there.

With the possible exception of Caterpillar, these companies have done nothing illegal. (Caterpillar settled with the IRS in 2022, paying no penalty.)[96] There is a difference between tax evasion, which is illegal, and tax avoidance, which is not. Emphasizing this distinction, Judge Learned Hand famously wrote:

> Anyone may arrange his affairs so that his taxes shall be as low as possible; he is not bound to choose that pattern which best pays the treasury. There is . . . nothing sinister in so arranging affairs as to keep taxes as low as possible. Everyone does it, rich and poor alike and all do right, for nobody owes any public duty to pay more than the law demands.

Still, it strikes many people as unfair when corporations seem to be dodging their fair share of the country's tax burden. That's probably why, when news of Starbucks's tax avoidance broke, the company voluntarily agreed to pay about $16 million in British taxes. "We believe that acting responsibly makes good business sense," says Corey duBrowa, senior vice president for global communications, "and payment of corporate tax in the U.K. is a good example of this ethos in action." Some business commentators applaud Starbucks. "Just because tax avoidance is legal," writes John Cassidy, "doesn't mean that it is right." Allan Sloan agrees; although lower taxes mean higher profits, "going to extraordinary lengths to avoid taxes helps undermine companies' long term-interest by hurting society and by giving average people yet another reason to detest Big Business."

The world's richest economies are now cooperating in an effort to curb the tax avoidance strategies used by multinational corporations. The American Tax Cut and Jobs Act, which passed in 2017 and largely went into effect in 2018, contains provisions that are meant to contribute to this effort. Along with dropping the corporate rate, it eliminated the provision in the tax code that allowed companies to defer taxation on overseas revenues. Essentially, the philosophy behind the law is to reduce the taxes that American corporations owe on their overseas earnings but to make it harder for them to avoid paying something—reducing the taxes owed but increasing the taxes collected. It's also meant to reduce the incentives for corporations to move operations out of the United States. How effective it will be remains to be seen.

It's worth noting, though, that some economists oppose corporate taxation in principle. They think only persons should be taxed. In their view, corporate taxation involves a kind of double taxation. Corporations pay tax on their income, which is then taxed again when it gets passed on to individuals in the form of dividends. Although the tax revenue that would be lost by abolishing the corporate income tax would have to be offset by higher taxation on individuals, doing so would, these economists believe, promote economic efficiency since companies would no longer spend so much time, energy, and money trying to avoid or reduce their taxes.

Discussion Questions

1. In your opinion, do corporations now pay their fair share of taxes? Explain why or why not. If not, what should be done about it?

2. Do corporations have a social responsibility not to exploit loopholes in the tax system or use accounting tricks to dodge taxes? Explain why or why not.

3. If a company like Apple is not acting illegally, is there anything wrong with its tax avoidance gimmicks? In general, is there anything wrong with either individuals or corporations arranging their affairs so as to minimize their taxes? Is that all that Apple was doing?

4. Why do you think Starbucks decided to pay voluntarily taxes it was not legally required to pay? Was this the right decision from the moral point of view? From the business point of view? Should Apple do something similar?

5. Should corporate taxation be abolished? Why or why not?

6. When you get a paycheck from work, you owe income tax. If you use some of the money that's left to pay a mechanic to repair your car, they'll owe income tax on what you pay them. Is this "double taxation"? How is it similar to or different from the double taxation that is said to affect corporate taxation?

7. Individual income from dividends and capital gains is now taxed at a lower rate than individual income from wages. Is this fair?

8. In order to avoid U.S. taxes, some long-standing American companies have renounced U.S. citizenship and reincorporated overseas, which they can do if, after a merger or acquisition, foreign shareholders own more than 20 percent of the company. Should companies be permitted to relocate for tax purposes? Is their doing so morally acceptable? Is it unpatriotic?

Chapter 6

Consumers

Learning Objectives

After completing this chapter, you should be able to:

1. Describe the current state of legal regulations meant to protect consumers from dangerous or defective products, manipulative or unfair pricing, incomplete or inaccurate labeling, and misleading or deceptive advertising.
2. Make and critically assess arguments both for imposing stricter regulations and easing existing regulations.
3. Make and critically assess arguments for different perspectives on the moral responsibilities of businesses toward their customers, for example, whether it is morally permissible for businesses to take advantage of the fact that the average person is prone to make certain sorts of mistakes in reasoning.

Introduction

The "Marlboro Man" Has Long Mesmerized People around the world, and few can deny the glamor of the ruggedly good-looking Marlboro cowboy, with boots, hat, chaps—and, of course, a cigarette in his mouth. Product of one of the most successful advertising campaigns in history, the Marlboro Man revolutionized the image of Marlboro cigarettes, making it the best-selling brand in the United States.

Everybody, of course, knows that smoking is hazardous to one's health. According to the Centers for Disease Control, 480,000 Americans die every year because of cigarettes, nearly one in five deaths in the United States.[1] Smoking increases the risk of stroke or coronary heart disease by two to four times and the risk of developing lung disease by over 25 times (with the increase slightly larger for women than for men).

Today, even the tobacco industry itself acknowledges the dangers of smoking. Tobacco company R. J. Reynolds admits as much on its website:

> Cigarette smoking is a leading cause of preventable deaths in the United States. Cigarette smoking significantly increases the risk of developing lung cancer, heart disease, chronic bronchitis, emphysema and other serious diseases and adverse health conditions. No tobacco product has been shown to be safe and without risks, and quitting tobacco use significantly reduces the risk for serious diseases.[2]

The tobacco industry was not always so forthcoming, however. For decades, they "blew smoke," publicly raising questions about the

> Everybody, of course, knows that smoking is hazardous to one's health—even the tobacco industry.

links between smoke and disease even though their own research clearly demonstrated their existence.[3] This is one reason why the federal government took the unprecedented step of bringing an anti-racketeering lawsuit against the large tobacco companies. The suit contended that cigarette manufacturers "have engaged in and executed . . . a massive 50-year scheme to defraud the public" by suppressing evidence that cigarette smoke contains carcinogens and that nicotine is addictive. In addition, the suit accused tobacco companies of marketing cigarettes to teenagers, agreeing among themselves not to develop safer cigarettes, and manipulating nicotine levels in cigarettes to create and sustain addiction. (For example, so-called low-tar and low-nicotine cigarettes, marketed as "light" or "ultra-light," were designed so that addicted smokers inhale as much nicotine as always.) After a nine-month trial, the government won its lawsuit in 2006—although not the $280 billion in damages it had sought. But U.S. District Court Judge Gladys Kessler did require cigarette manufacturers to correct their falsehoods; to desist from making incorrect, misleading, or deceptive statements about the health risks of cigarettes; and to disclose their marketing practices annually to government officials.

In 2009, Congress took things a step further by empowering the U.S. Federal Drug Administration (FDA) to regulate cigarettes—although not to outlaw smoking or ban nicotine altogether. Among other things, the FDA now has the legal authority to reduce nicotine content, to regulate

Buena Vista Pictures/courtesy Everett Collection

The movie **The Insider** brought to the screen the story of Jeffrey Wigand, who served as vice president for Research and Development for Brown & Williamson Tobacco Corporation. In an interview on TV news program **60 Minutes**, Wigand revealed that his former employer knew nicotine was addictive and intentionally manipulated the tobacco content of its cigarettes to increase the amount of nicotine they delivered.

the chemicals in cigarettes, and to restrict cigarette advertising even further. The law also bars tobacco flavorings (which are thought to lure first-time smokers), forbids marketing cigarettes as "light," "mild," or "low tar," and requires larger, more graphic warnings on cigarette packages. Meanwhile, smokers continue to sue cigarette manufacturers for injuries allegedly caused by their deadly habit. Despite the warnings that have been required on cigarette packs and ads since 1966, many smokers—or their estates—contend that they were addicted and couldn't stop. Many of these lawsuits have been successful, with juries penalizing tobacco companies with compensatory and punitive damage verdicts for millions, even billions, of dollars (although the companies often succeed in getting the largest of these judgments reduced or overturned on appeal, such as a $23 billion dollar judgment against R. J. Reynolds by a Florida jury that the judge reduced to $16.9 million). In response to this and to declining cigarette consumption in the United States and parts of Europe, the tobacco companies are marketing their wares more aggressively than ever in Asia and the developing world and fighting the efforts of poorer nations to reduce smoking through restrictions on the advertising, packaging, and sale of cigarettes.[4]

Given all this, it seems the world should welcome electronic cigarettes with open arms. E-cigarettes work by turning nicotine-infused liquid into vapor, which the user inhales or "vapes." Free of all the noxious substances that ordinary cigarettes contain, they don't pose the same health risks (although we're still learning about the health consequences of vaping).[5] They don't smell bad, and they don't pose a hazard to the health of bystanders. In effect, e-cigarettes allow consumers to get the pleasure that smokers get from the nicotine in cigarettes with less danger to their health (or that of others) than from smoking tobacco. There is also evidence that the use of e-cigarettes can help smokers to quit altogether. But not everyone is persuaded that they're a good thing, and health lobbyists have succeeded in getting a few cities and countries to impose restrictions on them. Nicotine is, after all, toxic, though probably no more dangerous than caffeine. It's also addictive. Critics of e-cigarettes claim that they allow smokers who might otherwise kick their habit to remain hooked by switching to vaping when it's not convenient to puff. But what really worries health lobbyists is that e-cigarettes might entice children or be a "gateway" to the real thing. More generally, they wish to discourage anything that even remotely resembles smoking or that might make it more socially acceptable. And the ads for vaping do make it seem cool. Meanwhile, the market for e-cigarettes is growing rapidly—by almost 50 percent during the COVID-19 pandemic.[6]

Vaping may be relatively safe, but ordinary cigarettes remain an especially dangerous product. Their manufacture, marketing, advertising, and sales raise a number of acute questions relevant to the consumer issues discussed in this chapter. For instance, what are the responsibilities to consumers of companies that sell potentially or (in the case of cigarettes) inherently harmful products? To what extent do manufacturers abuse advertising? When is advertising deceptive? Can advertisers create or at least stimulate desires for products that consumers would not otherwise want or would not otherwise want as much? How, if at all, should advertising be restricted? Are consumers sufficiently well informed about the products they buy? Are they misled by deceptive labeling and packaging?

In general, how far should society go in controlling the claims of advertisers, in regulating product packaging and labels, in monitoring product quality and price, and in upholding explicit standards of reliability and safety? What moral responsibilities do businesses have in these areas? In a market-oriented economic system, how do we balance the interests of business with the rights of consumers? How do we promote social well-being while still respecting the choices of individuals?

· · ·

Product Safety

Business's responsibility for understanding, providing for, and protecting the interests of consumers derives from the fact that they depend on business to satisfy their many and varied material needs and wants. This dependence is particularly true in our highly technological society, as it is characterized by a complex economy, automation, intense specialization, and urban concentration. These conditions contrast with those that prevailed in the United States when the country was primarily agrarian and people could satisfy most of their own needs. Today, we rely on others to provide the wherewithal for our survival and prosperity. We rarely make our own clothing, supply our own fuel, manufacture our own tools, or construct our own homes, and our food is more likely to come from thousands of miles away than from our own gardens.

The increasing complexity of today's economy and the multifaceted dependence of consumers on business for their survival and enrichment have heightened business's responsibilities to consumers—particularly in the area of product safety. From toys to tools, cars to baby cribs, consumers use countless products every day believing that neither they nor their loved ones will be harmed or injured by them. Consumers, however, lack the expertise to judge many of the sophisticated products they utilize. Being human, they also make mistakes in handling the things they buy—mistakes that the manufacturers of those products can often anticipate and make less likely. For these reasons, society must rely on the conscientious efforts of business to promote consumer safety. Government also plays a role in ensuring that that products we buy are safe, although here as in so many other spheres there's considerable debate about just how large its role should be.

Summary
The complexity of an advanced economy and the necessary dependence of consumers on business to satisfy their many wants increase business's responsibility for product safety.

The Legal Liability of Manufacturers

If any of us is injured by a defective product, we can sue the manufacturer of that product. We take this legal right for granted, but it didn't always exist. Before the landmark case of **MacPherson v. Buick Motor Car** in 1916, injured consumers could recover damages only from the retailer of the defective product—that is, from the party with whom they had actually done business. That made sense in a bygone day of small-scale, local capitalism. If your buggy crashed because the harness you bought from the local harness maker was defective, then your complaint was against him. By contrast, when a wheel fell off Donald MacPherson's Buick, the firm he had bought the Buick from hadn't actually made it.

Legal policy before *MacPherson* based a manufacturer's liability for damage caused by a defective product on the contractual relationship between the manufacturer and the purchaser (the "privity doctrine"). Their contractual relationship is simply the sale—that is, the exchange of money for a commodity of a certain description. But that contractual relationship is an important source of moral and legal responsibilities for the producer. It obligates business firms to provide customers with a product that lives up to the claims the firm makes about the product. Those claims shape customers' expectations about what they're buying and lead them to enter into the contract in the first place. The question in *MacPherson*, however, was whether a manufacturer's liability for defective products was limited to consumers with whom it had a direct contractual relationship.

The *MacPherson* decision from the New York Court of Appeals recognized the 20th-century economic reality of large manufacturing concerns and national systems of product distribution. Among other things, local retailers are not as likely as large manufacturers to be able to bear financial responsibility for defective products that injure others. One can also see the court moving in *MacPherson* to a "due-care" theory of the manufacturer's duties to consumers. **Due care** is the idea that consumers and sellers do not meet as equals and that the consumer's interests are particularly vulnerable to being harmed by the manufacturer, who has knowledge and expertise the consumer does not have. *MacPherson*, for instance, was in no position to have discovered the defective wheel before he purchased the Buick. According to the due-care view, then, manufacturers have an obligation, above and beyond any contract, to exercise due care to prevent the consumer from being injured by defective products.

The 1916 *MacPherson* case expanded the liability of manufacturers for injuries caused by defective products.

As the concept of due care spread, legal policy moved decisively beyond the old doctrine of ***caveat emptor***—literally "let the buyer beware"—which was seldom the guiding principle by the time of *MacPherson* anyway. Today, we associate *caveat emptor* with an era of patent medicines and outrageously false product claims. Although legally the doctrine of "let the buyer beware" was never upheld across the board, there was a time when consumers' legal responsibility to accept the consequences of their product choices was greater than it is today. Consumers were held to the ideal of being knowledgeable, shrewd, and skeptical. Because they freely chose whether to buy a certain product, they were expected to take the claims of manufacturers and salespeople with a grain of salt, to inspect any potential purchase carefully, to rely on their own judgment, and to accept any ill results of their decision to use a given product. In the first part of the 20th century, however, the courts repudiated this doctrine, largely on grounds of its unrealistic assumptions about consumer knowledge, competence, and behavior.

Strict Product Liability

Summary
The legal liability of manufacturers for injuries caused by defective products has evolved over the years. Today the courts have moved to the doctrine of strict liability, which holds the manufacturer of a product responsible for injuries suffered as a result of defects in the product, regardless of whether the manufacturer was negligent.

Despite its support for the due-care theory and for a broader view of manufacturer's liability, the *MacPherson* case still left the injured consumer with the burden of proving that the manufacturer had been negligent. Not only might such an assertion be difficult to prove, but also a product might be dangerously defective despite the manufacturer's having taken reasonable steps to avoid such a defect.

Beginning with the 1963 California case *Greenman v. Yuba Power Products*, this situation changed. In that landmark case, the court explicitly held that an injured consumer may be awarded damages without having to prove that the manufacturer of the defective product was negligent. Consumers, the court ruled, have a right to expect that the products they purchase are reasonably safe when used in the intended way. On the basis of these and hundreds of subsequent cases, the "strict liability" approach to product safety has come to dominate legal thinking.

The doctrine of **strict product liability** holds that the manufacturer of a product has legal responsibilities to compensate the user of that product for injuries suffered because the product's defective condition made it unreasonably dangerous regardless of whether the manufacturer was negligent in permitting that defect to occur. Under this doctrine, a consumer who purchased a defective product could conceivably win a judgment against a manufacturer who had adhered to the strictest possible quality control procedures. No matter how hard the manufacturer worked to prevent defective products from reaching the market, if as a result of bad luck one defective item slipped through, the fact that the manufacturer had not been negligent would not be an adequate defense. Strict liability, however, is not absolute liability. The product must be defective, and the consumer always has the responsibility to exercise care.

Critics of strict product liability contend that the doctrine is unfair. A firm that has exercised due care and taken reasonable precautions to avoid or eliminate foreseeable dangerous defects, they insist, should not be held liable for defects that are not its fault—that is, for defects that happen despite its best efforts to guard against them. To hold such a firm liable seems unjust.

Two broadly utilitarian considerations support strict product liability.

The argument for strict liability is basically utilitarian. *First*, its advocates contend that only such a policy will induce firms to bend over backward to guarantee product safety. Because they know they will be held liable for injurious defects no matter what, they will make every effort to enhance safety. *Second*, proponents of strict liability contend that the manufacturer is best able to bear the cost of injuries due to defects. Naturally, firms raise the price of their products to cover their legal costs (or pay for liability insurance). But defenders of strict liability do not disapprove of this. They see it as a perfectly reasonable way to spread the cost of injuries among all consumers of the product, rather than letting the cost fall on a single individual—a kind of insurance scheme.

Government Safety Regulation

These developments in product liability law set the general framework within which manufacturers must operate today. In addition, a number of government agencies have become involved in regulating product safety. Congress created one of the most important of these agencies in 1972 when it passed the Consumer Product Safety Act. This act empowers the **Consumer Product Safety Commission (CPSC)** to protect the public "against unreasonable risks of injury associated with consumer products." The five-member commission sets standards for products, bans products presenting undue risk of injury, and in general polices the entire consumer-product marketing process from manufacture to final sale.

In undertaking its policing function, the CPSC gathers data, conducts research, and aids consumers in evaluating product safety. It sets uniform standards and coordinates local, state, and federal product safety laws and enforcement. The commission's jurisdiction extends to more than 15,000 products, and it has the power to require recalls, public warnings, and refunds. Exceptionally risky products can be banned or seized. Rather than stressing punitive action, however, the commission emphasizes developing new standards and redesigning products to accommodate possible consumer misuse. It is less concerned with assigning liability than with avoiding injuries in the first place.

Aside from drugs and motor vehicles, however, most products—such as toys, tools, and appliances—go to the market without regulation.[7] Compared with many other developed countries, the United States regulates fewer products on grounds of safety, implicitly relying more on the tort system and the threat of private lawsuits to protect consumers and keep corporations in line. By contrast, the European Union follows a "better safe than sorry" approach and regulates products that haven't been definitively proved dangerous but that might cause harm. Europe bans some products (such as cheap Chinese cigarette lighters that can flare up and explode) that are readily available in the United States and regulates other products (such as decorative oil lamps) more closely than the United States does. Moreover, American safety regulators, unlike their European counterparts, frequently find themselves entangled in red tape, which hampers or prevents their defending consumers from unsafe products. Over 1,000 chemicals whose use in cosmetics is permitted in the United States are banned for this purpose in Europe.[8] (Europeans have access to a wider range of sunscreens, however, because in Europe these products are classified as cosmetics, whereas in the United States they're regulated as over-the-counter drugs.)[9]

Economic Costs

Although most product safety regulations bring obvious benefits, critics worry about the economic costs. New safety standards add millions of dollars to the cumulative price tag of various goods. Often, economists can estimate how many lives a regulation saves and then compare that number with the cost of implementing the rule. Different agencies use different figures for the value of a human life in deciding when a regulation is cost effective; this is the **value of statistical life** (VSL). For instance, the United States Environmental Protection Agency currently uses a value of $10.05 million in 2020 dollars.[10] The Department of Transportation's valuation is a bit higher; it was $11.6 million in 2020 and rose to $12.5 million in 2022.[11] Note that the VSL is meant to reflect an estimate of how much individuals value their own lives, based on how much they're willing to spend to avoid different risks, as opposed to a top-down political determination.

And what about recalls? Millions of automobiles are recalled every year for a variety of reasons; some years, automakers recall more vehicles than they sell. And recalls are expensive. A series of recalls—10 million vehicles in 2009–2010 and 7.4 million vehicles in 2012—cost Toyota billions of dollars, and the price of General Motors' 2014 recall of over 13 million vehicles because of defective ignition switches is likely to rival that. (On the other hand, auto dealers often like recalls because they give them an opportunity to renew relationships with owners and perhaps sell them a new car.)[12]

Consumer Choice

In addition to cost is the issue of consumer choice. Sometimes consumers dislike mandated safety technology. In 1974, for example, Congress legislated an interlock system that would require drivers to fasten their seat belts before their cars could move. No doubt the law would have saved lives, but a public outcry forced lawmakers to rescind it. Apparently, many

Safety regulations benefit consumers but raise the price of products. Is the expense always worth it?

drivers saw interlock systems as a nuisance and believed their inconvenience outweighed any gain in safety. More recently, an announcement that the CPSC was considering some form of regulation on gas stoves due to concerns about climate change and indoor air pollution prompted an outcry, with the House of Representatives approving a bill that would prevent the agency from banning these appliances.[13]

In other cases, safety regulations may prevent individuals from choosing to purchase a riskier, though less expensive, product. Take, for example, the notorious Ford Pinto with its unsafe gas tank (see Case 2.2). In 1978, after all the negative publicity, scores of lawsuits, and the trial of Ford Motor Company for reckless homicide, the sale of Pintos fell dramatically. Consumers evidently preferred a safer car for comparable money. But when the state of Oregon took all the Pintos out of its fleet because of safety concerns and sold them, at least one dealer reported brisk sales of the turned-in Pintos at their low, secondhand price. Some consumers were willing to accept the risks of a Pinto if the price was right.

Economists worry that preventing individuals from balancing safety against price is inefficient. Philosophers worry about interfering with people's freedom of choice. Take automobile safety again. Because smaller cars provide less protection than larger ones, people in small cars are less likely to survive accidents. Bigger, safer cars are more expensive, however, and many would prefer to spend less on their cars despite the increased risk. If only those cars that were as safe as, say, a Mercedes-Benz were allowed on the market, then there would be fewer deaths on the highways. But then fewer people could afford cars.

Preventing consumers from being able to choose a cheaper but riskier product can have both economic and ethical drawbacks.

Legal Paternalism

That example touches on the larger controversy over **legal paternalism**. The term "paternalism" comes from "*pater*," the Latin word for "father," and it describes the idea of treating an adult like a child by forcing them to do something "for their own good." No one doubts that the law rightly restrains people from harming or endangering other people, but a sizable number of moral theorists deny that laws should attempt to prevent people from running risks that affect only themselves. There is nothing paternalistic about requiring you to have working brakes in your car. This protects other people; without brakes, you are more likely to run over a pedestrian. But requiring you to wear a seat belt when you drive affects only you. Anti-paternalists would protest that forcing you to wear a seat belt violates your moral autonomy. Nonetheless, in the past hundred years state and federal governments have enacted thousands of paternalistic laws. In 2008, for example, California basically outlawed retail sales of raw, unpasteurized milk because of potential health risks, even though a number of consumers prefer it to pasteurized milk.[14]

There are various grounds on which philosophers and others have opposed legal paternalism. Some argue that adults can do a better job of deciding what's in their own interests, on the whole if not in every individual case, than anyone else can do for them. The philosopher most closely associated with this argument is John Stuart Mill, who famously wrote that "neither one person, nor any number of persons, is warranted in saying to another human creature of ripe years, that [they] shall not do with [their] life for [their] own benefit what [they choose] to do with it."[15] Some also argue that paternalistic laws give consumers a false sense of security that can make them less safety conscious. This is the so-called "lulling effect," and depending on its magnitude it might make paternalistic regulations less effective than expected or even counterproductive. For instance, requiring medications to be in bottles that are harder for children to open may result in parents' being less careful about keeping medication out of reach—and the fact that a pill bottle is harder for a child to open doesn't mean that it's impossible.[16] Or take seat belt laws. We know that if you're in a car that's involved in a serious accident then you're much more likely to survive if you're wearing a seat belt. However, there's some evidence that seat belt laws might result in more traffic accidents, and perhaps even—although this is more controversial and uncertain—more traffic fatalities on balance.[17] Why? Perhaps because drivers feel safer when wearing a seat belt and so are less attentive.

Four points might be made in reply. *First*, the safety of some products or some features of products (such as a car's tires) affects not only the consumer who purchases the product but third parties as well. Regulating these products or product features can be defended on nonpaternalistic grounds. *Second*, anti-paternalism gains plausibility from the view that individuals know their own interests better than anyone else does and that they're fully informed and able to advance those interests. But in the increasingly complex consumer world, that assumption is often doubtful. Whenever citizens lack knowledge and are unable to make intelligent comparisons and safety judgments, they may find it in their collective self-interest to set minimal safety standards. Such standards are particularly justifiable when few, if any, reasonable persons would want a product that did not satisfy those standards. Moreover, as philosopher Sarah Conly points out,

> Because of advances in psychology and behavioral economics, we now know more than we once did about how many of the instrumental errors that prevent people from reaching their goals are made. … We are all prone to 'cognitive bias', to glitches in thinking that lead us astray both when we are in the process of taking information in, and when we are using the information we do have to pick the best strategy for reaching our ends.[18]

> Four points about paternalism and safety regulations.

Third, even if the lulling effect is real, that doesn't mean that any given paternalistic regulation will do more harm than good, all things considered. It's a factor to take into consideration when proposing regulations, but only one factor among many. *Finally*, the controversy over legal paternalism pits the values of individual freedom and autonomy against social welfare. We may simply have to acknowledge that clash of values and be willing to make trade-offs. This doesn't imply a defense of paternalism across the board. In the end, one may have to examine paternalistic product safety legislation case by case and weigh the conflicting values and likely results.

How Effective Is Regulation?

American consumers usually assume that if a product is on the market, especially if it's something they ingest, then it has been certified as safe. That assumption can be mistaken, despite new federal food safety legislation enacted in 2011. There are serious gaps in the country's efforts to keep food free of contaminants like *E. coli* and salmonella.[19] The *E. coli* outbreak at Wendy's burger restaurants in 2022 that sickened 109 diners in six states is just one recent illustration of this point.[20] Unapproved drugs, to take another example, can linger on the market for years, either because they have been in use for so long that they have been "grandparented" (i.e., exempted) against regulatory review or due to a lack of enforcement by the **Food and Drug Administration (FDA)**.[21] For instance, Solvay first began manufacturing the hormone replacement Estratest in 1964, and millions of women have taken it over the years. But the drug remained under FDA review until 2009, when the company discontinued production (generic versions are still available), and was never officially approved.[22] Unfortunately, however, even FDA approval is no guarantee of safety as the scandal a few years ago over the high risk of heart attack from NSAID drug Vioxx and related painkillers revealed.

No government agency ensures that cosmetics and personal-care products are safe prior to their being sold, even though some are alleged to contain ingredients that are untested or known to be harmful.[23] Herbal remedies and dietary supplements are another source of concern. Although they represent an enormous—and enormously profitable—industry, they're exempt from the regulatory scrutiny applied to drugs.[24] The effectiveness of most herbal supplements is, at best, unsubstantiated. Worse, consumers have limited protection against contamination and mislabeling. When the CVS drugstore chain tested around 1,400 supplements that it had sold in 2019, it found that about 7 percent contained substances that weren't on the label.[25] Many cannabidiol (CBD) products contain less CBD than they claim, while some contain significant quantities of THC—the substance that is responsible for the cannabis "high" and that can't be legally sold in many parts of the United States (or indeed, according to federal law, anywhere in the country).

In some cases, public opinion and political considerations can interfere with regulatory efforts to protect consumers. The FDA has admitted, for example, that "extreme," "unusual," and persistent pressure from four New Jersey congressmen led the agency to approve a medical device that its scientific reviewers had repeatedly and unanimously ruled was unsafe.[26] Similarly, pressure from gun enthusiasts caused the CPSC to drop its effort to get Daisy Manufacturing to recall BB guns with a defective magazine that had contributed to the accidental shooting

Summary
Government agencies, such as the CPSC, have broad powers to regulate product safety, although the United States is less aggressive than the European Union about doing so. Critics contend that these regulations are costly and prevent individuals from choosing to purchase a riskier but less expensive product. This argument touches on the controversy over legal paternalism, the doctrine that the law may justifiably be used to restrict the freedom of individuals for their own good.

death of a teenage boy.[27] The same year, political pressure appears also to have led the FDA to override the recommendation of its panel of medical experts and to refuse to lift the ban on over-the-counter sales of the so-called "morning-after" pill, levonorgestrel. This decision stirred so much controversy that the FDA eventually relented and approved selling the pill to women over eighteen and then, two years later, to women over seventeen. In an unprecedented intervention, however, the Obama administration overruled that decision in 2011 only to reverse course in 2013 and permit over-the-counter sale of the morning-after contraceptive pill to any woman or girl, regardless of age.

Political pressure aside, the FDA, the CPSC, and other regulatory agencies frequently have difficulty fulfilling their many responsibilities. The 2004 shortage of flu vaccine, the massive 2007 recall of children's toys made in China with lead paint, and the salmonella outbreak of 2008 only underscored the difficulty that federal agencies have ensuring that products entering the country are safe.[28] And as in so many other areas, the COVID-19 pandemic only made existing problems worse. A 2021 government report says that while there have been "long-standing concerns" about the FDA's ability to inspect pharmaceutical plants in China and India, the suspension of inspections during the pandemic has resulted in a tremendous backlog.[29] Even when a regulatory agency recalls a product, it often ends up lingering on the shelves for years. Ask Walter Friedel: He spent four days in intensive care after breathing fumes from a do-it-yourself product to waterproof tile floors that he found at his local Home Depot, even though the CPSC had banned it a year earlier.[30]

Part of the reason for these regulatory lapses is underfunding. Adjusted for inflation, the CPSC has roughly half the budget that it did when it was created in 1972.[31] For instance, it has only half the employees it did in 1980,[32] and the FDA has lost nearly one-third of its inspectors since 2004.[33] Still, regulatory agencies do help to protect the interests of consumers and to pressure businesses to act responsibly. In addition to government regulation, of course, public opinion, media attention, pressure from consumer advocacy groups, and the prospect of class-action lawsuits prod companies to take product safety seriously.

Self-Regulation

Business dislikes regulation and consumer lawsuits or other pressure. But self-regulation sometimes falls short.

Businesspeople tend to be hostile both to regulation and to consumer lawsuits or other pressure. When it comes to safety, they generally prefer self-regulation, competition, and voluntary, industry-determined safety standards. Their point of view is certainly in keeping with the tenets of classical capitalism, and self-regulation is arguably an attractive ideal on both moral and economic grounds. However, self-regulation can easily become an instrument for subordinating consumer interests to profit making when the two goals clash. Under the guise of self-regulation, businesses can end up ignoring or minimizing their responsibilities to consumers.

For example, nothing enrages airplane passengers more than being stuck on a runway because of bad weather and congested terminals, waiting for hours to take off, with little to eat or drink, overflowing toilets, and poor ventilation. (One passenger, who became desperate after several hours of being trapped in a parked plane, made national news when he used his cell phone to call 911 to report that he and his fellow travelers were being held against their will. That call got authorities to empty the plane, but it also brought him a jail sentence.) In an effort to avoid regulation, the airlines successfully lobbied Congress to be allowed to solve the problem themselves. The result, however, was that only a few airlines developed any rules at all, and Congress was eventually forced to pass legislation forbidding them to hold passengers for more than four hours.[34]

Recently, however, some industries have reversed their usual stance and sought out federal regulation. Why the change of attitude? In the case of children's toys, retailers and manufacturers have sought regulation in the hope of reassuring customers, scared off by massive recalls, that their products are safe.[35] Other companies figure that they can use federal safety regulations to thwart competition from cheap foreign imports or as a way of heading off liability lawsuits and legal action by individual states.[36] Some "clean beauty" companies support increased regulation of the cosmetics industry.[37] Such regulations wouldn't change the way that companies who already prioritize product safety operate. Those who don't, though, might need to change their formulations and raise their prices.

Automobile Safety

The auto industry, however, has a long and consistent history of fighting against safety regulations. For example, it successfully lobbied the federal government to delay the requirement that new cars be equipped with air bags or automatic seat belts. Each year of the delay saved the industry millions of dollars. But the price paid by consumers was high: According to the National Highway Traffic Safety Administration (NHTSA), driving with your seat belt on in a car with air bags cuts in half your chance of dying in a crash.

When the law finally required passive restraint systems in new vehicles, Chrysler became (in 1989) the first U.S. auto manufacturer to install driver-side air bags in all its new models. Only five years earlier, Chrysler chairman Lee Iacocca had boasted in his autobiography of fighting against air bags since their invention in the mid-1960s. In 1971, he and Henry Ford II (then the top executives at Ford) met secretly with President Richard Nixon to persuade him to kill a pending Department of Transportation regulation requiring air bags in every new car sold in the United States.[38]

Decades earlier, Alfred Sloan decided not to fit Chevrolets with safety glass, one of the most important safety protections ever, in order to save money. Even after Ford began doing so, Sloan insisted, "It's not my responsibility to sell safety glass."[39] Today, too, automakers often resist the introduction of new safety measures. For a long time, the auto industry denied that car passengers are at greater risk from pickups or SUVs than from automobiles despite the fact that in a collision those larger vehicles can easily slide over the doorsills and bumpers of autos and pierce deep into their passenger compartments. Only under pressure from the NHTSA did the industry agree that, as of 2009, all SUVs and pickups would be built either lower to the ground or with an energy-absorbing beam that fits under the front and rear bumpers. A study released by the Insurance Institute for Highway Safety shows that an SUV that complies with these standards is 18 to 21 percent less likely to kill the driver of a passenger car in a front-to-front collision and 47 to 48 percent less likely to do so in a front-to-side collision. "To cut somebody's risk of death in half, that's huge," says one auto safety expert. "That's almost as good as seat belts. You're lucky if a new regulation gets you a 5 to 10 percent reduction in the death rate."[40]

The story is similar when it comes to tire pressure monitoring systems and electronic stability control. Although they clearly save lives, auto manufactures did not make them standard equipment in their vehicles until forced to do so by the NHTSA (in 2009 and 2012, respectively). Anti-lock brakes also reduce traffic fatalities because they greatly improve a car's ability to stop short without skidding. Although the technology has been around for years, anti-lock brakes are still not standard on vehicles built in the United States. The same is true of side-curtain air bags.

As car buyers have become better informed, however, automobile manufacturers are rethinking Iacocca's old bromide "Safety doesn't sell." For example, twenty carmakers signed on to a voluntary pledge to equip at least 95 percent of their light vehicles with automatic emergency braking by 2024, and fifteen had already done so by late 2022.[41] But even if safety does sometimes sell, for an industry to wait for marketplace demand before increasing safety standards can be irresponsible. If society always waited for marketplace demand before insisting on public health and safety regulations, then pasteurization of milk and sprinkler systems to suppress fires in public places would still be "options."

The Responsibilities of Business

Simply obeying laws and regulations does not exhaust the moral responsibilities of business in the area of consumer safety. The CPSC, for example, has long required toy manufacturers to analyze their products for choking hazards, and it has banned toys that small children can easily choke on. By contrast, until a few years ago no agency conducted safety testing of, or otherwise regulated or monitored, candy for its potential to choke children—even though many more children were choking to death on candy, particularly little gel candies, than on toys—and other food items that pose a choking hazard for young children go completely unreviewed.[42] However, this regulatory asymmetry between toy manufacturers and candy manufacturers marked no significant difference in their moral obligations. Regardless of what the law does or doesn't require, candy manufacturers have as great a responsibility as toy manufacturers do to minimize choking deaths.

Summary
Regulations help ensure that business meets its responsibilities to consumers, although many products are not as closely regulated as people think and political considerations sometimes interfere with the regulatory process. Businesspeople tend to favor self-regulation and government deregulation, but—as the auto industry shows—this sometimes provides insufficient consumer protection.

When it comes to consumer safety, the moral responsibilities of business go beyond merely obeying the law.

When it comes to product safety, the exact nature of business's moral responsibilities is difficult to specify because much depends on the particular product or service being provided. But attending to the following points would go a long way in helping business behave morally with respect to consumer safety:

1. **Business should give safety the priority warranted by the product.** This injunction is important because businesses often base safety considerations strictly on cost. If the margin of safety can be increased without significantly insulting budgetary considerations, fine; if not, then safety questions are shelved.

   Cost can't be ignored, of course, but neither can two other factors. One is the seriousness of the injury the product can cause. A police officer may seldom have to rely on a bulletproof vest, but the potential harm from a defective one is obvious. Yet Second Chance Body Armor suppressed evidence of a defect in its product because company executives feared that it would hurt plans for an initial stock offering.[43] The second factor to consider is the frequency of occurrence. Is a design flaw on a lawn mower, for example, likely to result in one customer out of a thousand—or one out of 2 million—cutting off a finger? The higher a product scores on either the seriousness or the frequency test (or both), the greater is the priority that needs to be placed on safety issues.

2. **Business should abandon the misconception that accidents occur exclusively as a result of product misuse and that it's thereby absolved of all responsibility.** At one time such a belief may have been valid, but in using today's highly sophisticated products, even people who follow product instructions explicitly sometimes still suffer injuries. In any case, the point is that the company shares responsibility for product safety with the consumer. Rather than insisting that consumers' abuse of products leads to most accidents and injuries, firms would probably accomplish more by carefully pointing out how their products can be used safely.

   A Pennsylvania court has endorsed this perspective. It awarded $11.3 million in damages to a twenty-year-old Philadelphia woman who was shot in the head when a handgun owned by her neighbor accidentally went off. The court determined that the shop that had sold the weapon should pay 30 percent of the damages because it had provided the buyer with no demonstration or written instructions for safe use of the gun.[44]

   Both manufacturers and retailers have an obligation to try to anticipate and minimize the ways their products can cause harm, whether or not those products are misused. For example, in a classic case, a four-year-old girl was seriously injured when she stood on an oven door to peek into a pot on top of the stove and her weight caused the stove to tip over. A manufacturer can reasonably foresee that a cook might place a heavy roasting pan on the oven door. If doing so caused the stove to tip over, a court would almost certainly find the stove's design defective. But should the manufacturer have foreseen the use of the door not as a shelf but as a step stool? The courts ruled that it should have.

   In the case of guns, manufacturers could make them safer with safety locks or design changes that would make them difficult for children to operate. They could also crack down on distributors and dealers who repeatedly sell weapons that end up in the hands of criminals (the police give gun makers the serial numbers of any of their guns used in crimes). Instead, the manufacturers contend that they have no responsibility to prevent illegal trafficking in their guns. "It's not for us to enforce the law," says the president of Browning, the gun manufacturer.[45]

3. **Business must monitor the manufacturing process itself.** This holds true as well for large companies that outsource all or part of a product's production to independent contractors. Frequently, firms' failure to control key variables during the manufacturing process results in product defects. Companies should periodically review working conditions and the competence of key personnel. At the design stage of the process, they need to predict ways the product might fail and the consequences of such failure. For production, companies ordinarily can select materials that have been pretested or certified as flawless. If a company fails to do this, then we must question its commitment to safety. Similar questions arise

when companies do not make use of available research about product safety. To answer some questions, a company may have to generate its own research. However, independent research groups ensure impartial and disinterested analysis and are usually more reliable than in-house studies.

Testing should be rigorous and simulate the toughest conditions. Tests shouldn't assume that the product will be used in exactly the way the manufacturer intends it to be used. Even established products should be tested. Neither a trouble-free history nor governmental approval of a product guarantees that it's free of defects.[46]

When a product moves into production, it's often changed in various ways. These changes should be documented and referred to some appropriate party, such as a safety engineer, for analysis. The firm must be scrupulous about coordinating department activities so manufacturing specifications are not changed without determining any potential dangers related to these changes.

4. **When a product is ready to be marketed, companies should have their product safety staff review their market strategy and advertising for potential safety problems.** This step is necessary because both product positioning and advertising influence how a product is used, which in turn affects the likelihood of safety problems. For example, all-terrain vehicles (ATVs) are marketed in a way that appeals to young people, who have comparatively little driving experience and a propensity to take risks. Yet ATVs result in more injuries per vehicle than cars do, and they cause more deaths and injuries than snowmobiles or personal watercraft. Every year, around 25,000 children are injured, and 100 killed, riding ATVs.[47] Or consider the feeder auger manufacturer whose promotional brochure stated that "even a child can do your feeding." The brochure had a photograph of the auger with its safety cover removed to show the auger's inner workings. When a young boy was injured while using the feeder auger with the safety cover removed, a jury found the promotional brochure misleading with respect to operating conditions and product safety.[48]

5. **When a product reaches the marketplace, firms should make available to consumers written information about the product's performance.** This information should include operating instructions, the product's safety features, conditions that will cause the product to fail, a complete list of the ways the product can be used, and a cautionary list of the ways it should not be used. Warnings must be specific. But no matter how specific they are, warnings are of little value if a consumer can't read them. St. Joseph Aspirin for Children is marketed in Spanish-speaking areas and is advertised in Spanish-language media. But you have to know English to read the crucial warning: "Children and teenagers should not use this medicine for chicken pox or flu symptoms before a doctor is consulted about Reye's Syndrome, a rare but serious illness reported to be associated with aspirin." Because his mother spoke only Spanish and couldn't read the label on the St. Joseph's box, little Jorge Ramirez of Modesto, California, contracted Reye's Syndrome. Today, he is blind, quadriplegic, and intellectually impaired.[49]

6. **Companies should investigate consumer complaints and do so quickly.** Federal law requires that manufacturers report all claims of potentially hazardous defects within twenty-four hours, even if it's unclear whether a recall is warranted. However, in at least three major cases, Mattel took months to gather information on reports of potentially hazardous problems with certain of its toys, collecting scores of consumer complaints in the meantime, before disclosing the problems to the CPSC. Despite having been fined twice for "knowingly" withholding information regarding safety defects that "created an unreasonable risk of serious injury or death," the company contends that it's right for it to proceed at its own pace regardless of what the law says.[50]

It's important for business to acknowledge and discharge its various product-safety responsibilities. But even if firms attend seriously to the above considerations, they can't guarantee an absolutely safe product. Some products are inherently hazardous, and some safety problems may be unforeseeable. Morally speaking, however, no one's asking for an accident- and injury-proof product, only that manufacturers do everything reasonable to approach that ideal.

Summary
To increase product safety, companies need to (1) give safety the priority necessitated by the product, (2) abandon the misconception that accidents are solely the result of consumer misuse, (3) monitor closely the manufacturing process, (4) review the safety implications of their marketing and advertising strategies, (5) provide consumers with full information about product performance, and (6) promptly investigate consumer complaints. Some successful companies already put a premium on safety.

The automotive industry offers some examples. On a Montana road, the tread on the left rear tire of Joseph Cartus's classic sports car separated, causing the car to flip and leaving his girlfriend disfigured and with brain damage. The tire had only 4,000 miles on it, but it was eleven years old, and as the NHTSA has now documented, even pristine tires deteriorate with age and become prone to sudden failure. "The age issue is the tire industry's dirty little secret," says one safety expert. While tires do have a numeric code which contains the year that they were manufactured, and while more carmakers are acknowledging that tires should be replaced after six years regardless of their tread level, tires do not have an expiration date. Tire makers are reluctant to address the age problem because it would create havoc with their distribution systems. New tires often sit around for two years or more before being sold, and if they had "use by" dates on them, consumers would do what they do when buying milk or meat, namely, refuse to buy anything other than the freshest item.[51]

Or consider the advent of "self-driving" cars. Cars have had cruise control, which allows them to maintain a constant speed, for decades. Today, though, several carmakers are introducing technology that purportedly allows cars to stay in their lanes and even to navigate city streets without the driver's needing to do anything. Leading the pack in this regard is Tesla. Human drivers are prone to being distracted and careless, a problem only made worse by cell phones, so in principle taking humans out of the equation could make driving safer. However, there is at least reason for concern about whether this technology is being put into use prematurely. In roughly one year, from May 2022 to June 2023, eleven people died in car crashes in which Tesla's Autopilot mode was being used.[52] There are allegedly patterns of issues with Autopilot including cars slamming on their brakes for no reason and rear-ending parked emergency vehicles. Tesla is clear that drivers are still supposed to be engaged and attentive using Autopilot, ready to take over in case it "glitches," but it may be unrealistic to expect drivers on long highway treks in a car that is apparently driving itself to remain alert enough to take over control in an instant. Online one can find videos of drivers engaged in all sorts of activities, even sleeping, while their cars speed down the highway. It's possible that Autopilot is preventing more collisions than it's contributing to, but this claim is hard to assess.[53]

Unfortunately, there are numerous other examples of companies and entire industries that play fast and loose with safety, resisting product improvements and dodging responsibility for consumer injury. But many companies do respond quickly to perceived or suspected hazards. Consider two examples of successful companies that placed a premium on product safety.[54]

Although some businesses fail to take safety seriously enough, others respond quickly to suspected hazards.

JCPenney and Burning Radios

Back in the early 1960s, a few of the radios sold by JCPenney were reported to have caught fire in customers' homes. JCPenney tested the radios and discovered a defective resistor in a few of them—less than 1 percent. Nonetheless, JCPenney informed the manufacturer, withdrew the entire line of radios, ran national ads informing the public of the danger, and offered immediate refunds. "This was before the Consumer Product Safety Commission even existed," said JCPenney vice chairman Robert Gill. "I guess some people might have thought we were crazy, and said that liability insurance was specifically designed to take care of such problems. But we felt we just could not sell that kind of product."

Johnson Wax and Fluorocarbons

In the mid-1970s, environmentalists became seriously alarmed at the possibility that fluorocarbons released from aerosol cans were depleting the earth's thin and fragile ozone layer. The media rapidly picked up the story, but nearly all manufacturers of aerosol cans denounced the scientific findings and stood by their products. The exception was Johnson Wax. The company acknowledged that the scientific questions were difficult to resolve, but it took seriously consumer concern about ozone depletion. Years before the FDA ban, Johnson Wax withdrew all its fluorocarbon products worldwide. "We picked up a lot of flak from other manufacturers," recalled company chairman Samuel Johnson, "and we lost business in some areas, but I don't have any question we were right. . . . Our belief is that as long as you can make do without a potentially hazardous material, why not do without it?"

Other Areas of Business Responsibility

Consumers are naturally concerned about product safety. No one wants to be injured by the products he or she uses. But safety is far from the only interest of consumers. The past forty years have seen a general increase in consumer awareness and an ever stronger consumer advocacy movement. One critical consumer issue has been advertising and its possible abuse, which is discussed in subsequent sections of this chapter. Three other areas of business responsibility—product quality, pricing, and labeling and packaging—are equally important and are taken equally seriously by the consumer movement.

Product Quality

The demand for high-quality products is closely related to a number of themes mentioned in the discussion of safety. Most people would agree that business bears a general responsibility to ensure that the quality of a product measures up to the claims made about it and to reasonable consumer expectations. They would undoubtedly see this responsibility as deriving primarily from the consumer's basic right to get what he or she pays for. Although high product quality can also be in a company's interest, sometimes business shirks this responsibility. For example, in 1973 new car bumpers had to withstand a 5-mile-per-hour collision with no damage. Ten years later, the auto industry succeeded in getting this quality standard lowered: The speed was cut in half, and damage to the bumpers themselves was no longer taken into account.

One way that business assumes responsibilities to consumers for product quality and reliability is through *warranties*, which are obligations to purchasers that sellers assume. Broadly speaking, there are two kinds of warranties: express and implied. **Express warranties** are the claims that sellers explicitly state—for example, that a product is "shrinkproof" or will require no maintenance for two years. The moral concern, of course, is whether a product lives up to its billing. Express warranties include assertions about the product's character, assurances of product durability, and any statements about the product on warranty cards, labels, wrappers, and packages or in the advertising of the product. Many companies offer detailed warranties that are very specific about what defects they cover.

Implied warranties include the claim, implicit in any sale, that a product is fit for its ordinary, intended use. The law calls this the implied warranty of **merchantability**. It's not a promise that the product will be perfect; rather, it's a guarantee that it will be of passable quality or suitable for the ordinary purpose for which it's used. Implied warranties can also be more specific—for example, when the seller knows that a buyer has a particular purpose in mind and is relying on the seller's superior skill or judgment to furnish goods adequate for that purpose.

The concept of an implied warranty is relevant to the case of Kodak's instant cameras. When Polaroid won a patent violation judgment against Kodak, Kodak was forced not only to stop selling its instant cameras but also to compensate previous purchasers, who could no longer obtain film for their cameras. Those purchasers had relied on the implicit claim that Kodak would not suddenly make its products obsolete.[55]

With or without warranties, however, consumers today are more militant than ever in their insistence on product quality and on getting exactly what they paid for. For example, when Ira Gore learned that his new car had been damaged and repainted before he took delivery, he sued BMW for having reduced his car's value by $4,000 and sought **punitive damages** based on the fact that BMW had sold 983 such "refinished" cars over a ten-year period. ("Punitive" damages are sometimes awarded in civil lawsuits as a form of punishment when the defendant is found to have acted especially badly, such as when they intentionally caused harm or acted recklessly. These damages are on top of whatever compensation the plaintiff receives to "make them whole" for the harm that they suffered.) An Alabama jury agreed with Gore. It viewed the practice as consumer fraud and awarded him $4 million in punitive damages—not bad recompense for an injury to his car that it had cost BMW only $601.78 to fix. The Alabama Supreme Court subsequently cut the award in half, and later the U.S. Supreme Court ordered Alabama to lower it still further, holding that $2 million is "grossly excessive" punishment for the minor economic injury Gore had suffered.[56] Although the Court's precedent-setting ruling cheered many corporations, it left no doubt that punitive damages are appropriate in product-quality cases like this. The only question is whether they're excessive.

Pricing

Have you ever wondered why a product sells at three for $10.00 or is priced at $6.99 rather than simply $7.00? Or why a product that retails for $9.80 on Monday is selling for $11.10 on Friday? The answer may have little to do with the conventional determinants of product price such as overhead, operating expenses, and the costs of materials and labor. More and more frequently, purely psychological factors enter into the price-setting equation.

For example, why would a retailer price T-shirts at $9.88 instead of $9.99? "When people see $9.99, they say, 'That's $10,'" explains the general sales manager of one company. "But $9.88 isn't $10. It's just psychological."[57] In fact, two-thirds of items on retail shelves have prices ending in nine because they appear lower to consumers than do prices in round numbers. On the other hand, that appearance of cheapness can sometimes backfire, which is why an upscale restaurant will sell its almond-crusted sea bass for $38, not $37.89. Strangely, the tendency to see round numbers as higher than fractional numbers sometimes holds even when the round number is actually less. For example, in one study where subjects were asked to make fast decisions about numbers, they judged $510,000 to be slightly higher than $511,534 and $400,000 as considerably higher than $401,298—a result that seems to be born out in subsequent studies of real-estate transactions.[58]

For many consumers, higher prices mean better products, so manufacturers arbitrarily raise the price of a product to give the impression of superior quality or exclusivity. But as often as not, the price is higher than the product's extra quality. For example, a few years ago Proctor-Silex's most expensive fabric iron sold for $54.95, a price $5 higher than the company's next most expensive model. However, its wholesale price was only $2.78 more, and the extra cost of producing the top model was less than $1.[59]

Manufacturers trade on human psychology when they sell similar or even substantially identical products at different prices. For example, Williams-Sonoma once offered a fancy breadmaker for $279. When it introduced a $429 model, it flopped, but sales of the less expensive model doubled. Why? Because in comparison, the $279 model looked like a good deal. Sometimes, however, the effect works the other way.[60] Heublein once raised the price of its Popov brand vodka about 10 percent. Why the price increase? Heublein sales representatives believed that consumers wanted a variety of vodka prices to choose from. Apparently, they were right: Even though Popov lost 1 percent of its market share, it increased its profits by 30 percent. Applying its theory further, Heublein offers vodka-drinkers an even more expensive vodka: Smirnoff. Yet, analysts insist that there is no qualitative difference among vodkas made in the United States.[61] In this case, the use of psychological pricing is closely related to the problem of pricing branded products higher than generic products that are otherwise indistinguishable. Consumers pay more assuming that the brand name or the higher price implies a better product.

Manipulative Pricing

Sometimes consumers are misled by prices that obscure a product's true cost, for example, with "three-for-two" offers or when airlines omit the taxes and other fees that make apparently cheap tickets much more expensive or that advertise one-way fares that are available only with the purchase of a round-trip ticket. Other times, hidden charges and surcharges, such as online booking charges and other stealth fees, can boost the consumer's actual cost significantly above the announced price: for example, charges for mounting and balancing when you buy tires; multiple taxes and services fees on cell-phone plans; "visitor" taxes and collision insurance on rental cars; "convenience" charges, processing fees, and shipping charges on concert tickets; and activation fees, monthly fees, inactivity fees, ATM withdrawal fees, and inquiry balance fees on prepaid debit cards. In addition, manufacturers often disguise price increases by reducing the quality or the quantity of the product—downsizing a "pound" of coffee to 13 ounces, for example, or shrinking a candy bar but not its price.

Promotional pricing can also be manipulative. Discount cards and "card specials" lure consumers into grocery stores such as Dominick's, Kroger, and Safeway, where customers often pay more for their food overall than they would at rival stores.[62] Sale-priced items have ballooned from 8 percent of U.S. retail sales in 1971 to as high as 78 percent in some sectors.[63] Although the discounts are deeper than ever these days, the initial mark-up has increased. Indeed, the product is often designed with the discount built in. This works, it seems, because buyers have little idea what goods are really worth, but they like feeling that they got a deal. Take a real example, provided by an industry consultant. A major retailer pays a supplier $14.50 for a sweater. It comes with a suggested retail price of $50. Although the retailer sells a few sweaters at that price, more sell at the first markdown price of $44.00, and the bulk sell at the final discount price of $21.99. All this is according to plan, with an average retail price of around $28 per sweater and a healthy profit margin for the retailer.[64]

Rebates, too, are a type of manipulative pricing. Most consumers dislike them. Satisfying the redemption rules and mailing them in are hassles. Sometimes the rebates are arbitrarily denied, and even when they're not, it usually takes weeks and weeks to receive the check. When a long-forgotten check does arrive, consumers sometimes toss it in the trash because it looks like junk mail. Companies love them, though. Rebates get consumers to focus on the discounted price of a product and then buy it at full price. And then, as one consultant explains, "anything less than 100 percent redemption is free money" for the company. With millions of rebates offered every year, that translates into more than $2 billion of extra revenue for retailers and their suppliers. Small wonder then that many consumers—and some state and federal authorities—suspect that companies design the rules to keep redemption rates down.[65]

A study of vacuum cleaner prices on Amazon.com uncovered a different sort of manipulative pricing. The prices on several different models were temporarily increased. During the period that the price was higher, the item listing would also include a "list price" that was even higher than the new selling price, creating the appearance that the vacuum was being discounted. When the price returned to its previous level, the list price would be removed from the listing.[66]

Some cases of manipulative pricing are not so obvious. For example, the pharmaceutical company Cephalon repeatedly raised the price of its popular narcolepsy drug Provigil to get patients and insurance companies to switch to a longer-acting version of it, called Nuvigil. That's because Cephalon's patent on Provigil was set to expire, after which the drug would face stiff competition from generic equivalents. Before that happened, the company wanted to make sure that Provigil users were taking Nuvigil instead because its patent—and the high profits that go with it—was still good for years to come.[67]

Many practical consumers think of these pricing practices and gimmicks as a nuisance or irritant that they must live with, not as something morally objectionable. But tricky or manipulative pricing does raise moral questions—not least about business's view of itself and its role in the community—that businesspeople and ethical theorists are now beginning to take seriously.

Tricky or manipulative pricing is not just a nuisance; it also raises moral questions.

Price Fixing

Much more attention has been devoted to price fixing, which despite its prevalence is widely recognized as a violation of the rules of the game in a market system whose ideal is open and fair price competition. **Horizontal price fixing** occurs when competitors agree to adhere to a set price schedule, not to cut prices below a certain minimum, or to restrict price advertising or the terms of sales, discounts, or rebates. For example, in 2012 three major publishers were found guilty of collusion in the pricing of e-books, and in 2013 Japanese and American officials uncovered more than a dozen separate price-fixing conspiracies among manufacturers of the auto parts sold to U.S. car makers, affecting more than 25 million vehicles over the years.[68] There is nothing illegal about businesses consciously charging the same prices as their competitors. It's the agreement to do so that violates the law.

Vertical price fixing takes place when manufactures and retailers—as opposed to direct competitors—agree to set prices. For example, a federal judge found Toys 'R Us guilty of conspiring to keep prices for Barbie, Mr. Potato Head, and other popular toys artificially high. The retail giant used its market clout to force Mattel, Hasbro, and other major toymakers

Summary
Business has obligations
to consumers that
go beyond safety:
Product quality must
live up to express and
implied warranties, and
prices should be fair.
In particular, business
should refrain from price
fixing, price gouging, and
manipulative pricing. In
assessing a particular
pricing practice, we
should ask whether it
would be good for our
socioeconomic system
as a whole if it were
widespread or generally
followed.

not to sell their toys to warehouse clubs like Sam's Club and Costco.[69] Sometimes it's the manufacturer, not the retailer, that engages in vertical price fixing. For example, Panasonic was found guilty of pressuring retailers such as Circuit City, Kmart, and Montgomery Ward into selling its products at the company's suggested retail price and not at a discount. Although manufacturers often suggest prices to their retailers, the retailers are supposed to be free to set their own prices, depending on the profit they foresee in the market.

Before 2007, any agreement between a manufacturer and a retailer to fix prices was illegal. That's when the U.S. Supreme Court reversed a 100-year-old precedent and held that minimum-retail-price agreements do not automatically violate the Sherman Antitrust Act.[70] In fact, some "resale price maintenance" agreements, the Court held, might even promote competition. It therefore instructed lower courts to adopt a case-by-case approach, forcing them to specify when such agreements unfairly disadvantage consumers and, more generally, when and why such price fixing is wrong. In response to the Court's decision, in 2009 Maryland passed a law that prohibits manufacturers from requiring retailers to charge minimum prices for their goods. Some other states are likely to do the same. In the meantime, small companies have sprung up that scour the web on behalf of clients such as Sony, Samsung, and Black & Decker, looking for retailers who are offering bargains below the minimum price set by the manufacturer. If the discounter is an authorized dealer, it's contractually bound to raise its price. If the seller is not an authorized dealer, other tactics are used, such as threatening people selling the product on eBay with trademark or copyright infringement.[71]

Horizontal price fixing, however, remains unambiguously outside the law. And it's easy to see why. When a handful of companies dominate a given market and conspire to charge artificially high prices, this clearly disadvantages consumers and subverts the principles of a market system. "It's tempting to see it as victimless because each customer is hurt only a little," says Mark Whitacre. "But it's bank robbery without a mask and gun." He knows what he is talking about, too, having blown the whistle on a global conspiracy to fix the price of lysine, an animal-feed additive (an episode that inspired the 2009 film, *The Informant!*).[72]

Of course, firms in an oligopolistic industry can tacitly agree not to compete with one another, thereby avoiding losses that might result from price-cutting competition. They can then play "follow the leader": Let the lead firm in the market raise its prices, and then the rest follow suit. The result is a laundered form of price fixing. Even when there is no tacit price fixing, the firms that dominate a field are often reluctant to compete on the basis of price. Nobody, they say to themselves, wants a price war, as if price competition were a threat to the market system rather than its lifeblood. Thus, familiar rivals such as Pepsi and Coca-Cola or McDonald's and Burger King usually prefer to compete by means of image and jingles rather than price.

Price Gouging

From the moral point of view, prices, like wages, should be just or fair. Merchants can't morally charge whatever they want or whatever they think the market will bear any more than employers can pay workers whatever they (the employers) wish or can get away with. In particular, price gouging is widely viewed as unethical, although what exactly constitutes price gouging is often debated.[73] Some define it as charging what the market will bear regardless of production costs. But that definition doesn't take into account supply and demand. Because they're in short supply, tickets for the World Series or houses in a popular neighborhood may command an extremely high price relative to their production costs, yet this does not constitute price gouging. **Price gouging** is better understood as a seller's exploiting a short-term situation in which buyers have few purchase options for a much-needed product by raising prices substantially. New York hotels that doubled or tripled their prices in the aftermath of the September 11, 2001, attacks engaged in this, as did oil companies, innkeepers, and merchants who took advantage of Hurricane Katrina to jack up their prices. Some jurisdictions make it illegal for retailers to raise their prices during a natural disaster or other emergency.

However, the morality or immorality of some instances of possible gouging seems open to debate. When Hurricane Fran hit Raleigh, North Carolina in 1996, residents lost power. Four men from a town outside of the hurricane zone bought many bags of ice for $1.70 per bag and

Although price gouging
is generally viewed
as unethical, there is
disagreement about what it
is and whether all instances
of it are wrong.

In May 2008, American Airlines, one of the industry's major carriers, started imposing a checked-bag fee. Other airlines promptly followed suit. What are consumers to think when a pricing policy instituted by one company is promptly adopted by others?

drove it to Raleigh, where they sold it for $7 per bag. Apparently, they had no trouble finding takers: plenty of people in Raleigh preferred paying $7 for a bag of ice to letting their food spoil. It might have been more noble for them to sell the ice for $1.70, or perhaps for just a little more (to cover transportation expenses). However, these four men would probably not have seen this as worthwhile. They had no more responsibility to help the people of Raleigh than anyone else; no one would have batted an eye had they simply stayed at home. They were only willing to rush ice to Raleigh for the prospect of a large profit. If you lived in Raleigh, which would you prefer: (1) to have a law against price gouging and no ice, or (2) the chance to buy a few $7 bags of ice and save food worth much more? (As it happened, the men were in fact arrested for price gouging. Much of the ice may have melted.) From a utilitarian standpoint, at least, an absolute bar on raising prices in response to emergencies may be hard to defend, since these price increases can motivate people to supply more of goods that are badly needed and to use these goods more efficiently—wasting less and thus leaving more for others.[74]

When a gas station raises the price of its current stock of gasoline because the wholesale price is scheduled to go up or when the big oil companies set the wholesale price of gasoline 10 to 19 cents a gallon higher in San Francisco than in Los Angeles because average household income is greater there,[75] that may not fit the definition of price gouging, but it strikes many people as unfair. So does the fact that Americans have to pay substantially more for medicines than do Canadians or Europeans. This is not a matter of cheap generics or illegal knockoffs. Brand-name drugs such as Lipitor, Zoloft, and Nexium cost 30 to 100 percent more in the United States than in Canada or Europe.[76]

Seventy-five days after initially introducing its iPhone, Apple decided to cut its price by $200. That might have sounded like good news for consumers, but it ignited loud protests from some of Apple's most devoted fans. That's because many of them had stood in long lines to purchase theirs and now felt like chumps. Maybe they weren't victims of price gouging in the traditional sense, but they believed they'd been exploited and they quickly let Steve Jobs hear about it. As a result, he apologized and issued early buyers a store credit for $100. That move was unprecedented, but it still left some of them unhappy. After all, a store credit is not the same as cash, and given the new, reduced price, Apple was still coming out $100 ahead.

In the end, the question "What is a fair price?" probably defies a precise answer. Still, one can approach an answer by assessing the factors on which the price is based and the process used to determine it. Certainly, factors such as the costs of material and production, operating and marketing expenses, and profit margin are relevant to price setting. One can also ask whether a seller's pricing practices try to exploit buyers by taking advantage of a lack of competition or some other buyer vulnerability or in some other way treat people as means rather than respecting them as ends in themselves. For instance, when it's unfair for sellers to take advantage of the fact that most people are prone to certain sorts of mistakes in their reasoning—what Sarah Conly calls "glitches." Also relevant is whether it would be good for our socioeconomic system as a whole if a particular pricing practice were widespread or generally followed.

Product price, of course, reflects in part the consuming public's judgment of the relative value of the article. Ideally, this judgment is formed in the open market in a free interplay between sellers and buyers. However, for this process to function satisfactorily, buyers must be in a position to exercise informed consent. As will be discussed further in Chapter 9, informed consent calls for deliberation and free choice, which require in turn that buyers understand all significant relevant facts about the goods and services they're purchasing. But consumers do not always receive the clear, accurate, and complete information about product quality and price that they need to make prudent choices.

Labeling and Packaging

Business's general responsibility to provide clear, accurate, and adequate product information undoubtedly applies to labeling and packaging. The reason is that, despite the billions of dollars spent annually on advertising, a product's label and package remain the consumer's primary source of product information. Often, however, labels and packages do not tell consumers what they need to know, or even what exactly they're getting. For example, many high-energy drinks do not list their caffeine content, and few cigarette cartons tell consumers which of the nearly 600 additives that manufacturers sometimes use have been added to their cigarettes. In other cases, the information supplied is exaggerated or inaccurate, as with the fuel-economy claims of some automobile makers.[77]

> Product labels and packages often fail to tell consumers what they need to know or even exactly what they're getting.

What information do consumers need to know? For instance, U.S. meatpackers have long opposed any regulations requiring country-of-origin labeling of beef, chicken, pork, and other meats. They argue that it's expensive and that the information is irrelevant. But many consumers prefer to buy meat from American ranches. Even more controversial is whether genetically modified (GM) food should be labeled as such. GM food is much more pervasive than most people realize. Food manufacturers contend that GM foods are indistinguishable from unaltered foods and pose absolutely no health risks. In their view, labeling them would only cause consumers unnecessary alarm. They think labeling should be required only when some health risk exists or there's a danger that the consumer might be misled about the product's characteristics. In contrast, some proponents of labeling call GM products "Frankenfood" and blame it, without any real evidence, for all sorts of ills. Others, however, favor labeling because they believe that consumers have a right to whatever information a significant number of them are interested in, whether it's rational or not for them to care about it.

Even when product labels provide pertinent information, they're often difficult to understand or even misleading, and what they omit may be more important than what they say. For example, organic milk often comes from cows that are not on pasture, and products that bear the label "organic" or "USDA organic" are not necessarily 100 percent organic but may contain the same kind of synthetics that conventional food processors use.[78] One-third of the fresh chicken sold in the United States is "plumped" with water, salt, and sometimes a seaweed extract called carrageenan that helps it retain the added water. Although chickens processed this way contain up to eight times as much sodium per serving, they're still labeled "all natural" or "100% natural." That's because water, salt, and carrageenan are natural ingredients, even though they're not naturally found in chicken.[79]

The FDA has no formal definition of "natural." To its credit, though, Ben & Jerry's has dropped the phrase "all natural" from its labels, after a health advocacy group complained that its ice cream contains alkalized cocoa, corn syrup, hydrogenated oil, and other ingredients that aren't natural. Equally confusing is environmental labeling. Manufacturers label products "biodegradable," "green," "environmentally safe," or "recyclable" without defining those terms or providing any scientific evidence to back them up. As environmental awareness has grown, so has the prevalence of "greenwashing"—the making of false or misleading environmental claims—by marketers.[80] And even the most socially and environmentally conscious consumers have difficulty distinguishing among "fair trade certified," "fairly traded," "Rainforest Alliance certified," "sustainable," and "certified sustainable." The label "Made in USA" is also ambiguous. The FTC says the label can go on goods that are "all or virtually all" made domestically, but it doesn't define "virtually." Some companies take it to mean that if 70 percent or more of the value of a product is made domestically, then it's American. California law, on the other hand, holds that if even one screw in a larger product is foreign made, then it's false advertising to say that it's U.S. made.[81]

The FDA's labeling requirements now oblige manufacturers of packaged foods to provide nutritional information that is clear, specific, and of benefit to health-conscious consumers, and the FDA has cracked down on grain and vegetable cooking oils that label themselves "cholesterol free." (Although it's true that only animal products or by-products contain cholesterol, cooking oils are often replete with saturated vegetable fats and hydrogenated oils, which the body converts into cholesterol.) The FDA also went after Procter & Gamble for labeling as "pure, squeezed, 100% orange juice" processed orange juice that is made from water, concentrated orange juice, pulp, and "orange essence." But Atkins-brand packaged foods continue to label items as "low-carb" because they're low in what Atkins calls "net carbs," even though their total carbohydrate count may be much higher. (The company's plain bagels, for example, contain only 7 grams worth of "net carbs" but 18 grams of "total carbs" while its blueberry muffins weigh in at 4 grams of "net" but 21 grams of "total" carbohydrates.)[82] In addition, companies frequently put serving sizes on their labels that are misleading because they're far smaller than the amount a typical consumer would eat or drink.

Labels can fool consumers in various ways. For example, the label on Aquafina, the bottled water, creates the false impression that its water comes from a mountain stream, and Gerber's Fruit Juice Snacks is packaged with images of a various fruits that the product does not contain. A particularly blatant example of label abuse was Sebastiani Vineyards' wine product, Domaine Chardonnay. "Chardonnay" has a high level of name recognition and a positive reputation among wine consumers. Unfortunately for them, however, there wasn't a drop of Chardonnay in Domaine Chardonnay, which was a blend of chenin blanc, sauvignon blanc, French Colombard, Riesling, and other grapes. After a public outcry when the wine was introduced, the Bureau of Alcohol, Tobacco, and Firearms required the company to redesign its label so that "Domaine Chardonnay" was in smaller letters at the bottom. Many people, however, felt that letting Sebastiani use the name of a grape varietal as a brand name was a travesty of labeling law when there was no Chardonnay in the bottle.

The question of misleading labels takes an interesting twist in the case of companies that choose to omit their corporate logo from products. For example, a brand called Cascadian Farm sells organic breakfast cereal, but from looking at the box you can't tell that it's actually made by General Mills. That's because General Mills is aiming the cereal at buyers who tend to eschew the brands of the big conglomerates. Similarly, you can't guess from reading the label of Blue Moon beer that it comes from Coors Brewing Company. This practice is spreading as big food and drink makers buy up the little brands that populate organic food stores or create their own "natural" products and boutique brands.

Food that doesn't come in packages can be labeled in misleading or confusing ways, too. For example, restaurants and steakhouses frequently describe their steaks as "prime" even though they're not "USDA prime beef," a label that designates the gold standard in beef and that inspectors award to only 3 percent of cattle carcasses (55 percent are graded "choice" and 42 percent "select" or below). As Wayne Schick, executive corporate chef for Columbus Mitchell Restaurants, which owns steakhouses in Michigan and Ohio, explains, "Prime is not the same as saying USDA prime. We're using it to mean superb, great, prime, premium, all of those things." He adds, "I agree it is confusing."[83]

Summary
Business also has a responsibility to provide product information that is accurate, clear, and understandable and that suffices to meet the needs of consumers. Product labels frequently fail to do this. Package shape, package terms, and quantity surcharges also sometimes mislead shoppers.

In addition to misleading labels, package shape can trick consumers by exploiting certain optical illusions. Tall and narrow cereal boxes look larger than short, squat ones that actually contain more cereal; shampoo bottles often have pinched waists to give the illusion of quantity; and canned fruits are packed in large quantities of syrup. Package terms such as *large*, *extra large*, *jumbo*, *economy size*, and *value pack* frequently confuse or mislead shoppers about what they're buying and how good a deal they're getting—especially when companies camouflage price increases by selling their products in packages that contain less than they used to.[84] Even when unit pricing allows shoppers to compare the relative prices of items, time-pressed buyers often err anyway.

This is part of the explanation of why many retailers are able to sell "economy size" items for a higher per-unit price than their smaller counterparts. Although consumers frequently compare prices between brands, they generally neglect to make intra-brand comparisons because they take it for granted that the larger the volume, the better the deal. "You assume 'bigger' is a better deal," says Tom Pirko, president of a beverage and food consulting company, "and that gives marketers an open door to take advantage of people."[85] These **quantity surcharges** are a much more widespread phenomenon than most people realize. They even crop up in online shopping, too, despite the fact that people shopping online have ready access to a calculator. One study found that between 15 and 20 percent of items for sale on Amazon.com exhibited quantity surcharges, especially those for common household items like coffee filters and pens.[86] Because quantity surcharges exploit a common consumer error, the practice raises at least two moral questions: Can it be justified as a conscious pricing policy, and can retailers ethically remain silent about its existence?

> Moral conduct in this area begins with a determination to provide consumers with what they need to know to make informed product choices.

In general, the moral issues involved in packaging and labeling, as in marketing as a whole, relate primarily to truth telling and consumer exploitation. Sound moral conduct in this area must rest on a strong desire to provide consumers with clear and usable information about the price, quality, and quantity of a product so that they can make intelligent comparisons and choices.

• • •

The Ethics of Advertising

We tend to take advertising for granted, yet its social and economic significance is difficult to exaggerate. Ads dominate our environment. Famous ones become part of our culture; their jingles dance in our heads, and their images haunt our dreams and shape our tastes. Advertising is also big business. Amazon spent over $13 billion in advertising in 2022, Comcast over $6 billion, and Procter & Gamble and Disney both over $5 billion.[87] Each of these corporations spent roughly half of its advertising budget on ads in traditional media like television and printed publications. The rest was spent on digital advertising.

When people are asked what advertising does, their first thought is often that it provides consumers with information about goods and services. In fact, advertising conveys very little information. Nor are most ads intended to do so. Except for classified ads, postings on eBay or Craig's List, and newspaper ads that give supermarket prices, very few advertisements offer any information of genuine use to the consumer. (Those wanting detailed product information must go to a magazine like *Consumer Reports*, which publishes objective and comparative studies of various products.) Instead, advertisements offer us jingles, rhymes, and attractive images.

The goal of advertising, of course, is to persuade us to buy the products that are being touted. Providing objective and comparative product information may be one way to do that, but it's not the only way, and judging from ads these days—which frequently say nothing at all about the product's qualities—it's not a very common way. The similarity among many competing products may be the explanation. One writer identifies the effort to distinguish among basically identical products as the "ethical, as well as economic, crux of the [advertising] industry"; another refers to it as the "persistent, underlying bad faith" of much American advertising.[88]

Deceptive Techniques

Because advertisers are trying to persuade people to buy their products and because straight product information is not necessarily the best way to do that, there is a natural temptation to obfuscate, misrepresent, or even lie. In an attempt to persuade, advertisers are prone to exploit ambiguity, conceal facts, exaggerate, and use psychological appeals.

Ambiguity

Ads that are ambiguous—that can be understood in two or more ways—can be deceiving. Continental Baking Company was charged with such **ambiguity** by the Federal Trade Commission (FTC). In ads for its Profile bread, Continental implied that eating the bread would lead to weight loss, and a large number of people interpreted the ad to mean that eating Profile bread really would cause them to lose weight. The fact was that Profile had about the same number of calories per ounce as other breads. However, because Profile was sliced thinner than most other breads, each slice contained seven fewer calories.

Likewise, for years consumers inferred from advertisements that Listerine mouthwash effectively fought bacteria and sore throats. Not so. Accordingly, the FTC ordered Listerine to run a multimillion-dollar disclaimer. And when Sara Lee began promoting its Light Classics desserts, the implicit message was that "light" meant the products contained fewer calories than other Sara Lee desserts. When pressed by investigators to support this implied claim, Sara Lee contended that "light" referred only to the texture of the product. In such cases, advertisers and manufacturers invariably deny that they intended consumers to draw false inferences, but sometimes the ambiguity is such that a reasonable person wouldn't infer anything else.

Aiding and abetting ambiguity is the use of **weasel words** to evade or retreat from a direct or forthright statement. Consider the weasel word *help*. Help means "aid" or "assist" and nothing else. Yet as one author has observed, "'help' is the one single word which, in all the annals of advertising, has done the most to say something that couldn't be said."[89] Because the word *help* is used to qualify, almost anything can be said after it. Thus, we're exposed to ads for products that "help keep us young," "help prevent cavities," and "help keep our houses germ-free." Consider for a moment how many times a day you hear or read phrases like these: helps stop, helps prevent, helps fight, helps overcome, helps you feel, and helps you look. And, of course, *help* is hardly the only weasel word. *Like, virtual* or *virtually, can be, up to* (as in "provides relief up to eight hours"), *as much as* (as in "saves as much as one gallon of gas"), and numerous other weasel words are used to imply what can't be said. Sometimes weasel words deprive the message of any meaning whatsoever, as when *up to* and *more* come together in "save up to 40 to 50 percent and more."

The fact that ads are open to interpretation doesn't exonerate advertisers from the obligation to provide clear information. Indeed, this fact intensifies their responsibility, because the more an ad is subject to interpretation the greater the danger that it will mislead consumers through ambiguity. Misleading ads exploit consumers, damaging their interests and costing them money, and they display a cavalier disregard for the truth. For these reasons ambiguity in ads is of serious moral concern.

Concealment of Facts

Advertisers who conceal facts suppress information that is unflattering to their products. They neglect to mention or they distract consumers' attention away from information, knowledge of which would probably make their products less desirable.

Shell resorted to **concealment of facts** when it advertised that its gasoline had "platformate" but neglected to mention that all other brands did too. Similarly, subway ads for the Bowery Bank in New York touted the fact that it's "federally insured," but so is almost every bank in the country. When peanut butter makers advertise their products as cholesterol free, they omit the fact that only animal products contain cholesterol and that peanut butter is rich in fat. Weight Watchers tells consumers that its frozen meals are without butter, chicken fat, or tropical oils but not that they're high in salt.

Because providing frank product information is not always the most effective way to sell something, advertisers are tempted to misrepresent and deceive.

Misleading ads exploit consumers and play fast and loose with the truth.

Likewise, advertisements for painkillers routinely conceal relevant information. For years, Bayer aspirin advertised that it contained "the ingredient that doctors recommend most." What was that ingredient? Aspirin. The advertising claim that "last year hospitals dispensed ten times as much Tylenol as the next four brands combined" does not disclose the fact that Johnson & Johnson supplies hospitals with Tylenol at a cost well below what consumers pay. Interestingly, American Home Products sued Johnson & Johnson on the grounds that the Tylenol ad falsely implies that it's more effective than competing products. But at the same time, American Home Products was advertising its Anacin-3 by claiming that "hospitals recommended acetaminophen, the aspirin-free pain reliever in Anacin-3, more than any other pain reliever"—without telling consumers that the acetaminophen hospitals recommend is, in fact, Tylenol.

Concealment of information occurs in a different way when newspaper or magazine advertisements are made to resemble editorials or news stories.[90] But however it takes place, concealment of pertinent facts can exploit people by misleading them; it also undermines truth telling. Unfortunately, truth rarely seems foremost in the minds of advertisers. For example, Coors continued to advertise its beer as brewed from "Rocky Mountain spring water" even after it opened plants outside Colorado that use local water. And Perrier advertised its bottled water as having bubbled up from underground springs decades after it had begun pumping the water up from the ground through a pipe and combining it with processed gas.

As one advertising-industry insider writes: "Inside the agency the basic approach is hardly conducive to truth telling. The usual thinking in forming a campaign is first what can we say, true or not, that will sell the product best? The second consideration is, how can we say it effectively and get away with it so that (1) people who buy won't feel let down by too big a promise that doesn't come true, and (2) the ads will avoid quick and certain censure by the FTC."[91] This observation shows the common tendency to equate what's legal with what's moral. It's precisely this outlook that leads to advertising behavior of dubious morality.

Examples of ads that conceal important facts are legion. A few years ago, ads for Campbell's vegetable soup showed pictures of a thick, rich brew calculated to whet even a gourmet's appetite. What the ads didn't show were clear glass marbles deposited in that bowl to give the soup the appearance of solidity. Similarly, a television ad for Volvo showed a row of cars being crushed by a big wheel truck, with only a Volvo remaining intact. What the ad neglected to say was that the Volvo had been reinforced and the other cars weakened. Ads run in travel magazines to encourage Americans to vacation in Bermuda have pictured people swimming or diving or sunning themselves on the beach—in Hawaii!

If business has an obligation to provide clear, accurate, and adequate information, we must wonder if it meets that charge when it hides facts germane to the consumer's purchase of a product. Concealing information raises serious moral concerns relative to truth telling and consumer exploitation. When consumers are deprived of relevant knowledge about a product, their choices are constricted and distorted.

If pushed further, the moral demand for full information challenges almost all advertising. Even the best advertisements never point out the negative features of their products or concede that there is no substantive difference between the product being advertised and its competitors, as is often the case. In this sense, they could be accused of concealing relevant information. Most advertisers would be shocked at the suggestion that honesty requires an objective presentation of the pros and cons of their products, and in fact consumers don't expect advertisers or salespeople to be impartial. Nevertheless, it's not clear why this moral value should not be relevant to assessing advertising. And it should be noted that retail salespeople, despite a sometimes negative reputation, often do approach this level of candor—at least when they're fortunate enough to sell a genuinely good and competitive product or when they do not work on commission.

In a broad sense, almost all advertising is vulnerable to the moral complaint that it conceals relevant information.

Exaggeration

Advertisers can mislead through **exaggeration**—that is, by making claims unsupported by evidence. Manufacturers of vitamins and other dietary supplements, such as Airborne, are notorious for exaggerating the possible benefits of their products. Some drug companies do the same. Ads for Propecia tell men, "Starting today, you need not face the fear of more hair loss."

But while Propecia can slow hair loss, it doesn't necessarily stop it. Similarly, the FDA found General Mills guilty of exaggerating the health benefits of eating Cheerios, which the company claimed "can lower your cholesterol by 4 percent." Nabisco's advertising of its 100 percent bran cereal as being "flavored with two naturally sweet fruit juices" is typical of exaggerated product claims. Although fig juice and prune juice have indeed been added to the product, they're its least significant ingredients in terms of weight; the primary sweetener is sugar. As in this case, exaggeration often goes hand-in-hand with concealed information. Until stopped by legal action, General Electric advertised its 90-watt Energy Choice bulb as an energy-saving replacement for a conventional 100-watt bulb. But there is nothing special about the GE bulb; it simply produces fewer lumens than a 100-watt bulb.

The line between such deliberate deception and puffery is not always clear. **Puffery** is the supposedly harmless use of superlatives and subjective praise in advertisements. Thus, advertisers frequently boast of the merits of their products by using words such as *best*, *finest*, or *most*, or phrases and slogans like *king of beers*, *breakfast of champions*, or *the ultimate driving machine*. In most instances, puffery appears innocuous, but sometimes it's downright misleading, as in the Dial soap ad that claimed Dial was "the most effective deodorant soap you can buy." When asked to substantiate that claim, the Armour-Dial company insisted that it was not claiming product superiority; all it meant was that Dial soap was as effective as any other soap.

The law permits puffery on the grounds that it doesn't deceive people. University of Wisconsin professor Ivan L. Preston, however, argues that puffery shouldn't be immune from regulation. Why? Because the public is often taken in by it. Consider the following pieces of puffery: "State Farm is all you need to know about life insurance," "Ford has a better idea," and "It's the real thing [Coca-Cola]." Although these statements may seem like meaningless verbal posturing, in one survey 22 percent of those sampled thought the first claim was "completely true" while 36 percent considered it "partly true." The second claim was judged "completely true" by 26 percent and "partly true" by 42 percent while 35 percent believed the third claim was "completely true" and 29 percent "partly true."[92] Moreover, argues Preston, if puffery didn't work, salespeople and advertisers wouldn't use it.[93]

> Although people are often taken in by puffery, the law permits it.

Psychological Appeals

A **psychological appeal** is a persuasive effort aimed primarily at emotion, not reason. This is potentially the advertising technique of greatest moral concern. An automobile ad that presents the product surrounded by people who look wealthy and successful taps into our need and desire for status. A life insurance ad that portrays a destitute family struggling in the aftermath of a provider's death tries to persuade through pity and fear. Reliance on such appeals is not automatically unethical, but it raises moral concerns because rarely do the products fully deliver what the ads promise.

Ads that rely extensively on pitches to power, prestige, sex, masculinity, femininity, acceptance, approval, and the like aim to sell more than a product. They're peddling psychological satisfaction. Perhaps the best example is the pervasive use of sexual pitches in ads:

Scene:	An artist's skylight studio.
	A young man lies nude, the bedsheets in disarray.
	He awakens to find a tender note on his pillow.
	The phone rings and he gets up to answer it.
Woman's voice:	You snore.
Artist (smiling):	And you always steal the covers.

More cozy patter between the two. Then a husky-voiced announcer intones: "Paco Rabanne. A cologne for men. What is remembered is up to you."

Some students of marketing claim that ads like these appeal to the subconscious mind of both marketer and consumer. Purdue University psychologist and marketing consultant Jacob Jacoby contends that marketers, like everyone else, carry around in their subconscious

Summary
Advertising tries to
persuade people
to buy products.
Because straight
product information is
not always the most
effective way to do this,
there is a temptation to
misrepresent. Ambiguity,
concealment of relevant
facts, exaggeration, and
psychological appeals
are among the morally
dubious techniques that
advertisers use.

sexual symbols that, intentionally or not, they use in ads. A case in point: the Newport cigarette "Alive with Pleasure" campaign. One campaign ad featured a woman riding the handlebars of a bicycle driven by a man. The main strut of the bike wheel stands vertically beneath her body. In Jacoby's view, such symbolism needs no interpretation.

Author Wilson Bryan Key, who has extensively researched the topic of subconscious marketing appeals, claims that many ads carry subliminal messages. **Subliminal advertising** is advertising that communicates at a level beneath conscious awareness, where, some psychologists claim, the vast reservoir of human motivation primarily resides. Most marketing experts deny that such advertising occurs or that ads with hidden messages can work. Key disagrees. Indeed, he goes so far as to claim: "It's virtually impossible to pick up a newspaper or magazine, turn on a radio or television set, read a promotional pamphlet or the telephone book, or shop through a supermarket without having your subconscious purposely massaged by some monstrously clever artist, photographer, writer, or technician."[94]

Concern with the serious nature of psychological appeals appears to have motivated the California Wine Institute to adopt an advertising code of standards.[95] The following restrictions are included:

> Wine advertising shall in no way suggest that wine be used in connection with operating motorized vehicles such as automobiles, motorcycles, boats, snowmobiles, or airplanes or any activities that require a high degree of alertness or physical coordination.

> [W]ine advertising shall not be placed in media with substantial underage appeal and shall not … [b]e placed on the premises of college and university campuses or in newspapers published by, or primarily for, a college or university.

> Wine advertising shall not degrade, demean, or objectify the human form, image or status of women, men, or of any ethnic, minority, religious or other group or sexual orientation. Advertising shall not exploit the human form, or feature sexually provocative images.

In adopting such a rigorous code of advertising ethics, the California Wine Institute rightly acknowledged the subtle implications and psychological nuances that affect the message that an ad communicates.

The Federal Trade Commission's Role

The **Federal Trade Commission (FTC)** was originally created in 1914 as an anti-trust weapon, but its mandate was expanded to include protecting consumers against deceptive advertising and fraudulent commercial practices. Although the FTC is not the only regulatory body monitoring advertisements, it's mainly thanks to the FTC that today we are spared the most blatant abuses of advertising.

One important question running through the FTC's history is relevant to all efforts to prohibit deceptive advertising: Is the FTC (or any other regulatory body) obligated to protect only reasonable, intelligent consumers who conduct themselves sensibly in the marketplace, or should it also protect careless, gullible, or ignorant consumers who are likely to make unwise decisions?[96] If the FTC uses the **reasonable-consumer standard**, it would prohibit only advertising claims that would deceive reasonable people. People who are taken in because they're more gullible or less bright than the average person would be unprotected. If the FTC uses the **gullible-consumer standard** and prohibits an advertisement that might mislead someone who is ill informed and naive, it would handle a lot more cases and greatly restrict advertising; but in spending its time and resources on such cases, it's not clear that the FTC would be proceeding in response to a substantial public interest, as it's legally charged with doing.

The reasonable-person standard was traditional in a variety of areas of the law long before the FTC was established. If you are sued for negligence, you can successfully defend yourself if you can establish that you behaved as a hypothetical reasonable person would have behaved under like circumstances. And, according to the law of misrepresentation, when you as a deceived consumer sue a seller on grounds that you were misled, then—assuming the deception is not proved to be intentional—you must establish that you were acting reasonably in relying on the false representation. If a reasonable person would not have been misled in like circumstances, you will not win your case. Ads that make claims that are obviously exaggerated or physically impossible would thus escape legal liability under the reasonable-person standard.

One decisive case in the legal transition away from the reasonable-person standard in matters of advertising, sales, and marketing was *FTC v. Standard Education* in 1937.[97] In this case, an encyclopedia company was charged by the FTC with a number of deceptive and misleading practices. The company's agents told potential customers that their names had been specially selected and that the encyclopedia they were being offered was being given away free as part of an advertising plan in return for use of their names for advertising purposes and in testimonials. The customer was only required to pay $69.50 for a series of looseleaf update volumes. Potential buyers were not told that both books and supplements regularly sold for $69.50.

In deciding the case, the U.S. Supreme Court considered the view of the appellate court, which had earlier dismissed the FTC's case. Writing for the appellate court, Judge Learned Hand had declared that the FTC was occupying itself with "trivial niceties" that only "divert attention from substantial evils." "We cannot take seriously the suggestion," he wrote, "that a man who is buying a set of books and a ten years' 'extension service' will be fatuous enough to be misled by the mere statement that the first are given away, and that he is paying only for the second." The Supreme Court itself, however, looked at the matter in a different light and held for the FTC and against Standard Education.

First, the Court noted that the practice had successfully deceived numerous victims, apparently including teachers, doctors, and college professors. But instead of resting its decision on the claim that a reasonable person might have been deceived, it advocated a change of standard to something like the ignorant-consumer standard:

> The fact that a false statement may be obviously false to those who are trained and experienced does not change its character, nor take away its power to deceive others less experienced. There is no duty resting upon a citizen to suspect the honesty of those with whom he transacts business. Laws are made to protect the trusting as well as the suspicious. The best element of business has long since decided that honesty should govern competitive enterprises, and that the rule of *caveat emptor* should not be relied upon to reward fraud and deception.

The decision in *FTC v. Standard Education*, as Ivan L. Preston notes, led the FTC to apply the gullible-person standard liberally, even in cases in which there was no intent to hoodwink consumers. In the 1940s, the FTC challenged ads in some cases in which it's difficult to believe that anyone could possibly have been deceived. For example, it issued a complaint against Clairol for advertising that its product would "color hair permanently" because some people might not know that new hair growth would still have its natural color, and it went after Bristol-Myers's Ipana toothpaste on the grounds that its "smile of beauty" slogan would lead some to believe that Ipana toothpaste would straighten their teeth. Eventually, however, the FTC abandoned the gullible-consumer standard in its extreme form and stopped trying to protect everyone from anything that might possibly deceive them. It now follows what might be called the "modified" gullible-consumer standard and protects consumers from ads that mislead significant numbers of people, whether those people acted reasonably or not.[98]

Still, deciding what is likely to be misleading to a significant number of consumers is not always easy. Consider these advertising claims, which are contested by some as deceptive: that Kraft Cheez Whiz is real cheese; that Chicken McNuggets are made from "whole breasts and thighs" (when they allegedly contain processed chicken skin as well and are fried in highly saturated beef fat); that ibuprofen causes stomach irritation (as Tylenol's ads seem to imply). Was it deceptive of Diet Coke to proclaim that it was sweetened "now with NutraSweet," even though the product also contained saccharin? Under legal pressure, Diet Coke changed its ads to read "NutraSweet blend." Is that phrase free of any misleading implications?

The 1937 *Standard Education* case moved the law away from the reasonable-person standard.

Summary
The FTC protects us from blatantly deceptive advertising. But it's debatable whether the FTC should ban only advertising that is likely to deceive reasonable people or whether it should protect careless or gullible consumers as well. The FTC now seeks to prohibit advertising that misleads a significant number of consumers, regardless of whether a reasonable person would have been taken in.

These days, the FTC follows what might be called the "modified" gullible-consumer standard.

Ads Directed at Children

The FTC has always looked after one special group of consumers without regard to how reasonable they are: children. Still, several consumer groups think the FTC has not done enough, and they advocate even stricter controls over advertisements that reach children.

Advertising is everywhere in a child's life. They see ads when they watch television, when they read magazines, when they visit kids' websites, and when they play games on tablets or the PC. They even see ads in their classrooms.[99] The ethical worry is that children, particularly young children, are naive and gullible and thus particularly vulnerable to advertisers' enticements. Consider, for example, ads in which children are shown, after eating a certain cereal, to have enough power to lift large playhouses. No adult would be misled by that ad, but children lack experience and independent judgment. This provides at least a prima facie case for protecting them.

Because of their susceptibility, children need special protection from being enticed and manipulated by advertising.

"Kids are the most pure consumers you could have," says one advertising expert. "They tend to interpret your ad literally. They are infinitely open." This problem is growing because the line between children's shows and the commercials that come with them is fading away. Children's entertainment features characters whose licensed images are stamped on toys, sheets, clothes, and food. Moreover, at the same time that movies and television shows are ever more tightly linked to the selling of toys and other items, commercials are becoming more like entertainment. Is it any wonder that many children perceive little difference between ads and television shows? As one nine-year-old sees it, the only distinction is that "commercials are shorter."

Furthermore, it's no longer just cereal, candy, and toys that are being advertised to children. Companies are directing ads for a wide range of products toward them, even those that the children aren't likely to buy themselves. They do this, first, because they know that children often influence the purchases that their families make. "We're relying on the kid to pester the mom to buy the product, rather than going straight to the mom," says Barbara A. Martino of Grey Advertising. Pursuing this strategy, marketing consultants study different ways that children nag and how effective their nagging styles are on different types of parents.[100] Karen Francis, a brand manager for Chevy, reports that even she was surprised how often parents tell her that their kids played a tie-breaking role in deciding which car to buy.[101] Naturally, advertisers argue that parents still have ultimate control over what gets purchased and what doesn't. But is the strategy of selling to parents by convincing the children a fair one? As one parent complains, "Brand awareness has been an incredibly abusive experience—the relentless requests to go to McDonald's [or] to see movies that are inappropriate for six-year-olds [but] that are advertised on kids' shows."

Summary
Advertising to children is big business, but children are particularly susceptible to the blandishments of advertising. Advertisers contend that parents still control what gets purchased and what doesn't. Critics, however, doubt the fairness of selling to parents by appealing to children.

A second reason that companies target children with ads for products that only adults are likely to buy is to create customers for the future. As Jackie Pate of Delta Air Lines puts it, "By building brand loyalty in children today, they'll be the adult passengers of the future." Ann Moore, chairman and CEO of Time Inc., which publishes *Sports Illustrated for Kids*, adds, "We believe children make brand decisions that will carry into their adult lives."[102] Although the magazine's readers are mostly between eight and fourteen years old, it sometimes features two-page spreads for automobiles.

Critics of the advertising industry believe that any sort of marketing aimed at children harms them and that it's wrong to treat children as "economic objects."[103] Advertisers dispute that this is what they do. They believe that advertising promotes choice and, thus, personal responsibility. Wallace S. Snyder of the American Advertising Federation contends that it's "ethical to advertise toys, sugar-loaded cereal or non-violent games to children . . . as long as it is *truthful* and as long as children understand the message."[104]

Issues Raised by Digital Advertising

Every year, companies move more of their advertising online, and it's no surprise that forecasts suggest that this trend will continue.[105] Digital or online ads raise some special moral concerns that aren't present with more traditional ads. When an ad appears in a magazine, everyone reading that issue sees the same ad. The same is true for television commercials, at least as of now. With digital ads, though, this isn't the case; two different people looking at the same website might see quite different ads. Online, advertisers are able to steer their ads toward people with particular characteristics. This lets them put their ads in front of the people who are most likely to be influenced by them. Men aren't likely to see ads for women's shoes online—at least not unless the ad is suggesting that shoes make an excellent gift.

This aspect of digital advertising raises some ethical issues over and above those that attach to traditional forms of advertising. First, there are issues about privacy. How do companies know which ads to "serve" to which consumers? The answer is that we're being constantly monitored by our technology. What webpages we look at, what TV programs we watch, what we say to our "smart speakers"—to advertisers, this is all valuable data that allows them to build up a profile of our interests and preferences. A tool company, say, can target its ads specifically to consumers who visit woodworking or home renovation websites.

One of the ethical issues that this sort of targeting raises concerns privacy. It's creepy enough to look at a product online and then see ads for it on every website that you visit for the next week. But it's even more concerning to think that advertisers essentially have dossiers on all of us that reflect our online activity. Track someone's web searches for a few weeks and you're likely to know more about them than many of their friends, including their sexual preferences and whether they have any embarrassing medical conditions. But it may not only be our online activity that is being tracked. Today, we're surrounded by devices with microphones: our cell phones, obviously, but also devices like Amazon Echoes or Google Nests; even many smart TVs include microphones and sometimes cameras. There is some uncertainty around when these devices are listening, what data they're gathering, and how that information us being used.[106]

Second, advertisers' ability to steer ads to specific consumers raises worries about the prospect of discrimination. Advertisers have a considerable ability to direct their ads towards—or away from—specific demographic groups, like members of specific racial and ethnic minorities.[107] Perhaps this is more concerning when it comes to ads for political candidates or employment opportunities than for commercial products. Still, at one point performing a Google search for a name that is more frequently associated with African Americans did make one more likely to see ads for services meant for individuals with arrest records.[108]

Third, there's the simple fact that targeted ads are more likely to be effective. When Apple allowed iPhone users to stop sharing data with advertisers, one mail-order bakery saw its revenue drop by more than 50 percent.[109] That illustrates how much more bang for the buck advertisers get from directing their ads to the individuals who are mostly like to be influenced by them. If we believe that ads frequently tempt us into buying things that we'd be better off without, then the fact that digital advertising is much more effective than "old-fashioned" advertising means that we can all expect to be induced to make bad choices more often.

Summary
Digital advertising raises special ethical issues. These include concerns over privacy, the prospect of discrimination by advertisers, and the greater effectiveness of targeted ads.

• • •

The Debate over Advertising

The controversy over advertising does not end with the issue of deceptive techniques and unfair advertising practices. Advertising provides little usable information to consumers. Advertisements almost always conceal relevant negative facts about their products, and they're frequently based on subtle appeals to psychological needs, which the products they peddle are unlikely to satisfy. These realities are the basis for some critics' wholesale repudiation of advertising on moral grounds. They also desire a less commercially polluted environment, one that does not continually reinforce materialistic values.

Consumer Needs

Some defenders of advertising take these points in stride. They concede that images of glamour, sex, or adventure sell products, but they argue that these images are what we, the consumers, want. We don't want just blue jeans; we want romance or sophistication or status with our blue jeans. By connecting products with important emotions and feelings, advertisements can also satisfy our deeper needs and wants. As one advertising executive puts it:

Advertising can show a consumer how a baby powder helps affirm her role as a nurturing mother—Johnson & Johnson's "The Language of Love." Or it can show a teenager how a soft drink helps assert his or her emerging independence—Pepsi's "The Choice of a New Generation."[110]

Harvard business professor Theodore Levitt has drawn an analogy between advertising and art. Both take liberties with reality, both deal in symbolic communication, and neither is interested in literal truth or in pure functionality. Rather, both art and advertising help us repackage the otherwise crude, drab, and generally oppressive reality that surrounds us. They create "illusions, symbols, and implications that promise more." They help us modify, transform, embellish, enrich, and reconstruct the world around us. "Without distortion, embellishment, and elaboration," Levitt writes, "life would be drab, dull, anguished, and at its existential worst." Advertising helps satisfy this legitimate human need. Its handsome packages and imaginative promises produce that "elevation of the spirit" that we want and need. Embellishment and distortion are therefore among advertising's socially desirable purposes. To criticize advertising on these counts, Levitt argues, is to overlook the real needs and values of human beings.[111]

Levitt's critics contend that even if advertising appeals to the same deep needs that art does, advertising promises satisfaction of those needs in the products it sells, and that promise is rarely kept. At the end of the day, blue jeans are still just blue jeans, and your love life will be unaffected by which soap you shower with. The imaginative, symbolic, and artistic content of advertising, which Levitt sees as answering real human needs, is viewed by critics as manipulating, distorting, and even creating those needs.

In his influential books *The Affluent Society* and *The New Industrial State*, the late John Kenneth Galbraith criticized advertising on exactly this point. Galbraith argued that the process of production today, with its expensive marketing campaigns, subtle advertising techniques, and sophisticated sales strategies, creates the very wants it then satisfies. In other words, producers create both the goods and the demand for those goods. If a new breakfast cereal or detergent were really wanted, Galbraith reasoned, why must so much money be spent trying to get the consumer to buy it? He thought it's obvious that "wants can be synthesized by advertising, catalyzed by salesmanship, and shaped by" discreet manipulations.

Galbraith believed that nowadays, instead of shaping the production process, consumer demand tends to be shaped by it.

Accordingly, Galbraith rejected the economist's traditional faith in **consumer sovereignty**: the idea that consumers should and do control the market through their purchases. Rather than independent consumer demand shaping production, as classical economic theory says it does, nowadays it's the other way around. Galbraith dubbed this the **dependence effect**: "As a society becomes increasingly affluent, wants are increasingly created by the process by which they are satisfied."[112]

One consequence, Galbraith thought, is that our system of production can't be defended on the ground that it's satisfying urgent or important wants. We can't defend production as satisfying wants if the production process itself creates those wants. "In the absence of the massive and artful persuasion that accompanies the management of demand," Galbraith argued,

> increasing abundance might well have reduced the interest of people in acquiring more goods. They would not have felt the need for multiplying the artifacts—autos, appliances, detergents, cosmetics—by which they were surrounded.[113]

Another consequence is our general preoccupation with material consumption. In particular, Galbraith claimed, our pursuit of private goods, continually reinforced by advertising, leads us to neglect important public goods and services. We need better schools, parks, artistic and recreational facilities; safer and cleaner cities and air; more efficient, less-crowded transportation systems. We are rich in the private production and use of goods, Galbraith thought, and starved in public services. In 2004, Galbraith summarized his long-held views this way:

> Belief in a market economy in which the consumer is sovereign is one of our most pervasive forms of fraud. Let no one try to sell without consumer management, control. As power over the innovation, manufacture, and sale of goods and services has passed to the producer and away from the consumer, the aggregate of this production has been the prime test of social achievement. . . . Not education or literature or the arts but the production of automobiles, including SUVs: Here is the modern measure of economic and therefore social achievement.[114]

Galbraith's critics have concentrated their fire on a couple of points. *First*, Galbraith never shows that advertising has the power he attributed to it. Advertising campaigns like that for Listerine in the 1920s, which successfully created the problem of "halitosis" in order to sell the new idea of "mouthwash," are rare. And even though in recent years pharmaceutical companies have found large profits in promoting new or exaggerated medical conditions with serious-sounding names—for example, "premenstrual dysphoric disorder" (premenstrual tension), "gastro-esophageal reflux disease" (heartburn), or "social anxiety disorder" (sadness)—and selling drugs to treat them,[115] most new products fail to win a permanent place in the hearts of consumers, despite heavy advertising. We are inundated with ads every day, but experiments suggest we no longer care much about them. Each of us sees an average of 1,600 advertisements a day, notices around 1,200 of them, and responds favorably or unfavorably to only about 12. We also appear to pay more attention to ads for products that we already have.

Second, critics have attacked Galbraith's assumption that the needs supposedly created by advertisers and producers are, as a result, "false" or "artificial" needs and therefore less worthy of satisfaction. Human needs, they stress, are always socially influenced and are never static. How are we to distinguish between "genuine" and "artificial" wants, and why should the latter be thought less important? Ads might produce a want that we would not otherwise have had without that want being in any way objectionable.

Although conclusive evidence is unavailable, critics of advertising continue to worry about its power to influence our lives and shape our culture and civilization. Even if producers can't create wants out of whole cloth, many worry that advertising can manipulate our existing desires—that it can stimulate certain desires, both at the expense of other, less materialistic desires and out of proportion to the likely satisfaction that fulfillment of those desires will bring.

Market Economics

Defenders of advertising are largely untroubled by these worries. They see advertising as an aspect of free competition in a competitive market, which ultimately works to the benefit of all. But this simple free-market defense of advertising has weaknesses. To begin with, advertising doesn't fit too well into the economist's model of the free market. Economists can prove, if we grant them enough assumptions, that free-market buying and selling lead to optimal results. (Technically, they lead to **Pareto optimality**, which means that no one person can be made better off without making someone else worse off.) One of those assumptions is that everyone has full and complete information, on the basis of which they then buy and sell. But if that were so, advertising would be pointless.

One might argue that advertising moves us closer to the ideal of full information, but there is good reason to doubt this. Even if we put aside the question of whether ads can create, shape, or manipulate wants, they do seem to enhance brand loyalty, which generally works to thwart price competition. A true brand-name consumer is willing to pay more for a product that is otherwise indistinguishable from its competitors. He or she buys a certain beer despite being unable to taste the difference between it and other beers.

More generally, critics of advertising stand the invisible-hand argument on its head. The goal of advertisers is to sell you products and to make money, not to promote your well-being. Rational demonstration of how a product will in fact enhance your well-being is not the only way advertisers can successfully persuade you to buy their products. Indeed, it's far from the most common technique. Critics charge, accordingly, that there is no reason to think that advertising even tends to increase the well-being of consumers.

Defenders of advertising may claim that, nonetheless, advertising is necessary for economic growth, which benefits us all. The truth of this claim, however, is open to debate. Critics maintain that advertising is a waste of resources and serves only to raise the price of advertised goods. Like Galbraith, they may also contend that advertising in general reinforces mindless consumerism. It corrupts our civilization and misdirects our society's economic effort toward private consumption and away from the public realm. The never-ending pursuit of material goods may also divert us as a society from the pursuit of a substantially shorter workday.[116]

Summary
Defenders of advertising view its imaginative, symbolic, and artistic content as answering real human needs. Critics maintain that advertising manipulates those needs or even creates artificial ones. John Kenneth Galbraith contended that today the same process that produces products also produces the demand for those products (the dependence effect). Galbraith argued, controversially, that advertising encourages a preoccupation with material goods and leads us to favor private consumption at the expense of important public goods and services.

Critics charge that because advertising's only goal is to persuade consumers to buy, there is no reason to think it enhances well-being.

Summary
Defenders of advertising see it as a necessary and desirable aspect of competition in a free-market system, a protected form of free speech, and a useful sponsor of the media, in particular, television. Critics challenge all three claims.

Free Speech and the Media

Two final issues should be briefly noted. Defenders of advertising claim that, despite these criticisms, advertising enjoys protection under the First Amendment as a form of speech. Legally, this claim probably requires qualification, especially in regard to radio and television, for which one must have a license to broadcast. Banning cigarette advertisements from television, for instance, did not run contrary to the U.S. Constitution. More important, even if we concede advertisers the legal right to free speech, not every exercise of that legal right is morally justifiable. If advertisements in general or of a certain type or for certain products were shown to have undesirable social consequences, or if certain sorts of ads relied on objectionable or nonrational persuasive techniques, then there would be a strong moral argument against such advertisements regardless of their legal status.

Advertising subsidizes the media, and that is a positive but far from conclusive consideration in its favor. But the very fact that broadcast television is free results in far more consumption than would otherwise be the case and probably, as many think, far more than is good for us. Although satellite and cable television have improved things, the mediocrity of much American television fare is hardly accidental. The networks need large audiences. Obviously, they can't run everyone's favorite type of program, because people's tastes differ, so they seek to reach a common denominator. There was a time when it looked like the shift away from broadcast and even cable television toward streaming service like Netflix might make a real difference to the sort of programs that are produced, with the prospect for successful shows that targeted specific niche audiences. Today, though, it's becoming less clear whether this change will happen. Streaming services are also starting to more strongly favor programs that appeal to broad and even global audiences.[117] It may be no coincidence that they're also starting to introduce ad-supported subscription options.

Study Corner

Key Terms and Concepts

ambiguity (in advertising)	*FTC v. Standard Education*	punitive damages
caveat emptor	gullible-consumer standard	quantity surcharges
concealment of facts (in advertising)	legal paternalism	reasonable-consumer standard
Consumer Product Safety Commission	*MacPherson v. Buick Motor Car*	strict product liability
consumer sovereignty	merchantability	subliminal advertising
dependence effect	pareto optimality	value of statistical life
due care	price fixing, horizontal and vertical	warranties, express and implied
exaggeration (in advertising)	price gouging	weasel words
Federal Trade Commission	psychological appeal (in advertising)	
Food and Drug Administration	puffery	

Points to Review

- issues raised by the manufacture, marketing, and advertising of cigarettes (pp. 159–160)

- importance of *MacPherson v. Buick Motor Car* (p. 161)

- why critics of strict product liability believe it's unfair (p. 162)

- two arguments in favor of strict product liability (p. 162)

- comparing lives saved versus costs of different regulations (p. 163)

- economic and philosophical worries about safety restrictions on consumer choice (pp. 163–164)

- four points to bear in mind about paternalism (pp. 164–165)

- examples of shortfalls in, and political interference with, safety regulations (pp. 165–166)

- what the auto industry's safety record illustrates (p. 167)

- six things business should do to increase product safety (pp. 168–169)

- old tires and self-driving cars versus burning radios and fluorocarbons as examples of questionable and responsible business conduct (p. 170)

- difference between express and implied warranties (p. 171)

- examples of manipulative pricing (pp. 172–173)

- types of price fixing (pp. 173–174)

- difficulty of defining price gouging and assessing its morality (pp. 174–176)

- examples of misleading labeling and packaging (pp. 176–178)

- examples of ambiguity, concealment of facts, exaggeration, and psychological appeals (pp. 179–182)

- how almost all advertising fails to provide full information (p. 180)

- the case against puffery (p. 181)

- reasonable-consumer standard versus gullible-consumer standard (p. 182)

- importance of *FTC v. Standard Education* (p. 183)

- why companies spend so much on advertising to children (p. 184)

- issues raised by ads directed at children (p. 184)

- issues raised by digital advertising (pp. 184–185)

- Levitt's defense of advertising (p. 186)

- Galbraith's "dependence effect" and his critique of advertising (pp. 186–187)

- two criticisms of Galbraith (p. 187)

- why advertising doesn't fit well with economists' model of the free market (p. 187)

For Further Reflection

1. What do you see as the pros and cons of government safety regulation?

2. Is business meeting its responsibilities to consumers with regard to the safety, quality, pricing, and labeling and packaging of its products? If not, how might it do better?

3. Is advertising a positive or socially desirable aspect of our economic system?

Case 6.1

Breast Implants

In The Last Few Decades, Silicone Has Become a Crucial Industrial product, playing a role in the manufacture of thousands of products, from lubricants to adhesive labels to Silly Putty. One of its medical uses, however, has been controversial—namely, as the gel used for breast implants. Dow Corning, which was founded in 1943 to produce silicones for commercial purposes, invented mammary prostheses in the 1960s. Since then, a million American women have had bags of silicone gel implanted in their breasts. For many of them, silicone implants are part of reconstructive surgery after breast cancer or other operations. However, by 1990 four out of five implants were for the cosmetic augmentation of normal, healthy breasts—a procedure that became increasingly popular in the 1980s as celebrities such as Cher and Jenny Jones spoke openly of their surgically enhanced breasts.

Today, however, what used to be a common elective operation is rarely performed.[118] The reason dates from the 1980s, when women with silicone breast implants first began reporting certain patterns of illness. There were stories of ruptured or leaky bags, although the estimates of the proportion of women affected ranged widely, from a low of only 1 to 5 percent to a high of 32 percent. And there were allegations that the silicone implants were responsible for various autoimmune disorders— such as rheumatoid arthritis, lupus erythematosus, and scleroderma— in which the body's immune system attacks its own connective tissue. Then, in 1991, a jury heard the case of Mariann Hopkins, who claimed that her implants had ruptured and released silicone gel, causing severe joint and muscle pain, weight loss, and fatigue. On the basis of documents suggesting that Dow Corning knew of the dangers of leaky bags, a San Francisco jury found the company guilty of negligence and fraud and awarded Hopkins $7.3 million.

When Dow Corning first sold breast implants in 1965, they were subject to no specific government regulations. In 1978, the FDA classified them as "Class II" devices, meaning that they did not need testing to remain on the market. In 1989, however, as worries about the dangers of silicone implants increased, the FDA reclassified them as "Class III" devices, and in 1991 it required all manufacturers to submit safety and effectiveness data. Although some FDA staff members were scathingly critical of the poor and inconclusive documentation submitted by the manufacturers, the FDA's advisory panel ruled that the implants were not a major threat to health. Based on public need, it voted to keep them on the market.

After the Hopkins case, however, David A. Kessler, the FDA's new chairman, called for a moratorium on breast implants. He asked doctors to stop performing the operation, but he told women who had already had the operation not to have the bags removed. Still, the moratorium terrified the women who had had breast implants, a few of whom tried in desperation to carve them out themselves, and it galvanized a political movement led by women who were upset about having been used, yet again, as guinea pigs for an unsafe medical procedure. For them, it was just one more episode in a long history of the mistreatment of women by a medical, scientific, and industrial establishment that refused to treat them as persons and take their needs seriously. The FDA moratorium also galvanized the legal forces marshaled against the manufacturers of silicone bags. By 1994, some 20,000 lawsuits had been filed against Dow Corning alone. Entrepreneurial lawyers organized most of these actions into a few large class-action suits so that their pooled legal resources would be more than a match for the manufacturers.

Meanwhile, Kessler instructed the FDA's advisory panel to re-study the breast implant question. Presented with a series of anecdotal reports about diseases that are not rare, the panel complained about the lack of hard scientific data. From the scientific point of view, the problem was how to distinguish coincidence from causation. For example, if connective-tissue disease strikes 1 percent of all women and if 1 million women have implants, then statistically one should expect that 10,000 women will have both implants and connective-tissue disease. So, if a woman develops the disease, can it correctly be said that it was caused by her breast implants? Moreover, not only does silicone appear to be chemically inert, but silicone from a ruptured breast implant will remain trapped inside a fibrous capsule of scar tissue. Nevertheless, on the basis of the panel's recommendation, the FDA ruled that silicone may be used only for reconstruction and that cosmetic breast augmentation must be done only with saline packs.

At that point the gulf between science, on the one hand, and the FDA and public opinion, on the other, began to widen further. A Mayo Clinic study published in the prestigious *New England Journal of Medicine* in June 1994 showed that there was no difference between women with breast implants and other women with respect to incidence of connective-tissue disease; by the summer of 1995, two larger studies had confirmed the Mayo Clinic's report. On top of that, the FBI and other investigators exposed several labs that were selling to lawyers and victims fraudulent test results purporting to show the presence of silicone in the blood of women with breast implants.

Lawyers and other advocates for the women with implants repudiate those studies, contending that the women have a new disease. To this contention, scientists respond that the description of the symptoms of this supposed disease keeps changing. Some say it looks like fibromyalgia, which is included in their studies. Many feminist activist groups distrust science; they believe that we should pay less attention to statistics and medical studies and greater attention to the women who have suffered. These women know what their bodies have been through, and they're convinced that their implants are responsible.

This reasoning, and the skepticism toward science and statistics that it represents, has swayed jurors. After Dow Corning filed bankruptcy in 1995, which brought to a halt the lawsuits against it, new lawsuits were filed against its parent company, Dow Chemical. The first of these resulted in a $14.1 million verdict against the company, despite the lack of scientific evidence. Disregarding the *New England Journal of Medicine* study, the jurors were convinced that this particular plaintiff's suffering somehow stemmed from her Dow-manufactured breast implant. A few years later, the women who said their silicone breast implants made them ill agreed to settle their claims against Dow Corning for $3.2 billion. The settlement is part of its bankruptcy reorganization plan and is similar to a settlement entered into earlier by 3M, Bristol-Myers Squibb, and other manufacturers of breast implants.

Update

In light of numerous studies that failed to find a link between implants and disease, in 2006 the FDA gave conditional approval to Mentor Corporation's application to produce silicone breast implants, thus effectively ending a thirteen-year ban on the use of silicone for cosmetic breast enhancements. However, concerns continue to be raised, and at least some of these have been borne out by research. In 2019, Allergan recalled its textured implants after they were found to put women at greater risk of anaplastic large cell lymphoma, a cancer of the immune system. The rough surface of the implants made them more likely to stay in place but may also have caused more inflammation. In 2021, the FDA placed a "black box warning" on breast implants informing patients and doctors that the products have been linked both to lymphoma and systemic diseases like autoimmune disorders and chronic fatigue.[119] It required surgeons to review these risks with patients before performing surgery. According to this warning, women who were treated for breast cancer may be at greater risk. In 2022, the FDA issued a further warning that breast implants may have been responsible for a small number of additional cancers that can form in the scar tissue that the surgery creates.

Discussion Questions

1. What does the breast implant controversy reveal about society's attitudes toward product safety, about the legal liability of manufacturers, and about the role of regulatory agencies like the FDA in protecting consumers? Is our society too cautious about product safety or not cautious enough?

2. Was the FDA justified in placing a moratorium on silicone breast implants and then halting them altogether for cosmetic purposes?

3. Was it irresponsible of the manufacturers of breast implants to have marketed them without first conclusively proving they were safe? If you were on the jury, would you have found Dow Corning or its parent company liable for the illnesses suffered by women who have had breast implants?

4. On safety matters, should the FDA or any regulatory agency err on the side of overprotection or underprotection? Some argue that in the case of new drugs or medical procedures in which the dangers are uncertain, consumers should be free to decide for themselves whether they wish to run the health risks associated with these products or services. Assess this argument.

5. Has the FDA's stance on breast implants been fair to women who would like breast augmentation but can't get it? Some people disapprove of cosmetic augmentation or believe it to be a frivolous operation. Do you think that attitudes like this played a role in the controversy over the safety of breast implants?

6. Someone who favors tighter regulation of breast implants might argue that many women choose augmentation only because social norms about beauty and sexual attractiveness attach undue significance to breast size. They might even question whether many women who choose augmentation do so entirely freely or only because of social pressure. Is this a good reason to regulate breast augmentation and implants more heavily than other medical procedures or other products that pose similar risks? Or does this line of argument implicitly depict women as less able to weigh risks and make decisions about their own lives?

Case 6.2
Hot Coffee at McDonald's

To Aficionados of the Bean, There's Nothing Like a Piping-Hot cup of java to get the day off to a good start, and nothing more insipid than lukewarm coffee. That's what McDonald's thought, anyway—until it learned differently, the hard and expensive way, when seventy-nine-year-old Stella Liebeck successfully sued the company after she was burned by a spilled cup of hot coffee that she'd bought at the drive-through window of her local McDonald's. The jury awarded her $160,000 in compensatory damages and a whopping $2.7 million in punitive damages. After the trial judge reduced the punitive damages to $480,000, she and McDonald's settled out of court for an undisclosed sum.[120]

Unlike the outcome of most other lawsuits, the hot-coffee verdict received nationwide attention, most of it unfavorable. To many ordinary people, the case epitomized the excesses of a legal system out of control. If hot coffee is dangerous, what's next: soft drinks that are too cold? To conservatives, the case represented the all-too-familiar failure of consumers to take responsibility for their own conduct, to blame business rather than themselves for their injuries. More policy-oriented pundits used the case as an occasion to call for reform of product liability law—in particular, to make winning frivolous suits more difficult and to restrict the punitive awards that juries can hand down.

However, those who examined the facts more closely learned that the Liebeck case was more complicated than it first appeared. For one thing, Liebeck was hospitalized for a week because of third-degree burns on her thighs and buttocks, which were serious enough to require skin grafting and leave permanent scars. After her injury, she initially requested $10,000 for medical expenses and an additional amount for pain and suffering. When McDonald's refused, she went to court, asking for $300,000. Lawyers for the company argued in response that McDonald's coffee was not unreasonably hot and that Liebeck was responsible for her own injuries.

The jury saw it differently, however. *First*, McDonald's served its coffee at 180–190 degrees Fahrenheit, significantly hotter than home-brewed coffee. The jury was persuaded that coffee at that temperature is both undrinkable and more dangerous than a reasonable consumer would expect. *Second*, before Liebeck's accident, the company had received over 700 complaints about burns from its coffee. In response to the complaints, McDonald's had in fact put a warning label on its cups and designed a tighter-fitting lid for them. Ironically, the new lid was part of the problem in the Liebeck case because she had held the coffee cup between her legs in an effort to pry it open.

Although the jury found that Liebeck was 20 percent responsible for her injuries, it also concluded that McDonald's had not done enough to warn consumers. The jury's $2.7 million punitive-damage award

was intended, jurors later said, to send a message to fast-food chains. Although the judge reduced the award—equivalent to only about two days' worth of coffee sales for McDonald's—he called McDonald's conduct "willful, wanton, reckless, and callous."

Discussion Questions

1. Is hot coffee so dangerous, as the jury thought? Should a reasonable consumer be expected to know that coffee can burn and to have assumed this risk? Is a warning label sufficient? Is our society too protective of consumers these days, or not protective enough?

2. In serving such hot coffee, did McDonald's act in a morally responsible way? What ideals, obligations, and effects should it have taken into consideration?

3. McDonald's claims that most consumers would prefer to have their coffee too hot rather than not hot enough. After all, if it's too hot, they can always wait a minute before drinking it. Suppose this is true. How does it affect McDonald's responsibilities? Given that McDonald's serves millions of cups of coffee every week, how important are a few hundred complaints about its coffee being too hot?

4. Was Liebeck only 20 percent responsible for her injuries? Do you agree with the amount of compensatory and punitive damages that the jury awarded her? If not, what would have been a fairer monetary award?

5. Should juries be permitted to award punitive damages in product liability cases? If so, should there be a limit to what they can award? Is it right for a jury to award punitive damages against one company in order to send a message to a whole industry?

Case 6.3
Closing the Deal

Now That She Had to, Jean Mcguire Wasn't Sure She Could. Not that she didn't understand what to do. Wright Boazman, sales director for Sunrise Land Developers, had made the step clear enough when he described a variety of effective "deal-closing techniques."

As Wright explained it, very often people actually want to buy a lot but suffer at the last minute from self-doubt and uncertainty. The inexperienced salesperson can misinterpret this hesitation as a lack of interest in a property. "But," as Wright pointed out, "in most cases it's just an expression of the normal reservations we all show when the time comes to sign our names on the dotted line."

In Wright's view, the job of a land salesperson was "to help the prospect make the decision to buy." He didn't mean to suggest that salespeople should misrepresent a piece of property or in any way mislead people about what they were purchasing. "The law prohibits this," he pointed out, "and personally I find such behavior repugnant. What I'm talking about is helping them buy a lot that they genuinely want and that you're convinced will be compatible with their needs and interests." For Wright Boazman, salespeople should serve as motivators, people who can provide whatever impulse was needed for prospects to close the deal.

In Wright's experience, one of the most effective closing techniques was what he termed "the other party." It goes something like this.

Suppose someone like Jean McGuire had a hot prospect, someone who was exhibiting real interest in a lot but who was having trouble deciding. To motivate the prospect into buying, Jean ought to tell the person that she wasn't even sure the lot was still available because a number of other salespeople were showing the same lot, and they could already have closed a deal on it. As Wright put it, "This first move generally increases the prospect's interest in the property, and more important to us, in closing the deal pronto."

Next Jean should say something like, "Why don't we go back to the office, and I'll call headquarters to find out the status of the lot?" Wright indicated that such a suggestion ordinarily "whets their appetite" even more. In addition, it turns prospects away from wondering whether they should purchase the land and toward hoping that it's still available.

When they return to the office, Jean should make a call in the presence of the prospect. The call, of course, would not be to "headquarters" but to a private office only yards from where she and the prospect sit. Wright or someone else would receive the call, and Jean should fake a conversation about the property's availability, punctuating her comments with contagious excitement about its desirability. When she hangs up, she should breathe a sigh of relief that the lot's still available—but barely. At any minute, Jean should explain anxiously, the lot could be "green-tagged," meaning that headquarters is expecting a call from another salesperson who's about to close a deal and will remove the lot from open stock. (An effective variation of this, Wright pointed out, would have Jean abruptly excuse herself on hanging up and dart over to another sales representative with whom she'd engage in a heated, although staged, debate about the availability of the property—loud enough, of course, for the prospect to hear. The intended effect, according to Wright, would be to place the prospect in a "now or never" frame of mind.)

Have you ever found yourself in a situation where you thought that you were being manipulated or felt pushed against your better judgment to purchase something?

Radius Images/Alamy Stock Photo

When Jean first heard about this and other closing techniques, she felt uneasy. Even though the property was everything it was represented to be and the law in her state allowed purchasers three days to change their minds after closing a deal, she instinctively objected to the use of psychological manipulation. Nevertheless, Jean never expressed her reservations to anyone, primarily because she didn't want to endanger her job, which, as a single mother with two children to support, she certainly needed. Besides, Jean had convinced herself that she could deal with closures more respectably than Wright and other salespeople might. But the truth was that, after six months of selling land for Sunrise, Jean's sales lagged far behind those of the other sales representatives. Whether she liked it or not, Jean had to admit she was losing a considerable number of sales because she couldn't close. And she couldn't close because, in Wright Boazman's words, she lacked technique. She wasn't using the psychological closing devices that he and others had found so successful.

Now as she drove back to the office with two hot prospects in hand, she wondered what to do.

....
Discussion Questions
....

1. Do you disapprove of this sales tactic, or is it a legitimate business technique? How might it be morally defended?

2. Suppose you knew either that the prospect would eventually decide to buy the property anyway or that it would genuinely be in the prospect's interest to buy it. Would that affect your moral assessment of this closing technique? Do customers have any grounds for complaining about this closing technique if the law allows them three days to change their minds?

3. What ideals, obligations, and effects must Jean consider? What interests and rights of the customer are at stake?

4. What weight should Jean give to self-interest in her deliberations? What do you think she should do? What would you do?

5. What rule, if any, would a rule utilitarian encourage real estate agents in this situation to follow? What should the realtors' professional code of ethics say about closing techniques?

Case 6.4
The Rise and Fall of Four Loko

If You're Serious about Your Partying, How Do You Manage to Keep awake when drinking late into the night? That question may seem absurd to some people, but it has long bedeviled club-hoppers and other revelers. Some of them drink cola on the side or mixed with alcohol; others favor Red Bull and vodka. Recently, however, a few entrepreneurial companies came to their aid, by combining alcohol and caffeine into one convenient package. Joose and Four Loko are two examples. The former added 54 milligrams, the latter 156 milligrams, of caffeine to a malt beverage that is 12 percent alcohol. (In comparison, a can of Coke contains 35 milligrams of caffeine, and an eight-ounce cup of coffee between 100 and 200 milligrams. Beer is usually around 5 percent alcohol and wine 12 percent.) Made with fruit flavors and packaged in bright colors, Joose and Four Loko were sold in large, 23.5-ounce cans.[121]

While these innovative products made some consumers happy, they soon alarmed colleges and health officials around the country when they led, or appeared to have led, to a growing number of intoxicated students and other young people landing in hospital emergency rooms, some with serious alcohol poisoning—for example, the New Jersey student who showed up in a local hospital with a blood alcohol level of 0.40 (at least four times the legal limit for driving a car) after drinking three cans of Four Loko and several shots of tequila in an hour. In response, several colleges and universities banned the drinks from their campuses or tried to warn students about their dangers. Peter Mercer, the president of Ramapo College, where the New Jersey student was enrolled, says, "I do not see any socially redeeming purpose being served by these beverages."

Senator Charles E. Schumer of New York calls Four Loko "a toxic and dangerous brew." Dr. Michael Reihart, an emergency room physician in Lancaster, Pennsylvania, agrees: "This is one of the most dangerous new alcohol concoctions I have ever seen." He adds, "It's a recipe for disaster because your body's natural defense is to get sleepy and not want to drink, but in this case you're tricking the body with caffeine." With these drinks, "you have a product where people don't appreciate how much alcohol they're consuming," says Rob McKenna, an attorney general in the state of Washington.

These concerns didn't dent the popularity of Four Loko, however. On a fan-operated Facebook page, for example, more than 25,000 people have displayed their support of the beverage, many posting photos of themselves with empty cans stacked or strewn about. Some say they like the drink because it doesn't take many to get intoxicated. Stores near many college campuses found themselves giving the beverages increased shelf space because of the high demand, especially after Four Loko expanded the flavors it offered. "You can get drunk for $5 all night," says Boston College junior, Christine Binko, though she doesn't like the cans littering the streets near the campus, and she thinks "it brings out the aggression in people." Many observers were worried by the colorful packaging of the beverages and the fact that they come in flavors like watermelon, blue raspberry, and lemon-lime. Senator Schumer, for one, charges that the beverages are "explicitly designed to attract under-age drinkers." And it's true that the brightly colored cans resemble iced tea, soda, or energy drink containers and can be mistaken for nonalcoholic beverages. "I've talked to parents who were shocked because the can was in their refrigerator and they didn't realize it was an alcoholic beverage," Dr. Reihart said. "It looks like every other energy drink out there."

Chris Hunter, the co-founder and managing partner of the company that owns Four Loko, believes that his product is being unfairly singled out and says that his company takes steps to prevent its product falling into the hands of minors. "Alcohol misuse and abuse and under-age drinking are issues the industry faces . . . The singling out or banning of one product is not going to solve that. Consumer education is what's going to do it."

Not wanting to wait for consumer education, Michigan and Washington banned prepackaged caffeinated alcoholic beverages in November 2010, and legislators in several other states were considering the same course of action. "Disappointed" by calls to ban the drink, Four Loko contended that its product is safe. "We want to open a dialogue to discuss specific concerns and try to reach solutions," a statement issued by the company said. "When consumed responsibly, our products are just as safe as any other alcoholic beverages." That dialogue never happened because, at the urging of Senator Schumer and other politicians, the FDA soon stepped in. It sent a warning to Four Loko and three other manufacturers that the caffeine added to their malt alcoholic beverages is an "unsafe food additive" and that the beverages are a "public health concern" because they mask the sensory clues that drinkers rely on to determine their level of intoxication. The products, the FDA ruled, can't remain on the market in their current form.

In response, some partygoers rushed to stack up on Four Loko before the ban went into effect. Four Loko, for its part, has released a new version of the drink, which now contains no caffeine. Sales of the new product, however, have been comparatively poor.

One of the beverages caught up in the FDA crackdown is Moonshot '69, a craft beer produced by tiny New Century Brewery, a one-person company run by Rhonda Kallman, a co-founder of Sam Adams. Because Moonshot '69 contains about 69 milligrams of caffeine, the FDA will no longer let Kallman produce it. That's because the caffeine was put directly into the beverage and not naturally occurring (as it would be if, say, the beer were brewed with coffee). But Moonshot '69 bears little resemblance to high-alcohol, high-caffeine malt beverages like Four Loko.

It's only 5 percent alcohol and comes in standard 12-ounce beer bottles, and no one would mistake it for an energy drink. "This is prohibition," complains Kallman. "It's devastating the company, and, as a U.S. citizen, I'm just flabbergasted." Stuck with $25,000 worth of inventory that she can't sell, Kallman says that instead of outlawing caffeinated alcoholic beverages across the board, the FDA should set parameters for alcoholic beverages with caffeine, including those where the caffeine comes from naturally occurring sources. "Give us a base line," she argues. "I'm happy to comply. Regulate, but don't ban. . . . I'm a responsible marketer who has more than twenty-five years in the business."

Discussion Questions

1. Are these drinks as dangerous as the critics maintain? How much of the problem is the caffeine, how much labeling and marketing, and how much is irresponsible behavior on the part of young drinkers? Are companies like Joose and Four Loko being singled out for social problems, in particular, alcohol abuse by young people, that are in fact much wider in scope?

2. Is Peter Mercer correct that caffeinated alcoholic beverages serve no "socially redeeming purpose"? Is that the proper test for determining whether society should permit a product to be sold? What about the fact that there is a market demand for these products?

3. Is the banning of Four Loko and kindred beverages an example of legal paternalism?

4. Should others measures—for example, consumer education, regulation of caffeine content, changes to product labeling and packaging—have been attempted before banning these beverages?

5. Did the FDA move too quickly or was it necessary for the agency to act swiftly (in Senator Schumer's words) "before more tragedies occur"? Do you think the FDA acted on the basis of scientific evidence or as a result of political pressure?

6. What responsibilities do the manufacturers of alcoholic beverages have? What steps, if any, should they take to see that their produces are not abused? Did Four Loko fall down in this respect? What about Moonshot '69?

Chapter 7

The Environment

Learning Objectives

After completing this chapter, you should be able to:

1. Identify many of the most important environmental problems faced by the United States and the world.

2. Explain some of the political and economic challenges that we face in attempting to address these problems.

3. Critically discuss the roles of businesses, governments, and individuals in creating these problems and in responding to them.

4. Compare and contrast of the major theoretical perspectives in environmental ethics and apply these perspectives in different environmental contexts.

5. Offer and critically analyze arguments for different positions in some of the ongoing debates in environmental ethics, such as the debate over the permissibility of our eating meat and using nonhuman animals in other ways.

Introduction

When Pressure Blew the Top Off a Deep-Sea Well That Had Been drilled by BP's oil rig Deepwater Horizon in 2010, causing an explosion and a fire that claimed the lives of eleven members of the rig's crew, the American public was astonished and then—as efforts to plug the hole (a mile below the ocean's surface) dragged on and on—dismayed and angry. And with good reason: In the four months it took to cap the well, 4.9 million barrels of oil were released into the Gulf of Mexico, about forty miles off the coast of Louisiana, wreaking environmental havoc and calling into question, yet again, the country's desperate dependence on petroleum. Over 1 million birds were killed. As terrible as that spill was ("the worst environmental disaster America has ever faced," said President Obama), the Gulf region faces other serious long-term threats: the continuing loss of wetlands, over-fishing, invasive species spread by climate change, and the deadening effect of fertilizers that flow down the Mississippi from Midwestern farms. There's also the looming danger of another Deepwater Horizon; in 2020, a bipartisan panel concluded that the United States was only slightly better prepared to deal with another catastrophic oil spill, despite important technological improvements made by oil companies.[1]

The public tends to overlook slow-moving environmental disasters and to ignore altogether smaller scale, less-spectacular calamities.

> ....
>
> **Humankind is even making a mess of outer space.**
>
> ....

For example, fifteen months before the crisis in the Gulf, there was little national attention when a coal ash pond ruptured and disgorged nearly a billion gallons of toxic sludge across 300 acres of eastern Tennessee, destroying homes, killing fish, and threatening the local water supply. The sludge, which contains heavy metals and toxic substances, such as cadmium, lead, mercury, and selenium, is a by-product of the coal that the Tennessee Valley Authority burns to produce electricity at its Kingston Fossil Plant. Some of the workers who cleaned up the Kingston disaster now claim to be suffering serious health conditions as a result of their exposure.[2] While the amount of coal ash that the United States produces has been cut almost in half since 2014, it still creates nearly 70 million tons per year. A coal ash pond doesn't need to rupture to be dangerous. Simple rainfall can leach toxins out of the ash and allow it to enter groundwater, water that people drink. Coal ash ponds are mostly in rural areas and often in areas predominantly inhabited by people of color. Ninety-four percent of regulated ponds lack a lining to protect groundwater; nearly half are not regulated at all.[3]

Coal production destroys mountains and abrades the countryside, and burning coal for energy damages the environment. It remains the world's leading source of electrical power, generating 34 percent of

A home that was flooded with toxic sludge following the coal ash spill at the Kingston Fossil Plant in Tennessee. Even if an environmental calamity like this does not directly affect our lives, should it still be a cause of concern? Are there indirect ways in which it may impact us or in which our conduct may have helped bring it about?

reaching 1.1°C above 1850–1900 in 2011–2020. … Human-caused climate change is already affecting many weather and climate extremes in every region across the globe."[8] Climate change has many manifestations that directly affect our lives. Sea level rise threatens the habitability of low-lying coastal areas or entire island-nations. Devastating wildfires destroy forests and houses. Because warmer air retains more moisture, many regions experience droughts while a few local areas are struck by rainfall so intense that it causes deadly floods. Homeowners are finding it increasingly difficult to buy property insurance in Florida, as a number of insurance companies have partially or entirely pulled out of that market and others have raised rates substantially. Why? The companies have determined that the chaotic climate has increased Florida's risk of destructive hurricanes to the point where insuring houses is no longer good business.[9]

The environment is thus a huge topic, but as one expert remarks, "the concerns of environmental ethics might begin with the food on our plate."[10] Fertilizers, herbicides, and pesticides: Agriculture uses hundreds of chemicals in crop production. Although chemically intensive agriculture has yielded many benefits, it's hard on the environment—because of what it consumes and because of its impact on the surrounding ecosystem. In addition to the ecological price we pay for what we eat, there's the risk of chemical residues left in food. One recent report depicts a "vicious cycle between chemical dependency and intensifying climate," as increasing pest pressures created by warmer temperatures lead farmers to apply more chemicals to their crops while these chemicals—often derived from petroleum—contribute to the warming.[11]

Nor are herbicides and pesticides the only problematic chemicals. Our bodies now contain measurable quantities of a wide range of unnatural metals and potentially hazardous substances, including polychlorinated biphenyls (PCBs), furans, dioxin, mercury, lead, benzene, and other nasty items.[12] Perfluorochemicals, for example, were introduced in 1956, primarily in Teflon and other nonstick products. In one recent study, 45 percent of the drinking water samples tested contained at least one of these nonbiodegradable "forever" chemicals.[13] They have been linked to metabolic disturbances, thyroid disease, and more than one form of cancer.[14]

the planet's electricity in 2020.[4] In the United States, it was still the source of 19 percent of the nation's electricity. (These figures might have been even higher if power use had not declined due to the pandemic.) The coal ash spill at Kingston Fossil thus encapsulates many of the environmental problems we face as the ill effects of our environmental recklessness come home to roost.

Our rivers and lakes are dirty, the oceans are unhealthy, and our air is unclean. The Earth's protective ozone layer is precarious. Lush forests are disappearing, and with them countless species of plants and animals. Wetlands are disappearing at an even faster rate; over a third just since 1970.[5] Groundwater is seriously depleted. As a result, the Earth is losing its capacity to continue to provide the goods we need, threatening our economic well-being and ultimately our survival—so concludes a mammoth United Nations (U.N.)–sponsored assessment of global ecosystems.[6] Humankind is even making a mess of outer space. The number of active satellites has increased rapidly; there are currently about 9,000, but this figure is expected to exceed 60,000 by 2030. But these satellites—and manned space vessels—are endangered by the estimated 100 trillion pieces of "space junk": fragments of old rockets and satellites, smashed bits of equipment, and other debris that orbit the planet at high speed. Only a small fraction of these artifacts are large enough for us to track.[7]

Yet we also face an environmental crisis larger than any of those that have been mentioned so far: the climate change that's been driven by our heavy use of fossil fuels like coal, oil, and natural gas. The latest report of the Intergovernmental Panel on Climate Change says it clearly: "Human activities, principally through emissions of greenhouse gases, have unequivocally caused global warming, with global surface temperature

One way chemicals enter our bodies is through our water, as various contaminants used in farming, manufacturing, and transportation run off into rivers, lakes, and underground reservoirs. In 1972, Congress passed the **Clean Water Act**, which proclaimed the goal of eliminating all water pollution by 1985. Since Congress acted, billions have been spent on pollution control. However, how the Clean Water Act should be interpreted and enforced has been politically and legally controversial. Legal rulings have made it more difficult for the **Environmental Protection Agency** (EPA) to go after companies that pollute the nation's waters.[15] For example, in a unanimous 2023 decision in *Sackett v. EPA*, the Supreme Court ruled that many wetlands fall outside the scope of the Clean Water Act.

Pollution even affects America's drinking water. In 2021, the British newspaper *The Guardian* ran a series titled "America's Water Crisis." Their investigation, conducted in conjunction with *Consumer Reports*, found that millions of Americans' drinking water falls short of federal standards, sometimes due to dangerous levels of contamination. Less economically advantaged and Latinx communities are disproportionately affected.[16] The investigation was conducted following the revelation that changes in 2014 to the water supply and water treatment processes in the predominantly African American city of Flint, Michigan—changes made by the state in the interest of reducing costs—had resulted in many residents drinking water that contained dangerous levels of lead (as well as the bacteria that causes "Legionnaires' disease").[17] Lead exposure has been linked to developmental difficulties in children, which is why the United States has phased out lead-based paint and leaded gasoline. Nine Michigan officials were indicted on criminal charges in connection with the Flint debacle.[18]

Pollutants also contaminate the air we breathe, despoiling vegetation and crops, corroding buildings and industrial materials, and threatening our lives and health. Each year, millions of pounds of hazardous materials, including tons of toxic chemicals, are emitted into the air.[19] In addition to that is the emission of nontoxic substances such as sulfur and nitrogen oxide, which are a major source of acid rain and of the smog that blankets so many cities, and of the dust, soot, smoke, and tiny drops of acid that create the fine-particle pollution known to be so dangerous to human health.

Thanks to the groundbreaking **Clean Air Act**, passed in 1970, our air is better than it would otherwise have been, and by most measures it's cleaner than it was fifty years ago. In particular, by banning lead as a fuel additive in gasoline, the act has reduced its presence in the air by nearly 90 percent. And the **Clean Air Act Amendments of 1990** require further measures be taken to fight smog, acid rain, and toxic emissions. But the fact remains: More than four decades after Congress first set a strict deadline for reducing air pollution to safe levels, more than 119.6 million people—roughly, 36 percent of the population—live where the air is often dangerous to breathe.[20] Although precise figures are impossible to obtain, there's little doubt that air pollution is responsible for thousands of deaths and millions of sick days every year because of air-related ailments such as asthma, emphysema, and lung cancer. Air pollution is especially harmful to young people, whose lungs are still developing. It also contributes to heart disease, and pregnant women residing in regions with significant air pollution are significantly more likely to give birth prematurely or to have a child with a low birth weight.

Surprisingly, some of the largest sources of pollution and environmental degradation are not at all exotic—for example, the tons and tons of salt that are spread on roads to make them passable in winter. As a result, streams and rivers in the east and north have seen their sodium and chloride concentrations skyrocket. "There's plenty of scientific evidence to suggest that freshwater ecosystems are being contaminated by salt from the use of things like road salt beyond the concentration which is safe for freshwater organisms and for human consumption," says Dr. Bill Hintz, a professor of environmental sciences at the University of Toledo.[21] But, unfortunately, salt is a very effective de-icer—and it's cheap.

Another mundane but extremely damaging source of pollution stems from the animals we raise for food. In fact, the ecological costs of producing beef, poultry, and pork are second only to those of the manufacture and use of cars and light trucks. In addition to the electrical energy, fuel, fertilizer, and pesticides consumed by the meat industry is the manure problem. Megafarms with tens or hundreds of thousands of animals have replaced factories as the biggest polluters of America's waterways. The United States generates close to 1.4 billion tons of animal manure every year—up to 20 times more than the annual production of human waste.[22] This waste wasn't a problem when small farms crisscrossed the nation and farmers used the manure as fertilizer. But giant farms with 100,000 hogs or a million chickens all defecating in the same place seriously damage the environment, with dangerous health consequences as parasites and bacteria seep into drinking water. Now scientists are also worrying about air pollution and the emission of methane and other noxious fumes from the disposal of animal waste.

Nuclear wastes, of course, are in a class by themselves. Over 88,000 metric tons of highly radioactive nuclear waste are stranded at nuclear sites across the country, waiting to be disposed of.[23] However, according to a presidential panel set up to study the issue, the U.S. nuclear waste disposal program has "all but broken down."[24] How we end up disposing of these wastes has to worry anyone who's sensitive to the legacy we leave future generations. Will the nuclear wastes we bury today return to haunt them tomorrow? And, as the crisis at the Fukushima Daiichi nuclear power plant in Japan brought vividly home to the world in 2011, the risk of accidents or even a meltdown at a nuclear reactor is real and potentially catastrophic. On the other hand, with energy consumption expected to grow by more than half over the next thirty years, we may need more, not fewer, nuclear reactors if we are to avoid calamitous climate change. Nuclear energy also means fewer deaths from air pollution.

The effort to fight climate change also depends on the greater use of electrical power—electric cars, electric lawnmowers, and so on. Even if the electricity comes from fossil-fuel-powered plants, having power generation happen at large central facilities is more efficient than operating innumerable small internal combustion engines. However, electrification requires batteries, generally "lithium ion" batteries. And producing these batteries also has a significant impact on the environment. In the United States, for instance, a new lithium mining project in Nevada is expected to use and potentially contaminate billions of gallons of groundwater.[25] Lithium extraction has also been blamed for the depletion of water resources and harm to indigenous communities in other parts of the world, for example, the Puna de Atacama region of South America.[26]

•••

Business and Ecology

To deal intelligently with the question of business's responsibilities for the environment, one must realize that as business uses energy and materials, discharges waste, and generates products and services, it's functioning within an ecological system. **Ecology** refers to the science of the interrelationships among organisms and their environments. The operative term is "interrelationships," implying that an interdependence exists among all entities in the environment. In particular, we must not forget that human beings are part of nature and thus intricately connected with and interrelated to the natural environment.

Ecosystems

In speaking about ecological matters, scientists frequently use the term **ecosystem**, which refers to a total ecological community, both living and nonliving. Webs of interdependency structure ecosystems. Predators and prey, producers and consumers, hosts and parasites are linked, creating interlocking mechanisms—checks and balances—that stabilize the system. A change in any one element can have ripple effects throughout the system.

For example, a decade after wolves were reintroduced into Yellowstone Park in the mid-1990s, their presence was discovered to have changed the behavior of elk.[27] Skittish of wolves, the elk now spend more time than they used to in places that afford a 360-degree view, and they shy away from rises or bluffs that conceal wolves. In those places, aspen, cottonwoods, and willow thickets have bounced back as a result. The trees, in turn, have stabilized the banks of streams, and by lowering the water temperature, their shade has improved the habitat for trout, resulting in more and bigger fish. Beavers, which eat willow and aspen, have also returned to the streams. So have yellow warblers, Lincoln sparrows, and other songbirds. When wolves kill an elk, they don't eat the whole carcass, so scavengers like magpies and ravens prosper. Coyotes, in contrast, have declined. The creatures they used to prey on—voles, mice, and other rodents—are flourishing, and their increased numbers have boosted the population of raptors and red foxes

Every living organism affects its environment, yet *Homo sapiens* possesses the power to upset dramatically the stability of natural ecosystems. In particular, many human commercial activities have unpredictable and disruptive consequences for ecosystems. For example, farmers in the Midwest use nitrogen fertilizer liberally. As mentioned earlier, excess nitrogen runs off their fields and finds its way into the Mississippi River and eventually into the Gulf of Mexico. There, in what has historically been the nation's best shrimping grounds, it has created what is known as the dead zone, where the water is devoid of life to about 10 feet below the surface. While the size of the dead zone varies by year, on average it covers around 5,300 square miles.[28]

Tampering with ecosystems, however, does not always have injurious effects. Sometimes unforeseen benefits result, as was true years ago when oil and gas drilling first expanded into the Gulf. Much to everyone's surprise, the operational docks, pipes, and platforms provided a better place for lower forms of life to attach themselves than the silt-laden sea ever did.[29] This in turn increased the fish catch in the area. But even in fortuitous instances like this, environmental intrusions affect the integrity of ecosystems. And that's the point. Because an ecosystem represents a delicate balance of interrelated entities, the introduction of any new element, whether biotic or abiotic, can disrupt it. And we are not usually so lucky in the results. Dr. Paul Ehrlich, one of the early exponents of ecological awareness, put the matter succinctly. "There are a number of ecological rules it would be wise for people to remember," Ehrlich said. "One of them is that there is no such thing as a free lunch. Another is that when we change something into something else, the new thing is usually more dangerous than what we had originally."[30]

As it produces the goods and services we need or want, business inevitably intrudes into ecosystems, but not all intrusions are free of risk or justifiable. In fact, precisely because of the interrelated nature of ecosystems and because intrusions so often have negative consequences, business must try to tread lightly, avoiding actions, practices, and policies with an undue impact on the environment. There's ample documentation to show that historically, business has been remiss in both recognizing and adequately discharging its obligations in this regard. Let's examine some attitudes that have been responsible for this.

Many commercial activities have unpredictable and often disruptive environmental consequences.

....

Summary
Ecology studies the interrelationships among organisms and their environments. Because of the interdependence of an ecosystem's elements and because intrusion into an ecosystem frequently creates unfavorable effects, business must be sensitive to its impacts on the physical environment.

....

Business's Traditional Attitudes toward the Environment

Several related attitudes, prevalent in our society in general and in business in particular, have led to or increased our environmental problems. One of these is the tendency to view the natural world as something that is free and without limit, something we can exploit, even squander, without regard to the future. Writer John Steinbeck once reflected on this attitude:

> I have often wondered at the savagery and thoughtlessness with which our early settlers approached this rich continent. They came at it as though it were an enemy, which of course it was. They burned the forests and changed the rainfall; they swept the buffalo from the plains, blasted the streams, set fire to the grass, and ran a reckless scythe through the virgin and noble timber. Perhaps they felt that it was limitless and could never be exhausted and that a man could move on to new wonders endlessly . . .
>
> This tendency toward irresponsibility persists in very many of us today; our rivers are poisoned by reckless dumping of sewage and toxic industrial wastes, the air of our cities is filthy and dangerous to breathe from the belching of uncontrolled products from combustion of coal, coke, oil, and gasoline. Our towns are girdled with wreckage and debris of our toys—our automobiles and our packaged pleasures. Through uninhibited spraying against one enemy we have destroyed the natural balances our survival requires. All these evils can and must be overcome if America and Americans are to survive; but many of us conduct ourselves as our ancestors did, stealing from the future for our clear and present profit.[31]

Traditionally, business has considered the environment to be a free, nearly limitless good. In other words, air, water, land, and other natural resources from coal to beavers (trapped almost to extinction for their pelts in the nineteenth century) were seen as available for business to use as it saw fit. In this context, pollution and the depletion of natural resources are two aspects of the same problem: Both involve using up natural resources that are limited. Pollution uses up clean air and water, just as extraction uses up the minerals or oil in the ground. The belief that both sorts of resources are unlimited and free promotes their wasteful consumption.

Garrett Hardin describes the consequences of this attitude in his well-known parable, the **tragedy of the commons**. Hardin asks us to imagine villagers who allow their animals to graze in the commons, the collectively shared village pasture. Even though it's in the interest of each person to permit their animals graze without limit on the public land, the result of doing so is that the commons is soon overgrazed, making it of no further grazing value to anyone.[32]

Today, the international fishing industry exemplifies Hardin's point: Over-fishing by ships armed with advanced technology is dramatically reducing the world's stock of fish, threatening to undermine the whole industry.[33] But the moral of Hardin's story is perfectly general: When it comes to "the commons"—that is, to public or communal goods such as air, water, and wilderness—problems arise as the result of individuals and companies following their own self-interest. Each believes that their own use of the commons has only a negligible effect, but the cumulative result can be the gradual destruction of the public domain, which is bad for everyone. In the tragedy of the commons we have the reverse of Adam Smith's invisible hand: Each person's pursuit of self-interest makes everyone worse off.

The tragedy of the commons also illustrates the more general point that there can be a difference between the private costs and the social costs of a business activity. Chapter 5 discussed this issue when it described what economists call "externalities," but it's worth reviewing the point in the present context.

Suppose a paper mill only partially treats the chemical wastes it releases into a lake that's used for fishing and recreational activities, thus saving on production costs. If the amount of effluent is great enough to reduce the fishing productivity of the lake, then while the mill's customers pay a lower price for its paper than they otherwise would, other people end up paying a higher price for fish. Moreover, the pollution may make the lake unfit for recreational activities such as swimming or for use as a source of potable water. The result is that other people are forced to absorb the cost of the mill's inadequate water-treatment system. Economists term this disparity between private industrial costs and public social costs an **externality**, or **spillover**. In viewing things strictly in terms of private industrial costs, business overlooks spillover. This is an economic problem because the price of the paper does not reflect the true cost of producing it. Paper is underpriced and overproduced, thus leading to a misallocation of resources.

Both pollution and the depletion of natural resources involve using up something that is in limited supply.

Summary

Traditionally, business has regarded the natural world as a free and unlimited good. Pollution and resource depletion are examples of situations in which each person's pursuit of self-interest can make everyone worse off (the "tragedy of the commons"). Business must be sensitive to possible disparities between its private economic costs and the social costs of its activities (the problem of externalities or spillovers).

This is also a moral problem because the purchasers of paper are not paying its full cost. Instead, part of the cost of producing paper is being unfairly imposed on other people.

The states of Texas and Oklahoma furnish a good example of environmental externalities. In recent years, vast amounts of wastewater from oil and gas exploration in these states have been buried deep in the ground along fault lines. This has produced numerous earthquakes in a part of the country where earthquakes were previously quite rare.[34] Most are very small, but some—like a 5.8 magnitude quake that struck Oklahoma in 2016 and a 4.1 magnitude quake in the same state in 2021—are significant if not catastrophic. Other neighboring states, including Kansas, have also been affected. While a lawsuit did result in some compensation for Oklahomans whose homes were damaged in the large 2016 earthquake, in general homeowners and others pay for such damages, either by paying directly for repairs or by purchasing increasingly expensive earthquake insurance. The beneficiaries of this oil and gas exploration are the energy companies and their customers, but while they reap the benefits of this activity a significant portion of its costs are being paid by others who have no choice in the matter.

One strategy for addressing negative externalities is to "internalize" the externalities by finding ways to shift the cost of the spillover effects back on to the people or companies producing them. Fencing what was once a common grazing area and giving everyone their own plot would be an example of this; if someone lets their animals overgraze their own field then they pay the entire price of this mistake, while the fields of their more prudent neighbors remain intact. Suppose that oil and gas companies had to pay the true costs of their activities themselves. Imagine, say, that they were required to provide earthquake insurance for all homeowners within some radius of their operations. If the price of this insurance would depend on the frequency of earthquakes, then this might provide them with an incentive to inject less water underground. This would be another example of internalizing externalities.

In sum, then, externalities or spillover effects, pursuit of private interest at the expense of the commons, and a view of the environment as a free good that can be consumed without limit have combined with an ignorance of ecology and of the often fragile interconnections and interdependencies of the natural world to create the serious environmental problems facing us today. Fortunately, however, the attitudes of many business leaders are changing. A growing number of them recognize the widespread and systemic nature of the environmental challenges we face and have begun rethinking the whole relation of business to the natural environment. They see sustainability as integral to their business mission. "Today," says Patrick Cescau, chief executive of Unilever, "social responsibility and environmental sustainability are core business competencies, not fringe activities."[35]

> Several factors have combined to create the serious environmental problems facing us today.

• • •

The Ethics of Environmental Protection

Much of what we do to reduce, eliminate, or avoid pollution and the depletion of scarce natural resources is in our collective self-interest. Many measures that we take—for example, recycling our cans or installing catalytic converters in our cars—are steps that benefit all of us, collectively and individually: Our air is more breathable and our landscapes less cluttered with garbage. But even if such measures benefit each and every one of us, there's still a **free-rider problem** because of the temptation to shirk individual responsibility. People or companies may rationalize that the little bit they add to the total pollution problem doesn't make any difference. They benefit from the efforts of others to prevent pollution but "ride for free" by not making the same effort themselves.

The unfairness here is obvious. Likewise, as explained in the previous section, the failure of companies to internalize their environmental "externalities" spells unfairness. Others are forced to pick up the tab when companies do not pay all the environmental costs involved in producing their own products. As mentioned in Chapter 5, those who adopt the broader view of corporate responsibility emphasize that business and the rest of society have an implicit social contract. This contract reflects what society hopes to achieve by allowing business to operate; it sets the "rules of the game" governing business activity. Companies that try to be free riders in environmental matters or that refuse to address the spillover or external costs of their business activity violate this contract.

So far, this chapter has emphasized that we need to view the environment differently if we are to improve our quality of life and even to continue to exist. And it has just stressed how the failure of an individual or business to play its part is unfair. Some moral theorists, like William T. Blackstone, have gone further to argue that each of us has a **right to a livable environment**. In Blackstone's view, this is a human right. "Each person," he argues, "has this right *qua* being human and because a livable environment is essential for one to fulfill his human capacities."[36] This right has emerged, he contends, as a result of changing environmental conditions, which affect the very possibility of human life as well as the possibility of realizing other human rights.

Recognition of a right to a livable environment would strengthen further the ethical reasons for business to respect the integrity of the natural world. In addition, recognition of this moral right would, Blackstone suggests, provide compelling grounds for establishing a legal right to a livable environment through legislation and even, perhaps, through a constitutional amendment or an environmental bill of rights. Doing this would, in turn, enhance our ability to go after polluters and other abusers of the natural environment.

Acknowledging a human right to a livable environment, however, leaves unsolved many of the difficult problems facing us. In the effort to conserve irreplaceable resources, to protect the environment from further degradation, and to restore it to its former quality, we are still faced with difficult choices, each with its economic and moral costs. The next section focuses on pollution control, but most of the points apply equally to other problems of environmental protection as well as to the conservation of scarce resources.

Summary
Companies that attempt to be free riders in environmental matters or that refuse to address the external costs of their business activities behave unfairly. Some philosophers maintain, further, that every human being has a right to a livable environment.

The Costs of Pollution Control

It's easy to say that we should do whatever it takes to improve the environment. Before this answer has any operational worth, however, we must consider a number of things. One is the quality of environment that we want. This can vary from an environment restored to its pristine state and fully protected from future harm to one minimally improved over its current condition. Then there's the question of precisely what is necessary to bring about the kind of environment we want. In some cases, we may lack the technological capacity to fully accomplish our environmental goals. Finally, an important concern in any determination of what should be done to improve the environment is a calculation of what it will cost.

To draw out this point, we must consider a major technique for determining the total costs of environmental improvement. **Cost–benefit analysis** is a device used to determine whether it's worthwhile to incur a particular cost—for instance, the cost of employing a particular pollution-control device. The general approach is to evaluate a project's direct and indirect costs and benefits, the difference being the net result for society. Suppose that the estimated environmental damage of operating a particular plant is $1 million per year, that closing the plant would have dire economic consequences for the community, and that the only technique that would permit the plant to operate in an environmentally nondamaging way would cost $6 million per year. In this case, cost–benefit analysis would rule against requiring the plant to introduce the new technique. If, however, the cost of the technique had been only $800,000, then cost–benefit analysis would have favored it.

Cost–benefit analysis can quickly get complicated. For example, to determine whether it would be worthwhile to initiate more stringent air-pollution standards for a particular industry, a multitude of factors must be considered. Possible costs might include lower corporate profits, higher prices for consumers, unfavorable effects on employment, and adverse consequences for the nation's balance of payments. On the side of anticipated benefits, a reduction in airborne particulates over urban areas would reduce illness and premature death from bronchitis, lung cancer, and other respiratory diseases by some determinate percentage. The increase in life expectancy would have to be estimated along with projected savings in medical costs and increases in productivity. In addition, diminished industrial discharges would mean reduced property and crop damage from air pollution, and that would save more money.

What do you see as the costs and benefits of wind turbines as a source of energy?

This example suggests the extreme difficulty of making reliable estimates of actual costs and benefits, of putting price tags on the different effects of the policy being considered. Any empirical prediction in a case like this is bound to be controversial. This problem is compounded by the fact that decision makers are unlikely to know for certain all future results of the policy being studied. Not only is estimating the likelihood of its various possible effects difficult, but also some future effects may be entirely unanticipated.

The new discipline of **ecological economics** is attempting to expand further the boundaries of environmental cost–benefit analysis by calculating the value of an ecosystem in terms of what it would cost to provide the benefits and services it now furnishes us—for example, the worth of a wetland in terms of the cost of constructing structures that provide the same flood control and storm protection that natural wetlands do.[37] Although conventional economists dismiss the idea of equating the value of something with its replacement cost rather than with what people are willing to pay for it, ecological economists respond that traditional market pricing fails to capture the economic benefits that nature provides, such as the nutrients that a forest recycles. In one study, for example, ecological economists established that a mangrove swamp in Thailand was worth 72 percent more when left intact to provide timber, charcoal, fish, and storm protection than when converted to a fish farm. "In every case we looked at," states Cambridge University biologist Andrew Balmford, "the loss of nature's services outweighed the benefits of development, often by large amounts."[38]

Even putting aside the debate over ecological economics, cost–benefit analyses of rival environmental policies will frequently prove controversial because they inevitably involve making value judgments about nonmonetary costs and benefits. Costs can include time, effort, discomfort, and lost opportunities. Benefits, too, can take numerous nonmonetary forms: health, comfort, enjoyment, scenic beauty, self-fulfillment, freedom from odor, and so on. These competing costs and benefits are often difficult to quantify. For example, some environmentalists may campaign for the preservation of a remote forest visited annually by only a handful of stalwart backpackers, whereas developers wish to convert it into a more accessible and frequented ski resort. Should the forest be preserved or should it be converted into a ski resort? Conflicting value judgments are at stake.

With the assistance of an economics consulting firm, the U.S. Department of the Interior asked Americans how much they're willing to shell out for environmental restoration. For instance, what would each consent to pay to restore the ecological balance of the Grand Canyon, even if few of them will actually see or truly understand the improvements: ten cents a month? A dollar a month? Ten dollars a month? The Interior Department used this technique

Summary
Pollution control has a price, and trade-offs must be made. Weighing environmental costs and benefits is often difficult, though. The new discipline of ecological economics and recent attempts to measure "non-use value" try to offer a wider perspective on environmental issues, but any kind of cost–benefit analysis inevitably involves controversial factual assessments and value judgments.

to justify reintroducing wolves into parts of Montana, Wyoming, and Idaho—a controversial move opposed by some taxpayers, ranchers, and consumers of beef. Some environmentalists applaud this attempt to calculate what economists call "non-use value," but others fear that the attempt to put a monetary price tag on ecosystems belittles the values they champion.[39]

An assessment of costs and benefits inevitably involves value judgments and factual uncertainties.

Although an analysis of cost-effectiveness may be necessary for determining the soundness of an environmental-preservation measure or a pollution-control project, it seems inevitable that any assessment of costs and benefits will be subject to various factual uncertainties and be significantly influenced by the values one holds. This is especially true in situations where environmental concerns clash. Windmills, for example, offer a clean, endlessly renewable source of energy, but they blemish the natural landscape, are sometimes noisy, and can chop up migratory birds. Likewise, plans to harvest solar power on a large scale would sacrifice hundreds of thousands of acres of wilderness and threaten some endangered species.[40] Technology that replaces wood fiber with calcium carbonate in the production of paper saves trees, but mining it sometimes despoils bucolic areas.[41] Natural gas burns more cleanly than other fossil fuels, but the new offshore terminals that process it kill sea life and put pressure on an already fragile marine ecosystem.[42] Even the simple question "Paper or plastic?" poses complicated environmental trade-offs.[43] Nor are cloth bags obviously better. According to a study by the Danish government, you would need to use a cotton grocery bag 7,100 times before its environmental impact would be lower than using disposable plastic bags that you reuse once (e.g., to line a trash can or to clean up after a dog).[44] Cotton is a water-intensive crop. This figure actually rises to 20,000 uses if the cotton is grown organically and hence less efficiently.

Who Should Pay the Costs?

The most comprehensive federal study of air-pollution rules shows the cost of compliance to be outweighed five to seven times by the economic benefits from reductions in hospitalization, emergency room visits, premature deaths, and lost workdays.[45] Indeed, over recent decades cleaner air has added nearly five months to average life expectancy in the United States.[46] In addition, of course, money spent to minimize pollution also benefits those paid to clean up or prevent the pollution. Indeed, restoring the environment or even just helping businesses and individuals adjust to climate change could well end up being the biggest economic enterprise of our times, a huge source of jobs, profits, and poverty alleviation. Still, environmental protection and restoration do not come cheap, and determining who should pay the necessary costs raises a tough question of social justice. Two popular answers to this question currently circulate: (1) Those responsible for causing the pollution ought to pay, and (2) those who stand to benefit from protection and restoration should pick up the tab.

Those Responsible

The claim that those responsible for causing the pollution ought to pay the costs of pollution control and environmental restoration seems eminently fair until one asks a simple question: Who, exactly, is responsible for the pollution? Who are the polluters?

Many people argue that big business is the chief polluter and therefore ought to bear the lion's share of the costs of environmental protection and restoration. Business probably has profited more than any other group from treating the environment as a free good, but consumers have also benefited by not having to pay higher costs for products. In fact, some would argue that consumers are primarily to blame for pollution because they create the demand for the products whose production impairs the environment. As Milton Friedman put it, "the people who use electricity are responsible for the smoke that comes out of the stacks of generating plants."[47] Therefore, the argument goes, it's consumers, not business, who should pay to protect and restore the environment. This argument can be extended globally. International agreements like the Kyoto Protocol, which became effective in 2005, look at greenhouse emissions on a country-by-country basis, requiring every participating nation to reduce the carbon dioxide (CO_2) produced within its borders. (CO_2 is a principal cause of global warming.) As the main producer of MP3 players, for example, China contributes significantly to global warming because manufacturing a single player releases about 17 pounds of CO_2 into the atmosphere.

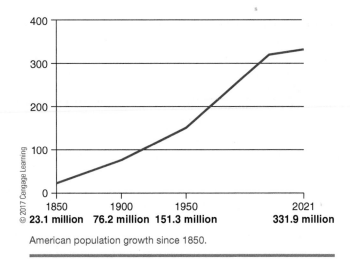

American population growth since 1850.

But if a Chinese factory makes something only to meet the demand of consumers in America, don't these consumers bear ultimate responsibility for the pollution that results?[48]

Actually, both versions of the polluter-should-pay-the-bill thesis—one attributing primary responsibility for pollution to big business, the other to consumers—largely ignore the manifold, deep-rooted causes of environmental degradation. Population growth and the increasing concentration of population in urban areas are two of them. In 1900, there were 76.2 million Americans; since then, the U.S. population has more than quadrupled, to 331.9 million. An increasingly urbanized nation, the United States is a long way from the rural, agriculturally oriented society it once was. Today, for example, the number of college students is more than three times the entire U.S. farm population, which has fallen from over 40 percent of the nation in 1900 to less than 2 percent today. More than 70 million Americans live in our ten largest metropolitan areas, and nearly half the population resides in metropolitan areas with populations of a million or more. Accompanying this tremendous growth and equally staggering level of urbanization is an ever-increasing demand for goods and services, natural resources, energy, and industrial production. Viewing the matter globally only underscores the point. The world's population has more than doubled since 1960 and is increasingly urbanized. Half the world's population lives in cities, and sixteen of the world's twenty largest cities are in developing countries.

Another root cause of environmental problems is rising affluence. As people get more money to spend, they buy and consume more tangible goods, discard them more quickly, and produce more waste, all of which put pressure on the environment, hastening its degradation. Americans today produce just under five pounds of garbage per person per day, almost 1,800 pounds per person per year.[49] We own more than 275 million motor vehicles—that's about a fifth of the global total—and are only making matters worse by our preference for big, gas-guzzling pickups, minivans, and sport-utility vehicles (SUVs), which emit significantly more CO_2 and nitrogen oxides (the main source of smog) than ordinary passenger cars do.[50] Naturally enough, people in less-developed countries aspire to the material lifestyle that Americans enjoy, and their rapidly growing economies are beginning to make this possible. But the environmental consequences of even a third of the world's population consuming as much and as wastefully as Americans do would be catastrophic.

Thus, the enemy in the war against environmental abuse turns out, in a sense, to be all of us. No solution to the question of who should pay the costs of pollution control can ignore this fact.

Those Who Would Benefit

The other popular reply to the payment question is that those who will benefit from environmental improvement should pay the costs.

Summary
Any equitable solution to the problem of who should bear the costs of environmental protection and restoration must recognize that all of us in some way contribute to the problem and benefit from environmental safeguards and improvements. Among the deep-rooted causes of environmental degradation are population growth, increasing urbanization, and rising affluence.

Workers in certain industries and people living in certain neighborhoods or regions benefit more than other people from environmental controls. The residents of the Los Angeles basin, for instance, gain more from stringently enforced auto-emission standards than do people living in a remote corner of Wyoming. The trouble with this argument, though, is that every individual, rich or poor, and every institution, large or small, stands to benefit in some way from environmental protection and restoration, albeit not necessarily to the same degree. As a result, the claim that those who will benefit should pay the costs is problematic because pollution touches everyone. This point holds true internationally. Improved environmental controls in China would undoubtedly benefit the Chinese people first and foremost; but the global warming to which this pollution contributes is a worldwide problem, and addressing it will benefit us all.

If, however, this position means that individuals and groups should pay to the degree that they will benefit, then one must wonder how this could possibly be determined. For example, changing the operation of the Glen Canyon Dam has raised electricity bills in the West, but it has reduced ecological damage to the Grand Canyon. Who benefits the most—local residents, visitors to the Grand Canyon, everyone who values this national resource—and how much should they pay?[51] But perhaps the most serious objection to this thesis is that it seems to leave out responsibility as a legitimate criterion. Pollution restrictions on American power plants in the Midwest benefit Canadians by reducing acid rain, but to make them pay the costs wouldn't seem fair. Some small island nations in the Pacific are in danger of disappearing under water if sea level rise due to climate change continues. Their resources are limited and their contributions to the problem are negligible. While they might benefit more than anyone from efforts to reduce greenhouse gas emissions, to ask them to pay more than a nominal amount to support these efforts would be the height of injustice.[52]

Any equitable solution to the problem of who should pay the bill for environmental cleanup should take into account responsibility as well as benefit. The preceding analysis suggests that, to a certain extent, we all share the blame for pollution and all stand to benefit from environmental improvement. This doesn't mean, however, that we can't pinpoint certain areas of industry as chronic polluters. Electric-power plants, for example, are one of the major sources of greenhouse gases, but not all plants are equally dirty. Old coal-burning plants that have resisted modernization produce a disproportionate share of the pollution. Likewise, some companies can be singled out as having particularly distressing environmental records.

When one reads reports that blame particular companies for the environmental track records, however, one should think critically about whether the responsibility or blame is being appropriately placed. Suppose that someone drives an SUV 10,000 miles a year, buying gasoline from a Shell station. Do we attribute the emissions coming out of their tailpipe to the driver or to the Royal Dutch Shell corporation? In recent years, various reports have included lists of corporations who are ostensibly the largest contributors to climate change, generally large petroleum companies. These reports ascribe the responsibility for the emissions generated by consumers when they drive cars, fly on airplanes, run their furnaces, and so forth to the corporations who supply the fuel.[53] If there's an argument for this sort of accounting, then there's also an argument for assigning individuals more responsibility for the emissions that their activities produce. Some responsibility might also be assigned to, say, local governments who have designed American cities in ways that encourage the use of private automobiles and carmakers who produce and promote oversized, inefficient vehicles. When it comes to a problem as large as global warming, there's plenty of blame to go around.

A fair and just program for assigning costs begins with a recognition that we all bear some responsibility for our environmental problems and that we all stand to benefit from correcting them. But even if we agree that it's only fair that everyone share the cost of environmental improvement, we can still wonder about how the bill ought to be paid. What would be the fairest and most effective way of handling those costs?

Although we all share some responsibility for pollution, certain companies and industries stand out as excessive polluters.

...

Achieving Our Environmental Goals

Without an environmentally informed citizenry making conscientious political, business, and consumer choices, it will prove impossible to reverse the degradation of our environment by halting pollution, stemming global warming, and reducing the utilization of natural resources to sustainable levels. Just as obviously, business and government must work together if we are to achieve our shared environmental goals. Government, in particular, has a crucial role to play by initiating programs that prod business to behave in more environmentally responsible ways. That's easy to see. The more challenging moral and economic task is to determine fair and effective methods for doing so.

Three distinct approaches to environmental protection are the use of regulations, the use of incentives, and the use of pricing mechanisms and pollution permits. Though similar in some respects, they carry different assumptions about the roles of government and business, as well as about what's fair and just. Each approach has distinct advantages and weaknesses; each raises some questions of social justice.

Regulations

The **regulatory approach** makes use of direct public regulation and control in determining how the pollution bill is paid. State and federal legislation and regulations formulated by agencies such as the EPA set environmental standards, which are then applied and enforced by those agencies, other regulatory bodies, and the courts. An emissions standard that, for example, prohibits industrial smokestacks from releasing more than a certain percentage of particulate matter would require plants exceeding that standard to comply with it by installing an appropriate pollution-control device.

A clear advantage to such a regulatory approach is that standards would be legally enforceable. Firms not meeting them could be fined or even shut down. Also, from the view of morality, such standards are fair in that they apply to all industries in the same way. There are, however, distinct disadvantages in this approach.

First, pollution statutes and regulations generally require polluters to use the strongest feasible means of pollution control. But that requires the EPA or some other regulatory body to investigate pollution-control technologies and economic conditions in each industry to find the best technology that companies can afford. Such studies may require tens of thousands of pages of documentation, and legal proceedings may be necessary before the courts give final approval to the regulation. Moreover, expecting the EPA to master the economics and technology of dozens of industries, from petrochemicals to steel to electric utilities, may be unreasonable. It's bound to make mistakes, asking more from some companies than they can ultimately achieve while letting others off too lightly.[54]

Second, although universal environmental standards are fair in the sense that they apply to all equally, this very fact raises questions about their effectiveness. In attempting to legislate realistic and reliable standards for all, will government end up with only diluted and inadequate regulations? Or consider areas where the environment is cleaner than government standards. In such cases, should an industry be allowed to pollute up to the maximum of the standard? The Supreme Court thinks not. In a case brought before it by the Sierra Club, the Court ruled that states with relatively clean air must prohibit industries from producing significant air pollution even when EPA standards are not violated. In this case, a firm was being forced to pay the costs of meeting an environmental standard that, in one sense, was sterner than what competitors were required to meet elsewhere. One can also question both the equity and the economic sense of requiring compliance with universal standards, without regard for the idiosyncratic nature of each industry or the particular circumstances of individual firms. Is it reasonable to force companies that cause different amounts of environmental damage to spend the same amount on pollution abatement? In one case, the courts required two paper mills on the West Coast to install expensive pollution-control equipment, even though their emissions were diluted effectively by the Pacific Ocean. It took a special act of Congress to rescue the mills.[55]

Although a regulatory approach is fair in the sense of setting legally enforced standards that apply equally to all, it has four drawbacks.

Summary
Regulation is the most familiar way of pursuing environmental goals, but requiring firms to use the strongest feasible means of pollution control is problematic. Although regulations treat all parties equally, this often comes at the cost of ignoring the special circumstances of particular industries and individual firms. Regulations also remove a company's incentive to do more than the law requires and can cause plants to shut down or relocate.

Third, regulation can also take away an industry's incentive to do more than the minimum required by law. No polluter has an incentive to discharge less muck than regulations allow. No entrepreneur has an incentive to devise technology that will bring pollution levels below the registered maximum. Moreover, firms have an incentive not to let the EPA know they can pollute less. Under the regulatory approach, a government agency may have the desire to regulate pollution but lack the information to do it efficiently. The position of industry is reversed: It may have the information and the technology but no desire to use it.[56]

Finally, there's the problem of displacement costs resulting from industrial relocation or shutdown due to environmental regulations. For example, Youngstown Sheet and Tube Company moved its corporate headquarters and some production lines to the Chicago area, thus eliminating 500 jobs in Youngstown, Ohio, and causing serious economic problems in nearby communities. One of the reasons for the transfer was the need to implement water-pollution controls, which depleted vital capital. Consider also the marginal firms that would fail while attempting to meet the costs of such standards. When air-pollution regulations were applied to a sixty-year-old cement plant in San Juan Bautista, California, the plant had to close because it was too obsolete to meet the standard economically. The shutdown seriously injured the economy of the little town, which had been supported primarily by the cement plant.

But if regulations are tougher for new entrants to an industry than for existing firms, as they often are, then new investment may be discouraged—even if newer plants would be cleaner than older ones. For example, a clause in the Clean Air Act exempts old coal-fired plants from complying with current emissions rules. As a result, much of America's electricity is produced by plants that are more than forty years old and far dirtier than newer plants would be.[57] Perhaps in 1970 it was fair not to force existing plants into compliance with new rules. But is it still fair? Clearly, a regulatory approach to environmental improvement, though having advantages, raises serious questions.

Incentives

A widely supported approach to the problem of cost allocation for environmental improvement is government investment, subsidy, and other economic incentives. For instance, government might give firms a tax break for purchasing (and using) pollution-control equipment, or it might offer matching grants to companies that install such devices. A different example is the "Future-Gen" project, launched in 2003. It commits the federal government to underwriting 80 percent of the $1 billion or so cost of industry's developing a cost-effective new generation of coal-fired plants that emit no greenhouse gases into the atmosphere.

In its "33/50 Program," the EPA tried a different approach. It asked 600 industrial facilities to reduce voluntarily their discharges of seventeen toxic contaminants, first by 33 percent, then by 50 percent. The incentive for firms to commit to the reductions was simply the public relations opportunities afforded by EPA press releases and outstanding performance awards—along with, perhaps, the firms' desire to stave off future regulatory action.

The advantage of an **incentive approach** is that it minimizes government interference in business and encourages voluntary action rather than coercing compliance, as in the case of regulation. By allowing firms to move at their own pace, it avoids the evident unfairness to firms that cannot meet regulatory standards and must either relocate or fail. In addition, whereas regulated standards often encourage only minimal legal compliance, an incentive approach provides an economic reason for going beyond the minimum. Firms have a financial inducement to do more than just meet EPA standards.

An incentives-based approach is likely to be slow and sometimes amounts to paying polluters not to pollute.

But incentives are not without disadvantages that bear moral overtones. *First*, as an essentially voluntary device, an incentive program is likely to be slow. Environmental problems that cry out for a solution may continue to fester. Incentive programs may allow urgently needed action to be postponed. *Second*, government incentive programs often amount to a subsidy for polluters, with polluting firms being paid not to pollute. Although this approach may sometimes address the economics of pollution more effectively than the regulatory approach, it nonetheless raises questions about the justice of benefiting not the victims of pollution but some of the egregious polluters. *Third*, incentive programs can be abused, and determining their cost-effectiveness can be problematic. Indeed, when promoted by business lobbyists and sectional political interests, the environmental gain they bring may not be worth the cost. For example, the United States spends billions upon billions to subsidize the conversion of corn to ethanol. The subsidy benefits agribusiness and other corporate interests, but its positive environmental impact is slight. Worse, by reducing the amount of food produced, the subsidy has helped drive up world food prices, with painful consequences for the poor.[58]

Special interests can distort incentive programs.

Pricing Mechanisms and Pollution Permits

A third approach to the cost-allocation problem involves programs designed to charge firms for the amount of pollution they produce. **Pricing mechanisms** spell out the cost for a specific kind of pollution. For instance, a carbon tax sets a price on CO_2 emissions. If feasible, prices might be tied to the amount of damage caused in a specific place at a specific time. For example, during the summer months in the Los Angeles basin, a firm might pay much higher charges for fly ash emitted into the environment than it would pay during the winter months. Whatever the set of prices, the more a firm pollutes, the more it pays.

One advantage of this approach is that it places the cost of pollution control squarely on the polluters. Pricing mechanisms penalize, rather than compensate, industrial polluters. For many people this is inherently fairer than incentive programs that subsidize companies that pollute. Also, because costs are internalized, firms are encouraged to do more than meet the minimal requirements established under a strict regulatory policy. Under this approach, a firm, in theory, could be charged for any amount of pollution and not just incur legal penalties whenever it exceeded an EPA standard. In effect, pollution costs would become production costs.

Instead of imposing a tax or a fee on the pollutants released into the environment, the government could charge companies for **pollution permits**, or it could auction off a limited number of permits. An even more market-oriented strategy, one called **cap and trade**, gives companies permits to discharge a limited amount of pollution and then to allow them to buy and sell the right to emit pollutants. With pollution permits, companies with low pollution levels can make money by selling their pollution rights to companies with poorer controls. Thus, each firm can estimate the relative costs of continuing to pollute as opposed to investing in cleaner procedures. The government can also set the precise amount of pollution it's prepared to allow, and by lowering the amount permitted over time the firm can reduce or even eliminate it.

Earlier in this chapter, it was noted that one possible solution to the problem of overgrazing on a common field is enclosure, using fences to give everyone their own private plot. The intention is to give individuals an incentive not to overgraze by internalizing what was previously an externality, so that each individual pays the full price if they let their animals eat so much grass that the turf is destroyed. The market-oriented approach to controlling pollution essentially takes this approach toward the atmosphere or a body of water. It's as if each company is given a certain "piece" of the air, say, that they're allowed either to pollute themselves or to sell to someone else. If companies squander their piece of the atmosphere by emitting the full amount of pollution that is allowed, then they pay a price since they lose the option to sell some of their piece of the atmosphere.

The EPA successfully experimented with this strategy in the 1970s when it gave oil refineries two years to reduce the allowable lead content in gasoline. Refineries received quotas on lead, which they could trade with one another. Later, the 1990 Clean Air Act Amendments adopted this approach with respect to the sulfur dioxide (SO_2) emissions of electric utilities. Though controversial at the time—the power industry insisted the SO_2 cuts were prohibitively costly and environmental groups derided the measure as a sham—the scheme surpassed its initial objectives and at a far lower cost than expected.[59] In 2008, ten northeastern states joined together to limit emissions from power plants within their borders by auctioning a limited number of permits to emit CO_2.[60] Meanwhile, a global market has emerged for trading carbon-emission credits because of the Kyoto Protocol on greenhouse gases.

Summary
Two other methods for protecting the environment are incentives and charges or permits for pollution. Each has advantages and disadvantages. Incentives can be slow to work and may amount to subsidizing polluters. Economists favor pricing mechanisms and pollution permits, but critics dislike the idea of turning pollution into a commodity to be bought and sold.

For both economic and scientific reasons, however, pricing mechanisms and pollution permits do not work well in all situations and for all environmental problems; dealing with mercury pollution is one example.[61] Still, economists generally favor using them wherever possible. However, they trouble many environmentalists. For one thing, the price tag for polluting seems arbitrary. How will effluent charges or permit prices be set? What is a fair price? Any decision seems bound to reflect debatable economic and value judgments. Moreover, environmentalists dislike the underlying principle of pricing mechanisms and pollution permits and view with suspicion anything that sounds like a license to pollute. They resent the implication that companies have a right to pollute, and they reject the notion that companies should be able to make money by selling that right to other firms. In fact, Michael J. Sandel, professor of government at Harvard, argues that it's immoral to buy the right to pollute. "Turning pollution into a commodity to be bought and sold removes the moral stigma that is properly associated with it," he says.[62]

In sum, although each of these approaches—regulations, incentives, pricing mechanisms, and pollution permits—has its advantages, none is without its weak points. Because there appears to be no single, ideal approach to all our environmental problems, a combination of regulations, incentives, effluent charges, and permits is probably called for. Any such combination must take into account not only effectiveness but also fairness to those who will have to foot the bill. Fairness in turn calls for input from all sectors of society, a deliberate commitment by all parties to work in concert, a sizable measure of good faith, and perhaps above all else a heightened sense of social justice. This is no mean challenge.

Measures to protect the environment often force firms to become more efficient.

Still, environmental protection isn't always a static or zero-sum trade-off, with a fixed economic price to be paid for the gains we want. One reason is that higher environmental standards and properly designed regulatory or other programs can pressure corporations to invest capital in newer, state-of-the-art manufacturing technology; this both reduces pollution and enhances productive efficiency. In addition, international data in a range of industrial sectors show that innovation can minimize or even eliminate the costs of conforming to tougher environmental standards by increasing productivity, lowering total costs, and improving product quality. The reason is that pollution is evidence of economic waste. The discharge of scrap, chemical wastes, toxic substances, or energy in the form of pollution is a sign that resources have been used inefficiently.

Consider some examples.[63] Environmental regulations forced Dow Chemical to redesign the production process at its complex in California to avoid storing chemical waste in evaporation ponds. Not only did the new process reduce waste, but the company also found that it could reuse part of it as raw material in other parts of the plant. For a cost of $250,000, Dow was soon saving $2.4 million each year. Likewise, when new environmental standards forced 3M to reduce the volume of solvents to be disposed of, the company found a way to avoid the use of solvents altogether, which yielded it an annual savings of more than $200,000. Most distillers of coal tar opposed regulations requiring them to reduce benzene emissions; they thought the only solution was to cover tar storage tanks with costly gas blankets. But Aristech Chemical Corporation found a way to remove benzene from tar in the first processing step. Instead of a cost increase, the company saved itself $3.3 million.

Summary
Environmental protection isn't a static or zero-sum trade-off. Higher environmental standards can pressure companies to invest in new technology, thus enhancing efficiency as well as reducing pollution. Many economists believe that measures to reduce greenhouse gas emissions may improve U.S. productivity in the long run.

Many other companies are finding that going green not only is environmentally responsible but also improves efficiency and saves them money, thus benefiting the bottom line.[64] At the end of the last century, a broad array of economists, led by Nobel laureates Kenneth J. Arrow and Robert M. Solow, urged that with regard to global warming, measures to reduce greenhouse gas emissions need not harm the economy and "may in fact improve U.S. productivity in the long run." This is because many innovative, energy-efficient technologies are just waiting for the right financial incentives to enter the market. And in many of these fields, U.S. industry was a leader.[65] More recently, analysts with the consulting firm McKinsey and Company observe that while America has ceded much of its leadership position to China and Europe, it still has an advantage in innovation that it could capitalize upon by doing more to encourage domestic firms to develop green technology.[66]

•••

Delving Deeper into Environmental Ethics

So far, our discussion of environmental ethics has focused on business's obligation to understand its environmental responsibilities, to acknowledge and internalize its externalities (or spillovers), and to avoid free riding. It has stressed the extent to which environmental protection is in our collective self-interest, and it has looked at the operational and moral dilemmas involved in dealing with the costs of pollution. The subject of environmental ethics can be pursued more deeply than this, however.

Global Environmental Fairness

For one thing, we need to consider our obligations to those who live outside our society. For example, the United States represents less than 5 percent of the world's population but consumes almost 17 percent of the world's energy (and 20 percent of the world's refined oil).[67] Americans also contribute far more than their proportional share to global warming, emitting close to 11 percent of all greenhouse gasses.[68] (China now accounts for more than 25 percent of greenhouse gas emissions, but its population is over four times that of the United States.) To add insult to unfairness, the United States exports much of its garbage (which it produces more of than any other nation) overseas, including old, "recycled" computers and other electronic equipment that now litter many poor nations.[69]

Tropical rain forests are of special concern. They're the Earth's richest, oldest, and most complex ecosystems. Tropical forests are major reservoirs of biodiversity, home to 40 to 50 percent of all types of living things, yet millions of acres of tropical rain forest are destroyed each year. Already half the globe's original rain forest has disappeared, and two-thirds of what remains is fragmented, making it more vulnerable to being cleared.[70] Tropical forests are often chopped down to provide farms for growing third-world populations, but the affluence of people in rich nations like the United States is responsible for much forest destruction. Central American forests are cleared in part for pasture land to make pet food and convenience food slightly cheaper in the United States. In response to the demand for beef and leather in the developed world, cattle ranches are carving into the Amazon rain forest.[71] Thus, a prosperous American living thousands of miles away may be the cause of more tropical forest destruction than a poor person living within the forest itself.

When it comes to global climate change, the issue is similar. From a historical perspective, the United States and other developed nations are responsible for the bulk of the greenhouse

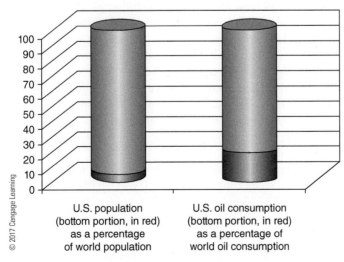

© 2017 Cengage Learning

The United States represents 4.23 percent of the world's population and consumes 20 percent of the world's refined oil. Is the United States obligated to reduce its oil consumption?

gasses that are destabilizing the world's climate and which stem from the industrialization that has brought those countries their extraordinary affluence. But it's the poorer nations, those that have done the least to cause the problem, that are suffering the most from it. They're also the least able to cope with it. One Bangladeshi says, "We are in a piece of land smaller than Denmark, with a population of 160 million, trying to cope with this extreme weather, trying to cope with the effect of emissions for which we are not responsible." And as was noted earlier, many small island nations in the South Pacific are worried simply about staying above water, now that rising sea levels threaten to submerge them.

The inequities of the world's environmental troubles thus raise the question of the nature and extent of the obligation, if any, of the advanced industrialized nations to assist poorer nations to deal with the effects of climate change and environmental degradation, which we—not they—have brought about. But our bloated levels of consumption and our dependence on foreign resources to satisfy our needs raise two further, equally pressing issues.

To satisfy its disproportionate consumption of nonrenewable resources, America turns to foreign lands. This raises two moral questions.

First is the question of how the continued availability of foreign resources is to be secured. Will our need for resources outside our territory lead us to try to control other countries, politically and economically, particularly in the Middle East and the developing world? To do so is morally risky, because political and economic domination almost always involves violations of the rights and interests of the dominated population, as well as of our own moral ideals and values.

Second is the question of whether any nation has a right to consume the world's irreplaceable resources at a rate so grossly out of proportion to the size of its population. Of course, we pay to consume oil and other resources that other nations own, but in the view of many, the fact that these nations acquiesce in our disproportionate consumption of resources does not resolve the moral problem of our doing so. Are we respecting the needs and interests of both our present co-inhabitants on this planet and the future generations who will live on Earth? This question is particularly burning now that scientists believe that human demand for natural resources has outstripped the biosphere's regenerative capacity.[72]

Obligations to Future Generations

Almost everybody feels intuitively that it would be wrong to empty the globe of resources or to irreparably contaminate the environment that we pass on to **future generations**. Certainly, there's a danger that we will do both of these things. But the question of what moral obligations we have to future generations is surprisingly difficult, and discussion among philosophers has not resolved all the important theoretical issues.

Can we talk meaningfully of future generations having a right that we not despoil the world they will inherit?

Even though most of us agree that it would be immoral to make the world uninhabitable for future people, can we talk meaningfully of those future generations having a right that we not do this? After all, our remote descendants are not yet alive and thus cannot claim a right to a livable environment. In fact, since these generations do not yet exist, they cannot at present, it seems, be said to have any interests at all. How can they then have rights?

Professor of philosophy Joel Feinberg argues, however, that whatever future human beings turn out to be like, they will have interests that we can affect, for better or worse, right now. Even though we do not know who the future people will be, we do know that they will have interests and what the general nature of those interests will be. This is enough, he contends, both to talk coherently about their having rights and to impose a duty on us not to leave ecological time bombs for them.

Feinberg concedes that it doesn't make sense to talk about future people having a right to be born. The child that you could conceive tonight, if you felt like it, cannot intelligibly be said to have a right to be born. (The idea that there could be such a right appears even more implausible when we remember that there might be indefinitely many children that a given couple could conceive in a given evening, since the precise timing of the procreative act may determine which sperm fertilizes the egg.) Thus, the rights of future generations are "contingent," says Feinberg, on those future people coming into existence. But this qualification does not affect his main contention: "The interests that [future people] are sure to have when they come into being . . . cry out for protection from invasions that can take place now."[73]

Even if we are persuaded that future generations have rights, we still do not know exactly what those rights are or how they're to be balanced against the interests and rights of present people. For example, how much economic growth must we sacrifice to try to prevent climate change from seriously damaging the lives and interests of future people? If we substantially injure future generations to gain some small benefit for ourselves, we are being as selfish and shortsighted as we would be by hurting other people today for some slight advantage for ourselves. Normally, however, if the benefits of some environmental policy outweigh the costs, then a strong case can be made for adopting the policy. But what if it's the present generation that receives the benefits and the future generations that pay the costs? Would it be unfair of us to adopt such a policy? Would doing so violate the rights of future people?

An additional puzzle is raised by the fact that policies we adopt will affect who's born in the future. Imagine that we must choose between two environmental policies, one of which would result in a slightly higher standard of living than the other over the next century. Given the differing effects of those policies on the specifics of people's lives, over time it would increasingly be true that people would marry different people under one policy than they would under the other. And even within the same marriages, children would increasingly be conceived at different times. The philosopher Derek Parfit observes that:

> Some of the people who are later born would owe their existence to our choice of one of the two policies. If we had chosen the other policy, these particular people would never have existed. And the proportion of those later born who owe their existence to our choice would, like ripples in a pool, steadily grow. We can plausibly assume that, after three centuries, there would be no one living in our community who would have been born whichever policy we chose.[74]

Parfit adds: "It may help to think about this question: How many of us could truly claim, 'Even if railways and motor cars had never been invented, I would still have been born'?"

This reasoning suggests that subsequent generations cannot complain about an environmental policy choice we make today that causes them to have fewer opportunities and a lower standard of living. If we had made a different choice, then those people would not have existed at all. It might be claimed, however, that we act immorally in causing people to exist whose rights to equal opportunity and to a standard of living at least on a par with ours cannot be fulfilled. But if those future people knew the facts, would they regret that we acted as we did?[75]

Perhaps it's a mistake to focus on the rights and interests of future people as individuals. Annette Baier argues that the important thing is to "recognize our obligations to consider the good of the continuing human community."[76] This stance suggests adopting a utilitarian perspective and seeking to maximize total human happiness through time. But a utilitarian approach is also not without problems. If our concern is with total happiness, we may be required to increase greatly the Earth's population. Even if individuals on an overcrowded Earth do not have much happiness, there may still be more total happiness than there would be if we followed a population-control policy that resulted in fewer but better-off people. This distasteful conclusion has led some utilitarians to modify their theory and maintain that with regard to population policy, we should aim for the highest average happiness rather than the highest total happiness. But this, too, is problematic because in theory one could, it seems, increase average happiness by eliminating unhappy people.

John Rawls has suggested another approach to the question of our obligations to future generations, an approach that reflects his general theory of justice (discussed in Chapter 3). He suggests that the members of each generation put themselves in the "original position." Then, without knowing what generation they belong to, they could decide what would be a just way of distributing resources between consecutive generations. They would have to balance how much they're willing to sacrifice for their descendants against how much they wish to inherit from their predecessors. In other words, the original position and the veil of ignorance might be used to determine our obligations to future generations—in particular, how much each generation should save for use by those who inherit the earth from it.[77]

Summary
America's bloated level of consumption puts a disproportionate strain on the world's resources. A broader view of environmental ethics considers our obligations to those in other societies as well as to future generations. Some philosophers argue that we must respect the right of future generations to inherit an environment that isn't seriously damaged, but talk of the rights of future people raises puzzles. Other ways of thinking about this issue are suggested by utilitarianism and the social contract theory of John Rawls.

The Value of Nature

A radical approach to environmental ethics challenges the human-centered assumption that preserving the environment is good only because it's good for us.

A more radical approach to environmental ethics goes beyond the question of our obligations to future generations. It challenges the human-centered approach adopted so far. Implicit in the discussion has been the assumption that preservation of the environment is good solely because it's good for human beings. This reflects a characteristic human attitude that nature has no intrinsic value, that it has value only because people value it. If human nature were different and none of us cared about the beauty of, say, the Grand Canyon, then the Grand Canyon would be without value.

Many writers on environmental issues do not recognize their **anthropocentric**, or human-oriented, bias. One who does is William F. Baxter. In discussing his approach to the pollution problem, Baxter mentions the fact that the use of DDT in food production is causing damage to the penguin population. He writes:

> My criteria are oriented to people, not penguins. Damage to penguins, or sugar pines, or geological marvels is, without more, simply irrelevant. . . . Penguins are important because people enjoy seeing them walk about rocks. . . . In short, my observations about environmental problems will be people-oriented. . . . I have no interest in preserving penguins for their own sake. . . .
>
> I reject the proposition that we *ought* to respect the "balance of nature" or to "preserve the environment" unless the reason for doing so, express or implied, is the benefit of man.[78]

Summary
Philosophers disagree about whether nature has intrinsic value. Adopting a human-oriented point of view, some theorists contend that the environment is valuable only because human beings value it. However, those adopting a naturalistic ethic believe that the value of nature isn't simply a function of human interests.

Contrast Baxter's position with what Holmes Rolston III calls the **naturalistic ethic**. Advocates of a naturalistic ethic contend, contrary to Baxter's view, "that some natural objects, such as whooping cranes, are morally considerable in their own right, apart from human interests, or that some ecosystems, perhaps the Great Smokies, have intrinsic values, such as aesthetic beauty, from which we derive a duty to respect these landscapes."[79] Human beings may value a mountain for a variety of reasons—because they can hike it, build ski lifts on it, mine the ore deep inside it, or simply because they like looking at it. According to a naturalistic ethic, however, the value of the mountain is more than a simple function of these human interests: Nature can have value in and of itself, apart from human beings. The people of Ecuador recently endorsed this idea by changing their constitution to recognize the ecosystem as having rights enforceable in court.[80]

Proponents of a naturalistic ethic contend that we have a particularly strong obligation to preserve species from extinction. Many environmentalists share this moral conviction, and it's easy to see why. According to some estimates, every year, 3,000 animal and plant species disappear, and the rate of extinction is accelerating so rapidly that over the next hundred years or so the earth could lose half its species.[81] Other scientists, however, believe these figures to be exaggerated.[82] But regardless of the exact rate of extinction, do species have value above and beyond the individuals that make them up? Scientists have formally identified around 2 million species, but we can be confident that there are many more that have yet to be discovered; estimates for the total number of species on Earth, including plants, animals, bacteria, and fungi, range from 8.7 million to over a billion.[83] How valuable is this diversity of species, and how far are we morally required to go in maintaining it?

Adopting a naturalistic ethic would change our way of looking at nature, but many philosophers are skeptical of the idea that nature has intrinsic value.

Adopting a naturalistic ethic would definitely alter our way of looking at nature and our understanding of our moral obligations to preserve and respect the natural environment. Many philosophers, however, doubt that nature has intrinsic value or that we can be said to have moral duties to nature. Having interests is a precondition, they contend, of something's having rights or of our having moral duties to that thing. Natural objects, however, have no interests. Can a rock meaningfully be said to have an interest in not being eroded or in not being smashed into smaller pieces?

Of course, plants and trees are different from rocks and streams: They're alive; we can talk intelligibly about what is good or bad for a tree, plant, or vegetable; and they can flourish or do poorly. Even so, philosophers who discuss moral rights generally hold that this isn't enough for plants to be said to have rights. To have rights, a thing must have genuine interests, and to have interests, most theorists contend, a thing must have beliefs and desires. Vegetative life, however, lacks any cognitive awareness. Claims to the contrary are biologically unsupportable.

Even if the plant world lacks rights, can it still have intrinsic value? Can we still have a moral obligation to respect that world and not abuse it? Or are the only morally relevant values the various interests of human beings and other sentient creatures? These are difficult questions. Among philosophers there's no consensus on how to answer them.

Our Treatment of Animals

Even someone who's unconvinced that nature or ecosystems matter morally in the sense of having intrinsic value may still believe that we have reasons to care about how we treat the environment beyond how this would affect humans. They may believe that animals matter morally, in a way that at least approximates the way that humans do. Above a certain level of complexity, animals do have at least rudimentary cognitive awareness. No owner of a cat or dog doubts that their pet has beliefs and desires. In line with this, many contemporary philosophers argue that because animals have genuine interests, they have genuine moral rights—despite the fact that they cannot claim their rights, that they cannot speak, that we cannot reason with them, and that they themselves lack a moral sense. Animals, it's more and more widely contended, do not have to be equal to human beings to have certain moral rights that we must respect.

Rather than talking about animals' rights, utilitarians would stress that higher animals are sentient—that is, that they're capable of feeling pain. Accordingly, there can be no justifiable reason for excluding their pleasures and pains from the overall utilitarian calculus. As Jeremy Bentham, one of the founders of utilitarianism, put it: "The question is not, Can they *reason*? nor, Can they *talk*? but, Can they *suffer*?"[84] Our actions have effects on animals, and these consequences cannot be ignored. When one is deciding, then, what the morally right course of action is, the pleasures and pains of animals must be considered, too. (Strictly speaking, it's only act utilitarians who would avoid talking about animals' having rights. As we saw earlier, while rights don't really have any place in act utilitarianism, rule utilitarians find it much easier to account for their existence. Like their act-utilitarian cousins, rule utilitarians will believe that animals' pleasures and pains must be included in the utilitarian calculus. But recall that rule utilitarians believe that the point of this calculus is to discover the ideal moral code, and they might well conclude that this code would include rules that require us to respect animals' rights.)

Business affects the welfare of animals very substantially. One way is through experimentation and the testing of products on animals. Critics such as Peter Singer, who was mentioned in Chapter 2, contend that the vast majority of experiments and tests cannot be justified on moral grounds. Consider the "LD 50" test, which used to be the standard method of testing new foodstuffs. The object of the test was to find the dosage level at which 50 percent of the test animals would die. Nearly all test animals became very sick before finally succumbing or surviving. When the substance was harmless, huge doses had to be forced into the animals, until in some cases the sheer volume killed them.[85]

In principle, utilitarians are willing to permit testing and experimentation on animals, provided the overall results justify their pain and suffering. Not only is this proviso frequently ignored, but human beings typically disregard altogether the price the animals must pay. Consider the actions of the pharmaceutical firm Merck Sharp and Dohme, which sought to import chimpanzees to test a vaccine for hepatitis B. Chimps are an endangered species and highly intelligent. Capturing juvenile chimps requires shooting the mother. One analyst assessed the situation this way:

> The world has a growing population of 4 billion people and a dwindling population of some 50,000 chimpanzees. Since the vaccine seems unusually innocuous, and since the disease is only rarely fatal, it would perhaps be more just if the larger population could find some way of solving its problem that was not to the detriment of the smaller.[86]

Factory Farming

Business's largest and most devastating impact on animals, however, is through the production of animal-related products—in particular, meat. Many of us still think of our chicken and beef as coming from something like the idyllic farms pictured in storybooks, where the animals roam

Many philosophers urge that animals have moral rights. Utilitarians, for their part, stress the moral necessity of taking into account animal pain and suffering.

contentedly and play with the farmer's children. But meat and egg production is big business. In 2021, almost 34 million heads of full-grown cattle, almost 400,000 calves, over 125 million pigs, and over 2.25 million sheep and lambs were slaughtered in the United States.[87] These numbers pale in comparison to the 8 billion chickens that Americans eat each year.[88] (Several hundred million chickens are used for laying eggs.) Shockingly, more than 20 million animals die in transport on their way to the slaughterhouse each year, often crowded into hot trucks.[89]

Today most of the animal products we eat are from "factory farms." According to the American Society for the Prevention of Cruelty to Animals,

> Nearly all meat chickens are raised indoors in large sheds containing 20,000 chickens (or more) crowded together on the shed floor. Due to the high concentration of birds living atop of their own waste without adequate ventilation, high ammonia levels develop—irritating eyes, throats and skin. … To keep them eating and growing, industrial farms restrict chickens' sleep by keeping the lights on almost all the time. As they grow, meat chickens become crowded together, competing for space. This constant interaction makes sleep even harder. As chickens die, their bodies are sometimes left among the living, adding to the stress and unhygienic conditions.[90]

The situation isn't much more pleasant for other varieties of animals in factory farms. Pigs, for instance, are at least as intelligent as dogs. Nevertheless,

> The United States raises around 120 million pigs for food each year, the vast majority of whom are raised in barren crates or pens at industrial-scale facilities without fresh air or sunlight. They live on hard, slatted floors that do not accommodate their natural urge to root. Ammonia fumes rise to dangerous, uncomfortable levels due to high concentrations of waste.[91]

The individuals involved in the meat and animal-products industries are not necessarily brutal, but the desire to cut business costs and to economize routinely leads to treatment of animals that can only be described as cruel. Fundamentally, in these industries animals are treated as natural resources. And the animal-products industries are a major part of our economy, employing over 500,000 American workers—often under conditions that not pleasant for the humans, either.[92]

Is It Wrong to Eat Meat?

Moral vegetarians are people who reject the eating of meat on moral grounds. Their argument is simple and powerful: The raising of animals for meat, especially with modern factory farming, sacrifices the most important and basic interests of animals simply to satisfy human tastes. Our preference for a Big Mac over a soybean burger is only a matter of taste and culture, as is our preference for shoes and accessories made of leather rather than some other materials. The extra pleasure we believe we get from eating the hamburger cannot justify the price the animals must pay, insist the moral vegetarians.

Peter Singer maintains that many people are guilty of arbitrarily distinguishing between human beings and other animals. Singer calls this **speciesism**, and he argues that it's analogous to (if not the same as) racism or sexism.[93] The racist or sexist treats some people as superior to others just because they belong to particular groups, when whatever differences might exist between the groups don't do anything to show that the members of one are more capable or worthy of consideration than members of the other. Similarly, the speciesist assumes that being a member of one species—*home sapiens*—by itself makes some beings vastly more worth of moral consideration than members of all others.

Singer says that in deciding how different creatures can permissibly be treated, we should be guided by their individual mental capacities, not their species membership. Most human beings do have mental capacities far beyond of those of other animals, and Singer agrees that this makes important differences to how they should be treated. The fact that a person has a desire to live, which requires concepts that most nonhuman animals lack, makes their life more valuable. However, Singer further argues, many animals' minds and feelings come close enough to ours that we can no longer justify eating them, given that today it's possible for most of us to

The desire of the meat and animal-products industries to economize leads to their treating animals in ways that many reject as cruel and immoral.

Summary
Through experimentation, testing, and the production of animal products, business has an enormous impact on the welfare of animals. The meat and animal-products industries rely on factory-farming techniques, which many describe as cruel and horrible. Because of these conditions, moral vegetarians argue that eating meat is wrong. There are signs that human indifference toward animal suffering and factory farming is changing.

eat healthy meat-free diets. The pleasure of eating steak, bacon, or chicken nuggets doesn't out-weigh the suffering imposed on the animals. To think that because we're humans we're some-how entitled to ignore their suffering would be speciesist.

Someone might believe, perhaps for religious reasons, that the distinction between humans and other species is deeper and more important than Singer believes. However, even a person who holds this view may still need to wrestle with the question of whether they can justify a meat-eating diet. Given that today a healthy meat-free diet is an option, can someone who eats meat—especially factory-farmed meat—still claim to be a good steward of the Earth and animals?

Would it be wrong to eat animals that were raised humanely, like those that run around freely and happily in children's picture books of farms? Unlike the lives of animals that we do in fact eat, the lives of such humanely raised animals, before being abruptly terminated, are not painful ones. Some philosophers would contend that it's permissible to raise animals for food if their lives are, on balance, positive. Other moral theorists challenge this view, contending that at least higher animals have a right to life and should not be killed.

This debate raises important philosophical issues, but it's also rather hypothetical. Given economic reality, mass production of meat at affordable prices currently dictates factory farm-ing, although increased consumer concern for animal welfare could conceivably change this economic logic. The important moral issue, in any case, is the real suffering and unhappy lives that billions of creatures experience on the way to our dinner tables. This often-overlooked aspect of environmental ethics raises profound and challenging questions for business and con-sumers alike.

There are hopeful signs that human attitudes toward animal suffering, in general, and factory farming, in particular, are changing. As of 2022, several states had passed laws or policies that were meant to improve animal welfare. Ten states have banned or will ban the use of gestation crates for pigs. Nine have prohibited the use of crates for veal calves. Ten have imposed many space requirements for chicken.[94] Companies are doing more, too. Hellman's Mayonnaise, for instance, contains only eggs that are from "cage-free" hens.[95] And some grocery store chains such as Whole Foods Markets sell only cage-free eggs and egg products.[96] But corporations don't always follow through on their public relations. In 2012, McDonald's announced that it would begin requiring its pork suppliers to phase out "gestation crates," the tiny pens that confine pregnant sows. However, in 2022 "corporate raider" Carl Icahn—an ani-mal welfare advocate—went public with claims that McDonald's is not following through on this promise because it's allowing its pork suppliers to keep sows in gestation crates for the first 4–6 weeks of their pregnancy, plus several additional weeks in slightly larger "farrowing" crates where they nurse piglets.[97] McDonald's maintains that it's honoring its earlier pledge, while Icahn asserts that what it promised the public was that its pork would be entirely crate free.

Study Corner

Key Terms and Concepts

anthropocentric	ecosystem	pollution permits
cap and trade	Environmental Protection Agency (EPA)	pricing mechanisms
Clean Air Act (1970)	externality (spillover)	regulatory approach
Clean Air Act Amendments of 1990	free-rider problem	right to a livable environment
Clean Water Act (1972)	future generations	speciesism
cost–benefit analysis	incentive approach	tragedy of the commons
ecological economics	moral vegetarians	
ecology	naturalistic ethic	

··

Points to Review

- progress against pollution since the Clean Air and Clean Water Acts (pp. 197–198)

- ecological costs of producing beef, poultry, and pork (p. 198)

- what the reintroduction of wolves into Yellowstone illustrates about ecosystems (p. 199)

- Ehrlich's two ecological rules (p. 199)

- pollution and resource depletion as two aspects of the same problem (p. 200)

- meaning and implications of the tragedy of the commons (p. 200)

- pollution as an externality (pp. 200–201)

- why free riding and failing to internalize externalities are unfair (p. 201)

- difficulties of cost–benefit analysis (pp. 202–203)

- what's new and different about ecological economics and estimates of "non-use value" (p. 203)

- deep-rooted causes of environmental degradation (p. 203)

- problems with the idea that those who benefit from environmental improvements should pay for them (pp. 205–206)

- four problems with regulations (pp. 207–208)

- the pros and cons of requiring old plants to meet new standards (p. 208)

- disadvantages of an incentive approach (pp. 208–209)

- what many environmentalists find troubling about pollution permits (p. 210)

- why higher environmental standards may increase efficiency and productivity (p. 210)

- disproportionate environmental impact of the United States (pp. 211–212)

- puzzles raised by the idea that future people have rights (pp. 212–213)

- implications of the fact that our policies affect who's born in the future (p. 213)

- utilitarian and Rawlsian approaches to future generations (p. 213)

- contrasting environmental ethics of William Baxter and Holmes Rolston (p. 214)

- Bentham on animal suffering (p. 215)

- why many consider factory farming cruel (pp. 215–216)

- moral vegetarianism and the question of the morality of killing animals (pp. 216–217)

- signs that attitudes toward animal suffering and factory farming are changing (p. 217)

··

For Further Reflection

1. What do you see as our most pressing environmental problems, and what role can and should business play in addressing them?

2. Can companies be truly green, committed to sustainability, *and* economically viable?

3. Do only human interests matter morally, or is the natural world intrinsically valuable? In your view, is our current treatment of animals, in particular, factory farming, morally legitimate?

Case 7.1
Risk Rating 2.0

Standard Homeowners' Insurance Doesn't Cover Damage Due to flooding. To protect against this risk, homeowners must have a separate flood policy. While many companies sell homeowners' policies, all flood policies come from the same place: the federal government, and more specifically, the Federal Emergency Management Agency (FEMA). American homeowners who live in flood zones and who have mortgages on their properties are often required by their lender to maintain a flood policy. Some homeowners who aren't required to carry flood insurance still do.

But for many years, selling flood insurance has been a money-losing proposition for FEMA.[98] The basic idea behind insurance is simple: it's to pool risk. Suppose that we can be reasonably sure that a certain percentage of a group of people will suffer an expensive problem, but we don't know in advance who it will be. They could all just take their chances, in which case most of them will be fine but a few may be financially devastated. Alternately, they could all contribute a modest amount of money to a central fund, with that money going to compensate the people who turn out to be unlucky. That way everyone loses a little, but no one is driven into bankruptcy. This is the basic idea behind car insurance, life insurance, health insurance, and so on.

Since there will be some administrative costs associated with insurance, the amount paid in must be a bit more than the amount paid out if the system is to be self-sustaining. When a private corporation is selling the insurance, it will expect the difference between revenues and payouts to be even greater than what's needed to cover its costs, since it will expect to make a profit for shareholders. As a government agency, FEMA isn't worried about making a profit. Still, at least at first glance, it seems reasonable to expect flood insurance to be financially neutral for FEMA, with revenues sufficient to cover payouts and administrative costs. Historically, however, this has not been the case.

To see why not, it's helpful to start with the fact that even though an insurer won't be certain who's going to file a claim in a given year, they can know that some people are more likely to do so than others. Where possible, insurers want to take account of this "actuarial risk" in setting rates, making those who are more likely to file a claim pay more into the pot. People who are older or in poor health must usually pay more for life insurance, if they can buy it at all. Young men tend to pay more for car insurance than young women because experience shows that on the whole they're more likely to have accidents, and a driver with a history of collisions is sure to see their rates increase. When higher insurance rates reflect people's life choices, making people who are more likely to file a claim pay more may seem perfectly fair. People who choose to drive aggressively should pay more for car insurance. But sometimes fairness seems to require insurers to ignore information about who's more likely to file a claim, especially when this is only true because the

people have already experienced bad luck. This is why the Affordable Care Act required insurers to stop denying coverage or charging higher rates for people with preexisting health conditions. Often, at least, preexisting conditions result from bad luck in the form of genetic issues or accidents.

With flood insurance, how likely one is to file a claim depends on whether one's house is in a spot that's likely to flood (and, of course, the size of any claim will depend at least in part on the value of one's home). Until recently, FEMA used a system of flood zones which designated different areas as having a high, moderate, or low risk of flooding. Other things being equal, those in high-risk zones paid more for flood insurance and those in low-risk zones paid less, if they had coverage at all.

Yet the rates that FEMA has charged did not reflect the actual risks that homeowners faced. This was true for a variety of reasons. First, the flood zone system ignored individual differences between houses that would affect their liability to flood. Second, the zones were based on models that did not take all sorts of flooding fully into account. Third, Congress had placed limits on FEMA's ability to price flood insurance at rates that reflected the true price of coverage. Essentially, flood insurance rates were higher on new homes, but the owners of older homes paid less than their actuarial risk would suggest they should. In effect, therefore, their flood insurance was being subsidized. Congress wanted the flood insurance program to cover its own costs, but they also wanted insurance to be affordable, and these goals are in tension. In fact, FEMA's National Flood Insurance Program (NFIP) was *not* solvent or able to cover its own costs; it ran a deficit of hundreds of millions of dollars per year.

FEMA began implementing a program called Risk Rating 2.0 in 2021, and it went fully into effect in 2022. Risk Rating 2.0 dispenses with the idea of flood zones, instead, pricing insurance for each house based on its individual flood risk. It more accurately models different varieties of flooding. And it aims to eliminate subsidies on flood insurance, with the goal of reaching the point where the NFIP is solvent. While the NFIP is not raising the rates of individual homeowners more than 18 percent per year, that might still amount to a large jump in a single year, and some homeowners might face 18 percent increases for multiple years in a row.

Risk Rating 2.0 will raise the price of living in a flood-prone area. Fewer new homes will be built in these places. Additionally, some people who own homes in these areas may have to sell them, and perhaps some people who want to sell will not be able to find buyers. These houses might be torn down or abandoned. These might not seem like bad outcomes, especially when one is thinking about expensive waterfront homes—which might be vacation homes. Why should the federal government, which is to say, taxpayers, subsidize some people's desire to be near water?

There's another predictable result of Risk Rating 2.0, which is that people who had been purchasing flood insurance even though they weren't required to may choose to drop their coverage. There's evidence that this is already happening; in the first few months after Risk Rating 2.0 came into effect, the number of policies issues by NFIP declined by 165,000.[99] If a major flooding event strikes, there will be fewer people entitled to insurance payouts. This may mean that more people will have no way to rebuild their homes and lives. It may also mean that there will be more pressure on FEMA and other agencies to offer other forms of disaster assistance.

Law Professor Alexander B. Lemann argues that while Risk Rating 2.0 may at first appear fair and equitable, this appearance is misleading.[100] First, Lemann points out that while some of the homes in highly flood-prone areas are expensive vacation getaways, many others are the primary residences of low-income families: "People who live in flood zones tend to have lower incomes than those living outside of them. Indeed, more than a quarter of NFIP policyholders in flood zones are classified as low income."

Second, Lemann contends that people who live in areas that are likely to flood don't always have much choice in the matter. We don't have good ways to communicate the risk of flooding clearly; people who haven't studied probability may not understand what it means to say that a given area is expected have a major flood once every 500 years. Moreover,

> We end up where we do thanks to some combination of family and work, and many residents of places like Houston, New Orleans, and Boston have found that the only neighborhoods they can afford are ones with a significant risk of flooding. If rising flood insurance premiums make such places unaffordable, residents might wonder with frustration where they are supposed to go.

In consequence, Lemann suggests, for many people, living in a place with a high risk of flooding is akin to a preexisting condition. It's a reflection of the fact that a person has already experienced bad luck in the form of limited opportunities, not a product of bad decision making for which people can rightly be made to pay the price.

Adding urgency to these issues is the fact that we can confidently predict that there will be more severe flooding in the future due to climate change, flooding produced by torrential downpours, rising sea levels, and storm surges generated by hurricanes. If some sort of change isn't made, then NFIP is going to lose even more money. However, Risk Rating 2.0 may make it much more expensive for homeowners to stay in homes that they bought decades ago, at a time when the risk that the property would flood was much lower than it is now.

In 2023, ten states and a number of cities and localities sued the federal government to block implementation of Risk Rating 2.0.[101] They argue that will destroy the property market and that it doesn't properly account for community efforts to mitigate flooding.

....
Discussion Questions
....

1. Should the federal government sell flood insurance, or should this be left to private corporations, as with other forms of insurance?

2. Should flood insurance always reflect the true cost of insuring a property against damage, or are there times in which it's appropriate for homeowners to pay less? For instance, should FEMA try to avoid situations in which people must leave their homes of many years because they can't afford flood insurance? Should it matter whether the risk of flooding has increased since they bought the house?

3. In some areas, Risk Rating 2.0 may result in entire neighborhoods becoming too expensive for their residents. How will this affect communities and the people who belong to them?

4 Some people have proposed that FEMA should consider the ability to pay in their pricing, which might mean that lower-income homeowners receive a subsidy on their flood insurance while wealthier homeowners pay even more. Would this be just?

5. Should the government be doing more to help those who are least well-off cope with the effects of climate change?

Case 7.2
Poverty and Pollution

It's Referred to as Brazil's "Valley of Death," and It May Be the Most polluted place on Earth. It lies about an hour's drive south of São Paulo, where the land suddenly drops 2,000 feet to a coastal plain. More than 100,000 people live in the valley, along with a variety of industrial plants that discharge thousands of tons of pollutants into the air every day. A reporter for *National Geographic* recalls that within an hour of his arrival in the valley, his chest began aching as the polluted air inflamed his bronchial tubes and restricted his breathing.[102]

The air in the valley is loaded with toxins—among them benzene, a known carcinogen. One in ten of the area's factory workers has a low white blood cell count, a possible precursor to leukemia. Infant mortality is 10 percent higher here than in the region as a whole.

Of the 40,000 urban residents in the valley municipality of Cubatão, nearly 13,000 suffer from respiratory disease.

Few of the local inhabitants complain, however. For them, the fumes smell of jobs. They also distrust bids to buy their property by local industry, which wants to expand, as well as government efforts to relocate them to free homesites on a landfill. One young mother says, "Yes, the children are often ill and sometimes can barely breathe. We want to live in another place, but we cannot afford to."

A university professor of public health, Dr. Oswaldo Campos, views the dirty air in Cubatão simply as the result of economic priorities. "Some say it is the price of progress," Campos comments, "but is it? Look who pays the price—the poor."[103]

Maybe the poor do pay the price of pollution, but there are those who believe that they should have more of it. One of them is Lawrence Summers, former director of the National Economic Council and a past president of Harvard University. He has argued that the bank should encourage the migration of dirty, polluting industries to the poorer, less-developed countries.[104] Why? First, Summers reasons, the costs of health-impairing pollution depend on the earnings forgone from increased injury and death. So polluting should be done in the countries with the lowest costs—that is, with the lowest wages. "The economic logic behind dumping a load of toxic waste in the lowest-wage country," he writes, "is impeccable."

Second, because pollution costs rise disproportionately as pollution increases, it makes sense to shift pollution from already dirty places such as Los Angeles to clean ones like the relatively underpopulated countries in Africa, whose air Summers describes as "vastly *under*-polluted." Third, people value a clean environment more as their incomes rise. If other things are equal, costs fall if pollution moves from affluent places to less-affluent places.

Critics charge that Summers views the world through "the distorting prism of market economics" and that his ideas are "a recipe for ruin." Not only do the critics want "greener" development in the third world, but also they're outraged by Summers's assumption that the value of a life—or of increases or decreases in life expectancy—can be measured in terms of per capita income. This premise implies that an American's life is worth that of a hundred Kenyans and that society should value an extra year of life for a middle-level manager more than it values an extra year for a blue-collar, production-line worker.

Some economists, however, believe that Summers's ideas are basically on the right track. They emphasize that environmental policy always involves trade-offs and that therefore we should seek a balance between costs and benefits. As a matter of fact, the greatest cause of misery in the third world is poverty. If environmental controls slow growth, then fewer people will be lifted out of poverty by economic development. For this reason, they argue, the richer countries should not impose their standards of environmental protection on poorer nations.

But even if economic growth is the cure for poverty, other economists now believe that sound environmental policy is necessary for durable growth, or at least that growth and environmental protection may not be incompatible. First, environmental damage can undermine economic productivity, and the health effects of pollution on a country's workforce reduce output. Second, poverty itself is an important cause of environmental damage because people living at subsistence levels are unable to invest in environmental protection. Finally, if economic growth and development are defined broadly enough, then enhanced environmental quality is part and parcel of the improvement in welfare that development must bring. For example, 1 billion people in developing countries lack access to clean water while 1.7 billion suffer from inadequate sanitation. Economic development for them means improving their environment.

Still, rich and poor countries tend to have different environmental agendas: Environmentalists in affluent nations worry about protecting endangered species, preserving biological diversity, saving the ozone layer, and preventing climate change, whereas their counterparts in poorer countries are more concerned with dirty air, dirty water, soil erosion, and deforestation. However, global warming—heretofore of concern mostly to people in the developed world—threatens to reverse the progress that the world's poorest nations are gradually making toward prosperity. Or so concludes a U.N. study.[105] It offers a detailed view of how poor areas, especially near the equator, are extremely vulnerable to the water shortages, droughts, flooding rains, and severe storms that increasing concentrations of greenhouse gases are projected to make more frequent, and the authors call on rich countries to do more to curb emissions linked to global warming and to help poorer nations leapfrog to energy sources that pollute less than coal and oil.

Update

According to a World Bank report, environmental conditions have improved in Cubatão, where, thanks to state action and an aroused population, pollution is no worse today than in other medium-size industrial cities in Brazil. True, it's no paradise, but some days you can see the sun, children are healthier, and fish are returning to the river (though their tissues are laced with toxic metals).[106]

Discussion Questions

1. What attitudes and values on the part of business and others lead to the creation of areas like the "valley of death"?

2. Should the third world have more pollution, as Lawrence Summers argues? Assess his argument that dirty industries should move to poorer and less-polluted areas.

3. Some say, "Pollution is the price of progress." Is this assertion correct? What is meant by "progress"? Who in fact pays the price? Explain the moral and the economic issues raised by the assertion. What are the connections between economic progress and development, on the one hand, and pollution controls and environmental protection, on the other?

4. Do human beings have a moral right to a livable environment? To a nonpolluted environment? It might be argued that if people in the "valley of death" don't complain and don't wish to move, then they accept the risks of living there and the polluters are not violating their rights. Assess this argument.

5. Assess the contention that people in the third world should learn from the errors of the West and seek development without pollution. Should there be uniform, global environmental standards, or should pollution-control standards be lower for less-developed countries?

6. Even though they will probably be hit hardest by it, poor nations are less able than are rich countries to deal with the consequences of global warming. As a result, do rich nations owe to it to poorer nations to curb their own emissions more than they otherwise would be inclined to do? Do they have an obligation to provide poorer nations with, or help them develop, greener industries and sources of energy? Explain why or why not.

Case 7.3
The Fight over the Redwoods

Dense Forests of Coastal Redwood Trees Once Covered 2.2 Million acres of Southern Oregon and Northern California. Today, only about 86,000 acres of virgin redwood forest remain. Most of this is in public parks and preserves, but about 6,000 acres of old-growth forest are privately owned—nearly all of it by the Pacific Lumber Company, headquartered in San Francisco.

Founded in 1869, Pacific Lumber owns 220,000 acres of the world's most productive timberland, including the old-growth redwoods. For years, the family-run company was a model of social responsibility and environmental awareness. Pacific Lumber paid its employees well, supported them in bad times, funded their pensions, and provided college scholarships for their children. It sold or donated nearly 20,000 acres of forest to the public, and instead of indiscriminate clear-cutting, the company logged its forests carefully and selectively. Throughout its history, the company harvested only about 2 percent of its trees annually, roughly equivalent to their growth rate. After other timber firms had logged all their old-growth stands, Pacific Lumber had a virtual monopoly on the highly durable lumber that comes from the heart of centuries-old redwood trees.[107]

Because Pacific Lumber was debt-free and resource-rich, its potential value drew attention on Wall Street, where the firm of Drexel Burnham Lambert suspected that the company was undervalued—and thus ripe for raiding. In 1985, Drexel hired a timber consultant to fly over Pacific Lumber's timberland to estimate its worth. With junk-bond financing arranged by its in-house expert, Michael Milken, Drexel assisted Charles Hurwitz, a Texas tycoon, and his firm, Maxxam, Inc., to take over Pacific Lumber for $900 million. After initially resisting the leveraged buyout, the timber company's directors eventually acquiesced, and by the end of the year Hurwitz and Maxxam had control of Pacific Lumber. At the time, Hurwitz was primary owner of United Financial Group, the parent company of United Savings Association of Texas. In exchange for Milken's

raising the money for the takeover of Pacific Lumber, Hurwitz had United Savings purchase huge amounts of risky junk bonds from Drexel. Three years later, the savings and loan failed, and taxpayers were stuck with a bill for $1.6 billion.

The takeover of Pacific Lumber left Maxxam with nearly $900 million in high-interest debt. To meet the interest payments, Maxxam terminated Pacific Lumber's pension plan and replaced it with annuities purchased from an insurance company owned by Hurwitz. Worse still, Maxxam tripled the rate of logging on Pacific Lumber's lands, and it was soon clear that Hurwitz intended to log the now-famous Headwaters forest, a 3,000-acre grove of virgin redwoods—the largest single stand of redwoods still in private hands. "It was the reason we were interested in Pacific Lumber," Hurwitz says. And one can see why. The value of the grove is astronomical: Milled into lumber, some of the trees are worth $100,000 each.

The potential lumber may be worth a fortune to Hurwitz, but environmentalists consider the Headwaters grove to be priceless as it is, and they stepped in to do battle with Hurwitz. They see the Headwaters forest with its 500- to 2,000-year-old trees as an intricate ecosystem that took millions of years to evolve, a web of animals and plants that depend not just on living trees but also on dead, fallen redwoods that provide wildlife habitat and reduce soil erosion. Some of these activists—including Darryl Cherney, a member of the environmental group Earth First!—have devoted their lives to stopping Hurwitz. Earth First! isn't a mainstream conservation organization; it has a reputation for destroying billboards, sabotaging bulldozers and lumber trucks, and spiking trees with nails that chew up the blades of saws. "Hurwitz is a latter-day robber baron," Cherney claimed. "The only thing that's negotiable . . . is the length of his jail sentence."

Other environmental organizations opposed Hurwitz in court. The Sierra Club Legal Defense Fund and the Environmental Protection

Information Center filed sixteen lawsuits against Pacific Lumber, giving the company's legal experts a run for their money. One of these suits bore fruit when a judge blocked the company's plan to harvest timber in a smaller old-growth forest known as Owl Creek Grove. The legal reason was protection of the marbled murrelet, a bird about the size of a thrush, which breeds in the forest and is close to extinction. The judge also noted that "after the logging of an old-growth forest, the original cathedral-like columns of trees do not regenerate for a period of 200 years." Pacific Lumber appealed the Owl Creek decision, but the ruling was upheld a year later. However, at the same time, the company won the right to appeal to another court to be allowed to harvest timber in the larger Headwaters forest. Meanwhile, both conservationists and a number of public officials were making strenuous efforts to acquire Headwaters and some surrounding redwood groves from Hurwitz.

Some environmentalists, however, worried that too much attention was being directed toward saving the 3,000-acre Headwaters grove while leaving Pacific Lumber free to log the rest of its land with abandon. They were less concerned about the murrelets in particular or even the redwoods themselves; rather, what disturbed them was the dismantling of an ancient and intricate ecosystem—an irreplaceable temperate rain forest, home to some 160 species of plants and animals. Their aim was to build a new style of forestry based on values other than board feet of lumber and dollars of profit. They sought sustainable forest management and a new resource ethic devoted to rebuilding and maintaining habitats for coho salmon, the murrelet, the weasel-like fisher, and the northern spotted owl. As a first step, these conservationists called for protection not just of the 3,000 Headwaters acres but also for an area nearly twenty times that amount, called the Headwaters Forest Complex. This tract included all the ancient redwoods that Hurwitz owned and large areas of previously logged forest. "We have a vision that's bigger than Headwaters," said Cecelia Lanman of the Environmental Protection Information Center.

Her vision was definitely more sweeping than that of the Pacific Lumber workers in Scotia, California, a village containing 272 company-owned homes. Because Hurwitz instituted stepped-up logging, which meant more jobs, his employees tended to side with him, not the environmentalists. Workers said that Hurwitz had reinvested more than $100 million in modernizing his mills and had kept up the tradition of paying college scholarships for their children. The environmentalists were the real threat, said one employee. "You've got a group of people who hate Mr. Hurwitz, and they're using the Endangered Species Act and anything they can to hurt him. And we're caught in the middle."

The Story Continues . . .

In 1999, Hurwitz signed a deal negotiated by Senator Dianne Feinstein and Deputy Interior Secretary John Garamendi. In exchange for a 7,500-acre tract that includes the Headwaters grove and 2,500 additional acres of old-growth forest, the U.S. government and the state of California agreed to pay Pacific Lumber $480 million (half of what Hurwitz originally spent for the entire company with its 220,000 acres of timberland). The agreement banned logging for fifty years on 8,000 other acres of company land in order to safeguard the murrelet, and it set up buffer zones to protect the river habitats of endangered coho salmon and steelhead trout. A Habitat Protection Plan regulated how and where Pacific Lumber could harvest timber on the rest of its land. However, because Hurwitz transferred the $868 million debt that still remained from his original hostile takeover of Pacific Lumber from Maxxam to Pacific Lumber itself, the company still needed to log as much as it could to make its interest payments.

Pacific Lumber, for its part, contended that state and federal agencies were so rigidly enforcing the habitat conservation plan that it couldn't cut enough lumber to keeps its mills running, and it decided to close down Scotia's 104-year-old mill. "We are being strangled by the operating restraints," said Robert Manne, president of Pacific Lumber, which are "not working to meet the company and its employees' economic needs." To this complaint, conservationists and governmental officials responded that Pacific Lumber, which continued to operate two smaller and much newer mills in neighboring towns, was scapegoating them for problems stemming from falling timber prices and the company's depletion of its old-growth redwood groves by clear-cutting. According to Paul Mason, president of a local environmental organization, "The lumber market is right in the tank, and that takes a bite out of your profit margin. The company has been operating at an unsustainable level for a number of years."

Whatever the exact cause, Pacific Lumber eventually declared bankruptcy, and in 2008, as part of a court-supervised reorganization plan, it was taken over by the Mendocino Redwood Company, a nine-year-old logging venture owned by Don and Doris Fisher, the founders of Gap. Environmentalists, state officials, and local residents were thrilled at the prospect of Pacific Lumber Company emerging from bankruptcy free of Hurwitz and Maxxam and able to reestablish itself as an environmentally responsible company practicing sustainable forestry. That's because, as U.S. bankruptcy judge Richard Schmidt explained, "MRC [is] an experienced, environmentally responsible operator with a proven track record, and whose experience in operating timberlands and working cooperatively with government regulators was uncontroverted."

As for the town of Scotia, the bankruptcy court awarded its 272 homes, two churches, hotel, and handful of commercial buildings to a hedge-fund group, Marathon Asset Management, which had been a big creditor of Pacific Lumber. Marathon executives say they're trying to do right by the residents, maintaining the homes and keeping rents reasonable. "We didn't want to fire everyone in the town and close it down, chop down the trees and call it a day," says Marathon's chief operating officer, Andrew Rabinowitz. As of 2015, the hedge fund had sold or put on the market the town hall and a few other buildings. Eventually, though, it wants to get out of the landlord business, sell the homes, and recover at least part of the $160 million it had been owed by Pacific Lumber.

....
Discussion Questions
....

1. Does an ancient redwood forest have value other than its economic one as potential lumber? If so, what is this value, and how is it to be weighed against the interests of a company like Maxxam? Are redwoods more important than jobs?

2. Is it morally permissible for private owners to do as they wish with the timberland they own? Explain why or why not. What's your assessment of Hurwitz? Is he a robber baron, a socially responsible businessperson, or something in between?

3. Were mainstream environmentalists right to try to thwart Hurwitz, or were they simply trying to impose their values on others? Does a radical group like Earth First! that engages in sabotage go too far, or do its ends justify its means?

4. Do we have a moral obligation to save old redwood forests? Can a forest have either moral or legal rights? Does an old-growth forest have value in and of itself, or is its value only a function of human interests? How valuable is a small but endangered species such as the murrelet?

5. Before its takeover by Hurwitz, did Pacific Lumber neglect its obligations to its stockholders by not logging at a faster rate? What would be a morally responsible policy for a timber company to follow? Do we need a new environmental resource ethic?

6. How would you respond to the argument that there's no need to try to save the Headwaters (or any other private) forest because there are already tens of thousands of acres of old-growth redwood forest in parks and preserves?

7. Was the deal that the U.S. government and the state of California struck with Pacific Lumber a fair and reasonable one? Did the taxpayers end up paying too much, as environmentalists think? Was Pacific Lumber squeezed too hard? What about Scotia and its laid-off workers?

Case 7.4
Palm Oil and Its Problems

Palm Oil Is One of Those Ubiquitous but Overlooked Products That have a hundred different uses. It comes from the oil palm tree (*Elaeis guineensis*), which originated in West Africa, but which by the mid-1800s was discovered to grow well in Malaysia and other countries in Southeast Asia. Back then, the oil was used for soap and to lubricate engines. By the mid-twentieth century, plantations dotted not only Malaysia but also Indonesia, which together now account for nine-tenths of the world's supply of palm oil. Today, the oil finds its way into many processed foods and into consumer products such as lipstick, shampoo, and shaving cream. Many Asian households cook with it, and recently it has come to be used as a biofuel, helping to make palm oil a $44 billion industry.[108]

Demand has pushed prices high and increased the number of palm-oil plantations. That in turn has contributed to needed economic growth in the countries that produce it, which is good news for them. But environmental groups are alarmed by the spread of palm-oil production, viewing it as damaging to wildlife and hazardous to the planet. In past decades, the area under cultivation for palm oil has mushroomed fifteenfold, eliminating peat land and forests in wide swathes of Malaysia and Indonesia. In fact, deforestation in Indonesia is so rapid that a recent U.N. report says that all of the country's forests could be gone by 2022. Destroying forests and peat land to slake the world's thirst for palm oil releases enormous quantities of carbon dioxide, thus contributing to climate change. In Sumatra and Borneo, palm-oil expansion also threatens the habitat of elephants, tigers, rhinos, and orangutans.

Awareness of the problem led to the establishment of the Roundtable on Sustainable Palm Oil (RSPO), a consortium of growers, processors, food companies, and nongovernmental organizations that was set up in 2004 to prod the industry into producing "sustainable" palm oil, that is, oil that could be certified as having been produced "without undue harm to the environment or society," in particular, without having involved the destruction of areas with "high conservation values." These areas include not just primary-growth forests, but also secondary and degraded forests that are "important for environmental conservation and community well-being."

But the Roundtable has proceeded slowly. Only 35 percent of RSPO growers have been certified, and none has been decertified for poor performance. Furthermore, an investigative report in *Bloomberg Businessweek* has revealed extensive abuse of workers on Indonesian palm oil plantations. "Every time an NGO shines light into the activities of an RSPO producer, it finds dirt," contends Tomasz Johnson of the London-based Environmental Investigation Agency. "Yet the RSPO hasn't displayed the ability or intent to exclude anyone."

Small wonder, then, that environmentalists are frustrated at the slow progress. Some of them have resorted to direct action. Greenpeace targeted Unilever, although the company uses only 4 percent of the world's palm oil, because some of its well-known brands (like Dove soap) include palm oil. In 2008, protestors stormed the company's London headquarters and demonstrated outside several of its facilities around the world with banners displaying slogans like "Unilever: Don't Destroy the Forests." Greenpeace also went after Nestlé, posting a video on YouTube that featured the bloody finger of an orangutan inside one of the company's Kit Kat candy bars.

Unilever quickly committed itself to using only palm oil certified as sustainable, and twenty other big companies, Procter & Gamble among them, rapidly followed suit. But Greenpeace wanted the company to go further and make sure that its suppliers weren't breaking the law. Unilever agreed, but doing so turned out to be problematic. "We found that, in one way or another, all of our suppliers have technically infringed either RSPO standards or Indonesian law," says Gavin Neath, a senior vice-president. "It isn't as easy as saying just pick the best. We are not in a position to do that. The industry almost certainly has to go through fundamental change."

Because it doesn't buy all that much palm oil, Nestlé hadn't anticipated being caught up in the controversy. A member of RSPO, it had been purchasing some sustainable oil but hadn't planned to utilize only sustainable oil until 2015. After first trying to stop the Greenpeace video, the company buckled because of the public response. It suspended all purchases from Sinar Mas, an Indonesian conglomerate known to be involved in the illegal clearing of forests and peat land. And it went further, hiring an independent auditor to review its supply chain and enable it to avoid "high-risk plantations or farms linked to deforestation."

Besides bad publicity and badgering from environmentalists, one factor in the change of policy at Unilever and Nestlé may have been the attitudes of their employees, many of whom are concerned about environmental issues. As the *Economist* magazine explains, "For years companies have been saying that a commitment to corporate social responsibility can improve the quality of staff that they can recruit. It follows that these recruits then care about the behavior of the company that employs them."

Despite these victories for environmentalists, much of the palm-oil industry has paid little attention, in part, because environmentalists have focused on a few well-known Western companies while ignoring Asian companies altogether. Verifying sustainability isn't as easy as it sounds either, because oil from different small plantations gets mixed together (and sustainable oil and unsustainable oil are indistinguishable).

An executive at one small cosmetics company, which has switched to coconut oil, says that there's "no such thing as sustainable palm oil: it doesn't exist." But for the world as a whole to get by with less palm oil is going to be expensive, and rival products also have some environmental drawbacks. On the other hand, deforestation is high on the agenda of the World Bank and United Nations, and various governments and nongovernmental organizations are getting involved. For example, a billion-dollar grant from Norway has induced Indonesia to declare a moratorium on clearing forests and to set up its own certification body. Some optimists argue that increased productivity can enable the palm-oil industry in Indonesia to continue to expand without destroying more forests, but that remains to be seen. In the meantime, the world's thirst for palm oil remains unslaked.

Discussion Questions

1. The word "sustainable" is tossed around a lot. What does it mean to you?

2. Is it fair for environmentalists to single out companies like Unilever and Nestlé that are more socially responsible than most and which are relatively small consumers of palm oil, or is this justified simply as a matter of strategy?

3. How far must corporations go to ensure that the various ingredients used in their products are produced in an environmentally satisfactory way? What if there aren't any truly sustainable options?

4. Can monitoring and self-regulation by industry groups like the Roundtable effectively address environmental issues, or will outside pressure always be needed? Was Greenpeace right to act as it did, or should it have tried to work with the companies in question?

5. Preventing deforestation is important, but once previously forested land has been cleared, whether six months ago or sixty years ago, is there anything wrong about using it to produce palm oil now?

6. Used as a biofuel, palm oil reduces our dependence on petroleum. How do we balance that against deforestation?

7. Developing countries like Indonesia are responding to increased demand for palm oil by Western consumers. Is it fair to the producer nations to insist that they restrict the expansion of this industry?

Chapter 8

The Workplace (1): Basic Issues

Learning Objectives

After completing this chapter, you should be able to:

1. Identify the moral issues to which some key personnel matters—hiring, promotions, discipline and discharge, and wages—give rise.

2. Make and evaluate arguments for different views about what morality demands from employers when these issues arise.

3. Discuss the role and history of unions in our economic system, their ideals and achievements, and the moral issues they raise.

4. Assess the desirability, from an ethical standpoint, of greater unionization of the American workforce and of legal measures meant to encourage unionization.

Introduction

A Manufacturer of Vinyl Replacement Windows, Republic Windows and Doors had been in business in Chicago for more than forty years. On December 2, 2008, however, it abruptly announced that it was bankrupt. The following day, the company told its 260 employees that it would permanently cease operations two days later, at which point their health coverage would end. The company also told the workers that they would not be receiving any severance pay or even their accrued vacation or sick pay.

Republic's workforce was represented by a labor union, the United Electrical, Radio and Machine Workers of America, which immediately filed a complaint charging that the company had violated federal law by failing to give sixty days' notice of a plant closure and that it owed the workers $1.5 million in severance and vacation pay and an extension of their medical benefits. Not content with this, however, Republic's workers quickly took more drastic measures. In a move reminiscent of the famous Flint Sit-Down Strike of 1936–1937 that led to the unionization of the U.S. auto industry, they voted to take over the company's plant and sit-in until their grievances were met. The country hadn't seen anything like it for decades, and there was an outpouring of support for the workers. People came by the occupied factory to offer food and donations, the Chicago police declined to intervene, and President-elect Barack Obama publicly sided with the workers.[1]

> Then the Public Learned that Republic's owners were not quite the innocent victims they claimed to be.

Why the popular support for the workers, who after all were seizing private property? One reason is that Bank of America had halted Republic's line of credit because of a downturn in sales and the harsh economic climate, thus making it impossible for the company to stay in business. This infuriated people across the nation because Bank of America had recently received $25 billion from the federal government precisely in order to provide it with the funds to continue making loans to businesses and thus help keep the country out of recession. And yet, here was a real American company, one that still made things, and the bank was forcing it to go under. The sit-in became a rallying point for all those who resented the government's bailing out Wall Street and the big banks while ordinary employees were left to fend for themselves. Then the public learned that Republic's owners were not quite the innocent victims they claimed to be. Before declaring bankruptcy, they had begun surreptitiously removing machinery from the factory and shipping it to a plant in Iowa belonging to a company that they had just purchased. Stopping the owners from gutting the factory was what really motivated Republic's workers to take it over.

Widespread media attention, demonstrations in Chicago and other cities, and political pressure resulted in the sit-in at Republic ending after just six days, when Bank of America and JP Morgan Chase agreed to loan Republic sufficient money to cover the workers' severance pay, earned

When Republic Windows and Doors announced bankruptcy and abruptly ceased operations, its workers occupied the plant. The discovery that Bank of America, the recent recipient of a federal government bailout, had closed the company's line of credit, making it impossible for it to continue operations, outraged many—as did the subsequent revelation that the company's owners had planned to strip the factory and move its machinery to another plant.

vacation pay, and an extension of their health benefits. Moreover, shortly after reading about the settlement, Kevin Surace, president and CEO of Serious Materials, a Sunnyvale, California, company that specializes in eco-friendly drywall and windows, decided to buy the plant. By March, he had closed the deal and rehired all of Republic's workers.[2]

But the story doesn't end there. In 2012, Serious Materials announced its own plan to close the factory. After another sit-down strike, some of the workers decided to purchase the factory themselves. Today, it operates as a worker-owned democratic cooperative under the name New Era Windows.[3]

The chapters in Part IV of this book discuss ethical issues that arise within companies, and especially in the relationship between employers and employees. It may be helpful to preface this material by drawing a contrast between two different ways of viewing this relationship.

On the first of these, employers and employees are essentially equally partners, on the same level morally. Employers ought to have as much freedom to decide who to offer positions to, and on what terms, as employees have to decide which job offers to accept. On this view, in its purest form, employers can attach whatever conditions to jobs they prefer, and employees or prospective employees can take or leave them. Companies would have a market incentive not to underpay employees or treat employees arbitrarily, since if they did, the best workers would go somewhere else. Still, people who hold this view tend to be skeptical that there's any standard that can be used to judge whether the compensation or other terms of a job are fair or just other than the fact that both parties agree to them.

On the other view, we can sometimes say that the terms of the employer/employee relationship are unfair and unjust even if both

parties did agree to them. The fact someone agreed to accept a job under certain conditions doesn't guarantee those terms are morally acceptable, according to this view. Perhaps they needed to take some job, and all their options involved exploitative terms. In principle, perhaps, it might be the employer rather than the employee who was forced to accept unfair terms, but in most labor markets it's far easier for employers to replace most employees than for these employees to find new jobs. This difference in bargaining power makes the possibility of employees exploiting their employers more theoretical than practical.

Very few people would subscribe to the first of these views in its purest form. Only the most doctrinaire libertarian would deny that the law ought to place *any* regulations on employment at all, and even they might still believe that there are moral limits on the terms that employers can offer. Still, there are people who believe that the limits that morality does place or that the law should place on employment are very minimal. They might agree that some terms of employment would be so outrageous as to be morally unacceptable, even if in some circumstances workers might be so desperate for money that they'd be willing to accept them. But they would think that it's unusual that workers in highly developed countries like the United States would face circumstances that dire. Absent these fairly unusual circumstances, they would maintain, if workers agreed to accept a job and their employer didn't deceive them about the nature of the work, the working conditions, or the compensation, then the workers are in no position to complain about unfair treatment. They knew what they were getting into, so to speak.

Others believe that morality places more stringent constraints on what constitutes "just work." Many people would (and do) say that even in the United States a substantial number of workers are being unjustly exploited to some degree. People who believe this will typically also favor robust legal restrictions on how employers may treat employees.

The discussion in the rest of the book won't aim for complete neutrality between these outlooks. It will assume that the fact that an employee agreed to work under certain conditions is not enough by itself to establish that those conditions are fair. Still, it's important to remember that claims about what fairness demands must be backed by reasons. Not every case in which workers wish some aspect of their jobs were different is one in which they're entitled to complain about unjust treatment.

One of the clearest illustrations of different ways in which the idea of just work can be understood can be found on college campuses. Over the last several decades, colleges and universities have begun to rely heavily on "adjunct" or "contingent" faculty, part-time instructors who are paid on a per-class basis and generally receive no benefits. Originally, adjunct positions generally went to working professionals for whom teaching was what we now call a "side gig" or to retired faculty members wanting to supplement their pensions. Today, however, many adjuncts support themselves and their families exclusively through part-time teaching; often this means teaching at more than one school. The pay is frequently quite low compared to that for full-time faculty, averaging less than $4,000 per course.[4] Adjuncts have little job security, because they're hired on a semester-by-semester basis. If a full-time instructor's class is canceled, they will often take over a class that had been assigned to an adjunct; typically, the adjunct will receive no compensation, even though they may have invested many hours in preparation. Universities often cope with tight budgets, so when a full-time faculty member leaves, the temptation to replace them with adjuncts rather than hire a new full-time instructor is strong. In 2021, almost half of the college and university instructors in the United States were adjuncts.

Today, the view that many adjuncts are being treated unfairly is very widespread among full-time faculty members and even university administrators. Despite this, however, few universities have so far taken the hard steps necessary to address "adjunctification": paying part-time faculty significantly more, sharply reducing their reliance on part-time faculty, and perhaps closing some graduate programs to reduce the number of people competing for faculty positions. Some of these steps would be expensive, requiring universities either to increase their revenues or to reduce other expenditures. Some scholars, though, have argued that since adjuncts are intelligent, highly educated people with many career options other than teaching, they aren't entitled to complain of unfair treatment if they continue to accept low-paying teaching jobs.[5] One response to this argument is that universities themselves encourage master's and Ph.D. students to believe that teaching is a noble profession, a "calling" rather than a mere job or career, and that abandoning the "life of the mind" in order to do other work would be shameful. Moreover, many people who teach as adjuncts may only have pursued a higher degree in the first place because their graduate program encouraged them to be unduly optimistic about the likelihood that they could find a full-time position. It's therefore wrong, this response continues, for universities to take advantage of the fact that people are reluctant to give up teaching to pursue other lines of work.[6]

· · ·

Civil Liberties in the Workplace

Employees have all sorts of job-related concerns. Generally speaking, they want to do well at their assignments, to get along with their colleagues, and to have their contributions to the organization recognized. Their job tasks, working conditions, wages and benefits, and the possibility of promotion are among the many things that occupy their day-to-day thoughts. Aside from the actual work that they're expected to perform, employees, being human, are naturally concerned about the way their organizations treat them. Frequently, they find that treatment to be morally deficient and complain that the organizations for which they work violate their moral rights and civil liberties.

Consider Lynne Gobbell, a machine operator who was fired for displaying a Democratic bumper sticker on her car, or John Stone, a car salesman who was fired by his Chicago Bears–loving boss for wearing a Green Bay Packers tie to work, or Michael Italie, who was fired from Goodwill Industries of South Florida—a charity meant to provide employment opportunities for people who have a hard time finding other work—because he ran to be elected mayor of Miami as a socialist. Then there's Louis MacIntire. A chemical engineer at DuPont for sixteen years, he was canned for writing a novel. Several characters in the book inveigh against various management abuses at the novel's fictional Logan Chemical Company and argue for a union for technical employees. Logan Chemical superficially resembles DuPont, and some of MacIntire's supervisors thought his veiled criticisms struck too close to home. MacIntire tried suing DuPont for violating his constitutional right of free speech, but the courts rejected his claim.[7] While the First Amendment protects Americans' freedom of speech, it prohibits censorship only by the government, not by companies or private individuals.

It's worth pausing a moment to be clear about what the issue here is. Taking any job means giving up some rights, at least during working hours. Committing to be in the office from 9 to 5 every day means giving up your right to free movement, for instance. No one supposes that employees should be completely free to exercise their civil liberties while they're "on the clock," say, by subjecting their coworkers or customers to political diatribes. Moreover, the fact that we have a right to do something doesn't mean that other people may never take the fact that we did it into account in how they treat us. If you make a statement that some people find offensive, then they're certainly allowed to criticize it, and morally speaking, they may also be free to cut you out of their social circle. But even given all this, we might still question whether or in what circumstances workers should be at risk of losing their jobs for things that they say or write. The threat of unemployment could chill speech as effectively as the threat of legal consequences, and a country in which the citizens are afraid to talk openly about politics or public affairs can hardly be a healthy democracy. This same basic reasoning could be extended to the exercise of other rights and liberties.

The questions of whether and how far employers are entitled to police the speech of their employees are especially pressing today because the rise of social media makes it so easy for people to post comments with little control over who sees them. According to employment lawyer Joyce Smithey, "In general, (employers) can fire you over what you put on social media, even if it's outside of work, even if it has nothing to do with work."[8] In a recent survey, 88 percent of hiring managers said that they would choose to fire employees over social media posts in at least some circumstances.[9] And many people have been fired as a result of what they've written on social media, although every case is different and the differences may be morally significant. Did the employee's social media activity take place during work hours? Was it from a company computer? Did the employee indicate where they worked? Did they identify themselves at all? Did they comment on their job, their employer, their customers, or their industry? Are they a high-ranking executive or a low-level hourly employee? Was their post merely unpopular, at least with their boss, or was it racist, sexist, homophobic? Was it "hate speech"? Was there one comment or a pattern? The answers to these questions and others like them may determine whether terminating an employee for what they post online is a regrettable necessity or an unreasonable intrusion into the employee's private life.

David W. Ewing, former editor of *Harvard Business Review*, sees the corporate invasion of employees' civil liberties as rampant and attacks it in scathing terms:

> In most . . . [corporate] organizations, during working hours, civil liberties are a will-o'- the-wisp. The Constitutional rights that employees have grown accustomed to in family, school, and church life generally must be left outdoors, like cars in the parking lot. As in totalitarian countries, from time to time a benevolent chief executive or department head may encourage speech, conscience, and privacy, but these scarcely can be called rights, for management can take them away at will. . . . It is fair to say that an enormous corporate archipelago has grown which, in terms of civil liberties, is as different from the rest of America as day is from night. In this archipelago . . . the system comes first, the individual second.[10]

Two historical factors, in Ewing's view, lie behind the absence of civil liberties and the prevalence of authoritarianism in the workplace. One of these factors is the rise of professional management and personnel engineering at the turn of the 20th century, following the emergence of large corporations. This shaped the attitudes of companies toward their employees in a way hardly conducive to respecting their rights. As Frederick Winslow Taylor, generally identified as the founder of "scientific management," bluntly put it, "In the past, the man has been first. In the future, the system must be first."

The other historical factor is that the law has traditionally given the employer a free hand in hiring and firing employees. In the 19th century, a Tennessee court expressed this doctrine in memorable form. Employers, the court held, "may dismiss their employees at will . . . for good cause, for no cause, or even for cause morally wrong, without thereby being guilty of legal wrong." The U.S. Supreme Court ratified this common-law principle in 1915, ruling that "an employer may discharge his employee for any reason, or for no reason." According to the Court, this "is an essential element of liberty."[11]

In addition, traditional common law requires that an employee be loyal to an employer, acting solely for the employer's benefit in matters connected to work. The employee is duty-bound not to act or speak disloyally, except when in pursuit of his or her own interests outside work. It's no wonder, then, that traditional employment law has hardly been supportive of the idea of freedom of speech and expression for employees. Against that background, the treatment of employees like Lynne Gobbell, Michael Italie, or Louis MacIntire and the refusal of the courts to see a free speech issue in cases like theirs are not surprising.

The emergence of professional management and personnel engineering promoted workplace authoritarianism.

So did the employer's traditional legal right to fire employees for no cause.

Summary

Writers such as David Ewing believe that too many corporations routinely violate the civil liberties of their employees. Historically, this authoritarianism stems from (1) the rise of professional management and personnel engineering and (2) the common-law doctrine that employees can be discharged without cause ("employment at will").

Current Trends

According to the common law tradition, then, unless there is an explicit contractual provision to the contrary, every employment is **employment at will,** and either side is free to terminate it at any time without advance notice or reason. (While giving two weeks' notice before resigning is customary, there's no legal requirement to this effect.) The majority of American workers are at-will employees: the major exceptions are those who do have explicit contracts specifying the reasons for which they can be terminated, public-sector workers (who, with limited exceptions, are not at-will employees), and the comparatively small number of people who work in parts of the country where at-will employment is not the law of the land.

The employment at will doctrine, however, has been modified in important ways. Some of these limitations are statutory. At the federal level, for example, the *Wagner Act* of 1935 (discussed later in this chapter) was, in this respect, a watershed. It prohibited firing workers because of union membership or union activities. The *Civil Rights Act of 1964* and subsequent legislation prohibit discrimination on the basis of race, religion, national origin, sex, or age. Equally important, employees in the public sector—that is, in federal, state, and local government—enjoy certain constitutional protections on the job. Some states and localities have also passed legislation that places limits on the ability of employers to terminate employees. An especially interesting example is the state of Montana, which is alone among the 50 states in having eliminated at-will employment altogether.[12] In Montana, a worker can only be fired for a "just cause," an idea that will be discussed more fully later in this chapter. Philadelphia abolished at-will employment for parking lot attendants in 2019, and New York City eliminated it for fast-food workers in 2021.

Courts, too, have placed some limits on the doctrine of at-will employment, including limits on employers' ability to terminate employees for exercising their civil liberties. This is especially true with respect to religious liberties. The U.S. Supreme Court, for instance, has ruled that a state cannot deny unemployment benefits to employees who are fired because they refuse to work on their Sabbath day, even if they aren't members of an organized religion, and several lower courts have held that employees can dress in accordance with their faith while at work and should be given times and places for prayer as long as this doesn't cause undue hardship to the employer.[13] In a unanimous 2023 decision, the U.S. Supreme Court ruled that employers can deny a worker's request for a religious accommodation only if granting the accommodation would "would result in substantial increased costs."[14]

Courts have also sometimes found in favor of employees when they were terminated for engaging in conduct that is required or encouraged by "public policy." This includes cases in which they employees were dismissed because of something that they said or wrote. Thus, for example, a federal jury held that Mobil Chemical Company had wrongfully dismissed one of its top environmental officials after he refused to perform acts that would have violated federal and state environmental laws. The jury ordered Mobil to pay $375,000 in compensatory damages and $1 million in punitive damages. Most states also recognize a "public policy" exception to the employment at-will doctrine, although this is generally construed narrowly.[15] Courts haven't found that public policy favors employees expressing their political views outside of work, for instance.

Thus, today, working people have protection against some forms of unjust termination, and many of them enjoy the assurance that they can expect due process and that at least some of their civil liberties and other moral rights will be respected on the job. However, it would be a mistake to suppose that there is a clear trend in favor of greater legal protection for these liberties and rights. For example, when Daniel Foley, district manager for Interactive Data Corporation, accurately reported to his employer that his new boss was under investigation by the FBI for embezzling funds on a former job, he was dismissed for "inadequate performance" three months later, despite a seven-year record of positive work reviews and a recent $6,700 bonus. Foley sued Interactive Data for wrongful termination, but the California Supreme Court decided that his dismissal did not violate the "public interest" and rejected his suit.

In 2006, the U.S. Supreme Court ruled that the Constitution does not protect public employees from retaliation by their supervisors for things they say in the performance of their work duties. Deputy District Attorney Richard Ceballos had urged his superiors to dismiss a pending criminal case because a police officer had allegedly lied to obtain a search warrant. His advice was rejected, and he was denied a promotion and transferred to a lesser position farther from his home. Writing for the majority in a 5-to-4 decision, Justice Anthony M. Kennedy distinguished between statements public employees make "pursuant to their official duties" and those they make as citizens contributing to the "civic discourse." The First Amendment may sometimes protect the second category but not the first.[16] (This decision concerns only public employees. For private-sector employees, recall, there is no general First Amendment protection at all.)

Thus, although the law seems to be gradually changing, leaving the common-law heritage of employer–employee doctrine behind, recent legal developments are complicated and not entirely consistent. The results not only depend on the details of each case but also vary from jurisdiction to jurisdiction and from court to court. As argued in Chapter 1, however, our moral obligations extend beyond merely keeping within the law.

> The law seems to be gradually moving away from employment at will, but our moral obligations are not limited to merely obeying the law.

True, some businesspeople not only support employment at will as a desirable legal policy but also embrace it as a moral doctrine. They reject the normative principle—accepted by most ordinary people—that employees should be fired only for a good reason, and they deny that employers have any obligations to their employees beyond those specified by law or by explicit legal contract. Their actions, if not their words, suggest that they view the people who work for them as lacking any meaningful moral rights, seeing them as fungible assets—as means rather than ends in themselves—to be used in whatever way is profitable. In short, they apply the same logic to hiring and firing employees as they do to installing or replacing equipment. But nowadays that is a minority perspective. More and more corporations are coming to acknowledge, and to design institutional procedures that respect, the rights and moral dignity of their employees. Moreover, the firms taking the lead in this regard are often among the most successful companies in the country.

This fact cuts against the old argument that corporate efficiency requires employees to sacrifice their civil liberties and other rights between the hours of 9 and 5. Without strict discipline and the firm maintenance of management prerogatives, it has been claimed, our economic system would come apart at the seams. An increasing body of evidence, however, suggests just the opposite. As Ewing writes:

> Civil liberties are far less of a threat to the requirements of effective management than are collective bargaining, labor-management committees, job enrichment, work participation, and a number of other schemes that industry takes for granted. Moreover, the companies that lead in encouraging rights—organizations such as . . . IBM . . . and Delta Air Lines—have healthier-looking bottom lines than the average corporation does.[17]

Companies that Look beyond the Bottom Line

Although under no legal compulsion to do so, a small but growing number of companies encourage employee questions and criticisms about company policies affecting the welfare of employees and the community. Microsoft is a leader in this respect. It hosts monthly virtual town halls, where CEO Satya Nadella takes questions from employees.[18] Senior leaders also answer questions on internal social media channels. Microsoft even sends a survey to some randomly selected employees each day—the "Daily Pulse"—to monitor employee attitudes.

Union contracts frequently require companies to set up grievance procedures and otherwise attempt to see that their members are guaranteed due process on the job. Some nonunionized companies do the same. For instance, some corporations have adopted the "peer review" system of managing grievances between workers and managers that General Electric devised (as a way of discouraging some of their plants from unionizing). Peers of the employee and the manager (usually more of the former) sit as a panel to decide which party is in the right.[19]

Respecting the rights and dignity of employees, in particular, by acknowledging their civil liberties and guaranteeing them due process, can work to a company's benefit by enhancing employee morale and, thus, the company's competitive performance. Summarizing volumes of research on human resources management and organizational behavior, Professor Bruce Barry writes that "employees who perceive that workplace procedures are fair are more likely to be satisfied with their jobs, to be committed to the organization, and to make extra contributions over and above job requirements. Evidence also links these justice perceptions with better work performance and with reduced levels of negative behaviors, such as workplace theft."[20] Hence, there is little basis for the widespread belief that efficient management is incompatible with a fair workplace environment.

Summary
Some very successful companies have taken the lead in respecting employees' rights. Corporate profits and efficient management are compatible with a workplace environment where employees aren't subject to being treated arbitrarily.

"What I absolutely believe is that honoring the people who do the work can produce stunning results for the company," says Sidney Harmon, CEO of Harmon International Industries. "If the people in the factory believe there's a real effort to help improve their skills, provide opportunities for advancement and job security, they can do things that will blow your mind."[21] Some business writers push this point even further. For example, Robert Levering and Milton Moskowitz argue that

> The authoritarian work style—long the standard operating procedure in business—has failed. That failure is at the root of the poor performance of U.S. companies and massive layoffs in the [past]. When management is disconnected from the people who work in the company, it becomes easy to fire those people. And when workers are disconnected from what they do, it becomes easy not to care about the product or service.[22]

Of course, a company that does not sincerely consider employee rights to be of inherent moral importance is not likely to reap the benefits of enhanced business performance. Trust, as more and more management theorists are saying, is the key here, and employees can tell the difference between a company that has a genuine regard for their welfare and a company that only pretends to have moral concern.[23]

···

Hiring

People make up organizations, and how an organization impinges on the lives of its members is a morally important matter. One obvious and very important way organizational conduct affects the welfare and rights of employees and potential employees is through personnel policies and procedures—that is, how the organization handles the hiring, firing, paying, and promoting of the people who work for it. These human resources procedures and policies structure an organization's basic relationship with its employees. This section on hiring and the next three sections—on promotions, discipline and discharge, and wages—look at some of the specific, morally relevant concerns to which any organization must be sensitive. Speaking generally, though, if a company's personnel decisions are to be fair, they must reflect policies and procedures that are based on criteria that are job related, clear and accessible, and applied equally.

Fair personnel policies and decisions must be based on criteria that are clear, job related, and applied equally.

A necessary task for almost any business is hiring. Employers strive to hire people who will enable the organization to produce the products or services it seeks to provide or to promote its other goals. Furthermore, the courts have used the principle of negligent hiring to broaden the liability of an employer for damage or injury caused by its employees—even after regular hours and away from the job site. For instance, Avis Rent-A-Car was required to pay $800,000 after a male employee raped a female employee; the jury found that the company had been negligent in hiring the man without thoroughly investigating his background.[24] Of course, hiring managers shouldn't overreact to the prospect of a negligent hiring suit. Employment attorney Maurice Emsellem cautions hiring managers against letting the fear of such lawsuits deter them from giving individuals with criminal records a second change, since research shows that there's no correlation between a criminal record and workplace misconduct.[25]

In making hiring decisions, employers must be careful to treat job applicants fairly. Determining what this involves is not always easy, but companies that put applicants on a "do not hire" list based on unverified secondhand reports or the impressions of people outside the company who have met the applicant are probably acting unjustly.[26] On the other hand, is it unfair when an applicant gets a leg up because he was referred by a current employee or a friend of the hiring manager?[27]

To bring out some of the moral issues in hiring, let's examine the principal steps it involves: screening, testing, and interviewing.

Screening

When firms recruit employees, they attempt to screen them—that is, to attract qualified applicants who have a good chance of succeeding at the job and to weed out applicants or potential applicants who are unlikely to work out. When done properly, **job screening** ensures a pool of competent candidates and guarantees that everyone has been dealt with fairly; when done improperly, it undermines effective recruitment and invites injustices into the hiring process.

Screening begins with a job description and a job specification. A **job description** lists all pertinent details about the content of a job, including its duties, responsibilities, working conditions, and physical requirements. A **job specification** describes the qualifications an employee needs, such as the pertinent skills, background, education, or work experience. Job descriptions and specifications must be complete and accurate. Otherwise, job candidates lack the necessary information for making informed decisions and can waste time and money pursuing jobs they aren't suited for. In addition, disappointment and unfairness can result if a position is inaccurately described or wrongly classified.

That sounds simple enough. But in an effort to attract strong job candidates, hiring officers can easily, perhaps even unintentionally, begin to exaggerate what the job offers in regard to opportunities, travel, the ability to work from home, the budget one will control, and so on. And exaggeration can grow into blatant distortion. One recruiter offers this sample lexicon: "Character building" means that the job stinks, "mentoring" translates into babysitting your staff, and "work team environment" denotes noisy cubicles.[28] Exaggerations such as these may start innocently, but some businesses clearly and intentionally cross the line—for example, by deliberately misclassifying hourly workers as salaried employees to avoid paying them overtime.[29]

Summary
Fairness in personnel matters requires that policies, standards, and decisions affecting workers be directly job related, based on clear and available criteria, and applied equally.

Wrongful Discrimination

One of the main moral concerns in screening is to avoid wrongful discrimination. For several decades, the law has forbidden discrimination against individuals on the basis of age, race, national origin, religion, or sex, and these factors should never be alluded to in job specifications or recruitment advertisements. Chapter 11 discusses the moral issues surrounding job discrimination, but it's clear that basing employment decisions on such factors almost always excludes potential employees on non-job-related grounds. Firms must therefore be careful to avoid job specifications that discriminate subtly ("excellent opportunity for college student") or employ gender-linked job terminology (e.g., "salesman" rather than "salesperson" or "waiter" rather than "server") that may discourage qualified candidates from applying.

Bona fide occupational qualifications (BFOQs) are job specifications to which the civil rights law does not apply. But BFOQs are very limited in scope. There are no BFOQs for race or color, and in the case of gender or sex, BFOQs exist only to allow for authenticity (a male model) and modesty (a woman for a women's locker room attendant). In line with this, the Equal Employment Opportunity Commission (EEOC) filed a sex discrimination lawsuit against the restaurant chain Hooters, well known for its buxom "Hooter Girl" waitresses, for hiring only women as servers. Hooters resisted the decision, claiming that the job position is legitimately defined as one that makes gender or sex relevant. After some unfavorable publicity, the EEOC quietly dropped the suit. (Shortly thereafter, however, Hooters did settle a lawsuit filed by men who at been denied employment at the chain, paying several million dollars and agreeing to create more non-server jobs open to men.)[30]

In validating job specifications, firms are not permitted to rely on the preferences of their customers as a reason for discriminatory employment practices. For example, the fact that for decades, airline passengers were accustomed to being attended to by young female flight attendants and may even have preferred them could not legally justify excluding men from this occupation. Similarly, a court has ruled that the fact that 20 percent of Domino's customers have a negative reaction to pizza deliverymen with beards does not constitute a substantial business justification for the company's no-beards rule. The EEOC holds that such rules discriminate against Black men, who sometimes suffer from a genetic skin disorder that makes shaving difficult and painful.

Since Congress passed the **Americans with Disabilities Act (ADA)**, which became effective for all firms with fifteen or more employees in 1994, employers must be careful not to screen out disabled applicants who have the capacity to carry out the job. The ADA is intended, among other things, to protect the rights of people with disabilities to obtain gainful employment, and it forbids employers from discriminating against employees or job applicants with disabilities when making employment decisions. Employers must also make "reasonable accommodations" for an employee or a job applicant with a disability as long as doing so doesn't inflict "undue hardship" on the business.

Although the general moral imperative here is clear, in practice, applying these concepts and making the appropriate determinations can be difficult. Respect for the rights of people with disabilities may sometimes have to be balanced against expense to the company or inconvenience to other employees, but the expense or inconvenience must be very great indeed if it's to outweigh the moral injury and financial loss being borne by the person who is denied a job opportunity because of disability. There are other moral and legal gray areas, too. For example, the ADA protects employees or job applicants who are addicted to drugs but who are in recovery. But can an employer justifiably refuse to rehire an employee who was terminated for active drug use if they are now in recovery? The Supreme Court has ruled that the ADA doesn't preclude such a policy.[31]

When screening potential employees, companies must also be careful to avoid unfairly excluding applicants on the basis of language, physical appearance, or lifestyle. And they should not automatically screen out potential employees because they lack qualifications that aren't really necessary or, contrariwise, are "overqualified" or because they have a gap in their employment history.

Language

Bilingual ability (English–Spanish, English–Vietnamese) may be a justifiable job specification in some areas of the United States, where such skills can be essential for successful job performance. But employers need to be aware of the danger of creating unnecessary specifications for a position, especially if they risk discriminating on the basis of national origin. Although the ability to communicate effectively in English is a common workplace requirement, it can impede the employment prospects of some workers. The EEOC has ruled in several cases that disqualifying a job applicant because the applicant has a pronounced foreign accent is unlawful national-origin bias unless it can be proved that the accent would hinder the job seeker's ability to perform the job. In line with this principle, the U.S. Court of Appeals in San Francisco determined that a heavy Filipino accent was a legitimate basis for rejecting an applicant for a job at a state department of motor vehicles office that required dealing with the public, even though the plaintiff had scored higher than all other candidates on a written examination.[32]

Physical Appearance

After one day, a Georgia employer changed its mind about a new employee because she "was overweight and had large breasts" and hired a smaller woman with less experience instead.[33] Though perfectly legal, the employer's conduct was morally questionable; at the very least, it was offensive and humiliating. In a handful of American cities, however, local ordinances prohibit discrimination against those who are short or overweight. On that basis, Jennifer Portnick brought a case against a San Francisco franchise of Jazzercise, a dance-fitness company. Portnick, who is 5 feet 8 inches tall and weighs 240 pounds, had applied for a job as an aerobics instructor, but Jazzercise rejected her application because it required instructors to have a "fit appearance." After the city of San Francisco sided with Portnick, Jazzercise revised its job criteria and now agrees that "it may be possible for people of varying weights to be fit."[34]

Lifestyle

Some employers wade into morally troubling waters by screening job applicants on the basis of lifestyle. For example, Multi-Developers Inc., a Georgia-based real-estate company, won't hire anyone who engages in recreational activities that are "high risk"—like motorcycling, skydiving, motor racing, mountain climbing, or flying one's own plane. In Indianapolis, Best Lock Corporation won't employ anyone who admits to taking even an occasional alcoholic drink. Other companies, such as Turner Broadcasting System, flatly refuse to hire smokers.[35] More and more companies are following suit.[36] They usually claim that doing so saves them money because employees who smoke have more health problems than nonsmokers. But many smokers resent being discriminated against as individuals on general statistical grounds. They suspect that what really underlies such policies is a holier-than-thou disapproval of smoking.

Educational Requirements

Ill-considered educational requirements are also potentially objectionable. Requiring more formal education than is truly needed for a job is unfair to less-educated candidates, who, as a result, aren't even considered for the position. One of them might, in fact, turn out to be the best person for the job, which means that the firm also stands to lose.

The other side of the coin is to deny an applicant consideration because they seem "overqualified" in education or experience. "I'd never feel comfortable putting a really high-level candidate into a lower-level position," says one information technology recruiter. "We don't want to take you on if we think you might jump ship."[37] To avoid getting flagged as overqualified, however, some job seekers now play down their credentials by omitting advanced degrees from their résumés, changing lofty job titles, shortening descriptions of work experience, or omitting awards or other significant achievements. After sending out 100 copies of her résumé in search of receptionist work and receiving no responses, Kristin Konopka dropped her master's degree and teaching experience from her résumé. The slimmed-down version quickly brought her three callbacks and two interviews. On the other hand, recruiters and hiring officers are worried about people dumbing down their résumés. "How do I know I can trust them later down the road if there's something on their résumé they decided to take off so they could have a better chance of getting a job?" asks one.[38]

To avoid hiring someone who may become bored or frustrated by the job or who is likely to depart for greener pastures at the first opportunity, firms are justified in raising the issue. But they shouldn't proceed on the basis of assumptions that may be unwarranted. The employment ranks are filled with people successfully doing jobs for which they are technically overqualified.

Gap in Employment History

As traditional gender roles change, more and more men are leaving the work world for personal reasons, such as to help raise children while their wives complete professional training. These men often face obstacles when they return to work. Employers assume that a man who quit work once for personal reasons may do so again. Moreover, "there's still a stigma associated with men who put parenting on an equal footing with their jobs," says sociologist Scott Coltrane.[39] Thus, discontinuity of employment cuts some men off from job consideration, as it has so often done to women.

"The hurdles men face returning to the job market are about three times greater" than those faced by women, says Charles Arons, president and chief executive officer for Casco Industries, a Los Angeles–based employment and recruiting firm. "There isn't a male I know of in an executive position who would accept raising kids as a legitimate excuse for not working for three years." Thomas Schumann, director of selection and placement for Dayton-based Mead Corporation, agrees. "If other qualified candidates are available," he says, "my guess is that a personnel manager would go with somebody who doesn't raise that question."[40]

Certainly, employers in highly technical or rapidly changing fields are warranted in suspecting that an individual's career interruption may have left him (or her) out of touch. But to automatically disqualify a candidate because of that seems arbitrary and unfair.

Summary
Misleading job descriptions and inaccurate job specifications deny applicants the information they need to make informed occupational decisions. Ordinarily, sex, age, race, national origin, and religion should not enter into personnel decisions. Discrimination against the disabled is now expressly forbidden by law. Screening on the basis of language, physical appearance, lifestyle, ill-considered educational requirements, or gaps in employment history may also be unfair.

Testing

Testing is an integral part of the hiring process, especially in large firms. Tests are generally designed to measure the applicant's verbal, quantitative, and logical skills. Aptitude tests help determine an applicant's suitability for a job; skill tests measure the applicant's proficiency in specific areas, such as writing ability, data entry, or arithmetic; personality tests help determine the applicant's maturity and sociability. In addition, some firms engaged in the design and assembly of precision equipment administer dexterity tests to determine how nimbly applicants can use their hands and fingers.

To be successful, a test must be valid. **Test validity** refers to whether test scores correlate with performance in some other activity—that is, whether the test measures the skill or ability it's intended to measure. Just as important, tests must be reliable. **Test reliability** refers to whether test results are replicable—that is, whether a subject's scores will remain relatively consistent from test to test (so that a test taker won't score high one day and low the next). Clearly, not all tests are both valid and reliable. Many are not able to measure desired qualities, and others exhibit a woefully low level of forecast accuracy. Some companies use tests that haven't been designed for their particular situation. Legitimizing tests can be an expensive and time-consuming project, but if tests are used, the companies using them are obliged to ensure their validity and reliability.

Even when tests are valid and reliable, they can be unfair—for example, if the tests are culturally biased or if the skills they measure are irrelevant to job performance. The U.S. Supreme Court took a stand on this issue in 1971 in the case of *Griggs v. Duke Power Company*.[41] The case involved thirteen African-American laborers who were denied promotions because they scored low on a company-sponsored intelligence test involving verbal and mathematical puzzles. In its decision, the Court ruled that the Civil Rights Act prohibits employers from requiring a high school education or the passing of a general intelligence test as a prerequisite for employment or promotion without demonstrating that the associated skills relate directly to job performance. The *Griggs* decision makes it clear that if an employment practice such as testing has an adverse impact (or unequal effect) on minority groups, then the burden of proof is on the employer to show the job-relatedness or business necessity of the test or other procedure. Duke Power Company couldn't do that.

In the aftermath of *Griggs* and other cases, many U.S. firms retreated from administering pre-employment tests because of doubts about their legal validity. In recent years, though, testing has made a comeback in both the public and the private sectors. Today, millions of job applicants are putting pencil to paper, or sitting down in front of a computer screen, to take skills tests, leadership tests, personality tests, loyalty tests, and tests to determine accident proneness—even tests to predict what an applicant's coworkers will think of him or her after a year on the job.[42] Management, of course, is seeking through testing to gain a potentially more productive group of workers whose skills, aptitudes, and attitudes match more closely the requirements of the job. The supposed objectivity of tests is often illusory, however. Chapter 9 will have more to say about testing when it discusses privacy, but clearly putting too much faith in tests can lead to arbitrary employment decisions, decisions that are unfair to candidates and not in the best interests of the company. Test results should therefore be treated as, at most, only one measure in an overall evaluative process. Indeed, many experts believe that even the best tests cannot substitute for face-to-face interviews.

Interviewing

When moral issues arise in interviewing, they almost always relate to the manner in which the interview was conducted. Human resources experts rightly caution against rudeness, coarseness, hostility, and condescension in interviewing job applicants. In guarding against these qualities, personnel managers would do well to focus on the humanity of the individuals who sit across the desk from them, mindful of the very human need that has brought those people into the office. This is especially true when the interviewer might not otherwise identify closely with the person being interviewed because of cultural or other differences. Interviewers must exercise care to avoid thoughtless comments that may hurt or insult the person being

Even tests that are valid and reliable can be unfair if culturally biased or irrelevant to job performance.

Summary
A test is valid if it measures what it's meant to measure and reliable when it provides reasonably consistent results. Tests that lack validity or reliability are unfair. Tests may also be unfair if they are culturally biased or if the skills they measure do not relate directly to job performance.

interviewed—such as a passing remark about a candidate's physical disability or personal situation (a single parent, for instance). A comment that an unthinking interviewer might consider innocent or even friendly could be experienced as distressing or intrusive by the person across the table. For example, it can be very uncomfortable for candidates when interviewers ask, as a surprising number of them do, about their political affiliation or how they intend to vote.[43]

Roland Wall, a job placement counselor for individuals with disabilities, describes taking a developmentally disabled client, with an IQ of about 70, for a job interview. The personnel manager emerged from the room in which Wall's client was taking an initial test along with several other job applicants. The personnel manager asked Wall where his client was and was amazed to learn that she had gone in along with the others for testing. "Really?" he said. "I didn't see one in there." This personnel manager is probably more sensitive about people with disabilities than many employers, given his willingness to interview Wall's client, yet he assumed that because she was mentally disabled, the applicant would look a certain way—would look like "one."[44]

Even though everyone suffers from conscious and unconscious biases and stereotypes, interviewers should strive to free themselves as much as possible from these "idols of the mind," as the English philosopher Francis Bacon (1561–1626) called them. As Bacon put it: "The human understanding is like a false mirror, which, receiving rays irregularly, distorts and discolors the nature of things by mingling its own nature with it."[45] In short, we view things, people included, through the lens of our own preconceptions. Interviewers need to keep this fact in mind. For example, until the 1970s classical music orchestras were almost entirely male. Once "blind" auditions were introduced, the percentage of women quintupled.[46]

Proponents of the new but increasingly popular **situational interview** claim that it predicts future job performance better than a standard interview does and also more accurately than résumé analysis, personality assessments, or pen-and-paper tests.[47] In situational interviews, job candidates have to engage in role playing in a mock office scenario. For example, they might have to face a company manager pretending to be a disgruntled customer. The company's interviewers watch and assess the candidates' performance: how they process the information given by "the customer," how they decide to handle the situation, the words they choose, and even their body language. Proponents of the technique believe that job candidates have a harder time putting on a false front during a situational interview than in a standard interview, but there's no escaping the fact that biases and preconceptions can affect the interviewers' assessment of the likely job performance of different candidates based on their role-playing skills.

Interviewers should try to free themselves from unconscious biases, stereotypes, and preconceptions.

Summary
Most moral concerns in interviewing relate to how the interview is conducted. Interviewers should focus on the humanity of the candidate and avoid allowing their personal biases to color their evaluations.

• • •

Promotions

It's no secret that factors besides job qualifications often determine promotions. How long you've been with a firm, how well you're liked, whom you know, even when you were last promoted—all these influence promotions in the real business world. As with hiring, the key moral ideal here is fairness. Nobody would seriously argue that promoting the unqualified is fair or justifiable. It's a breach of duty to owners, other employees, and ultimately the general public. But many reasonable people debate whether promoting by job qualification alone is the fairest thing to do. Are other criteria admissible? If so, when, and how much weight should those criteria carry? These are tough questions with no easy answers. To highlight the problem, we consider seniority, inbreeding, and nepotism, three factors that sometimes serve as bases for promotions.

Are seniority, inbreeding, and nepotism fair and reasonable bases for promotion?

Seniority

Seniority refers to longevity on a job or with a firm. Frequently, job transfers or promotions are made strictly on the basis of seniority, but this policy can be problematic. Imagine that personnel manager Manuel Rodriguez needs to fill the job of quality-control supervisor. Carol Balke seems slightly better qualified for the job than Jim Turner, except in one respect: Turner has been on the job for three years longer than Balke. Whom should Rodriguez promote to quality-control supervisor?

The answer isn't easy. Those who would argue for Carol Balke—opponents of seniority—would undoubtedly claim that the firm has an obligation to fill the job with the most-qualified person. In this way, the firm is best served and the most qualified are rewarded. Those advancing Turner's promotion—proponents of seniority—would contend that the company should be loyal to its senior employees, that it should reward them for faithful service. In this way, employees have an incentive to work hard and to remain with the firm. The difficulty of the question is compounded by the fact that seniority in itself does not necessarily indicate competence or loyalty.

Then there's the question of employee expectations. If employees expect seniority to count substantially, management can injure morale and productivity by overlooking it. True, worker morale might suffer equally should seniority alone determine promotions. Ambitious and competent workers might see little point in refining skills and developing talents when positions are doled out strictly on the basis of longevity.

Because work situations vary, specifying what part, if any, seniority ought to play in promotions seems impossible—all the more reason, therefore, for management to consider carefully its seniority policies. Of paramount importance is that management recognize that it must seek both to promote those who are capable and qualified and who will perform well and to honor employees who have made prolonged and constructive contributions to the organization. A policy that provides for promotions strictly on the basis of qualifications seems heartless, whereas one that promotes by seniority alone seems mindless. The challenge for management is how to blend these dual responsibilities in a way that is beneficial to the firm and fair to all concerned.

Inbreeding

All the cautions about seniority apply with equal force to **inbreeding**, the practice of promoting exclusively from within the firm. In theory, whenever managers must fill positions, they should look to competence—that is, the ability to perform the job in question, regardless of whether the candidate is inside or outside the firm. In this way management best fulfills its responsibilities to the organization.

In practice, however, managers must seriously consider the impact of outside recruitment on in-house morale as well as their obligations to current employees. Although outsiders can bring a fresh perspective and even shake up a stagnant company culture, insiders can resent being passed over for advancement. This is natural. Years of loyal service, often involving personal sacrifice, create a unique relationship between employer and employee and, with it, obligations of gratitude and respect. The eighteen years that Christina Zhuy has worked for National Textile establishes a relationship between her and the firm that does not exist between the company and an outsider it may be considering for the job Zhuy seeks. Some would argue that when determining promotions, management has a moral obligation to remember this loyalty as well as the possible negative effects on company morale of ignoring it, especially when outside recruitment departs from established policy.

Nepotism

Nepotism (from the Latin word for nephew) is the practice of showing favoritism to relatives and close friends. Suppose a manager promotes a relative, her niece, say, strictly because of the relationship between them. Such an action would raise a number of moral concerns, chief among them disregard of managerial responsibilities to the organization and of fairness to other employees.

Not all instances of nepotism raise serious moral concerns. For example, when a firm is strictly a family operation and has as its purpose providing work for family members, nepotistic practices are generally justified. Moreover, many people believe that it's unfair to exclude a person from consideration for a job or for a promotion just because they are a relative or friend of someone in the company. In fact, Advest Group, a brokerage firm, traditionally brings sons and daughters into the organization. "Good work ethics seem to run throughout families," says senior vice president Robert Rulevich.[48] But that is probably a minority view. Today, it's more common for companies to prohibit the employment of relatives or, at least, to restrict such employment to avoid situations in which one relative is supervising another.

Summary
Seniority, or longevity on the job, is not necessarily a measure of either ability or loyalty. The challenge for management is to promote the most competent while also recognizing long-term contributions to the company. Inbreeding, or promoting exclusively from within, presents similar challenges. Nepotism—showing favoritism to relatives or close friends—is not always objectionable, but it may slight managerial responsibilities to the organization and result in unfair treatment of other employees.

When it comes to senior executives, however, the matter may be different, because there's a long list of well-known, publicly traded companies that employ in lucrative positions the wives, children, and in-laws of their top managers or board members.[49] The companies in question contend that they hire and promote only on the basis of merit, but it's difficult to disagree with Charles Elson of the Center for Corporate Governance, who says, "It just doesn't look right." "It creates the appearance of a conflict of interest," adds Nell Minnow of the Corporate Library, a research firm focusing on corporate governance issues. "The burden of proof is on the company to prove it's an arms-length transaction, and that's hard to do."[50]

Even when a friend, a relative, or a spouse of a manager or some other high-ranking employee is qualified for a position or deserving of promotion, the decision can hurt company morale, breed resentment and jealousy, and create problems with regard to future placement, scheduling, or dismissal of the person. It can make him or her an object of distrust and hostility within the organization and even discourage qualified outsiders from seeking employment with the firm.

...

Discipline and Discharge

For an organization to function in an orderly, efficient, and productive way, managers and personnel departments establish guidelines for employee conduct based on performance factors such as punctuality, dependability, efficiency, cooperativeness, and adherence to the dress code and to other rules. This is not the place to examine the morality of specific rules and regulations; the organization's treatment of employees when infractions occur is our focus here. For example, it's one thing to speak with a person privately about some infraction and quite another to chastise or punish the person publicly. Also, trying to correct someone's behavior on a graduated basis, from oral warning to written reprimand to suspension or other punishment prior to dismissal, is different from firing someone for a first mistake. The point is that although discipline and discharge are inevitable and, indeed, necessary aspects of organizational life, they raise concerns about fairness, noninjury, and respect for persons in the way they're administered.

Two Basic Principles

To create an atmosphere of fairness, one in which rules and standards are equally applied, the principles of "just cause" and "due process" must operate. **Just cause** requires that reasons for discipline or discharge deal directly with job performance. In the law, according to John J. McCall,

> Typically, 'just cause' is defined loosely (e.g., as reasonable and job-related grounds for dismissal) and left to arbitrators or labor courts to define more precisely through their decisions. It is, however, clearly understood that union membership, race, sex, personal bias, political opinions, religion, or ethnicity are invalid reasons; theft, fighting on the job, drug use on the job, excessive absenteeism, or substandard performance are acceptable reasons.[51]

For example, Best Buy probably had a just cause for firing two Denver employees for tackling a shoplifter outside the store (who subsequently brandished a knife and escaped), even though they were celebrated as heroes in the local press.[52] It might not have been good public relations, but like most big retailers, the company has strict rules about approaching suspected shoplifters in order to minimize the risk of violence. On the other hand, Goodwill almost certainly didn't have a just cause for firing Michael Italie, given that there's no evidence that he engaged in any political activity in the workplace. Of course, although distinguishing between a job-related and a non-job-related issue is not always easy and can be controversial.

Even if dismissal is job-related, however, it may still be unreasonable. Consider, for example, the Bronx potato-packing plant that fired Angelica Valencia for refusing to work overtime even though she had a note from her doctor, who said she should only work eight hours a day because of a high-risk pregnancy. Was that reasonable?[53]

Just cause and due process are essential to the fair handling of disciplinary issues.

The second principle related to fair worker discipline and discharge is **due process**, which refers to the fairness of the procedures an organization uses to impose sanctions on employees. Of particular importance is that the rules be clear and specific, that they be administered consistently and without discrimination or favoritism, and that workers who have violated them be given a fair and impartial hearing. Due process requires both the hearing of grievances and the setting up of a step-by-step procedure by which an employee can appeal a managerial decision.

Dismissing Employees

It's useful to distinguish among three types of discharge. **Firing** is for-cause dismissal—the result of poor performance or misconduct. Firing can also be called **involuntary termination**. (A resignation can be described as a voluntary termination.) **Layoff** usually refers to the temporary unemployment experienced by hourly employees during periods when the firm needs fewer workers and implies that they are "subject to recall." **Position elimination** designates the permanent elimination of a job as a result of workforce reduction, plant closing, or departmental consolidation.

Before dismissing an employee, management should follow a rational and unbiased decision-making process and analyze carefully the reasons leading to that decision. The organization must ask itself whether its treatment of the employee follows the appropriate procedures for that type of discharge, as those procedures are outlined in the employee handbook, in a collective bargaining agreement, or in a corporate policy statement. In addition, the company must guard against preferential treatment. Have there been employees who behaved in the same way but were not let go?

Even strict compliance with established procedures and even-handedness may not ensure fairness. For example, unless it's stated otherwise in a contract or employees have union representation, a company may not (depending on the type of case and where it occurs) be legally obligated to give reasons for firing an employee or to give advance notice. Employers who terminate someone without notice or cause may have been strictly faithful to contractual agreement or to established practice. But have they been just? Have they acted morally?

In answering those questions, it's helpful to distinguish between two employer responsibilities. Employers bear the responsibility of terminating the employment of workers who fail to fulfill their contractual obligations, but they also are obliged to terminate these workers as painlessly as possible. In other words, although employers have the right to fire, this does not mean they have the right to fire an employee in whatever way they choose. Because firing can be psychologically as well as financially devastating to employees, management should take steps to ease its effects. Moreover, crass firings hurt a company's reputation and impair its ability to attract top-notch employees.[54]

The literature on personnel management provides many suggestions for handling the discharge of employees compassionately and humanely, ranging from the recommendation not to notify employees of termination on Fridays, birthdays, wedding anniversaries, or the day before a holiday, to various steps to respect the terminated employee's privacy and dignity.[55] A company should not notify employees of their dismissal by e-mail, nor should it give a longtime employee a pink slip, as General Dynamics did, on the day he returned to work after burying his six-year-old son.[56] And, certainly, no employer should do what John Patterson, former head of NCR, a computer company, once did. He fired an underperforming executive by taking his desk and chair outside, dousing it with kerosene, and setting it on fire in front of the poor man.[57] As a matter of policy, some companies routinely have security personnel immediately escort terminated employees out of the building to avoid their causing trouble. There are arguments for and against this practice: it's demeaning, but managers cannot responsibly ignore the possibility of workplace violence. In some cases, it may be desirable for security to be nearby but not visible.[58]

These days, many companies allow or even encourage employees to use their own smart phones and tablets for work-related activities. When they separate from the company, former employees are often surprised to find their phones or other devices wiped cleaned, their contents having been remotely erased by their former employer to secure company data.

Employers have the right to discharge employees who perform inadequately, but they should try to do so as painlessly as possible.

One ex-employee says that his iPhone looked "like it came straight from the factory." His apps, contacts, e-mail programs, family photos, and downloaded music had all vanished.[59]

One obvious thing employers can do to ease the trauma of firing is to provide sufficient notice. Although federal law requires companies to give sixty days' advance notice of plant closings, many companies ignore this legal obligation. Whenever employers have reason to suspect that employees will react to notice of their terminations in a hostile, destructive way, sufficient notice might merely take the form of severance pay. Morally speaking, what constitutes sufficient notice of termination depends primarily on the nature of the job, the availability of similar jobs, and the employee's length of service—not to mention the type of discharge and the reasons for it. Ideally, the length of notice should be spelled out in the work contract, as should the firm's policy with regard to severance pay and the maintenance of health insurance and other benefits after the end of employment.

For most people who have to do it, firing a worker is painfully difficult. To help managers with this unpleasant task, some large companies have counselors to help discharged employees deal with their emotions. Other companies seek the services of a displacement firm. For a fee, the firm sends in a specialist to work with the discharged employee to assess personal strengths and weaknesses, analyze the causes of the dismissal, and start planning a job search. Some companies grant laid-off staff continued access to employee-assistance programs that provide hotlines or counseling to deal with stress, depression, marital discord, and money problems.[60] They also try to include former employees in alumni networks, which can help them make new contacts and find jobs.

Companies that provide displacement and other services to discharged employees believe that doing so reduces resentment and possible litigation. Aiding terminated employees can prevent them from damaging a company's reputation with clients or potential future employees, and it can enhance the productivity and morale of employees who remain. Self-serving interests aside, however, companies that assist discharged employees and treat them with dignity deserve recognition for their attempt to ease the anguish of those who must do the firing and to help those who are terminated salvage both their interrupted careers and their self-respect.

Summary

Most moral issues in employee discipline and discharge concern how management carries out these unpleasant tasks. Just cause and due process are necessary for fair treatment. To ease the trauma associated with discharge, employers should provide sufficient warning, severance pay, and perhaps displacement counseling.

The 2009 movie *Up in the Air* relates the story of a corporate downsizer. What ethical obligations do you believe companies have to employees they terminate?

...

Wages

Every employer faces the problem of setting wage rates and establishing salaries. From the moral point of view, it's obvious that firms should pay a fair or just wage, but what constitutes a just wage?

Every job will have what we might call a **market wage**, which is the lowest level of pay at which employers are able to find adequate employees to fill the available jobs. The market wage will be determined by the supply of workers and the demand for their labor by employers. In a labor market where many people would like to do a given type of work, but only a few such jobs exist, the market wage may be comparatively low. With a large supply of potential workers and a low demand for their services, workers will essentially be competing to see who will work for the least amount of money. The "winners" will be hired. When many employers are competing for just a few qualified workers, in contrast, this will tend to drive the market wage up. Employers won't voluntarily hire people who cost the business more than they add to its bottom line, so the revenue that's generated by filling a position sets an upper limit on the market wage for that job.

The market wage is effectively a floor on how much workers are paid. If employers offer a wage below the local market wage for that type of work, they must assume that positions will go unfilled. But is it always permissible for employers to pay only the market wage and no more?

It's worth noting in passing that the law sometimes requires employers to pay more than the market wage. Federal law requires that businesses pay at least the minimum wage of $7.25 per hour (or $2.13 per hour for workers who receive tips). Some states have higher minimum wages; California, for instance, requires that employees receive at least $15.50. Some cities set even higher minimums than their states; in San Francisco, for instance, the minimum is $18.07. The minimum wage is not the only federal law governing wages. Since 1938, the Fair Labor Standards Act has required employers to pay overtime for every hour worked beyond forty in a week—a law that is violated when companies force employees to work off the clock or skip meal breaks.[61]

So, employers are sometimes legally required to pay workers more than the market rate. But the market wage for a job will often be above the legal minimum. We can still ask, in these cases, whether employers sometimes have a moral obligation to pay more than the market rate. As we saw at the beginning of the chapter, some people believe that as long as the employer and employee both agree to terms then those terms are fair. From that viewpoint, it would seem to be acceptable for employers to pay the market wage and no more. Recall that many people who hold this view are skeptical about whether there is any objective way to determine what the fair wage for a job is other than its being agreed to between the employer and employee.

Others, though, maintain that just because employers and employees both agree to a set of terms is no guarantee that those terms are fair. One side, which in practice usually means the workers, may have agreed to unfair terms only because they need to pay for food and shelter and the other options open to them are even less fair. As a result, even though they've agreed to work for a given wage it's still possible that they're being unfairly exploited. If many people are looking for work, then the market wage for some jobs may be so low as to be exploitative even if it's above the legal minimums. Paying the market wage and no more might be seen as unfairly taking advantage of the workers' poor prospects.

People who hold this second viewpoint usually don't imagine that there's any single magic formula that determines what a fair or just wage for work is. Instead, they point to a variety of questions that employers should consider in deciding how much to pay workers. These include:

1. **What is the law?** We saw in Chapter 1 that not all legal requirements are ethical requirements. Still, it seems implausible that an employer could be ethically justified in paying workers less than the legal minimum.

2. **What is the prevailing wage in the industry?** Employers who pay less than the prevailing wage will have a hard time finding workers, so they have prudential as well as moral reasons to take this into account. Still, they have to consider the possibility that the prevailing wage might be unfairly low.

3. **What is the community wage level?** Some communities have a higher cost of living than others. For example, it's more expensive to live in New York City than in Little Rock.

4. **What is the nature of the job itself?** Some jobs require more training, experience, and education than others. Some are stressful or very demanding, physically or emotionally. Some jobs are downright dangerous; others are viewed as demeaning or intrinsically undesirable. Risky, disagreeable, or unskilled jobs often attract the least-educated applicants and the most desperate for work, thus leading to possible worker exploitation.

5. **Is the job secure? What are its prospects?** Employment that promises little or no security fails to fulfill a basic need of employees. In such cases employers should seek to compensate workers through higher pay, better fringe benefits, or both. A secure job with a guarantee of regular work and excellent retirement benefits (such as a civil service position) may justify a more moderate wage. In addition, a relatively low salary may be acceptable for a job that is understood to be a stepping-stone to better positions inside the organization.

6. **What can the organization afford to pay?** A start-up company with minimal cash flow and a narrow profit margin may be unable to pay more than a minimum wage. A mature company with a secure market position might easily afford to pay better wages.

7. **What are other employees inside the organization earning for comparable work?** To avoid discrimination and unfairness in setting wage rates, it's important to look at what the organization is already paying its present employees for work of a similar nature. Gross salary disparities that are not warranted by the nature of the work, the experience required, or other objective considerations can also hurt employee morale.

8. **What is the value of the work to the organization?** It may not always be easy to quantify the size of the contribution that a given employee or position makes to a business. When this is possible, though, then we might think that if there's a large disparity between a worker's contribution and their compensation then this is reason to think that the employee is underpaid. Recall the discussion of adjunct instructors at the start of the chapter. Those who argue that adjuncts are being treated unfairly frequently point to the fact that a part-time instructor might easily receive no more than 10 percent of the tuition that students pay to take their courses.

Question 8 raises the possibility that employers might be justified in paying more productive workers more than others who hold the same job. Some people work harder or are more talented and thus contribute more to the organization, and many people today find the idea that these workers deserve higher pay familiar and intuitive plausible. To say that they deserve higher pay is to say more than that the market wage for superior workers is higher than it is for average ones, although that is certainly true; it's to say that their superior effort and/or talent is an ethically relevant factor. It's worth noting, though, that some critical questions could be asked about this idea. The philosopher John Stuart Mill, who we've already encountered several times, claims that paying more productive workers more is only perfectly just when their higher productivity results from differences in people's choices. In contrast, "when it depends on natural difference of strength or capacity, this principle of remuneration is in itself an injustice: it is giving to those who have; assigning most to those who are already most favoured by nature."[62]

A Living Wage

As mentioned earlier, many cities or counties and a handful of states have passed "living-wage" laws that raise the legally mandated minimum wage above federal requirements, sometimes by several dollars an hour. Often these laws apply only to businesses with city contracts, but some cities have extended them to cover all businesses above a certain size in the city's jurisdiction. In this context, a **living wage** is the amount of money a full-time employee needs to afford the necessities of life, support a family, and live above the poverty line.

How much money a person must make in order to earn a living wage will vary from community to community. Still, almost everywhere in the country it's impossible for a person who works full time but earns only the federally required minimum to pull himself or herself out

Summary
While some people believe that any wage that employers and employees agree upon is fair, others believe that workers may often be willing to agree to an unfairly low wage because their other options are even worse. People who hold this second view suggests that employers must consider a variety of questions in order to determine what level of compensation would be just.

of poverty, let alone support a family. This fact galvanizes the living-wage movement. Its supporters argue that employers have a moral obligation to pay a living wage, and they ground their case on the utilitarian injunction to promote human welfare, on the Kantian principle of respect for human dignity, or on the commonsense idea that some wages are so low as to be inherently exploitative. MIT economics professor Amy K. Glasmeier has created an online tool, the Living Wage calculator, to estimate a living wage anywhere in the United States (https://livingwage.mit.edu).

Various moral considerations support the idea that businesses should pay a living wage.

Opponents of a mandated living wage argue that it's bad policy, favoring instead either eliminating or at least reducing the minimum wage.[63] They contend that living-wage laws are hard on local companies because they raise the cost of doing business. Such laws can also cost taxpayers money because local government must pay more for the goods and services it uses. Moreover, raising the price of anything inevitably lowers the demand for it. Hence, opponents argue, living-wage laws only serve to reduce the number of jobs. They also contend that living-wage advocates exaggerate the number of employees trying to support families on the minimum wage. Many low-wage workers are teenagers, living at home. Raising their wages won't help to reduce poverty. Moreover, they argue, if poverty is the issue, then this problem should be addressed by government programs, not by interfering in the marketplace and setting wages by fiat.

Critics of living-wage laws believe they cost jobs.

Standard economic theory affirms the principle that raising the minimum wage will, other things being equal, lower the demand for minimum-wage labor, thus putting some people at the bottom end of the scale out of work. These people also may be hurt if higher wages attract more skilled people to compete for those jobs. The real world, however, is complicated, and empirical evidence suggests that, in practice, increasing the minimum wage does not necessarily cost jobs or hurt the poor more than it helps them.[64] Living-wage advocates also insist that even if those laws do lead to some job loss, it's still wrong to offer people employment that does not meet this standard. It's worth it for a community to have better-paying jobs even if there are fewer jobs as a result. Moreover, advocates of living-wage laws contend that business really can afford to pay better wages and that in this day of growing economic inequality, it's important to pressure them to do so.

· · ·

Labor Unions

This chapter and Chapter 9 are concerned with a number of moral issues that arise in the workplace between employer and employees, and no discussion of the workplace should overlook one institution that has done much to shape employer–employee relations in modern economies, influencing the terms and conditions of employment and shaping the environment in which people work—namely, labor unions. Accordingly, this section briefly examines the history and economic role of unions, the ideals that motivate them, and some of the moral dilemmas they raise.

History of the Union Movement

Unions have increased the security and standard of living of working people and contributed to social stability and economic growth.

In a famous remark, Franklin D. Roosevelt said that free and independent labor unions are characteristic of a free and democratic modern nation. Many economists and students of the union movement go on to give it primary credit for raising the standard of living and increasing the security of working people in the United States. They argue that almost all the benefits enjoyed by employees today, whether they happen to be in unions or not, can be traced to union victories or to union-backed legislation. At the same time, the higher wages, paid vacations, health benefits, retirement programs, and increased job security that unions have brought have, in turn, contributed to social stability in the country and, through enhanced demand, to economic growth itself. Yet as the history of the labor movement reveals, employers have opposed unionization and union demands at almost every step of the way—often with violence.

Yet employers have resisted unions at every step.

Just as the roots of capitalism can be traced to the handicraft guilds, so the earliest efforts of American unionism can be found in the craft unions of the 18th century. At that time, groups of skilled artisans—carpenters, shoemakers, tailors, and the like—formed secret societies for two basic reasons: to equalize their relationship with their employers and to professionalize their crafts. They agreed on acceptable wages and working hours and pledged not to work for any employer who didn't provide them, and they set minimal admission standards for their crafts. They also agreed to keep their allegiance secret—and for good reason. Until the second half of the 19th century, the courts frequently convicted workers of criminal conspiracy merely for joining together, even if no strike or other illegal activity took place.

Labor historians generally consider the Knights of Labor, established in 1869, to be the first truly national trade union. The Knights endeavored to call together all workers, skilled and unskilled, Black and White, male and female, into one mighty association. The Knights were followed by the American Federation of Labor (AFL). Founded in 1886, the AFL united the great national craft unions, such as iron- and steelworkers, boilermakers, tailors, coal miners, and printers, in a closely knit organizational alliance. Appealing to better-paid skilled workers, the AFL soon surpassed the Knights, and the latter eventually faded away. Under the temperate leadership of Samuel Gompers, the AFL's membership reached 500,000 within seven years, growing to around 2 million by 1917.

During this period, companies routinely used the 1890 Sherman Act, which outlawed business monopolies, to obtain anti-strike injunctions from the courts on the grounds that strikes illegally restrained trade. Usually, it was sufficient merely for a company to allege that a strike might cause harm, and it was rewarded with an injunction, which made union organizing exceedingly difficult. However, with the stock-market crash of 1929 and the Great Depression that followed, public sympathy shifted toward workers. In 1932, Congress passed the *Norris–LaGuardia Act*, which prohibited federal injunctions in nonviolent labor disputes. Then in 1935 it enacted the **National Labor Relations Act** (also called the **Wagner Act**). The most important of all our labor laws, it guarantees employees the right to organize and join unions and to bargain collectively through representatives of their own choosing. The Wagner Act prohibits employers from interfering with employees trying to organize unions, from attempting to gain control over labor unions, from treating union workers differently from nonunion workers, and from refusing to bargain with union representatives. Under the National Labor Relations Act, there are two main ways for workers to form a union. One is for a majority of the workers at a company to demonstrate their desire for a union by signing up to join it (**card check**). Alternatively, if 30 percent or more of the workers sign a petition requesting union representation, then an election is organized and employees vote by secret ballot whether to have a union. However, employers can refuse to recognize a union chosen by majority signup and can demand an election instead.

The Wagner Act helped increase union membership to almost 12 million by the end of World War II in 1945. Most of these members belonged to the Congress of Industrial Organizations (CIO), an offshoot of the AFL that brought together various workers—auto, sheet metal, steel, and so on—into industry-wide unions. The distinct advantage of the CIO over the AFL was that CIO unions could call a firm's entire workforce out on strike rather than just its skilled workers.

Increasing union strength raised public suspicions and fears of union power. Many businesspeople and political critics encouraged these worries and quickly pointed to the wave of strikes after World War II as evidence of union abuse of power. In 1947 a newly elected Republican Congress passed the **Taft–Hartley Act**, which amended the National Labor Relations Act. Taft–Hartley outlaws *closed shops* (which hire only union members) and permits individual states to ban *union shops* (which require employees to join the union within a specified time after being hired). In 2017, Kentucky became the most recent of the so-called **right-to-work states**, with **open-shop laws** on their books. These laws prohibit union contracts requiring all employees on a job site to either join the union or pay the equivalent of union dues once hired. Taft–Hartley also prohibits various labor practices designated as unfair, such as sympathetic strikes and secondary boycotts (discussed later in this chapter).

The Situation of Unions Today

In 1955, the AFL and the CIO merged to form the **AFL-CIO**. Since then, unions have attempted to increase membership by recruiting outside basic industry—for example, in education, government, white-collar professions, and service jobs. But they have been only moderately successful. For the past twenty years, union membership has been falling, both absolutely and as a percentage of the workforce, especially outside of government. Whereas unions represented 36 percent of the private-sector workforce in the 1950s, today only 6 percent of private-sector workers are union members. Just over 33 percent of public-sector workers are in unions, which means that all together overall, just over 10 percent of American wage and salary workers are unionized. This is the lowest number on record.[65] Union membership as a percentage of the workforce is at its lowest level in the United States since 1916, substantially below what it is in Japan and most Western nations—for instance, Australia, Belgium, France, Germany, the Netherlands, and the United Kingdom.

Unions have been more and more on the defensive over the last few decades, as the industries in which they have traditionally been based have declined. The number of days lost to strikes, for instance, has been at a record low, and many unions have been forced to go along with decreases in wages and benefits. Meanwhile, the general political climate has been unfavorable to labor for the past three decades. President Reagan set the anti-union tone back in the 1980s when he fired nearly 12,000 striking air traffic controllers and broke their union. The union had been considered powerful, but it was soundly defeated. Pushed by business interests, in recent years the federal government has moved to tighten its regulation of unions and to restrict their ability to organize.[66] And several states that had been considered pro-labor, such as Wisconsin, Indiana, and West Virginia, have recently passed anti-union legislation.

On the legal front, labor unions suffered a major setback when the U.S. Supreme Court ruled that private employers could "replace permanently" striking workers, even though the 1935 Wagner Act makes it illegal for employers to retaliate against workers who go on strike by "firing" them. Whatever the terminology, if workers risk losing their jobs because of a strike, then the balance of power in collective bargaining is dramatically altered. Instead of negotiating in good faith, a company can now provoke a strike, hire new workers to replace the pickets, and cut costs. And management has done exactly that in a number of cases, as many corporations have grown increasingly and aggressively anti-union.

Employers hire anti-union management consultants, hold mandatory anti-union meetings, show anti-union videos at work, have supervisors meet individually with employees to disparage unions, and distribute anti-union leaflets at work or mail them to employees' homes.[67] They try to break existing unions or prevent their formation by harassing and even firing pro-union workers and by waging vigorous, often illegal anti-union campaigns. For example, if a Walmart store thinks its employees may be planning to organize a union, corporate headquarters dispatches a union-busting team by corporate jet to deal with the problem. When, after somehow dodging the corporate police, the meat-cutting department of a Texas Walmart voted to join the Union of Food and Commercial Workers, the company responded a week later by closing the department and firing the offending employees. And it shuttered a whole store in Quebec a few months after it became the only unionized Walmart in North America.[68] It's not surprising, then, that nearly half of the country's nonunion workers—more than 60 million—would like to join a union if they could.[69]

Some years ago, Richard Edwards and Michael Podgursky summarized labor's situation in words that still largely hold true today:

> Bargaining structures built up over many years are crumbling and collapsing. . . . Rising product market competition, deregulation, and technological changes; adverse labor force dynamics; worsening public policy; and the legacy of the long stagnation have thrust the labor movement into a qualitatively new stage. This new period is characterized . . . by: (a) greater corporate mobility, power, and militancy; (b) ineffective labor law and a growing indifference, and in some cases, outright opposition of the government towards organized labor and collective bargaining; and (c) a waning belief in unions as the agents of working class interests. In these hostile circumstances, American unions face a difficult and troubling future.[70]

In recent years, unions have been on the defensive.

Summary
Working people struggled for decades to form unions and win their legal recognition. Although unions are responsible, directly or indirectly, for many of the benefits employees today enjoy, a changing economy, hostile political environment, and aggressive anti-union policies have weakened them. Still, there are positive signs for unions.

However, periods of economic crisis and dislocation, when accompanied by high corporate profits and a public perception of greed and unfairness, sometimes lead to increased unionization and stronger labor organizations. Some think that may begin to happen now. In fact, there are several recent positive signs for unions.

Consider, for instance, the state of Michigan. In 2012, Michigan adopted a right-to-work law. In 2023, however, that law was repealed. It had been over 50 years since a state last moved out of the right-to-work camp. Recent polling also indicates that public attitudes are changing, with over 70 percent of Americans now indicating their support for unions.[71] The last time that support was that high was 1965. There have also been several recent cases where workers were successful in unionizing despite strong corporate resistance. The first Amazon warehouse was unionized in 2022, in Staten Island, New York, as were an Apple store in Maryland and over 300 Starbucks stores.[72] In September of 2023, for the first time ever, the UAW initiated simultaneous strikes against all three unionized American carmakers at once: Ford, General Motors, and Stellantis (Chrysler). The union's bid to win significantly higher wages, greater job security, and other concessions was largely successful. That same year, strikes by the Screen Actors Guild–American Federation of Television and Radio Artists and the Writers Guild of America succeeded in winning better compensation and protection against replacement by artificial intelligence for actors and writers.

Union Ideals

From the beginning, unions have fought to protect workers from abuses of power at the hands of employers. Employers have tremendous power over individual workers. They can hire and fire, relocate and reassign, set work hours and wages, and create rules and control working conditions. Acting individually, a worker rarely is an employer's equal in negotiating any of these items. As we have already noted, in most labor markets, employers have far more bargaining power than workers. The position of most workers acting independently is further weakened by their lack of capital, occupational limitations, and personal and family needs. Furthermore, whereas employers obviously need workers, they rarely need any particular worker. They can, generally speaking, select whomever they want, for whatever reasons they choose.

Interestingly, Adam Smith himself recognized this fundamental imbalance in his classic *The Wealth of Nations*. Regarding the respective bargaining power of workers and their "masters," or employers, he wrote that "upon all ordinary occasions" employers "have the advantage in the dispute, and force the other into a compliance with their terms."

> The masters, being fewer in number, can combine much more easily. . . . We have no acts of parliament against combining to lower the price of work; but many against combining to raise it. In all such disputes the masters can hold out much longer. . . . Though they did not employ a single workman, [employers] could generally live a year or two upon the stocks which they have already acquired. Many workmen could not subsist a week, few could subsist a month, and scarce any a year without employment. In the long run the workman may be as necessary to his master as his master is to him, but the necessity is not so immediate.[73]

In an attempt, then, to redress the balance of power in their dealings with employers, workers band together. In acting as a single body, a union, workers in effect make employers dependent on them in a way that no individual worker can. The result is a rough equality or mutual dependence, which serves as the basis for *collective bargaining*—negotiations between the representatives of organized workers and their employers over things such as wages, hours, rules, work conditions, and, increasingly, participation in decisions affecting the workplace. As the World Bank and others have recognized, by giving workers a collective voice, unions do not just push up wages. They also can improve productivity and efficiency, promote stability in the workforce, and make government less likely to meddle in the labor market.

Certainly no one can object to unionism's initial and overriding impulse: to protect workers from abuse and give them a voice in matters that affect their lives. Indeed, those two goals reflect two lofty moral ideals: noninjury and autonomy. Ironically, it's out of respect for these ideals that some individuals criticize modern unions.

Unions seek to protect workers and give them a voice. Some people, however, base their criticism of unions on these same ideals.

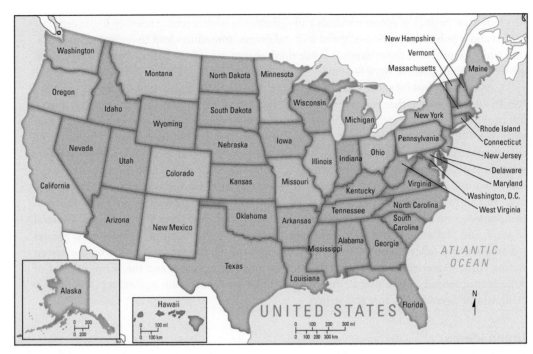

This map shows the states (in green) where employees at unionized workplaces can be required to be members of the union (or to pay dues or fees to the union) as a condition of employment and the states where the law forbids this.

The critics argue that union shops infringe on the autonomy and right of association of individual workers. Even if workers are not required to join the union but only to pay union dues or its equivalent, the critics contend, this still infringes on their freedom. In addition, evidence suggests that unionized companies sometimes treat nonunion personnel less favorably than they treat union members. Some workers have gone to court to argue that favoritism to union members is discriminatory and unlawful. Whether it is or not, it certainly raises a moral question about the right to determine for oneself organizational membership and participation.

Taking the union's viewpoint reveals competing ideals and other consequences that must be considered. *First*, there is organized labor's ideal of solidarity, which is vital to collective bargaining and to winning worker equality. Union proponents point to the fact that workers in unionized workplaces earn more than nonunionized workers and that per capita personal income is higher in states with free collective bargaining than in right-to-work states. For instance, of the twenty-six right-to-work states, only one—Virginia—has an average personal income above the national average of $59,428.[74] Practically speaking, if workers receive union benefits without having to pay dues, then they lack an incentive to join the union, which greatly weakens the union's ability to improve wages and strengthen workers' rights.

Second, there is a question of fairness. Is it fair for a nonunion worker to enjoy the benefits won by union members—often at great personal and organizational expense? This question arises most clearly when employees don't have to join the union but must nevertheless pay the equivalent of union dues. This policy is designed to eliminate free riders while respecting the individual worker's freedom of choice. Opponents claim that it does not so much eliminate free riders as create forced passengers.

Union Tactics

The tactics unions use to try to get management to accept their demands also raise moral issues.

Direct Strikes

By withholding their labor in a strike, workers try to compel an employer to meet their demands.

The legal right to strike is labor's most potent tool in labor–management negotiations. A strike occurs when an organized body of workers withholds its labor in an effort to pressure the employer to comply with its demands. On libertarian principles, it's clear that employees have a right to agree among themselves to stop working for an employer. However, because strikes can cause financial injuries to both employer and employee, inconvenience and perhaps worse to consumers, and economic dislocations in society, they raise serious moral questions. On the other hand, sometimes workers cannot obtain justice and fair play in the workplace in any other way. Austin Fagothey and Milton A. Gonsalves suggest the following conditions of a justified strike:[75]

1. **Just cause.** Strikes are justified only if the reasons for them are serious and job related. Certainly, inadequate pay, excessive hours, and dangerous and unhealthful working conditions are legitimate worker grievances and provide just cause for a strike. Minor workplace irritants, political ambition, and petty jealousies or personal likes and dislikes do not constitute just cause and thus cannot justify a strike.

2. **Proper authorization.** For a strike to be legitimate, it must be duly authorized. This means, first, that workers themselves must freely reach the decision without coercion and intimidation. Second, if the workers are organized, then the proposed strike must receive union backing (although this condition becomes difficult to apply when the local union chapter and the national organization don't see eye-to-eye).

3. **Last resort.** To be justified, a strike must come as a last resort. This condition acknowledges the serious potential harm of strikes. A basic moral principle is that we should always use the least injurious means available to accomplish the good we desire. Since there is an array of less drastic collective-bargaining tactics that can and usually do achieve worker objectives, all these should be exhausted before a strike is called.

Even when a strike is warranted, however, not every means of implementing it is morally justified. In general, non-violent picketing and an attempt by striking workers to publicize their cause and peacefully persuade others not to cross the picket line are moral means of striking. Physical violence, threats, intimidation, and sabotage are not. More controversially, Fagothey and Gonsalves argue that if workers have the right to withhold their labor and strike, then employers have a right to fill their jobs with other workers but not with professional strikebreakers, whose presence incites violence and whose function extends beyond doing work to denying strikers justice and the right to organize.

The preceding discussion deals with **direct strikes**—that is, cessation of work by employees with the same industrial grievance. There is, however, another kind of strike, far more controversial than the direct strike: the sympathetic strike.

Sympathetic Strikes

A **sympathetic strike** occurs when workers who have no particular grievance of their own decide to strike in support of others. Sympathetic strikes can even take on global proportions, as when American dockside workers refused to unload freighters from the Soviet Union to show support of the Solidarity movement in Poland. Frequently, the sympathetic strike involves several groups of workers belonging to different unions but employed by the same company. Acting on a grievance, one group strikes. But because it's so small, it enlists the aid of the other groups; it asks them to engage in a sympathetic strike. In circumstances like this, a sympathetic strike does not seem to differ in any morally significant way from a direct strike. Indeed, it could be argued that the affiliated groups have obligations of loyalty and beneficence to join the strike. It's true, of course, that the sympathetic strikers do not have personal grievances, but they do have the same unjust employer, and they're in a position to help remedy that injustice by withholding their labor.[76]

On the other hand, however, sometimes sympathetic strikes involve employees who work for a different employer striking in support of other workers. Such strikes differ significantly from direct strikes or sympathetic strikes against the same employer. For one thing, the employers being struck out of sympathy may be perfectly innocent victims whose treatment of workers is beyond reproach. They may have lived up to their end of the work contract, only to have their workers break it.

Summary
Unions attempt to protect workers from abuse and give them a voice in matters that affect their lives. Critics charge that forcing workers to join unions infringes on autonomy and the right of association. They allege that union workers receive discriminatory and unlawful favoritism. In response, union sympathizers stress fairness and the importance of solidarity.

Summary
Direct strikes may be justified when there is just cause and proper authorization and when they're called as a last resort. Because they involve the cessation of work in support of other workers with a grievance, sympathetic strikes raise distinct moral concerns.

Sympathetic strikes can be very effective, however. J. P. Stevens & Co., once the second-largest company in the U.S. textile industry, fought unionization for decades. The company engaged in a variety of flagrantly unfair labor practices and refused to recognize or bargain collectively with the union despite various court orders to do so.[77] During a boycott of J. P. Stevens products, United Auto Workers (UAW) members at a General Motors plant in Canada refused to install J. P. Stevens carpeting in the cars they were producing, thus shutting down the assembly line. In less than half a day, J. P. Stevens carpeting was gone from the plant. Had U.S. workers done something similar, both they and the textile workers union would have been subject to legal action, but J. P. Stevens would not have been able to refuse to bargain as long as it did.

Boycotts and Corporate Campaigns

Besides strikes, unions also use boycotts to support their demands. A **primary boycott** occurs when union members and their supporters refuse to buy products from a company being struck. A **secondary boycott** occurs when people refuse to patronize companies that handle products of struck companies. The Taft–Hartley Act prohibits unions from organizing secondary boycotts. However, because agricultural laborers are not covered by the Wagner Act, Taft–Hartley doesn't apply to them, so the United Farm Workers union was legally able to use this tactic successfully in the 1960s and 1970s.

The express purpose of any boycott is the same as that of a strike: to hurt the employer or company financially and thus strengthen the union's bargaining position. In general, a boycott is justifiable when it meets the same conditions as a strike. In the case of the secondary boycott, which is like a sympathetic strike, the damage is extended to those whose only offense may be that they're handling the products of the unjust employer—and perhaps they're handling them out of financial necessity. In such cases, Fagothey and Gonsalves reject secondary boycotts. But this assessment seems too automatic and doesn't allow us to weigh the likely harms and benefits in particular cases.[78]

A relatively new pressure tactic by organized labor is the so-called **corporate campaign**, in which unions enlist the cooperation of a company's creditors to pressure the company to allow its employees to unionize or to comply with other union demands. For example, several unions united to mount a corporate campaign to force Washington Gas Company to settle a dispute with the International Union of Gasworkers. The Teamsters, the Service Employees International Union, the Laborers' International Union, and the Communications Workers of America joined forces with several local unions to pressure Crestar Bank—where Washington Gas had a line of credit—to intervene on the union side. To lean on Crestar, the unions had at their disposal pension funds, payroll accounts, normal operating capital for their organizations, and even the mortgages on their buildings. Crestar complained that it was only caught in the middle. "We are not a party to the dispute," said spokesman Barry Koling. "We are neutral with respect to the issues between them." But union spokesman Jorge Rivera responded, "We judge our business partners by their actions concerning workers."[79]

At the heart of the corporate campaign is the issue of corporate governance. In pressuring financial institutions with mass withdrawals and cancellations of policies, unions and administrators of public employee pension funds are trying to influence those institutions' policies and business relationships. And when the financial institutions accede to union demands, they in turn pressure the recalcitrant company to change its business policies. The harshest critics of the corporate campaign call it corporate blackmail. Its champions view it as an effective way to get financial institutions and companies to become good corporate citizens. Such tactics, they say, are necessary at a time when wages are stagnating, economic inequality is increasing, and management has been so successful at exploiting labor laws and regulations to undermine unions and thwart their recruitment efforts.

Like a strike, a boycott tries to strengthen the union's bargaining position. A secondary boycott is analogous to a sympathetic strike.

Summary
Primary boycotts seem morally comparable to direct strikes, and secondary boycotts analogous to sympathetic strikes. In corporate campaigns, unions enlist the cooperation of a company's creditors to pressure the company to permit unionization or agree to union demands.

Study Corner

Key Terms and Concepts

AFL-CIO
Americans with Disabilities Act (ADA)
bona fide occupational qualifications
   (BFOQs)
card check
corporate campaign
direct strike
due process
employment at will
firing
inbreeding

involuntary termination
job description
job screening
job specification
just cause
layoff
living wage
market wage
National Labor Relations Act
nepotism
open-shop laws

position elimination
primary boycott
right-to-work state
secondary boycott
seniority
situational interview
sympathetic strike
Taft–Hartley Act
test reliability
test validity
Wagner Act

Points to Review

- two historical factors behind workplace authoritarianism (p. 229)
- why efficiency doesn't require sacrificing employees' civil liberties and rights (p. 231)
- importance of job descriptions and job specifications (p. 233)
- potentially unfair bases of screening (pp. 233–235)
- requirements of the ADA (p. 234)
- ways in which employment tests can be unfair (p. 236)
- Supreme Court's decision in *Griggs v. Duke Power Company* (p. 236)
- what we can learn from Francis Bacon (p. 237)
- pros and cons of nepotism, inbreeding, and promotion on the basis of seniority (pp. 237–239)
- two key principles related to discipline and discharge (pp. 239–240)

- three types of discharge (p. 240)
- eight questions to ask when assessing the fairness of wages (pp. 242–243)
- considerations for and against living-wage laws (pp. 243–244)
- historical development of unions (pp. 244–245)
- situation of unions today (pp. 246–247)
- what Adam Smith had to say about workers and masters (p. 247)
- the goals and ideals of unions (pp. 247–248)
- what the critics of unions say (p. 248)
- different types of strikes and boycotts (pp. 248–250)

For Further Reflection

1. Give examples, if possible, from your own employment experiences, of companies' respecting the rights of employees and of companies' failing to do so.

2. When it comes to a company's personnel policies and procedures—that is, how it handles the hiring, firing, promoting, and paying of the people who work for it—what do you see as the most important moral principles for it to bear in mind?

3. Explain why you either support or disapprove of unions.

Case 8.1
The Dean's Dilemma

"I Just Don't Know How I'm Supposed to Do This," Said Dean Jane Morris. As the dean of the College of Arts and Sciences at Lake Afton University, Dr. Morris had administrative responsibility for numerous academic departments, from Anthropology to Zoology. She was, in some ways, the victim of her own success. She had argued to her boss, Provost Angela Gaff, that professors' salaries in Arts and Sciences were woefully deficient and that the College's payroll needed to be increased so that she could offer raises. The Provost had listened. However, she had only been able to find $100,000 in money for raises to be distributed, somehow, among the College's 250 full-time faculty members. Now Dean Morris had to decide how to allocate this money.

"We have some serious inequities in salaries now," pointed out Associate Dean Jamal Price. "We've gone years without being able to offer real raises. We haven't even kept up with inflation. In fact, the starting salaries of the new professors we're hiring have been going up at a faster rate than the salaries of faculty who are already here. As a result, we're paying new faculty nearly as much as we are people who have been good faculty members for decades. Sometimes we're paying them even more. So we don't just have salary compression, we have salary inversion. That's demoralizing for people who feel like their loyalty to the institution isn't being rewarded."

"But we have to pay new faculty that much or else they'll take jobs somewhere else," replied Dean Morris. "The only way to prevent compression is to settle for hiring new faculty who are much less qualified. And compression isn't the only factor we need to consider in assigning raises. Our salaries are just not competitive with those at our peer schools, especially in some departments. It's worst in Chemistry, for whatever reason. Many of our most senior chemistry faculty are making no more than 70 percent of what their counterparts at similar schools make. Some of the gaps are in the tens of thousands of dollars."

"But the chemists are still among our most highly paid faculty members," answered the other associate dean, Frank Diaz. "They aren't having any real trouble making ends meet. I don't see how we justify giving any of them raises when the faculty in Art or History are barely scraping by. Professor Goodbody in Chemistry just bought a Tesla. Meanwhile, I saw the front end of Professor Sole's rusted-out Volvo nearly fall off when she hit a speed bump in the parking lot. But it's not just that she needs more money. She works just as hard teaching art history as Professor Goodbody does teaching chemistry. It doesn't seem fair that she's paid far less."

"That's the market," Morris pointed out. "Chemistry professors get paid more than art history professors at every university. And there's a reason, which is that they have other options. Someone with a Ph.D. in chemistry can make far more money than nearly any university can pay by working for a chemical company. And this means that we must pay at least as much as we do to get them to come here. Outside of a few museum jobs, art historians just don't have many alternatives. We need to compete with other universities to hire them, but we don't need to compete with massive corporations. It's just supply and demand."

"And there's another factor that we need to think about," Dr. Morris continued. "Merit. When I was a faculty member, we got raises nearly every year that were tied to our performance evaluations. Some years they were bigger and some years they were smaller, but our top performers were always rewarded. For the last fifteen years the raises that we've been able to offer have been so small that we haven't worried about merit. We just gave everyone the same raise across the board. At the time, this made sense; people who get smaller-than-average raises are always offended, and when the average raise is only 2 percent the high performers don't get enough money to feel valued anyway. So why bother? Still, after fifteen years of this the salaries of some of our best teachers and researchers aren't that much higher than those of faculty who are just doing the minimum—except when they've had offers from other schools that we've had to match."

"That's a good point about counteroffers," said Price. "The Provost always says that we should think strategically. Maybe we need to consider how we can use this money to make ourselves a stronger college. And that means giving the money to the people who we think are most likely to get offers somewhere else—the 'flight risks.' After all, a lot of times we're not able to match the offers that other schools make. We could be proactive rather than reactive. Giving someone a modest raise now might keep them from going on the job market at all. It might save us from needing to offer them a much larger raise to keep them—especially since we might not be able to offer enough."

"That's approach is so unfair," Diaz shot back. "We know that faculty are less likely to leave if they have partners with careers of their own or kids in school. How can we penalize people for putting down roots and having families? In fact, even merit raises penalize people for having lives outside of work. We should reward productivity to a point, obviously, but we shouldn't make people feel like the only way to get a raise is to work sixty hours a week."

"You're both making valid points," said Morris. "That's why I'm stuck. There are multiple factors to consider, each of which seems important. There are so many different problems that I feel like I should address: compression within departments, uncompetitive salaries, real financial need by some faculty members, pay discrepancies between departments, unrewarded merit, and the risk of our people getting poached by other schools. Each one of these is a different lens to look at the problem through, and which lens I use will determine who gets a raise. Yet I have to choose. Looking at a problem through too many lenses at once just makes everything blurry, and trying to take all these factors into account would be too complicated. I'm tempted just to give everyone the same raise to avoid needing to make a decision."

"I'm not sure that this would spare you from making a choice," pointed out Price. "You'd still have to decide what counts as the 'same raise.' Would that mean giving everyone $4,000 or raising their salary by the same percentage? Anyway, whatever we decide, we have to decide soon. The Provost said that she needs a decision by tomorrow. Otherwise, she might give the money to the business school."

"I wonder how the business dean would resolve this," mused Morris.

The Dean's executive assistant, Doris Lane, listened to the discussion in silence. She knew that the faculty at Lake Afton worked hard and cared about their students. But she also knew that many were only on campus a few hours a week, just long enough to teach and hold office hours, with much of their work being done at home or in coffeeshops at times of their own choosing. Some even taught online and never came to campus at all. She also knew that the full-time faculty were much better paid than the office staff, who were at work in person from nine to five every day. She couldn't help but think how many of their lives could be changed by $100,000 in raises.

Discussion Questions

1. What do fairness and justice require in this case? Is it fairer or more just to prioritize helping the faculty who the smallest paychecks, those who are paid least relative to peers at comparable universities, those who are paid less than faculty in the same department who have fewer years of service, or those who have had the best job performance? Why?

2. How should Dean Morris balance producing "good results" like improving the lives of the lowest-paid professors in her college or keeping faculty from applying for other jobs against doing what is fair or just?

3. Dean Morris notes that "the market" dictates that faculty in some departments must be paid much more than those in others. Should she take these market forces as a given in assigning raises or does justice require that she ignores them—or even that she actively tries to counteract them?

4. Is Diaz right to worry that prioritizing the faculty who seem mostly likely to leave for raises unfairly penalizes professors for having other people in their lives in ways that make it harder to move? Is he right to raise the related worry that basing raises on merit unfairly penalizes faculty who aren't "workaholics"?

5. Is Lane right to wonder whether Lake Afton might be prioritizing the wrong group of employees? Assume that the school's office staff have far less education than its faculty. Assume also, though, that as a group their lives started out very differently—for example, that far more of the faculty than the staff had parents who were college graduates. Does the Provost's decision to dedicate this money to raises for faculty rather than staff only offer more benefits to those who are already more fortunate?

6. Recall the discussion of adjunct faculty from the introduction to this chapter. Assume that Lake Afton employs numerous adjuncts. How should the reasons to improve their situation be weighed against the reasons to increase the pay of full-time faculty?

Case 8.2

Web Porn at Work

Al Smetana Is the Founding President of a Medium-Size, Midwestern manufacturing firm, Rayburn Unlimited. He's proud of the way his company has grown, and done so on the basis of an organizational culture committed to honesty, integrity, and the intrinsic value of each individual. But now those values are being put to the test.

It began when Al learned that an employee had tapped into the company's computer system and figured out how to read people's e-mail and to learn what websites they visited. Determining who the culprit was wasn't difficult. When confronted about it, the employee admitted what he had done. Al immediately terminated his employment. But as he left, the employee said angrily, "Just ask Lindley about his computer usage," referring to Craig Lindley, associate vice president for human

resources and an old friend of Al's. Although Al didn't trust the discharged employee, he was disturbed by his comment and reluctant to let it go. So, he called Craig Lindley into his office and asked him about it.

After a few minutes of gentle questioning, Craig started weeping. When he recovered himself, he explained that for the past year or so he had been hooked on pornography on the web and at the office sometimes spent an hour or so a day looking at it. Al asked him whether his wife knew. Craig said she didn't. He was too ashamed of his habit to talk to her or anybody else about it. Al then told him to take the rest of the day off, to think the matter over, and to return to Al's office the next morning. When Craig left, Al stood and looked out the window, silently asking himself what he should do.[80]

Discussion Questions

1. Is Craig Lindley's behavior a sign of some psychological problem that Rayburn Unlimited should help him overcome, perhaps with personal counseling? Or is dismissal called for? Should Al Smetana fire Craig to send a message to other employees not to misuse company time and resources?

2. Does Al have just cause for dismissing Craig? Does it matter whether or not Rayburn Unlimited has an explicit policy regarding computer use? Suppose it has such a policy and Craig violated it. Does that settle the matter? Would it affect your judgment of the case if Craig had helped draw up that policy?

3. Does the fact that Craig is a valued member of the company with a long record of service make a difference? Or that he is a personal friend of Al's?

4. Was it right for Al to have asked Craig about his computer usage in the first place? Did he violate Craig's privacy or civil liberties?

5. Because Al fired the employee who violated the company's computer system, would it be inconsistent or unfair of him to treat Craig any differently?

6. Al Smetana and Rayburn Unlimited are committed to honesty and integrity (the upholding of which seems to support dismissal) and the intrinsic worth of each individual (which might argue for more lenient treatment). Are these values in conflict? What would you do if you were Al?

Case 8.3

Speaking Out about Malt

When Mary Davis, Associate Vice President for Plant Management at Whitewater Brewing Company, wrote an article for a large metropolitan newspaper in her state, she hadn't realized where it would lead. At first, she was thrilled to see her words published. Then she was just worried about keeping her job.

It all started when her husband, Bob, who was working on his MBA, talked her into taking an evening class with him. She did and, to her surprise, really got into the course, spending most of her weekends that semester working on her term project—a study of wine and beer marketing. Among other things her essay discussed those respectable wine companies like E. & J. Gallo (the nation's largest) that market cheap, fortified wines such as Thunderbird and Night Train Express. With an alcohol content 50 percent greater and a price far less than regular wine, these screw-top wines are seldom advertised and rarely seen outside poor neighborhoods, but they represent a multimillion-dollar industry. Low-income alcoholics are their major consumers, a fact that evidently embarrasses Gallo, because it doesn't even put its company name on the label.

Mary's essay went on to raise some moral questions about the marketing of malt liquor, a beer brewed with sugar for an extra punch of alcohol. It has been around for about forty years; what is relatively new is the larger size of the container. A few years ago, the industry introduced malt liquor in 40-ounce bottles that sell for about $3. Packing an alcohol content roughly equivalent to six 12-ounce beers or five cocktails, 40s quickly became the favorite high of many inner-city teenagers. Ads for competing brands stress potency—"It's got more" or "The Real Power"—and often use gang slang. Get "your girl in the mood quicker and get your jimmy thicker," raps Ice Cube in a commercial for St. Ides malt liquor. Like baggy pants and baseball caps turned backward, 40s soon moved from the inner city to the suburbs. Teenage drinkers like the quick drunk, and this worries drug counselors. They call 40s "liquid crack" and "date rape brew."

Mary's instructor liked her article and encouraged her to rewrite it for the newspaper. The problem was that Whitewater also brews a malt liquor, called Rafter, which it had recently started offering in a 40-ounce bottle. True, Mary's article mentioned Whitewater's brand only in passing, but top management was distressed by her criticisms of the whole industry, which, they thought, damaged its image and increased the likelihood of further state and federal regulation. The board of directors thought Mary had acted irresponsibly, and Ralph Jenkins, the CEO, had written her a memo on the board's behalf instructing her not to comment publicly about malt liquor without first clearing her remarks with him. Mary was hurt and angry.

"I admit that the way the newspaper edited my essay and played up the malt liquor aspect made it more sensationalistic," Mary explained to her colleague Susan Montoya, "but everything I said was true."

"I'm sure it was factual," replied Susan, "but the company thought the slant was negative. I mean, lots of ordinary people drink Rafter."

"I know that. Bob even drinks it sometimes. I don't know why they're so upset about my article. I barely mentioned Rafter. Anyway, it's not like Rafter is a big moneymaker. Most of our other beers outsell it."

"Well," continued Susan, "the company is really touchy about the whole issue. They think the product is under political attack these days and that you were disloyal."

"That's not true," Mary replied. "I'm no troublemaker, and I have always worked hard for Whitewater. But I do think they and the other companies are wrong to market malt liquor the way they do. It only makes a bad situation worse."

The next day Mary met with Ralph Jenkins and told him that she felt Whitewater was "invading," as she put it, her rights as a citizen. In fact, she had been invited to speak about wine and beer marketing at a local high school as part of its antidrug campaign. She intended to keep her speaking engagement and would not subject her remarks to company censorship.

Jenkins listened but didn't say much, simply repeating what he had already written in his memo. But two days later Mary received what was, in effect, an ultimatum. She must either conform with his original order or submit her resignation.

Discussion Questions

1. Do you think Mary Davis acted irresponsibly or disloyally? Does Whitewater have a legitimate concern about her speaking out on this issue? Does the company have a right to abridge her freedom of expression?

2. Is your answer to question 1 affected by whether you agree or disagree with the views Mary Davis expressed?

3. Should there be any limits on an employee's freedom of expression? If not, why not? If so, under what circumstances is a company justified in restricting an employee's right to speak out?

4. The case presentation doesn't specify whether the newspaper article identified Mary Davis as an employee of Whitewater. Is that a relevant issue? Does it matter what position in the company Mary Davis holds?

5. What do you think Mary Davis ought to do? What moral considerations should she weigh? Does she have conflicting obligations? If so, what are they?

6. Is the company right to be worried about what Mary Davis writes or says, or is the board of directors exaggerating the potential harm to Whitewater of her discussing these issues?

7. Assume a CEO like Ralph Jenkins is legitimately worried that an employee is making damaging statements about the company. How should the CEO handle the situation? Is discharge or some sort of discipline called for? Should the company adopt a formal policy regarding employee speech? If so, what policy would you recommend?

8. Compare and contrast Mary Davis's situation with that of Michael Italie. Are any of the differences between the two morally significant?

Case 8.4

Have Gun, Will Travel . . . to Work

Organizational Theorists and Employee Advocates Frequently emphasize the importance, from both a moral and a practical point of view, of companies' respecting the rights of their employees. Many employees spend long hours at work and remain tethered to the job by phone or computer even when they're off-site; not just their careers but also their friendships, social identity, and emotional lives are tied up with their work. All the more reason, it seems, that companies should recognize and respect their moral, political, and legal rights. But enshrined in our Constitution is one right that frequently gets overlooked in discussions of the workplace: the right to bear arms.[81]

In 2002 Weyerhaeuser, the Seattle-based timber-products company, fired several employees at an Oklahoma plant who were discovered to have violated company policy by keeping guns in their vehicles. Their dismissal provoked a response from the National Rifle Association (NRA) and other gun-rights advocates, which began lobbying for legislation that would make it illegal for companies to bar employees from leaving guns in their cars in company parking lots. And with some success:

Although no state requires companies to allow workers to carry weapons into the workplace, twenty-two states have now passed laws guaranteeing them the right to keep guns in their cars. Gun advocates argue that licensed gun owners should have access to their weapons in case they need them on the trek to and from work. If an employer can ban guns from workers' cars, "it would be a wrecking ball to the Second Amendment" of the U.S. Constitution, says Wayne LaPierre, executive vice president of the NRA.

Brian Siebel, a senior attorney at the Brady Center to Prevent Gun Violence, thinks otherwise. He sees these laws as "a systematic attempt to force guns into every nook and cranny in society and prohibit anyone, whether it's private employers or college campuses . . . from barring guns from their premises." But that's not how UCLA law professor Eugene Volokh looks at it. "It's part of the general movement," he says, "to allow people to have guns for self-defense not only at home, but in public places where they're most likely needed." For his part, LaPierre of the NRA contends that the legal right of people to have guns for personal protection is largely nullified if employers can ban guns from the parking lot. "Saying you can protect yourself with a firearm when you get off work late at night," he argues, "is meaningless if you can't keep it in the trunk of your car when you're at work."

Interpreting the somewhat ambiguous language of the Second Amendment is not easy. It only says, "A well-regulated Militia, being necessary to the security of a free State, the right of the people to keep and bear Arms, shall not be infringed." All jurists agree, however, that the Second Amendment does not make all forms of gun control unconstitutional and that, like the rest of the Bill of Rights, it places restrictions only on what government, not private parties, may do.

In particular, the Second Amendment does not give gun owners a constitutionally protected right to carry their weapons onto somebody else's private property against the wishes of the owner. "If I said to somebody, 'You can't bring your gun into my house,' that person's rights would not be violated," explains Mark Tushnet, a Harvard law professor. For this reason, the American Bar Association sides with business owners and endorses "the traditional property rights of private employers and other private property owners to exclude" people with firearms. Steve Halverson, president of a Jacksonville, Florida, construction company agrees that business owners should be allowed to decide whether to allow weapons in their parking lots. "The larger issue is property rights," he says, "and whether you as a homeowner and I as a business owner ought to have the right to say what comes onto our property." However, Tennessee state senator Paul Stanley, a Republican sponsor of legislation requiring that guns be allowed in company parking lots, begs to differ. "I respect property and business rights," he says. "But I also think that some issues need to overshadow this. . . . We have a right to keep and bear arms." Other gun advocates think that the property-rights argument is a red herring. Corporations are not individuals, they argue, but artificial legal entities, whose "rights" are entirely at the discretion of the state. What's really going on, they think, is that some companies have an anti-gun political agenda.

Property rights, however, aren't the only thing that companies are concerned about. Business and other organizations have a widely acknowledged duty to keep their workplaces—and their employees—as safe as possible, and that means, many of them believe, keeping their campuses free of weapons. There are over 700 workplace homicides per year; and in a recent survey, more than one-third of employers reported violent incidents at work. Having guns anywhere in the vicinity, many employers worry, can only make volatile situations more deadly. "There's no need to allow guns [into] parking lots," says the Brady Center's Siebel. "The increased risks are obvious." Steve Halveson drives that point home, too. "I object to anyone telling me that we can't . . . take steps necessary to protect our employees." For him it's no different from banning guns from his construction sites or requiring workers to wear hard hats. "The context is worker safety, and that's why it's important."

Discussion Questions

1. Do you have not only a legal right but also a moral right to own a gun? Assume that either the Second Amendment or state law gives you a legal right to keep a gun in your car when you drive. Do you also have a moral right to do this? Do you have either a moral or a legal right to park a car with a loaded gun in a privately owned public parking lot regardless of what the lot's owner wants?

2. In your view, do employees have either a moral or a legal right to park cars with guns in them in the company parking lot? If so, what about the property rights and safety concerns of employers? If employees don't have this right, would it be good policy for companies to allow them to stow guns in their cars anyway? Do companies have good grounds for being concerned about weapons in their parking lots?

3. Do you agree with the NRA that if companies ban guns from their parking lots, this restriction would take "a wrecking ball to the Second Amendment" or nullify the right of people to have weapons for self-defense? Explain why or why not. In your view, have gun advocates been guilty of politicizing this issue? Do you think state legislatures are right to get involved, or should the matter be left to companies and employees to settle?

4. Because the workplace is the company's private property, the company could choose, if it wished, to allow employees to bring guns not only into the parking lot but also into the workplace itself. Are there ever circumstances in which doing so might be reasonable? Or would the presence of guns automatically violate the rights of other employees to be guaranteed a safe working environment?

5. What would a libertarian say about this issue? What considerations would a utilitarian have to take into account? What conclusion might they draw?

6. If you were on a company's board of directors, what policy would you recommend regarding handguns, rifles, or other weapons in employees' cars? In making your recommendation, what factors would you take into account? Would it make a difference how large the company was, the nature of its workforce, or where it was located? If you support banning firearms from the parking lot, what steps, if any, do you think the company should take to enforce that policy?

7. Explain whether (and why) you agree or disagree with the following argument: "If employees have a right to keep guns in the parking lot, then they also have a right to bring them into workplace. After all, we're only talking about licensed, responsible owners, and the same rationale applies: An employee might need a weapon for self-protection. What if a lunatic starts shooting up the company?"

Case 8.5

Union Discrimination

The National Right to Work Legal Defense Foundation Is One of several anti-union organizations that have been active in recent years. The "right to work," in this context, means the alleged right of an individual to work without being obliged to join a union or pay union dues. To put it the other way around, it means that companies cannot sign contracts with unions agreeing to hire only workers who are willing to join the union or at least to pay the equivalent of union dues.

What follows is one of the Foundation's advertisements, titled "Job Discrimination . . . It Still Exists":[82]

Paul Robertson is not a member of a persecuted minority. But he has experienced blatant discrimination all the same because he has chosen not to join a union.

Paul Robertson is a working man, a skilled licensed electrician with more than twenty years experience. He found out the hard way how a big company and a big union can discriminate on the job.

Paul was hired by the Bechtel Power Corporation to work on their Jim Bridger Power Plant project in the Rock Springs, Wyoming, area. Only three months later, he was fired, supposedly because of a reduction in force.

But during the week preceding his discharge, Bechtel hired at least nineteen union electricians referred by the local union and retained at least sixty-five unlicensed electricians.

A determined Paul Robertson filed unfair labor practice charges against the company and the union.

An administrative law judge ruled and was upheld by the full National Labor Relations Board that the union and the employer had indeed discriminated. The judge ordered that Robertson and seven other electricians be given the back pay they would have earned if they had been treated fairly.

The NLRB later reversed part of its decision, but Paul Robertson did not give up. With the help of the National Right to Work Legal Defense Foundation, he appealed the Board's decision to the U.S. Court of Appeals, arguing that hiring hall favoritism is discriminatory and unlawful.

Paul Robertson was fortunate. He found experienced legal help—all important because the case dragged on for nearly four years in the courts and the union still refused to obey the NLRB's back-pay order.

The National Right to Work Legal Defense Foundation is helping everyone it can—currently in more than seventy-five cases involving academic and political freedom, protection from union violence, and other fundamental rights. But it would like to do even more.

If you'd like to help workers like Paul Robertson write to: The National Right to Work Legal Defense Foundation. . . .

Discussion Questions

1. Assuming the Foundation's description of the case is accurate, was Paul Robertson treated unfairly? Was this a case of discrimination? If Robertson was an "at-will" employee, does he have any legitimate grounds for complaint?

2. Does it make a difference to your assessment of the case whether someone like Robertson knows, when he accepts a job, that he must join the union or that nonunion employees will be the first to be laid off?

3. If union employees negotiate a contract with management, part of which specifies that management will not hire non-union employees, does this violate anyone's rights? Would a libertarian agree that the resulting union shop was perfectly acceptable?

4. Presumably Paul Robertson could have joined the union, but he chose not to. What principle, if any, do you think he was fighting for? Assess the union charge that people like Paul Robertson are "free riders" who want the benefits and wages that unionization has brought but try to avoid paying the dues that make those benefits and wages possible.

5. What do you see as the likely motivations of Bechtel Power and the union? How would they justify their conduct?

6. Why did the Foundation run this ad? Is the ad anti-union propaganda? Do you think the Foundation is sincerely interested in the rights of individual workers? Or is it simply interested in weakening unions vis-à-vis management?

7. Assess union shops from the moral point of view. What conflicting rights, interests, and ideals are at stake? What are the positive and negative consequences of permitting union shops?

Chapter 9

The Workplace (2): Today's Challenges

After completing this chapter, you should be able to:

1. Explain the nature of privacy and the problems of organizational influence over private decisions.
2. Explore the moral issues raised by the use of polygraph, personality, and drug tests and by the monitoring of employees in the workplace.
3. Analyze the ethical issues surrounding the conditions under which people work—in particular, health and safety conditions, styles of management, and provision of day-care facilities and family leave.
4. Critically discuss the causes of job satisfaction and dissatisfaction and the prospects for enhancing the quality of work life.

Introduction

It Was a Routine Business Day for Eastern Airlines—Until It received an anonymous tip that some of its baggage handlers at Miami International Airport were using drugs. Eastern quickly sprang into action, ordering security guards to round up the ten employees then at work in the airport's plane-loading area. The employees were marched between two rows of guards and into waiting vans—"like terrorists," a lawsuit later claimed—all in full view of other employees and passengers. After questioning the workers, suspicious supervisors put them on a bus, once again in front of onlookers, and took them to a hospital. There the employees were given an ultimatum: Either take a urine test or be fired on the spot.

The baggage handlers were union members, but they caved in and took the test. All ten of them tested negative (that is, free of drugs), but they weren't happy about what they'd been through. Not long afterward, they filed suit against the airline in federal court, seeking damages of $30,000 each on charges of invasion of privacy, defamation, and intentional infliction of emotional distress. Eastern has since gone out of business, but the case represents in dramatic form one of the major issues dividing employers and employees today: **privacy**. Companies are delving further into employees' personal lives than ever before, claiming

> ....
> **Companies are Delving further into employees' personal lives than ever before . . .**
> ....

the need to monitor their behavior and probe into their health and habits. Workers are resisting ever more adamantly, fighting back for the right to be left alone.

In 1928, U.S. Supreme Court justice Louis D. Brandeis described the right to privacy, or "the right to be let alone," as "the most comprehensive of rights and the right most valued by civilized men." He was referring to the Fourth Amendment's guarantee that citizens are protected against illegal searches and seizures by government. Today, many Americans are resisting invasions of their privacy not just by government agencies or pesky telemarketers but also by intrusive employers. And not without reason: American workers' privacy enjoys considerably less legal protection than that of their European counterparts.[1]

It's not only ordinary employees, either, whose privacy companies sometimes fail to respect, as the world learned when the Hewlett-Packard (H-P) boardroom exploded in controversy. Concerned about leaks of confidential company information to the *Wall Street Journal* from someone on H-P's board of directors, board chairwoman Patricia Dunn had authorized the company's legal and security personnel to investigate. They did, and at a meeting of the board a few months later, the culprit was disclosed. Board member Jay Keyworth admitted to the group that he was the leaker but refused to resign. However, his friend and fellow board member Tom Perkins, a Silicon Valley venture capitalist, was so outraged at H-P's snooping into the phone records of board members that he resigned on the spot and stormed out of the meeting. End of story? Not quite. Perkins managed to get the ear of California's attorney general and other law-enforcement agencies, which launched an investigation into the legality of H-P's spy tactics—in particular, its "pretexting" or use of false pretenses to obtain phone records and other personal information. This eventually led to a congressional hearing, recriminations, and denial of responsibility by various H-P executives, and, finally, criminal charges against Dunn and several underlings.[2]

Businesses and other organizations frequently believe, as Eastern Airlines and Hewlett-Packard evidently did, that they have a compelling need to know about the lives and conduct of their employees, whether on or off the job—a need that they believe justifies invading their privacy. Employees, however, tend to think otherwise, and more and more frequently these days they're responding by asserting a right to a personal sphere not subject to the needs, interests, or curiosity of their employers. "I don't think politicians and corporate executives realize how strongly Americans feel about it," says a San Francisco lawyer who specializes in employee lawsuits. "It's not a liberal or a conservative issue, and the fear of abuse doesn't emanate from personnel policies. It's coming out of the larger, impersonal notion that workers are fungible, expendable items."[3]

Chapter 8 examined personnel policies and procedures, trade unions, the state of civil liberties on the job, and the efforts of some successful companies to respect the rights, dignity, and moral integrity of their workers. This chapter also focuses on moral issues that emerge in the workplace. It looks in detail at one crucial civil liberty—the right to privacy—and at the ethical choices it poses inside the organization. The remainder of the chapter examines several other topics that are stirring up controversy in today's workplace.

Organizational Influence in Private Lives

Privacy is widely acknowledged to be a fundamental right, yet corporate behavior and policies often threaten privacy, especially in the case of employees. One way this happens is through the release of personal information about employees. The data banks and personnel files of business and nonbusiness organizations contain an immense amount of private information, the disclosure of which can seriously violate employees' rights. Most firms guard their files closely and restrict the type of material that they can contain in the first place, but the potential for abuse is still great. Although a complicated set of laws and court rulings limits access to such information, a wide range of snoops still manage, legitimately or illegitimately, to get their hands on it.

As a related matter, more employees are successfully suing their former bosses for passing on damaging information to prospective employers. The courts have traditionally considered this sort of information exchange between employers to be "privileged," but companies can lose this protection by giving information to too many people or by making false reports. Due to fear of defamation suits, in fact, many organizations now refuse to reveal anything about former employees except their dates of employment. Such reticence obviously makes it more difficult for companies to screen job applicants.

More significant are the threats to privacy that can arise on the job itself. For example, some bosses unhesitatingly rummage through the files of their workers, even when they are marked "private." Some companies routinely eavesdrop on their employees' phone calls, and a majority of them read their employees' e-mail and monitor their use of the Internet.[4] Voice mail isn't safe, either, as Michael Huttcut, a manager of a McDonald's outlet in St. Louis, learned the hard way. He was having an affair with a coworker, and the romantic voice-mail messages he sent her were retrieved and played by his boss. When Huttcut complained, he was fired.[5] Other companies secretly quiz managers—or even call in private investigators—to gain knowledge about the personal habits and behavior of workers who call in sick.[6] Meanwhile, GPS technology lets companies track employees when they are in their company vehicles—often without their knowledge.[7]

How would you feel about being asked to supply a urine sample for drug testing by an employer?

Equally important is the way organizations attempt to influence behavior that ought properly to be left to the discretion of their employees—in particular, by trying to impose their own values on their workers. For example, Walmart fired Lauren Allen, who was married but separated from her husband, for dating a coworker, who was single. Walmart says that it "strongly believes in and supports the 'family unit'" and that the conduct of Allen and her coworker violated the company's rules.[8] Or consider the case of Virginia Rulon-Miller, a marketing manager in IBM's office products division. She made the mistake of falling in love. A week after receiving a 13.3 percent pay raise, she was called on the carpet for dating Matt Blum, a former IBM account manager who had gone to work for a competitor. She and Blum had begun dating when Blum was at IBM, and he still played on the IBM softball team. IBM told Rulon-Miller to give up Blum or be demoted. "I was so steeped in IBM culture," she says, "that I was going to break up with Matt." But the next day, before she had a chance to do anything, she was dismissed. Even though IBM's decision was based on written policy governing conflicts of interest, a California jury decided that Rulon-Miller's privacy had been invaded. It awarded her $300,000.

A year later, however, the Oregon Supreme Court upheld JCPenney's firing of a merchandising manager for dating another employee. He claimed that his right to privacy had been violated. Although it may seem harsh to fire an employee on the basis of personal lifestyle, the Oregon court said, private firms aren't barred from discriminating against workers for their choice of mates. And a federal district court permitted the firing of a New Mexico employee with an excellent work record because she was married to a worker at a competing supermarket.[9]

It's not only in affairs of the heart that companies sometimes intrude into the personal sphere of employees by imposing their values on them or telling them what to think or do in matters that bear little relation to their jobs. Some executives, for example, find themselves pressured to contribute cash to their company's political action committee.[10] And now that the Supreme Court's 2010 *Citizens United* decision has freed companies to use corporate money to endorse and campaign for political candidates, many of them are urging—some would say pressuring—their employees to vote for specific politicians.[11] It's hard to wear a pin or sport a bumper sticker or voice your support for a candidate against whom your company is campaigning.

The Importance of Privacy

Our concern for privacy has three aspects.

Both in the workplace and in general, our concern for privacy seems to have at least three dimensions to it. *First*, we want to control intimate or personal information about ourselves and not permit it to be freely available to everyone. We are concerned to limit the people who have certain kinds of knowledge about us, to control the means by which they can acquire it, and to restrict those to whom they may disclose it. *Second*, we wish to keep certain thoughts, feelings, and behavior free from the scrutiny, monitoring, or observation of strangers. We don't want our private selves to be on public display. *Third*, we value being able to make certain personal decisions autonomously. We seek to preserve and protect a sphere in which we can choose to think and act for ourselves, free from the illegitimate influence of our employers and others.

There is, however, no consensus among philosophers or lawyers about how precisely to define the concept of privacy, how far the right to privacy extends, or how to balance a concern for privacy against other moral considerations. All of us would agree, nonetheless, that we have a clear right to keep private certain areas of our lives and that we need to have our privacy respected if we are to function as complete, self-governing agents.

Even when a genuine privacy right is identified, the strength of that right depends on circumstances—in particular, on competing rights and interests. Privacy is not an absolute value. Corporations and other organizations often have legitimate interests that may conflict with the privacy concerns of employees. Determining when organizational infringement on a person's private sphere is morally justifiable is, of course, precisely the question at issue.

As a general rule, though, whenever an organization infringes on what would normally be considered the personal sphere of an individual, it bears the burden of establishing the legitimacy of that infringement. The fact that a firm thinks an action or policy is justifiable does not, of course, make it so. The firm must show both that it has some legitimate interest at stake and that the steps it's taking to protect that interest are reasonable and morally permissible. But what are the areas of legitimate organizational influence over the individual?

> The burden is on the organization to establish the legitimacy of encroaching on the personal sphere of the individual.

Legitimate and Illegitimate Influence

Employers are naturally and legitimately interested in anything that significantly influences employee work performance. What constitutes a significant influence on work performance, however, is often debatable.

Take, for example, the area of dress and grooming. A roofing company has a legitimate interest in the type and quality of shoes its workers wear because footwear affects safety and job performance. And perhaps specialty clothing stores such as Gap, Polo Ralph Lauren, and Abercrombie & Fitch have legitimate grounds for requiring their employees to dress in the store's latest styles. However, it's not clear that Enterprise Rent-A-Car had legitimate grounds for requiring employee Angela Garrett to remove the red tints from her hair because they weren't "appropriate" for an African American person.[12] Likewise, it's questionable whether a genuine corporate interest was at stake when an airline ticket agent was fired for refusing to wear makeup or when American Airlines forbade a Black employee from wearing her hair in corn rows because the company claimed the style clashed with the company's corporate image

The general proposition that a firm has a legitimate interest only in employee behavior that significantly influences work performance applies equally to **off-the-job conduct**. Bank of America probably ran afoul of this guideline when it fired Michael Thomasson, a legal secretary, for working as an exotic dancer at a club during his off-hours. After a coworker read a personal letter Thomasson had written on a company computer that mentioned his job as an exotic dancer, a group of bank employees, including several of Thomasson's supervisors, went to see him perform. Two weeks later he was dismissed—despite a record of positive job evaluations and a recent merit raise.[13]

> A firm has a legitimate interest in employee conduct off the job only if it affects work performance.

Years ago, Henry Ford made his autoworkers' wages conditional on their good behavior outside the factory. He had 150 inspectors whose job was to keep tabs on his employees' hygiene and housekeeping habits. And Milton Hershey, another famous business leader, used to tour Hershey, Pennsylvania, the chocolate-manufacturing town, to make sure his workers were keeping up their lawns. He even hired private detectives to find out who was throwing trash in Hershey Park.[14] These days, it's easy to say that Ford and Hershey crossed the line and were poking their noses into aspects of their employees' lives that had nothing to do with their jobs. In other cases, though, determining when off-the-job conduct bears on job performance can be difficult.

How would you decide the following case? In an off-the-job fight, a plant guard drew a gun on his antagonist. Although no one was injured, the guard's employer viewed the incident as grounds for dismissal. The employer reasoned that such an action indicated a lack of judgment by the guard. Do you think the employer had a right to fire the guard under those circumstances? The courts did. By contrast, consider the employee who sold a small amount of marijuana to an undercover agent, or the employee who made obscene phone calls to the teenage daughter of a client. Their employers fired them, but the employees were reinstated by an arbitrator or the court.

Then there's the amorphous area of company image and the question of whether it can be affected by off-the-job conduct. For example, the image a firm wishes to project might be hurt by the political activities of a corporate executive but probably not by what a lower-profile

Summary
Individuals have a right to privacy, in particular, a right to control certain information about themselves, to shelter aspects of their lives from public scrutiny, and to make personal decisions autonomously, free from illegitimate influence. Whenever an organization infringes on an individual's personal sphere, it must justify that infringement.

production worker on an assembly line does. To be sure, companies and other organizations have a legitimate interest in protecting their good names, and the off-duty conduct of any employee could conceivably damage an organization's reputation. But in practice, damage is often difficult to establish. For example, two IRS agents were suspended for mooning a group of women after leaving a bar. Would you agree with their suspension? An arbitrator didn't and revoked it. He couldn't see that their conduct damaged the IRS's reputation.[15] In 2005, Isac Aguero was photographed by the local newspaper drinking a Bud Light one Saturday night, as part of coverage of the city's nightlife. Unfortunately, he worked for a distributor of a rival beer, and Monday morning he was fired[16] Is it plausible to suppose that a company's image is hurt by a lower-level employee's being seen using a competitor's product off-duty and out of uniform?

Obviously, we can't spell out exactly when off-duty conduct affects company image in some material way, any more than we can say precisely what constitutes a significant influence on job performance. But that doesn't prevent us from being able to judge that, in many cases, organizations step beyond legitimate boundaries and interfere with what should properly be personal decisions by their employees. That interference can take many forms, but two are worth looking at more closely.

Involvement in Civic Activities

To enhance their image in the community, businesses and other organizations have long prodded their employees to donate to charitable causes during company-led fund-raising drives or encouraged them to participate in **civic activities** off the job—for example, by running for the local school board or joining community service organizations, such as Kiwanis, Lions, or Rotary. Moreover, the past decade has seen a boom in corporate-sponsored employee volunteer programs, with more and more firms encouraging employees to spend off-duty hours helping out at designated charities or donning a company T-shirt and pitching in on Saturdays at some company-run philanthropic project.[17]

There's no question that the trend toward corporate volunteer programs has been good for society. One in four adults does at least some volunteer work, and corporate programs have probably drawn many of them into doing so. But such programs can collide with accelerating job demands, forcing employees to spend valued off-duty time away from their families and fueling employee resentment and burnout. Moreover, the programs can raise moral questions, especially as the pressure to participate increases. Some employers have "unwritten rules" requiring volunteer work; other companies award employees with points for approved volunteer work on their performance evaluations. Employees also have been downgraded, disciplined, or even fired for not contributing the "suggested" amount of money to the United Way or other charitable causes sponsored by the firm. The pressure can be real, too, when the boss solicits donations for their favorite charity or goes cubicle to cubicle with a sign-up sheet for Girl Scout cookies.[18]

Employee volunteer programs and other corporate-sponsored civic activities sometimes infringe on the right to privacy.

By striving too hard for a do-gooder image, a company can thus be guilty of attempting to influence the personal choices and off-the-job behavior of employees in ways that constitute an invasion of privacy. By explicitly or implicitly requiring employees to associate themselves with a particular activity, group, or cause, firms are telling workers what to believe, what values to support, and what goals to promote outside work.

Wellness Programs

Wellness programs, which push employees toward healthier lifestyles, are now a common feature of the corporate landscape. These paternalistic programs are aimed at helping employees live longer and improve their health and productivity. The programs teach them about nutrition, exercise, stress, and heart disease and encourage them to give up smoking, eat more healthfully, moderate their drinking, and work out in the company gym or join a company sports team after work.[19]

Wellness programs try to make fitness part of the corporate culture, and that goal seems innocent enough. But some companies are making employees pay more for their health care benefits if they are overweight, have high blood pressure, or don't exercise.[20] And employees have been fired for having a drink at home or for refusing to take a test to prove they're nonsmokers.[21] In 2022, the American Association of Retired Persons and Yale University settled a $1.29 million dollar lawsuit over Yale's practice of leveling a $25 per week surcharge on employees who opted out of its wellness program.[22] Other organizations offer employees financial incentives for agreeing to complete health questionnaires, undergo comprehensive health assessments, or even work with a health coach. Whether it's an incentive or a surcharge, critics see it as a kind of "privacy tax." Those with good salaries may be able to afford to protect their privacy, but what about receptionists, file clerks, or other employees earning only a modest wage?[23]

Some companies are now intruding further into the personal sphere by bringing employees' families into wellness programs.[24] Others are trying to improve the mental health of their employees as well, seeking not only to combat depression, anxiety, and other psychological problems but also to promote positive thinking, coping under pressure, and "mental fitness" in an effort to increase creativity and productivity. Although this sounds enlightened and humane, it's often the companies themselves that are to blame for stressful work environments conducive to poor mental health. Moreover, many employees worry about their employers delving into their psychological and emotional lives. Can companies be trusted with the information they receive? Or will it find its way into annual appraisals or be held over employees' heads by manipulative managers? "I think employers are going to get deeper and deeper into the wellness business," says Professor Alan F. Westin of Columbia University. "This is going to throw up a series of profound ethical and legal dilemmas about how they should do it and what we don't want them to do."[25]

* * *

Testing and Monitoring

It's no secret that firms frequently seek, store, and communicate information about employees, often highly personal information. The previous section examined privacy and organizational encroachment on employees' personal lives. This section focuses on two common methods of obtaining information about employees: monitoring them on the job and subjecting them to various tests—in particular, polygraph tests, personality tests, and drug tests. Before beginning this discussion, however, we need to look briefly at the concept of informed consent.

Informed Consent

Certainly, no employee is ever compelled to take a lie-detector, personality, or genetic screening test in the sense that someone physically threatens them and says, "Take the test or else." But compulsion, like freedom, comes in degrees. Obviously if workers submit to an honesty exam or to a test for genetic disorders, then they agree to do so. But is their assent valid and legitimate? Does it constitute informed consent? That's the issue, and it's an altogether reasonable issue to raise because information collected on workers is often intimately personal and private and, when used carelessly, can injure them.

Informed consent implies deliberation and free choice. Workers must understand what they are agreeing to, including its full ramifications, and must voluntarily choose it. Deliberation requires not only the availability of facts but also a full understanding of them. Workers must be allowed to deliberate on the basis of enough usable information, information that they can understand. But usable information is not of itself enough to guarantee informed consent. Free choice is also important—the *consent* part is as significant as the *informed* part of informed consent.

Everyone agrees that for consent to be legitimate, it must be voluntary. Workers must willingly agree to the privacy-invading procedure. They must also be in a position to act voluntarily. One big factor that affects the voluntariness of consent is the pressure, expressed and implied, exerted on employees to conform to organizational policy. Especially when the pressure to conform is reinforced with implicit threats of reprisal, it can effectively undercut the voluntariness of consent. That is obvious in the case of job applicants asked to undergo some invasion of their privacy. They can either submit or look for work elsewhere.

Summary
A firm is legitimately interested in whatever significantly influences job performance, but some companies intrude where they shouldn't. Organizations may be invading privacy when they interfere with employees' off-the-job conduct or pressure them to contribute to charities, do volunteer work, or participate in wellness programs.

Summary
Companies often gather highly personal information about employees. The critical issue here is informed consent, which implies deliberation and free choice. Deliberation requires that employees be provided all significant facts concerning the information-gathering procedure and understand its consequences. Free choice entails that the decision to participate must be voluntary and uncoerced.

The concept of informed consent implies deliberation and free choice.

Polygraph Tests

When an individual is disturbed by a question, certain detectable physiological changes occur. The person's heart may begin to race, blood pressure may rise, and respiration may increase. The polygraph simultaneously records changes in these physiological processes and, thus, is often used in lie detection. But the use of **polygraph tests** rests on at least three assumptions that can be questioned.[26]

The *first* assumption is that lying triggers an involuntary, distinctive response that truth telling does not. But this is not necessarily the case. What the polygraph can do is record that the respondent was more disturbed by one question than by another, but it cannot determine why the person was disturbed. Perhaps the question made the person feel guilty or angry or frightened, but deception does not necessarily lurk behind the emotional response.

Second, it's assumed that polygraphs are extraordinarily accurate. Lynn March, president of the American Polygraph Association, says that "when administered correctly by qualified operators, the tests are accurate more than 90 percent of the time."[27] But David T. Lykken, a psychiatry professor, claims that this boast is not borne out by three scientifically credible studies of the accuracy of polygraphs used on actual criminal suspects. The accuracies obtained by qualified operators in these experiments were 63, 39, and 55 percent.[28] Whether the polygraph is accurate 90 percent of the time or less, the conclusion is the same: It cannot reveal with certainty whether a person is or is not telling the truth.

The *third* major assumption about polygraphs is that they cannot be beaten. Lykken, for one, suggests otherwise. The easiest way to beat the polygraph, the psychiatrist claims, is by augmenting your response to the control question by some form of covert self-stimulation, like biting your tongue. Not everybody believes this. Defenders of the polygraph contend that liars can't fool skilled operators of the machine. But even if the polygraph generally catches the guilty, it will also generate a disturbing number of **false positives**—that is, it will falsely identify as liars people who are telling the truth.

To understand this, suppose that the polygraph is 95 percent accurate in both directions, that is, in 5 percent of the cases in which someone is lying the polygraph will report that they're telling the truth and in 5 percent of the cases in which they're actually telling the truth the polygraph will report that they're lying. Suppose further, for the sake of illustration, that at a large corporation with an in-house theft problem one out of every fifty employees is stealing from their employer. If the corporation has 1,000 employees, then 20 will be crooks and 980 will be honest. If every employee is tested, then the test, being only 95 percent accurate, will identify nineteen of the twenty crooks; one will escape detection. But the test will also identify 5 percent of the company's 980 innocent employees as liars; 49 people will be falsely accused. By firing all those who fail the polygraph, a company might succeed in weeding out the guilty, but it would also seriously harm many innocent employees.

In addition to these considerations, polygraphs infringe on privacy. As professor of politics Christopher Pyle says, they violate "the privacy of beliefs and associations, the freedom from unreasonable searches, the privilege against self-accusation, and the presumption of innocence."[29] That is not to say employers never have the right to abridge privacy or employees never have an obligation to reveal themselves. In important cases of in-house theft or corporate espionage, employers may be justified in using a polygraph as a last resort. But the threat to privacy remains.

The moral concerns embedded in the use of polygraphs suggest three points—in addition to the question of informed consent—to consider in evaluating their use in the workplace:

1. The information the organization seeks should be clearly and significantly related to the job. This caveat harks back to a determination of the legitimate areas of organizational influence over the individual.

2. Not only should the organization have job-related grounds for using the polygraph, but these must be compelling enough to justify violating the individual's privacy and psychic freedom. At the very least, the organization must have no viable alternative way of getting extremely important information or must have exhausted other, less intrusive means first.

3. Assuming the grounds for using the polygraph are sufficiently compelling, we must also be concerned about the sort of information being gathered, who will have access to it, and how it will be disposed of. Normally, not only the results but also the fact that a person is being tested at all should be kept confidential. And it's always important to treat that person respectfully.

Responding to moral concerns about polygraphs as well as to their practical and statistical limitations, Congress passed the **Employee Polygraph Protection Act**. It prohibits most private employers from using lie detectors in the hiring process. Private security firms are exempted from this provision of the law, along with drug companies, contractors with certain government agencies, and selected others. The law permits the use of polygraphs in "ongoing investigations of economic loss or injury," but it provides a number of procedural safeguards. For instance, the employer must explain the test's purpose to the employee and the reason why they were selected to take it. The worker also has a right to consult with someone who will explain the workings and limitations of the machine. Ultimately, the worker retains the option not to submit to the test, and no one can be fired on the basis of a lie-detector test "without other supporting evidence."

Scientists, however, are experimenting with new techniques for detecting dishonesty, such as magnetic resonance imaging, "cognosensors," and electroencephalography (EEG), all of which look directly at brain activity to see who is lying and who is not.[30] Although these techniques are not yet foolproof, their proponents believe that they promise to prove far more accurate than the antiquated polygraph. Look for them soon at a workplace near you.

Summary
Polygraph tests can infringe employee privacy. Moreover, their accuracy and underlying assumptions are open to question, and they can generate false positives. Their use in employment situations is now legally restricted.

Personality Tests

Companies often wish to determine whether prospective employees are emotionally mature, get along well with others, have a good work ethic, and, more generally, whether they would fit in with the organization, so they sometimes administer **personality tests**. One of the most popular of these tests, the Myers–Briggs Type Indicator, is purportedly used by 88 percent of *Fortune* 500 companies, even though the Meyers–Briggs company says that it's unethical to use the test for hiring.[31] Personality tests such as the Myers–Briggs can reveal highly personal information, and they often intrude into areas of our lives and thoughts that we normally consider private. Consent is usually less than fully voluntary because personality tests are generally part of a battery of tests that job applicants must take if they wish to be considered for a position.

Used properly, personality tests help screen applicants for jobs and current employees for particular assignments by indicating areas of adequacy and inadequacy. In theory, they simplify the complexities of business life by reducing the amount of decision-making involved in determining whether an individual has the personal characteristics appropriate for a given position. But one key premise underlying such tests is questionable. That premise is that all individuals can usefully and validly be categorized on the basis of a relatively small number of personality characteristics. In fact, test designers typically believe that one's overall personality is shaped by only five factors and that these factors, which they seek to measure, account for "99 percent of the differences in human behavior."[32] However, the possession of a personality trait or characteristic is not an all-or-nothing thing, nor is it something that is permanently fixed. Most of us possess a variety of traits in various degrees, and social circumstances often influence the characteristics we display and the talents we develop. When organizations attempt to categorize employees in terms of their personalities, they simplify human nature and may miss their employees' true potential.

The supposition that individuals can be categorized based on a small number of personality traits is questionable.

Personality tests also screen for organizational compatibility, sometimes functioning to eliminate prospective employees whose individuality or creativity may be exactly what the firm needs. Some companies, for example, seek employees who are extremely submissive to authority. Thus, when writer Barbara Ehrenreich submitted to a personality test for a job at Walmart, she was reprimanded for getting the "wrong" answer when she agreed only "strongly" with the proposition "All rules have to be followed to the letter at all times." The correct answer

Summary
Personality tests help businesses screen candidates and match individuals to appropriate jobs. But their use rests on some questionable psychological premises, and they can invade privacy and reinforce conformity.

was "totally agree."[33] When used to secure complete conformity to organizational values, goals, and philosophy, personality tests heighten the danger that organizations by nature represent to individual freedom and moral autonomy.

Then, of course, there's the intrusive nature of the questions. Questions like "Does driving give you a sense of power?" "Do you like a lot of excitement in your life?" or "If you could, would you work as an entertainer in Las Vegas?" may seem innocuous, but what about a personality test that delves into your love life or that asks men, "Was there ever a time in your life when you liked to play with dolls?" One disgruntled test taker complained about "questions you wouldn't even answer for your own mother, if she asked you."[34] Worse, many of the tests asking these questions have little or no research to back them up or have not been validated for use in pre-employment situations. Even those who favor testing admit as much. John Kamp, an industrial psychologist, points out that even intelligent businesspeople can be swayed by a good marketing pitch from companies that peddle invalid or unreliable tests. "That's the unfortunate thing," he says. "A person with a slick pitch and no real research behind their tests can have a good business."[35]

Drug Testing

Drug testing first became a live issue for some sports fans when the National Collegiate Athletic Association (NCAA) began banning college football players from postseason bowl competition based on the results of steroid testing. But political and legal battles over the drug testing of employees have raged for years. At one time, numerous companies warmly embraced testing. A study published in the *Journal of the American Medical Association* supported doing so. It showed that postal workers who tested positive for drug use in a pre-employment urine test were at least 50 percent more likely to be fired, injured, disciplined, or absent than those who tested negative.[36] Nevertheless, far fewer companies drug test new or current employees than in the past. More than two-thirds of corporations once employed drug testing, but a 2021 survey by the Bureau of Labor Statistics found that only 16.1 percent continue to do so.[37] Moreover, many companies that still require drug tests are no longer testing for cannabis, a reflection of this drug's growing social and legal acceptability.[38]

In principle, testing employees to determine whether they are using illegal drugs raises the same questions that other tests raise: Is there informed consent? How reliable are the tests? Is testing really pertinent to the job in question? Are the interests of the firm significant enough to justify encroaching on the privacy of the individual? But rather than reiterate these issues, all of which are important and relevant, this section limits itself to four additional remarks:

1. Most drug tests work differently from tests for alcohol. By using a breathalyzer or blood draw, it's possible to tell how much alcohol someone has in their system at that time and hence to infer how impaired they are. In contrast, drug tests conducted using urine or hair samples measure metabolites that drugs leave in the body, and these by-products may be present days or weeks after the last time that the drug was consumed—long after the its effects have dissipated. The fact that someone who takes a drug test at work tests positive doesn't mean that they showed up to work under the drug's influence.

2. Drugs differ, so one must carefully consider both what drugs one is testing for and why. Steroids, for instance, are a problem for the NCAA but not for IBM. And it's difficult to believe that Ford Meter Box was warranted in urine testing employees for nicotine in order to root out smokers.[39] To be defensible, drug testing must be pertinent to employee performance, and there must be a lot at stake. Testing airline pilots for alcohol consumption is one thing; testing the baggage handlers is something else. To go on a fishing trip in search of possible employee drug abuse when there is no evidence of a problem and no significant danger seems unreasonable.

3. Drug abuse by an individual is a serious problem, generally calling for medical and psychological assistance rather than punitive action. The moral assessment of any program of drug testing must rest in part on the potential consequences for those taking the test: Will they face immediate dismissal and potential criminal proceedings or therapy and

a chance to retain their positions? To put the issue another way, when an organization initiates a testing program, does it approach this solely as a kind of punitive function? Or is it also responsive to the needs and problems of individual employees? Some business writers argue that voluntary, nonpunitive drug assistance programs are far more cost-effective for companies, in any case, than testing initiatives.[40]

4. Any drug-testing program, assuming it's warranted, must be careful to respect the dignity and rights of the persons to be tested. Some alternatives to body-fluid testing are less invasive of employee privacy. Due process must also be followed, including advance notification of testing as well as procedures for retesting and appealing test results. All possible steps should be taken to ensure individual privacy.

Monitoring Employees on the Job

Many major employers routinely monitor the performance of their employees through the computers and telephones they use. They check the number of keystrokes that employees engaged in word processing enter during the day and record or listen in on calls handled by customer service agents. The Electronic Communications Privacy Act of 1986 restricts the government or unauthorized parties from eavesdropping on e-mail, fax transmissions, and cell phone conversations. The law applies to employers, but it allows exceptions when the consent of employees has been obtained, when the organization owns or maintains the system, or when there is a legitimate business purpose for the surveillance. Workers don't necessarily resent this monitoring, if it's in the open. "I don't think people mind having their work checked," said Morton Bahr, president of the Communications Workers of America. "It's the secretiveness of it" that bothers employees.[41]

According to one recent survey, over three-quarters of employers record employees' voice mail, e-mail, or phone calls; review their computer files; or even videotape them.[42] Over half of employees in the survey report feeling anxious about this surveillance. In 2006, an Ohio firm took things a step further when it embedded RFID (radio frequency identification) chips in the arms of two employees to monitor them when they accessed secured areas—the first known case of a company's electronically tagging workers.[43] Tightening security and overseeing customer service are not the only reasons companies monitor their employees. Some companies, for example, check employees' computers to see whether they exceed the allotted time for lunch or work breaks; others listen in on phone conversations and examine e-mail messages to catch employees conducting personal business on company time. The shift to remote work during and after the COVID-19 pandemic exacerbated employers' monitoring of employees. When ResumeBuilder.com surveyed 1,000 business leaders at firms with remote or hybrid workforces in 2023, the "vast majority" reported using technology to monitor employees and over one-third required employees to be on a live video feed.[44] Some employers have started paying employees only for the time that their monitoring software can determine that the employee is working, which means that employees may not get paid for reading printouts, thinking, or other activities that their computers don't register.[45]

"What are they going to think up to do to us next?" wonders one employee. "It's scary. I'll bet no one monitors the phones or e-mail of CEOs and other top executives." Nancy Flynn, executive director of ePolicy Institute, agrees with that sentiment. "In a lot of organizations," she says, "the senior executives are immune from [electronic] monitoring."[46] If so, this raises a basic moral objection. As explained in Chapter 1 and again in Chapter 2's discussion of Kant, if we make a moral judgment, we must be willing to make the same judgment in any similar set of circumstances. These executives, however, are apparently willing to apply to others a policy that they are unwilling to have applied to themselves.

When in-house theft, sabotage, or other threatening conduct occurs, organizations frequently install monitoring devices—two-way mirrors, cameras, and electronic recorders—to apprehend the employees who are responsible. But monitoring suspected trouble spots or private acts can create moral problems. Consider the two employees of Sheraton Boston Hotel who were secretly videotaped changing clothes in the locker room during a hunt for a drug dealer. They weren't suspects, just bystanders.[47]

Summary
Drug testing raises questions of test reliability and job relevance. Companies must also consider whether drug testing is really necessary and, if so, design such programs to respect the rights and dignity of employees as much as possible. They must also determine how to respond appropriately to individuals who fail the test.

Summary
Monitoring employees may be necessary, but it can be abused and it can violate privacy.

Notifying employees of
workplace monitoring does
not constitute consent.

As with personality, polygraph, and drug tests, the **monitoring of employees** often gathers personal information without informed consent. Organizations frequently confuse notification of such practices with employee consent, but notification alone does not constitute agreement. When employee restrooms, dressing rooms, locker rooms, and other private places are bugged or video-taped, an obvious and serious threat to privacy exists—posted notices notwithstanding. It's true that in some cases surveillance devices may be the only way to apprehend the guilty. Nevertheless, they often can do more harm than good by violating the privacy of the vast majority of innocent employees. Obviously, even more serious moral questions arise when monitoring devices are used not exclusively for officially designated purposes but also for cajoling, harassing, or snooping on employees (sometimes with the goal of thwarting them from organizing unions).[48]

· · ·

Working Conditions

In a broad sense, the conditions under which people work include personnel policies and procedures, as well as the extent to which an organization is committed to respecting the rights and privacy of its employees. This section, however, examines three other aspects of working conditions: health and safety on the job, styles of management, and the organization's parental leave and day-care arrangements.

Health and Safety

The year is 2013: A fire at a propane plant in Florida triggers multiple explosions, injuring 8 workers, some critically; a petrochemical plant southeast of Baton Rouge, Louisiana, explodes, killing 2 workers and injuring 114; and an earth-shattering blast at a fertilizer plant in the town of West, Texas, kills 15 people, injures 160, and lays waste to the surrounding neighborhood. Among the 150 damaged or destroyed buildings are a middle school, a nursing home, a community hospital, and an apartment complex. The year 2010 wasn't a good year for safety, either. In the deadliest coal mine incident in forty years, twenty-nine coal miners perished in a Massey Energy coal mine in West Virginia. And as you'll recall from Chapter 7, 2010 was also the year that the BP oil rig Deepwater Horizon exploded off the coast of Louisiana, leaving eleven workers dead and releasing millions of gallons of oil into the Gulf of Mexico.

These tragic episodes gained media coverage across the country, and some of them will remain seared in our memories for a long time. But most workplace deaths gather little or no publicity. For example, the national media ignored altogether the deaths of twenty-one-year-old Dennis Claypool and eighteen-year-old Mark DeMoss, who suffocated while working inside a tanker trailer at a trucking company outside Chicago. The two didn't know that the tanker had recently been cleaned with nitrogen, which removes oxygen from the air. A freak accident? Each year, close to 150 workers die in such "confined space" incidents.[49]

The scope of occupational hazards remains incredible and generally unrecognized. In a given year, about 5,000 workers are killed on the job.[50] Deaths are just part of the problem. According to the Bureau of Labor Statistics, in 2020 American workers suffered 266,530 sprains, strains, and tears at work. Some of these no doubt resulted from their 211,640 falls, slips, and trips. And researchers believe that government statistics actually undercount workplace injuries and illnesses.[51]

Employers clearly have a moral obligation not to expose workers to needless risks or to negligently or recklessly endanger their lives or health. In the case of a drilling company that lowered a twenty-three-year-old worker to the bottom of a 33-foot-deep, 18-inch-wide hole, where he then suffocated, a Los Angeles county prosecutor put it this way: "Our opinion is you can't risk somebody's life to save a few bucks. That's the bottom line."[52] Issues of legal liability aside, however, employers are not morally responsible for all workplace accidents. Sometimes coworkers are negligent or act irresponsibly, and sometimes the victims themselves may have behaved irresponsibly or failed to exercise due care. Sometimes, as people often say, accidents "just happen." Moreover, nothing in life is free of risk, and we often judge the risk worth taking (for example, when we choose to drive a car). And in some circumstances or in certain occupations, an injured worker can reasonably be said to have voluntarily assumed the risk. But although there is some truth in all these points, they are somewhat misleading about the nature of accidents.

To begin with **assumption of risk**, the proposition that Dennis Claypool, Mark DeMoss, or the young Los Angeles man who died at the bottom of the shaft can be inferred to have freely and knowingly decided to gamble with their lives is dubious, to say the least. Voluntary assumption of risk presupposes informed consent. As we have noted, that would require the worker to have been fully informed of the danger and to have freely chosen to assume it, which is rarely true of workers who are just doing what the boss tells them to do. Informed consent entails that employees have a moral right to refuse work when it exposes them to imminent danger and that employers are wrong to reprimand or otherwise retaliate against them for doing so. The U.S. Supreme Court has acknowledged the **right to refuse dangerous work** to be a legal right, too. In a crucial workplace decision, it ruled in favor of two employees of Whirlpool Corporation who had refused to follow their foreman's order to undertake activities they considered unsafe.[53] Of course, what constitutes an "imminent" danger may sometimes be open to debate, and workers should always behave reasonably and, when trying to avoid a perceived danger, take the least disruptive course of action open to them.

> Voluntary assumption of risk presupposes informed consent. Employees have a right to refuse dangerous work.

Employers, for their part, should inform workers of any life-threatening hazards, and, indeed, a number of states make that a legal requirement. Still, employees are often unaware of the dangers they face, many of which may be long-term, rather than imminent, hazards. Take the electronics industry, for example. It may look safe in comparison with other occupations, but behind its clean, high-tech image lurk health hazards for workers—in particular, the chemical toxins that are indispensable to the manufacture of computer chips. One workplace toxin causing concern recently is beryllium, a miracle metal—one-third the weight of aluminum yet six times stiffer than steel—which is used in a number of products these days, including computers, cell phones, and golf clubs. It's also found in coal, including the ground coal residue that's blasted at the hulls of ships as an abrasive scouring agent. More toxic than plutonium, a few millionths of a gram of beryllium can trigger an immune system attack and fatally damage the lungs and other organs. The federal government moved to tighten the standards that limit the permissible workplace exposure to beryllium in early 2017. Later that year, though, it exempted the shipbuilding and construction industries from these new standards.[54]

Putting aside assumption of risk and the right to know about and refuse hazardous work, we turn now to the causes of workplace accidents. As previously stated, it seems that accidents often result not from direct employer malfeasance but rather from employee blunders, coworker negligence, or just plain bad luck with nobody at fault. According to safety experts, though, this way of thinking is inaccurate. Industrial accidents don't just happen. They are caused—by inadequate worker training, sloppy procedures, lack of understanding of the job, improper tools and equipment, hazardous work environments, poor equipment maintenance, and overly tight scheduling.[55] And these are all matters that fall within the purview of the employer. For example, when a worker falls to his death from the tenth floor of a construction site because he wasn't wearing the required safety harness, the accident almost certainly has causes that go beyond poor judgment on his part.[56] Or consider the case of Michael Rodriguez. When some heavy machinery crushed his ankle, he was unable to leave his workplace and get to the hospital for several hours. That's because, until unfavorable publicity forced a policy change, Walmart would lock its employees in at night, and there was no one on duty with a key.[57]

> Accidents don't just happen. They result from poor job practices and workplace environments that fail to prioritize safety.

Workplace injuries, most experts believe, are related not to shortcomings in technology but rather to unsafe human behavior resulting from poor job practices, bad management, and a workplace environment that fails to put safety first. The key to a safer workplace, says risk-management consultant Beth Rogers, is not engineering but changing the company's "hidden culture"—the "unspoken rules that are adhered to"—to a culture that is proactively oriented toward safety.[58] As evidence for what Rogers is saying, consider two of the cases mentioned at the beginning of this section. With a long history of industrial mishaps, including a deadly refinery explosion in Texas five years earlier that killed 15 people and injured 170, BP had a

Summary

Employers have a moral obligation not to expose workers to needless risk, and employees have a right to know about and refuse hazardous work. Although industrial accidents sometimes seem to result from employee recklessness or to "just happen," experts believe that they are caused by factors that are under the control of the company.

reputation within the industry for subordinating safety management to aggressive growth. It's not surprising, then, that managers ignored the safety concerns expressed by crew members before the Deepwater Horizon oil rig blew up.[59] Likewise, Massey Energy had a long record of safety violations and a history of playing cat-and-mouse with regulators. Its West Virginia mine was known to be a "ticking time bomb."[60]

OSHA

With the 1970 Occupational Safety and Health Act, the prime responsibility for regulating working conditions passed from the states to the federal government. The thrust of the act is "to ensure so far as possible every working man and woman in the nation safe and healthful working conditions," and it places a duty on employers to provide a workplace "free from recognized hazards that are causing or are likely to cause death or serious injury." In its early years, the **Occupational Safety and Health Administration (OSHA)**, created by the act, added to its own troubles by promulgating some rules that seemed trivial and nitpicking—for example, detailed guidelines regulating toilet seats and the belts to be worn by telephone line workers.[61] Fortunately, most of those rules have been repealed, but controversies have raged over how far OSHA should go in the cause of safety. The organization seeks to require only safeguards that are feasible. It has, for example, never attempted to entirely eliminate toxins in the workplace. But is "feasibility" to be understood in a broad economic and technological sense or must the gains in safety outweigh the costs that particular companies must bear? And how are those costs and gains to be measured? Sometimes, even when union and industry representatives have agreed on new safety measures, politicians have prevented OSHA from introducing them because of ideological opposition to regulation.[62]

With limited resources—despite a recent surge in hiring, it still has fewer than 1,900 inspectors to monitor 8 million workplaces—OSHA has always faced a daunting task. Its performance has been spotty.[63] For instance, the fertilizer plant mentioned earlier that exploded in West, Texas, had not been visited by OSHA for twenty-eight years.[64] Worse, the relationship between OSHA and the businesses and industries it regulates has often been too cozy. Consider the case of Stephen Golab, a fifty-nine-year-old immigrant from Poland who worked for a year stirring tanks of sodium cyanide at the Film Recovery Services plant in Elk Grove, Illinois. One day he became dizzy from the cyanide fumes, went into convulsions, and died. OSHA then inspected the plant and fined Film Recovery Services $4,855 for twenty safety violations. OSHA subsequently cut the fine in half. In contrast, the state attorney general for Cook County filed criminal charges. Three company officials were convicted of murder and fourteen counts of reckless conduct. The company itself was also found guilty of manslaughter and reckless conduct and fined $24,000.[65]

Since the Golab case, budget cuts have shrunk OSHA's staff further and inspections and citations have dropped. For example, an examination of 1,242 cases in which the agency itself concluded that workers had died because of their employer's "willful" safety violations revealed that in 93 percent of those cases OSHA declined to prosecute. At least seventy of those employers willfully violated safety laws again, resulting in more deaths. Yet even those repeat offenders were rarely prosecuted.[66] Why the leniency? "A simple lack of guts and political will," says John T. Phillips, a former regional OSHA administrator.[67] Congress, however, is at least partly responsible. It has pushed the agency from rule making and enforcement to helping businesses comply with federal requirements. As a result, critics call OSHA a "toothless tiger" that has moved from "beat cop to social worker."[68]

New Health Challenges

One problem that both OSHA and business need to address is the epidemic of occupational injury and illness known as **musculoskeletal disorders**. In offices and factories across the country, millions of workers suffer from aching backs, crippled fingers, sore wrists, and other problems caused or aggravated by their jobs. Every year, carpal tunnel syndrome, low back pain, sciatica, tendinitis, and other musculoskeletal disorders cause hundreds of thousands of workers to miss time on the job.

Numb fingers, swollen knuckles, and aching wrists from the constant repetition of awkward hand and arm movements may sound like minor complaints, but they are anything but trivial to the many employees who suffer from them. Ask Janie Jue of San Francisco. For seventeen years she keyed in up to 48,000 strokes a day on an automatic letter-sorting machine. Today, even picking up a book or a coffee pot sends bolts of pain tearing up her hand and arm. "I wish I could work," she says, "but it hurts from my elbow to my fingertips."[69] "For many years," remarks one expert, "it was just considered a cost of doing business. If you did certain jobs, you would end up with hands crippled at the end of your career. That's not acceptable in this country any more."[70]

No longer associated only with manufacturing, musculoskeletal disorders are also rampant among white-collar office workers, especially those who spend all day at a computer. The redesign of jobs, adjustable chairs, training in the proper use of computer terminals, and other preventive measures can often reduce the problem. In the meantime, it's not only the employees who are suffering. Musculoskeletal disorders decrease productivity and dampen morale, and having a skilled worker go out on long-term disability and vocational rehabilitation can cost a company a small fortune. Nevertheless, various employer groups and business lobbies continue to fight vigorously any step toward ergonomic regulation, even thwarting a thirteen-year effort by the National Safety Council to draft voluntary guidelines for preventing repetitive-motion injuries.[71]

An aspect of work life over which OSHA exercises little direct control is the shifts people work. Yet a team of scientists from Harvard and Stanford universities believes that the health and productivity of 25 million Americans whose work hours change regularly could be measurably improved if employers scheduled shift changes to conform with the body's natural and adjustable sleep cycles. This is particularly important given that sleep deprivation and fatigue are prime causes of industrial accidents and cost employers billions a year in absences, accidents, and diminished productivity.[72]

Related to fatigue is an aspect of work we have only recently begun to appreciate fully—the health implications of **job stress**. In a 2023 survey conducted by the American Psychological Association, 77 percent of workers reported that they had experienced work-related stress in the last month, and 57 percent reported that they were experiencing negative effects from work-related stress, including emotional exhaustion and irritability with coworkers and customers.[73] One reason, of course, is the long hours many Americans put in. Furthermore, technology leashes many employees to the job even when they're at home. As a result, says Donald I. Tepas, a professor of industrial psychology, "the distinction between work and nonwork time is getting fuzzier all the time."[74]

The relation between workplace stress and ill health is now well established. In fact, scientists have ascertained that stressful job conditions diminish mental health and damage physical functioning as much as smoking does.[75] Workers who report being stressed incur significantly higher health care costs than do other employees. Revamping working environments that produce stress and helping employees to learn to cope with stress are among the major health challenges that are facing American businesses now and for years to come.

Summary
The scope of occupational hazards, including musculoskeletal disorders, shift work, fatigue, and stress, and the numbers of employees harmed by work-related injuries and illness are greater than many people think. OSHA's enforcement of existing regulations has too often been lax.

Management Styles

How managers conduct themselves on the job—**management styles**—can do more to enhance or diminish the work environment than any other facet of employer–employee relations. Indeed, a poor relationship with their immediate supervisor is the most common reason people give for leaving a job; office politics comes second.[76] "Management creates the conditions in which most adults spend half their waking lives," wrote Thomas A. Stewart, editor of *Harvard Business Review*. "Bad management makes lives miserable."[77] In survey after survey, employees rank honest communication, personal recognition, and respectful treatment as more important than good pay. Unfortunately, according to a Columbia University psychologist, millions of workers suffer from bosses who are abusive, dictatorial, devious, dishonest, manipulative, and inhumane.[78] Some research estimates that bad management which fails to keep employees engaged costs the United States $960 billion and $1.2 trillion annually. (Globally, the figure is an astronomical $7 trillion, about 10 percent of the entire world's productivity.)[79]

Nothing affects work environment more than the style and quality of management.

This workplace reality runs contrary to the teachings of almost all management theorists. For example, in his classic work *The Human Side of Enterprise*, Douglas McGregor described two styles of management, which he called "Theory X" and "Theory Y." Theory X managers believe that workers dislike work and will do everything they can to avoid it.[80] These managers insist that the average person wishes to avoid responsibility, lacks ambition, and values security over everything else. Accordingly, they believe they must coerce and bully workers into conformity with organizational objectives. In contrast, McGregor advocated a Theory Y management style. Theory Y managers assume that employees basically like work and view it as something natural and potentially enjoyable. They believe that workers are motivated as much by pride and a desire for self-fulfillment as by money and job security and that workers don't dodge responsibility but accept it and even seek it out.

Since the publication of McGregor's book, other management writers have pursued this line of thought and described other management styles—including Theory Z, which touts Japanese-style respect for workers. More recently, some theorists have advocated a management style that eschews a masculine, hierarchical, aggressive, analytic, winner-take-all approach in favor of a more personal, empathetic, and collaborative style, thought to be characteristic of, and more congenial to, women.

This is not the place to discuss different theories of management, but clearly the management styles recommended by different writers, as well as the management styles actually adopted by different bosses, rest on implicit or explicit assumptions about human nature. However, no set of assumptions about human nature is absolutely correct or incorrect, nor is there one perfectly right way to manage. But that's precisely the point. Problems inevitably arise when managers routinize their leadership style, regardless of the needs, abilities, and predilections of their particular employees. When managers ignore individual differences, they risk creating a work atmosphere that's distressing to workers and less productive than it might be. Moreover, implicit assumptions about human nature can easily become self-reinforcing because people tend to behave as they are treated. Thus, managers who treat employees as if they were incapable of taking initiative or thinking for themselves will probably end up with employees who don't take initiative or think for themselves. Managers, therefore, must carefully examine their preconceptions when determining the most appropriate leadership style to adopt in their workplace. That is easier said than done for most managers. Research shows that managers frequently overestimate their skills and rarely display self-doubt.[81] And those who have been successful can be the most rigid. "With the success they've achieved," says Michael Feiner of the Columbia Business School, "bosses can come to believe that their way is the right way, the best way—perhaps the only way."[82]

Summary
Management style greatly affects the work environment. Managers who operate with rigid assumptions about human nature or who devote themselves to infighting and political maneuvering damage employees' interests.

A different problem of management style, which also has moral overtones, stems from the bureaucratic character of many American corporations. One aspect of this problem is that corporate America may simply have more administrators and managers than it needs (a criticism that's also frequently made about universities). According to a 2016 analysis, "the cost of excess bureaucracy in the U.S. economy amounts to more than $3 trillion in lost economic output, or about 17% of GDP."[83] A second aspect is that managers' incentives may not always align with the good of the corporation. Corporate bureaucracies often create an environment in which managers and other executives must pay excessive attention to hierarchy—often hoarding information and keeping subordinates in the dark—and in which they are tempted to put personal ambition ahead of other things and spend their energy trying to move up the company ladder. "Corporate infighting," "management power struggles," "maneuvering and politics and power grabbing," and "Machiavellian intrigues" are the phrases one business observer, H. Ross Perot, used to describe the reality of corporate life.[84]

Day Care and Family Leave

One area often overlooked in discussions of working conditions is the provision of family leave and child-care services for workers with children. The need for both is steadily growing as more and more women enter the paid labor force. Women's participation in the labor force has nearly doubled since 1960; today, women hold more than half of all professional and management positions.[85] In 1960, only 18.6 percent of married women with children under age six were in the paid labor force; today, the figure is nearly 68 percent.[86] Despite these statistics, the United States lags behind many industrialized nations in the provision of child care. The Norwegian government subsidizes child care by spending over $29,000 per child annually.[87] Slovenia spends over $11,000; Chile spends over $8,000.[88] Those countries, like many others, view child care as a national responsibility. In contrast, in the United States child care is treated as a private rather than a public good; the federal government spends only $500 per child each year.

The situation is even more striking with respect to family leave, which is a broad term meant to encompass several different types of leaves available to new parents. **Maternity leave** is offered to new mothers, and sometimes only birth mothers, while **paternity leave** is for new fathers. Gender-neutral **parental leave** is sometimes available to let one parent stay at home longer after paternity or maternity leave has run out. Only thirteen states and the District of Columbia have passed laws requiring any *paid* family leave, and in some of these states the laws have yet to go into effect.[89] At the federal level, the United States guarantees only *unpaid* time off for pregnancy or for personal or family illness (and then only if you work for a company with more than fifty employees). This makes the United States an outlier. In fact, the very few other countries not to have national paid family leave requirements are much smaller than the United States and not nearly as wealthy or industrialized: Papua New Guinea, the Marshall Islands, Micronesia, Nauru, Palau, and Tonga.[90] (Some countries require only paid maternity leave, but more than half the countries in the world require paid paternity leave as well.) Of course, American companies can offer family leave even in states where this isn't mandated. Today, about 40 percent of American companies offer maternity leave, with slightly fewer offering paternity or parental leave.[91]

Given that women in our society continue to bear the primary responsibility for child rearing, their increasing participation in the paid workforce generates a growing demand for reasonable maternity-leave policies and affordable child-care services. Nor is that demand likely to diminish. Many families are unable to make satisfactory child-care arrangements, either because the services are unavailable or because the parents cannot afford them. An estimated 7.7 million children are thus left alone without any supervision while their parents work.[92] The need for child-care services is particularly acute among single-parent families, 71 percent of which are headed by women.[93] Single mothers have a higher rate of participation in the labor force than do married mothers. Nevertheless, many of them are too poor to pay for satisfactory child-care services. At the same time, the general societal move toward men's participation in child care creates more demand for paternity leave as well, and making paternity and parental leave available to more men is probably a prerequisite of shifting more responsibility for parental care onto them.

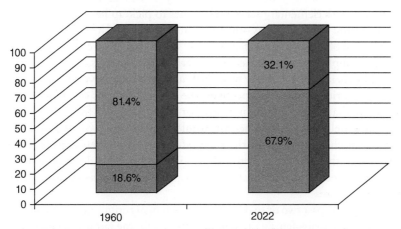

Percentage (in orange) of married women with children under age six in the paid labor force in 1960 and in 2022.

Business and Child Care

Some companies try hard to help with employee child care.[94] Campbell Soup Co., for example, offers on-site **day care**, as does hotel chain Marriott (at its global headquarters, in Maryland, not at individual hotels) and Tyson Foods (at some locations). However, nationally only 6 percent of American employers provide day care at or near their operations.[95] Other companies subsidize their employees' child care expenses, although again they're a distinct minority.[96]

Large businesses are in a good position to assist in the provision of child-care services, and the need for it is there, given the paucity of government funding. Viewed from a broader perspective, day-care arrangements set up by companies themselves or by several companies together in the same area can be socially cost-effective. With in-house day-care arrangements, parents need not make special trips to pick up and drop off their children. Because the parents are not far away, they can have more interaction with their children. Depending on the specific organization of work and the firm's flexibility, parents could share in the actual running of the child-care facility at assigned intervals during the course of their working day. Hewlett-Packard took an innovative step in this regard when, in conjunction with the local school district, it set up kindergarten and first-grade classes on company grounds for the children of employees. Some other companies now do the same thing.[97]

Some business writers argue that offering child care as a fringe benefit and dealing as flexibly as possible with employees' family needs can prove advantageous for most employers. Such policies can be cost-effective in the narrower sense by decreasing absenteeism, boosting morale and loyalty to the firm, enhancing productivity, and attracting new recruits. A growing body of empirical research demonstrates the bottom-line benefits for companies that promote their employees' well-being and engage their hearts and minds with family-friendly policies.[98] This is an important consideration.

Assistance with child care and flexible, family-oriented policies can be cost-effective.

Three Moral Concerns

Even more important are three underlying moral considerations.

Even more important are the underlying moral issues. *First,* women have a right to compete on an equal terrain with men. The legal requirement that large firms provide at least unpaid maternity leave and reinstatement respects that right. Whether companies should also provide paid maternity leave is more controversial, although one might argue that paid leave is necessary to give substance to that right. Or one might defend such a policy on the utilitarian ground that it would enhance total social welfare. As mentioned, many organizations find it in their interest to provide paid leave and flexible work arrangements so that they can attract better and more-talented employees, and some are working hard at luring stay-at-home moms back to work.[99] On the other hand, the trend toward tough performance standards and no-fault absence policies can penalize workers for missing work regardless of the reason. That happened to Tanya Frazier, office manager for a payroll company in Burbank, California. After receiving a call from her daughter's elementary school telling her to pick up her flu-stricken nine-year-old, she stayed home from work for a day—and was fired because of it. She claims she had missed work only a handful of days that year, but her boss says he was tired of her taking so much time off.[100] Even when employees aren't sacked, their performance appraisal, year-end bonus, or raise can be affected by their taking a legally protected, unpaid family leave.[101]

Second, from various ethical perspectives, the development of our potential capacities is a moral ideal—perhaps even a human right. For that reason, or from the point of view of promoting human well-being, many theorists would contend that women should not be forced to choose between childbearing and the successful pursuit of their careers. If employment circumstances force them to do so, and if those circumstances could reasonably be changed, then we have not lived up to the ideal of treating those women as persons whose goals are worthy of respect.

Third, although the past two or so decades have seen many criticisms of, and attempts to move beyond, the traditional male–female division of labor within the family, there can be little doubt that the world of work tends to reproduce those patterns. For instance, as mentioned in Chapter 8, men who leave work to help raise children often face enormous hurdles when returning to the job market. It seems clear that many fathers today feel hampered by work arrangements that pit meaningful career advancement against a fully developed family life.[102] Enhanced opportunities

Summary
Day-care services and reasonable parental-leave policies also affect working conditions. Despite the genuine need for and the ethical importance of both day care and flexible work arrangements for parents, only a handful of companies strive seriously to provide them.

for part-time employment and job sharing, along with generous parental-leave arrangements and flexible, affordable, and accessible firm-sponsored child-care facilities—even efforts to facilitate workplace lactation by nursing mothers—can assist all employees in achieving a more personally desirable balance between paid work and family relations.

The moral value here is not to promote any single vision of the good life but rather to permit individuals, couples, and families as much autonomy as possible, given other social goals. They should be able to define the good life for themselves and to seek the arrangement of work and personal relations that makes that life possible. Firm-affiliated child-care services and other institutional arrangements that accommodate parental needs clearly promote this moral goal.

• • •

Redesigning Work

Chapter 4 looked at alienation under capitalism and changing attitudes toward work in America. It remains true that many, perhaps even most, employees are at least somewhat dissatisfied with their jobs. Any investigation of the moral issues arising around the workplace and any discussion of the challenges facing business today must confront this basic problem and consider ways of improving the quality of work life.

> Business must confront the fact of widespread job dissatisfaction and consider ways of improving the quality of work life.

Dissatisfaction on the Job

In the early 1970s, the federal government conducted a major study of work in America, the basic findings of which remain relevant.[103] The *Work in America* report identified three chief sources of worker dissatisfaction. The first was industry's preoccupation with quantity, not quality; the rigidity of rules and regulations; and the fracturing of work into the smallest possible tasks, together with the monotonous repetition of those tasks. The second source of dissatisfaction was the lack of opportunities to be one's own boss. The third source of dissatisfaction was "bigness": More people today work for large corporations than ever before.

The *Work in America* survey reported similar sources of dissatisfaction in the managerial ranks. One out of three middle managers at that time was willing to join a union. Moreover, just as industrial workers voiced general complaints about work, so did middle managers. Some resented having so little influence in their organizations; others objected to the organization's goals, policies, and ways of operating. Still other managers complained about the tension, frustration, and infighting that intraorganizational competition can breed. Beyond these complaints, the *Work in America* survey reported that many managers felt like cogs in a machine, like parts that could and would be replaced when a better part came along.

More contemporary empirical research on American job satisfaction is somewhat ambiguous. A 2023 Pew study found that 51 percent of workers were "extremely" or "very" satisfied with their jobs.[104] The Conference Board, a business policy organization, found in the same year that just over 62 percent of American workers were satisfied with their jobs—about two percentage points higher than in 2022.[105] However, a 2022 Gallup poll reached somewhat more pessimistic conclusions.[106] It found that only 32 percent of American workers were "engaged" with their work. Eighteen percent were "actively disengaged," meaning that they tended to undermine their colleagues and employers and shirk their duties whenever possible. Whatever the statistics, if industry is to improve productivity, enhance customer satisfaction, and be more competitive, it must seriously confront these attitudes and the sources of employee dissatisfaction. It must devise ways to make work more satisfying and to improve the quality of work life.

Factors Affecting Job Satisfaction

As early as the 1920s, researchers began to realize that workers would be more productive if management met those needs that money cannot buy. Managers at the Hawthorne factory of Western Electric Company were conducting experiments to determine the effect of the work environment on worker productivity. In the literature of work motivation, these studies have become known as the Hawthorne studies. What they discovered has been termed the **Hawthorne effect**.

Researchers at the Hawthorne plant chose a few employees to work in an experimental area, apart from the thousands of employees in the rest of the factory. Every effort was made to improve working conditions, from painting walls a cheerful color to making lights brighter. Worker productivity increased with each improvement. Then the experimenters decided to reverse the process. For example, lights were made dimmer. To everyone's surprise, productivity continued to increase.

The conclusion the researchers drew was that workers were producing more because they were receiving attention. Instead of feeling that they were spokes in an organizational wheel, they felt important and recognized. The attention had the effect of heightening their sense of personal identity and feeling of control over their work environment. Recognition of this effect can help management increase worker motivation and job satisfaction and also increase the organization's productivity.

Subsequent research corroborates and deepens the Hawthorne results.[107] In studying the problem of poor worker motivation, influential management theorist Frederick Herzberg discovered that the factors that promote **job satisfaction** differed from those producing job dissatisfaction. Herzberg found that although job dissatisfaction frequently arises from extrinsic problems (such as pay, supervision, working conditions, and leadership styles), resolving those extrinsic problems does not necessarily produce satisfied workers. The reason, Herzberg contends, is that worker satisfaction depends on such intrinsic factors as a sense of accomplishment, responsibility, recognition, self-development, and self-expression.[108] Recent surveys add support to Herzberg's findings. When employees at all occupational levels are asked to rank what is important to them, they list interesting work; sufficient help, support, and information to accomplish the job; enough authority to carry out the work; good pay; the opportunity to develop special skills; job security; and a chance to see the results of their work. Other research shows that what makes people content is being respected by members of groups they respect. In line with this, Roger Martin, dean of the school of management at the University of Toronto, argues that employees are happiest when they are respected members of a team they admire and when the team and company are respected by the outside world.[109]

Importance of Job Satisfaction

Numerous mental-health problems stem from a lack of job satisfaction—low self-esteem, anxiety, impaired interpersonal relations, and psychosomatic ailments such as ulcers and hypertension—especially in low-status, boring, unchallenging jobs that offer little autonomy. In fact, although having a job is better for one's mental health than being unemployed, being in a bad job is worse than having no job at all.[110] Furthermore, dreary, unchallenging jobs tend to inhibit intellectual growth and the pursuit of richer, more fulfilling activities outside work. Even worse, researchers have found that workers in boring, passive jobs are 33 to 35 percent more likely to die prematurely than workers in active jobs. Stressful work that offers little decision-making opportunity makes an untimely demise even more likely.[111] In contrast, job satisfaction is strongly linked to longevity.[112]

Because the design of work materially affects the total well-being of workers, work content and job satisfaction are paramount moral concerns. But if we also assume that a happier, more contented worker is generally a more productive one, then it follows that business has an economic reason as well as a moral obligation to devise ways, in concert with labor and perhaps even government, to improve the quality of work life.

Improving Work Life

This book isn't the place for determining precisely what measures firms should take to improve employees' work lives. For some firms, it may mean less supervision and more autonomy for workers. For others, it may mean offering opportunities to develop and refine skills. Still other firms might try to provide workers with greater participation in the conception, design, and execution of their work—that is, with greater responsibility and a deeper sense of achievement.

Granting workers new responsibilities and respect can benefit the entire organization. Randy Pennington, vice president of Performance Systems Corporation, tells of a friend who showed an ad for a new American car to a Japanese businessperson. The ad said that the car "set a new standard for quality because it was examined by 34 different quality inspectors." "Now, *this*," he said to his Japanese colleague, "is what we need to compete with you. Imagine: 34 quality inspectors!" The colleague looked at the ad, smiled, and said, "You don't need 34 inspectors to get quality. You just need everyone who works on the car to be proud of the work. Then you'll need only one inspector."[113]

Thawing the antagonistic worker–boss relations that characterize many plants isn't always easy. Some union members are wary of "being co-opted and looking like management flunkies."[114] Investigators believe that the success of workplace reform efforts depends on the ability of the organization to reinforce high levels of trust. To the extent that it does so, organizational performance can improve. But, warns William Cooke, professor at Wayne State University and author of a book on workplace reform, "if [workers] perceive management as doing this without due consideration for the welfare of employees . . . it will have the potential of destroying the efforts altogether."[115]

After Gerard Arpey took over as CEO of American Airlines, the company began the arduous but ambitious process of developing better and more stable working relations between managers and employees, something that had long eluded American Airlines. In an apparently successful effort to end adversarial relations with the unions, Arpey created new structures of consultancy across the company, captured in the slogans "Involve before Deciding. Discuss before Implementing. Share before Announcing." "We are trying to make our unions our business partners," Arpey says. "It is not about sitting around the campfire singing Kumbaya."[116] (Arpey resigned in 2011 over his opposition to American's declaring bankruptcy, a move that the airline's unions also opposed.)

Transportation company Patriot Rail offers a more recent example of constructive union–management relations. When CEO John Fenton collaborated with the stevedores' union to improve working conditions—replacing the old van used to ferry workers around the job site with air-conditioned buses and providing an indoor place that the workers could eat indoors, among other measures—the turn around was immediate. Freight damage claims dropped 70 percent and the time needed to load trucks dropped by more than half.[117] At American Airlines and Patriot Rail, the ideals of improved work atmosphere, employee participation, and job security appear to have meshed nicely with the goal of increased productivity.

At American Airlines and Patriot Rail, the ideals of improved work atmosphere, employee participation, and job security appear to have meshed nicely with the goal of increased productivity. The same is true at BMW, which also gives its creative and motivated workforce a share of the profits.[118] Not only is productivity 5 to 10 percent greater in companies with profit sharing, but productivity is also consistently higher in enterprises with an organized program of worker participation.[119] This is in line with the views of experts who insist that worker-friendly companies outperform traditional command-and-control employers. They argue that new organizational structures and work practices that put a premium on collaboration and cooperation are fundamental to the nation's future economic success.[120]

A range of social and economic research supports that conclusion, but there is no watertight guarantee that worker participation and an improved quality of work life will always boost productivity. For example, although diversifying tasks may make work more satisfying, Japanese carmakers reduced the number of rejects on their assembly line not by diversifying but by standardizing the cars produced. And some years ago, Volkswagen found that its productivity and quality were higher when production consisted solely of the standard Rabbit model than when other models were introduced. Job-enlargement programs, by definition, add to the variety of tasks the worker is assigned; job-enrichment programs add some planning, designing, and scheduling to the operative worker's tasks. Both programs may slow output in some cases. Also, worker involvement in production management may not fit well, some argue, with the two other ingredients that managers and management consultants see as essential for manufacturing efficiency: a just-in-time approach to eliminate waste and rigorous statistical process control to improve quality.

Employee involvement, however, is essential to work elimination programs—programs that eliminate wasteful and unnecessary tasks, thus enhancing job satisfaction while making the organization leaner and more productive. This is particularly important as competition

Summary
Studies report extensive job dissatisfaction at all levels. Various factors influence satisfaction and dissatisfaction on the job. Redesigning the work process and increasing employee responsibility and participation can enhance the quality of work life, the well-being of workers, and even productivity.

Worker participation can increase productivity. Worker-friendly companies tend to outperform traditional command-and-control employers.

pressures manufacturers in the car industry and elsewhere to move to smaller, more flexible factories. Still, the possibility of a conflict between the obligation to make work more satisfying and the goal of increasing productivity will likely be at the heart of moral decisions in this area for years to come. To resolve them will require a cooperative effort by labor and management, rooted in the recognition that trade-offs are inevitable.

Study Corner

Key Terms and Concepts

assumption of risk	job satisfaction	off-the-job conduct
civic activities	job stress	parental leave
day care	management styles	paternity leave
drug testing	maternity leave	personality tests
Employee Polygraph Protection Act	monitoring of employees	polygraph tests
false positives	musculoskeletal disorders	privacy
Hawthorne effect	Occupational Safety and Health	right to refuse dangerous work
informed consent	Administration (OSHA)	wellness programs

Points to Review

- examples of business actions that encroach upon privacy (pp. 259–260)
- three dimensions of privacy (p. 260)
- difficulties of determining when companies have a legitimate interest in employee conduct, on and off the job (pp. 261–262)
- privacy issues raised by company-sponsored civic activities and wellness programs (pp. 262–263)
- what informed consent implies (p. 263)
- debatable assumptions behind polygraphs (p. 264)
- problem of false positives (p. 264)
- three points to consider in evaluating workplace use of polygraphs (pp. 264–265)
- one questionable assumption of personality tests (p. 265)
- four points about drug testing (pp. 266–267)

- assumption of risk and the right to refuse hazardous work (p. 269)
- what causes accidents (p. 269)
- the key to workplace safety (pp. 269–270)
- OSHA's spotty record (p. 270)
- new health challenges in the workplace (pp. 270–271)
- management theories and human nature (pp. 271–272)
- corporate record on child care (p. 274)
- three moral reasons to accommodate employees' parental and family needs (pp. 274–275)
- the Hawthorne experiment and the factors affecting job satisfaction (pp. 275–276)
- health effects of job dissatisfaction (p. 276)
- effect of participation and improved quality of work life on productivity (pp. 276–278)

For Further Reflection

1. How important is privacy to you personally? Describe a situation, work-related or otherwise, in which you felt your privacy was threatened.
2. Describe your experiences with drug testing or personality testing. Have you or has anyone you know been subjected to job monitoring that seemed too intrusive?
3. Does business have a responsibility to provide employees with more satisfying work lives? Or to better accommodate their family needs?

Case 9.1
Unprofessional Conduct?

Teaching Elementary School Children With Intellectual Disabilities requires skill, patience, and devotion, and those who undertake this task are among the unsung heroes of our society. Their difficult and challenging work rarely brings the prestige or financial rewards it deserves. Mrs. Pettit was one of those dedicated teachers. Licensed to teach in California, she had been working with children with intellectual disabilities for over thirteen years when her career came to an abrupt end. Throughout that career, her competence was never questioned, and the evaluations of her school principal were always positive.

Teaching was not Pettit's only interest, however. She and her husband viewed with favor various "nonconventional sexual lifestyles," including "wife swapping." Because so-called sexual liberation was a hot topic at the time, the Pettits were invited to discuss their ideas on two local television shows. Although they wore disguises, at least one fellow teacher recognized them and discussed Mrs. Pettit's views with colleagues. A year later Pettit, then forty-eight years old, and her husband joined "The Swingers," a private club in Los Angeles that sponsored parties intended to promote diverse sexual activities among its members. An undercover police officer, Sergeant Berk, visited one of those parties at a private residence. Amid a welter of sexual activity, he observed Mrs. Pettit engaged in sexual activity with three different men in a one-hour period.

Pettit was arrested and charged with oral copulation, which at the time—1973—contravened the California Penal Code (although now it does only if one of the parties is under eighteen). After a plea bargain was arranged, she pleaded guilty to the misdemeanor of outraging public decency and paid a fine. The school district renewed her teaching contract the next academic year, but two years later, disciplinary proceedings were initiated against her. The State Board of Education found no reason to complain about her services as a teacher, and it conceded that she was unlikely to repeat her sexual misconduct. But the Board revoked her elementary school life diploma—that is, her license to teach—on the ground that by engaging in immoral and unprofessional conduct at the party, she had demonstrated that she was unfit to teach.

Pettit fought the loss of her license all the way to the California Supreme Court, which upheld the decision of the Board of Education.[121] In an earlier case, the court had reversed the firing of a public school teacher for unspecified "homosexual conduct," concluding that a teacher's actions could not constitute "immoral or unprofessional conduct" or "moral turpitude" unless there was clear evidence of unfitness to teach. But Pettit's case was different, the court hastened to explain.

The conduct in the earlier case had not been criminal, oral copulation had not been involved, and the conduct had been private. Further, in that case the Board had acted with insufficient evidence of unfitness to teach; by contrast, three school administrators had testified that in their opinion, Pettit's conduct proved her unfit to teach. These experts worried that she would inject her views of sexual morality into the classroom, and they doubted that she could act as a moral example to the children she taught. Yet teachers, the court reaffirmed, are supposed to serve as exemplars, and the Education Code makes it a statutory duty of teachers to "endeavor to impress upon the minds of the pupils the principles of morality . . . and to instruct them in manners and morals."

In a vigorous dissent, Justice Tobringer rejected the opinion of the majority, arguing that no evidence had established that Pettit was not fit to teach. The three experts didn't consider her record; they couldn't point to any past misconduct with students, nor did they suggest any reason to anticipate future problems. They simply assumed that the fact of her sexual acts at the "swingers" party itself demonstrated that she would be unable to set a proper example or to teach her pupils moral principles.

Such an attitude is unrealistic, Tobringer argued, when studies show that 75 to 80 percent of the women of Pettit's educational level and age range engage in oral copulation. The majority opinion "is blind to the reality of sexual behavior" and unrealistically assumes that "teachers in their private lives should exemplify Victorian principles of sexual morality." Pettit's actions were private and could not have affected her teaching ability. Had there not been clandestine surveillance of the party, the whole issue would never have arisen.

Discussion Questions

1. In concerning itself with Pettit's off-the-job conduct, did the Board of Education violate her right to privacy? Or was its concern with her lifestyle legitimate and employment related?

2. Was Pettit's behavior "unprofessional"? Was it "immoral"? Did it show a "lack of fitness" to teach? Explain how you understand the terms in quotation marks.

3. Was the Board of Education justified in firing Pettit? Explain.

4. Was the court's verdict consistent with its earlier handling of the case of the gay male teacher?

5. If teachers perform competently in the classroom, should they also be required to be moral exemplars in their private lives? Are employees in other occupations expected to provide a moral example—either on or off the job?

6. Which of the following, in your view, would show unprofessional conduct, immorality, or lack of fitness to teach: drunken driving, smoking marijuana, advocating the use of marijuana, forging a check, resisting arrest for disorderly conduct and assaulting a police officer, being discovered in a compromising position with a student, propositioning a student, cheating on income tax, calling attention to your sexual proclivities?

7. Under what conditions do employers have a legitimate interest in their employees' off-the-job conduct?

Case 9.2
Testing for Honesty

At Christmas Time, Holiday Shoppers Drop All Sorts of Things Into the Salvation Army's red kettles: diamond rings, lottery tickets, casino chips—even Viagra.[122] Most people, of course, put in coins and dollar bills. Some years ago, however, one of the Army's local branches found that money also seemed to be disappearing out of its kettles. Worried about theft by its kettle workers, Army officials sought the assistance of Dr. John Jones, director of research for London House Management Consultants.

London House is one of several companies that market honesty tests for prospective employees.[123] Employee theft is a serious problem for many companies. Honesty-test makers say the best way to deal with it is before workers are hired—by subjecting them to a pre-employment psychological test that will identify those prospective employees who are likely to steal.

James Walls, one of the founders of Stanton Corporation, which has offered written honesty tests for twenty-five years, says that dishonest job applicants are clever at hoodwinking potential employers in a job interview. "They have a way of conducting themselves that is probably superior to the low-risk person. They have learned what it takes to be accepted and how to overcome the normal interview strategy," he says. "The high-risk person will get hired unless there is a way to screen him." For this reason, Walls maintains, written, objective tests are needed to weed out the crooks.

Millions of written honesty tests are given annually, thanks to congressional restrictions on polygraph testing. In addition to being legal, honesty tests are also economical because they cost only a fraction of what polygraph tests cost. Furthermore, honesty tests are easily administered at the workplace and can be quickly evaluated by the test maker. The tests also are nondiscriminatory because the race, gender, or ethnicity of applicants has no significant impact on scores.

A typical test begins with some cautionary remarks. Test takers are told to be truthful because dishonesty can be detected, and they are warned that incomplete answers will be considered incorrect, as will any unanswered questions. Then applicants ordinarily sign a waiver permitting the results to be shown to their prospective employer and authorizing the testing agency to check out their answers. Sometimes, however, prospective employees are not told that they are being tested for honesty, only that they are being asked questions about their background. James Walls justifies this lack of candor by saying that within a few questions it's obvious that the test deals with attitudes toward honesty. "The test is very transparent, it's not subtle."

Some questions do indeed seem transparent—for example, "If you found $100 that was lost by a bank truck on the street yesterday, would you turn the money over to the bank, even though you knew for sure there was no reward?" But other questions are more controversial: "Have you ever had an argument with someone and later wished you

had said something else?" If you were to answer no, you would be on your way to failing. Other questions that may face the test taker are "How strong is your conscience?" "How often do you feel guilty?" "Do you always tell the truth?" "Do you occasionally have thoughts you wouldn't want made public?" "Does everyone steal a little?" "Do you enjoy stories of successful crimes?" "Have you ever been so intrigued by the cleverness of a thief that you hoped the person would escape detection?" Or consider questions like "Is an employee who takes it easy at work cheating his employer?" or "Do you think a person should be fired by a company if it's found that he helped employees cheat the company out of overtime once in a while?" These ask you for your reaction to hypothetical dishonest situations. "If you are a particularly kind-hearted person who isn't sufficiently punitive, you fail," says Lewis Maltby, director of the workplace rights office at the American Civil Liberties Union. "Mother Teresa would never pass some of these tests."

A big part of some tests is a behavioral history of the applicant. Applicants are asked to reveal the nature, frequency, and quantity of specific drug use, if any. They also must indicate if they have ever engaged in drunk driving, illegal gambling, traffic violations, forgery, vandalism, and a host of other unseemly behaviors. They must also state their opinions about the social acceptability of drinking alcohol and using other drugs.

Some testing companies go further in this direction. Instead of honesty exams, they offer tests designed to draw a general psychological profile of the applicant, claiming that this sort of analysis can predict more accurately than either the polygraph or the typical honesty test how the person will perform on the job. Keith M. Halperin, a psychologist with Personnel Decision, Inc. (PDI), a company that offers such tests, complains that most paper-and-pencil honesty tests are simply written equivalents of the polygraph. They ask applicants whether they have stolen from their employers, how much they have taken, and other questions directly related to honesty. "But why," asks Halperin, "would an applicant who is dishonest enough to steal from an employer be honest enough to admit it on a written test?" It's more difficult for applicants to fake their responses to PDI's tests, Halperin contends.

Not everyone is persuaded. Phyllis Bassett, vice president of James Bassett Company of Cincinnati, believes tests developed by psychologists that do not ask directly about the applicant's past honesty are poor predictors of future trustworthiness. This may be because, as some psychologists report, "it is very difficult for dishonest people to fake honesty." One reason is that thieves tend to believe that "everybody does it" and that therefore it would be implausible for them to deny stealing. In general, those who market honesty exams boast of their validity and reliability, as established by field studies. They insist that the tests do make a difference, and that they enable employers to ferret out potential troublemakers—as in the Salvation Army case.

Dr. Jones administered London House's PSI to eighty kettler applicants, which happened to be the number that the particular theft-ridden center needed. The PSIs were not scored, and the eighty applicants were hired with no screening. Throughout the fund-raising month between Thanksgiving and Christmas, the center kept a record of each kettler's daily receipts. After the Christmas season, the tests were scored and divided into "recommended" and "not recommended" for employment. After accounting for the peculiarities of each collection neighborhood, Jones discovered that those kettlers the PSI had not recommended turned in on the average $17 per day less than those the PSI had recommended. Based on this analysis, he estimated the center's loss to employee theft during the fund drive at $20,000.

The list of psychological-test enthusiasts is growing by leaps and bounds, but the tests have plenty of detractors. Many psychologists believe the tests often lack validity or reliability, and the American Psychological Association favors the establishment of federal standards for written honesty exams. But the chief critics of honesty and other psychological exams are the people who have to take them. They complain about having to reveal some of the most intimate details of their lives and opinions.

For example, until an employee filed suit, Rent-A-Center, a Texas corporation, asked both job applicants and employees being considered for promotion true–false questions like these: "I have never indulged in any unusual sex practices," "I am very strongly attracted by members of my own sex," "I go to church almost every week," and "I have difficulty in starting or holding my bowel movements." A manager who was fired for complaining about the test says, "It was ridiculous. The test asked if I loved tall women. How was I supposed to answer that? My wife is 5 feet 3 inches." A spokesman for Rent-A-Center argues that its questionnaire is not unusual and that many other firms use it. Firms who use tests like Rent-A-Center's believe that no one's privacy is being invaded because employees and job applicants can always refuse to take the test.

Discussion Questions

1. Describe how you'd feel if you had to take a psychological test or an honesty test either as an employee or as a precondition for employment. Under what conditions, if any, would you take such a test?

2. How useful or informative do you think such tests are? Is their use a reasonable business policy? Assuming that tests like those described are valid and reliable, are they fair? Explain.

3. Do you think tests like these invade privacy and, if so, that this invasion is justified? Explain why or why not.

4. What ideals, obligations, and effects must be considered in using psychological tests as pre-employment screens? In your view, which is the most important consideration?

5. If you were an employer, would you require either employees or job applicants to pass an honesty exam? Explain the moral principles that support your position.

6. What do you think a business's reaction would be if the government required its executive officers to submit to an honesty test as a precondition for the company's getting a government contract? If, in your opinion, the business would object, does it have any moral grounds for subjecting workers to comparable tests?

7. Utilitarians would not find anything inherently objectionable about psychological tests as long as the interests of all parties were taken into account and given equal consideration before such tests were made a pre-employment screen. Do you think this is generally the case?

8. Should there be a law prohibiting or regulating psychological tests as a pre-employment screen? Should a decision to use these tests be made jointly by management and labor, or is testing for employment an exclusive employer's right?

Case 9.3
She Snoops to Conquer

Jean Fanuchi, Manager of a Moderately Large Department Store, was worried. Shrinkage in the costume jewelry department had continued to rise for the third consecutive month. In fact, this time it had nearly wiped out the department's net profit in sales. Worse, it couldn't be attributed to damage or improper handling of markdowns or even to shoplifting. The only other possibility was in-house theft.

Fanuchi ordered chief of security Matt Katwalski to instruct his security people to keep a special eye on jewelry department employees as they went about their business. She also instructed that packages, purses, and other containers employees carried with them be searched when workers left the store. When these measures failed to turn up any leads, Katwalski suggested they hire a couple of plainclothes officers to observe the store's guards. Fanuchi agreed. But still nothing turned up.

"We're going to have to install a hidden camera at the checkout station in the jewelry department," Katwalski informed the manager.

"I don't know," Fanuchi replied.

"Of course," said Katwalski, "it won't be cheap. But you don't want this problem spreading to other departments, do you?" Fanuchi didn't.

"One other thing," Katwalski said. "I think we should install some microphones in the restroom, stockroom, and employee lounge."

"You mean snoop on our own employees?" Fanuchi asked, surprised.

"We could pick up something that could crack this thing wide open," Katwalski explained.

"But what if our employees found out? How would they feel, being spied on? And then there's the public to consider. Who knows how they'd react? Why, they'd probably think that if we are spying on our own workers, we were surely spying on them. No, Matt," Fanuchi decided. "Frankly, this whole approach troubles me."

"Okay, Ms. Fanuchi, but if it was my store . . ."

Fanuchi cut in, "No."

"You're the boss," said Katwalski.

When the shrinkage continued, Fanuchi finally gave in. She ordered Katwalski to have the camera and microphones installed. Within ten days the camera had nabbed the culprit.

The microphones contributed nothing to the apprehension of the thief. But because of them, Fanuchi and Katwalski learned that at least one store employee was selling marijuana and perhaps hard drugs, that one was planning to quit without notice, that three were getting food

stamps fraudulently, and that one buyer was out to discredit Fanuchi. In solving their shrinkage problem, the pair had unwittingly raised another: What should they do with the information they had gathered while catching the thief?[124]

Discussion Questions

1. If you were Jean Fanuchi, how would you feel about your decision to order the installation of the viewing and listening devices? What other options did she have? Did she overlook any moral considerations or possible consequences?

2. Do employees have a right not to be spied on? If you were an employee at Fanuchi's store, would you think your privacy had been wrongly invaded?

3. How would you assess Fanuchi's actions if you were the owner of the store? Whose interests are more important in this case—the employer's or the employees'?

4. Do you think Fanuchi acted immorally? Why or why not? Evaluate her action by appeal to ethical principles.

5. How should Fanuchi and Katwalski handle the information they've gathered about their employees? What ideals, obligations, or effects are relevant to your answer?

Case 9.4
Protecting the Unborn at Work

The Unobtrusive Factory Sits Behind a Hill-Side Shopping Center in the small college town of Bennington, Vermont. Inside, the men and women make lead automobile batteries for Sears, Goodyear, and other companies. However, until the 1990s, none of the women employed there were able to have children. The reason was simple. The company, Johnson Controls, Inc., refused to hire any who could.[125]

Why? Because tiny toxic particles of lead and lead oxide fill the air inside the plant. According to the company, the levels of lead are low enough for adults but too high for children and fetuses. Numerous scientific studies have shown that lead can damage the brain and central nervous system of a fetus. Moreover, lead lingers in the bloodstream, which means that fetuses can be affected by it even if a woman limits her exposure to lead after she learns she is pregnant. Because of this, Johnson Controls decided that it would exclude women at all fourteen of its factories from jobs that entail high exposure to lead—unless they could prove that they couldn't become pregnant. The company made no exceptions for celibate women or women who used contraceptives. The company's position was simple: "The issue is protecting the health of unborn children."

Johnson Controls' stance was in line with the national Centers for Disease Control's recommendation that women of childbearing age be excluded from jobs involving significant lead exposure. Because by law its standards must be "feasible," Occupational Safety and Health Administration (OSHA) regulations permit chemicals in the workplace that are known to cause harm both to fetuses and to some adult employees. But OSHA holds that employers have a general duty to reduce the hazards of the workplace as far as possible. On this basis, employers such as Olin Corporation, American Cyanamid, General Motors, Monsanto, Allied Chemical, Gulf Oil, and B. F. Goodrich also adopted policies excluding women from chemical plant jobs judged to be hazardous to their potential offspring.

Unfortunately, there are relatively few scientific studies of the effect of exposure to toxic manufacturing chemicals on workers' reproductive health. Only a small percentage of the workplace chemicals with a potential for damaging reproduction have been evaluated, and each year many new chemicals are introduced into factories. Although employers are obviously dealing with many unknowns, no one doubts that they have a moral and legal obligation to control and limit these risks as best they can. Lawsuits and even criminal sanctions have battered companies that have managed hazardous chemicals irresponsibly. Monsanto Chemical Company, for example, agreed to pay $1.5 million to six employees because exposure to a chemical additive used for rubber production allegedly gave them bladder cancer. Fetal protection policies aren't just dictated by management, though. "Women who become pregnant," the *New York Times* reports, "are beginning to demand the right to transfer out of jobs they believe to be hazardous, even when there is only sketchy scientific evidence of any hazard."

But many women were unhappy about the decision of Johnson Controls. They worried that fetal protection policies would be used to exclude women from more and more workplaces on the grounds that different chemical substances or certain tasks such as heavy lifting might be potential causes of miscarriage and fetal injury. In line with this, the United Automobile Workers, which represents many of the Johnson employees, sought to overturn the U.S. Court of Appeals decision that judged Johnson's policy to be "reasonably necessary to the industrial safety-based concern of protecting the unborn child from lead exposure." The union contends, to the contrary, that the policy discriminates against women, jeopardizing their hard-won gains in male-dominated industries.

Many women's advocates see the issue in slightly different terms. They believe policies like that of Johnson Controls challenge a woman's right not only to control her fetus but to control her unfertilized eggs as well. In addition, such policies infringe on privacy: By taking a job at Johnson, a woman was in effect telling the world that she was sterile. And there is also the fundamental question of who knows what is best for a woman.

After bearing two children, Cheryl Chalifoux had a doctor block her fallopian tubes so that she couldn't become pregnant again. Although career advancement wasn't the reason she made her decision, it did enable her to switch from a factory job paying $6.34 an hour to one at Johnson's Bennington plant paying $15 an hour. Still, she says that the policy was unfair and degrading. "It's your body," she complains. "They're implying they're doing it for your own good." Cheryl Cook, also a mother of two who had surgery for the same reason, joined Chalifoux in leaving the other company to work for Johnson Controls. She says, "I work right in the lead. I make the oxide. But you should choose for yourself. Myself, I wouldn't go in there if I could get pregnant. But they don't trust you."

Isabelle Katz Pizler, director of women's rights at the American Civil Liberties Union, agrees. "Since time immemorial," she says, "the excuse for keeping women in their place has been because of their role in producing the next generation. The attitude of Johnson Controls is: 'We know better than you. We can't allow women to make this decision. We have to make it for them.'" And the ACLU has argued in court that "since no activity is risk-free, deference to an employer's analysis of fetal risk could limit women's participation in nearly every area of economic life."

To this, the company responded that it has a moral obligation to the parties that cannot participate in the woman's decisions—namely, the unfertilized ovum and the fetus. In addition, the company has an obligation to stockholders, who would bear the brunt of lawsuits brought by employees' children born with congenital disabilities, nervous system disorders, or other ailments that lead can cause.

Joseph A. Kinney, executive director of the National Safe Workplace Institute in Chicago, sides with Johnson Controls, but only because he believes that letting women assume the burden of their safety

ZUMA Press, Inc./Alamy Stock Photo

Should pregnant police officers or military personnel be allowed to be in situations that endanger the life of their unborn child?

undermines OSHA's responsibility to mandate workplace safety rules. "The discrimination side of the issue needs to be resolved," Kinney says. "But the ideal thing is to regulate lead out of the workplace and any other toxin that poses fetal damage."

However, the U.S. Supreme Court ruled unanimously that the fetal protection policy at Johnson Controls violated the Civil Rights Act of 1964, which prohibits sex discrimination in employment.[126] Pointing to evidence that lead affects sperm and can thus harm the offspring of men exposed to it at the time of conception, the Court stated:

> Respondent does not seek to protect the unconceived children of all its employees. Despite evidence in the record about the debilitating effect of lead exposure on the male reproductive system, Johnson Controls is concerned only with the harms that may befall the unborn offspring of its female employees. . . . [The company's policy is] discriminatory because it requires only a female employee to produce proof that she is not capable of reproducing.

The Court was divided over whether fetal protection policies could ever be legally justified. Justice Harry A. Blackmun, writing for a majority of the Court, declared that they could not, that the Civil Rights Act prohibited all such policies:

> Decisions about the welfare of future children must be left to the parents who conceive, bear, support and raise them rather than to the employers who hire those parents. Women as capable of doing their jobs as their male counterparts may not be forced to choose between having a child and having a job.

Referring to the Pregnancy Discrimination Act of 1978, which amended the 1964 Civil Rights Act and prohibits employment discrimination on the basis of pregnancy or potential pregnancy, Blackmun added:

> Employment late in pregnancy often imposes risks on the unborn child, but Congress indicated that the employer may take into account only the woman's ability to get her job done.

A minority of the justices, however, were unwilling to go so far, and in a concurring opinion, Justice Byron R. White wrote that "common sense tells us that it is part of the normal operation of business concerns to avoid causing injury to third parties as well as to employees." But he added that, in his view, a fetal protection policy would not be defensible unless an employer also addressed other known occupational health risks.

Discussion Questions

1. Do you agree that Johnson Controls' fetal protection policy discriminated against women? Do pregnant women have a moral—not just a legal—right to work with lead?

2. Suppose exposure to lead did not affect sperm or the male reproductive system. Would Johnson's policy still have been discriminatory? Would it hamper women's efforts to win equality in the workplace?

3. Can there be a nondiscriminatory fetal protection policy? Is Justice White correct in arguing that companies have an obligation to avoid causing injury to fetuses just as they do to other "third parties"?

4. Suppose a company forbids any employee capable of reproducing from working with lead. Would such a policy wrongly interfere with employees' freedom of choice? Would it be an invasion of their privacy? Would it be fair to employees who are fertile but plan to have no children?

5. Evaluate fetal protection policies from the egoistic, utilitarian, and Kantian perspectives. What rights are involved? What are the likely benefits and harms of such policies?

6. If they are fully informed, do employees with a certain medical condition have a right to work at jobs that can be hazardous to the health of people in their condition? Or can company policy or OSHA regulations justifiably prevent them from doing so for their own good?

7. Would you agree with Joseph Kinney that the real issue is the need to remove toxins from the workplace? Is this a realistic goal?

Case 9.5

Swedish Daddies

Years Ago, Famous Economist Paul Samuelson Quipped that "women are just men with less money." He was referring to the financially dependent position of women at that time, when they were unlikely to be employed outside the home and, if they were, were likely to earn substantially less than men. That has now changed for the better. Although women have yet to achieve full equity at the highest levels of business, they constitute nearly half the U.S. workforce, and across the economy the pay disparity between men and women is at least diminishing. Moreover, with the decline of manufacturing and the growing importance of the service sector in today's economy, brain power matters more than brawn. Here, women can compete as well as men, and they have proved their value to employers over and over again. In fact, they now outnumber men in professional and managerial positions. And with women continuing to graduate from college at a higher rate and in greater numbers than men, their future looks bright.[127]

Nevertheless, many women feel forced to choose between motherhood and a high-powered career. Jobs that offer the hours and flexibility that suit women with family responsibilities tend to pay less, while the most financially rewarding jobs frequently require brutal hours and total commitment to the job. And the higher you go, the rougher it gets. Not only must those who want to fight their way to the top of the corporate world work long, grueling hours, but they are also often expected to gain experience working in different departments and divisions and even in different countries. That tends to rule out women with family commitments. As a result, women with children, especially single mothers, earn less on average than men do, while childless women earn almost as much as men.

Over the years, some business writers have argued that we should simply accept this fact and that companies should distinguish between the career-primary woman and the career-and-family woman. Those in the first category put their careers first. They remain single or childless or, if they do have children, are satisfied to have other people's help to raise them. The automatic association of all women with babies is unfair to these women, argues Felice N. Schwartz, an organizer and advocate for working women. "The secret to dealing with such women," she writes, "is to recognize them early, accept them, and clear artificial barriers from their path to the top."

The majority of women, however, fall into the second category. They want to pursue genuine careers while participating actively in the rearing of their children. Most of them, Schwartz and others believe, are willing to trade some career growth and compensation for freedom from the constant pressure to work long hours and weekends. By forcing these women to choose between family and career, companies lose a valuable resource and a competitive advantage. Instead, firms must plan for and manage maternity leave, they must provide the flexibility to help career-and-family women be maximally productive, and they must take an active role in providing family support and in making high-quality, affordable child care available to all women. In other words, companies should provide women with the option of a comfortable but slower "mommy track."

Although distinguishing between career-primary women and career-and-family women seems reasonable and humane, there's rarely any mention of fathers or of shared parental responsibility for raising children. The mommy track idea also takes for granted the existing values, structures, and biases of a corporate world that is still male dominated. As authors Barbara Ehrenreich and Deidre English write, "Eventually it is the corporate culture itself that needs to slow down to a human pace . . . [and end] workloads that are incompatible with family life."

One country that is trying to push things in a new direction is Sweden. Whereas America stands almost alone in the world in not guaranteeing women paid maternity leave, Sweden provides sixteen months paid leave per child, with the costs shared between the employer and the government. However—and this is what is novel—at least two of these months are reserved for fathers. No father is forced to take baby leave, but the leave is nontransferable so It's "use it or lose it." And more and more men are using it. In fact, more than eight in ten Swedish fathers now take advantage of parental leave. And some Swedish politicians are arguing that more months—perhaps half of them—should be exclusively for fathers. Germany has now followed Sweden's lead. In 2007 it began guaranteeing fathers two months' paternity leave. No country, however, has gone further toward parental equity than Iceland. It reserves three months of parental leave for the father and three months for the mother and allows parents to share an additional three months.

In the meantime, the paternity-leave law is helping to redefine masculinity in Sweden. Take game warden Mikael Karlson. A former soldier who owns a snowmobile, two hunting dogs, and five guns, in many ways he embodies a familiar masculine stereotype. Cradling his two-month-old baby girl in his arms, he says he cannot imagine not taking parental leave. "Everyone does it." Not only does his wife agree, but she says that he never looks more attractive to her than "when he is in the forest with his rifle over his shoulder and the baby on his back." Some men admit that they were unsure of themselves at first—the cooking, cleaning, and sleepless nights—but that they adjusted to it and even liked it. One Swedish father calls it a "life-changing experience."

"Many men no longer want to be identified just by their jobs," says Bengt Westerberg, who as deputy prime minister helped to bring the law about. "Many women now expect their husbands to take at least some time off with the children." "Now men can have it all—a successful career and being a responsible daddy," adds Birgitta Ohlsson, another government minister. "It's a new kind of manly. It's more wholesome." Some also think the paternity-leave law is the reason that the divorce rate in Sweden has declined in recent years.

There are, however, stories of companies' discouraging men from taking long baby leaves, and managers admit that parental leave can be disruptive. Still, by and large, Swedish business has adapted, and many companies find that a family-friendly work environment helps them attract talented employees. "Graduates used to look for big paychecks," says one human resources manager. "Now they want work–life balance."

Many men in the United States would like a better balance between work life and family life, too. But even when paternity leave is an option, men are reluctant to take it. One reason is the attitude of their colleagues and employers, who tend to believe that, for men, work should come first. And, indeed, a recent study has found that fathers who are active care-givers are seen as distracted and less dedicated and that they are more likely than the so-called traditional fathers to be teased and insulted at work, accused of being "wimpy" or "henpecked" by their wives. Because of this or because they do not put their jobs first, they earn lower salaries than do men in traditional breadwinner roles.[128]

Discussion Questions

1. If you have, or plan to have, children, what sort of balance do you seek between career and family life? Do you believe that the mindset of corporate America is conducive to the type of work-and-family arrangement that would suit you?

2. Should the United States require companies to provide paid maternity leave? Should it assist them to do so? What about paternity leave?

3. Do companies already have a mommy track, whether they call it that or not? Is the idea a good one? Is it somehow discriminatory against women? Against men?

4. Should men be more actively involved in childrearing? If not, why not? If so, what steps, if any, should either business or society take to encourage this?

5. Should special organizational arrangements be made for workers who wish to combine career and child raising? If so, identify the steps that companies can take to accommodate parental needs more effectively.

6. Does a firm have an obligation to give employees the flexibility to work out the particular balance of career and family that is right for them? Or does this go beyond the social responsibilities of business?

7. Can paid maternity or paternity leave make sense from a business point of view, even if it's not subsidized by the government?

Chapter 10

Moral Choices Facing Employees

Learning Objectives

After completing this chapter, you should be able to:

1. Contrast different perspectives on employees' obligation to demonstrate loyalty to the firm.

2. Recognize conflicts of interest and explain why they should be avoided when possible.

3. Explain what is morally problematic about the illegitimate use of one's official position for private gain, especially through insider trading or access to proprietary data.

4. Explain the moral perils of domestic and foreign bribery and the factors to consider in determining the morality of giving and receiving gifts in a business context.

5. Apply the procedure for moral decision making recommended in Chapter 2 to cases in which employees have conflicting moral duties or divided loyalties.

6. Analyze cases in which employees report unfavorable news about their firms to determine whether the employees were whistle-blowers, and if so, whether they were justified in "blowing the whistle."

7. Describe the factors that employees should take into account in situations in which morality and self-interest seem to pull them in different directions.

Introduction

When His Eldest Daughter Asked Him, "Why Don't You Just Do what they want?," George Betancourt wasn't sure how he should answer. Betancourt was a senior engineer at Northeast Utilities, which operates five nuclear power plants in New England, and all he had done was to speak up and express his professional judgment. Now Northeast wanted him to shut up. First, Northeast's human resources officer had called him in. After complaining that Betancourt wasn't being a "team player," she described to him the company's termination policies. Three weeks later, Betancourt was informed he was being reassigned. "We'd like to help you, George," Eric DeBarba, vice president of technical services, told him. "But you've got to start thinking company."[1]

George Galatis was the Northeast engineer on whose behalf Betancourt had spoken up. Galatis had discovered what he considered to be a glaring safety problem at Northeast's Millstone No. 1 plant. In an effort to save downtime (and hence money) during the refueling process, the plant's procedures routinely violated federal guidelines and pushed its spent-fuel pool well beyond its design capacity. For eighteen months, Galatis's supervisors denied the problem existed

> Galatis had discovered
> what he considered
> to be a glaring safety
> problem at Northeast's
> Millstone No. 1 plant.

and refused to report it to the Nuclear Regulatory Commission (NRC). Northeast brought in a series of outside experts to prove Galatis wrong, but the consultants ended up agreeing with him. Within the company, Betancourt backed up Galatis's safety concerns. When Northeast finally began to acknowledge a possible problem, it didn't move fast enough to satisfy Galatis. Two years after he first raised his safety concerns, he finally took the case directly to the NRC, only to learn that it had known about the unsafe procedures for years. He also discovered evidence that suggested collusion between Northeast and NRC officials to subordinate safety to profitability.

As a result of going to the NRC, Galatis experienced "subtle forms of harassment, retaliation, and intimidation." He wasn't being paranoid. Two dozen Millstone No. 1 employees claimed they were fired or demoted for raising safety concerns. Some of his colleagues sided with the company, however, accusing Galatis of aiding anti-nuclear activists and trying to take away their livelihood. But Galatis didn't stop. He hired a lawyer who specializes in representing whistle-blowers and kept after the NRC. With the lawyer's help, the public spotlight was focused on Millstone No. 1. Local politicians began asking questions. Even though the NRC ignored Galatis, it ended up validating his concerns, and Millstone No. 1 was shut down. Citing chronic safety concerns, employee harassment, and a "historic emphasis on cost savings vs. performance," the NRC also put Northeast's other two Millstone plants on its high-scrutiny "watch list." And a new NRC head vowed to shake up the regulatory body itself.

Galatis and Betancourt managed to hang on to their jobs, but their careers came to a standstill. "The two Georges had better watch their backs," says one engineer. "Up at Northeast, they've got long memories." A disillusioned Galatis says, "If I had it to do over again, I wouldn't."

For someone in the same position of George Galatis or George Betancourt, two general issues come up. *First* is the question of where an employee's overall moral duty lies. For a professional engineer to go public with documented safety concerns may seem to be a more straightforward moral decision than that faced by an employee who suspects irregularities, unsafe procedures, or wrongdoing in an area unrelated to their own job. In that case, the employee may possibly have

conflicting moral obligations. Furthermore, if an employee reports such irregularities to the appropriate authority, the employee must then decide whether they are morally obligated to pursue the matter further. Again, other moral considerations come into play.

Second, once they have decided that they ought to blow the whistle, employees must face the possible negative consequences. Galatis and Betancourt are skilled, mature, and respected professionals, with established records and good credentials; in terms of employment options, they may have had less to risk than do potential whistle-blowers who are just starting their careers or who have limited job options or heavy financial obligations. This is not simply a tug-of-war between moral duty and self-interest. Most moral theorists would agree that depending on the circumstances, certain personal sacrifices might be so great that a person cannot reasonably be morally obliged to make them.

These two themes—determining one's moral responsibility amid a welter of conflicting demands and paying the personal costs that can be incurred from living up to one's obligations—recur throughout this chapter.

Obligations to the Firm

When you accept employment, you generally agree to perform certain tasks, usually during certain specified hours, in exchange for financial remuneration. Whether oral or written, implicit or explicit, a contract governs your employment relationship and provides the basic framework for understanding the reciprocal obligations between you and your employer. Your employment contract determines what you are supposed to do or accomplish for your employer, and it may cover other matters ranging from parking privileges to your dress and deportment while carrying out your responsibilities. The terms of your employment contract may be specific and detailed or vague and open-ended.

The employment contract governs the employer–employee relationship and provides the framework for understanding the respective obligations of employer and employee.

Loyalty to the Company

Because you are hired to work for your employer, you have an obligation, when acting on behalf of the organization, to promote your employer's interests. Insofar as you are acting as an agent of your employer, the traditional law of agency places you under a legal obligation to act loyally and in good faith and to carry out all lawful instructions. For example, Polo Ralph Lauren successfully sued a sales clerk for violating the clerk's duty of loyalty by letting a friend buy clothes with an employee discount and with merchandise credits made out to fictitious people. The employee argued that he was such a low-level employee that he had no duty of loyalty, but the court disagreed.[2] However, it would be morally mistaken to view employees simply as agents of their employers or to expect them to subordinate entirely their autonomy and private lives to the organization. Morality requires neither blind loyalty nor total submission to the organization.

Some writers deny that employees have any obligation of loyalty to the company, even a prima facie obligation, "because companies are not the kind of things that are properly objects of loyalty." Why not? Because a business firm functions to make money, the argument goes, self-interest is all that binds it together, whereas "loyalty depends on ties that demand self-sacrifice with no expectation of reward."[3] From this perspective, then, one can owe loyalty to family, friends, or country but not to a corporation; employees simply work to get paid and are misguided if they see themselves as owing loyalty to the company.

However, the notion of **company loyalty** is commonplace, and most people find it a coherent and legitimate concept. For the many employees who willingly make sacrifices for the organization above and beyond their job descriptions, loyalty is a real and important value. Indeed, it is not clear how well any business or organization could function without employee loyalty, and certainly most companies want more than minimal time and effort from their employees. Loyalty, though, is a two-way street, and most employees believe that it's up to the company to earn and retain their loyalty.

Arguably, some obligations of loyalty simply come with the job—for example, the obligation to warn the organization of danger, the obligation to act in a way that protects its legitimate interests, and the obligation to cooperate actively in the furtherance of legitimate corporate goals. To be sure, many businesses demand more than this in the name of loyalty. They may expect employees to defend the company if it is maligned, to mentor coworkers, to work overtime when the company needs it, to accept a transfer if it is necessary for the good of the organization, or to demonstrate their commitment to it in countless other ways. Being loyal in these ways may be important to an employee, even if it is not morally required. In addition, employees, like other individuals, can come to identify with the groups they are part of, accepting group goals and norms as their own. Some moral theorists believe not only that loyalty to the group can become an important value for the individual employee, but also that in the appropriate circumstances the process of group identification can create an additional obligation of loyalty that the employee otherwise would not have.[4]

> Although some writers deny that employees owe loyalty to the company, most people find company loyalty a coherent and legitimate concept.

Conflicts of Interest

Even the most loyal employees can find that their interests collide with those of the organization. You want to dress one way, but the organization requires you to dress another way; you'd prefer to show up for work at noon, but the company expects you to be present at 8 A.M.; you'd like to receive $75,000 for your services, but the organization pays you a fraction of that figure. The reward, autonomy, and self-fulfillment that workers seek aren't always compatible with the demands of the organization. Whatever the matter in question, the perspectives of employee and employer can differ.

Sometimes, this clash of goals and desires can take the serious form of a conflict of interest. In an organization, a **conflict of interest** arises when employees at any level have special or private interests that are substantial enough to interfere with their job duties—that is, when

Are employees who publicly protest wages or working conditions being disloyal to their employer?

Summary
The employment
contract creates
various obligations
to one's employer. In
addition, employees
often feel loyalty to
the organization.
Conflicts of interest arise
when employees have
a personal interest in a
transaction substantial
enough that it might be
expected to affect their
judgment or lead them to
act against the interests
of the organization.

their personal interests lead them, or might be anticipated to lead them, to make decisions or to act in ways that are detrimental to their employer's interests. That was certainly the case when Enron's former chief financial officer, Andrew Fastow, represented the company in negotiations with several firms of which he was a managing partner (and, as a result, eventually earned millions of dollars from the deals).

As mentioned, the work contract is the primary source of an organization's right to expect employees to act on its behalf in a way that is unprejudiced by their personal interests. In general, if the contents of the work agreement are legal and if the employee freely consents to them, then they are under an obligation to fulfill the terms of the agreement. Implicit in any work contract is the assumption that employees will not sacrifice the interests of the organization for personal advantage. Of course, individuals may seek to benefit from being employed with a certain business or organization, but in discharging their contractual duties, employees should not subordinate the welfare of the organization to their own gain.

When an employee's private interests run counter to the interests of their employer in some significant way—or, to put the point differently, when those interests are likely to interfere with the employee's ability to exercise proper judgment on behalf of the organization—a conflict of interest exists. The danger, then, is that those interests will lead the employee to sacrifice the interests of their employer. For example, Bart Erdman, sales manager for Leisure Sports World, gives all his firm's promotional work to Impact Advertising because its chief officer is Erdman's brother-in-law. As a result, Leisure Sports World pays about 15 percent more in advertising costs than it would if its work went to another agency. Here, Erdman has allowed his decisions as an employee to be influenced by his personal interests, to the detriment of Leisure Sports World. Note that Erdman's interest is not financial; conflicts of interest can take various forms.

Suppose that Erdman does not throw all of his company's promotional work to his brother-in-law; rather, he gives the firm's business to his brother-in-law only when he sincerely believes that doing so is best for Leisure Sports World. Nevertheless, a conflict of interest can still be said to exist. Because of his brother-in-law, Erdman still has a private interest in his business dealings for Leisure Sports World that could possibly lead him to act against the interests of the company. In other words, there is a danger that Bart's judgment may not be as objective as it should be.

Conflicts of interest are
morally worrisome even
if the employee doesn't
act to the detriment of the
employer.

Conflicts of interest are morally worrisome not only when an employee acts to the detriment of the organization but also when the employee's private interests are significant enough that they could tempt the person to do so. Indeed, research shows that conflicts of interest can unconsciously distort the decisions of even very honest people.[5] That's why alarm bells went off when *Businessweek* disclosed that two members of the audit committee at Qwest Communications—already under fire for dubious accounting practices—directed companies with million-dollar contracts with Qwest, thus raising questions about their ability to exercise independent judgment.[6] Even the appearance of impropriety can undermine trust and erode the confidence that others are entitled to have in the impartiality and objectivity of one's decisions. The revelation that some Supreme Court justices had accepted gifts and hospitality from wealthy individuals who have had or might in the future have business before the Court damaged the Court's credibility, despite the absence of direct evidence that this affected their decisions. The situation is still rife with conflicts of interest.

By definition, to have a conflict of interest is to be in a morally risky situation; that is why employees should promptly extricate themselves from such conflicts or avoid them in the first place. But deciding when an employee's private interests are substantial enough for the situation to constitute a conflict of interest can be difficult. Equally difficult can be deciding exactly how the person should deal with a specific conflict. Sometimes people are encouraged simply to disclose the conflict to those relying on their judgment, thus preventing deception and allowing those relying on them to adjust their reliance accordingly. That is often good counsel, but it doesn't end the conflict of interest. Moreover, it's no panacea. Supposedly, if I tell you that I have a financial reason for skewing my advice to you, you'll take that into account and everything will be fine. Unfortunately, however, experimental evidence suggests that even when informed that the advice they're receiving may be biased, people fail to discount it as much as they should.[7] Moreover, those who disclose a conflict of interest often end up giving more biased advice than those who do not disclose.[8]

Finally, it is worth mentioning auditors. They face a different sort of conflict, namely, between their duty to report the truth and their running successful businesses. That's because they are hired and paid by the companies that they are supposed to audit. It's one of the reasons credit-rating agencies were so generous, to put it mildly, in their grading of many financial products in the run-up to the subprime mortgage crisis. A large Harvard study has now confirmed what one might have guessed: When auditors are paid by a third party, they report more accurately.[9]

Financial Investments

Conflicts of interest may exist when employees have financial investments in suppliers, customers, or distributors with whom their organizations do business. During the dot-com boom, executives at high-tech firms often owned stock in other young companies in the same or closely related fields. Those tangled financial relationships sometimes produced conflicts of interest. For example, eight executives at EMC were heavily invested in the start-up StorageNetworks. They recommended it to their clients, and those referrals quickly grew to 40 percent of the younger company's business. But as StorageNetworks got larger and as EMC expanded its own services division, the two companies found themselves competing, leading some at EMC to complain that the other firm was poaching its employees and interfering with its customer relationships. Today, EMC says the impact on business was negligible. But a former board member maintains that the eight executives were recommending StorageNetworks when they should have been pushing EMC equipment: "No question, it had an impact on their day-to-day decisions. It was a tremendous financial incentive."[10]

How much of a financial investment does it take to create a conflict of interest? There's no simple answer. Certainly, it is acceptable to own stock in large publicly held corporations, such as Coca-Cola or Hewlett-Packard, that are listed on the stock exchange and whose stock price is unlikely to be influenced by your company's buying their products or not. Sometimes companies limit the percentage of outstanding stock their employees may own in a potential supplier, customer, distributor, or competitor (usually up to 10 percent). But in the EMC case, the eight executives owned shares of StorageNetworks before the company went public, and with the latter's stock rocketing from 50 cents a share to over $90, adhering to the 10 percent rule wouldn't have prevented the problem. Frequently, companies require key officials to disclose all outside interests that could cloud their judgment or adversely affect their ability to promote the organization's interests. That's important, but as previously mentioned, full disclosure alone doesn't make the conflict disappear; further steps should probably still be taken. Organizations need a detailed policy, customized to reflect their needs and interests, that spells out the limits of permissible outside financial investments and what employees should do when they have possible conflicts of interest. Because such a policy can affect the financial well-being of those who fall under it, however, it should be open to negotiation just as employee compensation is.

Summary
When employees have financial investments in suppliers, customers, or distributors with whom their organization does business, conflicts of interest can arise. Company policy usually determines the permissible limits of such financial interests.

• • •

Abuse of Official Position

The use of one's official position for personal gain always raises moral concerns and questions because of the likelihood that one is violating one's obligations to the firm or organization. Examples of **abuse of official position** range from misusing expense accounts to billing the company for unnecessary travel and from using subordinates for work outside the firm to exploiting a position of trust within an organization to enhance one's own financial leverage and holdings. Executives who use corporate funds for private purposes like health club memberships, extravagant parties, vacation travel, or remodeling their homes are guilty of abusing their official position, as were Bernard J. Ebbers of WorldCom, John Legere of Global Crossing, and L. Dennis Kozlowski of Tyco International, who used their high positions to borrow huge amounts of money at below-market rates—in Ebbers's case over $400 million— from the companies they worked for.[11]

Using one's official position for personal gain is likely to violate one's obligations to the organization.

Insider Trading

One common way of abusing one's official position is through **insider trading**: the buying or selling of stocks (or other financial securities) by business "insiders" on the basis of information that has not yet been made public and is likely to affect the price of the stock.[12] For example, as soon as he learned that the Food and Drug Administration (FDA) was not going to approve his company's highly touted cancer drug Erbitux, Dr. Sam Waksal, CEO of ImClone Systems at the time, knew its stock would plummet. Before the FDA's decision was made public, Waksal quickly but quietly sold his stock in the company and told his father and one of his daughters to do so as well. He is also alleged to have passed the word on to his friend Martha Stewart, who dumped her ImClone stock the day before the FDA announced its decision. One doesn't have to profit personally to cross the line, however. For example, the wife of Genentech's president and chief executive officer was charged with insider trading for providing confidential information to her brother. Before the biotechnology firm was partly acquired by another company, she told her brother that "some good things were about to happen" to the company and suggested that he buy a few thousand dollars' worth of stock, even if he had to borrow the funds. She also advised him to keep the purchase secret and make it in the name of a "trustworthy" friend.

Inside traders ordinarily defend their actions by claiming that they don't injure anyone. It's true that trading by insiders on the basis of nonpublic information seldom directly harms anyone. But moral concerns arise from indirect injury, as well as from direct. As one author puts it, "What causes injury or loss to outsiders is not what the insiders knew or did; rather it is what [the outsiders] themselves did not know. It is their own lack of knowledge which exposes them to risk of loss or denies them an opportunity to make a profit."[13] Case in point: the famous Texas Gulf Sulphur stock scandal.

When test drilling by Texas Gulf indicated a rich deposit of ore near Timmins, Ontario, some officials at Texas Gulf attempted to play down the potential worth of the Timmins property in a press release by describing it as only a prospect. But four days later a second press release termed the Timmins property a major discovery. In the interim, inside investors made a handsome personal profit through stock purchases. At the same time, stockholders who unloaded stock after the first press release or who sold the stock short, anticipating its price would fall, lost money.

In December 2013, a jury found Michael Steinberg, a trader at SAC Capital Advisors, guilty of insider trading. Some consider insider trading a victimless crime. Do you agree?

The Securities and Exchange Commission (SEC), which is charged with policing the stock market, subsequently charged that a group of insiders—including Texas Gulf directors, officers, and employees—had violated the disclosure section of the Securities Exchange Act of 1934 by purchasing stock in the company while withholding information about the rich ore strike the company had made. The courts upheld the charge, finding that the first press release was "misleading to the reasonable investor using due care."[14] As a result, the courts not only ordered the insiders to pay into a special court-administered account all the money they had made but also directed them to repay profits made by outsiders whom they had tipped off. The courts then used this account to compensate people who had lost money by selling their Texas Gulf Sulphur stock on the basis of the first press release.

Insiders and "Misappropriation"

Insider dealings raise intriguing questions. When can employees buy and sell securities in their own companies? How much information must they disclose to stockholders about the firm's plans and prospects? When must this information be disclosed? There's also the question: Who is considered an insider? Corporate executives, directors, officers, and other key employees are certainly insiders. But what about outsiders whom a company temporarily employs, such as accountants, lawyers, and contractors? Or what about those who just happen upon inside information?

In its effort to police the marketplace, the SEC has interpreted "insider" in a broad sense to mean anyone who buys or sells stock based on nonpublic information—whether or not the person is a corporate officer or otherwise linked to the company whose stock is being bought or sold. However, in 1980 the U.S. Supreme Court challenged the SEC's broad conception of insider trading in the case of Vincent Chiarella, a financial printer who traded on information he culled from documents passing through his shop. The Court ruled that Chiarella was not an insider with fiduciary responsibilities and thus had not violated the Securities Exchange Act. The Court reinforced its decision three years later when it reversed the conviction of securities analyst Raymond Dirks, who advised several of his clients to dump their shares in a company that he was about to blow the whistle on for fraud. In so ruling, the Court held that there is nothing improper about an outsider's using information, as long as the information is not obtained from an insider who breaches a legal duty to the corporation's shareholders for personal gain or to show favor to friends.

Since then the SEC has developed a new tactic, arguing that people who trade on confidential information but who are not, strictly speaking, company insiders are guilty of insider trading if they have "misappropriated" sensitive information. Although some appellate courts had rejected the SEC's approach, in 1997 the Supreme Court endorsed the misappropriation theory of insider trading in **U.S. v. O'Hagan**, thus upholding one of the SEC's main legal weapons against insider trading. In this case, James O'Hagan, a lawyer, had reaped a $4.3 million profit after learning that a company represented by his law firm was planning a hostile takeover of another company. O'Hagan had not worked on the case himself, but he had—the Court ruled—misappropriated confidential information belonging to his firm and its client. Writing for the majority, Justice Ruth Bader Ginsburg stressed that the Court's decision reflected the "animating purpose" of the Securities Exchange Act, namely, "to insure honest securities markets and thereby promote investor confidence."

Conflicting Perspectives on Insider Trading

Arthur Levitt, Jr., chairman of the Securities and Exchange Commission at the time, applauds the Court's O'Hagan decision, stating that it "reaffirms the SEC's effort to make the stock market fair to all people, whether you're a Wall Street veteran or a Main Street newcomer."[15] Law professor Henry Manne, however, sees nothing inherently wrong with insider trading and thinks the SEC should stay totally out of the insider-trading field. "The use of insider information should be governed by private contractual relationships," he believes, such as those between a corporation and its personnel or among the partners and associates of a law firm.[16]

Some business theorists dispute the need to outlaw insider trading.

Summary

Insider trading is the buying or selling of stocks on the basis of nonpublic information likely to affect stock prices. Insider trading seems unfair; it can injure other investors and undermine public confidence in the stock market. In practice, determining what counts as insider trading is not always easy, but it typically involves misappropriating sensitive information. Although some writers defend insider trading as performing a necessary and desirable economic function, executives who do it are putting their own interests before those of the company and its shareholders.

At the core of this disagreement are two opposed perspectives on what makes the market work. Levitt and like-minded analysts contend that the marketplace can work only if it is perceived as being honest and offering equal investment opportunity. Insider trading, they argue, makes that impossible. Those who think like Manne believe that permitting insiders to trade is good for the market because it accelerates the flow of positive or negative information about the stock to other shareholders and investors. As a result, this information is more quickly reflected in the stock's price, which is healthy for the market. They also believe that permitting insider trading can benefit a company by providing employees an incentive to invent new products, put together deals, or otherwise create new information that will increase the value of a company's stock.

Contrary to the view expressed by Manne, however, it's difficult to believe that insider trading does much to promote genuine market efficiency. That's because insiders hoard information, profiting on the lag between when they start buying or selling and when the rest of the market learns what the insiders already know. In addition, insiders can benefit from negative, not just positive, information about the company they work for; this creates a dangerous incentive for them to act in ways that hurt it. Even if insider trading does promote market efficiency in some cases, this fact would have to be weighed against its moral drawbacks.

Insider trading makes some ordinary investors worse off than they would have been if they had had the same information. This strikes many people as unfair. True, it's not always unfair for one party to a transaction to know more than another, but insider traders often do seem to be taking unfair advantage of outsiders. Moreover, as Justice Ginsburg and Arthur Levitt suggest, widespread perception that "the game is rigged" would discourage ordinary investors from buying stocks. Even more important, when executives engage in insider trading, they are putting their own interests ahead of their shareholders, thus violating the fiduciary responsibility that is central to business management. All employees, but especially company insiders, have a duty to act in the interests of the firm and its shareholders, but many ways of profiting from insider information do not benefit the company at all—indeed, they may damage its interests.[17]

The information that employees garner within the company is not always the kind that affects stock prices. Sometimes the information concerns highly sensitive data related to company research, technology, product development, and so on. How employees treat such secret or classified data can also raise important moral issues.

Proprietary Data

Companies guard information that can affect their competitive standing with all the zealousness of a bulldog guarding a ham bone. This is especially true of high-tech firms. A typical example is Lexar Media, which sued Toshiba for abusing its business relation with Lexar and passing the latter's confidential flash-memory technology to SanDisk, one of its competitors.[18] But even in the low-tech world, spats over **proprietary data** break out all the time. Procter & Gamble (P&G), for example, once sued three rival food chains for allegedly using the patented baking technique in its Duncan Hines brand of chocolate-chip cookies to make "infringing cookies." P&G further claimed that these companies had spied at a sales presentation and at cookie plants. One of the defendants, Frito-Lay, admitted to sending a worker to photograph the outside of a Duncan Hines bakery. But it denied telling the man's college-age son to walk into the plant and ask for some unbaked cookie dough—which the enterprising youth did, and got.[19]

Trade Secrets

When novel information is patented or copyrighted, it is legally protected but not secret. Others may have access to the information, but they are forbidden to use it (without permission) for the life of the patent or copyright. When a company patents a process, as Kleenex, for example, did many years ago with pop-up tissues, the company has a monopoly on that process. Until the patent expires, no other firm may compete in the production of pop-up facial tissues. Although on the face of it this rule violates the ideal of a free market and would appear to slow the spread of new processes and technology, patents and copyrights are generally defended on the ground that without them technological innovation would be hampered. Individuals and companies would not be willing to invest in the development of a new process if other firms could immediately exploit any new invention without having invested in developing it.

Although patent law is complicated and patents are not easy to acquire, what it means for something to be patented is well defined legally. By contrast, the concept of a trade secret is broad and imprecise. The standard legal definition says that a **trade secret** is "any formula, pattern, device, or compilation of information which is used in one's business and which gives him an opportunity to obtain an advantage over competitors who do not know or use it."[20] Virtually any information that is not generally known (or whose utility is not recognized) is eligible for classification as a trade secret, as long as such information is valuable to its possessor and is treated confidentially. Most states have laws against the theft of trade secrets, and the **Economic Espionage Act** of 1996 makes it a federal crime. By contrast with patents and copyrights, one does not have to declare or register something as a trade secret for it to be protected. Trade secrets, however, do not enjoy the same protection as patented information. The formula for Coca-Cola, for instance, is secret, as is the recipe for KFC's "finger-lickin' good" chicken, but neither is patented. No competitor has yet succeeded in figuring them out by "reverse engineering," but if your company managed to do so, then it would be entitled to use this information itself.

There are at least three arguments for legally protecting trade secrets: (1) Trade secrets are the intellectual property of the company, (2) the theft of trade secrets is unfair competition, and (3) employees who disclose trade secrets violate the confidentiality owed to their employers.[21] In individual cases, what constitutes intellectual property, unfair competition, or a violation of confidentiality is often controversial. But clearly, one of the biggest challenges facing an organization can be to prevent its trade secrets and proprietary data from being misused by employees who leave the company.

Employees Who Join a Competitor

Employees who leave the company are often privy to confidential or proprietary information, which their new employer can sometimes take unfair advantage of. For example, Starwood Hotels and Resorts charged that when some of its executives left to take high-profile jobs at Hilton Hotels, they brought with them documents that helped Hilton create a new luxury-hotel brand.[22] Or take Thomas' English Muffins. It sued to stop a former employee from going to work for rival company Hostess. He was one of only seven executives who knew the secret, the company said, to producing the muffins' distinctive "nooks and crannies" and their ability to toast up crunchy on the outside and soft on the inside.[23] And Mattel, maker of the famous Barbie doll, sued MGA Entertainment for having gotten the idea for its popular Bratz doll line from a designer it had hired away from Mattel and who had originally conceived the idea while working there.[24] The problem posed by employees who quit to work for a competitor is especially troublesome for high-tech firms because their employees are so prone to job-hopping (at one point, the job tenure of an executive in the software industry was estimated to be a scant twenty-two months)[25] and because of the difficulty of separating trade secrets from the technical know-how, experience, and skill that are part of the employee's own intellect and talents.

A classic case involved Donald Wohlgemuth, who worked in the spacesuit department of B.F. Goodrich in Akron, Ohio.[26] Eventually, Wohlgemuth became general manager of the spacesuit division and learned Goodrich's highly classified spacesuit technology for the Apollo flights. Shortly thereafter, Wohlgemuth, desiring a higher salary, joined Goodrich's competitor, International Latex Corporation in Dover, Delaware, as manager of engineering for the industrial area that included making spacesuits in competition with Goodrich. Goodrich protested by seeking a court order restraining Wohlgemuth from working for Latex or for any other company in the space field. The Court of Appeals of Ohio denied Goodrich's request for an injunction, respecting Wohlgemuth's right to choose his employer, but it did provide an injunction restraining Wohlgemuth from revealing Goodrich's trade secrets.

Almost any information that is not generally known can be classified as a trade secret if it is valuable to its possessor and treated confidentially.

Three arguments for legally protecting trade secrets.

Proprietary data cases sometimes pit the firm's right to protect its secrets against an employee's right to seek employment wherever they choose.

Cases like Wohlgemuth's pit a firm's right to protect its secrets against an employee's right to seek employment wherever they choose. As a result, the moral dilemmas that arise in proprietary data cases are not easily resolved. For one thing, the trade secrets that companies seek to protect have often become an integral part of the departing employee's total job skills and capabilities. These may, for instance, manifest themselves simply in a subconscious or intuitive sense of what will or will not work in the laboratory. Wohlgemuth's total intellectual capacity included the information, experience, and technical skills acquired at his former workplace. Goodrich might be justified in claiming much of Wohlgemuth's intellectual capacity as its corporate property, but it is difficult to see how he could divest himself of it.

Sometimes, companies require employees to sign contracts restricting their ability to get a job with, or start, a competing company within a certain geographical radius or for a certain time. Although employers have legitimate interests to protect, sometimes such **noncompete agreements** can go too far. Consider hair stylist Daniel McKinnon, who was prohibited from working for another salon, even after he had been fired by his original employer.[27] Because they can conflict with freedom of employment, however, not all such noncompete contracts are legally valid. In 2016, sandwich chain Jimmy Johns agreed to stop requiring employees at their restaurants to sign noncompete agreements after they were sued by the attorneys general of New York and Illinois.[28] Moreover, some believe that such contracts decrease employee motivation, discourage innovation, and reduce economic efficiency.[29] Even without them, however, companies sometimes sue departing employees, as Essex Temporary Services did when Frank Cumbo and ten colleagues left the organization to start a competing business. Essex filed a second suit against six other employees who quit a few months later to join the new firm of Lerner, Cumbo, and Associates.[30]

Summary
Proprietary data are an organization's classified or secret information. Problems arise as employees with access to sensitive information and trade secrets quit and take jobs with competitors. Proprietary data issues pose a conflict between two legitimate rights: the right of employers to keep certain information secret and the right of individuals to work where they choose.

The underlying issue of fairness isn't, of course, just a legal question. Frank Cumbo claims that he didn't take any information from Essex that couldn't be found in a phone book. That's relevant to assessing the morality of his conduct, but one would have to know all the details to determine if he wrongly took advantage of information, connections, or business know-how that he had acquired at Essex. In the Goodrich case, it appears that Donald Wohlgemuth didn't take this moral question very seriously. When asked whether he had acted ethically in leaving Goodrich for a competitor, he replied, "Loyalty and ethics have their price, and International Latex has paid the price."[31]

· · ·

Bribes and Kickbacks

In a professional or organizational context, to **bribe** someone is to pay the person to violate their official duties; that is, to perform an action that is inconsistent with the person's work contract or job responsibilities or with the nature of the work the person has been hired to do. Although usually financial, the payment can be anything that is of value to the recipient. Offering a bribe is wrong because it is an inducement to act dishonestly, to disregard one's duties, or to betray a trust—for example, tendering cash to a building inspector to ignore a code violation. For the same reasons, it is wrong to accept a bribe. This is true even if one happens to end up not doing what one was bribed to do.[32]

Thus, employees working in a facilities management department of a Ford plant in Germany acted dishonestly and violated their duties to the company when they participated in bribery by accepting "material benefits" from suppliers in exchange for preferential treatment and for drafting fraudulent invoices.[33] Or take the case of Norman Rothberg, an accountant working at ZZZZ Best Carpet Cleaning Company in the Los Angeles area. When he learned that ZZZZ Best had falsified accounts on insurance restoration jobs, he passed on the information to the accounting firm of Ernst & Whinney, which was overseeing ZZZZ Best's planned multimillion-dollar acquisition of another carpet-cleaning chain. When an investigation began, Rothberg accepted $17,000 from ZZZZ Best officials to back off from his initial reports.[34] Rothberg's conduct was wrong because he received money in exchange for violating his responsibilities as an accountant. By contrast, a server who accepts a gratuity for providing good service to a customer in a restaurant is not accepting a bribe, for she is not violating her duties.

However, the situation would be different if she took money in exchange for not charging the customer for the drinks he ordered. Bribery can, of course, be less blatant than in the Rothberg case—for example, a contractor who charges a company executive only a nominal fee for building her a home patio on the tacit understanding that the executive will see that her company accepts the contractor's bid for an important project.

Bribery sometimes takes the form of a **kickback**, which is a percentage payment to a person able to influence or control a source of income. Thus, Alicia Rocha, sales representative for Sisyphus Books, offers a textbook-selection committee member in a large school district a percentage of the handsome commission she stands to make if a Sisyphus civics text is adopted. The money the committee member receives for the preferred consideration is a kickback. A flagrant case of kickbacks involved American executives of the Honda Motor Company. For years they pocketed millions in bribes and kickbacks from local car dealers; in return, the dealers received permission to open lucrative dealerships and had no trouble obtaining models that were in scarce supply and could be sold at a large profit.[35] More recently, Allergan was alleged to have paid kickbacks to doctors for prescribing the wrinkle-smoothing drug Botox for unapproved medical uses.[36]

The Foreign Corrupt Practices Act

Bribery is generally illegal in the United States, but U.S. companies have a history of paying off foreign officials for business favors. Such acts were declared illegal in the **Foreign Corrupt Practices Act (FCPA)** of 1977, which was passed in the wake of the discovery that nearly 400 U.S. companies, including Exxon, Gulf Oil, and United Brands, had made such payments. Egregious within this sordid pattern of international bribery were Lockheed Aircraft Corporation's secret payoffs to foreign politicians to get aircraft contracts. Lest one understate the effects of such bribery, it is worth noting that revelations of Lockheed bribes in Japan caused a government crisis there, and that in Holland, Prince Bernhard was forced to resign his government duties after admitting that he took a $1 million payoff from Lockheed.

In 1977, the FCPA made it illegal for American companies to engage in bribery overseas.

The FCPA provides stiff fines and prison sentences for corporate officials engaging in bribery overseas and requires corporations to establish strict accounting and auditing controls to guard against the creation of slush funds from which bribes can be paid. The FCPA does not, however, prohibit **grease payments** to the employees of foreign governments who have primarily clerical or ministerial responsibilities. These payments are sometimes necessary to ensure that the recipients carry out their normal job duties. On the other hand, the FCPA makes no distinction between bribery and extortion. A company is extorted by a foreign official if, for instance, the official threatens to violate the company's rights, perhaps by closing down a plant on some legal pretext, unless the official is paid off.

One company caught violating the FCPA was Ashland Oil. Under its then-CEO Orin Atkins, Ashland had agreed to pay an entity controlled by an Omani government official approximately $29 million for a majority interest in Midlands Chrome, Inc.—a price far higher than it was worth—for the purpose of obtaining crude oil at a highly favorable price. When Atkins proposed the acquisition of Midlands Chrome to his board of directors, he said that although the acquisition was a high-risk project, it "had the potential for being more than offset by a potential crude oil contract." Midlands Chrome did not in fact prove particularly profitable, but the Omani government awarded Ashland a contract for 20,000 barrels a day for one year at a $3-per-barrel discount from the regular selling price—a discount worth $21.9 million.[37] More recently, Johnson & Johnson has admitted that its subsidiaries bribed doctors and hospital administrators in Greece, Poland, and Romania to order the company's surgical products, and Walmart acknowledged that its Mexican subsidiary paid government officials to gain the necessary permits for expanding its operations there. In 2014, Alcoa paid $384 million to settle allegations of bribery in Bahrain, and bribery charges involving bags of cash, jewelry, and tours of the Grand Canyon for foreign officials cost Hewlett-Packard $108 million in fines. Around the same time Ralph Lauren and Archer Daniels Midland were fined for bribes paid by subsidiaries, respectively, in Argentina and in Germany and Ukraine. In those two cases, the companies discovered the misconduct themselves and reported it to authorities.[38]

Summary

A bribe is payment in some form for an act that runs counter to the work contract or the nature of the work one has been hired to perform. The Foreign Corrupt Practices Act prohibits corporations from engaging in bribery overseas. Critics charge that the FCPA puts American firms at a disadvantage and imposes U.S. standards on foreign countries. However, bribery can injure individuals, competitors, and political institutions. It also hurts economic growth and damages the free-market system.

The argument that the FCPA wrongly imposes U.S. standards on foreign countries is weak.

The Case against Overseas Bribery

The FCPA has been weakened by amendments that expand the exemption for grease payments and offer corporations more defenses against prosecution. In 1998, however, the law was extended to include bribery by foreign firms on American territory, and, thanks to the Federal Sentencing Guidelines, penalties are now stiffer than those originally specified by the FCPA. Moreover, according to attorney Robert Anello, "Department of Justice officials appear poised for an increase in enforcement of the Foreign Corruption Practices Act in 2023."[39] Critics of the FCPA disapprove of this. They insist that the law puts American corporations at a competitive disadvantage in relation to foreign firms whose governments permit them to bribe. For example, in response to a Senate probe into corrupt activities by oil companies in Africa, an oil executive complained that if his company chose to take the moral high road, "Someone [else] will come [in]. The French will, the Russians will, Petronas [of Malaysia] will."[40] Alexandra Wrage of Trace International, a business ethics group based in Washington, D.C., is sympathetic. "The lack of a level playing field is an enormous competitive advantage for non-U.S. companies," she says. "U.S. companies feel like they are in the cross-hairs, which is a good thing for anti-bribery enforcement, but it comes at a pretty high cost."[41]

Such reasoning, however, can be a way of rationalizing conduct that is morally indefensible. For one thing, competition is often not a factor at all. For example, when United Brands paid a Honduran official a $1.25 million bribe, it was to gain a reduction in the country's business export tax, not to win a contract that might have gone to a foreign competitor. Moreover, when, before passage of the FCPA, U.S. firms did use bribery to beat out competitors, their competitors were usually other U.S. companies.[42] Furthermore, studies show that the FCPA has been at most a minor disincentive to export expansion. Even in nations where the FCPA is alleged to have hurt American business, there has been no statistically discernible effect on U.S. market share. In fact, since passage of the FCPA, U.S. trade with bribe-prone countries has outpaced U.S. trade with other countries.[43]

Thirty-seven countries, including all the world's industrialized nations, have now passed domestic legislation implementing the **OECD** (Organization for Economic Co-operation and Development) **Anti-Bribery Convention**, a formal treaty that outlaws bribing public officials in foreign business transactions and sets up review and monitoring mechanisms. As a result, these days, many nations are going after overseas bribery as zealously as the United States does. A Munich court, for example, fined Siemens AG, the German giant, nearly $300 million for trying to win contracts by bribing officials in Nigeria, Russia, and Libya.[44] The OECD Convention has been reinforced by separate European anti-corruption conventions, various industry-specific agreements, and by the efforts of the United Nations, World Bank, and International Monetary Fund to combat corruption. Even China is getting more aggressive about enforcing its anti-bribery laws.[45]

These developments make it doubtful that the FCPA puts American business at a competitive disadvantage. Furthermore, companies like Reebok, Google, and Novo Nordisk have prospered in emerging markets without getting their hands dirty, and the Swedish company IKEA has done well in Russia despite having to fight hard against corruption (for example, by threatening to halt its expansion there, firing managers who pay bribes, and even buying its own generators to thwart officials attempting to extort it by holding up its access to electricity).[46] But even if the FCPA does handicap U.S. firms and cause them to lose exports, that fact would have to be carefully weighed against the ample documentary evidence of the serious harm done to individuals, companies, and governments as a result of systematic bribery overseas.

A frequently heard argument against the FCPA is that the law imposes U.S. standards on foreign countries and that bribery and payoffs are common business practices in other nations. But that argument is too glib, especially when it comes from those who don't really have a working knowledge of another culture. In some other nations, to be sure, bribery does seem more widespread than it is here, but that doesn't imply that bribery is considered morally acceptable even in those nations. (Drug dealing is not morally acceptable here, even though it is, unfortunately, widespread.) If other countries really did consider bribery and related practices to be morally acceptable, then presumably the people engaging in them would not mind having this fact publicized. But it is difficult to find a real-life example of foreign officials willing to let the public know they accept bribes.

Certainly, the FCPA reflects our own moral standards, but those standards are not simply matters of taste (like clothing styles) or completely arbitrary (like our decision to drive on the right, whereas the British drive on the left). Good, objective arguments can be given against bribery and related corrupt practices because they are intended to induce people inside a business or other organization to make a decision that would not be justifiable according to normal business or other criteria. For example, by encouraging on nonmarket grounds the purchase of inferior goods or the payment of an exorbitant price, bribery can clearly injure a variety of legitimate interests—from stockholders to consumers, from taxpayers to other businesses. It subverts market competition by giving advantage in a way that is not directly or indirectly product related.

There is nothing "relative" about the damage that such corruption can do to a society. Studies show that the more corrupt a nation is, the less investment there is and the slower its economic growth.[47] If we were to permit U.S. companies to engage in bribery overseas, we would be encouraging in other countries practices that we consider too harmful to tolerate at home. Moreover, even an occasional corporate bribe overseas can foster bribery and kickbacks at home and lead employees to subordinate the interest of the organization to their own private gain. Corruption is difficult to cordon off; once a company engages in it, corruption can easily spread throughout the organization.

> Permitting U.S. companies to engage in foreign bribery would be encouraging something in other countries that we consider too harmful to tolerate at home.

The multiple impacts of bribery can be succinctly drawn out in one final case, which involved Bethlehem Steel Corporation, once the nation's second-largest steel company. Bethlehem was convicted of bribery and other corrupt practices for paying ship owners' representatives, including officers of the Colombian Navy, to steer ships needing repairs to Bethlehem's eight shipyards. Thus, competitive bidding for the contracts was effectively eliminated, various members of the Colombian Navy were corrupted, and the Colombian government presumably ended up paying more for the repair work than it had to. Beyond that, Bethlehem generated the money for the payoffs by padding bills and skimming profits from legitimate shipyard repair work. Thus, unsuspecting clients of Bethlehem were made to pay the bill for Bethlehem's bribery.

· · ·

Gifts and Entertainment

Business gifts and entertainment of clients and business associates are familiar parts of the business world. Normally, giving someone a small gift or taking the person out for a nice meal is a gesture of good will or friendship and can help cement a relationship between two people. Unlike a bribe, it involves no quid pro quo or expectation that the recipient will do something specific in return. But gifts do tend to create a sense of gratitude in the recipient, who may feel obligated to reciprocate in some way. For this reason, in a business context gifts can raise conflict-of-interest problems and even border on bribery. Knowing where to draw the line here is not always easy. But one thing is clear: Those who cross that line, wittingly or not, can end up in big trouble. Ask the former General Services Administration (GSA) official who pleaded guilty to a criminal charge of accepting free lunches from a subsidiary of BellSouth Corporation, which was seeking a telephone contract with the GSA.

The federal government provides its procurement officers with two days of lectures and case-study discussions on the ethics of government contracting. Procurement officers, for example, are taught that they may accept an invitation to speak before a trade association consisting of the contractors they buy from, but they must decline the $50 honorarium, whatever the topic of their talk. They also must refuse a ticket for their transportation to the meeting, although they may be permitted to accept lunch as a guest seated at the head of the table, if this is compatible with the policy of their particular agency.

For people in the business world, the rules are not so cut-and-dried, and some of them manage to ignore altogether the conflict-of-interest issues that gifts create. Consider Colin Dalzell, an executive at MCI Systemhouse. Just before it went public, the e-biz software maker Commerce One offered Dalzell, who had done business with it, a chance to buy its shares. He did, and in one day made a profit of $40,000, which he used to buy a 1965 Cobra racing-car kit. Dalzell says that he had a long, established relationship with Commerce One and that the payment wasn't enough to influence his future dealings with it.[48] But most companies and most businesspeople view behavior like his as morally problematic, to say the least.

Determining the morality of giving and receiving gifts in a business situation can be challenging. But there are several factors a conscientious businessperson should take into account:

1. **What is the value of the gift?** Is the gift of nominal value or is it substantial enough to influence a business decision? Undoubtedly, definitions of "nominal" and "substantial" are open to interpretation and are often influenced by situational and cultural variables. Nevertheless, many organizations consider a gift worth less than $25 and given infrequently—perhaps once a year—only nominal but view anything larger or more frequent as problematic. Although this standard won't fit all cases, it does indicate that accepting even a rather inexpensive present might be deemed inappropriate. And, indeed, it's been shown that even small gifts can sometimes be surprisingly influential.[49]

2. **What is the purpose of the gift?** Dick Zolezzi, a department store manager, accepts small gifts such as USB flash drives from an electronics firm. He insists that the transactions are harmless and that he doesn't intend to give the firm any preferential treatment in store advertising displays. As long as the gifts are not intended or received as bribes, remain nominal, and are given only occasionally, there doesn't appear to be a problem. But it would be important to ascertain the electronics firm's intention in giving the gifts. Is it to influence how Zolezzi lays out displays? Does Zolezzi himself expect them as palm-greasing before he'll ensure that the firm receives equal promotional treatment? If so, extortion may be involved. Relevant to the question of purpose is whether a gift has some business purpose or reflects a customary business practice. For example, appointment books, calendars, or pens and pencils with the donor's logo imprinted on them serve to advertise a firm. Golf clubs or the use of a holiday home in Hawaii rarely serve this purpose.

3. **What are the circumstances under which the gift was given or received?** A gift given during the holiday season, for a store opening, or to signal other special events is circumstantially different from one unattached to any special event. Whether the gift was given openly or secretly should also be considered. An open gift, say, with the donor's name embossed on it, raises fewer questions than a gift known only to the donor and the recipient.

Summary
The following considerations are relevant in determining the moral acceptability of gift giving and receiving: the value of the gift, its purpose, the circumstances under which it is given, the position of the person receiving the gift, accepted business practice, company policy, and what the law says.

4. **What is the position or decision-making authority of the person receiving the gift?** Is the person in a position to affect materially a business decision on behalf of the gift giver? In other words, could the recipient's opinion, influence, or decision result in preferential treatment for the donor? Another important point is whether the recipient has made it clear to the donor that the gift won't influence their action one way or the other.

5. **What is the accepted business practice in the industry?** Is this the customary way of conducting this kind of business? Monetary gifts and tips are standard practice in numerous service industries. Their purpose is not only to reward good service but to ensure it again. But it's not customary to tip the head of the produce department in a supermarket so that the person will put aside the best tomatoes for you. When gratuities or the giving of certain kinds of gifts are an integral, publicly acknowledged aspect of customary business practice, they are far less likely to pose moral questions.

6. **What is the company's policy?** Many firms explicitly limit or even forbid altogether the giving or receiving of gifts. Walmart, for example, doesn't permit employees to accept anything from companies doing business with it, not even a cup of coffee, and Kmart

required not only its managers but also its vendors, suppliers, and real-estate associates to sign a no-gifts policy.[50] When such a policy exists, the giving or receiving of a gift is almost certainly wrong.

7. **What is the law?** Certain federal, state, or local government employees may be legally forbidden from receiving gifts from firms with which they do business. Sometimes the law also regulates gift giving in specific industries. For example, the Securities and Exchange Commission fined Fidelity Investments, the mutual fund company, because some of its traders had accepted gifts from brokers seeking to do business with it.[51] And several title insurance companies violated Washington state law by lavishing pro-basketball tickets and other goodies on bankers, builders, and representatives of real-estate companies as a way of drumming up referrals.[52] When gift transactions violate the law, they are clearly unacceptable.

Related to gift giving is the practice of entertaining. Some companies distinguish entertainment from gifts as follows: If you can eat it or drink it on the spot, it's entertainment. In general, entertainment should be interpreted more sympathetically than gifts because it usually occurs within the context of doing business in a social situation. Still, the morality of entertainment should be evaluated along the same lines as gifts—that is, with respect to value, purpose, circumstances, position of the recipient, accepted business practice, company policy, and the law. In each case, the ultimate moral judgment hinges largely on whether an objective party could reasonably suspect that the gift or entertainment might influence the recipient's judgment or lead him or her to act other than in the best interest of the firm.

> The same seven considerations are also relevant to the moral evaluation of business entertainment.

· · ·

Conflicting Obligations

Consider the following situations:

> An employee knows that a coworker occasionally sips whiskey on the job. Should she inform the boss?

> A dishwasher observes that the restaurant's chef often reheats three- or four-day-old food and serves it as fresh. When he informs the manager, he is told to forget it. What should the dishwasher do?

> A consulting engineer discovers a defect in a structure that is about to be sold. If the owner will not disclose the defect to the potential purchaser, should the engineer do so?

> A clerical worker learns that the personnel department has authorized hirings that violate the firm's anti-nepotism rules and neglect its affirmative action commitments. What should she do about it?

> On a regular basis, a secretary is asked by her boss to lie to his wife about his whereabouts. "If my wife telephones," he instructs her, "tell her that I'm calling on a client." In fact, as the secretary well knows, the boss is having an affair with another woman. What should the secretary do?

Such cases are not unusual, but they are different from the ones previously considered in this chapter because they involve workers caught in the crossfire of competing ethical concerns and moral responsibilities. Should the employee ensure the welfare of the organization by reporting the fellow worker who drinks, or should she be loyal to her coworker and say nothing? Should the dishwasher go public with what he knows, or should he simply forget the matter? Should the secretary carry out her boss's instructions, or should she tell his wife the truth? In each case, the employee may experience conflicting obligations, diverging ideals, and divided loyalties.

Many of the difficult moral decisions that employees sometimes face involve such conflicts. How are they to be resolved? According to the procedure recommended in Chapter 2, our moral decisions should take into account our specific obligations, the effects or consequences

Recall from Chapter 2 that our moral decisions should take into account the relevant obligations, ideals, and effects.

Summary
Balancing our obligations to employer or organization, to friends and coworkers, and to third parties outside the organization can create conflicts and divided loyalties. In resolving such moral conflicts, we must identify the relevant obligations, effects, and ideals and decide where the emphasis among them should lie.

Two simple things can help keep our moral decisions free from rationalization.

of the different actions open to us, and any important ideals that our actions would support or undermine. To begin with consequences, remember that even staunch nonconsequentialists acknowledge that the likely results of our actions are relevant to their moral assessment and that we have some duty to promote human well-being. In general, the fuller our understanding of the possible results of the different actions we might take in the specific situation before us— that is, the better we understand the exact ramifications of the alternatives—the more likely we are to make a sound moral decision. Reflecting on the effects of these different courses of action can help us understand what ideals are at stake and determine the exact strength of the more specific obligations we have.

The impact of our actions on significant moral ideals must always be considered. Any serious moral decision should take into account the various ideals advanced or respected, ignored or hindered, by the alternative courses of conduct open to us. In addition, our moral choices are often strongly influenced by the personal weight we place on the different values at stake in a specific situation. Sometimes those values can point in different directions, as when our simultaneous commitment to professional excellence, personal integrity, and loyalty to friends pulls us in different ways.

Finally, any responsible moral decision must, of course, take into account the more specific obligations we have—in particular, those obligations that are a function of the particular relationships, roles, or circumstances we happen to be in. This chapter has already discussed the obligations employees have to the organization based on a freely negotiated work contract, and it is easy to see that employees have moral obligations arising from the business, professional, or organizational roles they have assumed. For example, teachers have an obligation to grade fairly, bartenders to refrain from over-serving intoxicated customers, engineers to guarantee the safety of their projects, and accountants to certify that financial statements present data fairly and according to generally accepted accounting principles. Because of their role responsibilities, an auditor who suspects some irregularity has an obligation to get to the bottom of the matter, an obligation that is probably lacking when an ordinary employee has a hunch that something is not in order in another department.

Thus, employees have certain general duties to their employers, and because of the specific business, professional, or organizational responsibilities they have assumed, they may have other, more precise role-based obligations. In addition, employees are human beings with moral responsibilities to friends, family, and coworkers—to those flesh-and-blood people with whom their lives are intertwined, both inside and outside the workplace. These ongoing relationships are the source of important moral obligations.

What about the obligations of employees to other parties or to society in general? In particular, what obligations do employees have to people with whom they have no relationship and for whom they have no specific professional, organizational, or other role responsibility? Here, different moral theories may steer us in slightly different directions, but simply as a matter of ordinary commonsense morality it is clear that employees—like everyone else—have certain elementary duties to other people. Of particular significance are the obligations to avoid injuring others and to be truthful and fair.

When faced with a moral decision, then, employees should follow the two-step procedure set forth in Chapter 2: identifying the relevant obligations, effects, and ideals, and then trying to decide where the emphasis should lie among these considerations. There is nothing mechanical about this process, but when we weigh moral decisions, two simple things can help us to keep our deliberations free from the various rationalizations to which we are all prone. *First*, we can ask ourselves whether we would be willing to read an account of our actions in the newspaper. Is the course of action we are considering one that we would be willing to defend publicly? *Second*, discussing a moral dilemma or ethical problem with a friend can often help us avoid bias and gain a better perspective. People by themselves, and especially when emotionally involved in a situation, sometimes focus unduly on one or two points, ignoring other relevant factors. Input from others can keep us from overlooking pertinent considerations, thus helping us make a better, more objective moral judgment.

As the preceding discussion mentioned, employees sometimes learn about the illegal or immoral actions of a supervisor or firm. When an employee tries to correct the situation within institutional channels and is thwarted, a central moral question emerges: Should the employee

The workers at the Fukushima Daiichi nuclear power plant took an enormous risk by staying at the plant to try to prevent a nuclear meltdown after a devastating earthquake and tsunami hit Japan in March 2011. In making this decision, what moral considerations do you think influenced them?

go public with the information? Should a worker who is ordered to do something illegal or immoral, or who knows of the illegal or immoral behavior of a supervisor or organization, inform the public?

• • •
Whistle-Blowing

Morris H. Baslow, a middle-aged biologist and father of three, won't forget the day he dropped an envelope in the mail to Thomas B. Yost, an administrative law judge with the Environmental Protection Agency (EPA). Later that day, Baslow was fired from his job with Lawler, Matusky & Skelly Engineers, an engineering consulting firm hired by Consolidated Edison (Con Ed) of New York to help it blunt EPA demands. The EPA was insisting that the power company's generating plants on the Hudson River had to have cooling towers to protect fish from the excessively warm water that it was discharging into the river.

Baslow claimed that the documents he sent showed that Con Ed and Lawler, Matusky & Skelly had knowingly submitted to the EPA invalid and misleading data, giving the false impression that the long-term effects of the utility's effluent on fish were negligible. On the basis of his own research, Baslow believed that the fish could be significantly harmed by the warm-water discharge. He said that for two years he tried to get his employers to listen, but they wouldn't.

Shortly after being fired, Baslow sent seventy-one company documents supporting his allegation to the EPA, the federal Energy Regulatory Commission, and the U.S. Justice Department. In the month following those disclosures, Baslow's employers accused him of stealing the documents and sued him for defamation. Baslow countersued, citing the Clean Water Act, which protects consultants from reprisals for reporting findings prejudicial to their employers and clients.

Summary
Employees have duties to their employers, and they may also have other obligations based on the business or professional roles and responsibilities they have assumed. In addition, they have the same elementary moral obligations that all human beings have—including the obligation not to injure others and to be truthful and fair.

A year later, Lawler, Matusky & Skelly dropped all legal action against Baslow and gave him a cash settlement, reportedly of around $100,000. In return, Baslow wrote to the EPA and other government agencies, withdrawing his charges of wrongdoing and perjury but not recanting his own scientific conclusions. Asked why he finally accepted the cash payment, the unemployed Baslow said, "I've had to bear the brunt of this financially by myself. . . . I just wish somebody had listened to me six months ago."[53]

Other whistle-blowers express similar sentiments, even when they have been proved right. Microbiologist David Franklin blew the whistle on Warner-Lambert for promoting its epilepsy drug Neurontin for off-label uses such as migraines, hiccups, and bipolar disorder. Among other things, the company paid doctors to listen to pitches for uses of Neurontin that lacked FDA approval and even treated them to luxury trips to Hawaii and to the Olympics. (Although doctors are free to prescribe drugs for uses not on their FDA-approved label, the agency forbids companies from promoting their drugs for off-label uses.) After a lengthy legal battle, Franklin was completely vindicated when Warner-Lambert pled guilty and agreed to pay more than $430 million to settle the Justice Department's claims against it. As part of the settlement, Franklin even received a multimillion-dollar reward under the False Claims Act, originally passed in 1863 to crack down on Civil War profiteering. Still, says Franklin, "This has been the most disruptive thing I can imagine can take place in anyone's life."[54]

Or talk to David Graham, an FDA researcher, who endured rebukes and harassment from superiors for first investigating and then exposing the risk of heart attack that the painkiller Vioxx poses. "I can guarantee you, there are other whistle-blowers at the FDA," says Graham. "Fear has them by the throat. And they struggle with their conscience and they struggle with the wrong they see, and they are paralyzed by their fear. They are looking to see—can that Graham fellow get away with committing the truth? It remains to be seen whether I can." He adds, "Please understand, I am not a hero, and I'm not endowed with extraordinary courage."[55] For his part, David Franklin offers the following advice to potential whistle-blowers: "People who are in the position I was need to think about their own futures and how they feel about themselves and what their kids look up to and why they got into this business in the first place," he says. "That's where the endurance of the thing comes into play."[56]

The Baslow, Franklin, and Graham cases illustrate the ethical issues and personal risks facing employees who blow the whistle on what they perceive as organizational misconduct. We now address three more specific questions: What exactly is whistle-blowing? What motivates whistle-blowers to do what they do? When is one morally justified in blowing the whistle?

The Definition of Whistle-Blowing

Whistle-blowing refers to an employee informing the public about the illegal or immoral behavior of an employer or an organization. One expert defines whistle-blowing more fully as

> A practice in which employees who know that their company is engaged in activities that (a) cause unnecessary harm, (b) are in violation of human rights, (c) are illegal, (d) run counter to the defined purpose of the institution, or (e) are otherwise immoral inform the public or some governmental agency of those activities.[57]

Another business ethicist spells out the concept in a somewhat different way:

> Whistle-blowing is the voluntary release of nonpublic information, as a moral protest, by a member or former member of an organization outside the normal channels of communication to an appropriate audience about illegal and/or immoral conduct in the organization or conduct in the organization that is opposed in some significant way to the public interest.[58]

These definitions, although not identical, clearly limit the scope of what constitutes whistle-blowing. Whistle-blowing is something that can be done only by a (past or present) member of an organization. An investigative reporter, for example, who exposes corporate malfeasance is not a whistle-blower. Nor is an employee who spreads gossip about in-house gaffes and indiscretions, thus abusing confidentiality and acting disloyally to colleagues and to the organization. By contrast, whistle-blowing involves exposing activities that are harmful, immoral, or contrary to the public interest or to the legitimate goals and purposes of the organization. It does not encompass sabotage or taking retaliatory action against the

Summary
Whistle-blowing refers to an employee's informing the public about the illegal or immoral behavior of an employer or organization. Whistle-blowers frequently act out of a sense of professional responsibility.

employer or firm, but it does require going outside normal channels, typically, to the media or some external agency. (Most writers on the subject, however, hold that there can also be internal whistle-blowing, which is the disclosure of inappropriate conduct to someone inside the organization, especially when doing so is contrary to standard procedure or outside the normal chain of command.)

What Motivates Whistle-Blowers?

Professor of philosophy Norman Bowie correctly points out that today's discussion of whistle-blowing parallels the discussion of **civil disobedience** in the 1960s.[59] Just as practitioners of civil disobedience of that time felt their duty to obey the law was overridden by other moral obligations, so the whistle-blower believes that the public interest morally outweighs loyalty to colleagues and their own duties to the organization. Coleen Rowley, for example, was a veteran Federal Bureau of Investigation (FBI) agent with twenty-one years of experience who had never worked anywhere else—indeed, she had wanted to be an agent ever since she was in the fifth grade. When she decided to go public with evidence that her bosses had failed to follow up on information that might have thwarted the terrorist attacks of September 11, 2001, and were now misleading the public about what the FBI had known, her desire to do what was right took precedence over her lifelong love of the Bureau. Although whistle-blowers such as Rowley are often stigmatized as "disloyal," many of them see themselves as acting in the best interests of the organization.

> Whistle-blowers believe that the public interest can be more important than loyalty to the organization.

What motivates whistle-blowers? Often, it's simply a sense of professional responsibility. Take F. Barron Stone, for example. He warned his bosses at Duke Power that they were overcharging ratepayers in the Carolinas. When they wouldn't listen, he told state regulators. That triggered an investigation, which led to Duke Power's agreeing to change its accounting procedures and reimburse customers. "I was just doing my job" is all Stone says.[60] Or consider Cynthia Cooper. An internal auditor at WorldCom, she got wind that some of the company's divisions were engaged in crooked accounting practices. She raised the matter with the firm's external auditor, Arthur Andersen, but it assured her there was no problem. When she didn't drop the issue, WorldCom's chief financial officer Scott Sullivan told her that everything was fine and she should back off. Troubled and suspicious about what was going on, Cooper ignored Sullivan's order. She and her team began doing what the external auditor was supposed to do. For weeks and weeks, they pored over company books, working late at night to avoid detection by management, before eventually exposing the accounting scams Sullivan and others were involved in. "I'm not a hero," she told friends and colleagues. "I'm just doing my job."[61]

In the case of Noreen Harrington, the motivation was a little different. A veteran of the mutual fund industry, she resigned from Stern Asset Management because her in-house complaints about improper transactions were disregarded. But she had no intention of telling authorities. Then a year later, her older sister asked her for advice about her 401(k). She had lost a lot of money and wasn't sure that she would be able to retire. "All of a sudden, I thought about this from a different vantage point," Harrington explains. "I saw one face—my sister's face—and then I saw the faces of everyone whose only asset was a 401(k). At that point I felt the need to try to make the regulators look into [these] abuses." That's when she called the office of Eliot Spitzer, then the New York State attorney general, who was on a crusade to clean up the mutual fund industry.[62]

When Is Whistle-Blowing Justified?

Although the motivations of whistle-blowers such as F. Barron Stone, Cynthia Cooper, and Noreen Harrington are honorable and praiseworthy, whistle-blowing itself is a morally problematic action, as Professor Sissela Bok reminds us.[63] The whistle can be blown in error or malice, privacy invaded, confidentiality violated, and trust undermined. Not least, publicly accusing others of wrongdoing can be very destructive and brings with it an obligation to be fair to the persons accused. In addition, internal prying and mutual suspicion make it difficult for any organization to function. And, finally, one must bear in mind that whistle-blowers are only human beings, not saints, and they sometimes have their own self-serving agenda.[64]

In developing his analogy with civil disobedience, Professor Bowie proposes several conditions that must be met for an act of whistle-blowing to be morally justified.[65] These conditions may not be the last word on this controversial subject, but they do provide a good starting point for further debate over the morality of whistle-blowing. According to Bowie, whistle-blowing is morally justified if and only if the following circumstances apply:

1. **It is done from an appropriate moral motive.** For an act of whistle-blowing to be justified, it must be motivated by a desire to expose unnecessary harm, illegal or immoral actions, or conduct counter to the public good or the defined purpose of the organization. Desire for attention or profit or the exercise of one's general tendency toward stirring up trouble is not a justification for whistle-blowing.

   Although, as Chapter 2 explained, the question of motive is an important one in Kantian ethics, not all moral theorists would agree with Bowie's first condition. Might not an employee be justified in blowing the whistle on serious wrongdoing by the employer, even if the employee's real motivation was the desire for revenge? Granted that the motivation was ignoble, the action itself might nonetheless have been the morally right one. An action can still be morally justified, say some theorists, even when it is done for the wrong reason. Still, many people were troubled to learn that the whistle-blowing paralegal who provided anti-tobacco lawyers with crucial documents about a tobacco company's secret studies on the health dangers of cigarettes was paid more than $100,000 by the lawyers.[66] It is also problematic when government awards entice people who are themselves wrongdoers to blow the whistle on others in return for a large reward.[67]

2. **The whistle-blower, except in special circumstances, has exhausted all internal channels for dissent before going public.** The duty of loyalty to the firm obligates workers to seek an internal remedy before informing the public of a misdeed. This is an important consideration. In some cases, however, the attempt to exhaust internal channels may result in dangerous delays or expose the would-be whistle-blower to retaliation. When the personal risks are great, some writers recommend going outside official channels and blowing the whistle anonymously.[68]

3. **The whistle-blower has compelling evidence that wrongful actions have been ordered or have occurred.** General allegations, such as that a company is "not operating in the best interests of the public" or is "systematically sabotaging the competition," won't do. The whistle-blower must be specific, and the charges must be backed up. What constitutes "compelling evidence" can be debated, but employees can ask themselves whether the evidence is strong enough that any reasonable person in possession of it would be convinced that an illegal or immoral activity has happened or is likely to happen.

4. **The whistle-blower has acted after careful analysis of the danger: How serious is the moral violation? How immediate is the problem? How great is the danger?** These criteria focus on the nature of the wrongdoing. Owing loyalty to employers, employees should blow the whistle only for grave legal or moral matters. The greater the harm or the more serious the wrongdoing, the more likely is the whistle-blowing to be justified. Additionally, employees should consider the time factor. The greater the time before the violation is to occur, the more likely it is that the firm's own internal mechanisms will prevent it, whereas the more imminent a violation, the more justified is the whistle-blowing.

5. **The whistle-blowing has some likelihood of success.** This criterion recognizes that the probability of remedying an immoral or illegal action is an important consideration. Sometimes the chances are good; other times they're slim. Probably most cases fall somewhere between these extremes. In general, given the potential harmful effects, whistle-blowing that stands no chance of success is less justified than that with some prospect of succeeding. Even so, sometimes merely drawing attention to an objectionable practice, although it may fail to improve the specific situation (perhaps because the events disclosed happened in the past), encourages government and society to be more watchful of certain behavior.

Summary
An act of whistle-blowing can be presumed to be morally justified if it is done from a moral motive; if the whistle-blower has, if possible, exhausted internal channels before going public; if the whistle-blower has compelling evidence; if the whistle-blower has carefully analyzed the dangers; and if the whistle-blowing has some chance of success.

The phrase "morally justified" can be ambiguous, and the preceding discussion does not explicitly distinguish between situations in which whistle-blowing is morally permissible and situations in which it is also morally required (in the sense that one would act wrongly if one failed to blow the whistle). Factors 3, 4, and 5 are particularly relevant to determining this. Speaking generally, though, if the harm in question is great enough and if an employee is well positioned to prevent it by blowing the whistle on the organization, then they may well be morally obligated—not just morally justified or morally permitted—to do so.

• • •

Self-Interest and Moral Obligation

For many employees, protecting themselves or safeguarding their jobs is the primary factor in deciding whether to put third-party interests above those of the firm. Concern with **self-interest** in cases that pit loyalty to the company against other obligations is altogether understandable and even warranted. After all, workers who subordinate the organization's interests to an outside party's expose themselves to charges of disloyalty, disciplinary action, freezes in job status, forced relocations, and even dismissal. Furthermore, even when an employee successfully blows the whistle, they can be blacklisted in an industry. Given the potential harm to self and family that employees risk in honoring obligations to third parties, it is perfectly legitimate to inquire about the weight that considerations of self-interest should be given in resolving cases of conflicting obligations.

Sadly, there is no clear, unequivocal answer to this question. Moral theorists and society as a whole do distinguish between **prudential reasons** and moral reasons. "Prudential" (from the word *prudence*) refers here to considerations of self-interest; "moral" refers here to considerations of the interests of others and the demands of morality. Chapter 1 explained that it is possible for prudential and moral considerations to pull us in different directions. One way of looking at their relationship is this: If prudential concerns outweigh moral ones, then employees may do what is in their own best interest. If moral reasons override prudential ones, then workers should honor their obligations to others.

> Some theorists believe that prudential concerns sometimes outweigh moral ones.

Consider the case of a cashier at a truck stop who is asked to write up phony meal receipts so truckers can get a larger expense reimbursement from their employers than they really deserve. The cashier doesn't think this is right, so she complains to the manager. The manager explains that the restaurant is largely dependent on trucker business and that this is a good way to ensure it. The cashier is ordered to do the truckers' bidding and thus to act dishonestly and in a way that is unfair and harmful to the trucking companies. Given these moral considerations, the cashier ought to refuse, and perhaps she should even report the conduct to the trucking companies.

But let's suppose that the cashier happens to be a single mother with only a high school education. She lacks occupational skills and stands little chance of getting another job in an economy that is depressed—for months, she was unemployed before landing her present position. With no other means of support, the consequences of job loss for her would be serious indeed. Now, given this scenario and given that the wrongdoing at issue is relatively minor, prudential concerns would probably take legitimate precedence over moral ones. In other words, the cashier would be justified in "going along" with the practice, at least on a temporary basis.

Some moral theorists would agree with this conclusion but analyze the case somewhat differently. They think it is incorrect to say that in some circumstances we may permit prudential considerations to outweigh moral considerations. There is no neutral perspective outside both morality and self-interest from which one can make such a judgment. Furthermore, they would say that, by definition, nothing can outweigh the demands of morality.

> Other theorists say that nothing can outweigh morality but that morality itself does not require us to make large sacrifices to right small wrongs.

Does that mean the cashier should refuse to do what her manager wants and, thus, lose her job? Not necessarily. Morality does not, these theorists contend, require us to make large sacrifices to right small wrongs. Writing up inaccurate receipts does violate some basic moral principles, and the cashier has some moral obligation not to go along with it. But morality does not, all things considered, require her—under the present circumstances—to take a course of action that would spell job loss. She should, however, take less drastic steps to end the practice (like continuing to talk to her boss and the truckers about it) and perhaps eventually find other work. Thus, according to this way of thinking, the cashier is not sacrificing morality to self-interest in "going along" for a while. The idea is that morality does not impose obligations on us without regard to their cost; it does not, under the present circumstances, demand an immediate resignation by the cashier.

Whichever way one looks at it, the question of balancing our moral obligations to others and our own self-interest is particularly relevant to whistle-blowing. On the one hand, in situations in which whistle-blowing threatens one's livelihood and career, prudential concerns may properly be taken into account in deciding what one should do, all things considered. This doesn't mean that if the worker blows the whistle despite compelling prudential reasons not to, they acted immorally. On the contrary, such an action could be highly moral. (As Chapter 2 explained, ethical theorists term such actions *supererogatory*, meaning that they are, so to speak, above and beyond the call of duty.) On the other hand, when the moral concerns are great (for example, when the lives of others are at stake), elementary morality and personal integrity can require people to make substantial sacrifices.

Two further points are pertinent here. *First*, an evaluation of prudential reasons obviously is colored by one's temperament and perceptions of self-interest. Each of us has a tendency to magnify potential threats to our livelihood or career. Exaggerating the costs to ourselves of acting otherwise makes it easier to rationalize away the damage we are doing to others. In the business world, for instance, people talk about the survival of the firm as if it were literally a matter of life and death. Going out of business is the worst thing that can happen to a firm, but the people who make it up will live on and get other jobs. Keeping the company alive (let alone competitive or profitable) cannot justify seriously injuring innocent people.

> Exaggerating the costs to ourselves allows us to rationalize away the damage we are doing to others.

Not only do we tend to exaggerate the importance of self-interested considerations, but also most of us have been socialized to heed authority. As a result, we are disinclined to question the orders of someone above us, especially when the authority is an employer or supervisor with power to influence our lives for better or worse. It's easy for us to assume that any boat rocking will be very harmful, even self-destructive.

It follows, then, that each of us has an obligation to perform a kind of character or personality audit. Do we follow authority blindly? Do we suffer from moral tunnel vision on the job? Do we mindlessly do what is demanded of us, oblivious to the impact of our cooperation and actions on outside parties? Have we given enough attention to our possible roles as accomplices in the immoral undoing of other individuals, businesses, and social institutions? Do we have a balanced view of our own interests versus those of others? Do we have substantial evidence for believing that our livelihoods are really threatened, or is that belief based more on an exaggeration of the facts? Have we been imaginative in trying to balance prudential and moral concerns? Have we sought to find some middle ground, or have we set up a false "self–other" dilemma in which our own interests and those of others are erroneously viewed as incompatible? These are just some of the questions that a personal inventory should include if we are to combat the all-too-human tendency to stack the deck in favor of prudential reasons whenever they are pitted against moral ones.

> We all have an interest in encouraging people to act in non-self-interested ways.

A *second* point about the relationship between prudential and moral considerations concerns our collective interest in protecting the welfare of society by encouraging people to act in non-self-interested ways. As we have seen, in some cases considerations of self-interest may mean that one does not have an overriding obligation to blow the whistle. When that is the case, how can society be protected from wrongdoing? Is its welfare to be left to those few heroic souls willing to perform supererogatory actions? And even when employees have a clear duty to blow the whistle, the personal risk involved may, human nature being what it is, keep them from doing the right thing. Who protects society then? The only realistic and reasonable approach, it seems, is to restructure our legal, business, and social institutions so that acting in a morally responsible way no longer brings the severe penalty that it often does. Whether people do what they know to be right—whether they act in a way that respects others and protects their important interests—is not simply a matter of their conscience and the strength of their moral convictions. It is also a function of the environment in which they must act and the incentives and disincentives they face.

Protecting Those Who Do the Right Thing

Although a hodgepodge of legal precedents and state and federal legislation already afforded some assistance to employees who blow the whistle, the **Sarbanes-Oxley Act** of 2002 marked an important advance. The act provides sweeping new legal protection for employees who report possible securities fraud, making it unlawful for companies to "discharge, demote, suspend, threaten, harass, or in any other manner discriminate against" them. Fired workers can sue, and they are guaranteed the right to a jury trial instead of having to endure months or years of administrative hearings. In addition, the Labor Department can order companies to rehire terminated whistle-blowers with no court hearings whatsoever. Moreover, executives who retaliate against employees who report possible violations of *any* federal law now face imprisonment for up to ten years.

Unfortunately, Sarbanes-Oxley came too late to help Christine Casey. After a few years working at Mattel, Casey was assigned by the toymaker to develop a system to allocate production among its factories. But she soon discovered that Mattel's official sales forecasts were so high that managers routinely ignored the numbers. "It was a joke around the office," she says. Managers kept two sets of figures and would telephone around to find out what they should really tell their factories to produce. Casey went to a company director with a proposal to fix the numbers and help the company forecast profits more accurately. She then began experiencing hostility from company executives, received her first negative performance review, and was shunted off to a tiny cubicle, stripped of most of her work responsibilities. When Mattel's chief financial officer ignored her concerns, and its human resources department turned a blind eye to her mistreatment, she telephoned the SEC. Although Mattel later had to pay $122 million to shareholders who sued it for deliberately inflating its sales forecasts, Casey lost her wrongful-termination suit against the company for having harassed her into resigning. She has little chance of getting a job like the one she lost because big companies routinely check job applicants' litigation history.[69]

It is not enough, however, merely to change the law. Corporate attitudes need to change as well. In America, *The Economist* magazine writes, "it is almost always thought cheaper to fire whistle-blowers than to listen to them, despite years of legislation designed to achieve the opposite."[70] Lehman Brothers is a good illustration. A few days after Lehman Brothers' vice president Matthew Lee sent a letter to top management pointing out serious irregularities in the company's books—in particular, their completely unrealistic appraisals of assets—he was pulled out of a meeting and fired on the spot. Two months later, Lehman Brothers was forced to file bankruptcy (the largest in U.S. history) and was quickly liquidated. Examples such as this make Kris Kolesnik, director of the National Whistleblower Center, pessimistic. "No matter how many protections whistleblower laws have created over the years," he says, "the system always seems to defeat them."[71]

In the long run, however, organizations benefit more from encouraging employees to come forward with their ethical concerns than they do from ignoring possible wrongdoing and retaliating against those who raise awkward queries. Openness and a receptive attitude toward moral questioning by employees give the organization a chance to take corrective action. This can save it money (by rooting out embezzlement, say, or forestalling litigation) or at least—as recent scandals make clear—help it to head off worse trouble when the problems bothering employees eventually leak out to the public. This is especially true on Wall Street now that financial reform legislation passed in 2010 gives potential whistle-blowers a strong incentive for providing information to the SEC: between 10 and 30 percent of any fines or penalties over $1 million.[72]

To discharge their moral responsibilities and safeguard their own interests, companies need to develop explicit, proactive whistle-blowing policies. At a minimum, these policies should state that employees aware of possible wrongdoing have a responsibility to disclose that information; specific individuals or groups outside the chain of command should be designated to hear those concerns; employees who in good faith disclose perceived wrongdoing should be protected from adverse employment consequences; and there should be a fair and impartial investigative process. Some large companies also hire outside vendors to set up software systems, websites, or toll-free call centers for employees to alert them anonymously to ethical

Summary
Prudential considerations based on self-interest can conflict with moral considerations, which take into account the interests of others. Some sacrifices of self-interest would be so great that moral considerations must give way to prudential ones. But employees must avoid the temptation to exaggerate prudential concerns, thereby rationalizing away any individual moral responsibility to third parties. Legislation and changes in corporate culture can reduce the personal sacrifices that whistle-blowers must make.

Companies need to develop explicit, proactive whistle-blower policies.

problems.[73] Then, of course, there must be follow-through. In these ways, management can create organizational procedures and a corporate culture that make it less likely that employees will be forced to blow the whistle externally.

Study Corner

Key Terms and Concepts

abuse of official position

bribe

business gifts and entertainment

civil disobedience

company loyalty

conflict of interest

Economic Espionage Act

Foreign Corrupt Practices Act (FCPA)

grease payments

insider trading

kickback

noncompete agreements

OECD Anti-Bribery Convention

proprietary data

prudential reasons

Sarbanes-Oxley Act

self-interest

trade secret

U.S. v. O'Hagan

whistle-blowing

Points to Review

- two issues facing someone like George Galatis or George Betancourt (p. 288)
- importance of the work contract (p. 288)
- why some writers reject the idea of company loyalty (p. 288)
- why conflicts of interest are a moral problem (p. 290)
- why disclosing a conflict of interest doesn't necessarily solve the problem (p. 290)
- financial investments as possible conflicts of interest (p. 291)
- examples of abuse of official position (p. 291)
- significance of the Chiarella and Dirks cases (p. 293)
- the Supreme Court's position on insider trading in *U.S. v. O'Hagan* (p. 293)
- arguments for and against insider trading (pp. 293–294)
- differences between a patented idea or process and a trade secret (pp. 294–295)
- three arguments for legally protecting trade secrets (p. 295)

- issues raised by the Wohlgemuth/Goodrich case (pp. 295–296)
- FCPA's handling of grease payments and extortion (p. 297)
- pros and cons of the FCPA (p. 297)
- seven factors relevant to determining the morality of business gifts and entertainment (pp. 300–301)
- procedure recommended in Chapter 2 for making moral decisions (pp. 301–302)
- two ways of trying to keep your moral decisions free from rationalization (p. 302)
- the analogy between civil disobedience and whistle-blowing (p. 305)
- why whistle-blowing can be morally problematic (p. 305)
- five factors to consider when morally evaluating whistle-blowing (p. 306)
- self-interest and the demands of morality (pp. 307–308)
- how to reduce the personal sacrifices that whistle-blowers must often make (pp. 309–310)

For Further Reflection

1. What does the concept of company loyalty mean to you? Does it still make sense today?

2. Have you ever experienced a conflict of interest or been tempted to do something that you thought went against your job responsibilities? Describe an employment- or business-related situation where your self-interest diverged from what you believed to be morally right.

3. When, if ever, is an employee justified in blowing the whistle? What do you see as the most important factors that they need to consider in deciding whether to blow the whistle?

Case 10.1

Changing Jobs and Changing Loyalties

Cynthia Martinez Was Thrilled When She First Received the Job offer from David Newhoff at Crytex Systems. She had long admired Crytex, both as an industry leader and as an ideal employer, and the position the company was offering her was perfect. "It's just what I've always wanted," she told her husband, Tom, as they uncorked a bottle of champagne. But as she and Tom talked, he raised a few questions that began to trouble her.

"What about the big project you're working on at Altrue right now? It'll take three months to see that through," Tom reminded her. "The company has a lot riding on it, and you've always said that you're the driving force behind the project. If you bolt, Altrue is going to be in a real jam."

Cynthia explained that she had mentioned the project to David Newhoff. "He said he could understand that I'd like to see it through, but Crytex needs someone right now. He gave me a couple of days to think it over, but it's my big chance."

Tom looked at her thoughtfully and responded, "But Newhoff doesn't quite get it. It's not just that you'd like to see it through. It's that you'd be letting your whole project team down. They probably couldn't do it without you, at least not the way it needs to be done. Besides, Cyn, remember what you said about that guy who quit the Altrue branch in Baltimore."

"That was different," Cynthia responded. "He took an existing account with him when he went to another firm. It was like ripping Altrue off. I'm not going to rip them off, but I don't figure I owe them anything extra. It's just business. You know perfectly well that if Altrue could save some money by laying me off, the company wouldn't hesitate."

"I think you're rationalizing," Tom said. "You've done well at Altrue, and the company has always treated you fairly. Anyway, the issue is what's right for you to do, not what the company would or wouldn't do. Crytex is Altrue's big competitor. It's like you're switching sides. Besides, it's not just a matter of loyalty to the company, but to the people you work with. I know we could use the extra money, and it would be a great step for you, but still . . ."

They continued to mull things over together, but the champagne no longer tasted quite as good. Fortunately, she and Tom never really argued about things they didn't see eye to eye on, and Tom wasn't the kind of guy who would try to tell her what she should or shouldn't do. But their conversation had started her wondering whether she really should accept that Crytex job she wanted so much.

Discussion Questions

1. What should Cynthia do? What ideals, obligations, and effects should she take into account when making her decision?

2. Would it be unprofessional of Cynthia to drop everything and move to Crytex? Would it show a lack of integrity? Could moving abruptly to Crytex have negative career consequences for her?

3. Is it morally wrong, morally permissible, or morally required for Cynthia to take the new job? Examine Cynthia's choice from a utilitarian point of view. How would Kant and Ross look at her situation?

4. What does loyalty to the company mean, and how important is it, morally? Under what circumstances, if any, do employees owe loyalty to their employers? When, if ever, do they owe loyalty to their coworkers?

Case 10.2

A Textbook Conflict of Interest

Dr. Melvina Kahn Is Chair of the Accounting Department at Lake Afton University. One of her many responsibilities is reviewing the opinion surveys that students complete for the courses that her department offers. She's noticed that last semester three students complained about the price of the introductory accounting text assigned by one of the faculty members in her department, Dr. Larry Jestmore.

Dr. Jestmore is the book's author. She has asked him to stop by her office to discuss the student comments.

"Thanks for coming to see me, Larry. I'm sure you've noticed that some students are unhappy with the cost of the textbook that you're requiring them to buy. Have you given any thought to finding a cheaper alternative?"

"I saw the comments, but I don't really see the issue," Dr. Jestmore replied. "Accounting textbooks aren't cheap, even when students only rent them for the semester or sell them back to the bookstore at the end of the term. But my book isn't the most expensive. The price is about average; at worst, it's a little more than average. In fact, the intro text that Karen Feleppa requires her students to buy costs a few dollars more. Did her students complain?"

"Interestingly, no. And that makes the me think that it's not the price alone that your students were responding to. Karen isn't the author of the book she uses, but you're requiring students to buy a text that you wrote yourself. They may feel like you have a conflict of interest, since when they buy the book you receive a percentage of the purchase price."

"It's a very small percentage; I only make a few dollars from each book sold, and only from new copies. When a student buys a used book, I don't see a dime. That means that I only make any real money once every few years, when a new edition comes out."

"I understand," Dr. Kahn said, nodding her head. "Still, on the surface it does look like a straightforward conflict of interest. Your job is to choose a book based on what's best for your students, yet you stand to gain if you require them to buy your own book."

"But I am doing what's best for my students," Dr. Jestmore protested. "Maybe I can't say that my book is objectively better than all the other accounting textbooks out there. I'm not sure that any book is objectively best. But what I'm sure of is that I can teach more effectively from my textbook then I could any other. It perfectly suits my approach to the class. And several instructors at other schools use it, too; they seem to think it's pretty good."

"Some instructors have gotten away from using textbooks altogether," Dr. Kahn pointed out. "Have you considering teaching the class using 'open educational resources' that your students could access freely?"

"I've seen some of the free resources for teaching accounting that are available. I even use them, in some of my more advanced classes. So far, though, I haven't found a free alternative that I could teach Accounting 101 from nearly as well as I can my own book. I agree with you that my job is to do what's best for my students. But I take that to mean that I should offer them the best accounting class that I can, not the cheapest—at least as long as the cost is within reason. If I can offer them a better learning experience using my book than I could using any other, and if the book's price isn't excessive compared to its competitors, then I don't see how you can fault me."

Dr. Kahn thanked Dr. Jestmore for meeting with her. After he left, she considered whether the Accounting Department needs a policy about instructors requiring students to use books that they wrote.

Discussion Questions

1. Did Dr. Jestmore have a conflict of interest in this case?

2. Given the information that you have, does it seem that Dr. Jestmore was wrong to assign his own textbook? Should Dr. Kahn implement a policy that forbids instructors from assigning their own textbooks, or at least a policy that requires them to receive special approval to do so?

3. How should instructors weigh price against quality and features in choosing textbooks?

4. Instructors receive free "desk copies" of textbooks that they assign, and in fact publishers often send them unsolicited free copies of textbooks in the hopes that they'll adopt these books in their courses. Does this alone create a worrisome conflict of interest?

5. How could Dr. Jestmore address student concerns about his requiring his own textbook while continuing to use the book?

Case 10.3
Inside Traders or Astute Observers?

In 2009, Federal Authorities Broke Up the Biggest Insider-Trading ring ever. Originally focused on the Galleon Group hedge fund, the investigation soon unraveled a complicated network of nearly two dozen traders, analysts, and lawyers at several different companies who were engaged in a criminal conspiracy to buy insider information, usually about pending corporate acquisitions. Using throw-away cell phones to avoid detection, they had netted $20 million in illegal profits. Allegedly at the center of it all was ringmaster Zvi Goffer of the Schottenfeld Group and later Galleon, nicknamed "Octopussy" because his arms reached out

to so many sources of information. Among those caught up in the federal dragnet was a senior vice president at IBM, Robert Moffat, who had been induced by his lover into divulging confidential information, which she then passed on to the head of Galleon Group.

Since that case, the Securities and Exchange Commission (SEC) has been pushing hard against securities fraud in general and insider trading in particular, using informants, wiretaps, and sophisticated software tools to make a number of prominent arrests. "Illegal insider trading is rampant and may even be on the rise," says Preet Bharara, the U.S. attorney in Manhattan. A main target of recent investigations has been the so-called expert network firms that arose in response to an SEC rule in 2000 that banned companies from selectively divulging significant information, such as upcoming earnings reports, to favored analysts. These firms purport to offer "independent investment research" but routinely deliver inside information on revenue numbers and sales forecasts. In Bharara's view, however, it's not just about prosecuting the big fish on Wall Street: "The people cheating the system include bad actors not only at Wall Street firms, but also at Main Street companies." However, some think the SEC is now pushing too hard and too far.

Take the case of Gary Griffiths and Cliff Steffes, who worked in a rail yard owned by Florida East Coast Railways in Jacksonville, Florida. The SEC charged them with making more than $1 million by trading on inside information, specifically, on the information that their company was going to be sold. How did they do it? After all, one of them is a mechanical engineer, the other a trainman—not your usual corporate insiders. The answer is simply that they were observant. According to the SEC, the two noticed that "there were an unusual number of daytime tours" of the rail yard with "people dressed in business attire." Although they were not told anything, officially or unofficially, Griffiths and Steffes had a hunch that something was up. Along with members of their families, they bet that a deal was in the works by buying tens of thousands of call options on the company's stocks. That gave them the right to buy the stock at its current price at some future date. (Purchasers of call options make money if the stock increases in value because they can then buy it at its earlier, lower price. If the stock decreases in value, then the buyers simply don't exercise the options; they're out only whatever they paid for the options.) In this case, when Fortress Investment Group acquired Florida East Coast Railways, the value of the latter's stock shot up, and Griffiths, Steffes, and their families were able to cash in big-time.

Critics of the SEC say that it is going beyond making sure that insiders are not abusing their positions or violating their fiduciary duties. Joel M. Cohen, a partner at the law firm of Gibson, Dunn & Crutcher, has written that the SEC is moving from "deterring and punishing those who abuse special relationships at the expense of shareholders into a murkier area . . . [of] policing general financial unfairness." Other business observers agree with him that the SEC shouldn't focus on trying to make the markets "feel" fair to everyone.

For its part, the SEC contends that Gary Griffiths and Cliff Steffes were more than just observant. After the tours began, they had heard "rail yard employees . . . expressing concerns that [it] was being sold, and that their jobs could be affected by the sale." It also claims that Griffiths was asked to make a list of all the locomotives, freight cars, trailers, and containers owned by the company, along with their current value, something he had never been asked to do before. "Is all of that material information?" asks *New York Times* business columnist Andrew Ross Sorkin. "Clearly, it is nonpublic. But without being told directly that a deal was in the works, did the men actually have inside information? What would have happened if there had been no deal? Or if the company was later sold for a price below its prevailing stock market value?" And as Joel Cohen points out, in most cases, "if you overhear something and divine from the conversation that Party A is about to buy Party B, and you buy Party B, that's fine. You can do that."

On the other hand, both Griffiths and Steffes had signed the company's code of conduct, which states that employees cannot trade on or disseminate material nonpublic information. So maybe they breached a fiduciary duty after all. Or maybe they were just alert employees, who happened to be good guessers and—until the SEC showed up, anyway—very lucky.[74]

Update

After the SEC charged Griffiths, Steffes, and four members of Steffes's family with insider trading, Griffiths and one of Steffes's relatives signed agreements with the SEC to avoid prosecution. Although neither admitted guilt, they agreed to pay fines of $120,000 and $240,000, respectively. The other defendants went to trial in 2014 but were acquitted by a jury.

....
Discussion Questions
....

1. Did Griffiths and Steffes violate any legal or moral duties toward their employer? Did they act unfairly in some way?

2. Were they "insiders"? If so, explain why. If not, does that imply that they cannot be guilty of insider trading or that what they did was morally permissible?

3. Should the law prohibit employees acting as Griffiths and Steffes did? Explain why or why not. If actions like theirs are tolerated, will it diminish people's faith in the fairness of the stock market? Would permitting it set a bad precedent in other cases?

4. Putting legal technicalities aside, did Griffiths and Steffes act unethically? Explain the facts and moral principles that support your answer.

5. In your view, is insider trading a serious moral problem? Explain why or why not. Should we legalize insider trading, as some argue, and simply let different companies decide how they want to deal with the issue?

6. Suppose Griffiths and Steffes were not employees of Florida East Coast Railways, but merely lived across the street and guessed what was going on. Could they still be guilty of insider trading?

7. Assuming that insider trading should remain outlawed, does prosecuting Griffiths and Steffes represent a wise use of the SEC's resources, or should it ignore cases like this?

Case 10.4
The Housing Allowance

Wilson Mutambara Grew Up in the Slums Outside Stanley, Capital of the sub-Saharan African country of Rambia.[75] Through talent, hard work, and luck, he made it through secondary school and won a scholarship to study in the United States. He eventually received an MBA and went to work for NewCom, a cellular telephone service. After three years in the company's Atlanta office, Wilson was given an opportunity to return to Rambia, where NewCom was setting up a local cellular service. Eager to be home, Wilson Mutambara couldn't say yes fast enough.

NewCom provides its employees in Rambia with a monthly allowance of up to $2,000 for rent, utilities, and servants. By Western standards, most of the housing in Stanley is poor quality, and many of its neighborhoods are unsafe. By providing the allowance, NewCom's intention is to see that its employees live in areas that are safe and convenient and that they live in a style that is appropriate to the company's image.

To claim their housing allowance, NewCom's employees in Rambia are supposed to turn in receipts, and every month Wilson Mutambara turned in an itemized statement for $2,000 from his landlord. Nobody at NewCom thought it was unusual that Wilson never entertained his coworkers at home. After all, he worked long hours and traveled frequently on business. However, after Wilson had been in Rambia for about fifteen months, one of his coworkers, Dale Garman, was chatting with a Rambian customer, who referred in passing to Wilson as a person living in Old Town. Garman knew Old Town was one of the slums outside Stanley, but he kept his surprise to himself and decided not to mention this information to anyone else until he could independently confirm it. This wasn't difficult for him to do. Wilson was indeed living in Old Town in the home of some relatives. The house itself couldn't have rented for more than $300, even if Wilson had the whole place to himself, which he clearly didn't. Dale reported what he had learned to Wilson's supervisor, Barbara Weston.

When Weston confronted him about the matter, Wilson admitted that the place did rent for a "little less" than $2,000, but he vigorously defended his action this way: "Every other NewCom employee in Rambia receives $2,000 a month. If I live economically, why should I be penalized? I should receive the same as everyone else." In response, Weston pointed out that NewCom wanted to guarantee that its employees had safe, high-quality housing that was in keeping with the image that the company wanted to project. Wilson's housing arrangements were "unseemly," she said, and not in keeping with his professional standing. Moreover, they reflected poorly on the company. To this, Wilson Mutambara retorted: "I'm not just a NewCom employee; I'm also a Rambian. It's not unsafe for me to live in this neighborhood, and it's insulting to be told that the area I grew up in is 'unseemly' or inappropriate for a company employee."

Barbara Weston pointed out that the monthly receipts he submitted had been falsified. "Yes," he admitted, "but that's common practice in Rambia. Nobody thinks twice about it." However, she pressed the point, arguing that he had a duty to NewCom, which he had violated. As the discussion continued, Mutambara became less confident and more and more distraught. Finally, on the verge of tears, he pleaded, "Barbara, you just don't understand what's expected of me as a Rambian or the pressure I'm under. I save every penny I have to pay school fees for eight nieces and nephews. I owe it to my family to try to give those children the same chance I had. My relatives would never understand my living in a big house instead of helping them. I'm just doing what I have to do."

Discussion Questions

1. Did Wilson Mutambara act wrongly? Explain why or why not. Assess each of the arguments he gives in his own defense. What other courses of action were open to him? What would you have done in his place?

2. Was Dale Garman right to confirm the information he had received and to report the matter? Was it morally required of him to do so?

3. What should Barbara Weston and NewCom do? Should Wilson be ordered to move out of Old Town and into more appropriate housing? Should he be terminated for having falsified his housing receipts? If not, should he be punished in some other way?

4. Is NewCom unfairly imposing its own ethnocentric values on Wilson Mutambara? Is the company's housing policy fair and reasonable? Is it culturally biased?

Case 10.5
Ethically Dubious Conduct

Brenda Franklin Has Worked at Allied Tech for Nearly Eight Years. It's a large company, but she likes it and enjoys the friendly work environment. When she tacked her list onto the bulletin board outside her office, she didn't intend to make things less friendly. In fact, she didn't expect her list to attract much attention at all.

It had all started the week before when she joined a group of coworkers for their weekly lunch get-together, where they always talked about all sorts of things. This time, they had gotten into a long political discussion, with several people at the table going on at great length about dishonesty, conflicts of interest, and shady dealings among politicians and corporate leaders. "If this country is going to get on the right track, we need people whose integrity is above reproach," Harry Benton had said to nods of approval around the table, followed by a further round of complaints about corruption and corner-cutting by the powerful.

Brenda hadn't said much at the time, but she thought she sniffed a whiff of hypocrisy. Later that night, after pondering the group's discussion, she typed up her list of "Ethically Dubious Employee Conduct." The next day she posted it outside her door.

Harry Benton was the first one to stick his head in the office. "My, my, aren't we smug?" was all he said before he disappeared. Later that morning, her friend Karen dropped by. "You don't really think it's immoral to take a pad of paper home, do you?" she asked. Brenda said no, but she didn't think one could just take it for granted that it was okay to take company property. She and Karen chatted more about the list. On and off that week, almost everyone she spoke with alluded to the list or commented on some of its items. They didn't object to her posting it, although they seemed to think it was a little strange. One day outside the building, however, an employee she knew only by sight asked Brenda sarcastically whether she was planning on turning people in for "moral violations." Brenda ignored him.

Now she was anticipating her group's weekly lunch. She had little doubt about what the topic of discussion would be, as she again glanced over her list:

Ethically Dubious Employee Conduct

1. Taking office supplies home for your personal use.

2. Using the telephone for personal, long-distance phone calls.

3. Making personal copies on the office machine.

4. Charging the postage on your personal mail to the company.

5. Making nonbusiness trips in a company car.

6. On a company business trip: staying in the most expensive hotel, taking taxis when you could walk, including wine as food on your expense tab, taking your spouse along at company expense.

7. Using your office computer to shop online, trade stocks, view pornography, or e-mail friends on company time.

Are open-plan work premises likely to prevent employee theft?

picturelibrary/Alamy Stock Photo

8. Calling in sick when you need personal time.

9. Taking half the afternoon off when you're supposedly on business outside the office.

10. Directing company business to vendors who are friends or relatives.

11. Providing preferential service to corporate customers who have taken you out to lunch.

Discussion Questions

1. Review each item on Brenda's list and assess the conduct in question. Do you find it morally acceptable, morally unacceptable, or somewhere in between? Explain.

2. Examine Brenda's list from both the utilitarian and the Kantian perspectives. What arguments can be given for and against the conduct on her list? Is the rightness or wrongness of some items a matter of degree? Can an action (such as taking a pad of paper) be both trivial and wrong?

3. Someone might argue that some of the things listed as ethically dubious are really employee entitlements. Assess this contention.

4. How would you respond to the argument that if the company doesn't do anything to stop the conduct on Brenda's list, then it has only itself to blame? What about the argument that none of the things on the list are wrong unless the company has an explicit rule against it?

5. What obligations do employees have to their employers? Do companies have moral rights that employees can violate? What moral difference, if any, is there between taking something that belongs to an individual and taking something that belongs to a company?

6. What, if anything, can we learn about an employee's character based on whether they do or do not do the things on Brenda's list? Would you admire someone who scrupulously avoids doing any of these ethically dubious things, or would you think the person is self-righteous?

7. What should Brenda do when she finds a fellow employee engaging in what she considers ethically dubious conduct?

Chapter 11

Job Discrimination

Learning Objectives

After completing this chapter, you should be able to:

1. Identify the meaning of job discrimination and its different forms.
2. Characterize statistical and attitudinal evidence of discrimination and explain its relevance.
3. Explain the historical and legal context of affirmative action.
4. Make and assess moral arguments for and against affirmative action.
5. Make and assess moral arguments for and against comparable worth.
6. Distinguish the different forms that sexual harassment in employment takes, characterize the grounds on which sexual harassment is illegal, and explain why it's morally impermissible.

Introduction

In 2022, The National Football League Announced That Going forward each team must have at least one offensive coach who is a female or a member of a racial or ethnic minority.[1] This was a strengthening of the NFL's "Rooney Rule," named after former Pittsburgh Steelers owner Dan Rooney, which is intended to diversify the coaching ranks. When the rule was initially adopted in 2003, it had required only that teams must interview a diverse candidate for head coaching vacancies. Additional interviewing requirements had been imposed over time, expanding the number of positions the rule covers and the number of diverse candidates who must be interviewed, but 2022 marked the first time that the NFL imposed a requirement on who teams hire. (It also marked the first time that the rule mentioned female candidates.)

The success of the Rooney Rule in its first 20 years is open to debate. At the start of the 2023 season there were only three African-American head coaches in professional football, one head coach who identifies as biracial, and one head coach who is Hispanic. The league and several teams are also embroiled in a lawsuit filed by former Miami Dolphins head coach Brian Flores, who alleges that the NFL is biased against coaches of color and that teams offer non-White candidates who aren't being seriously considered "sham" interviews in order to comply with the Rooney Rule.[2]

If some believe that the NFL is still doing too little to increase the diversity of its coaches, however, then it is still doing more than college football. If you want to understand why some have said that

> ....
>
> **Most Commentators agree that the old-boys' network among athletic directors and coaches is part of the problem.**
>
> ....

college football needs its own Rooney Rule, a good place to start is with the experience of former Notre Dame coach Tyrone Willingham. When Notre Dame hired Willingham back in 2002, he was its first Black coach in any sport; moreover, signing him made Notre Dame the only top-notch football team in the nation with a Black coach. At the time only five coaches in the NCAA's top football division were Black. Today, the situation is a little better. Fifteen of the 130 schools in the NCAA's Football Bowl Subdivision—just under 12 percent—now have Black head coaches. An additional ten schools have head coaches who aren't White. (The Football Bowl Subdivision is the highest level of college football, comprising those Division I schools who aspire to be selected for "bowl games" at the end of the season.) However, fewer schools at the lower levels of competition have non-White coaches. All told, only 78 of the 626 college head coaches are not White: 12.5 percent.[3] These 2022 figures omit historically Black colleges and universities (HBCUs), but including these only raises the percentage of non-White coaches to 18 percent. For comparison, 40 percent of college football players are Black while 44 percent are White.

What explains this imbalance? Experts suggest several answers. At many universities, football is the biggest moneymaking sport, and search committees may fear that boosters and alumni will donate less if the head coach is a person of color. Another reason may be that Black men are often passed over for decision-making positions early in their athletic careers.

Athletes of color are underrepresented at the quarterback position, for instance, and African-American assistant coaches may be relegated to recruiting or smoothing out race relations rather than calling plays. In addition, the dearth of coaches of color may result in athletes of color failing to consider coaching as a possible career.

Finally, most commentators agree that the old-boys' network among athletic directors and coaches is part of the problem. Athletic directors, naturally enough, tend to look to people they know to fill coaching positions. "Athletic directors, to the extent that they're [White], generally have contacts who are also [White], and they use those contacts as they engage in searches at the informal level," says sociologist Jay Oakley of the University of Colorado at Colorado Springs. And 83 percent of athletic directors are White.

In the case of Willingham, it's no secret that he wasn't Notre Dame's first choice. The university had initially hired George O'Leary, who resigned five days later when it became known that he had lied on his résumé about his academic and athletic background. In discussing the appointment, Notre Dame athletic director Kevin White explained that he had been charmed by O'Leary's Irish-American background and his rah-rah style. O'Leary was like "something out of central casting," White said. In other words, the flamboyant O'Leary matched Kevin White's stereotypic image of what a Notre Dame coach should be. Sports columnist Mark Purdy writes that White's remark "basically confirms that athletic directors—at Notre Dame and too many other places—really do look for middle-aged [White] guys as the top choices for the top jobs. And that's depressing." It's to Notre Dame's credit, however, that after the O'Leary debacle, it took a second look at Willingham.

Unfortunately, the story doesn't end happily there. Three years later, Notre Dame fired Willingham. Football recruitment was solid, the team's morale was strong—it was on its way to a postseason bowl— and its academic performance had never been better. But that season, the squad had posted only a 6–5 record, and Notre Dame desperately wanted its team to rejoin the elite of college football. A case of job discrimination? It's difficult to say, but at the time some sportswriters and other observers thought so—including the university's outgoing president, Father Edward A. Malloy, who said the decision to fire Willingham was an embarrassment to the university. That's because Willingham's overall record was a respectable 21–15, and Notre Dame, which claims to adhere to higher values than other schools, had never before dismissed a coach only three years into a five-year contract. In fact, Willingham's record was better than the three-year marks of his two predecessors, who both had kept their jobs.

As it turned out, three years later Willingham's successor, Charlie Weis, had a 22–15 record—almost identical to Willingham's—but Notre Dame retained him for another two years, during which he posted a 13–12 record. On the other hand, after leaving Notre Dame, Willingham spent four years coaching the University of Washington, where he had a poor 6–29 record. Looking back, sportswriter Jon Wilner says, "I don't think Willingham was treated differently because he was [Black]. I think he was treated differently by Notre Dame because he was different, and being [Black] was not an insignificant part of that difference." As Wilner sees it, Willingham wasn't a Notre Dame guy. He had no ties to South Bend, and his reserved personality "wasn't the type to make boosters and trustees feel comfortable and important—to make them feel like the head coach was one of them." By contrast, "Weiss is one of them. He's a [White] guy who went to Notre Dame."

Most people oppose racial or sexual bias and reject job discrimination as immoral. But, as the paucity of coaches who are people of color or women reveals, explicit prejudice and overt discrimination are only part of the problem. Even open-minded people may operate on implicit assumptions that work to the disadvantage of women and people of color and many who believe themselves to be unprejudiced harbor unconscious racist or sexist attitudes.

Barack Obama gave an important speech on America's racial divisions during his 2008 presidential campaign. While he characterized the view that White "racism is endemic" as "profoundly

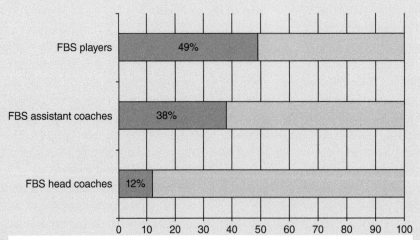

There are significant disparities between the percentages of Black players, Black assistant coaches, and Black head coaches in the Football Bowl Subdivision (FBS) level of college football.

distorted," Obama nevertheless reminded his audience about the country's history of discrimination and the present-day consequences of that history:

> As William Faulkner once wrote, "The past isn't dead and buried. In fact, it isn't even past." We . . . need to remind ourselves that so many of the disparities that exist in the African-American community today can be directly traced to inequalities passed on from an earlier generation that suffered under the brutal legacy of slavery and Jim Crow.
>
> Segregated schools were, and are, inferior schools; we still haven't fixed them, fifty years after *Brown v. Board of Education,* and the inferior education they provided, then and now, helps explain the pervasive achievement gap between today's black and white students.
>
> Legalized discrimination—where blacks were prevented, often through violence, from owning property, or loans were not granted to African-American business owners, or black homeowners could not access FHA mortgages, or blacks were excluded from unions, or the police force, or fire departments—meant that black families could not amass any meaningful wealth to bequeath to future generations. That history helps explain the wealth and income gap between black and white, and the concentrated pockets of poverty that persist in so many of today's urban and rural communities.
>
> A lack of economic opportunity among black men, and the shame and frustration that came from not being able to provide for one's family, contributed to the erosion of black families. . . . And the lack of basic services in so many urban black neighborhoods . . . helped create a cycle of violence, blight, and neglect that continue to haunt us.
>
> . . . What's remarkable is not how many failed in the face of discrimination, but rather how many men and women overcame the odds. . . . But for all those who scratched and clawed their way to get a piece of the American Dream, there were many who didn't make it—those who were ultimately defeated, in one way or another, by discrimination. That legacy of defeat was passed on to future generations—those young men . . . who we see standing on street corners or languishing in our prisons, without hope or prospects for the future.[4]

We must bear the history that Obama describes in mind as we explore the issue of job discrimination.

· · ·

The Meaning of Job Discrimination

To discriminate in employment is to make an adverse decision regarding an employee or a job applicant based on their membership in a certain group.[5] More specifically, **job discrimination** occurs when (1) an employment decision in some way harms or disadvantages an employee or a job applicant; (2) the decision is based on the person's membership in a certain group rather than on individual merit; and (3) the decision rests on prejudice, false stereotypes, or the assumption that the group in question is in some way inferior and thus does not deserve equal treatment. Because historically most discrimination in the American workplace has been aimed at women and at racial or ethnic minorities such as African Americans and Hispanics, the following discussion focuses on those groups.

Job discrimination can take different forms. It can be individual or institutional, and it can be either intentional or unwitting. Individuals, for instance, sometimes intentionally discriminate out of personal prejudice or on the basis of stereotypes. For example, an executive at Rent-A-Center, the nation's largest rent-to-own furniture and home appliance company, purposely disregarded job applications from women because he believed that they "should be home taking care of their husbands and children."[6]

Individuals also may discriminate because they unthinkingly or unconsciously accept traditional practices or stereotypes. For example, suppose that the merit-pay recommendations of a Walmart manager are influenced by the manager's implicit assumption that male employees are career oriented and have families to support, whereas female employees are there just to make a little extra money.[7] If the (presumably male) manager is unaware that this bias affects his decisions, his actions would fall into this category. Unconscious bias explains the fact that when researchers change a male name to a female name or a "White-sounding" name (say, Emily Walsh or Greg Baker) to a "Black-sounding" name (say, Lakisha Washington or Jamal Jones) on otherwise identical (but fictional) résumés, they receive fewer call-backs—even though hiring managers opine that qualified candidates who are women or people of color have a leg up because recruiters are seeking diversity.[8]

Job discrimination takes different forms.

Institutions discriminate. Sometimes they do so explicitly and intentionally—for example, employment agencies that screen out workers who are African Americans, Latinx, or older workers, and others at the request of their corporate clients,[9] or the Shoney's restaurants that color-coded job applications to separate Black from White applicants and that directed Black applicants, if hired, into kitchen jobs so that they would not be seen from the dining room.[10] Sometimes the routine operating procedures of a company reflect stereotypes and prejudiced practices that the company is not fully aware of. That seems to have been the case at Abercrombie & Fitch, which paid $50 million to settle a class-action job-discrimination lawsuit. The suit charged that in trying to cultivate its distinctive retail image, the company put people of color in less visible jobs and hired a disproportionately White sales force. The same is alleged to have been true at Wet Seal.[11] Or, to take another example, for years the FBI routinely transferred Hispanic agents around the country on temporary, low-level assignments where a knowledge of Spanish was needed; the agents functioned as little more than assistants to non-Hispanic colleagues. Hispanic agents dubbed this the "taco circuit" and claimed that it adversely affected their opportunities for promotion. A federal court agreed with them that the practice was indeed discriminatory.[12]

In addition, institutional practices that appear neutral and nondiscriminatory may harm members of groups that have been discriminated against in the past. When membership in an all-White craft union, for instance, requires nomination by those who are already members, racial exclusion is likely to result even if the motivation of those who do the nominating is purely nepotistic and results from no racially motivated ill will or stereotyping. Similarly, when USAir had a special backdoor hiring channel for pilots recommended by employees or friends of the company, only White pilots were ever hired this way.[13] Although the policy may look racially neutral, it produced disparate outcomes. Institutional procedures like these may not involve job discrimination in the narrow sense, but they clearly work to the disadvantage of women and minority groups, denying them full equality of opportunity.

There are strong moral arguments against job discrimination on racial or sexual grounds.

From a variety of moral perspectives there are compelling arguments against job discrimination on racial or sexual grounds. Since discrimination involves false assumptions about the inferiority of a certain group and harms individual members of that group, utilitarians would reject it because of its ill effects on total human welfare. Kantians would clearly repudiate it as failing to respect people as ends in themselves. Universalizing the maxim underlying discriminatory practices is practically impossible. No people who now discriminate would be willing to accept such treatment themselves. Discrimination on grounds of sex or race also violates people's basic moral rights and mocks the ideal of human moral equality. Furthermore, such discrimination is unjust. To use Rawls's theory as an illustration, parties in the original position would clearly choose for themselves the principle of equal opportunity.

There are no respectable arguments in favor of racial and sexual discrimination. Whatever racist or sexist attitudes people might actually have, few people today are prepared to defend job discrimination publicly, any more than someone would publicly defend slavery or advocate repealing the Nineteenth Amendment (which gave women the right to vote). This attitude toward job discrimination is reflected in legal and political efforts to develop programs to root it out and to ameliorate the results of past discrimination.

Before looking at those programs, however, and at the relevant legal history, we need to examine the relative positions of White and non-White people and of men and women in the American workplace to see what they reveal about ongoing discrimination.

⋯

Evidence of Discrimination

When investigators sent equally qualified young White and Black men to apply for entry-level jobs in Chicago and Washington, D.C., the results clearly showed racial discrimination against young African-American men.[14] Subsequent studies have confirmed that result.[15] In fact, one of them found that White applicants were more successful than Black applicants even when they had criminal records and the otherwise-identical Black applicants did not.[16] Similarly, Hispanic and African-American individuals are more likely to be turned down for home mortgages or to pay higher interest rates than are White individuals at the same income level.[17] The same is true for auto loans.[18] (It's worth noting that experts disagree over whether these disparities are best explained by racial bias.)[19]

Job discrimination certainly exists, but determining how widespread it is isn't easy. However, when statistics indicate that women and people of color play an unequal role in the work world and when endemic attitudes, practices, and policies are biased in ways that seem to account for the skewed statistics, then there is good reason to believe that job discrimination is a pervasive problem.

Statistical Evidence

People of color are disproportionately affected by poverty in the United States.[20] A plurality of Americans who live in poverty are White; in other words, more people who live in poverty are White rather than members of some other race. (This is true even if individuals who describe themselves as both White and Hispanic are excluded.) Nevertheless, while African-American people constitute 13.5 percent of the population of the United States, they make up just over 20 percent of the population in poverty. While just under 20 percent of the American population is Hispanic, just under 30 percent of the people who live in poverty are. Native Americans represent just over 1 percent of the total population but over 2 percent of the "poverty population."

The median wealth of White households today is many times that of Hispanic households or African-American households—$187,300 versus $31,700 for Hispanic households and $14,100 for African-American households.[21] At the same time, the median income of African-American families is only 65 percent, and that of Hispanic families only 77 percent, the median income of non-Hispanic White households.[22] Unemployment also hits some underrepresented communities hard; in 2021, for instance, the unemployment rate for Black or African-American people was 8.6 percent, for Native Americans and Inuit 8.2 percent, and for Hispanics or Latinx Americans 6.8 percent. In contrast, the unemployment rate for White Americans was 4.7 percent.[23]

There are also racial disparities in the types of jobs that Americans do. In 2019, Black workers represented 12.8 percent of the workforce, but only 10 percent of professionals were Black.[24] Drill down into specific categories of professionals and the disparities are even more glaring. Black professionals held 20.5 percent of community and social service positions, but they constituted under 7 percent of workers in the legal field, only 6 percent of scientists, and under 6 percent of employees in architecture and engineering. Hispanic or Latinx individuals made up over 17 percent of the workforce but less than 10 percent of the professional workforce. Hispanic and Latinx professionals were also clustered in community and social service roles and underrepresented in other professional fields.

Along with racial inequalities in rates of employment and in family income and wealth, these occupational disparities between Black and White individuals take on even greater importance because of the role that social networking and help from family and friends play in landing a good job. "Such favoritism has a strong racial component," says Nancy DiTomaso, a professor at Rutgers Business School. "It's a powerful, hidden force driving [racial] inequality in the United States."[25]

Women, too, are clustered in poorer-paying jobs—the so-called **pink-collar occupations.** They tend to work as librarians, nurses, elementary school teachers, salesclerks, secretaries, bank tellers, and waitresses—jobs that generally pay less than traditionally male occupations such as electrician, plumber, auto mechanic, shipping clerk, and truck driver. In the real world of work, the top-paying occupations have been, and to a large extent continue to be, almost exclusively male preserves. For example, in 2020 only 34.5 percent of dentists were women, compared to 94 percent of dental hygienists.[26] This actually represents a significant increase in the proportion of women dentists over decades past.

Over time, the across-the-board wage gap between men and women has shrunk slightly, but only slightly. In 1992, women who worked full-time made 75 percent of what men earned; they now make 83 percent.[27] Note that this figure reflects the median annual pay of all women who work at least 35 hours a week compared to that of all men who work at least 35 hours a

Summary
Discrimination In employment occurs when decisions adversely affect employees or job applicants because they are members of a group that is an object of prejudice or false stereotypes or is viewed as inferior and not deserving of equal treatment. Discrimination can be individual or institutional, intentional or unintentional. From various moral perspectives, there are strong arguments against job discrimination.

Summary
Studies reveal the persistence of discrimination in American life, and statistical evidence shows wide economic disparities between White people and people of color. It also shows significant occupational and income differences between White men on the one hand and women and people of color on the other.

week, without respect to what jobs they do or even how many hours per week they work; it doesn't mean that on average women earn only 83 percent of men in the same line of work. However, within nearly all broad occupational categories, men do earn more than women.[28] Female respiratory therapists make 93 cents for every dollar made by their male counterparts. Female truck drivers make 64 cents for every dollar earned by men. There are some exceptions. For instance, women who work as barbers—a separate category from hairdressers and hairstylists—make on average 8 percent more than men. But the U.S. Department of Labor divides the workforce into over 300 distinct occupational categories, and women outearn men in only 14. Barbering is actually the only example of an occupation where women outearn men in a field where most workers are men.

A discussion of gender discrimination in the workplace wouldn't be complete without mention of the discrimination faced by members of the transgender community. Surveys shows that roughly half of transgender individuals believe that they experience workplace discrimination and harassment (e.g., misgendering) on a regular basis.[29] One trans woman who works as a teacher describes her experience in this way: "Students were being removed from my class, rumors were spread about me, and it just wasn't a great place to be working anymore."

In recent decades both women and people of color have made considerable inroads into white-collar and professional ranks, but few have made it to the very top of their professions—as a glance at the companies that make up the Fortune 500 confirms. In 2023, 52 chief executives were women, an all-time high but still barely over 10 percent of the total.[30] The situation for Black executives is similar; there were only 8 African-American Fortune 500 CEOs.[31] Until Franklin Raines became CEO of Fannie Mae in 1999, no African American had ever been in charge of a Fortune 500 company. And it was only in 2009, when Ursula Burns took the helm at Xerox, that an African-American woman became a Fortune 500 CEO.

Attitudinal Evidence

Although some would disagree, statistics alone do not conclusively establish discrimination because one can always argue that other things account for the disparities in income and position between men and women and between White and non-White people. The U.S. Supreme Court, in fact, has stated that "no matter how stark the numerical disparity of the employer's work force," statistical evidence by itself does not prove discrimination.[32] But when widespread attitudes and institutional practices and policies are taken into account, they point to discrimination as a significant cause of the statistical disparities.

Take the case of Bari-Ellen Roberts. In 1990, she left an $80,000-a-year job at Chase Manhattan Bank to join Texaco's finance department. A White friend, whose husband worked for the company, had assured her that "Texaco's changing" and that the company was "looking for [Blacks]." Her new job was closer to home and held the promise of overseas assignments, but her friend was mistaken about Texaco's having changed. Soon after she arrived, Roberts found herself subjected to demeaning racial comments from colleagues and superiors (for example, one referred to her as a "little colored girl"). They couldn't understand why Roberts found such remarks offensive. A report on diversity that she and some other Black employees were asked to prepare was summarily dismissed with the comment "the next thing you know we'll have Black Panthers running down the halls." And a supervisor downgraded her performance record because he thought she was "uppity."[33]

Fed up with a "plague of racial insults" and "egregious acts of bigotry," she and several other Black employees filed a discrimination suit citing "the poisonous racial atmosphere" at Texaco. Texaco settled the suit for $141 million in retroactive raises after the news media got hold of a tape recording of an executive strategy session at Texaco. In the meeting, one official referred to Black employees as "black jelly beans," saying, "This diversity thing, you know how all the black jelly beans stick together," to which another responded, "That's funny. All the black jelly beans seem to be stuck at the bottom of the bag." One of Roberts's supervisors said, "I can't punch her [Roberts] in the face, so I play mind games with her." The executives were also heard agreeing to shred incriminating personnel records.

Consider some other well-known instances of job discrimination. In a precedent-setting 1980 case, Elizabeth Hishon sued King & Spalding, a big Atlanta law firm, contending that the firm's sexism prevented her from attaining partner status, causing her to be terminated as a result. (The case was eventually settled out of court.) Ten years later, Nancy O'Mara Ezold became the first woman to win a sex-discrimination case against a law firm in a partnership decision. Around that same time, another legal precedent was set when Price Waterhouse, the accounting firm, was ordered to give a partnership and back pay to Ann Hopkins, against whom it had discriminated. And in 2002 the federal Equal Employment Opportunity Commission filed its first sex-discrimination lawsuit against a major Wall Street firm, alleging that Morgan Stanley fired Allison Schieffelin, one of its top bond dealers, for complaining about pay discrimination.

Of particular interest here are the discriminatory attitudes and policies revealed by these cases. In the Ezold case, the judge found that the prominent Philadelphia law firm for which she had worked had applied tougher standards to women seeking partnerships than to men. Ezold said, "It wasn't just that similarly situated men were treated better than me, which is the double-standard idea. Another thing that came out of the trial was that in the year preceding the partnership decision, [the firm] assigned me to less complex cases and to fewer partners than it did men, so that I was denied the exposure that was critical to the partnership decision."[34]

In Ann Hopkins's case, sex stereotyping was at the root of the discrimination. Though she was considered an outstanding worker, Price Waterhouse denied her the position because she was allegedly an abrasive and overbearing manager. Coworkers referred to her as "macho," advised her to go to charm school, and intimated that she was overcompensating for being a woman. One partner in the firm even told her that she should "walk more femininely, talk more femininely, dress more femininely, wear makeup, have her hair styled, and wear jewelry." Hopkins argued, and the court agreed, that comments like these revealed underlying sexism at the firm and that her strident manner and occasional cursing would have been overlooked if she had been a man.[35] The same issue came up in the case of Schieffelin, who was viewed by her firm as insubordinate, verbally abusive, and "physically threatening."

As for the Hishon decision, the case is noteworthy because the defendants expressed no specific complaints about Hishon's work. They apparently denied her a partnership based on a general feeling that "she just didn't fit in." In the words of another woman who had been an associate at King & Spalding, "If you can't discuss the Virginia–North Carolina basketball game, you're an outcast."[36] Her pithy comment speaks volumes about how deep-seated attitudes operate against women and people of color in the workplace.

Women entering male turf, or people of color of either sex going into a predominantly White work environment, can find themselves uncomfortably being measured by a White male value system. Here's how Florence Blair, a twenty-five-year-old African-American woman, described working as a civil engineer at Corning Glass Works:

> As a minority woman, you are just so different from everyone else you encounter. . . . I went through a long period of isolation. . . . When I came here, I didn't have a lot in common with the [White] males I was working with. I didn't play golf, I didn't drink beer, I didn't hunt. All these things I had no frame of reference to.
>
> You need to do your job on a certain technical level, but a lot of things you do on the job come down to socializing and how well you mesh with people. Sometimes I look at my role as making people feel comfortable with me.
>
> Sometimes it's disheartening. You think why do I have to spend all of my time and energy making them feel comfortable with me when they're not reciprocating?[37]

Similarly, an executive who is a woman of color says: "I struggle with the idea of 'professionalism.' It feels like a [White] construct used to judge if I belong. Yet, I know it is how I get evaluated, so I do it."[38]

Surveys support the evidence of these cases. Over the years, they have indicated that sex stereotyping and sexist assumptions are widespread in business. Psychological experiments show that, even when they state that it doesn't matter to them, both men and women tend to prefer bosses who are men.[39] Male managers frequently assume that women place family demands

Women and people of color often find themselves measured by a White male value system.

Summary

Evidence of biased attitudes and sexist or racist assumptions also points to significant job discrimination in the workplace. As they try to fit into a work world dominated by White men, women and people of color can be disadvantaged by stereotypes, false preconceptions, and prejudiced attitudes.

above work considerations, that they lack the necessary drive to succeed in business, that they take negative feedback personally rather than professionally, and that they are too emotional to be good managers. Even worse, researchers have found that women internalize many of the stereotypes that men have of them as less-effective leaders despite the well-established fact that there is little difference between the leadership styles of successful male and female bosses.[40] This can lead to a phenomenon known as **stereotype threat**, in which a person's anxiety over the possibility that they will conform to a negative stereotype about their social group hinders their performance.

When it comes to race, the stereotypes can be even more damaging. Many White individuals, even very well-educated ones, still accept the canard that Black people are less intelligent than White people. Psychologists at a number of universities have also documented that most White people harbor hidden racial biases that they are unaware of and do not consciously agree with.[41]

Myths, stereotypes, false preconceptions, and biased attitudes victimize both women and people of color in the world of work, leading to decisions that disadvantage them in all aspects of their careers. This is especially true when companies give managers too much discretion in hiring, task assignment, promotion, and pay. In such circumstances, writes sociology professor William T. Bielby, all people unknowingly revert to stereotypes in making decisions: "The tendency to invoke gender stereotypes in making judgments about people is rapid and automatic. As a result, people are unaware of how stereotypes affect their perceptions and behavior," including "individuals whose personal beliefs are relatively free of prejudice."[42] Commenting on racial stereotypes, business consultant Edward W. Jones, Jr., writes:

> All people possess stereotypes, which act like shorthand to avoid mental overload. . . . Most of the time stereotypes are mere shadow images rooted in one's history and deep in the subconscious. But they are very powerful. For example, in controlled experiments the mere insertion of the word *black* into a sentence has resulted in people changing their responses to a statement.
>
> One reason for the power of stereotypes is their circularity. People seek to confirm their expectations and resist contradictory evidence, so we cling to beliefs and stereotypes that become self-fulfilling. If, for example, a [White] administrator makes a mistake, his boss is likely to tell him, "That's OK. Everybody's entitled to one goof." If, however, a [Black] counterpart commits the same error, the boss thinks, "I knew he couldn't do it. The guy is incompetent." The stereotype reinforces itself.[43]

Laws guaranteeing equality of opportunity are one response to the problem of discrimination. A more controversial response is affirmative action.

Taken together with the statistics, the attitudes, assumptions, and practices reviewed here provide powerful evidence of ongoing discrimination against women and people of color in the American workplace. Recognizing the existence of such discrimination and believing for a variety of reasons that it is wrong, we have as a nation passed laws to provide equality of opportunity to women and members of underrepresented groups. Such laws expressly forbid discrimination in recruitment, screening, promotion, compensation, and firing. But anti-discrimination laws do not address the present-day effects of past discrimination. To remedy the effects of past discrimination and counteract visceral racism and sexism, some companies and institutions have adopted stronger and more controversial affirmative action measures.

· · ·

Affirmative Action: The Legal Context

In 1954, the U.S. Supreme Court decided in the case of ***Brown v. Board of Education*** that racially segregated schooling is unconstitutional. In doing so, the Court conclusively rejected the older doctrine that "separate but equal" facilities are legally permissible. Not only were segregated facilities in the South unequal, the Court found, but also the very idea of separation of the races, based as it was on a belief in Black racial inferiority, inherently led to unequal treatment. That decision helped launch the civil rights movement in this country. One fruit of that movement was a series of federal laws and orders that attempt to safeguard the right of each person to equal treatment in employment.

The changes began in 1961, when President John F. Kennedy signed Executive Order 10925, which decreed that federal contractors should "take affirmative action to ensure that applicants are employed without regard to their race, creed, color, or national origin." In 1963, the Equal Pay Act was passed by Congress. Aimed especially at wage discrimination against women, it guaranteed the right to equal pay for equal work. That was followed by the **Civil Rights Act of 1964** (later amended by the Equal Employment Opportunity Act of 1972). Applying to all employers, both public and private, with fifteen or more employees, it prohibits all forms of discrimination based on race, color, sex, religion, or national origin. Title VII, the most important section of the act, prohibits discrimination in employment. It says:

> It shall be an unlawful employment practice for an employer (1) to fail or refuse to hire or to discharge any individual, or otherwise discriminate against any individual with respect to his compensation, terms, conditions, or privileges of employment, because of such individual's race, color, religion, sex, or national origin; or (2) to limit, segregate, or classify his employees or applicants for employment in any way that would deprive or tend to deprive any individual of employment opportunities or otherwise adversely affect his status as an employee, because of such individual's race, color, religion, sex, or national origin.

Employers may violate Title VII not only if they treat an individual differently because of sex, race, religion, color, or national origin (**disparate treatment**) but also if they have a rule or practice that, although not discriminatory on its face, excludes or adversely affects too many people of a particular sex, race, or other protected category (**disparate impact**). Disparate impact, however, does not automatically establish discrimination. In particular, if the employer can show that the practice in question was a legitimate, job-related business necessity, then it does not break the law. Avoiding job discrimination, though, can sometimes pose tricky dilemmas. Fearing a lawsuit, the City of New Haven threw out the results of an exam it had developed for determining which firefighters to promote to lieutenant or captain because of its disparate impact: No Black firefighters scored high enough to win promotion. However, the White firefighters who had done well on the exam sued the city. In 2009, the Supreme Court sided with them, ruling that discarding the test discriminated against them on grounds of race—it was a form of disparate treatment.[44]

There have in fact been a number of important Supreme Court cases that required the Court to develop interpretations of Title VII. In 2020, it issued rulings in a trio of such cases—*Bostock v. Clayton County*, *Altitude Express, Inc. v. Zarda*, and *R.G. & G.R. Harris Funeral Homes Inc. v. Equal Employment Opportunity Commission*, which were decided together.[45] With a 6–3 majority, the Court ruled that Title VII protection extends to LGBTQ+ individuals, since to discriminate against someone based on their sexual orientation or gender identity is to discriminate against them based on their sex. As Justice Neil Gorsuch's majority opinion states, "An employer who fires an individual for being homosexual or transgender fires that person for traits or actions it would not have questioned in members of a different sex. Sex plays a necessary and undisguisable role in the decision, exactly what Title VII forbids."

Congress has gone beyond the 1964 Civil Rights Act to outlaw other forms of job discrimination as well. Of particular importance are the Age Discrimination in Employment Act (1967, amended in 1978) and the Americans with Disabilities Act (1990), which extends to people with disabilities the same rights to equal employment opportunities that the Civil Rights Act of 1964 guarantees to women and people of color. In addition, several acts and executive orders regulate government contractors and subcontractors and require equal opportunities for veterans. All of these acts are enforced through the **Equal Employment Opportunity Commission (EEOC)**.

Affirmative Action Programs

By the late 1960s and early 1970s, companies contracting with the federal government (first in construction and then generally) were required to develop **affirmative action programs**, designed to correct imbalances in employment that exist directly as a result of past discrimination. These programs reflected the courts' recognition that job discrimination can

Summary
The Civil Rights Act of 1964 forbids discrimination in employment on the basis of race, color, sex, religion, or national origin. Employment practices that involve disparate treatment or disparate impact can violate the law. Subsequent legislation also forbids discrimination based on age or disability.

exist even in the absence of conscious intent to discriminate.[46] Affirmative action riders were added, with various degrees of specificity, to a large number of federal programs. Many state and local bodies adopted comparable requirements.

It's important to understand that true affirmative action programs involve positive steps toward including members of underrepresented groups that go beyond merely offering equal opportunity, that is, not discriminating against them. Only governmental agencies and larger companies that are government contractors or subcontractors are legally required to have affirmative policies, although other companies may choose to do so voluntarily as the NFL has done with the Rooney Rule. Employers with affirmative action policies are expected to survey current employment of women and people of color by department and job classification. Whenever underrepresentation of these groups is evident, companies are to develop goals and timetables to improve in each area of underrepresentation. They should then develop specific programs to achieve these goals, establish an internal audit system to monitor them, and evaluate progress in each aspect of the program. Finally, companies are encouraged to develop supportive in-house and community programs to combat discrimination.

There is a common misconception that by definition affirmative action involves quotas that require that particular percentages of jobs be filled by members of marginalized groups. In fact, however, federal contractors are not permitted to add quotas to their affirmative action programs.[47] Those rare cases in which affirmative action in employment takes the form of quotas generally involve instances in which governmental agencies like police departments are found to have engaged in pervasive discrimination that has not been corrected by less rigid forms of affirmative action.[48]

We saw earlier that Texaco was forced to pay its Black employees $141 million, the largest race-discrimination settlement in history, because the company had discriminated against qualified African Americans by refusing to promote them or pay them comparable salaries. In 2010, a jury found Novartis guilty of discriminating against female sales employees in pay and promotions, requiring it to pay $3.3 million in compensatory and $250 million in punitive damages. Lawsuits have also exposed discriminatory pay practices at many other companies, including Mitsubishi, Home Depot, Merrill Lynch, American Express, Walmart, and Boeing. Other firms are guilty of ignoring the spirit of equal employment opportunity even if they don't violate the letter of the law. For example, some companies forbid their employees from speaking Spanish among themselves even when their jobs do not require English proficiency or dealing with the public; others have made no effort to expand employment opportunities for women or people of color.

> Many large corporations find that diversity benefits the bottom line.

Yet today, many large corporations not only accept the necessity of equal opportunity employment and even affirmative action but also find that the bottom line benefits when they make themselves more diverse. According to research conducted by the consulting firm McKinsey & Company,

> [C]ompanies in the top quartile of gender diversity on executive teams were 25 percent more likely to experience above-average profitability than peer companies in the fourth quartile. … In the case of ethnic and cultural diversity, the findings are equally compelling. We found that companies in the top quartile outperformed those in the fourth by 36 percent in terms of profitability.[49]

Equal employment opportunity and affirmative action expand the pool of talent available to corporations. They foster the inclusion of a wider range of perspectives in decision making. They also allow corporations to reach out to a demographically wider customer base and make them better able to compete both in the global marketplace and in an increasingly multicultural environment at home.

However, despite the strong business case for diversity, genuine equality of opportunity has yet to be achieved in the corporate world. Moreover, many Americans oppose affirmative action. Critics of affirmative action charge that, in practice, it means illegal quotas, preferential treatment of African Americans and women, and even reverse discrimination against White men. In the 1960s and early 1970s, federal courts dismissed legal challenges to affirmative action, and in 1972 Congress gave it increased legislative validity by passing the Equal Employment Opportunity Act. Eventually, however, the Supreme Court had to address the question.

Summary
Affirmative action programs aim to correct racial imbalances existing as a result of past discrimination. Today, many companies believe that they benefit from affirmative action by becoming more diverse. Critics charge, however, that in practice affirmative action has often meant preferential treatment of women and people of color and even reverse discrimination against White men.

The Supreme Court's Position

The U.S. Supreme Court's first major ruling on affirmative action was in 1978, in the case of ***Bakke v. Regents of the University of California***. Allan Bakke, a White man, applied for admission to the medical school at the University of California at Davis. At the time almost all its medical students were White. To help remedy this situation, Davis's affirmative action program set aside for applicants of color 16 out of its 100 entrance places. If qualified applicants of color could not be found, those places were not to be filled. In addition to the special admissions process, applicants of color were free to compete through the regular admissions process for the unrestricted 84 positions. When Bakke was refused admission, he sued the University of California, contending that he had been discriminated against because he would have won admission if those 16 places had not been withdrawn from open competition and reserved for people of color. Bakke's grades, placement-test scores, and so on were higher than those of several applicants "of color who were admitted. The university did not deny this but defended its program as legally permissible and socially necessary affirmative action.

Bakke won his case, although it was a close, 5-to-4 decision. In announcing the judgment of the Court, Justice Lewis F. Powell's opinion rejected explicit racial criteria setting rigid quotas and excluding nonpreferred groups from competition. At the same time, Powell held that the selection process can take race and ethnic origin into account as one factor and pointed to Harvard's admission program as a model. In such a program, "race or ethnic background may be deemed a 'plus' in a particular applicant's file, yet it does not insulate the individual from comparison with all other candidates for the available seats."

A year later, in *United Steelworkers of America v. Weber*, the Supreme Court took up the issue again. At Kaiser Aluminum's Gramercy, Louisiana, plant, only 5 out of 273 skilled craft workers were Black, although the local workforce was 39 percent Black. Kaiser therefore entered into an agreement with the United Steelworkers to train employees from its workforce for these craft positions on the basis of seniority, except that 50 percent of the positions would be reserved for African-American employees until their percentage in these jobs approximated the percentage of African Americans in the local workforce. The program was challenged in court, and the case eventually reached the Supreme Court, which upheld Kaiser's affirmative action program. In delivering the court's opinion, Justice William Brennan made clear that legal prohibition of racial discrimination does not prevent "private, voluntary, race-conscious affirmative action plans." Kaiser's program, he wrote, "does not unnecessarily trammel the interest of the [White] employees. . . . Moreover, the plan is a temporary measure . . . simply to eliminate a manifest racial imbalance."

A few years later, though, the Supreme Court upheld seniority over affirmative action in *Memphis Firefighters v. Stotts*. When financial difficulties forced the city to lay off firefighters, it respected the customary practice of "last hired, first to be let go," even though that undermined its recent efforts to increase the number of Black firefighters. After reviewing the case, the Supreme Court ruled that seniority systems are racially neutral and that the city may not lay off White workers to save the jobs of Black workers with less seniority. However, the court reaffirmed the principle of affirmative action in 1987, this time in a case concerning women. In *Johnson v. Transportation Agency*, it held that considerations of sex were permissible as one factor in promoting Diane Joyce, a female county employee, to the position of road dispatcher over an equally qualified male employee, Paul Johnson. In summing up the Court's position, Justice Brennan stated that the promotion of Joyce "was made pursuant to an affirmative action plan that represents a moderate, flexible, case-by-case approach to effecting a gradual improvement in the representation of minorities and women in the Agency's work force."

Since then, however, the Court has grown more antagonistic to affirmative action programs. For example, in *City of Richmond v. Croson*, the Court invalidated a Richmond, Virginia, law that channeled 30 percent of public-works funds to minority-owned construction companies (refer to Case 11.1). In *Adarand Constructors v. Pena*, the Supreme Court examined a federal program that provided financial incentives for contractors to hire "socially or economically disadvantaged" subcontractors. In her majority opinion in the 5-to-4 decision, Justice Sandra

Summary
Although the legal situation is complex, in a series of rulings over the years a majority of the Court has upheld the general principle of affirmative action, as long as such programs are moderate and flexible. Race can legitimately be taken into account in employment-related decisions, but only as one among several factors. Affirmative action programs that rely on rigid and unreasonable quotas or that impose excessive hardship on present employees are illegal.

Day O'Connor affirmed the principle that "federal racial classification, like those of a State, must serve a compelling government interest, and must be narrowly tailored to further that interest." Accordingly, all government action based on race should be subjected to "the strictest judicial scrutiny" to ensure that no individual's right to equal protection has been violated. The Court then sent the case back to a lower court for rehearing.

In addition to O'Connor's majority opinion, however, five other justices wrote opinions in the *Adarand* case, and these reveal a range of perspectives on affirmative action. For instance, Justice David Souter criticized the Court for departing from past practice, reminding his colleagues that it is well established "that constitutional authority to remedy past discrimination is not limited to the power to forbid its continuation, but extends to eliminating those effects that would otherwise persist and skew the operation of public systems even in the absence of current intent to practice any discrimination."

In his dissenting opinion, Justice John Paul Stevens also defended the general principle of affirmative action:

> There is no moral or constitutional equivalence between a policy that is designed to perpetuate a caste system and one that seeks to eradicate racial subordination. . . .
>
> A decision by representatives of the majority to discriminate against the members of a minority race is fundamentally different from those same representatives' decision to impose incidental costs on the majority of their constituents in order to provide a benefit to a disadvantaged minority. Indeed, as I have previously argued, the former is virtually always repugnant to the principles of a free and democratic society, whereas the latter is, in some circumstances, entirely consistent with the ideal of equality.

However, Justice Clarence Thomas explicitly challenged Stevens's position. In an opinion concurring with the majority's judgment, he asserted that

> there is a "moral and constitutional equivalence" between laws designed to subjugate a race and those that distribute benefits on the basis of race in order to foster some current notion of equality. Government cannot make us equal; it can only recognize, respect, and protect us as equal before the law. . . .
>
> In my mind, government-sponsored racial discrimination based on benign prejudice is just as noxious as discrimination inspired by malicious prejudice. In each instance, it is racial discrimination, plain and simple.

The Supreme Court's most recent rulings are decidedly hostile to the principle and practice of affirmative action.

In its most recent rulings on the topic, the Court has been decidedly hostile to the principle and practice of affirmative action. In *Grutter v. Bollinger* the Court upheld, by a 5-to-4 majority, the affirmative action program at the University of Michigan's law school. Citing testimony from various business and military leaders, who urged that diversity is essential to the country's economy and security, the Court ruled that the state has a "compelling interest" in promoting educational diversity and that the law school's method of doing so was "narrowly tailored" to meet that interest. Under the law school's "highly individualized" and "holistic" approach, "belonging to certain minority groups" was a "plus factor" in evaluating potential students, but it was possible for a White student who was likely to make a particularly interesting contribution to the law school's academic climate to beat out a non-White student with better grades and test scores. But in *Gratz v. Bollinger*, a companion case, a different majority of justices ruled, 6 to 3, that Michigan's undergraduate affirmative action program was unconstitutionally rigid and mechanistic because it gave members of underrepresented groups an automatic 20-point bonus on the 150-point scale used to rank applicants.

In 2023, in deciding a further pair of cases on affirmative action in university admissions, the Court effectively overruled both *Bakke* and *Grutter* without formally reversing them. In *Students for Fair Admissions v. Harvard* and *Students for Fair Admissions v. University of North Carolina*, the Court held that the use of race-based affirmative action in admissions at these elite universities violated both the Equal Protection Clause of the Fourteenth Amendment and the Civil Rights Act.[50] The cases were filed by Students for Fair Admissions, an advocacy group, on behalf of unnamed Asian-American students whose applications had been rejected by these schools (whose admissions procedures did not treat Asians as an underrepresented group). In his majority opinion in the Harvard case, Chief Justice John Roberts wrote:

> [T]the Harvard and UNC admissions programs cannot be reconciled with the guarantees of the Equal Protection Clause. Both programs lack sufficiently focused and measurable objectives warranting the use of race, unavoidably employ race in a negative manner, involve racial stereotyping, and lack meaningful endpoints. We have never permitted admissions programs to work in that way, and we will not do so today.

In a dissenting opinion, Justice Sonia Sotomayor responded:

> Today, the Court concludes that indifference to race is the only constitutionally permissible means to achieve racial equality in college admissions. That interpretation of the Fourteenth Amendment is not only contrary to precedent and the entire teachings of our history … but is also grounded in the illusion that racial inequality was a problem of a different generation. Entrenched racial inequality remains a reality today. That is true for society writ large and, more specifically, for Harvard and the University of North Carolina (UNC), two institutions with a long history of racial exclusion. Ignoring race will not equalize a society that is racially unequal. What was true in the 1860s, and again in 1954, is true today: Equality requires acknowledgment of inequality.

The rulings in these cases applied only to affirmative action in higher education. However, according to attorneys Esther G. Lander & Amanda S. McGinn,

> [A]lthough the Harvard Opinion does not change the landscape for private employers, where the use of affirmative action is already extremely limited, employers should anticipate increased scrutiny and challenges to their workplace affirmative action plans and diversity initiatives. Employers should therefore review their practices to ensure they are being carried out in a manner that is not vulnerable to attack under Title VII and the Supreme Court's teachings.[51]

• • •

Affirmative Action: The Moral Issues

Understanding the Supreme Court's evolving position on affirmative action is important, because the Court sets the legal context in which business operates and lets employers know what they are and are not legally permitted to do. But legal decisions by themselves do not exhaust the relevant moral issues. Are affirmative action programs morally permissible? Are they morally obligatory? Knowing the state of the law is not enough by itself to answer these ethical questions. Indeed, it is a safe bet that the Supreme Court's own decisions are influenced not only by technical legal issues but also by how the justices answer them.

Before evaluating arguments for and against affirmative action, one needs to know what is being debated. *Affirmative action* here means programs taking the race or sex of employees or job candidates into account as part of an effort to correct imbalances in employment that exist as a result of past discrimination, either in the company itself or in the larger society. To keep the discussion relevant, it's limited to affirmative action programs that might realistically be expected to be upheld by the Supreme Court. Excluded are programs that establish rigid, permanent quotas or that hire and promote unqualified persons. Included are programs that hire or promote a woman or person of color who might not otherwise, according to established but reasonable criteria, be the best-qualified candidate.

A final word about terminology: Critics of affirmative action often label it "reverse discrimination." According to the definition offered earlier, job discrimination involves prejudice, inaccurate stereotypes, or the assumption that a certain group is inferior and deserves unequal treatment. Typically, none of this is true about affirmative action programs. As philosopher Ronald Dworkin has written, while affirmative action treats the members of different groups unequally, it still treats them "as equals," that is, without judging that some are superior to others in virtue of the groups to which they belong.[52] The effect of the affirmative action policy that resulted in Bakke's being rejected from the UC Davis medical school might look similar to that of the segregationist admissions policies and practices that excluded students of color from many universities. However, the rationales and motivations behind these policies are entirely different.

Arguments for Affirmative Action

1. Compensatory justice demands affirmative action programs.

POINT: "As groups, women and peoples of color have historically been discriminated against, often viciously. As individuals and as a nation, we can't ignore the sins of our fathers and mothers. In fact, we have an obligation to do something to help repair the wrongs of the past. Affirmative action in employment is one sound way to do this."

COUNTERPOINT: "People today can't be expected to atone for the sins of the past. We're not responsible for them, and in any case, we wouldn't be compensating those who rightly deserve it. Young African Americans and women coming for their first job have never suffered employment discrimination. Their parents and grandparents may deserve compensation, but why should today's candidates receive any special consideration? No one should discriminate against them, of course, but they should have to compete openly and on their merits, just like everybody else."

2. Affirmative action is necessary to permit fairer competition.

POINT: "Even if young Black people and young women today have not themselves suffered job discrimination, Black individuals in particular have suffered all the disadvantages of growing up in families that have been affected by discrimination. In our racist society, they have suffered from inferior schools and poor environment. In addition, as victims of society's prejudiced attitudes and stereotype threat, some young people of color and young women may have been hampered by a lack of self-confidence and self-respect. Plus, it's likely that implicit biases influence the evaluation of candidates by hiring managers, even managers who are sincerely committed to equal opportunity. Taking race and sex into account makes job competition fairer by keeping White men from having a competitive edge that they don't really deserve."

COUNTERPOINT: "Your point is better when applied to people of color than to women, it seems to me, but I'm still not persuaded. You overlook the fact that there are a lot of disadvantaged White people out there, too. Is an employer going to have to investigate everyone's life history to see who had to overcome the most obstacles? I think an employer has a right to seek the best-qualified candidate without trying to make life fair for everybody. And isn't the best-qualified person entitled to get the job or the promotion?"

3. Affirmative action is necessary to break the cycle that keeps peoples of color and women locked into low-paying, low-prestige jobs.

POINT: "You advocate neutral, nondiscriminatory employment practices, as if we could just ignore our whole history of racial and sexual discrimination. Statistics show that members of the African-American community have been trapped in a socioeconomically subordinate position. If we want to break that pattern and eventually heal the racial rifts in our country, we've got to adopt vigorous affirmative action programs that push more African-American individuals into middle-class jobs. Even assuming racism were dead in our society, with mere nondiscrimination alone it would take a hundred years or more for Black people to equalize their position."

COUNTERPOINT: "You ignore the fact that affirmative action has its costs, too. You talk about healing the racial rifts in our country, but affirmative action programs make everybody more racially conscious. They also cause resentment and frustration among White men. Many peoples of color and women also resent being advanced on grounds other than merit. Finally, if you hire and promote people faster and farther than they merit, you're only asking for problems."

Arguments Against Affirmative Action

1. Affirmative action injures White men and infringes their rights.

POINT: "Even moderate affirmative action programs injure the White men who are made to bear their brunt. Affirmative action violates their right to be judged as individuals

Summary
The moral issues surrounding affirmative action are controversial. Its defenders argue that compensatory justice demands affirmative action programs, that affirmative action is needed to permit fairer competition, and that affirmative action is necessary to break the cycle that keeps people of color and women locked into poor-paying, low-prestige jobs.

based on their own actions and abilities. In general, there's no reason to think that the White men who miss out on opportunities because of affirmative action are either guilty of discrimination themselves or the beneficiaries of past discrimination. It's unfair to make certain specific White men pay the price for our country's history of injustice when they are neither responsible for that history nor the ones who have gained the most from it."

COUNTERPOINT: "Jobs are scarce resources, and society may distribute these in a way that furthers its legitimate ends—like breaking the cycle of poverty for historically marginalized peoples. I admit that with affirmative action programs White men do not have as many advantages as they did before, and I'm against extreme programs that disregard their interests altogether. But their interests have to be balanced against society's interest in promoting these programs. This may not be entirely fair to the people who miss out on opportunities because of affirmative action. However, society is still fairer on the whole with affirmative action than without."

2. **Affirmative action itself violates the principle of equality.**

POINT: "Affirmative action programs are intended to enhance racial and sexual equality, but you can't do that by treating people unequally. If equality is the goal, it must be the means, too. With affirmative action programs, you consider race and sex as factors but that is the very thing that has caused so much harm in the past and that affirmative action itself is hoping to get rid of."

COUNTERPOINT: "Maybe an analogy will be helpful here. Ideally, light will enter our eyes without being distorted. That's how we see most clearly. Eyeglasses and contact lenses introduce distortions. Does that mean that no one should wear them? Obviously not. Some people have issues like astigmatisms that distort light on its way into the eye, and they need corrective lenses. One distortion counteracts the others—maybe not perfectly, but enough to improve one's sight. Perhaps eyeglasses and contact lenses would be unnecessary in an ideal world, but in the real world they're essential. In an ideal world, we wouldn't need affirmative action, which introduces a sort of distortion into the hiring or admission process, but in the real world we do because that distortion is counteracting others— albeit imperfectly."

3. **Nondiscrimination will achieve our social goals; stronger affirmative action is unnecessary.**

POINT: "The 1964 Civil Rights Act unequivocally outlaws job discrimination, and numerous employees and job candidates have won discrimination cases before the EEOC or in court. We need to insist on rigorous enforcement of the law. Also, employers should continue to recruit in a way that attracts applicants from historically marginalized groups and to make sure that their screening and review practices do not involve any implicit racist or sexist assumptions. And they should monitor their internal procedures and the behavior of their White male employees to root out any discriminatory behavior. Stronger affirmative action measures, in particular taking race or sex into account in employment matters, are unnecessary. They only bring undesirable results."

COUNTERPOINT: "Without affirmative action, progress often stops. The percentage of people of color and women employed by those subject to federal affirmative action requirements has risen much higher than it has elsewhere. Take the example of Alabama. In the late 1960s, a federal court found that only 27 out of the state's 3,000 clerical and managerial employees were African American. Federal Judge Frank Johnson ordered extensive recruiting of Black employees, as well as the hiring of the few specifically identified Black people who could prove they were victims of discrimination. Nothing happened. Another suit was filed, this time just against the state police, and this time a 50 percent hiring quota was imposed, until Black officers reached 25 percent of the force. As a result, Alabama's state police quickly became the most thoroughly integrated state police force in the country."[53]

Summary
Critics of affirmative action argue that affirmative action injures White men and infringes their rights, that affirmative action itself violates the principle of equality, and that nondiscrimination (without affirmative action) will suffice to achieve our social goals.

Fred Schilling / United States Supreme Court

The newest U.S. Supreme Court justice, Ketanji Brown Jackson, was sworn into office in June 2022. Today, American presidents seem to be under political pressure to ensure that peoples of color and women are represented on the Supreme Court. Is this desire for diversity a kind of affirmative action?

The debate over affirmative action is not the only controversy connected with job discrimination. Two other issues, both primarily concerning women, have been the topic of recent moral, legal, and political discussion: the issue of comparable worth and the problem of sexual harassment on the job.

• • •

Comparable Worth

Louise Peterson was a licensed practical nurse at Western State Hospital in Tacoma, Washington. For supervising the daily care of sixty men convicted of sex crimes, she was paid $192 a month less than the hospital's groundskeepers and $700 a month less than men doing work similar to hers at Washington state prisons. Convinced of the inequity of the state's pay scale, Peterson filed a suit claiming that she and other women were being discriminated against because men of similar skills and training and with similar responsibilities were being paid significantly more. A federal judge found Washington guilty of sex discrimination and ordered the state to reimburse its female employees a whopping $838 million in back pay.

Although an appellate court later overturned that ruling, the state of Washington began a program intended to raise the pay for government jobs typically considered "women's work." Even though the program had flaws,[54] it helped raise to national prominence the doctrine of comparable worth and signaled a dramatic escalation in women's fight for equal employment rights.

In essence, the doctrine of **comparable worth** holds that women and men should be paid on the same scale not only for doing the same or equivalent jobs but also for doing different jobs involving comparable skill, effort, working conditions, and responsibility. Advocates of comparable worth point to the substantial statistical evidence demonstrating that women are in more low-paying jobs than men. They also note the consistent relationship between the percentage of women in an occupation and the salaries in that occupation: The more women dominate an occupation, the less it pays.[55] Comparable-worth advocates contend that women

Summary

Comparable worth is the idea that women and men should be paid on the same scale for doing different jobs if they involve equivalent skill, effort, and responsibility. Advocates of comparable worth say that women have been shunted into low-paying jobs, that they suffer from a discriminatory labor market, and that justice requires that they receive equal pay for doing jobs of equal worth.

have been shunted into a small number of pink-collar occupations and that a biased and discriminatory wage system has kept their pay below that of men in occupations involving comparable demands.

As comparable-worth advocates see it, justice demands that women receive equal pay for doing work of comparable value. Jobs should be objectively evaluated in terms of the education, skills, and experience required and in terms of responsibilities, working conditions, and other relevant factors. This is typically done using a point system. Equivalent jobs—those scoring equal or nearly equal numbers of points—should receive equivalent salaries, even if the labor market would otherwise put them on different pay scales. So, if a given employer determined that truck drivers and administrative assistants have comparably demanding jobs, all-things-considered, then they would need to be on the same pay scale even though the market wages of these two occupations might be very different. If truck drivers are currently paid more, and if the company doesn't think that it can lower their pay, then comparable worth would require the company to raise the pay of administrative assistants.

Some comparable-worth advocates further argue that when women have not received equivalent pay for jobs of comparable worth, justice requires that employers pay them reparation damages for the money they have lost. That would be expensive. But whether pay adjustments are retroactive or not, all comparable-worth programs envision adjusting the salary schedules of women upward rather than the pay of men downward.

Opponents of comparable worth insist that women, desiring flexible schedules and less taxing jobs, have freely chosen lower-paying occupations and thus are not entitled to any readjustment in pay scales. Phyllis Schlafly, for one, calls comparable worth "basically a conspiracy theory of jobs. . . . It asserts that, first, a massive societal male conspiracy has segregated or ghetto-ized women into particular occupations by excluding them from others; and then, second, devalued the women's job by paying them lower wages than other occupations held primarily by men." She adds: "For two decades, at least, women have been free to go into any occupation. . . . But most women continue to choose traditional, rather than non-traditional, jobs. This is their own free choice. Nobody makes them do it."[56]

Others who are sympathetic to the concept of comparable worth worry about its implementation. How are different jobs to be evaluated and compared, they wonder. "How do you determine the intrinsic value of one job and then compare it to another?" asks Linda Chavez, former staff director of the Commission on Civil Rights. She points out that "for 200 years, this has been done by the free marketplace. It's as good an alternative as those being suggested by comparable-worth advocates. I'm not sure the legislative bodies or courts can do any better."[57] Job evaluation studies, however, are common in the public sector, and many private companies also utilize them to determine the skill, effort, responsibility, and working conditions that characterize different job categories and, hence, the wages appropriate to them. However, even if reasonably objective judgments of comparability are possible, opponents worry about the price tag: Revising salaries could cost a medium-size company millions of dollars in increased pay and benefits.

Advocates of comparable worth respond to those criticisms by pointing to statistical evidence demonstrating gender-linked pay inequities, some of which have already been cited in this chapter, as well as to the reality of visceral sexism in the workplace and to the thousands of cases every year involving workplace discrimination against women. They reject the idea that women end up in jobs that pay less than comparable jobs held by men because of their free choice. Rather, discrimination distorts the operation of the labor market and needs to be corrected. They also point out that even if there's a sense in which women are nominally choosing to cluster in the pink-collar jobs, the choice may not be an entirely free one. Young girls are still often socialized to believe that some future careers are more appropriate for them than others. They're also socialized to believe that they'll be the primary caregiver for their children, which has implications for what sorts of careers they consider. Some women may also choose to work pink-collar jobs because they anticipate that otherwise they'll face workplace discrimination and harassment.

Proponents of comparable worth believe that women have been directed into certain occupations and held back by a biased wage system.

Opponents insist that women have freely chosen lower-paying occupations.

Summary
Opponents of comparable worth claim that women have freely chosen their occupations and are not entitled to compensation. They contend that only the market can and should determine the value of different jobs and that revising pay scales would be expensive.

Moreover, proponents of comparable worth reject the argument that implementing comparable worth would be prohibitively expensive. They point to Minnesota, which phased in a comparable-worth program over several years so that the state incurred an expense of only about 1 percent a year. But the core of their argument remains an appeal to fairness and equity, which, they insist, shouldn't be sacrificed on the altar of economics.

The comparable-worth issue continues to engender controversy because, as one commentator puts it, "The issue pits against each other two cherished American values: the ethics of nondiscrimination versus the free enterprise system."[58] The federal courts have not explicitly accepted the doctrine of comparable worth, even when they've rendered legal decisions that seem to support it. One form of job discrimination against women that the courts agree about, however, is sexual harassment.

...

Sexual Harassment

Sexual harassment—we hear about it all the time. In 2017, women began using the hashtag #MeToo on social media to indicate that they had been victims of sexual harassment or assault. This amplified the "Me Too" movement that had been initiated by African-American activist Tarana Burke several years earlier. Numerous powerful men lost positions as a result of being accused of sexual harassment, especially in the entertainment industry.[59] Movie producer Harvey Weinstein, who was convicted of several criminal offenses including rape, was the most notorious example. Others included morning show host Matt Lauer and PBS television host Charlie Rose. But sexual harassment is not merely a matter of a few rich and powerful men misbehaving. It is a form of sexual discrimination that violates Title VII of the Civil Rights Act, and between the 2018 and 2021 fiscal years the EEOC received over 27,000 sexual harassment complaints.[60] Many cases go unreported. No large American corporation or organization has escaped the issue. Indeed, charges of sexual harassment have cost some of them a small fortune. In the late 1990s, for instance, Ford paid $7.75 million and Mitsubishi $34 million to settle class-action sexual-harassment lawsuits against them. According to the Supreme Court, men as well as women can be victims of sexual harassment.[61] The focus here is on women, however, because they are the ones who suffer most from it. One survey found that 38 percent of women report having been harassed at work.[62]

Critics may find it odd that sexual harassment is viewed by the courts as a kind of sex discrimination. If an infatuated supervisor harasses only the female employee who is the object of his desire, is his misconduct really best understood as discrimination against women? He does not bother women in general, only this particular individual. In viewing sexual harassment as a violation of the 1964 Civil Rights Act, however, the courts are rightly acknowledging that such behavior, and the larger social patterns that reinforce it, rest on male attitudes and assumptions that work against women.

Accepting this viewpoint still leaves puzzles, however. Assume that the infatuated supervisor is a woman and the employee a man. Are we to interpret this situation as sex discrimination, considering that it does not take place against a social backdrop of exploitation and discrimination against men? Or imagine an employer who sexually harasses employees of all genders. Does the absence of discrimination mean that there's no sexual harassment?

These conceptual puzzles have to do with the law's interpretation of sexual harassment as a kind of sex discrimination. Practically speaking, this interpretation has benefited women and brought them better and fairer treatment on the job, but it clearly has its limits. Legally speaking, the most important aspect of sexual harassment may be that it represents discrimination, but it is doubtful that discrimination is morally the worst aspect of sexual harassment. (By analogy, compare the fact that often the only grounds on which the federal government can put a murderer on trial is on the charge of having violated the civil rights of their victim. The charge of violating the victim's civil rights doesn't get to the heart of the murderer's wrongdoing, even if it is the only violation of federal as opposed to state law.)

Legally, sexual harassment is a form of discrimination. But that may not be the worst aspect of it, morally speaking.

The Definition of Sexual Harassment

What exactly is sexual harassment? According to the EEOC, **sexual harassment** involves "unwelcome sexual advances, requests for sexual favors, and other verbal or physical conduct of a sexual nature." Catherine A. MacKinnon, author of *Sexual Harassment of Working Women*, describes sexual harassment as "sexual attention imposed on someone who is not in a position to refuse it." Alan K. Campbell, former director of the Federal Office of Personnel Management, defines it as "deliberate or repeated unsolicited verbal comments, gestures, or physical contact of a sexual nature which are unwelcome."[63] Here is a fuller statement of the EEOC definition that reflects the way most courts understand sexual harassment:

> Unwelcome sexual advances, requests for sexual favors, and other verbal or physical conduct of a sexual nature constitute sexual harassment when (1) submission to such conduct is made either explicitly or implicitly a term or condition of an individual's employment, (2) submission to or rejection of such conduct by an individual is used as the basis for employment decisions affecting such individual, or (3) such conduct has the purpose or effect of substantially interfering with an individual's work performance or creating an intimidating, hostile, or offensive working environment.

Sexual harassment divides into two types: "quid pro quo" and "hostile work environment." The phrase *quid pro quo* refers to giving something in return for something else; translated from Latin, it means "this for that." **Quid-pro-quo harassment** occurs when a supervisor makes an employee's employment opportunities conditional on the employee's entering into a sexual relationship with, or granting sexual favors to, the supervisor. Sexual threats are an example— in their crudest form, "You'd better agree to sleep with me if you want to keep your job." The immorality of such threats seems clear. In threatening harm, they are coercive and violate the rights of the person being threatened, certainly depriving them of equal treatment on the job. Obviously, such threats can be seriously damaging, psychologically and otherwise, and hence are morally wrong. The numbered clauses (1) and (2) in the EEOC definition of sexual harassment refer to quid-pro-quo harassment.

Sexual offers are another species of quid-pro-quo sexual harassment: "If you sleep with me, I'm sure I can help you advance more quickly in the firm." Often such offers harbor an implied threat, and, unlike with genuine offers, the employee may risk something by turning them down. Larry May and John Hughes have argued that such offers by a male employer to a female employee put her in a worse position than she was in before and are therefore coercive. Even sexual offers with no hint of retaliation, they contend, change the female employee's working environment in an undesirable way.[64] In the case of both threats and offers, the supervisor is attempting to exploit the power imbalance between him and the employee.

The second kind of sexual harassment—**hostile-work-environment harassment**— is broader, but it may be more important because it is so pervasive. This form of sexual harassment is behavior of a sexual nature that is distressing to women and interferes with their ability to perform on the job, even when the behavior is not an attempt to pressure the woman for sexual favors. Sexual innuendos; sexually explicit e-mails; leering at or ogling a woman; sexist remarks about women's bodies, clothing, or sexual activities; the posting of sexually suggestive or pornographic pictures; raunchy office banter; and unnecessary touching, patting, or other physical conduct can all constitute sexual harassment. Such behavior is humiliating and degrading to its victim. It interferes with their peace of mind and undermines their work performance. The third numbered clause in the EEOC definition obviously refers to hostile-work-environment harassment.

Legally, an employee is not required to prove that she was psychologically damaged or unable to work in order to establish sexual harassment. On the other hand, an isolated or occasional sexist remark or innuendo does not constitute harassment. To qualify as harassment, the objectionable behavior must be persistent. The same holds for racial slurs and epithets. An ethnic joke by itself does not constitute discriminatory harassment, but a concerted pattern of "excessive and opprobrious" racially derogatory remarks and related abuse does violate the law.[65]

There are two types of sexual harassment.

Summary
Sexual harassment is widespread. It includes unwelcome sexual advances and other conduct of a sexual nature when either (1) employment decisions are based on submission to it (quid pro quo) or (2) such conduct substantially interferes with an individual's work performance (hostile work environment). The law treats sexual harassment is a kind of discrimination.

Human beings are sexual creatures, and when people work together, there may be sexual undertones to their interactions. With the right persons and at the appropriate times, many people can enjoy sexual references, sex-related humor, or flirtation with co-workers. Many married couples met in the workplace, which is unsurprising given the number of hours spent there. It's not necessary that a serious and professional work environment be entirely free from sexuality, nor is this an achievable goal.

When, then, is behavior objectionable or offensive enough to constitute harassment? What one person views as innocent fun or a friendly overture may be understood as objectionable or demeaning by someone else. Comments that one person appreciates or enjoys may be distressing to another. Who can decide what is right? In the case of sexual harassment, who determines what is objectionable or offensive?

To answer that question, the courts ask what the hypothetical "reasonable person" would find offensive if the person were a woman in that situation. What matters morally, however, is to respect each person's choices and wishes. Even if the other people in the office like it when the boss gives them a little hug, it would still be wrong to hug the one person who is made uncomfortable. If the behavior is unwanted—that is, if the person doesn't like it—then persisting in it is wrong. The fact that objectionable behavior must be persistent and repeated to be sexual harassment allows for the possibility that people can honestly misread coworkers' signals or misjudge their likely response to a sexual innuendo, a joke, or a friendly pat. That may be excusable; what is not excusable is persisting in the behavior once you know it's unwelcome.

Some lower courts have extended the concept of sexual harassment to include **sexual favoritism**, upholding the claims of women to have been discriminated against because the boss was sleeping not with them but with one or more other employees. That seems to stretch the concept of sexual harassment almost to the breaking point, because the rights of the complaining employee have not been violated. Her employment opportunities have not been made contingent on her acquiescing to her employer's sexual wishes. However, the women who entered into sexual relations with their supervisor may have benefited from doing so, possibly at the expense of the employee who had no such relationship with the boss. Moreover, such conduct by a supervisor can create a sexually charged work environment that interferes with the ability of other employees to do their job. It also reinforces beliefs that demean women and perpetuate discrimination against them because, in the words of one judge, "a message is conveyed that managers view women as sexual playthings."[66]

Dealing With Sexual Harassment

Neither the wrongness nor the illegality of sexual harassment requires that the harassing conduct be by the employee's supervisor. This is particularly relevant in hostile-work-environment cases, in which the harassment a person endures may come from coworkers. Furthermore, companies can be held legally liable for harassing behavior by their employees even if they are unaware of it, especially in cases of quid-pro-quo harassment by supervisors. In hostile-work-environment cases, companies can escape liability if they can show that (1) they took reasonable steps to prevent and promptly correct sexually harassing behavior and (2) the employee unreasonably failed to take advantage of the preventive or corrective procedures established by the company. This fact gives companies an incentive to be proactive, and many have responded by developing comprehensive programs to educate employees about, and to protect them from, sexual harassment. Legal issues aside, companies clearly have a moral obligation to provide a work environment in which employees are free from sexual harassment. They need to be alert to the possibility of sexual harassment, take reasonable steps to prevent it, and deal with it swiftly and fairly should it occur.

Practically speaking, what should an employee do if they encounter sexual harassment? *First,* if they are comfortable doing so then they can make it clear that the behavior is unwanted.[67] That may be more difficult to do than it sounds, because most of us like to please others and do not want to be thought to be "prudes" or to lack a sense of humor. The employee may wish to be tactful and even pleasant in rejecting behavior they find

---

In sexual harassment cases, the courts look to what a reasonable person would find offensive. But what matters morally is to respect each person's choices and wishes.

Summary
Employees encountering sexually harassing behavior from coworkers should make it clear that the behavior is unwanted. If it persists, harassed employees should document the behavior and report it to the appropriate person or office in the organization. In the case of sexual threats or offers from supervisors, they should do this immediately. If internal channels are ineffective, employees should seek legal advice.

What you should do if you encounter sexual harassment.

inappropriate, especially if they think the offending party is well intentioned. *Second,* if the behavior persists, the employee should try to document it by keeping a record of what has occurred, who was involved, and when it happened. If others have witnessed some of the incidents, then that will help to document the case.

Third, the employee should complain to the appropriate supervisor, sticking to the facts and presenting allegations as objectively as possible. The employee should do this immediately in the case of sexual threats or offers by supervisors. In the case of inappropriate behavior by coworkers, an employee who has experienced harassment should generally wait to see if it persists despite having told the offending party that they object. If complaining to the immediate supervisor does not bring quick action, then the employee must try whatever other channel is available within the organization—the grievance committee, for example, or the chief executive's office.

Fourth, if internal complaints do not bring results, then the employee should seriously consider seeing a lawyer and learning in detail what legal options are available. Many employees try to ignore sexual harassment, but the evidence suggests that in most cases it continues or grows worse. When sexual threats or offers are involved, a significant number of victims are subject to unwarranted reprimands, increased workloads, or other reprisals. The employee must remember, too, that they have both a moral and a legal right to work in an environment free from sexual harassment.

Study Corner

Key Terms and Concepts

affirmative action programs
Bakke v. Regents of the University of California
Brown v. Board of Education
Civil Rights Act of 1964
comparable worth

Equal Employment Opportunity Commission (EEOC)
disparate impact
disparate treatment
hostile-work-environment harassment
job discrimination

pink-collar occupations
quid-pro-quo harassment
sexual favoritism
sexual harassment
stereotype threat

Points to Review

- what the case of Notre Dame and Willingham illustrates (pp. 317–318)
- three defining features of job discrimination (p. 319)
- four different forms of job discrimination (p. 319)
- moral arguments against job discrimination (p. 320)
- statistical evidence of inequality (pp. 321–322)
- attitudes that victimize women like Ezold, Hopkins, and Hishon (pp. 323–324)
- how stereotypes can lead to discrimination (pp. 323–324)
- what was decided in *Brown v. Board of Education* (p. 324)
- what the Civil Rights Act says about discrimination (p. 325)

- the difference between disparate treatment and disparate impact (p. 325)
- the difference between equal opportunity and affirmative action (p. 326)
- why many companies believe in affirmative action (p. 326)
- where the Supreme Court stands on affirmative action (pp. 327–329)
- what's misleading about calling affirmative action "reverse discrimination" (p. 329)
- three arguments for affirmative action (p. 330)
- three arguments against affirmative action (pp. 330–331)

- what the doctrine of comparable worth requires employers to do (pp. 332–333)
- arguments for and against comparable worth (pp. 333–334)
- what's puzzling about viewing sexual harassment as sex discrimination (p. 334)
- two types of sexual harassment (p. 335)

- who decides what is sexual harassment (p. 336)
- sexual favoritism as a possible form of sexual harassment (p. 336)
- how companies can escape legal liability for hostile-work-environment claims (p. 336)
- four things to do when you encounter sexual harassment (pp. 336–337)

For Further Reflection

1. In your view, how pervasive is job discrimination these days? Have you or anyone you've known experienced some form of it?
2. Do you think affirmative action programs are misguided, or are they justifiable and socially beneficial? Which side of the comparable-worth issue are you on?
3. Why is sexual harassment so distressingly common?

Case 11.1

Subcontract Set-Asides

Richmond, Virginia, The Former Capital of The Confederacy, Is not the sort of place one would normally associate with controversial efforts at affirmative action. But aware of its legacy of racial discrimination and wanting to do something about it, the Richmond City Council adopted what it called the Minority Business Utilization Plan—a plan that eventually brought it before the U.S. Supreme Court.

The plan, which the council adopted by a 5-to-2 vote after a public hearing, required contractors to whom the city awarded construction contracts to subcontract at least 30 percent of the dollar amount of their contracts to minority business enterprises (MBEs). A business was defined as an MBE if non-White individuals controlled at least 51 percent of it, and a minority-owned business from anywhere in the United States could qualify as an MBE subcontractor. (The 30 percent set-aside did not apply to construction contracts awarded to minority contractors in the first place.)

Proponents of the set-aside provision relied on a study that indicated that whereas the general population of Richmond was 50 percent African American, only 0.67 percent of the city's construction contracts had been

awarded to minority businesses. Council member Marsh, a proponent of the ordinance, made the following statement:

> I have been practicing law in this community since 1961, and I am familiar with the practices in the construction industry in this area, in the state, and around the nation. And I can say without equivocation, that the general conduct of the construction industry . . . is one in which race discrimination and exclusion on the basis of race is widespread.

Opponents questioned both the wisdom and the legality of the ordinance. They argued that the disparity between people of color in the population of Richmond and the low number of contracts awarded to MBEs did not prove racial discrimination in the construction industry. They also questioned whether there were enough MBEs in the Richmond area to satisfy the 30 percent requirement.

The city's plan was in effect for five years. During that time, it was challenged in the courts. A federal district court upheld the set-aside ordinance, stating that the city council's "findings [were] sufficient to ensure that, in adopting the Plan, it was remedying the present effects of past discrimination in the construction industry." However, the case was appealed to the Supreme Court, which ruled in *City of Richmond v. Croson* that the Richmond plan was in violation of the equal protection clause of the Fourteenth Amendment.[68] In delivering the opinion of the majority of the Court, Justice Sandra Day O'Connor argued that Richmond had not supported its plan with sufficient evidence of past discrimination in the city's construction industry:

> A generalized assertion that there has been past discrimination in an entire industry provides no guidance for a legislative body to determine the precise scope of the injury it seeks to remedy. It "has no logical stopping point." . . . "Relief" for such an ill-defined wrong could extend until the percentage of public contracts awarded to MBEs in Richmond mirrored the percentage of minorities in the population as a whole.
>
> [The City of Richmond] argues that it is attempting to remedy various forms of past discrimination that are alleged to be responsible for the small number of minority businesses in the local contracting industry. . . . While there is no doubt that the sorry history of both private and public discrimination in this country has contributed to a lack of opportunities for [Black] entrepreneurs, this observation, standing alone, cannot justify a rigid quota in the awarding of public contracts in Richmond, Virginia. Like the claim that discrimination in primary and secondary schooling justifies a rigid racial preference in medical school admissions, an amorphous claim that there has been past discrimination cannot justify the use of an unyielding racial quota.
>
> It is sheer speculation how many minority firms there would be in Richmond absent past societal discrimination, just as it was sheer speculation how many minority medical students would have been admitted to the medical school at Davis absent past discrimination in educational opportunities. Defining these sorts of injuries as "identified discrimination" would give local governments license to create a patchwork of racial preferences based on statistical generalizations about any particular field of endeavor.
>
> These defects are readily apparent in this case. The 30% quota cannot in any realistic sense be tied to any injury suffered by anyone. . . .
>
> In sum, none of the evidence presented by the city points to any identified discrimination in the Richmond construction industry. We, therefore, hold that the city has failed to demonstrate a compelling interest in apportioning public contracting opportunities on the basis of race. To accept Richmond's claim that past societal discrimination alone can serve as the basis for rigid racial preference would be to open the door to competing claims for "remedial relief" for every disadvantaged group. The dream of a Nation of equal citizens in a society where race is irrelevant to personal opportunity and achievement would be lost in a mosaic of shifting preferences based on inherently unmeasurable claims of past wrongs. . . . We think such a result would be contrary to both the letter and spirit of a constitutional provision whose central command is equality.

But the Court's decision was not unanimous, and Justice Thurgood Marshall was joined by Justices William Brennan and Harry Blackmun in dissenting vigorously to the opinion of the majority. Justice Marshall wrote:

The essence of the majority's position is that Richmond has failed to . . . prove that past discrimination has impeded minorities from joining or participating fully in Richmond's construction contracting industry. I find deep irony in second-guessing Richmond's judgment on this point. As much as any municipality in the United States, Richmond knows what racial discrimination is; a century of decisions by this and other federal courts has richly documented the city's disgraceful history of public and private racial discrimination. In any event, the Richmond City Council has supported its determination that minorities have been wrongly excluded from local construction contracting. Its proof includes statistics showing that minority-owned businesses have received virtually no city contracting dollars; . . . testimony by municipal officials that discrimination has been widespread in the local construction industry; and . . . federal studies . . . which showed that pervasive discrimination in the Nation's tight-knit construction industry had operated to exclude minorities from public contracting. These are precisely the types of statistical and testimonial evidence which, until today, this Court has credited in cases approving of race-conscious measures designed to remedy past discrimination.

Discussion Questions

1. What was the Richmond City Council trying to accomplish with its Minority Business Utilization Plan? If you had been a member of the council, would you have voted for the plan?

2. What are the pros and cons of a plan like Richmond's? Will it have good consequences? Does it infringe on anyone's rights? What conflicting moral principles, ideals, and values are at stake?

3. Do you believe that there was sufficient evidence of racial discrimination to justify the city's plan? Who is right about this—Justice O'Connor or Justice Marshall?

4. Justice O'Connor and the majority of the Court seem to believe that there must be some specific, identifiable individuals who have been discriminated against before race-conscious measures can be adopted to remedy past discrimination. Do you agree that affirmative action measures must meet this standard?

5. In light of the fact that no federal statute specifically bars racial discrimination in private domestic commercial transactions between two business firms, and given the evidence that racism is an obstacle to African-American business success,[69] what obligation, if any, does state, local, or federal government have to assist minority-owned companies?

6. What measures could Richmond have taken that would have increased opportunities for businesses owned by people of color but would not have involved racial quotas? Would such measures be as effective as the original plan?

Case 11.2
Hoop Dreams

In Basketball, Talent Plus Hard Work Equals Success. That's an equation that holds true for everyone, and in recent years, dedicated female athletes have raised women's basketball to new heights and won the allegiance of many new fans.[70]

But what about their coaches? Do any obstacles stand between them and their dreams? Marianne Stanley didn't think so when she began coaching women's basketball for the University of Southern California, where she earned $64,000 a year—a fair sum, one might think, but less than half that of her counterpart, George Raveling, who coached the men's team. True, Raveling had been coaching for thirty-one years, had been an assistant on the U.S. Olympic team, and was twice named coach of the year. But Stanley was no slouch. She had been a head coach for sixteen years and won three national championships. In her last two years at USC, she had win–loss records of 23–8 and 22–7, which compared favorably with Raveling's 19–10 and 24–6.

So when her initial four-year contract expired, Marianne Stanley sought pay parity with Raveling. Stanley knew that Raveling was also earning tens of thousands of dollars in perks, but she was willing to overlook that and settle for an equal base salary of $135,000. Instead, USC offered Stanley a three-year contract starting at $88,000 and increasing to $100,000. When she rejected that offer, USC countered with a one-year contract for $96,000. Stanley declined the offer and left USC, her hoop dreams diminished, although she later began coaching at UC Berkeley, where her salary was equivalent to that of the men's coach.

For his part, George Raveling didn't mind Stanley's making as much money as he did. But he understood why USC paid him more. He was, after all, a hot property, and if USC was going to prevent his being lured away by some other university trying to boost its basketball program, then it had to pay him a high salary. By contrast, Marianne Stanley didn't have any other job offers.

Too bad, one might say, but that's how the market works in a capitalist society. But what if the market itself is discriminatory? Defenders of comparable worth argue that it is and that coaches like Stanley can't negotiate for comparable salaries because women's basketball isn't valued as highly as men's basketball. And it's college administrators, they argue, who are to blame for that. As one feminist puts it:

> The women didn't get the advertising and marketing dollars. They didn't get the PR. Then when fans weren't showing up, the TV stations weren't carrying the games and other universities weren't fighting over the best coaches, administrators told the women that, because they and their sport didn't draw as much attention as men, they shouldn't be paid as much.

In response, defenders of USC deny that it or any other university is responsible for the fact that men's sports are big revenue earners and women's sports are not. The higher pay for those who coach men simply reflects that social and cultural reality, which is something college administrators have no control over. If someone like Marianne Stanley wants to enter the big leagues, then she should coach men.

Still, many find it distressing that even though 40 percent of American athletic participants are female, their sports get less respect and less attention—to be specific, less than 5 percent of all media coverage and only 1.62 percent of sporting airtime on big networks.[71] Shouldn't universities try to combat this, at least by paying equivalent salaries to the coaches of men's and women's teams?

Update

Sadly, sometimes even those who have fought against discrimination can discriminate against others. Just a few years after Marianne Stanley assumed her head coaching position at UC Berkeley, one of the assistant coaches, Sharrona Alexander, filed suit against the university, alleging that Stanley told her to get an abortion or lose her job. Stanley denied the abortion allegation, but admitted that she did ask Alexander to resign because of her pregnancy. Either way, a champion of women's rights was guilty of trampling on someone else's hoop dreams. Ironically, Stanley herself played college basketball when she was pregnant (returning to practice eleven days after her daughter was born) and went on, single and with a toddler, to coach Old Dominion University to three national championships. Moreover, some sports commentators believe that, far from being a handicap, motherhood can give a coach an edge in recruiting because the parents of prospective recruits prefer their daughters to be coached by women who, when they say that they treat their teams as family, know what they are talking about. In addition, Arizona State coach Charli Turner Thorne says, because "you're taking young ladies at a very formative time, you have to play the parent role." She adds, "There's absolutely no doubt [motherhood] makes me a better coach."

Discussion Questions

1. The doctrine of comparable worth holds that men and women should be paid the same wage for doing jobs of equal skill, effort, and responsibility. Were Marianne Stanley and George Raveling doing work of comparable value?

2. Was Stanley treated unfairly or in some way discriminated against? Should USC have offered to pay her more?

3. Why do sports played by men tend to be more popular and generate more revenue than sports played by women? Are female athletes—and their coaches—disadvantaged? Are they discriminated against? If so, who is responsible for this discrimination, and do colleges and universities have an obligation to do something about it?

4. Should universities like USC base their coaching salaries entirely on market considerations? Or should they pay the coaches of men's and women's sports comparable salaries based on experience, skill, and performance?

5. Respond to the argument that because men are free to coach women's teams and women to coach men's teams, there is nothing discriminatory in the fact that one job pays more than the other.

6. Was Sharrona Alexander's pregnancy likely to have adversely affected her coaching performance? If so, was Marianne Stanley wrong to ask her to resign? How should Stanley have handled the situation?

Case 11.3

Raising the Ante

Having Spearheaded The Women's Cause on Behalf of Equal pay for jobs of equal value, Phyllis Warren was elated when the board decided to readjust salaries. Its decision meant Phyllis and the other women employed by the manufacturing firm would receive pay equivalent to men doing work of comparable worth. But in a larger sense it constituted an admission of guilt by the board, acknowledgment of a history blemished by implicit sexual discrimination.

In the euphoria that followed the board's decision, neither Phyllis nor any of the other activists thought much about the implied admission of female exploitation. But some weeks later, Herm Leggett, a sales dispatcher, half-jokingly suggested to Phyllis over lunch that she shouldn't stop with equal pay now. Phyllis asked Herm what he meant.

"Back pay," Herm said without hesitation. "If they're readjusting salaries for women," he explained, "they obviously know that salaries are out of line and have been for some time." Then he asked her pointedly, "How long you been here, Phyl?" Eleven years, she told him. "If those statistics you folks were passing around last month are accurate," Herm said, "then I'd say you've been losing about $2,000 a year, or $22,000 over eleven years." Then he added with a laugh, "Not counting interest, of course."

"Why not?" Phyllis thought. Why shouldn't she and other women who'd suffered past inequities be reimbursed?

That night Phyllis called a few of the other women and suggested that they press the board for back pay. Some said they were satisfied and didn't think they should force the issue. Others thought the firm had been fair in readjusting the salary schedule, and they were willing to let bygones be bygones. Still others thought that any further efforts might, in fact, roll back the board's favorable decision. Yet a nucleus agreed that workers who had been unfairly treated in the past ought to receive compensation. They decided, however, that

because their ranks were divided, they shouldn't wage as intense an in-house campaign as previously but instead take the issue directly to the board, while it might still be inhaling deeply the fresh air of social responsibility.

The following Wednesday, Phyllis and four other women presented their case to the board, intentionally giving the impression that they enjoyed as much support from other workers as they had the last time they appeared before it. Although this wasn't true, Phyllis suggested it as an effective strategic ploy.

Phyllis's presentation had hardly ended when board members began making their feelings known. One called her proposal "industrial blackmail." "No sooner do we try to right an injustice," he said testily, "than you take our good faith and threaten to beat us over the head with it unless we comply with your request."

Another member just as vigorously argued that the current board couldn't be held accountable for the actions, policies, and decisions of previous boards. "Sure," he said, "we're empowered to alter policies as we see fit and as conditions change to chart new directions. And we've done that. But to expect us to bear the full financial liability of decisions we never made is totally unrealistic—and unfair."

Still another member wondered where it would all end. "If we agree," he asked, "will you then suggest we should track down all those women who ever worked for us and provide them compensation?" Phyllis said no, but the board should readjust retirement benefits for those affected.

At this point the board asked Phyllis if she had any idea what her proposal would cost the firm. "Whatever it is, it's a small price to pay for righting wrong," she said firmly.

"But is it a small price to pay for severely damaging our profit picture?" one of the members asked. Then he added, "I needn't remind you that our profit outlook directly affects what we can offer our current employees in terms of salary and fringe benefits. It directly affects our ability to revise our salary schedule." Finally, he asked Phyllis whether she'd accept the board's reducing everyone's current compensation to meet what Phyllis termed the board's "obligation to the past."

Despite its decided opposition to Phyllis's proposal, the board agreed to consider it and render a decision at its next meeting. As a final broadside, Phyllis hinted that, if the board didn't comply with the committee's request, the committee was prepared to pursue legal action.

Discussion Questions

1. If you were a board member, how would you vote? Why?
2. What moral principles are involved in this case?
3. Do you think Phyllis Warren was unfair in taking advantage of the board's implied admission of salary discrimination on the basis of sex? Why or why not?
4. Do you think Phyllis was wrong in giving the board the impression that her proposal enjoyed broad support? Why or why not?
5. If the board rejects the committee's request, do you think the committee ought to sue? Give reasons.

Case 11.4

Consenting to Sexual Harassment

In The Case of *Vinson v. Taylor*, Heard Before the Federal District Court for the District of Columbia, Mechelle Vinson alleged that Sidney Taylor, her supervisor at Capital City Federal Savings and Loan, had sexually harassed her.[72] But the facts of the case were contested.

In court, Vinson testified that about a year after she began working at the bank, Taylor asked her to have sexual relations with him. She claimed that Taylor said she "owed" him because he had obtained the job for her. Although she turned down Taylor at first, she eventually became involved with him. She and Taylor engaged in sexual relations, she said, both during and after business hours, in the remaining three years she worked at the bank. The encounters included intercourse in a bank vault and in a storage area in the bank basement. Vinson also testified that Taylor often actually "assaulted or raped" her. She contended that she was forced to submit to Taylor or jeopardize her employment.

Taylor, for his part, denied the allegations. He testified that he had never had sex with Vinson. On the contrary, he alleged that Vinson had made advances toward him and that he had declined them. He contended that Vinson had brought the charges against him to "get even" because of a work-related dispute.

In its ruling on the case, the court held that if Vinson and Taylor had engaged in a sexual relationship, that relationship was voluntary on the part of Vinson and was not employment related. The court also held that Capital City Federal Savings and Loan did not have "notice" of the alleged harassment and was therefore not liable. Although Taylor was Vinson's supervisor, the court reasoned that notice to him was not notice to the bank.

Vinson appealed the case, and the Court of Appeals held that the district court had erred in three ways. First, the district court had overlooked the fact that there are two possible kinds of sexual harassment. Writing for the majority, Chief Judge Spottswood Robinson distinguished cases in which the victim's continued employment or promotion is conditioned on giving in to sexual demands and those cases in which the victim must tolerate a "substantially discriminatory work environment." The lower court had failed to consider whether Vinson's case involved harassment of the second kind.

Second, the higher court also overruled the district court's finding that because Vinson voluntarily engaged in a sexual relationship with Taylor, she was not a victim of sexual harassment. Voluntariness on Vinson's part had "no bearing," the judge wrote, on "whether Taylor made Vinson's toleration of sexual harassment a condition of her employment." Third, the Court of Appeals held that any discriminatory activity by a supervisor is attributable to the employer, regardless of whether the employer had specific notice.

In his dissent to the decision by the Court of Appeals, Judge Robert Bork rejected the majority's claim that "voluntariness" did not automatically rule out harassment. He argued that this position would have the result of depriving the accused person of any defense, because he could no longer establish that the supposed victim was really "a willing participant." Judge Bork contended further that an employer should not be held vicariously liable for a supervisor's acts that it didn't know about.

Eventually the case arrived at the U.S. Supreme Court, which upheld the majority verdict of the Court of Appeals, stating that:

> [T]he fact that sex-related conduct was "voluntary," in the sense that the complainant was not forced to participate against her will, is not a defense to a sexual harassment suit brought under Title VII. The gravamen of any sexual harassment claim is that the alleged

In the movie *North Country*, Charlize Theron plays a character who has no choice but to take on a miner's job in order to survive as the mother of two. Confronted with unrelenting verbal and physical abuse at the hands of her male coworkers, she fights back and ultimately wins a sexual harassment lawsuit.

sexual advances were "unwelcome.". . . The correct inquiry is whether respondent by her conduct indicated that the alleged sexual advances were unwelcome, not whether her actual participation in sexual intercourse was voluntary.

The Court, however, rejected the Court of Appeals's position that employers are strictly liable for the acts of their supervisors, regardless of the particular circumstances.[73]

Discussion Questions

1. According to her own testimony, Vinson acquiesced to Taylor's sexual demands. In this sense her behavior was "voluntary." Does the voluntariness of her behavior mean that she had "consented" to Taylor's advances? Does it mean that they were "welcome"? Do you agree that Vinson's acquiescence shows there was no sexual harassment? Which court was right about this? Defend your position.

2. In your opinion, under what circumstances would acquiescence be a defense to charges of sexual harassment? When would it not be a defense? Can you formulate a general rule for deciding such cases?

3. Assuming the truth of Vinson's version of the case, do you think her employer, Capital City Federal Savings and Loan, should be held liable for sexual harassment it was not aware of? Should the employer have been aware of it? Does the fact that Taylor was a supervisor make a difference? In general, when should an employer be liable for harassment?

4. What steps do you think Vinson should have taken when Taylor first pressed her for sex? Should she be blamed for having given in to him? Assuming that there was sexual harassment despite her acquiescence, does her going along with Taylor make her partly responsible or mitigate Taylor's wrongdoing?

5. In court, Vinson's allegations were countered by Taylor's version of the facts. Will there always be a "your word against mine" problem in sexual harassment cases? What could Vinson have done to strengthen her case?

Case 11.5
Facial Discrimination

Scene: A Conference Room of a Branch Office of Allied Products, Inc., where Tom, Frank, and Alice have been interviewing college students for summer internships.

Tom: Did you see that last candidate? Jeez, was he sorry looking.

Frank: Too gangly to work here, that's for sure. And those thick glasses didn't help. Still, he wasn't as unattractive as that young woman you hired last summer. What was her name . . . Allison? Remember that hair of hers? It wasn't surprising we had to let her go.

Alice: Come on, Frank. Don't be so hung up on looks. That last guy seemed to know his stuff, and he certainly was enthusiastic about working for Allied.

Frank: Hey, don't get me wrong, Alice. I know you don't have to be beautiful to work for Allied—after all, look at Tom here. Still, with a face like that guy's, you got to wonder.

Tom: Wisecracks aside, Alice, Frank's got a point. Studies show that it's natural for people to discriminate on the basis of looks. I've read that even babies will look at a face that's pretty longer than one that's not.

Alice: I know that. Studies also show that people attribute positive characteristics to people they find attractive and that they treat unattractive people worse than other people in lots of ways. For example, strangers are less likely to do small favors for unattractive people than they are for attractive people, and even parents and teachers have lower expectations for unattractive or odd-looking children. Attractive people also earn more money than average-looking people. So what this really boils down to is implicit discrimination.

Tom: That's what I'm saying. It's natural. Besides, it's not illegal to discriminate on the basis of appearance.

Frank: That's right. You wouldn't want us to hire somebody with green hair and rings in his nose and put him out at the front desk, would you? This is a business, not a freak show.

Alice: Hey, slow down, guys. First, it may be natural and it may even be legal to favor good-looking people, but that doesn't make it right. And second, I'm not talking about grooming or dress. It's your choice to dye your hair and decorate your face,

and if you don't fit in because of that, that's your fault. But the guy we talked to today didn't choose to be unattractive, so why hold it against him?

Frank: I suppose next you'll be telling us that we should have kept Allison on last summer just because she was unattractive.

Alice: No, I'm not saying you have to give preferential treatment to unattractive people. But I think that nobody in the office cut her any slack. If she'd been born with a different nose or different teeth things would have worked out okay, but people took one look at her and prejudged her to be a loser.

Tom: Seriously, though, Alice, a number of our interns have to interact with the public, and people can be put off by having to deal with people who are unattractive or even very short. So why aren't an employee's looks a job-relevant issue?

Alice: No, I think that as long as the person is clean and well groomed, then the public shouldn't be put off by having to deal with someone who is unattractive or unusual looking. It's unreasonable.

Tom: That's what you say. But what if the public is "unreasonable"? What if they prefer companies with attractive or at least normal-looking employees?

Alice: It's still irrelevant. It's the same as if a company had customers who didn't like dealing with Black people. That's no reason for it not to hire Black people.

Tom: Yeah, I can see that.

Frank: Okay, but what about this guy? Do we have to offer him an internship?

Discussion Questions

1. How frequently are people discriminated against based on their looks? Is it a serious problem in job situations? What about the fact that students give more positive course evaluation rankings to attractive professors?[74] (The website RateMyProfessor.com used to invite students to rate professors specifically on their appearance, with those rated most attractive being awarded a chili pepper emoji.)

2. Assess the argument that there is nothing wrong with "facial discrimination"—that it simply reflects the fact that human beings are naturally attracted to, or repelled by, other human beings on the basis of their physical characteristics.

3. Under what circumstances is physical attractiveness a job-related employment criterion? Is it relevant to being a salesperson, a flight attendant, or a receptionist?

4. What arguments can be given for and against a law preventing job discrimination on the basis of immutable aspects of one's appearance?

5. Assess the argument that because "ugly" or unusual-looking people have it tougher throughout their lives than do attractive people, we should give them preferential treatment whenever we can—for example, in job situations—to make up for the disadvantages they've suffered and to help level the playing field.

6. Are businesses morally obligated to try to prevent or reduce appearance discrimination in the workplace? What steps can they take?

Suggestions for Further Reading

Chapter 1

Theranos

John Carreyrou, *Bad Blood: Secrets and Lies in a Silicon Valley Startup* (Vintage: New York, 2020), is an account of the Theranos scandal from the journalist who broke the story.

Ethics

James Rachels and Stuart Rachels, *The Elements of Moral Philosophy*, 7th ed. (New York: McGraw-Hill, 2011), and Louis P. Pojman, *How Should I Live?* (Belmont, Calif.: Wadsworth, 2005), are excellent, clear introductions.

George Sher, ed., *Moral Philosophy: Selected Readings*, 2nd ed. (Belmont, Calif.: Wadsworth, 2000), and Louis P. Pojman, ed., *Ethical Theory: Classical and Contemporary Readings*, 5th ed. (Belmont, Calif.: Wadsworth, 2007), offer more advanced readings on various topics in moral philosophy.

Moral Reasoning

Patrick Hurley, *A Concise Introduction to Logic,* 11th ed. (Belmont, Calif.: Wadsworth, 2012), is a good introduction to all the main areas of logic.

Joel Rudinow and Vincent Barry, *Invitation to Critical Thinking,* 6th ed. (Belmont, Calif.: Wadsworth, 2008), provides a guide to argument assessment.

Business and Morality

Both Richard T. De George, *Business Ethics*, 7th ed. (New York: Macmillan, 2009), and Manuel G. Velasquez, *Business Ethics*, 7th ed. (Upper Saddle River, N.J.: Prentice Hall, 2012), contain useful introductions to moral philosophy in relation to business, as does Robert Audi's lucid and succinct book, *Business Ethics and Ethical Business* (New York: Oxford University Press, 2009). Two valuable reference works are *The Blackwell Encyclopedia of Management, vol. 2: Business Ethics*, 2nd ed., eds. Patricia Werhane and R. Edward Freeman (Malden, Mass.: Blackwell, 2005), and the five-volume *SAGE Encyclopedia of Business Ethics and Society*, 2nd ed., ed. Robert W. Kolb (Los Angeles: SAGE Publications, 2018). Robert E. Frederick, ed., *A Companion to Business Ethics* (Malden, Mass.: Blackwell, 1999), and George G. Brenkert and Tom L. Beauchamp, eds., *The Oxford Handbook of Business Ethics* (New York: Oxford University Press, 2010), are collections of essays by different authors on all aspects of business ethics. Fritz Allhoff and Anand Vaidya's three-volume *Business Ethics* (London: SAGE, 2005) reprints ninety-six important essays on business and professional ethics. Eugene Heath and Byron Kaldis, eds., *Wealth, Commerce, and Philosophy: Foundational Thinkers and Business Ethics* (Chicago: University of Chicago Press, 2017), contains essays on what twenty great philosophers, including Aristotle, Confucius, Hobbes, Mill, and Rawls, thought about the morality of commerce and business.

Four good sources of advanced work in business ethics are *Business and Professional Ethics Journal*, *Business and Society Review*, *Business Ethics Quarterly*, and the *Journal of Business Ethics*.

Chapter 2

Tom L. Beauchamp, *Philosophical Ethics,* 3rd ed. (New York: McGraw-Hill, 2001), is an introductory text with selected readings covering classical ethical theories, rights, and the nature of morality.

Heimir Geirsson and Margaret R. Holmgren, eds., *Ethical Theory: A Concise Anthology*, 2nd ed. (Peterborough, Ontario: Broadview, 2010); Judith A. Boss, ed., *Perspectives on Ethics,* 2nd ed. (New York: McGraw-Hill, 2003); and Mark Timmons, ed., *Conduct and Character,* 6th ed. (Belmont, Calif.: Wadsworth, 2011), provide good selections of readings on egoism, relativism, utilitarianism, Kantianism, and other normative theories.

Bernard Gert, *Common Morality: Deciding What to Do* (New York: Oxford University Press, 2004), provides a lucid account of the moral system that implicitly guides thoughtful people's everyday moral decisions.

Hugh LaFollette, ed., *The Blackwell Guide to Ethical Theory* (Oxford: Blackwell, 2000), and Peter Singer, ed., *A Companion to Ethics* (Oxford: Blackwell, 1991), are comprehensive reference works with survey essays by many individual authors.

William H. Shaw, *Contemporary Ethics: Taking Account of Utilitarianism* (Oxford: Blackwell, 1999), sympathetically examines the utilitarian approach to ethics.

Jeffrey D. Smith, ed., *Normative Theory and Business Ethics* (Lanham, Md.: Rowman & Littlefield, 2009), is a useful collection probing the normative foundations of business ethics from various theoretical perspectives.

Mark Timmons, *Moral Theory: An Introduction*, 2nd ed. (Lanham, Md.: Rowman & Littlefield, 2013), provides a clear and accessible survey of all the major moral theories.

In addition to these books, there are some excellent free online resources that contain numerous readings on different ethical theories and perspectives. *The Stanford Encyclopedia for Philosophy* (https://plato.stanford.edu/), edited by Edward N. Zalta and Uri Nodelman, contains the most detailed readings, some of which might be challenging for readers new to philosophy.

The *1000-Word Philosophy: An Introductory Anthology* (https://1000wordphilosophy.com/) offers more accessible, albeit far less comprehensive, entries. The *Internet Encyclopedia of Philosophy* (https://iep.utm.edu/), edited by James Fieser and Bradley Dowden, is intermediate between the other two resources in both respects.

Chapter 3

John Arthur and William H. Shaw, eds., *Justice and Economic Distribution,* 2nd ed. (Englewood Cliffs, N.J.: Prentice Hall, 1991), contains substantial extracts from Rawls's *A Theory of Justice* and Nozick's *Anarchy, State, and Utopia*, contemporary presentations of the utilitarian approach to economic justice and various other essays on the topic.

Anthony B. Atkinson, *Inequality: What Can Be Done?* (Cambridge, Mass.: Harvard University Press, 2015), examines the meaning and causes of inequality and proposes ways of reducing it.

"For Richer, for Poorer: Special Report on the World Economy," *Economist,* October 13, 2012, discusses issues of equality and inequality around the world.

Justin Fox, "Piketty's 'Capital,' in a Lot Less Than 696 Pages," *Harvard Business Review* (April 24, 2014), https://hbr.org/2014/04/pikettys-capital-in-a-lot-less-than-696-pages, is a readable summary of a major but massive book on capital and wealth.

John Isbister, *Capitalism and Justice: Envisioning Social and Economic Fairness* (Bloomfield, Conn.: Kumarian Press, 2001), discusses in a readable but thoughtful way a number of questions of justice in the real world, such as income distribution, taxation, welfare, and foreign aid.

Will Kymlicka, *Contemporary Political Philosophy,* 2nd ed. (Oxford: Oxford University Press, 2001), covers the major schools of contemporary political thought and their competing views of justice and community.

Jeffrey Moriarty, "Do CEOs Get Paid Too Much?" *Business Ethics Quarterly* 15 (April 2005), argues that they do, according to the leading theories of justice in wages.

Liam Murphy and Thomas Nagel, *The Myth of Ownership: Taxes and Justice* (New York: Oxford University Press, 2002), explores the justice of different tax policies in the light of contemporary moral and political philosophy.

David K. Shipler, *The Working Poor: Invisible in America* (New York: Random House, 2004), and Barbara Ehrenreich, *Nickel and Dimed: On (Not) Getting by in America* (New York: Henry Holt, 2001), are two vivid accounts of those forgotten Americans who work hard but barely manage to keep their heads above water.

Joseph Stiglitz, *The Price of Inequality: How Today's Divided Society Endangers Our Future* (New York: Norton, 2012), explores the various facets of inequality and their implications for our society. Stiglitz is a winner of the Nobel Prize in Economics.

Richard Wilkenson and Kate Pickett, *The Spirit Level: Why Greater Equality Makes Societies Stronger* (New York: Bloomsbury, 2009), argues that societies with greater economic equality have fewer social problems and greater well-being.

Chapter 4

Elizabeth Anderson, *Hijacked: How Neoliberalism Turned the Work Ethic against Workers and How Workers Can Take It Back* (Cambridge: Cambridge University Press, 2023), suggests that there has been a historical struggle over the work ethic, specifically over whether this ethic should serve the interests of workers or capitalists. Anderson, one of the leading American social and political philosophers, holds that currently the pendulum has swung in favor of capitalists but calls for the struggle to be taken up again.

William J. Baumol, Robert E. Litan, and Carl J. Schramm, *Good Capitalism, Bad Capitalism, and the Economics of Growth and Prosperity* (New Haven, Conn.: Yale University Press, 2007), distinguishes four different forms of contemporary capitalism, focusing on the essential role of entrepreneurship.

John Douglas Bishop, ed., *Ethics and Capitalism* (Toronto: University of Toronto Press, 2000), is a collection of thought-provoking essays. Bishop's own contribution to the volume, "Ethics and Capitalism: A Guide to the Issues," is a valuable survey of the nature of capitalism and the key ethical issues it gives rise to.

Alan S. Blinder, *After the Music Stopped: The Financial Crisis, the Response, and the Work Ahead* (New York: Penguin, 2013), is a lucid and balanced account, by a leading economist, of the 2008 meltdown and its aftermath.

Todd G. Buchholz, *New Ideas from Dead Economists*, rev. ed. (New York: Penguin, 2007), and Randy Charles Epping, *The 21st Century Economy: A Beginner's Guide* (New York: Vintage, 2009), are balanced and readable guides to modern economic thought applied to today's economy.

Ann E. Cudd and Nancy Holstrom, *Capitalism: For and Against* (New York: Cambridge University Press, 2011), presents opposing sides of the debate over capitalism, with each author arguing from a feminist perspective.

Helen McCabe, *John Stuart Mill, Socialist* (Montreal: McGill-Queens University Press, 2021), examines the views on socialism and capitalism of one of the historical philosophers who features most prominently in this textbook.

Christopher Meyer and Julie Kirby, "Runaway Capitalism," *Harvard Business Review*, January–February 2013, argues that contemporary capitalism has taken two good ideas—competition and the importance of return on equity—too far.

Robert B. Reich, *Supercapitalism: The Transformation of Business, Democracy, and Everyday Life* (New York: Knopf, 2007), is a well-written analysis of contemporary American capitalism, its clash with democracy, and problems our society faces.

David Schweickart, *After Capitalism* (Lanham, Md.: Rowman & Littlefield, 2002), is an argument for worker-control socialism.

Walter E. Williams, *The State against Blacks*, 3rd ed. (New York: New Press, 1982), makes the provocative argument that government regulations like professional licensing requirements and minimum wage laws work to the disadvantage of Black citizens. Williams was an African-American free-market economist.

Chapter 5

Joel Bakan, *The Corporation: The Pathological Pursuit of Profit and Power* (New York: Free Press, 2004), is a scaring though rather one-sided indictment of the modern corporation (and the basis of a documentary film of the same title).

Norman E. Bowie, "Organizational Integrity and Moral Climates," in George G. Brenkert and Tom L. Beauchamp, eds., *The Oxford Handbook of Business Ethics* (New York: Oxford University Press, 2010), is an insightful discussion of the factors that strengthen organizational integrity.

John R. Danley, "Corporate Moral Agency," in Robert E. Frederick, ed., *A Companion to Business Ethics* (Malden, Mass.: Blackwell, 1999), reviews the philosophical literature on this difficult topic with particular attention to the influential views of Peter French.

Peter A. French, *Collective and Corporate Responsibility* (New York: Columbia University Press, 1984), analyzes the philosophical issues involved in assigning moral responsibility to corporations and other collectivities. French's *Corporate Ethics* (Ft. Worth, Tex.: Harcourt Brace, 1996) looks at a wider range of moral issues involving corporations.

James Willard Hurst, *The Legitimacy of the Business Corporation in Law of the United States 1780–1970* (Charlottesville: University of Virginia Press, 1970), traces the legal history of the American corporation.

Robert Jackall, *Moral Mazes: The World of Corporate Managers* (Oxford: Oxford University Press, 2008), illustrates the sorts of moral problems that corporate leaders face and how they deal with them. Jackall is a sociologist, and the book reflects extensive interviews with managers at two major corporations (whose names are changed). The original edition was published in 1988.

Thomas M. Jones and Will Felps, "Shareholder Wealth Maximization and Social Welfare: A Utilitarian Critique," *Business Ethics Quarterly* 23:2 (April 2013), critiques the idea that maximizing shareholder wealth maximizes social welfare.

Steve May, George Cheney, and Juliet Roper, eds., *The Debate over Corporate Social Responsibility* (New York: Oxford University Press, 2007), and Andrew Crane, Abagail McWilliams, Dirk Matten, Jeremy Moon, and Donald S. Siegel, eds., *The Oxford Handbook of Corporate Social Responsibility* (New York: Oxford University Press, 2008), are advanced collections of essays by business theorists and social scientists.

John Micklethwait and Adrian Wooldridge, *The Company: A Short History of a Revolutionary Idea* (New York: Modern Library, 2003), is a readable, well-informed history of the corporation from its earliest beginnings to recent scandals.

Lynn Stout, *The Shareholder Value Myth* (San Francisco: Berrett-Koehler, 2012), argues that putting shareholders first harms investors, corporations, and the public.

David Vogel, *The Market for Virtue: The Potential and Limits of Corporate Social Responsibility* (Washington, D.C.: Brookings Institution, 2005), provides an insightful analysis and balanced assessment of the growing corporate social responsibility movement.

Thomas I. White, ed., *Business Ethics: A Philosophical Reader* (New York: Macmillan, 1993), contains useful essays on corporate personhood and responsibility in Chapter 6 and on the punishment of corporations in Chapter 7.

Chapter 6

Robert L. Arrington, "Advertising and Behavior Control," *Journal of Business Ethics* 1 (February 1982); John Waide, "The Making of Self and World in Advertising," *Journal of Business Ethics* 6 (February 1987); Roger Crisp, "Persuasive Advertising, Autonomy, and the Creation of Desire," *Journal of Business Ethics* 6 (July 1987); Richard L. Lippke, "Advertising and the Social Conditions of Autonomy," *Business and Professional Ethics Journal* 8 (Winter 1989); and Andrew Gustafson, "Advertising's Impact on Morality in Society: Influencing Habits and Desires of Consumers," *Business and Society Review* 106 (Fall 2001), are influential philosophical discussions of advertising. Timothy Aylsworth, "Autonomy and Manipulation: Refining the Argument against Persuasive Advertising," *Journal of Business Ethics* 175 (February 2022), continues the conversation.

David M. Holley, "A Moral Evaluation of Sales Practices," *Business and Professional Ethics Journal* 5 (Fall 1987), is a seminal discussion of the ethics of sales. Holley revisits the subject in "Information Disclosure in Sales," *Journal of Business Ethics* 17 (April 1998), and replies to Thomas L. Carson in "Alternative Approaches to Applied Ethics: A Response to Carson's Critique," *Business Ethics Quarterly* 12 (January 2002).

Peter Katel, "Consumer Safety: Do Government Regulations Need More Power?" in *Issues for Debate in Corporate Social Responsibility: Selections from CQ Researcher* (Thousand Oaks, Calif.: SAGE, 2010), is an informative survey.

Patrick E. Murphy, Gene R. Laczniak, Norman E. Bowie, and Thomas A. Klein, *Ethical Marketing* (Upper Saddle River, N.J.: Prentice Hall, 2005), and George G. Brenkert, *Marketing Ethics* (New York: Wiley Blackwell, 2008), survey a variety of issues in marketing ethics, including researching and segmenting markets, product management, distribution and pricing, and sales.

Juliet Schor, *Born to Buy: The Commercialized Child and the New Consumer Culture* (New York: Simon & Schuster, 2005), is a well-researched critique of the ruthless targeting of children by advertisers and of their induction into consumerism.

Kim Bartel Sheehan, *Controversies in Contemporary Advertising,* 2nd ed. (Thousand Oaks, Calif.: SAGE, 2014), examines a wide range of ethical and other issues in advertising.

Edward Spence and Brett Van Heekeren, *Advertising Ethics* (Upper Saddle River, N.J.: Prentice Hall, 2005), is a succinct and stimulating discussion of, among other issues, truth in advertising, endorsements and testimonials, targeted advertising, and stereotyping.

Chapter 7

Robin Attfield, *Environmental Ethics* (Malden, Mass.: Blackwell, 2003), and Joseph R. DesJardins, *Environmental Ethics,* 5th ed. (Belmont, Calif.: Wadsworth, 2013), are good introductions to environmental ethics.

Stephen Gardiner, Simon Caney, Dale Jamieson, and Henry Shue, eds., *Climate Ethics: Essential Readings* (New York: Oxford University Press, 2010), provides intelligent and probing essays examining this issue in terms of justice, policy, and individual responsibility.

Panl Hawken, *The Ecology of Commerce,* rev. ed. (New York: Harper, 2010), argues that business can be transformed to lead the way in solving our sustainability problems.

Dale Jamieson, *Reason in a Dark Time: Why the Struggle against Climate Change Failed—And What It Means for Our Future* (Oxford: Oxford University Press, 2014), addresses the moral and philosophical implications of climate change and our attempts to respond to it.

Dale E. Miller and Ben Eggleston, eds., *Moral Theory and Climate Change: Ethical Perspectives on a Warming Planet* (New York: Routledge, 2020), is a collection of essays by philosophers describing what different ethical theories have to say about how we should respond to the changing climate.

Lisa H. Newton, Catherine K. Dillingham, and Joanne Cody, *Watersheds: Classic Cases in Environmental Ethics,* 4th ed. (Belmont, Calif.: Wadsworth, 2006), offers ten detailed and insightful environmental case studies.

William D. Nordhaus, "Why the Global Warming Skeptics Are Wrong," *New York Review of Books,* March 22, 2012, is an eminent economist's informed but readable rejoinder to skeptics of global warming.

Holmes Rolston III, *A New Environmental Ethics: The New Millennium for Life on Earth* (New York: Routledge, 2012), is a recent work from an important environmental philosopher.

Mark Sagoff, *The Economy of the Earth: Philosophy, Law, and the Environment,* 2nd ed. (New York: Cambridge University Press, 2008), is an insightful discussion of environmental policy.

Peter Singer, *Animal Liberation,* 3rd ed. (New York: HarperCollins, 2002), is a seminal work advocating a radical change in our treatment of animals; Gary L. Francione, *Introduction to Animal Rights: Your Child or the Dog?* (Philadelphia: Temple University Press, 2000), offers a provocative but very readable critique of our treatment of animals.

James Sterba, ed., *Earth Ethics: Introductory Readings on Animal Rights and Environmental Ethics,* 3rd ed. (Upper Saddle River, N.J.: Prentice Hall, 2009), is an excellent, wide-ranging collection of essays representing different environmental and philosophical approaches.

Chapter 8

Bruce Barry, *Speechless: The Erosion of Free Speech in the American Workplace* (San Francisco: Berrett-Koehler, 2007), is a balanced, well-written study, rich with examples, that advocates for greater freedom of expression in today's workplace.

Ronald Duska, "Employee Rights," in Robert E. Frederick, ed., *A Companion to Business Ethics* (Malden, Mass.: Blackwell, 1999), discusses the nature of rights in general and the specific rights claimed for employees in recent times.

Gertrude Ezorsky, *Freedom in the Workplace?* (Ithaca, N.Y.: Cornell University Press, 2007), argues that many contemporary philosophers and social scientists hold conceptions of freedom that are too limited to account for the reality of workplace unfreedom.

Thomas Geoghegan, *Which Side Are You On? Trying to Be for Labor When It's Flat on Its Back,* rev. ed. (New York: New Press, 2004), is the insightful and entertaining memoir of a labor lawyer.

Louis Maltby, *Can They Do That? Retaking Our Fundamental Rights in the Workplace* (New York: Penguin, 2009), exposes our lack of rights at work and suggests steps we can take.

Dale E. Miller, "Terminating Employees for Their Political Speech," *Business and Society Review* 109 (June 2004), argues that employers are morally permitted to fire employees for political speech only under certain conditions. It discusses both the case of Michael Italie and case study 8.3, "Speaking Out about Malt."

Priscilla Murolo, A. B. Chitty, and Joe Sacco, *From the Folks Who Brought You the Weekend: A Short, Illustrated History of Labor in the United States* (New York: New Press, 2001), is a readable and informative account of the struggles of working people in America.

David Sirota, Louis A. Mischkind, and Michael Irwin Meltzer, *The Enthusiastic Employee: How Companies Profit by Giving Workers What They Want* (Philadelphia: Wharton School, 2005), presents years of research demonstrating the relationship between high employee morale and strong financial performance.

Alan Strudler, "Confucian Skepticism about Workplace Rights," *Business Ethics Quarterly* 18, no. 1 (January 2008), defends workplace rights while acknowledging the strength of the Confucian critique.

Matt Vidal and David Kusnet, *Organizing Prosperity* (Washington, D.C.: Economic Policy Institute, 2009), uses case studies to argue that unions bring widespread social and economic benefits.

Chapter 9

David Barstow and Lowell Bergman, "Dangerous Business," *New York Times,* January 8, 9, and 10, 2003, is a disturbing, detailed investigative report on the company with the worst safety record in the United States.

Douglas Birsch, "The Universal Drug Testing of Employees," *Business and Professional Ethics Journal* 14 (Fall 1995); Michael Cranford, "Drug Testing and the Right to Privacy," *Journal of Business Ethics* 17 (November 1998); and John R. Rowan, "Limitations on the Moral Permissibility of Employee Drug Testing," *Business and Professional Ethics Journal* 19 (Summer 2000), examine the ethics of drug-testing employees.

Robert J. Dewar, *A Savage Factory: An Eyewitness Account of the Auto Industry's Self-Destruction* (Bloomington, Ind.: Authorhouse, 2009), is an inside look at factory life and the problems of the auto industry by a former Ford factory foreman.

Gertrude Ezorsky, ed., *Moral Rights in the Workplace* (Albany: State University of New York Press, 1987), is an older, but good collection of articles on the right to meaningful work, occupational health and safety, employee privacy, unions, industrial flight, and related topics.

Laura P. Hartman, "Technology and Ethics: Privacy in the Workplace," *Business and Society Review* 106 (Spring 2001), examines employee privacy in light of today's technology, current law, and ethics.

Sylvia Ann Hewlett, "Executive Women and the Myth of Having It All," *Harvard Business Review* 80 (April 2002), discusses the factors that prevent successful career women from having children.

John Kaler, "Understanding Participation," *Journal of Business Ethics* 21 (September 2000), discusses different types of employee participation, and John J. McCall, "Employee Voice in Corporate Governance," *Business Ethics Quarterly* 11 (January 2001), argues for a strong employee right to co-determine corporate policy.

Robert Mayer, "Is There a Right to Workplace Democracy?" *Social Theory and Practice* 26 (Summer 2000), argues on nonlibertarian grounds against such a right.

Adam D. Moore, "Employee Monitoring and Computer Technology," *Business Ethics Quarterly* 10 (July 2000), discusses the tension between privacy and evaluative surveillance.

Kim Parker, Juliana Horowitz, and Rachel Minkin, "How the Coronavirus Outbreak Has—and Hasn't—Changed the Way Americans Work," *Pew Research* (December 9, 2020), examines how the pandemic affected Americans' working lives.

Social Philosophy and Policy 17 (Summer 2000), special issue on "The Right to Privacy," is an insightful but advanced collection of readings.

Chapter 10

Sissela Bok, *Secrets* (New York: Vintage, 1983), includes insightful writing on trade secrets and patents in Chapter 10 and on whistle-blowing in Chapter 14.

George G. Brenkert, "Whistle-Blowing, Moral Integrity, and Organizational Ethics," in George G. Brenkert and Tom L. Beauchamp, eds., *The Oxford Handbook of Business Ethics* (New York: Oxford University Press, 2010), is an intelligent, well-argued survey of the issues that whistle-blowing raises. Two interesting recent discussions are James Rocha and Edward Song, "Pre-emptive Anonymous Whistle-Blowing," *Public Affairs Quarterly* 26 (October 2012), and Scott R. Paeth, "The Responsibility to Lie and the Obligation to Report," *Journal of Business Ethics* 112 (January 2013).

Thomas L. Carson, "Conflicts of Interest," *Journal of Business Ethics* (May 1994), analyzes the concept and discusses the wrongness of conflicts of interest. Also useful is Michael Davis, "Conflict of Interest Revisited," *Business and Professional Ethics Journal* 12 (Winter 1993).

Cynthia Cooper, *Extraordinary Circumstances: The Journey of a Corporate Whistleblower* (Hoboken, N.J.: Wiley, 2008), uses her personal story to explain what we can learn from the WorldCom scandal.

Roger Parloff, "The Gray Art of Not Quite Insider Trading," *Fortune,* September 2, 2013, discusses the fuzzy parameters of insider-trading law.

Brian Schrag, "The Moral Significance of Employee Loyalty," *Business Ethics Quarterly* 11 (January 2001), discusses the meaning of loyalty and whether it is good for either the employee or the employer.

Martin Snoeyenbos, Robert Almeder, and James Humber, eds., *Business Ethics,* 3rd ed. (Buffalo, N.Y.: Prometheus, 2001), provides in part 3 essays and cases on conflict of interest, gifts and payoffs, patents, and trade secrets.

Alan Strudler, "The Moral Problem in Insider Trading," in George G. Brenkert and Tom L. Beauchamp, eds., *The Oxford Handbook of Business Ethics* (New York: Oxford University Press, 2010), is a clear and thoughtful analysis of the wrongness of insider trading.

Chapter 11

Affirmative Action

Steven M. Cahn, ed., *The Affirmative Action Debate,* 2nd ed. (New York: Routledge, 2002); Francis Beckwith and Todd E. Jones, eds., *Affirmative Action: Social Justice or Reverse Discrimination?* (Buffalo, N.Y.: Prometheus, 1997); and George E. Curry, ed., *The Affirmative Action Debate* (Reading, Mass.: Addison-Wesley, 1996), are good sources of essays both for and against affirmative action.

Gertrude Ezorksy, *Racism and Justice: The Case for Affirmative Action* (Ithaca, N.Y.: Cornell University Press, 1991), provides a succinct, well-informed defense, whereas Louis P. Pojman, "The Case against Affirmative Action," in William H. Shaw, ed., *Social and Personal Ethics,* 8th ed. (Belmont, Calif.: Wadsworth, 2014), is a robust critique. Philosophers Carl Cohen and James P. Sterba debate the issue in their valuable book *Affirmative Action and Racial Preference* (New York: Oxford University Press, 2003).

Comparable Worth

Laura Pincus and Bill Shaw, "Comparable Worth: An Economic and Ethical Analysis," *Journal of Business Ethics* 17 (April 1998), presents opposing views on pursuing comparable worth as a matter of public policy.

Helen Remick and Ronnie J. Steinberg, "Comparable Worth and Wage Discrimination," and Robert L. Simon, "Comparable Pay for Comparable Work?" in Tom L. Beauchamp and Norman E. Bowie, eds., *Ethical Theory and Business,* 4th ed. (Englewood Cliffs, N.J.: Prentice Hall, 1993), provide a clear and thorough introduction to the comparable-worth debate.

Race in America

How Race Is Lived in America (New York: Henry Holt, 2001), a collection of personal narratives and conversations produced by the *New York Times,* probes race relations from various individual perspectives.

Nikole Hannah-Jones, Caitlin Roper, Ilena Silverman, and Jake Silverstein, eds., *The 1619 Project: A New Origin Story* (New York: One World, 2021), is a well-known and controversial series of essays that reconsiders the role of race and slavery in American history.

Glenn Loury, *The Anatomy of Racial Inequality* (Cambridge, Mass.: Harvard University Press, 2002), examines the complex reality of "racial stigma" and the self-replicating patterns of racial stereotypes that rationalize and sustain discrimination.

Barack Obama, *Dreams from My Father: A Story of Race and Inheritance* (New York: Random House, 1996), is a thoughtful, self-reflective memoir of growing up with a biracial identity, written before the author's entry into politics.

Sexual Harassment

Augustus B. Cochran III, *Sexual Harassment and the Law: The Mechelle Vinson Case* (Lawrence, Kans.: University of Kansas Press, 2004), examines the origin, context, and impact of this landmark case.

Linda Gordon Howard, *The Sexual Harassment Handbook* (Franklin Lakes, N.J.: Career Press, 2007), is a thorough, intelligent guide for both employers and employees.

Linda LeMoncheck and Mane Hajdin, *Sexual Harassment: A Debate* (Totowa, N.J.: Rowman & Littlefield, 1997), probes the philosophical and ethical issues.

Linda LeMoncheck and James Sterba, eds., *Sexual Harassment: Issues and Answers* (New York: Oxford University Press, 2001), contains fifty-seven popular and scholarly perspectives on this complex topic.

Workplace Discrimination

Daniel S. Hamermesh, *Beauty Pays: Why Attractive People Are More Successful* (Princeton, N.J.: Princeton University Press, 2011), examines the role that appearance plays in the workplace.

D. W. Haslett, "Workplace Discrimination, Good Cause, and Color Blindness," *Journal of Value Inquiry* 36 (March 2002), provides a helpful theory of what constitutes unethical discrimination in the workplace.

Herminia Ibarra, Robin Ely, and Deborah Kolb, "Women Rising: The Unseen Barriers," *Harvard Business Review,* September 2013, discusses "second-generation" gender bias in the workplace.

Elizabeth Kristen, "Addressing the Problem of Weight Discrimination in Employment," *California Law Review* 90 (January 2002), argues that job discrimination against the overweight is a serious problem that the law should address.

Andrew Valls, "The Libertarian Case for Affirmative Action," *Social Theory and Practice* 25 (Summer 1999), argues that affirmative action programs intended to benefit African Americans can be justified on the basis of the libertarian theory developed in Robert Nozick's *Anarchy, State, and Utopia.*

Notes

Chapter 1

1. For more on Theranos, see Carreyrou's *Bad Blood: Secrets and Lies in a Silicon Valley Startup* (Vintage: New York, 2020), which is the source of most of the information in this section.
2. Cicero, *Selected Works* (London: Penguin, 1971), 177–180.
3. For some further thoughts on the defining characteristics of moral standards, see Bernard Gert and Joshua Gert, "The Definition of Morality," *The Stanford Encyclopedia of Philosophy* (Fall 2020), ed. Edward N. Zalta, https://plato.stanford.edu/archives/fall2020/entries/morality-definition.
4. Martin Luther King, Jr., "Letter from Birmingham Jail," in *Why We Can't Wait* (New York: Harper & Row, 1963), 85.
5. Although the Security and Exchange Commission enacted a "Best Interest Regulation" in 2019, the standard that it imposes on brokers is actually rather lower. (Patrick Temple-West, "Warren, Waters Blast SEC Financial Advice Rule as Wall Street Cheers," *Politico*, June 5, 2019, https://www.politico.com/story/2019/06/05/warren-waters-blast-sec-financial-advice-rule-as-wall-street-cheers-1507335.)
6. Aaron Greff, "Publicly Traded Firms Paid Dividends, Bought Their Own Stock After Receiving PPP Loans to Pay Employees," *The Washington Post*, September 24, 2022.
7. "The Good, the Bad, and Their Corporate Codes of Ethics: Enron, Sarbanes-Oxley, and the Problems with Legislating Good Behavior," *Harvard Law Review*, May 2003, 2128.
8. *Evangelii Gaudium* (available at www.vatican.va); "Pope's Voice Is Resonating in the Capitol," *New York Times*, January 6, 2014, A1.
9. More sophisticated versions of moral relativism than the one discussed here may not suffer from all these problems. For a more in-depth discussion, see Chris Gowans, "Moral Relativism," *The Stanford Encyclopedia of Philosophy* (Spring 2021), ed. Edward N. Zalta, https://plato.stanford.edu/archives/spr2021/entries/moral-relativism/.
10. Albert Z. Carr, "Is Business Bluffing Ethical?" *Harvard Business Review* 46 (January–February 1968): 143–153.
11. Ibid., 145.
12. Richard B. Brandt, *A Theory of the Good and the Right* (New York: Oxford University Press, 1979), 165–170.
13. Joseph L. Badaracco, Jr. and Allen P. Webb, "Business Ethics: A View from the Trenches," *California Management Review* 37 (Winter 1995): 8.
14. Ibid., 10.
15. ECI, "2021 Global Business Ethics Report Survey," https://www.ethics.org/global-business-ethics-survey/.
16. See Solomon E. Asch, "Opinion and Social Pressure," *Scientific American*, November 1955, 31–35.
17. See Malcolm Gladwell, *The Tipping Point* (Boston: Little, Brown, 2000), 27–28; John M. Doris, *Lack of Character* (Cambridge: Cambridge University Press, 2002), 28–29, 32–33.
18. Lynn Sharp Paine, "Managing for Organizational Integrity," *Harvard Business Review* 72 (March–April 1994): 108.
19. "US Airways' Unwritten Policy," *USA Today*, July 22, 2011, 5B; news stories at www.USAirlinePilots.org; and Tom Reed, "US Airways Captain Escorted from Airport," *The Street*, July 25, 2011 (online).
20. Tom Regan, *Defending Animal Rights* (Urbana: University of Illinois Press, 2001), 45.
21. The facts and quotations reported in this case are based on Mark Dowie's essays in *Mother Jones* (November 1979) and on Russell Mokhiber, *Corporate Crime and Violence* (San Francisco: Sierra Club Books, 1988), 181–195.
22. "EPA Petitioned to Halt Export of U.S.-Banned Pesticides to Developing Countries Unless Approved by Their Governments" (March 8, 2023), https://biologicaldiversity.org/w/news/press-releases/epa-petitioned-to-halt-export-of-us-banned-pesticides-to-developing-countries-unless-approved-by-their-governments-2023-03-08/.
23. The website of the nongovernmental organization Basel Action Network is an excellent resource for current information about the Convention (https://www.ban.org/).
24. This case is based on "Debtor's Dilemma: Pay the Mortgage or Walk Away," *New York Times*, December 19, 2009, A22; "No Aid or Rebound in Sight, More Homeowners Just Walk Away," *New York Times*, February 2, 2010, A1; and James Surowiecki, "The Financial Page: Living by Default," *New Yorker*, December 19 and 26, 2011, 44. See also the Reuters news story, "The Rich Homeowners Who Just Walk Away," *South China Morning Post*, February 20, 2012, B10.
25. The material for this case has been drawn from Kermit Vandivier, "Why Should My Conscience Bother Me?" in Robert Heilbroner, ed., *In the Name of Profit* (New York: Doubleday, 1972), 3–31. For a discussion skeptical of Vandivier's version of these events, see John H. Fielder, "Give Goodrich a Break," *Business and Professional Ethics Journal* 7 (Spring 1988): 3–24. John M. Darley discusses the Goodrich case in his informative essay, "How Organizations Socialize Individuals into Evildoing," in David M. Messick and Ann E. Tenbrunsel, eds., *Codes of Conduct: Behavioral Research into Business Ethics* (New York: Sage, 1996), 13–41.

Chapter 2

1. T. M. Scanlon, *What We Owe to Each Other* (Cambridge, Mass.: Harvard University Press, 1998), 197–198.
2. Bernard Williams, *Ethics and the Limits of Philosophy* (Cambridge, Mass.: Harvard University Press, 1985), 16.
3. For more on the trolley problem see Gabriel Andrade, "How Useful Is the Trolley Problem," *The Prindle Post* (May 25, 2018), https://www.prindleinstitute.org/2018/05/just-how-useful-is-the-trolley-problem/.

4. "Anonymous 'Hero' Saves Driver from Flaming Semi Truck in Rockcastle Co., Ky," *WDRB.com* (May 14, 2018), https://www.wdrb.com/news/anonymous-hero-saves-driver-from-flaming-semi-truck-in-rockcastle-co-ky/article_315722fd-5242-5a96-88e0-2e0075d01fcc.html.

5. For more about this see Dale E. Miller, "John Stuart Mill on The Good Life: Higher-Quality Pleasures," *1,000-Word Philosophy* (September 26, 2020), https://1000wordphilosophy.com/2020/09/26/john-stuart-mill-on-the-good-life-higher-quality-pleasures/.

6. Richard B. Brandt, "Toward a Credible Form of Utilitarianism," in Hector-Neri Castañeda and George Nakhnikian, eds., *Morality and the Language of Conduct* (Detroit: Wayne State University Press, 1963), 109–110.

7. *The Ones Who Walk Away from Omelas* (Mankato: Creative Education, 1993).

8. Adam Smith, *The Wealth of Nations* (New York: Modern Library, 1985), 223–225.

9. Kurt Eichenwald, "Commissions Are Many, Profits Few," *New York Times*, May 24, 1993, C1.

10. Immanuel Kant, *Practical Philosophy*, ed. M. J. Gregor (Cambridge: Cambridge University Press, 1996), 611–615.

11. See, in particular, W. D. Ross, *The Right and the Good* (London: Oxford University Press, 1930).

12. Ross, *The Right and the Good*, 21.

13. Ibid., 30.

14. Richard B. Brandt, "The Real and Alleged Problems of Utilitarianism," *Hastings Center Report* (April 1983): 38.

15. Ibid., 42.

16. Ibid.

17. John Austin, *The Province of Jurisprudence Determined*, ed. W. E. Rumble (Cambridge: Cambridge University Press, 1995), 49.

18. Vincent Ryan Ruggiero, *The Moral Imperative* (Port Washington, N.Y.: Alfred, 1973).

19. "Against Zoos," *Morality's Progress: Essays on Humans, Other Animals, and the Rest of Nature* (Oxford: Clarendon, 2002), 166–175.

20. https://www.aza.org/what-is-accreditation

21. https://www.aza.org/partnerships-visitor-demographics?locale=en

22. This case study is based on Douglas Birsch and John H. Fielder, eds., *The Ford Pinto Case* (Albany, N.Y.: SUNY Press, 1994). For a recent discussion, see John R. Danley, "Polishing Up the Pinto: Legal Liability, Moral Blame, and Risk," *Business Ethics Quarterly* 15, no. 2 (April 2005): 205–236. On G.M.'s ignition switches, see "In G.M. Recalls, Inaction and a Trail of Fatal Crashes," *New York Times*, March 3, 2014, B1; Floyd Norris, "History Gives Other Cases of G.M.'s Behavior," *New York Times*, March 28, 2014, B1; "303 Deaths Seen in G.M. Cars with Failed Air Bags," *New York Times*, March 14, 2014, B1; and "Documents Show G.M. Kept Silent on Fatal Crashes," *New York Times*, July 14, 2014, A1.

23. This and the following three paragraphs are based on T. W. Zimmerer and P. L. Preston, "Plasma International," in R. D. Hay, E. R. Gray, and J. E. Gates, eds., *Business and Society* (Cincinnati: South-Western, 1976). The remainder of the case draws on Peter Singer, "Rights and the Market," in John Arthur and William H. Shaw, eds., *Justice and Economic Distribution*, 2nd ed. (Englewood Cliffs, N.J.: Prentice Hall, 1991); and Richard M. Titmuss, *The Gift Relationship* (London: Allen & Unwin, 1972).

24. Barry Schwartz, "The Dark Side of Incentives," *Business Week*, November 23, 2009, 84.

25. Singer, "Rights and the Market." Reprinted by permission of the author. See also "Blood Donation—Altruism or Profit?," *British Medical Journal*, May 4, 1996, 1114; and "Economics Focus: Looking Good by Doing Good," *Economist*, January 17, 2009, 76.

26. Uri Gneezy and Aldo Rustichini, "A Fine Is a Price," *Journal of Legal Studies* 29 (January 2000): 1–17.

27. "Kidney Shortage Inspires a Radical Idea: Organ Sales," *Wall Street Journal*, November 13, 2007, A1. See also, Gary S. Becker and Julio J. Elias, "Cash for Kidneys," *Wall Street Journal*, January 18–19, 2014, C1.

28. James Stacey Taylor, *Stakes and Kidneys: Why Markets in Human Body Parts Are Morally Imperative* (Aldershot: Ashgate, 2005), 165–187.

29. William Saletan, "How Did Steve Jobs Get His Liver?," *Slate* (January 19, 2011), https://slate.com/technology/2011/01/steve-jobs-liver-transplant-did-he-game-the-system.html.

Chapter 3

1. Josh Biven and Jori Kandra, "CEO pay has skyrocketed 1,460% since 1978" (October 4, 2022), https://www.epi.org/publication/ceo-pay-in-2021/.

2. Juliana Menasce Horowitz, Ruth Igielnik, and Rakesh Kochhar, "Most Americans Say There Is Too Much Economic Inequality in the U.S., but Fewer Than Half Call It a Top Priority" (January 9, 2022), https://www.pewresearch.org/social-trends/2020/01/09/most-americans-say-there-is-too-much-economic-inequality-in-the-u-s-but-fewer-than-half-call-it-a-top-priority/.

3. Jessica Semega and Melissa Kollar, "Income in the United States: 2021" (September 13, 2022), https://www.census.gov/library/publications/2022/demo/p60-276.html.

4. https://data.worldbank.org/indicator/SI.POV.GINI?most_recent_value_desc=false.

5. "The Distribution of Household Income, 2019" (November 15, 2022), https://www.cbo.gov/publication/58353.

6. ABC News, "Warren Buffett and His Secretary on Their Tax Rates" (January 25, 2012), https://abcnews.go.com/blogs/business/2012/01/warren-buffett-and-his-secretary-talk-taxes.

7. Horowitz, Igielnik, and Kochhar, "Most Americans Say There Is Too Much Economic Inequality in the U.S., But Fewer Than Half Call It a Top Priority."

8. *Capital in the Twenty-First Century*, translated by Arthur Goldhammer (Cambridge, MA: Belknap, 2017).

9. Jedda Fernandez, "Walmart Owners' Net Worth: How Rich Are the Walmart Family Members?," *International Business Times* (January 24, 2023), https://www.ibtimes.com/walmart-owners-net-worth-how-rich-are-walmart-family-members-3660264.

10. Katie Jones, "Ranked: The Social Mobility of 82 Countries," *Visual Capitalis* (February 7, 2020), https://www.visualcapitalist.com/ranked-the-social-mobility-of-82-countries/.

11. John Stuart Mill, *Utilitarianism* (Indianapolis: Bobbs-Merrill, 1957), 71.

12. Michael Walzer, *Spheres of Justice* (New York: Basic Books, 1983). See also Jon Elster, *Local Justice: How Institutions Allocate Scarce Goods and Necessary Burdens* (New York: Sage, 1992).

13. Walzer, *Spheres of Justice*, 6.

14. Ibid., 10.

15. Mill, *Utilitarianism*, 66.

16. Ibid., 73.

17. Ibid., 71.

18. Ibid.

19. Ibid.

20. Ibid.

21. Mill, *Principles of Political Economy*, ed. Sir William Ashley (Fairfield, N.J.: Augustus M. Kelley, 1987), 211.

22. See, for example, Rosamond Hutt, "Sweden Is a Top Performer on Well-Being. Here's Why," *World Economic Forum* (May 31, 2019), https://www.weforum.org/agenda/2019/05/sweden-is-a-top-performer-on-well-being-here-s-why/.

23. Richard B. Brandt, *A Theory of the Good and the Right* (New York: Oxford University Press, 1979), 312–313.

24. John Stuart Mill, *Principles of Political Economy*, 764.

25. Ibid., 763.

26. Ibid., 772–773.

27. Ibid., 792.

28. John Hospers, *Libertarianism* (Los Angeles: Nash, 1971), 5.

29. Robert Nozick, *Anarchy, State, and Utopia* (New York: Basic Books, 1974).

30. John Locke, "Second Treatise," *Two Treatises of Government*, § 38 https://www.nlnrac.org/earlymodern/locke/documents/second-treatise.

31. Nozick, *Anarchy, State, and Utopia*, 161.

32. Ibid., 163.

33. Amartya Sen, *Development as Freedom* (New Delhi: Oxford University Press, 1999), ch. 7. See also Amartya Sen, *Poverty and Famines* (New York: Oxford University Press, 1981); and Jean Drèze and Amartya Sen, *Hunger and Public Action* (Oxford: Oxford University Press, 1989).

34. Sen, *Development as Freedom*, 167, 170–171.

35. Lawrence C. Becker and Kenneth Kipnis, eds., *Property: Cases, Concepts, Critiques* (Englewood Cliffs, N.J.: Prentice Hall, 1984), 3–5.

36. John Locke, "First Treatise," *Two Treatises of Government*, § 42, https://www.nlnrac.org/earlymodern/locke/documents/first-treatise-of-government.

37. John Rawls, *A Theory of Justice*, rev. ed. (Cambridge, Mass.: Harvard University Press, 1999). For subsequent developments in Rawls's thinking, see John Rawls, *Political Liberalism* (New York: Columbia University Press, 1993); and *Justice as Fairness: A Restatement* (Cambridge, Mass.: Harvard University Press, 2001).

38. Rawls, *A Theory of Justice*, 266; cf. *Political Liberalism*, 291.

39. Rawls, *Political Liberalism*, 6; cf. *A Theory of Justice*, 53, 72, 266.

40. John Rawls, "Justice as Fairness," *Philosophical Review* 67 (April 1958): 167.

41. Rawls, *A Theory of Justice*, 3–4.

42. Rawls, "Justice as Fairness," 168.

43. *Political Liberalism*, 265–266.

44. *A Theory of Justice*, 89.

45. Ibid., 87.

46. *Anarchy, State, and Utopia*, 231.

47. "'Ideal Theory' as Ideology," *Hypatia* 20:3 (Summer 2005), 165–84.

48. This case study is based on "Government Says It's Too Nice for Them to Call Home," *New York Times*, January 30, 2005, sec. 1, 25; "Case for the Public Good Collides with Private Rights," *Financial Times*, February 14, 2005, 14; "Clear the Way, Fellows," *New York Times*, May 8, 2005, sec. 1, 25; and "Justices Uphold Taking Property for Developing," *New York Times*, June 24, 2005, A1.

49. "Eminent Domain: Is It Only Hope for Inner Cities?" *Wall Street Journal*, October 5, 2005, B1; and "Eminent Domain Revisited: A Minnesota Case," *New York Times*, October 5, 2005, C10.

50. See Justice Thomas's dissent to the denial of certiorari, 594 U.S. ____ (2021), https://www.supremecourt.gov/opinions/20pdf/20-1214_7lh8.pdf.

51. "Trends in College Pricing and Student Aid 2022," https://research.collegeboard.org/trends/college-pricing.

52. Brianna McGurran, "College Tuition Inflation: Compare the Cost of College Over Time," *Forbes* (March 28, 2022), https://buffalonews.com/lifestyles/parenting/college-tuition-inflation-compare-the-cost-of-college-over-time/article_a2002c76-91f5-5614-9c4b-6382bcd10923.html.

53. Nick Anderson and Danielle Douglas-Gabriel, "The Next Inflation-Driven Worry: Rising College Tuition" (August 12, 2022), https://www.washingtonpost.com/education/2022/08/12/college-tuition-inflation-prices/.

54. Melanie Hanson, "Pell Grant Statistics," https://educationdata.org/pell-grant-statistics.

55. Raymond AlQaisi, "College Affordability Challenges Persist for Students from Low-income Backgrounds" (October 25, 2022), https://www.ncan.org/news/620206/College-Affordability-Challenges-Persist-for-Students-from-Low-income-Backgrounds.htm.

56. "Exploring the Effects of Tuition Increases on Racial/Ethnic Diversity at Public Colleges and Universities," *Research in Higher Education* 60 (2019), 18–43.

57. Kellie Woodhouse, "Lazy Rivers and Student Debt," *Inside Higher Ed* (June 14, 2015), https://www.insidehighered.com/news/2015/06/15/are-lazy-rivers-and-climbing-walls-driving-cost-college.

58. Robert Morse and Eric Brooks, "A More Detailed Look at the Ranking Factors," *U.S. News and World Report* (September 11, 2022), https://www.usnews.com/education/best-colleges/articles/ranking-criteria-and-weights.

59. Caroline Simon, "Bureaucrats and Buildings: The Case for Why College Is So Expensive," *Forbes* (September 5, 2017), https://www.forbes.com/sites/carolinesimon/2017/09/05/bureaucrats-and-buildings-the-case-for-why-college-is-so-expensive/?sh=229a71c0456a.

60. Phillip Levine, "How Much Does College Really Cost?" *The Chronicle of Higher Education* (April 25, 2022), https://www.chronicle.com/article/how-much-does-college-really-cost.

61. Michael Mitchell, Michael Leachman, and Matt Saenz, "State Higher Education Funding Cuts Have Pushed Costs to Students, Worsened Inequality" (October 24, 2019), 10, https://www.cbpp.org/research/state-budget-and-tax/state-higher-education-funding-cuts-have-pushed-costs-to-students.

62. "The Higher Ed Funding Rollercoaster: State Funding of Higher Education During Financial Crises" (October 25, 2022), 3, https://www.nea.org/he_funding_report.

63. John Creamer, Emily A. Shrider, Kalee Burns, and Frances Chen, *Poverty in the United States: 2021* (September 2022), https://www.census.gov/library/publications/2022/demo/p60-277.html.

64. Ieshia Haynie, "Childhood Poverty, Living Below the Line," *The SES Indicator* (June 2014), https://www.apa.org/pi/ses/resources/indicator/2014/06/childhood-poverty.

65. Jennifer Sheehy-Skeffington and Jessica Rea, "How Poverty Affects People's Decision-Making Processes" (February 2017), https://www.lse.ac.uk/PBS/Research/Research-Articles/How-poverty-affects-peoples-decision-making-processes.

66. Alisha Coleman-Jensen, Matthew P. Rabbitt, Christian A. Gregory, and Anita Singh, "Household Food Security in the United States in 2021" (September 2022), https://www.ers.usda.gov/publications/pub-details/?pubid=104655.

67. "State of Homelessness" (December 19, 2022), https://www.usich.gov/fsp/state-of-homelessness.

68. U.S. Bureau of Labor Statistics, "A Profile of the Working Poor, 2020," https://www.bls.gov/opub/reports/working-poor/2020/home.htm.

69. Finatopia, "Minimum Wage vs Inflation," https://www.finatopia.com/data/minimum-wage.

70. Robert Pear, "Welfare Buying Power Wanes, Report Says," *San Francisco Chronicle*, November 19, 1996, A9.

71. U.S. Census Bureau, *Statistical Abstract of the United States: 1998* (Washington, D.C.: U.S. Government Printing Office, 1997), 390.

72. Aditi Shrivastava and Gina Azito Thompson, "TANF Cash Assistance Should Reach Millions More Families to Lessen Hardship" (February 18, 2022), https://www.cbpp.org/research/income-security/tanf-cash-assistance-should-reach-millions-more-families-to-lessen.

73. H. Luke Shaefer, Pinghui Wu, and Kathryn Edin, "Can Poverty in America Be Compared to Conditions in the World's Poorest Countries?," *National Poverty Center Working Paper Series* (August 2016), https://npc.umich.edu/publications/working_papers/.

74. https://confrontingpoverty.org/poverty-facts-and-myths/americas-poor-are-worse-off-than-elsewhere/.

75. AEI Brookings, "Opportunity, Responsibility, and Security" (December 3, 2015), https://www.brookings.edu/research/opportunity-responsibility-and-security-a-consensus-plan-for-reducing-poverty-and-restoring-the-american-dream/.

Chapter 4

1. Matthew Yglesias, "Denmark's Prime Minister Says Bernie Sanders Is Wrong to Call His Country Socialist," *Vox* (October 31, 2015), https://www.vox.com/2015/10/31/9650030/denmark-prime-minister-bernie-sanders.

2. For a succinct treatment of the rise of the Fugger dynasty, see Ned M. Cross, Robert C. Lamm, and Rudy H. Turk, *The Search for Personal Freedom* (Dubuque, Iowa: W. C. Brown, 1972), 12. For a curious legacy of the Fuggers, see "In This Picturesque Village, the Rent Hasn't Been Raised Since 1520," *Wall Street Journal*, December 26, 2008, A1.

3. John Micklethwait and Adrian Wooldridge, *The Company: A Short History of a Revolutionary Idea* (New York: Modern Library, 2003), xv.

4. Robert Heilbroner, *The Worldly Philosophers*, 5th ed. (New York: Simon & Schuster, 1980), 22–23.

5. Adam Smith, *The Wealth of Nations* (New York: Modern Library, 1985), 16.

6. Ibid., 223–225.

7. Alan Reynolds, "The Smoot-Hawley Tariff and the Great Depression," *Cato At Liberty* (May 7, 2016), https://www.cato.org/blog/smoot-hawley-tariff-great-depression.

8. Quoted by Joseph E. Stiglitz, "A Fair Deal for the World," *New York Review of Books*, May 23, 2002, 28.

9. Robert Heilbroner, *The Economic Problem* (Englewood Cliffs, N.J.: Prentice Hall, 1972), 725.

10. Ed Diener et al., "Subjective Well-Being: Three Decades of Progress," *Psychological Bulletin* 125, no. 2 (1999): 228; Richard A. Easterlin, "The Economics of Happiness," *Daedalus* (Spring 2004): 31; and Robert H. Frank, "How Not to Buy Happiness," *Daedalus* (Spring 2004): 70. See also "Money Can't Buy Me Love," *Economist*, June 16, 2012, 34.

11. Adam Smith, *The Theory of Moral Sentiments*, eds. D. D. Raphael and A. L. Macfie (Oxford: Oxford University Press), 1976.

12. "The Next Society: A Survey of the Near Future," *Economist*, November 3, 2001, 16.

13. https://www.transtats.bts.gov/; Meininger's International, "Concentration in the Beer Market" (20 August 2021), https://www.meiningers-international.com/wine/news-analysis/concentration-beer-market#:~:text=Only%20ten%20companies%20account%20for%20two%20thirds%20of%20global%20beer%20production.&text=The%20ten%20largest%20breweries%20in,1.235m%20hectolitres%20of%20beer.

14. "Fortune 500," https://fortune.com/ranking/fortune500/2022/; Bureau of Economic Analysis, "Gross Domestic Product, Fourth Quarter and Year 2022 (Third Estimate), GDP by Industry, and Corporate Profits" March 30, 2023), https://www.bea.gov/news/2023/gross-domestic-product-fourth-quarter-and-year-2022-third-estimate-gdp-industry-and.

15. Matt O'Brien and the Associated Press, "Microsoft Steps Up to Antitrust Fight with FTC Over $69 Billion Activision Acquisition" (December 23, 2022), https://fortune.com/2022/12/23/microsoft-steps-up-to-antitrust-fight-with-ftc-over-69-billion-activision-acquisition/.

16. Robert B. Carson, *Business Issues Today: Alternative Perspectives* (New York: St. Martin's, 1982), 29.
17. Lee Drutman, "How Corporate Lobbyists Conquered American Democracy," *The Atlantic* (April 20, 2015), https://www.theatlantic.com/business/archive/2015/04/how-corporate-lobbyists-conquered-american-democracy/390822/.
18. Congressional Research Service, "Domestic Steel Manufacturing: Overview and Prospects" (May 17, 2022), https://crsreports.congress.gov/product/pdf/R/R47107.
19. Colin Grabow, "Candy-Coated Cartel: Time to Kill the U.S. Sugar Program," *Cato Institute Policy Analysis* 837 (April 10, 2018), https://www.cato.org/policy-analysis/candy-coated-cartel-time-kill-us-sugar-program.
20. Chuck Abbot, "Record-High Ag Subsidies to Supply 39% of Farm Income," *Successful Farming* (December 2, 2020), https://www.agriculture.com/news/business/record-high-ag-subsidies-to-supply-39-of-farm-income.
21. Associated Press, "EPA Seeks to Mandate More Use of Ethanol and Other Biofuels" (December 1, 2022), https://www.npr.org/2022/12/01/1140203082/epa-seeks-to-mandate-more-use-of-ethanol-and-other-biofuels.
22. Ana Swenson, "The CHIPS Act Is About More Than Chips: Here's What's in It," *New York Times* (February 28, 2023), https://www.nytimes.com/2023/02/28/business/economy/chips-act-childcare.html.
23. David Biello, "Obama Has Done More for Clean Energy Than You Think," *Scientific American* (September 8, 2015), https://www.scientificamerican.com/article/obama-has-done-more-for-clean-energy-than-you-think/.
24. Government Accountability Office, "Corporate Income Tax: Effective Rates Before and After 2017 Law Change" (December 14, 2022), https://www.gao.gov/products/gao-23-105384.
25. Ryan Koronowski, Jessica Vela, and Zahir Rasheed, "These 19 Fortune 100 Companies Paid Next to Nothing—or Nothing at All—in Taxes in 2021," Center for American Progress (April 26, 2022), https://www.americanprogress.org/article/these-19-fortune-100-companies-paid-next-to-nothing-or-nothing-at-all-in-taxes-in-2021/.
26. Alan Greenblatt, "Tax Incentives: The Losing Gamble States and Cities Keep Making," *Governing* (February 25, 2020), https://www.governing.com/finance/tax-incentives-the-losing-gamble-states-and-cities-keep-making.html.
27. See, for instance, Hans von der Burchard and Giorgio Leali, "Germany and France Join Forces against Biden in Subsidy Battle," *Politico* (November 22, 2022), https://www.politico.eu/article/germany-france-biden-green-subsidy-inflation-reduction-act-robert-habeck-bruno-le-maire/.
28. Quoted in "Economic Focus: Competition Is All," *Economist*, December 6, 2003, 70.
29. Alfie Kohn, *No Contest: The Case against Competition* (Boston: Houghton Mifflin, 1986), 46–55. This paragraph and the next are based on Chapter 3, "Is Competition More Productive?"
30. John F. Burns, "Soviet Food Shortages: Grumbling and Excuses," *New York Times* (January 15, 1982), https://www.nytimes.com/1982/01/15/world/soviet-food-shortages-grumbling-and-excuses.html.
31. Hedrick Smith, "The Russian Auto Market," *New York Times* (October 8, 1972), https://www.nytimes.com/1972/10/08/archives/the-russian-auto-market-no-tradeins-no-imports-no-options-and-you.html.
32. This extract is from *Karl Marx: Early Writings*, translated by T. B. Bottomore, 1963. Used with permission of McGraw-Hill Book Company.
33. Studs Terkel, "How I Am a Worker," in Leonard Silk, ed., *Capitalism: The Moving Target* (New York: Quadrangle, 1974), 68–69. Reprinted by permission of the *New York Times*.
34. Robert Nozick, *Anarchy, State, and Utopia*, pp. 246–250.
35. McKinsey & Company, "Delivering the US Manufacturing Renaissance" (August 29, 2022), https://www.mckinsey.com/capabilities/operations/our-insights/delivering-the-us-manufacturing-renaissance.
36. Quoted in "The Hollow Corporation," *Business Week*, March 3, 1986.
37. Josh Bivens, "Updated Employment Multipliers for the U.S. Economy," Economic Policy Institute (January 23, 2019), https://www.epi.org/publication/updated-employment-multipliers-for-the-u-s-economy/?utm_source=Economic+Policy+Institute&utm_campaign=a9c273dba0-EMAIL_CAMPAIGN_2019_02_01_08_47&utm_medium=email&utm_term=0_e7c5826c50-a9c273dba0-59992185&mc_cid=a9c273dba0&mc_eid=32141f5ffe.
38. Susan Helper, Timothy Krueger, and Howard Wial, "Why Does Manufacturing Matter? Which Manufacturing Matters? A Policy Framework," Brookings Institute (February 2012), https://www.brookings.edu/wp-content/uploads/2016/06/0222_manufacturing_helper_krueger_wial.pdf.
39. Andrea Shalal, "80 Countries Are Hoarding Medical Supplies – Here's Why It Damages the Global Response to COVID-19," World Economic Forum (April 24, 2020), https://www.weforum.org/agenda/2020/04/wto-report-80-countries-limiting-exports-medical-supplies/.
40. Su-Lin Tan, "China Could Reopen in March, But Zero-Covid Has Shaken Confidence in Supply Chains, Economist Says" CNBC (November 30, 2022), https://www.cnbc.com/2022/11/30/economist-chinas-zero-covid-has-shaken-confidence-in-supply-chains.html.
41. John Keilman, "America Is Back in the Factory Business," *Wall Street Journal* (April 8, 2023), https://www.wsj.com/articles/american-manufacturing-factory-jobs-comeback-3ce0c52c.
42. Ben Casselman, "The White-Collar Job Apocalypse That Didn't Happen," *New York Times* (September 27, 2019), https://www.nytimes.com/2019/09/27/business/economy/jobs-offshoring.html; Jack Kelly, "How Offshoring and Artificial Intelligence Threaten U.S. White-Collar Workers," *Forbes* (April 12, 2023), https://www.forbes.com/sites/jackkelly/2023/04/12/how-offshoring-and-artificial-intelligence-threaten-us-white-collar-workers/?sh=63c54d2b42a1.
43. Quoted in "Shaking Up Trade Theory," *Business Week* (February 2, 2003), 118. For an advanced discussion, see Paul A. Samuelson, "Where Ricardo and Mill Rebut and Confirm Arguments of Mainstream Economists Supporting Globalization," *Journal of Economic Perspectives* 18, no. 3 (Summer 2004): 135–146. See also William J. Baumol, "Errors in Economics and Their Consequences," *Social Research* 72, no. 1 (Spring 2005): 183–184, 186–192.
44. Bureau of Economic Analysis, "U.S. International Trade in Goods and Services, December and Annual 2022" (February 7, 2023), https://www.bea.gov/news/2023/us-international-trade-in-goods-and-services-december-and-annual-2022#:~:text=The%20goods%20and%20services%20deficit%20was%203.7%20percent%20of%20current,from%203.6%20percent%20in%202021.&text=Exports%20of%20goods%20increased%20%24324.2,and%20materials%20increased%20%24190.9%20billion.

45. "Inside the Banks," *Economist*, January 24, 2009, 13; and "When a Flow Becomes a Flood," *Economist*, January 24, 2009, 74–76.

46. Brad W. Setser, "What Would Happen If China Started Selling Off Its Treasury Portfolio?" Council on Foreign Relations (June 21, 2018), https://www.cfr.org/blog/what-would-happen-if-china-started-selling-its-treasury-portfolio.

47. Eric Beech, "Trump Picks 'Death by China' Author for Trade Advisory Role," Reuters (December 21, 2016), https://www.reuters.com/article/us-usa-trump-navarro/trump-picks-death-by-china-author-for-trade-advisory-role-idUSKBN14A27N.

48. Christina Wilkie, "Biden and Sanders' Fight Over Trade Is a War for the Future of the Democratic Party," CNBC (March 9, 2020), https://www.cnbc.com/2020/03/09/biden-vs-sanders-trade-fight-is-war-for-future-of-democratic-party.html.

49. "Corporations to the Rescue? Not So Fast," *Wall Street Journal*, July 14, 2004, C1; "Tired of Playing Quarters," *Wall Street Journal*, September 14, 2004, B2; and "Call to End Quarterly Guidance 'Obsession,'" *Financial Times*, July 24, 2006, 1. See also Lynn Stout, *The Shareholder Value Myth* (San Francisco: Berrett-Koehler, 2012), 63–73.

50. See "China Steps Up Pressure on Western Rivals," *Financial Times*, October 13, 2004, 5; Adam Segal, "Is America Losing Its Edge?" *Foreign Affairs* (November–December 2004), 2–8; Thomas Bleha, "Down to the Wire," *Foreign Affairs* (May–June 2005), 111–124; and "Can America Keep Up?" *Business Week*, March 27, 2006, 48–56.

51. Adrian Slywotsky and Richard Wise, "Resist the Urge to Merge," *Wall Street Journal*, July 16, 2002, B2.

52. Francesco Guerra, "A Need to Reconnect," *Financial Times*, March 13, 2009, 9. See also "Shareholder Value Re-Evaluated," *Financial Times*, March 16, 2009, 8; and Justin Fox, "Stop Spoiling the Shareholders," *Atlantic*, July–August 2013, 30.

53. "Greenspan Issues Hopeful Outlook as Stocks Sink," *Wall Street Journal*, July 17, 2002, A1.

54. "Excerpts from President's Speech," *Wall Street Journal*, July 10, 2002, A8; and Bill Staub, "A Matter of Greed," *Rocky Mountain News*, July 5, 2002, 3B.

55. Majorie Kelly, "Waving Goodbye to the Invisible Hand," *Business Ethics* (March–April 2002): 5.

56. These figures are for 2021 "Average Annual Hours Actually Worked per Worker," *OECD.Stat (June 2023),* https://stats.oecd.org/index.aspx?DataSetCode=ANHRS.

57. Sherwood Ross, "Workers Fearful of Being Laid Off," *San Jose Mercury News*, December 17, 1995, 2PC.

58. Matt Gonzales, "Nearly Half of Workers Are 'Definitely Looking' to Work Remotely," Society for Human Resource Management (June 13, 2022), https://www.shrm.org/resourcesandtools/hr-topics/behavioral-competencies/global-and-cultural-effectiveness/pages/nearly-half-of-workers-are-definitely-looking-to-work-remotely.aspx.

59. Joseph Fuller and William Kerr "The Great Resignation Didn't Start with the Pandemic," *Harvard Business Review* (March 23, 2022), https://hbr.org/2022/03/the-great-resignation-didnt-start-with-the-pandemic.

60. These quotes are from Lauren Aratani, "Goodbye to the Job: How the Pandemic Changed Americans' Attitude to Work," *The Guardian* (November 28, 2021), https://www.theguardian.com/money/2021/nov/28/goodbye-to-job-how-the-pandemic-changed-americans-attitude-to-work.

61. "Future of Work Reinvented," Gartner (no date), https://www.gartner.com/en/insights/future-of-work.

62. Edward Segal, "How Companies Can Respond to the Rising Tide of the Great Resignation," *Forbes* (January 12, 2022), https://www.forbes.com/sites/edwardsegal/2022/01/12/how-companies-can-respond-to-the-rising-tide-of-the-great-resignation/?sh=58dea1673d54.

63. Lauren Aratani, "Goodbye to the Job: How the Pandemic Changed Americans' Attitude to Work," *Guardian* (November 28, 2021), https://www.theguardian.com/money/2021/nov/28/goodbye-to-job-how-the-pandemic-changed-americans-attitude-to-work.

64. Noah Sheidlower, "Big City Restaurants and Bars Are Missing Office Workers' Spending on Mondays and Fridays," CNBC (February 24, 2023), https://www.cnbc.com/2023/02/24/big-city-restaurants-bars-hybrid-work.html.

65. This case study draws on "How to Fix Bangladesh's Factories," *Bloomberg Businessweek*, May 6–12, 2013, 10; "$40 Million in Aid Set for Bangladesh Garment Workers," *New York Times*, December 24, 2013, A1; "First Companies Give to Fund for Victims of Bangladeshi Clothing Factory Collapse," *New York Times*, February 24, 2014, A4; "Battling for a Safer Bangladesh," *New York Times*, April 22, 2104, B1; and John Miller, "After Horror, Change?" *Dollars & Sense*, September /October 2014, 9–11.

66. Nathasha Sheriff Wells and Chana Rosenthal, "A Broken Partnership: How Clothing Brands Exploit Suppliers and Harm Workers—And What Can Be Done About It," NYU Stern (April 2003), https://bhr.stern.nyu.edu/manufacturing-buyersupplier-2023.

67. "Memo from the Editor," *Medical Economics*, November 7, 1988.

68. For more examples and further discussion of occupational licensure, see "Informer," *Forbes*, April 26, 2004; "The New Unions," *Forbes*, February 25, 2008, 100; "Equine Dentists Shine in Court," *Wall Street Journal*, November 13–14, 2010, A5; and "A License to Shampoo: Jobs Needing State Approval Rise," *Wall Street Journal*, February 7, 2011, A1.

69. See the chapter entitled "Occupational Licensure" in Milton Friedman, *Capitalism and Freedom* (Chicago: University of Chicago Press, 1962), in particular, 149.

70. Atul Gawande, "Piecework," *New Yorker*, April 4, 2005, 44; "Patients' Costs Skyrocket; Specialists' Incomes Soar," *New York Times*, January 18, 2013, A1; and "Medicine's Top Earners Are Not the M.D.s," *New York Times*, May 17, 2014 (online).

71. "Competition and Cutbacks Hurt Foreign Doctors in U.S.," *New York Times*, November 7, 1995, B15.

72. Ibid.

73. U.S. Census Bureau, *Statistical Abstract of the United States: 2012* (Washington, D.C.: U.S. Government Printing Office, 2011), Table 1347.

74. "The Coming Shortage of Doctors," *Wall Street Journal*, November 5, 2009, A19; and "After Years of Quiet, Expecting a Surge in U.S. Medical Schools," *New York Times*, February 15, 2010, A1. See also "How to Beat the Doctor Shortage," *AARP Bulletin*, March 2013, 14.

75. Bernard Gert, "Licensing Professions," *Business and Professional Ethics Journal* 1 (Summer 1982): 52; and Donald Weinert, "Commentary," *Business and Professional Ethics Journal* 1 (Summer 1982): 62.

76. "Dubious Claims for H1N1 Cures are Rife Online," *New York Times*, November 6, 2009 (online).

77. Andrea Salcedo, "Medical Board Suspends PA's License, Claiming He Prescribed Ivermectin and 'Harassed' Hospitals to Do the Same," *Washington Post* (October 20, 2021), https://www.washingtonpost.com/nation/2021/10/20/washington-suspends-physician-assistant-license-ivermectin/.

78. Tessa Weinberg, "Missouri Governor Signs Law Shielding Doctors Prescribing Ivermectin, Hydroxychloroquine," *Missouri Independent* (June 7, 2022), https://missouriindependent.com/briefs/missouri-governor-signs-law-shielding-doctors-prescribing-ivermectin-hydroxychloroquine/.

79. United States Government Accountability Office, "Federal Social Safety Net Programs: Millions of Full-Time Workers Rely on Federal Health Care and Food Assistance Programs" (October 2020), https://www.sanders.senate.gov/wp-content/uploads/taxpayers-subsidize-poverty-wages-at-large-corporations-gao-finds.pdf

80. Maggie Fitzgerald, "Amazon Has 'Destroyed the Retail Industry' So US Should Look into Its Practices, Mnuchin Says," CNBC (July 24, 2019), https://www.cnbc.com/2019/07/24/amazon-has-destroyed-the-retail-industry-so-us-should-look-into-its-practices-sec-mnuchin-says.html.

81. Sophie Nieto-Munoz, "Excessive Injuries, Low Pay at Amazon Warehouses Cause High Turnover, Report Claims," *New Jersey Monitor* (June 23, 2022), https://newjerseymonitor.com/2022/06/23/excessive-injuries-low-pay-at-amazon-warehouses-cause-high-turnover-report-claims/.

82. Jodi Kantor, Karen Weise and Grace Ashford, "Inside Amazon's Worst Human Resources Problem," *New York Times* (October 24, 2021), https://www.nytimes.com/2021/10/24/technology/amazon-employee-leave-errors.html.

83. Annie Palmer, "Amazon Hikes Pay for Warehouse and Delivery Workers," CNBC (September 28, 2022), https://www.cnbc.com/2022/09/28/amazon-Hikes-Pay-for-Warehouse-and-Delivery-Workers.html.

84. James W. Sheehy, "New Work Ethic Is Frightening," *Personnel Journal* (June 1990), is the source of this case.

85. See Jia Wertz, "Shoplifting Has Become A $100 Billion Problem For Retailers," *Forbes* (November 20, 2022), https://www.forbes.com/sites/jiawertz/2022/11/20/shoplifting-has-become-a-100-billion-problem-for-retailers/?sh=26b6113b2d62.

86. Barry Rosen, "Why 'Quiet Quitting' Is a Loud Call for a Better Social Contract at Work," *Forbes* (November 23, 2022), https://www.forbes.com/sites/forbesbusinesscouncil/2022/11/23/why-quiet-quitting-is-a-loud-call-for-a-better-social-contract-at-work/?sh=1840af9bdb29.

87. Jim Detert, "Let's Call Quiet Quitting What It Often Is: Calibrated Contributing," *MIT Sloan Management Review* (Winter 2023), 1–3.

88. Sarah Green Carmichael, "Quiet Quitting Is the Fakest of Fake Workplace Trends," *Washington Post* (September 27, 2022), https://www.washingtonpost.com/business/quiet-quitting-is-the-fakest-of-fake-workplace-trends/2022/09/27/bbf5e354-3e5c-11ed-8c6e-9386bd7cd826_story.html.

89. This case study draws on Joe Nocera, "Let's Start Paying College Athletes," *New York Times*, December 30, 2011 (online); Jeffrey Dorfman, "Pay College Athletes? They're Already Paid Up to $125,000 per Year," *Forbes*, August 29, 2013 (online); Jonathan Mahler, "The Case for Higher Earning," *Bloomberg Businessweek*, January 6–12, 2014, 8–9; Dennis Dodd, "Paying Athletes Figures to Be Key Issue at Annual NCAA Convention," *CBSSports.com*, January 15, 2014; "College Players Granted Right to Form Union," *New York Times*, March 26, 2014 (online); "Justice for Jocks," *Economist*, August 16, 2014, 12; and "What Made College Football More Like the Pros? $7.3 Billion, for a Start," *New York Times*, December 30, 2014 (online).

90. 141 S. Ct. 2141 (2021), https://www.supremecourt.gov/opinions/20pdf/20-512_gfbh.pdf.

91. Cole Clayburn, "Name, Image, Likeness: What College Athletes Should Know About NCAA Rules," *U.S. News and World Report* (March 2, 2023), https://www.usnews.com/education/best-colleges/articles/name-image-likeness-what-college-athletes-should-know-about-ncaa-rules.

Chapter 5

1. John McDermott, *Corporate Society: Class, Property, and Contemporary Capitalism* (Boulder, Colo.: Westview, 1991), 4.

2. The figures in this paragraph come from *Fortune* magazine's 2023 ranking of "Fortune 500" companies, https://fortune.com/ranking/fortune500/2023/search/, and its 2022 ranking of "Global 500" companies, https://fortune.com/ranking/global500/2022/search/.

3. Anthony J. Parisi, "How Exxon Rules Its Great Empire," *San Francisco Chronicle*, August 5, 1980, 27.

4. Quoted in Larry D. Soderquist, Linda O. Smiddy, A. A. Sommer, Jr., and Pat K. Chew, *Corporate Law and Practice*, 2nd ed. (New York: Practicing Law Institute, 1999), 11.

5. Thomas Donaldson, *Corporations and Morality* (Englewood Cliffs, N.J.: Prentice Hall, 1982), 4.

6. David E. Schrader, "The Oddness of Corporate Ownership," *Journal of Social Philosophy* 27 (Fall 1996): 106.

7. Donaldson, *Corporations and Morality*, 5.

8. Ibid., 3.

9. "Prosecutor's Dilemma," *Economist*, June 15, 2002, 76.

10. Parisi, "How Exxon Rules," 38.

11. See Kenneth Goodpaster and John B. Matthews, Jr., "Can a Corporation Have a Conscience?" *Harvard Business Review* 60 (January–February 1982): 132–141.

12. Donaldson, *Corporations and Morality*, 10.

13. See Peter A. French, "The Corporation as a Moral Person," *American Philosophical Quarterly* 16 (July 1979): 207–215; and French, "Corporate Moral Agency," in P. H. Werhane and R. E. Freeman, eds., *The Blackwell Encyclopedia of Management*, Vol. 2: *Business Ethics*, 2nd ed. (Malden, Mass.: Blackwell, 2005), 123–125.

14. See Manuel G. Velasquez, "Why Corporations Are Not Morally Responsible for Anything They Do," *Business and Professional Ethics Journal* 2 (Spring 1983), 1–18; and Velasquez, "Debunking Corporate Moral Responsibility," *Business Ethics Quarterly* 13 (October 2003), 531–562.

15. "After a Decade, SAC Capital Blinks," *New York Times*, November 5, 2013, B1.

16. Quoted in Goodpaster and Matthews, "Can a Corporation Have a Conscience?," 141.

17. Jeffrey L. Seglin, "A Safer World for Mea Culpas," *New York Times*, March 21, 1999, sec. 3, 4. See also "Mattel Seeks to Placate China with Apology on Toys," *Wall Street Journal*, September 22–23, 2007, A1.

18. Quoted in Clarence C. Walton, *Corporate Social Responsibilities* (Belmont, Calif.: Wadsworth, 1967), 169–170.

19. Quoted in Bernard D. Nossiter, *The Mythmakers: An Essay on Power and Wealth* (Boston: Houghton Mifflin, 1964), 100.

20. Milton Friedman, *Capitalism and Freedom* (Chicago: University of Chicago Press, 1962), 133.

21. Theodore Levitt, "The Dangers of Social Responsibility," *Harvard Business Review* 36 (September–October 1958): 41–50.

22. Aneel Karnani, "The Case against Corporate Social Responsibility," *Wall Street Journal*, August 23, 2010, R1.

23. Milton Friedman, "The Social Responsibility of Business Is to Increase Its Profits," *New York Times Magazine*, September 13, 1970, 33, 126. For a recent endorsement of Friedman's position, see Henry G. Manne, "Milton Friedman Was Right," *Wall Street Journal*, November 24, 2006, A12.

24. Friedman, "Social Responsibility," 124.

25. Quoted in Robert B. Reich, *Supercapitalism: The Transformation of Business, Democracy, and Everyday Life* (New York: Knopf, 2007), 45.

26. Reprinted from Keith Davis, "Five Propositions for Social Responsibility," *Business Horizons* 18 (June 1975): 20. Copyright © 1975 by the Foundation for the School of Business at Indiana University. Used with permission.

27. John Kay, "Business Leaders Have No Natural Authority," *Financial Times*, April 5, 2005, 17.

28. James Surowiecki, "The Financial Page: A Fair Day's Wage," *New Yorker*, February 9, 2015, 22.

29. Robert Kuttner, "The Great American Pension-Fund Robbery," *Business Week*, September 8, 2003, 24. "The Corporate Tax Game," *Business Week*, March 31, 2003, 79–83. See also "Google Has Made $11.1 Billion Overseas since 2007. It Paid Just 2.4% in Taxes. And That's Legal," *Bloomberg Businessweek*, October 25–31, 2010, 43.

30. Kay, "Business Leaders," 17.

31. Melvin Anshen, "Changing the Social Contract: A Role for Business," *Columbia Journal of World Business* 5, no. 6 (November–December 1970): 6–14, and Melvin Anshen, *Corporate Strategies for Social Performance* (New York: Free Press, 1980). See also James E. Post, Anne T. Lawrence, and James Weber, *Business and Society: Corporate Strategy, Public Policy, Ethics*, 10th ed. (New York: McGraw-Hill, 2002), 16–17.

32. Anshen, "Changing the Social Contract," 10.

33. Davis, "Five Propositions for Social Responsibility," 22.

34. Just Capital, "Annual Survey: In an Unstable Economic Environment, Workers and Wages Are More Important Than Ever to the American Public" (September 15, 2022), https://justcapital.com/reports/2022-survey-workers-and -wages-are-more-important-than-ever-to-the-american-public/.

35. Thomas Donaldson, "Defining the Value of Doing Good Business," *Financial Times* (supplement on "Mastering Corporate Governance"), June 3, 2005, 2. See also the Goldman Sachs report, "Shaping the New Rules of Competition" (July 2007), prepared for the U.N. Global Compact (July 2007), www.unglobalcompact.org.

36. John R. Boatwright, *Blackwell Encyclopedic Dictionary of Business Ethics*, eds. Patricia R. Werhane and R. Edward Freeman (Malden, Mass.: Blackwell, 1996), 278.

37. Friedman, "The Social Responsibility of Business," 122.

38. Ibid.

39. Thomas J. White III, "Benefit Corporations: Increased Oversight through Creation of the Benefit Corporation Commission," *Journal of Legislation* 41 (2015), https://scholarship.law.nd.edu/jleg/vol41/iss2/6/.

40. Lynn Stout, *The Shareholder Value Myth* (San Francisco: Berrett-Koehler, 2012), 37.

41. Adolf A. Berle, Jr. and Gardiner C. Means, *The Modern Corporation and Private Property* (New York: Macmillan, 1932).

42. Quoted in "Design by Committee," *Economist*, June 15, 2002, 71. See also James Surowiecki, "The Financial Page: Board Stiff," *New Yorker*, June 1, 2009 (online); James B. Stewart, "Bad Directors and Why They Aren't Thrown Out," *New York Times*, March 29, 2013; and the references in note 43 below.

43. Josh Bivens and Jori Kandra, "CEO Pay has Skyrocketed 1,460% since 1978," Economic Policy Institute (October 4, 2022), https://www.epi.org/publication/ceo-pay-in-2021/.

44. Laurent Back and Daniel Metzger, "Are Shareholder Votes Rigged," Harvard Law School Forum on Corporate Governance (January 4, 2017), https://corpgov.law.harvard.edu/2017/01/04/are-shareholder-votes-rigged/.

45. "Revising a Boardroom Legacy," *New York Times*, September 28, 2007, C5. On the difficulty of firing CEOs, see John Cassidy, "The CEO's New Armor," *Condé Nast Portfolio* (June 2008): 56–59.

46. Quoted in Reich, *Supercapitalism*, 75.

47. "As California Starved for Energy, U.S. Business Had a Feast," *Wall Street Journal*, September 16, 2002, A1; and "How Energy Traders Turned Bonanza into an Epic Bust," *Wall Street Journal*, December 31, 2002, A1. For recent developments, see "California Restarts Daily Electricity Auction," *Wall Street Journal*, March 30, 2009, A2; and "California Revisits Power Shopping," *Wall Street Journal*, March 13–14, 2010, A3.

48. Clifford Krauss, Manny Fernandez, Ivan Penn, and Rick Rojas, "How Texas' Drive for Energy Independence Set It Up for Disaster," *New York Times*, February 21, 2021, https://www.nytimes.com/2021/02/21/us/texas-electricity-ercot -blackouts.html.

49. Quoted in Mark S. Schwartz, "Beyond the Bottom Line: A Shifting Paradigm for Business?" in Julian Friedland, ed., *Doing Well and Doing Good: The Human Face of the New Capitalism* (Charlotte, N.C.: Information Age Publishing, 2009), 136.

50. Ibid.

51. "The Corporate Givers," *Business Week*, November 29, 2004, 102–103. See also "Luxury Brands Fail to Make Ethical Grade," *Financial Times*, November 7, 2007, 2; Linda K. Treviño and Katherine A. Nelson, *Managing Business Ethics: Straight Talk about How to Do It Right*, 4th ed. (Hoboken, N.J.: Wiley, 2007), 31; "Does Being Ethical Pay?," *Wall Street Journal*, May 12, 2008, R4; and "Give and Take," *Economist*, February 13, 2010, 68.

52. Peter Georgescu, "Doing the Right Thing Is Just Profitable," *Forbes*, July 26, 2017, https://www.forbes.com/sites /petergeorgescu/2017/07/26/doing-the-right-thing-is-just-profitable/?sh=21ca86c47488.

53. Quoted by John Micklethwait and Adrian Wooldridge, *The Company* (New York: Modern Library, 2003), 182.
54. Robert B. Reich, "How to Avoid These Layoffs," *New York Times*, January 4, 1996, A13. See also Robert B. Reich, "No Obligations," *Condé Nast Portfolio* (January 2008): 39; Reich, *Supercapitalism*, ch. 5; and Karnani, "The Case against Corporate Social Responsibility."
55. "When Business Is Good," *New York Times*, February 22, 2011, B1.
56. Reich, *Supercapitalism*, 197–199.
57. "From a Handout to a Hand Up," *Financial Times*, February 3, 2005, 3. For a different example, see "Goldman Launches '10,000 Women' Drive," *Financial Times*, March 6, 2008, 6; and "Goldman's Conspicuous Compassion," *Condé Nast Portfolio* (November 2008): 54–61.
58. Levitt, "The Dangers of Social Responsibility," 44. See also George G. Brenkert, "Private Corporations and Public Welfare," *Public Affairs Quarterly* 6 (April 1992): 155–168.
59. Davis, "Five Propositions for Social Responsibility," 20.
60. Paul F. Camenisch, "Business Ethics: On Getting to the Heart of the Matter," *Business and Professional Ethics Journal* 1 (Fall 1981): 59–69.
61. "The Cecil Rhodes of Chocolate-Chip Cookies," *Economist*, May 25, 1996, 74.
62. "Good Citizens of the Community," *Business Ethics: The Magazine of Corporate Responsibility* 16 (March–April 2002): 9. See also "The Corporate Donors," *Business Week*, December 1, 2003, 92; and "How Companies Dig Deep," *Business Week*, November 26, 2007, 52.
63. Camenisch, "Business Ethics."
64. See Christopher D. Stone, *Where the Law Ends* (New York: Harper & Row, 1975), ch. 11. For other problems of overreliance on legal rules, see Michael L. Michael, "Business Ethics: The Law of Rules," *Business Ethics Quarterly* 16 (October 2006): 475–504.
65. Kenneth J. Arrow, "Social Responsibility and Economic Efficiency," *Public Policy* 21 (Summer 1973).
66. Milton Snoeyenbos and Barbara Caley, "Managing Ethics," in Milton Snoeyenbos, Robert Almeder, and James Humber, eds., *Business Ethics*, 3rd ed. (Buffalo, N.Y.: Prometheus, 2001), 143. See also Betsy Stevens, "Corporate Ethical Codes: Effective Instruments for Influencing Behavior," *Journal of Business Ethics* 78, no. 4 (April 2008): 601–609.
67. Snoeyenbos and Caley, "Managing Ethics," 141.
68. Gillian Flynn, "Make Employee Ethics Your Business," *Personnel Journal* (June 1995).
69. "Organisations, Too, Can Be Put on the Couch," *Financial Times*, June 20, 2003, 12.
70. Boris Groysberg, Jeremiah Lee, Jesse Price, and J. Yo-Jud Cheng, "The Leader's Guide to Corporate Culture," *Harvard Business Review* 96 (January–February 2018): 46.
71. "When Something Is Rotten," *Economist*, July 27, 2002, 53.
72. "Donaldson Laments U.S. Chiefs' Lack of Ethical Leadership," *Financial Times*, September 20, 2004, 1.
73. Lynn Sharp Paine, "Managing for Organizational Integrity," *Harvard Business Review* 72 (March–April 1994): 107–108.
74. "Culture at Fannie Mae Led to Fraud," *Financial Times*, February 24, 2006, 17.
75. "Learning the Lingo," *Economist*, January 11, 2014, 72.
76. "Businesses Are Signing Up for Ethics 101," *Business Week*, February 15, 1988, 56. See also "Adding Ethics to the Core Curriculum," *CRO: Corporate Responsibility Officer* (September–October 2007): 43.
77. Sandra Waddock and Neil Smith, "Corporate Responsibility Audits: Doing Well by Doing Good," *Sloan Management Review* 41 (Winter 2000): 75–83.
78. Scot J. Paltrow, "Brokers Who Break the Rules," *Los Angeles Times*, July 1, 1992, A1.
79. "GE to Release Audit of Ethical Violations," *Financial Times*, May 19, 2005, 19.
80. "Businesses Are Signing Up," 56.
81. "Lessons Thomas Still Could Learn," *New York Times*, October 24, 2007, C1.
82. *Economist*, April 8, 1995, 57; and August 19, 1995, 56.
83. This case is based on new stories and commentary in the *Financial Times*, September 8 and 12, 2005, February 23, 2006, and November 7, 2007; in the *New York Times*, September 8 and October 24, 2005, and January 6 and February 9, 2006; in the *Wall Street Journal*, November 7, 2007; and in Reich, *Supercapitalism*, 199. See also "Microsoft in China," *Fortune*, July 23, 2007, 84. For further discussion and analysis, see G. Elijah Dunn and Neil Haddow, "Just Doing Business or Doing Just Business: Google, Microsoft, Yahoo! and the Business of Censoring China's Internet," *Journal of Business Ethics* 79, no. 3 (May 2008): 219–234. On Google in China, see "A Heated Debate at the Top," *Wall Street Journal*, January 14, 2010, A14; "The Chinese Disconnection," *New York Times*, January 14, 2010, B1; "Stance by China to Limit Google Is Risk by Beijing," *New York Times*, March 24, 2010, B1; "Google Takes on Beijing Censors," *South China Morning Post*, June 2, 2012, A6; and "Google's Dropped Anti-Censorship Warning Marks Quiet Defeat in China," *Guardian* (U.K.), January 7, 2013 (online).
84. Xinmei Shen, "Google Executive Says Company Is Committed to Hong Kong Amid Fear of Search Engine Pull-Out over Potential Protest Song Ban," *South China Morning Post* (June 15, 2023), https://www.scmp.com/tech/big-tech/article/3224224/google-executive-says-company-committed-hong-kong-amid-fear-search-engine-pull-out-over-potential.
85. Jeb Su, "Confirmed: Google Terminated Project Dragonfly, Its Censored Chinese Search Engine," *Forbes* (July 19, 2019), https://www.forbes.com/sites/jeanbaptiste/2019/07/19/confirmed-google-terminated-project-dragonfly-its-censored-chinese-search-engine/?sh=3b585e807e84.
86. Dara Kerr, "Twitter once Muzzled Russian and Chinese State Propaganda. That's over Now," NPR (April 21, 2023), https://www.npr.org/2023/04/21/1171193551/twitter-once-muzzled-russian-and-chinese-state-propaganda-thats-over-now.
87. Sui-Lee Wee, "Giving in to China, U.S. Airlines Drop Taiwan (in Name at Least)," *New York Times*, July 25, 2018, https://www.nytimes.com/2018/07/25/business/taiwan-american-airlines-china.html.
88. Simon Denyer, "Gap Apologizes to China over Map on T-shirt that Omits Taiwan, South China Sea," *Washington Post* (May 15, 2018).

89. Aris Angelis, Roman Polyakov, Olivier J. Wouters, Els Torreele, and Martin McKee, "High Drug Prices Are Not Justified by Industry's Spending on Research and Development," *BMJ* 380 (February 15, 2023), http://dx.doi.org/10.1136/bmj-2022-071710.

90. Richard G. Frank and Kathleen Hannick, "5 Things to Understand about Pharmaceutical R&D," Brookings Institute (June 2, 2022), https://www.brookings.edu/blog/usc-brookings-schaeffer-on-health-policy/2022/06/02/five-things-to-understand-about-pharmaceutical-rd/.

91. Rebecca Robbins and Sheryl Gay Stolberg, "How a Drugmaker Profited by Slow-Walking a Promising H.I.V. Therapy," *New York Times,* July 23, 2023, https://www.nytimes.com/2023/07/22/business/gilead-hiv-drug-tenofovir.html.

92. "Untapped opportunity: The Growing Potential of Clinical Trials in Georgia," Pharmaceutical Technology (June 30, 2022), https://www.pharmaceutical-technology.com/sponsored/untapped-opportunity-the-growing-potential-of-clinical-trials-in-georgia/.

93. For more on this case, see "Just How Far Does First Amendment Protection Go?," *Wall Street Journal*, January 10, 2003, B1; "Suit against Nike Raises Free Speech Questions," *San Jose Mercury News*, April 21, 2003, 1A; "Free Speech or False Advertising?," *Business Week*, April 28, 2003, 69; and Robert J. Samuelson, "The Tax on Free Speech," *Newsweek*, July 24, 2003, 41.

94. Daniel Bunn and Cecilia Perez Weigel, "Sources of U.S. Tax Revenue by Tax Type," Tax Foundation (February 27, 2023), https://taxfoundation.org/publications/sources-government-revenue-united-states/#:~:text=Corporate%20income%20taxes%20accounted,U.S.%20tax%20revenue%20in%202021.&text=Source%3A%20OECD%2C%20%E2%80%9CRevenue%20Statistics,OECD%20Countries%3A%20Comparative%20Tables.%E2%80%9D.

95. This case study draws on James Livingston, "If Companies Are People…," *New York Times*, April 15, 2013, A19; "Billions in Taxes Avoided by Apple, U.S. Inquiry Finds," *New York Times*, May 21, 2013, A1; Eduardo Porter, "The Trouble with Taxing Corporations," *New York Times*, May 29, 2013, B1; Graham Bowley, "The Corporate Tax Game," *New York Times*, May 3, 2013, B7; "G-20 Backs Plan to Curb Tax Avoidance," *New York Times*, July 19, 2013 (online); John Cassidy, "Just Because Tax Avoidance Is Legal Doesn't Mean It Is Right," *Fortune*, July 1, 2013, 42; Allan Sloan, "Why We Need Leaders with Some Sense of Shame," *Fortune*, November 18, 2013, 81; Floyd Norris, "Switching Names to Save on Taxes," *New York Times*, April 4, 2014, B1; Allan Sloan, "Positively Un-American," *Fortune*, July 21, 2014, 62–70; and Eduardo Porter, "Tax Tactics Threaten Public Funds," *New York Times*, October 2, 2014, B1.

96. Denny Jacob and Bob Tita, "Caterpillar Settles Tax Dispute with IRS, Will Pay No Penalties," *Wall Street Journal,* September 8, 2022, https://www.wsj.com/articles/caterpillar-settles-tax-dispute-with-irs-will-pay-no-penalties-11662680622.

Chapter 6

1. "Health Effects of Cigarette Smoking," Centers for Disease Control and Prevention (October 29, 2021), https://www.cdc.gov/tobacco/data_statistics/fact_sheets/health_effects/effects_cig_smoking/.

2. "Addressing the Issues in an Open and Objective Manner," https://rjrt.com/tobacco-use-health/.

3. K. Michael Cummings, Anthony Brown, and Richard O'Connor, "The Cigarette Controversy," *Cancer Epidemiology, Biomarkers & Prevention* 16 (2007), 1070–1076, https://doi.org/10.1158/1055-9965.EPI-06-0912.

4. "Philip Morris Readies Global Tobacco Blitz," *Wall Street Journal*, January 29, 2008, A1; "Philip Morris Unbound," *Business Week*, May 4, 2009, 39–42; "Tobacco Firms' Strategy Limits Poorer Nations' Smoking Laws," *New York Times*, December 13, 2013 (online). See also "Running Out of Puff," *Economist*, January 25, 2014, 53.

5. "'Vaping' Increases Odds of Asthma and COPD," Johns Hopkins Medicine (January 7, 2020), https://www.hopkinsmedicine.org/news/newsroom/news-releases/vaping-increases-odds-of-asthma-and-copd.

6. Molly Bohannon, "E-Cigarette Sales Skyrocket 50% during Pandemic—But FDA Restrictions Showed Some Success," *Forbes*, June 22, 2023, https://www.forbes.com/sites/mollybohannon/2023/06/22/e-cigarette-sales-skyrocket-50-during-pandemic-but-fda-restrictions-showed-some-success/?sh=7804bc083f9b.

7. "Teenage Shooting Opens a Window on Safety Agency," *Wall Street Journal*, April 29, 2004, https://www.wsj.com/articles/SB108319481417696735. For an interesting example, see "U.S. Probes Off-Road Vehicles after a String of Accidents," *Wall Street Journal*, November 4, 2008, A1.

8. Oliver Milman, "US Cosmetics Are Full of Chemicals Banned by Europe—Why?" (May 22, 2019), https://www.theguardian.com/us-news/2019/may/22/chemicals-in-cosmetics-us-restricted-eu. Note that this doesn't mean that all these chemicals can be found in American cosmetics.

9. Fiona Rutherford, "Why the US Has Fewer Sunscreen Options Than Europe" (June 23, 2022), https://www.bloomberg.com/news/newsletters/2022-06-23/why-the-us-has-fewer-sunscreen-options-than-europe.

10. Dylan Matthews, "The Tricky Business of Putting a Dollar Value on a Human Life," *Vox*, December 22, 2022, https://www.vox.com/future-perfect/23449849/social-cost-carbon-value-statistical-life-epa.

11. "Departmental Guidance on Valuation of a Statistical Life in Economic Analysis," U.S. Department of Transportation (March 23, 2021), https://www.transportation.gov/office-policy/transportation-policy/revised-departmental-guidance-on-valuation-of-a-statistical-life-in-economic-analysis.

12. "What Do You Recall?," *Economist*, April 5, 2014, 56; "An Increase in Vehicle Recalls Extends beyond Just General Motors," *New York Times*, May 30, 2014, B4; and Holman W. Jenkins, Jr., "Your Car Recalled? Buy a New One!," *Wall Street Journal*, July 5–6, 2014, A13.

13. Rachel Frazin, "House Votes to Restrict Feds from Banning or Regulating Gas Stoves" (June 13, 2023), https://thehill.com/homenews/house/4047484-house-votes-to-restrict-feds-from-banning-or-regulating-gas-stoves/.

14. "Tough New Standards for State's Raw Milk," *San Francisco Chronicle*, October 26, 2007, A1. See also "Raw Deal," *Economist*, June 12, 2010, 36.

15. John Stuart Mill, *On Liberty* (1859), https://www.gutenberg.org/files/34901/34901-h/34901-h.htm#Page_140.

16. W. Kip Viscusi, "The Lulling Effect: The Impact of Child-Resistant Packaging on Aspirin and Analgesic Ingestions," *American Economic Review* 74 (May 1984): 324–327.

17. See, for example, Christopher Garbacz, "Do Front-Seat Belt Laws Put Rear-Seat Passengers at Risk?" *Population Research and Policy Review* 11 (1992): 157–168, https://doi.org/10.1007/BF00125536.

18. Sarah Conly, "Coercive Paternalism in Health Care: Against Freedom of Choice," *Public Health Ethics* 6 (2013): 241–245, https://doi.org/10.1093/phe/pht025.

19. Helena Bottenmiller Evich, "The FDA's Food Failure," *Politico*, April 8, 2022, https://www.politico.com/interactives/2022/fda-fails-regulate-food-health-safety-hazards/. Many Red Flags Preceded a Recall," *New York Times*, October 23, 2007, C1; "Food Safety Officials to Review Procedures after Lapses in Recall of Tainted Beef," *New York Times*, October 5, 2007, A18; "Agency Orders Largest Recall of Ground Beef," *New York Times*, February 18, 2008, A1. See also "The Burger That Shattered Her Life," *New York Times*, October 4, 2009, 1.

20. "E.coli Outbreak with Unknown Food Source," Centers for Disease Control and Prevention (October 2, 2022), https://www.cdc.gov/ecoli/2022/o157h7-08-22/index.html.

21. While the FDA is challenging manufacturers who try market unapproved drugs on the grounds that they are old enough be grandparented in—which would require that they were in use in just the same form prior to 1938 Food, Drug, and Cosmetic Act—they may still be used by compounding pharmacies that create customized drug formulations for individual patients. Lloyd V. Allen, Jr., "Compounding and Unapproved Drugs," *Eureka*, June 24, 2013, https://www.criver.com/eureka/compounding-and-unapproved-drugs.

22. "Unapproved Drugs Linger on the Market," *Wall Street Journal*, March 20, 2003, A4. See also "What's Behind an F.D.A. Stamp?" *New York Times*, September 30, 2008, D3. Solvay stopped manufacturing Estratest in 2009, but generic versions are still available.

23. "Irene Lopez, "Are Harmful Chemicals Hiding in Your Cosmetics?," Radiance by WebMD (September 9, 2021), https://www.webmd.com/beauty/features/harmful-chemicals-in-your-cosmetics.

24. Jasmine Wang, Peter Jacobs, and Hannah Pugh, "Is Your Dietary Supplement Safe?" *The Regulatory Review* (February 27, 2021), https://www.theregreview.org/2021/02/27/saturday-seminar-is-dietary-supplement-safe/.

25. C. Michael White, "Natural Supplements Can Be Dangerously Contaminated, or Not Even Have the Specified Ingredients," *The Conversation*, February 14, 2020, https://theconversation.com/natural-supplements-can-be-dangerously-contaminated-or-not-even-have-the-specified-ingredients-131021.

26. "F.D.A. Admits Role of Politics in Safety Case," *New York Times*, September 25, 2009, A1.

27. "Teenage Shooting," A1.

28. "Behind Flu-Vaccine Shortage: Struggle to Police Drugs Globally," *Wall Street Journal*, November 5, 2004, A1; "U.S. Orders New China Toy Recall," *Wall Street Journal*, November 8, 2007, A3; "Salmonella Outbreak Exposes Food-Safety Flaws," *Wall Street Journal*, July 23, 2008, A2.

29. "Drug Safety: FDA's Future Inspection Plans Need to Address Issues Presented by COVID-19 Backlog," United States Government Accountability Office (March 4, 2021), https://www.gao.gov/assets/gao-21-409t.pdf.

30. "Dangerous Sealer Stayed on Shelves after Recall," *New York Times*, October 8, 2007 (online); "Tire Recalls Show Flaws in the System," *Wall Street Journal*, November 7, 2007, D1; "Safety Agency Faces Scrutiny amid Changes," *New York Times*, September 2, 2007 (online).

31. Michael E. Lemov, "A Failed Consumer Safety Law: Will Congress Fix It?," *The Hill*, February 27, 2022, https://thehill.com/blogs/congress-blog/politics/596009-a-failed-consumer-safety-law-will-congress-fix-it/.

32. "The Financial Page: Parsing Paulson," *New Yorker*, April 28, 2008, 26.

33. "Where's the Food Safety Net?" *Business Week*, June 23, 2008, 34.

34. "No Limit for Waits on Runways," *New York Times*, September 26, 2007, C1; "From Paradise to Perdition on the Tarmac," *Wall Street Journal*, April 28, 2009, D1.

35. "Toy Makers Seek Standards for U.S. Safety," *New York Times*, September 7, 2007, C1.

36. "In Turnaround, Industries Seek U.S. Regulation," *New York Times,* September 16, 2007 (online); "Retailers Face the Test of Testing," *Wall Street Journal*, November 26, 2007, A6.

37. Ambreen Ali, "Federal Regulations Are Finally Taking Aim at the 'Wild West' of Clean Beauty," *Fortune* (July 4, 2022), https://fortune.com/2022/07/04/federal-regulations-are-finally-taking-aim-at-the-wild-west-of-clean-beauty/.

38. Dan Oldenburg, "Chrysler's Reversal in Airbag Debate," *San Francisco Chronicle*, August 23, 1989, in "Business Briefing," 9.

39. Quoted by N. Craig Smith, "Arguments for and against Corporate Social Responsibility," in Fritz Allhoff and Anand Vaidya, eds., *Business Ethics, Vol. 1: Ethical Theory, Distributive Justice, and Corporate Social Responsibility* (London: Sage, 2005), 305.

40. "Gains Seen in Redesign of S.U.V.'s," *New York Times*, February 3, 2006, C1.

41. "Three More Automakers Fulfill Pledge to Make Autobrake Nearly Universal," Insurance Institute for Highway Safety /Highway Loss Data Institute (December 8, 2022), https://www.iihs.org/news/detail/three-more-automakers-fulfill-pledge-to-make-autobrake-nearly-universal.

42. "Dangerous Candies," *San Jose Mercury News*, June 13, 2002, 1A; "Pediatricians Urge Labels on Food That Can Choke," *New York Times*, May 25, 2010, D1.

43. "Witness Says Police-Vest Maker Ignored Safety Concerns," *Wall Street Journal*, November 15, 2004, C1.

44. "Gun Dealer Is Held Liable in Accident for Not Teaching Customer Safe Use," *Wall Street Journal*, June 6, 1989, B10.

45. "Gun Makers Saw No Role in Curbing Improper Sales," *New York Times*, May 28, 2013, A1. See also "New 'Personalized' Gun May Trigger Old Law," *Wall Street Journal*, November 21, 2013, A8.

46. Marisa Manley, "Products Liability: You're More Exposed Than You Think," *Harvard Business Review* 65 (September–October 1987): 28–29, and "High Court Eases Way to Liability Lawsuits," *Wall Street Journal*, March 5, 2009, A1.

47. John Topping, "2021 Report of Deaths and Injuries Involving Off-Highway Vehicles with More than Two Wheels," Consumer Product Safety Commission (November 2021), https://www.cpsc.gov/s3fs-public/2021-Report-of-Deaths-and-Injuries-Invoving-Off-Highway-Vehicles-with-more-than-Two-Wheels.pdf. Strictly speaking, these numbers include not only ATVs, which feature handlebars and saddle seats, but also similar vehicles with steering wheels and side-by-side seating.

48. Melvyn A. J. Menezes, "Ethical Issues in Product Policy," in N. Craig Smith and John A. Quelch, eds., *Ethics in Marketing* (Homewood, Ill.: Irwin, 1993), 286.

49. "Child Contracts Reye's Syndrome," *ACLU News* (San Francisco), July–August 1993, 1.

50. "Safety Agency, Mattel Clash over Disclosures," *Wall Street Journal*, September 4, 2007, A1.

51. "Expiration Dates Sought for Tires," *Wall Street Journal*, September 22, 2003, A8; and "Tires Get an Expiration Date," *Wall Street Journal*, May 31, 2005, D1.

52. Faiz Siddiqui and Jeremy B. Merrill, "17 Fatalities, 736 Crashes: The Shocking Toll of Tesla's Autopilot," *Washington Post* (June 10, 2023), https://www.washingtonpost.com/technology/2023/06/10/tesla-autopilot-crashes-elon-musk/.

53. Cade Metz, "How Safe Are Systems Like Tesla's Autopilot? No One Knows," *New York Times*, June 8, 2022, https://www.nytimes.com/2022/06/08/technology/tesla-autopilot-safety-data.html.

54. These Are Taken from Tad Tuleja, *Beyond the Bottom Line* (New York: Penguin, 1987), 77–78.

55. Smith and Quelch, *Ethics in Marketing*, 337–339.

56. "For First Time, Justices Reject Punitive Awards," *New York Times*, May 21, 1996, C1.

57. Jeffrey H. Birnbaum, "Pricing of Product Is Still an Art, Often Having Little Link to Costs," *Wall Street Journal*, November 25, 1981, sec. 2, 29.

58. "Investors, Look before You Leap into the Market," *Santa Cruz Sentinel*, April 25, 2010, D4.

59. Birnbaum, "Pricing of Product."

60. "Why the Price Is Rarely Right," *Bloomberg Businessweek*, February 1–8, 2010, 77.

61. "Pricing of Product." See also Matthew Miller, "Absolute Chaos," *Forbes*, December 13, 2004.

62. "The Discount Cards That Don't Save You Money," *Wall Street Journal*, January 21, 2003, D1.

63. "Markdown Lowdown," *Fortune*, January 12, 2004, 40.

64. "Black Friday: A Retail Illusion," *Wall Street Journal*, November 26, 2013, B1.

65. "The Great Rebate Runaround," *Business Week*, December 5, 2005, 34–37.

66. Sungsik Park, Man Xie, and Jinhong Xie, "Framing Price Increase as Discount: A New Manipulation of Reference Price," *Marketing Science* 42 (January–February 2023), 37–47, https://doi.org/10.1287/mksc.2022.1402.

67. "How a Drug Maker Tries to Outwit Generics," *Wall Street Journal*, November 8, 2008, B1.

68. "Companies Admit They Fixed Prices of Car Parts," *New York Times*, September 27, 2013, B1.

69. *San Francisco Chronicle*, October 1, 1997, A3.

70. "Supreme Court Lifts Ban on Minimum Retail Pricing," *New York Times*, June 29, 2007, C1.

71. "Discounters, Monitors Face Battle on Minimum Pricing," *Wall Street Journal*, December 4, 2008, A1. See also "State Law Targets 'Minimum Pricing,'" *Wall Street Journal*, April 28, 2009, D1; and "The Fight over Who Can Determine Prices at the Online Mall," *New York Times*, February 8, 2010, B1.

72. "Just One More Fix," *Economist*, March 29, 2014, 67.

73. See the debate between Jeremy Snyder and Matt Zwolinski in *Business Ethics Quarterly* 19, no. 2 (April 2009).

74. Matt Zwolinski, "The Ethics of Price Gouging," *Business Ethics Quarterly* 18 (July 2008): 347–378.

75. *San Francisco Chronicle*, May 9, 1997, A1.

76. "Why Do We Pay More?" *Business Week*, August 11, 2003, 26–27. See also Donald L. Barlett and James B. Steele, "Why We Pay So Much for Drugs," *Time*, February 2, 2004.

77. "U.S. Punishes Hyundai, Kia on Fuel Claims," *Wall Street Journal*, November 4, 2014, B1.

78. "What Is Organic?" *New York Times*, November 1, 2005, C1.

79. Melinda Beck, "The Fine Print: What's Really in a Lot of 'Healthy' Foods," *Wall Street Journal*, May 5, 2009, D1.

80. Scot Case, "Not Paint-by-Numbers," *CRO: Corporate Responsibility Officer* (November–December 2007): 52; TerraChoice Environmental Marketing, "The Six Sins of Greenwashing" (November 2007), www.terrachoice.com; and "'Greenwash' Hype Fails to Sway Consumers," *Financial Times*, May 1, 2009, 18.

81. "For Factories, Tougher to Say 'Made in USA,'" *Wall Street Journal*, October 1, 2014, B1.

82. "Let Them Eat Carbs," *Wall Street Journal*, July 26, 2004, B1.

83. "Steakhouse Confidential," *Wall Street Journal*, October 8–9, 2005, P4.

84. "Food Inflation Kept Hidden in Tinier Bags," *New York Times*, March 29, 2011, A1.

85. Michael J. McCarthy, "Taking the Value Out of Value-Sized," *Wall Street Journal*, August 14, 2002, D1. See also Omprakash K. Gupta and Anna S. Rominger, "Blind Man's Bluff: The Ethics of Quantity Surcharges," *Journal of Business Ethics* 15 (1996): 1299–1312.

86. Hooman Estelami, "Incidence and Magnitude of Quantity Surcharges and Quantity Discounts in Online Shopping," *Journal of Consumer Affairs* 2 (2018): 517–539, DOI: 10.1111/joca.12174.

87. Bradley Johnson, Kevin Brown, and Joy R. Lee, "The 25 Biggest US Advertisers, Ranked—Leading National Advertisers 2023," *Ad Age* (June 26, 2023), https://adage.com/article/datacenter/25-biggest-us-advertisers-include-amazon-comcast-and-pg/2497386.

88. Roger Draper, "The Faithless Shepherd," *New York Review of Books*, June 26, 1986, 17.

89. Paul Stevens, "Weasel Words: God's Little Helpers," in Paul A. Eschhol, Alfred A. Rosa, and Virginia P. Clark, eds., *Language Awareness* (New York: St. Martin's Press, 1974), 156.

90. "A Magazine Labels as News an Ad for Its Own Products," *New York Times*, January 17, 2014, B6.

91. Samm Sinclair Baker, *The Permissible Lie* (New York: World, 1968), 16.

92. Ivan L. Preston, *The Great American Blow-Up: Puffery in Advertising and Selling*, rev. ed. (Madison: University of Wisconsin Press, 1996), 181.

93. Ibid., 24.

94. Wilson Bryan Key, *Subliminal Seduction* (New York: New American Library, 1973), 11. See also Martin Lindstrom, *Buyology: Truth and Lies about Why We Buy* (New York: Doubleday, 2008), especially chap. 4, and "Retail Therapy," *Economist*, December 17, 2011, 111.

95. https://wineinstitute.org/our-work/responsibility/social/ad-code/#:~:text=Wine%20advertising%20is%20intended%20 for,persons%20below%20legal%20drinking%20age.

96. Preston, *Great American Blow-Up*, 113–123.

97. 302 U.S. 112 (1937).

98. Preston, *Great American Blow-Up*, 122–123.

99. Tim Walker, "Commercialism in Schools: No Windfall for Districts and Students Pay a Huge Price," *NEA News*, November 4, 2015, https://www.nea.org/advocating-for-change/new-from-nea/commercialism-schools-no-windfall-districts -and-students-pay-huge-price.

100. Joel Bakan, *The Corporation* (New York: Free Press, 2004), 119–120.

101. "Hey Kid, Buy This"; "This Is the Car We Want, Mommy," *Wall Street Journal*, November 6, 2007, D1.

102. Lisa J. Moore, "The Littlest Consumers," *San Francisco Chronicle*, January 13, 1991, in "This World," 8.

103. "Cookie Monster Crumbles," *Economist*, November 23, 2013, 61.

104. Wallace S. Snyder, "Ethics in Advertising: The Players, the Rules, the Scorecard," *Business and Professional Ethics Journal* 22 (Spring 2003): 41.

105. Bradley Johnson, "Forecasters Predict Ad Growth as Recession Looms—Leading National Advertisers 2023," *Ad Age* (June 26, 2023), https://adage.com/article/datacenter/forecasters-predict-ad-growth-recession-looms/2497381.

106. Kate O'Flaherty, "What Your Smart TV Knows about You—And How to Stop It Harvesting Data," *The Guardian*, January 29, 2022, https://www.theguardian.com/technology/2022/jan/29/what-your-smart-tv-knows-about-you-and-how-to-stop -it-harvesting-data#:~:text=Microphones%20and%20software%20are%20listening,is%20another%20issue%20to%20 consider; Tatum Hunter, "Ask Help Desk: No, Your Phone Isn't Listening to Your Conversations. Seriously," *Washington Post* (November 12, 2021), https://www.washingtonpost.com/technology/2021/11/12/phone-audio-targeting-privacy/.

107. Jinyan Zang, "Solving the Problem of Racially Discriminatory Advertising on Facebook," Brookings Institute (October 19, 2021), https://www.brookings.edu/articles/solving-the-problem-of-racially-discriminatory-advertising-on-facebook/.

108. Alyssa Newcomb, "Google Ad Delivery Can Show 'Racial Bias,' Says Harvard Study," *ABC News*, February 6, 2013, https:// abcnews.go.com/Technology/google-ad-delivery-shows-racial-bias-study-harvard/story?id=18419075.

109. Brian X. Chen, "The Battle for Digital Privacy Is Reshaping the Internet," *New York Times*, September 16, 2021, https://www.nytimes.com/2021/09/16/technology/digital-privacy.html.

110. Randall Rothenberg, "Executives Defending Their Craft," *New York Times*, May 22, 1989, C7. See also "Retail Therapy."

111. Theodore Levitt, "The Morality (?) of Advertising," *Harvard Business Review* 48 (July–August 1970): 84–92.

112. John Kenneth Galbraith, *The Affluent Society*, 3rd ed. (New York: Houghton Mifflin, 1976), 131.

113. John Kenneth Galbraith, *The New Industrial State* (New York: Signet, 1967), 219.

114. John Kenneth Galbraith, *The Economics of Innocent Fraud* (Boston: Houghton Mifflin, 2004), 12.

115. Marcia Angell, "Drug Companies and Doctors: A Story of Corruption," *New York Review of Books*, January 15, 2009, 10–12. See also "Ask Your Doctor If This Ad Is Right for You," *Business Week*, November 16, 2009, 78.

116. See Al Gini, "Work, Identity, and Self: How We Are Formed by the Work We Do," *Journal of Business Ethics* 17 (May 1998): 711.

117. Lucas Shaw, "Streaming Is Starting to Look a Lot Like Cable TV" (August 14, 2022), https://www.bloomberg.com/news /newsletters/2022-08-14/streaming-is-starting-to-look-a-lot-like-cable-tv.

118. This case study is based on the *Frontline* program "Breast Implants on Trial," aired on PBS, February 27, 1996. For background details, see Anne T. Lawrence, "Dow Corning and the Silicone Breast Implant Controversy," in John R. Boatright, ed., *Cases in Ethics and the Conduct of Business* (Englewood Cliffs, N.J.: Prentice Hall, 1995).

119. Roni Caryn Rabin, "Patients Must Be Warned of Breast Implant Risks, F.D.A. Says," *New York Times*, October 27, 2021, https://www.nytimes.com/2021/10/27/health/breast-implants-cancer-fda.html; "Breast Implants May Be Linked to Additional Cancers, F.D.A. Warns," *New York Times*, September 28, 2022, https://www.nytimes.com/2022/09/08/health /breast-implants-cancer.html.

120. For more on this case, see the video "Retro Report: Scalded by Coffee, then News Media" (October 21, 2013), www .nytimes.com.

121. This case study is based on "Doctors Point to Caffeinated Alcoholic Drinks' Dangers" and "A Mix Attractive to Students and Partygoers," *New York Times*, October 27, 2010, A12; "Second State Bans Caffeinated Alcoholic Drinks," *New York Times*, November 11, 2010, A23; and "Beer with Kick Is Caught in F.D.A.'s Net," *New York Times*, November 29, 2010, A17.

Chapter 7

1. Peter Coy, "The Coast Is Not Clear," *Bloomberg Businessweek*, August 16–29, 2010, 50; Lisa Friedman, "Ten Years after Deepwater Horizon, U.S. Is Still Vulnerable to Catastrophic Spills," *New York Times*, April 19, 2020, https://www.nytimes .com/2020/04/19/climate/deepwater-horizon-anniversary.html.

2. Austyn Gaffney, "Hundreds of Workers Who Cleaned Up the Country's Worst Coal Ash Spill Are Now Sick and Dying," National Resource Defence Council (December 17, 2018), https://www.nrdc.org/stories/hundreds-workers-who-cleaned -countrys-worst-coal-ash-spill-are-now-sick-and-dying.

3. Austyn Gaffney, "As Enforcement Lags, Toxic Coal Ash Keeps Polluting U.S. Water," *Yale Environment 360*, March 23, 2023, https://e360.yale.edu/features/coal-ash-united-states-epa-rule.

4. Dave Jones, "2021 Global Electricity Review," Ember (March 2021), https://ember-climate.org/insights/research /global-electricity-review-2021/#supporting-material.

5. Convention on Wetlands, "Global Wetland Outlook: Special Edition 2021 (Gland, Switzerland: Secretariat of the Convention on Wetlands, 2021), https://www.ramsar.org/resources/publications/global-wetland-outlook.

6. See the *Millennium Ecosystem Assessment Synthesis Report* (March 2005), https://www.millenniumassessment.org/en /Synthesis.aspx; and *Global Environment Outlook* 5 (2012), published by the United Nations Environment Program and available at https://www.unep.org/geo/geo-resources/geo-5.

7. Imogen E. Napper, Alasdair J. Davies, Moriba Jah, Kimberley R. Miner, Richard C. Thompson, Melissa Quinn, and Heather J. Koldewey, "Protect Earth's Orbit: Avoid High Seas Mistakes," *Science* 379 (March 10, 2023): 990–991.

8. Intergovernmental Panel on Climate Change, "Climate Change 2023 Synthesis Report: Summary for Policymakers" (2023), https://www.ipcc.ch/report/sixth-assessment-report-cycle/.

9. Jedidajah Otte, "Florida Rocked by Home Insurance Crisis: 'I May Have to Sell Up and Move'," *Guardian*, July 15, 2023, https://www.theguardian.com/us-news/2023/jul/15/florida-hurricane-insurance-crisis-climate.

10. Tom Regan, ed., *Earthbound: Introductory Essays in Environmental Ethics* (New York: Random House, 1984), 3.

11. Pesticide Action Network, "Pesticides and Climate Change: A Vicious Cycle" (Winter 2022–2023), https://www.panna.org/resources/pesticides-and-climate-change-a-vicious-cycle/.

12. For details, consult "Toxic America," *San Francisco Chronicle*, March 28, 2004, E1; George F. Canor, *Legally Poisoned: How the Law Puts Us at Risk from Toxicants* (Cambridge, Mass.: Harvard University Press, 2011); and "The Chemicals That Stick Around in Your System," *Wall Street Journal*, March 4, 2014, D1.

13. Kelly L. Smalling et al., "Per- and Polyfluoroalkyl Substances (PFAS) in United States Tapwater: Comparison of Underserved Private-Well and Public-Supply Exposures and Associated Health Implications," *Environment International* 178 (August 2023), https://doi.org/10.1016/j.envint.2023.108033.

14. Jesse A. Goodrich et al., "Metabolic Signatures of Youth Exposure to Mixtures of Per- and Polyfluoroalkyl Substances: A Multi-cohort Study," *Environmental Health Perspectives* 131 (February 2023), https://doi.org/10.1289/EHP11372.

15. "Rulings Restrict Clean Water Act, Hampering E.P.A.," *New York Times*, March 1, 2010, A1; Nina Totenberg, "The Supreme Court Has Narrowed the Scope of the Clean Water Act," *All Things Considered*, May 25, 2023, https://www.npr.org/2023/05/25/1178150234/supreme-court-epa-clean-water-act.

16. Emily Holden, Caty Enders, Niko Kommenda and Vivian Ho, "More than 25m Drink from the Worst US Water Systems, with Latinos Most Exposed," *Guardian*, February 26, 2021, https://www.theguardian.com/us-news/2021/feb/26/worst-us-water-systems-latinos-most-exposed.

17. National Resource Defense Council, "Flint Water Crisis: Everything You Need to Know" (November 8, 2018), https://www.nrdc.orgstories/flint-water-crisis-everything-you-need-know#summary.

18. Kathleen Gray and Julie Bosman, "Nine Michigan Leaders Face Charges in Water Crisis That Roiled Flint" (January 14, 2021), https://www.nytimes.com/2021/01/14/us/rick-snyder-flint-water-charges.html.

19. Environmental Protection Agency, *2021 Toxic Release Inventory (TRI) National Analysis* (March 2023), https://www.epa.gov/trinationalanalysis.

20. American Lung Association, "State of the Air 2023," https://www.lung.org/research/sota.

21. Jenny Gross, "Road Salt Works. But It's Also Bad for the Environment," *New York Times* (January 7, 2022), https://www.nytimes.com/2022/01/07/climate/road-salt-water-supply.html.

22. Jenny Splitter, "America Has a Manure Problem, and the Miracle Solution Being Touted Isn't All That It Seems," *Guardian*, January 20, 2022, https://www.theguardian.com/us-news/2022/jan/20/manure-natural-gas-pipeline-factory-farms-greenwashing.

23. Allison Macfarlane and Rodney C. Ewing, "Nuclear Waste Is Piling Up. Does the U.S. Have a Plan?" *Scientific American*, March 6, 2023, https://www.scientificamerican.com/article/nuclear-waste-is-piling-up-does-the-u-s-have-a-plan/#:~:text=About%2088%2C000%20metric%20tons%20of,de%20facto%20permanent%20disposal%20facilities.

24. "Nuclear Waste Piles Up—in Budget Deficit," *New York Times*, August 9, 2011, A3.

25. Ivan Penn and Eric Lipton, "The Lithium Gold Rush: Inside the Race to Power Electric Vehicles," *New York Times*, May 6, 2021, https://www.nytimes.com/2021/05/06/business/lithium-mining-race.html.

26. National Resource Defense Council, "Exhausted: How We Can Stop Lithium Mining from Depleting Water Resources, Draining Wetlands, and Harming Communities in South America" (2022), https://www.nrdc.org/resources/exhausted-how-we-can-stop-lithium-mining-depleting-water-resources-draining-wetlands-and.

27. This paragraph is based on "Hunting Habits of Yellowstone Wolves Change Ecological Balance in Park," *New York Times*, October 18, 2005, D3. See also "Gray Wolves Rebound, to Neighbors' Unease," *Wall Street Journal*, May 29–30, 2010, A3. For a discussion of the effect of global warming on the ecology of Yellowstone, see "In a Warmer Yellowstone Park, a Shifting Environmental Balance," *New York Times*, March 18, 2008, D3. For another example of complicated ecological interactions, see "For Polar Bears, a Climate Change Twist," *New York Times*, September 22, 2014 (online).

28. "Trading System Tackles Waste," *Wall Street Journal*, February 20, 2014, A3.

29. See "Reefer Madness," *Economist*, June 14, 2014, 29.

30. "*Playboy* Interview: Dr. Paul Ehrlich," *Playboy* (August 1970): 56.

31. John Steinbeck, *America and Americans* (New York: Viking Press, 1966), 127.

32. Garrett Hardin, "The Tragedy of the Commons," *Science* 162 (December 13, 1968): 1243–1248.

33. "How to Stop Fisherman Fishing," *Economist*, February 25, 2012, 14; and "Lost Property," *Economist*, February 25, 2012, 57–58. See also "Troubled Waters: A Special Report on the Sea," *Economist*, January 3, 2009, 10–13.

34. J. David Goodman, "In Texas Oil Country, an Unfamiliar Threat: Earthquakes," *New York Times*, January 28, 2023, https://www.nytimes.com/2023/01/28/us/texas-earthquakes-fracking.html; Curtis Kilman, "3 Energy Firms Settle Earthquake-Damage Lawsuits Stemming from Pawnee Temblors," *Tulsa World*, December 28, 2022, https://tulsaworld.com/news/state-and-regional/crime-and-courts/3-energy-firms-settle-earthquake-damage-lawsuits-stemming-from-pawnee-temblors/article_bb0e5208-86ca-11ed-95f3-eb6c898b7c67.html.

35. Quoted in Joseph R. DesJardins, *An Introduction to Business Ethics*, 4th ed. (New York: McGraw-Hill, 2011), 237.

36. William T. Blackstone, "Ethics and Ecology," in William T. Blackstone, ed., *Philosophy and Environmental Crisis* (Athens: University of Georgia Press, 1974).

37. Sharon Begley, "Furry Math? Market Has Failed to Capture the True Value of Nature," *Wall Street Journal*, August 9, 2002, B1. See also "Are You Being Served?" *Economist*, April 23, 2005, 76–78; and Matt Jenkins, "Mother Nature's Sum," *Miller-McCune*, October 2008, 44–53. For a critical assessment of ecological economics, see Mark Sagoff, "Locke Was Right: Nature Has Little Economic Value," *Philosophy and Public Policy Quarterly* 25, no. 3 (Summer 2005): 2–11.

38. Begley, "Furry Math?" B1.

39. "Would You Pay More to Let Nature Thrive?" *San Jose Mercury News*, October 4, 1994, 1A. For the doubts of an economist, see Amartya Sen, "The Discipline of Cost-Benefit Analysis," *Journal of Legal Studies* 29 (June 2000): 946–950.

40. On windmills, see "Debate over Wind Power Creates Environmental Rift," *New York Times*, June 6, 2006, A14; "Not on My Beach, Please," *Economist*, August 21, 2010, 47; and "Wind Farms in Maine Stir a Power Struggle," *Wall Street Journal*, December 24, 2013, A3. On solar power, see "Environmentalists in a Clash of Goals," *New York Times*, March 24, 2009, A17.

41. "In Vermont, a Mine Pits 2 Green Goals against Each Other," *Wall Street Journal*, October 7, 2003, A1.

42. "A Real Energy Boom," *Sierra*, March–April 2006, 13.

43. "Paper or Plastic? A Lawyer's Answer Sends Him from Hero to Pariah," *Wall Street Journal*, March 28, 2011, A1.

44. Ministry of Environment and Food of Denmark, "Life Cycle Assessment of Grocery Carrier Bags" (February 2018), https://www2.mst.dk/udgiv/publications/2018/02/978-87-93614-73-4.pdf.

45. "Clean-Air Rules Worth It, Says White House Study," *San Jose Mercury News*, September 27, 2003, 7A. But on the value of introducing tighter ozone restrictions, see "EPA again Delays Tighter Ozone Restrictions," *Wall Street Journal*, December 9, 2010, A4.

46. "Cleaner Air Has Boosted Life Spans," *Wall Street Journal*, January 22, 2009, A14.

47. As quoted in Joanna B. Ciulla, Clancy Martin, and Robert C. Solomon, eds., *Honest Work: A Business Ethics Reader* (New York: Oxford University Press, 2007), 483.

48. "Why China Could Blame Its CO$_2$ on West," *Wall Street Journal*, November 12, 2007, A3. See also "Chinese Polluters Point to Western Demand," *Business Week*, April 6, 2009, 76, and "China Is also an Exporter of Pollution to the Western U.S., Study Finds," *New York Times*, January 21, 2014.

49. United States Environmental Protection Agency, "National Overview: Facts and Figures on Materials, Wastes and Recycling" (December 3, 2022), https://www.epa.gov/facts-and-figures-about-materials-waste-and-recycling/national-overview-facts-and-figures-materials#Trends1960-Today.

50. Lyle Daly, "How Many Cars Are in the U.S.? Car Ownership Statistics 2022," *Motley Fool's Ascent*, July 21, 2022, https://www.fool.com/the-ascent/research/car-ownership-statistics/.

51. "Would You Pay More?" 1A.

52. Lagipoiva Cherelle Jackson, "Amid Rising Seas, Island Nations Push for Legal Protection," *PBS Newshour*, September 30, 2022, https://www.pbs.org/newshour/world/amid-rising-seas-island-nations-push-for-legal-protection.

53. For example, Matthew Taylor and Jonathan Watts, "Revealed: The 20 Firms behind a Third of All Carbon Emissions," *Guardian* (October 9, 2019), https://www.theguardian.com/environment/2019/oct/09/revealed-20-firms-third-carbon-emissions.

54. "Grime and Punishment," *New Republic*, February 20, 1989, 7.

55. Ibid.

56. Ibid., 8.

57. "Environmental Enemy No. 1," *Economist*, July 6, 2002, 11. See also "Dirty Secret: Coal Plants Could Be Much Cleaner," *New York Times*, May 22, 2005, sec. 3, 1; and "Cap and Fade," *New York Times*, December 7, 2009, A27.

58. "Political Pressure Keeps Cash Flowing into Ethanol's Tanks," *Financial Times*, October 12, 2008, 6; Elizabeth Chiles Shelburne, "The Great Disruption," *Atlantic Monthly*, September 2008, 28–29. See also "Ethanol Tanks," *Economist*, October 24, 2009, 72.

59. "How Many Planets? A Survey of the Global Environment," *Economist*, July 6, 2002, 16.

60. "Efforts to Curtail Emissions Gain," *Wall Street Journal*, September 22, 2008, A13.

61. Paul Krugman, "The Mercury Scandal," *New York Times*, April 6, 2004 (online). See also "On the Air," *New Yorker*, May 3, 2004, 33; and "Mapping Mercury," *Scientific American*, September 2005, 20–21.

62. Michael J. Sandel, "It's Immoral to Buy the Right to Pollute," *New York Times*, December 15, 1997, A19.

63. Michael E. Porter and Claas van der Linde, "Green and Competitive: Ending the Stalemate," *Harvard Business Review* 73 (September–October 1995): 125–126, 128–129.

64. Isabel Contreras an Christopher Helman, "Green Growth 50: Learning from Companies Boosting Profits While Cutting Emissions," *Forbes* (November 16, 2021), https://www.forbes.com/sites/isabelcontreras/2021/11/16/growing-green-50-companies-that-raised-profits-while-cutting-emissions/?sh=78599228e125.

65. "Yes, Global Warming," *International Herald Tribune*, February 2, 1997, 8.

66. Laura Corb, Kimberly Henderson, Amy Wagner, and Selena Wang-Thomas, "Climate Tech Competitiveness: Can the United States Raise Its Game?" McKinsey & Company (October 2022), https://www.mckinsey.com/industries/public-sector/our-insights/climate-tech-competitiveness-can-the-united-states-raise-its-game#/.

67. University of Michigan Center for Sustainable Systems, "U.S. Energy System" (September 2022), https://css.umich.edu/publications/factsheets/energy/us-energy-system-factsheet; Robert Rapier, "The World's Top 10 Oil Producers and Consumers," *Forbes*, June 26, 2020, https://www.forbes.com/sites/rrapier/2020/06/26/the-worlds-top-10-oil-producers-and-oil-consumers/?sh=77207c822303.

68. Emma Newburger, "China's Greenhouse Gas Emissions Exceed Those of U.S. and Developed Countries Combined, Report Says," CNBC (May 6, 2021), https://www.cnbc.com/2021/05/06/chinas-greenhouse-gas-emissions-exceed-us-developed-world-report.html.

69. Brook Larmer, "E-Waste Offers an Economic Opportunity as Well as Toxicity," *New York Times Magazine*, July 5, 2018, https://www.nytimes.com/2018/07/05/magazine/e-waste-offers-an-economic-opportunity-as-well-as-toxicity.html.

70. "Seeing the Wood: A Special Report on Forests," *Economist*, September 25, 2010, 4. See also "Fiddling While the Amazon Burns," *Economist*, December 3, 2011, 49, and "Special Report: Biodiversity," *Economist*, September, 14, 2013, 13–15.

71. "Consumer Link to Rainforest Destruction," *Financial Times*, June 1, 2009, 3; Terrence McCoy and Júlia Ledur, "Devouring the Rainforest," *Washington Post*, April 29, 2022, https://www.washingtonpost.com/world/interactive/2022/amazon-beef-deforestation-brazil/.

72. Mathis Wackernagel et al., "Tracking the Ecological Overshoot of the Human Economy," *Proceedings of the National Academy of Sciences* 99 (June 27, 2002): 9266. See also "UN Warns of Rapid Decay of Environment," *New York Times*, October 26, 2007, A8; and "Study Warns of Gloomy Future for Resources," *Financial Times*, October 26, 2007, 3.

73. Joel Feinberg, "The Rights of Animals and Unborn Generations," in Tom L. Beauchamp and Norman E. Bowie, eds., *Ethical Theory and Business*, 2nd ed. (Englewood Cliffs, N.J.: Prentice Hall, 1983), 435.

74. Derek Parfit, *Reasons and Persons* (New York: Oxford University Press, 1986), 361.

75. Ibid., 365.

76. Annette Baier, "The Rights of Past and Future Persons," in Joseph R. DesJardins and John J. McCall, eds., *Contemporary Issues in Business Ethics* (Belmont, Calif.: Wadsworth, 1985), 501.

77. See John Rawls, *A Theory of Justice*, rev. ed. (Cambridge, Mass.: Harvard University Press, 1999), 251–258.

78. William F. Baxter, *People or Penguins: The Case for Optimal Pollution* (New York: Columbia University Press, 1974), ch. 1.

79. Holmes Rolston III, "Just Environmental Business," in Tom Regan, ed., *Just Business: New Introductory Essays in Business Ethics* (New York: Random House, 1984), 325.

80. Patrick Greenfield, "Plans to Mine Ecuador Forest Violate Rights of Nature, Court Rules," *Guardian* December 2, 2021, https://www.theguardian.com/environment/2021/dec/02/plan-to-mine-in-ecuador-forest-violate-rights-of-nature-court-rules-aoe#:~:text=In%20a%20landmark%20ruling%2C%20the,the%20brown%2Dheaded%20spider%20monkey%2C.

81. Steven M. Meyer, "End of the Wild," *Boston Review* (April–May 2004): 20. See also "Watching the Numbers and Charting the Losses—of Species," *New York Times*, October 15, 2008, A30; and "A Conversation with Stuart L. Pimm," *New York Times*, November 4, 2008, D2.

82. "Special Report: Biodiversity," 6.

83. Camilo Mora, et al., "How Many Species Are There on Earth and in the Ocean?," *PLoS Biology* 9 (August 2011), https://doi:10.1371/journal.pbio.1001127; Brendan B. Larsen, et al., "Inordinate Fondness Multiplied and Redistributed: The Number of Species on Earth and the New Pie of Life," *Quarterly Review of Biology* 92 (September 2017), https://doi.org/10.1086/693564.

84. Jeremy Bentham, *An Introduction to the Principles of Morals and Legislation* (1789), ch. 17, sec. 2.

85. Peter Singer, *Practical Ethics*, 2nd ed. (Cambridge: Cambridge University Press, 1993), 65–66.

86. Quoted by Rolston, "Just Environmental Business," 340.

87. United States Department of Agriculture, "Livestock Slaughter: 2021 Summary" (April 2022), https://usda.library.cornell.edu/concern/publications/r207tp32d.

88. Kelsey Piper, "How Chickens Took over America's Dinner Plates, in One Chart," *Vox*, February 19, 2021), https://www.vox.com/future-perfect/22287530/chicken-beef-factory-farming-plant-based-meats.

89. Sophie Kevany, "More than 20 Million Farm Animals Die on Way to Abattoir in US Every Year," *Guardian*, June 15, 2022, https://www.theguardian.com/environment/2022/jun/15/more-than-20-million-farm-animals-die-on-way-to-abattoir-in-us-every-year.

90. American Society for the Prevention of Cruelty to Animals, "How Factory Farming Hurts Animals" (n.d.), https://www.aspca.org/protecting-farm-animals/animals-factory-farms#Chickens.

91. American Society for the Prevention of Cruelty to Animals, "How Factory Farming Hurts Animals" (n.d.), https://www.aspca.org/protecting-farm-animals/animals-factory-farms#Pigs.

92. United States Department of Agriculture, "Ag and Food Sectors and the Economy" (January 26, 2023), https://www.ers.usda.gov/data-products/ag-and-food-statistics-charting-the-essentials/ag-and-food-sectors-and-the-economy/.

93. Singer, *Practical Ethics*, 274–75.

94. Danielle J. Ufer, "Farm Animal Welfare Policies Cover Breeding Sows, Veal Calves, or Laying Hens in 14 U.S. States," United States Department of Agriculture Economic Research Service (April 24, 2023), https://www.ers.usda.gov/amber-waves/2023/april/farm-animal-welfare-policies-cover-breeding-sows-veal-calves-or-laying-hens-in-14-u-s-states/.

95. Hellman's "We Care about Sustainability" (n.d.), https://www.hellmanns.com/us/en/we-care-about-sustainably-sourced-ingredients.html.

96. Whole Foods, "Our Standard for Eggs: Beyond Cage-Free" (n.d.), https://www.wholefoodsmarket.com/quality-standards/egg-standards.

97. Kenny Torrella, "The Corporate Raider Taking Aim at McDonald's over the Treatment of Pigs," *Vox*, March 3, 2022, https://www.vox.com/future-perfect/22958698/mcdonalds-icahn-pork-pigs-gestation-crates-animal-welfare.

98. Much of the factual information in this case study comes from the Congressional Research Service, "Options for Making the National Flood Insurance Program More Affordable" (December 23, 2021), https://crsreports.congress.gov/product/pdf/R/R47000/2.

99. Christopher Flavelle, "Hurricane Ian's Toll Is Severe. Lack of Insurance Will Make It Worse," *New York Times*, September 29, 2022, https://www.nytimes.com/2022/09/29/climate/hurricane-ian-flood-insurance.html.

100. Alexander B. Lemann, "Raising Flood Insurance Premiums Sounds Fair. It Isn't," *Slate*, October 1, 2021, https://slate.com/news-and-politics/2021/10/flood-insurance-premium-fema-risk-rating.html.

101. Debbie Elliott, "10 States and Scores of Local Governments sue FEMA over Higher Flood Insurance Rates," National Public Radio (June 1, 2023), https://www.npr.org/2023/06/01/1179573166/fema-lawsuit-flood-insurance-rate-hikes.

102. See Noel Grove, "Air: An Atmosphere of Uncertainty," *National Geographic* 171, no. 4 (April 1987): 502–537.

103. Ibid.

104. The following paragraphs are based on "Let Them Eat Pollution," *Economist*, February 8, 1992, 66; "Pollution and the Poor," *Economist*, February 15, 1992, 18; "Economics Brief: A Greener Bank," *Economist*, May 23, 1992, 79; and "A Great Leap Forward," *Economist*, May 11, 2002. See also "How Green Is Their Growth," *Economist*, January 28, 2008, 57.

105. "U.N. Warns of Climate-Related Setbacks," *New York Times*, November 28, 2007, A6. See also "Where Climate Change Hurts Most," *U.S. News & World Report*, April 2009, 52–53; "A Bad Climate for Development," *Economist*, September 19, 2009, 69; and "Shoots, Greens, and Leaves," *Economist*, June 10, 2012, 58–60.

106. David R. Wheeler, *Greening Industry* (New York: Oxford University Press, 1999), ch. 5.

107. The primary source for this case study is Elliot Diringer, "Cutting a Deal on Redwoods," *San Francisco Chronicle*, September 4, 1996, A1. See also "Timber!" *Fortune*, December 12, 2005, 102–106. The final section is based on news stories in *San Francisco Chronicle*, March 3, 1999, A1; *New York Times*, March 3, 1999, A1, and March 6, 1999, A7; *Economist*, March 6, 1999, 30; *San Jose Mercury News*, December 8, 2001, 21A; *Wall Street Journal*, June 6, 2008; and *San Francisco Chronicle*, June 7, 2008; Josh Harrison, "Out of the Woods," *Mother Jones*, November–December 2008, 62–64, 99; and "Hedge-Fund Firm Goes to Town in California," *Wall Street Journal*, December 28–29, 2013, B1.

108. This case study is based on "Briefing: The Campaign against Palm Oil," *Economist*, June 26, 2010, 71–73; see also "Nestlé Learns to See the Wood for the Trees," *Financial Times*, June 1, 2010, 11; "A Rebel without a Cause Sells Out to Palm Oil," *South China Morning Post* (Hong Kong), December 11, 2011, 10; E. Benjamin Skinner, "Asia's Better Harvest: The Hidden Human Toll of the Palm Oil Boom," *Bloomberg Businessweek*, July 22–28, 2013, 63–65; and the website of the Roundtable for Sustainable Palm Oil (www.rspo.org).

Chapter 8

1. "In Factory Sit-In, an Anger Spread Wide," *New York Times*, December 7, 2009 (online).

2. Mike Cassidy, "Serious Materials' Purchase of Chicago Window Factory a Bright Spot in Dismal Economy," *MercuryNews.com*, February 27, 2009 (online); "New Owners Will Reopen Plant in Sit-In," *New York Times*, February 27, 2009, A15.

3. New Era Windows, "Our Story," n.d., https://newerawindows.com/Content/our-story_Z03ejZ.html.

4. American Association of University Professors, "The Annual Report on the Economic Status of the Profession, 2022–23" (June 2023), https://www.aaup.org/report/annual-report-economic-status-profession-2022-23.

5. Jason Brennan and Phillip Magness, "Are Adjunct Faculty Exploited: Some Grounds for Skepticism," *Journal of Business Ethics* 152 (2018): 53–71, https://doi.org/10.1007/s10551-016-3322-4.

6. Scott Hill and Justin Klocksiem, "Adjuncts Are Exploited," *Philosophia* 50 (2022): 1153–73, https://doi.org/10.1007/s11406-021-00425-4.

7. Bruce Barry, "The Cringing and the Craven: Freedom of Expression in, Around, and Beyond the Workplace," *Business Ethics Quarterly* 17, no. 1 (April 2007): 263; "Man Fired for Wearing Packers Tie Back at Work—for Rival Car Dealer," *Chicago Sun-Times*, January 26, 2011 (online); Timothy Noah, "Can Your Boss Fire You for Your Political Beliefs?," *Slate*, July 1, 2002, https://slate.com/news-and-politics/2002/07/can-your-boss-fire-you-for-your-political-beliefs.html; David W. Ewing, "Civil Liberties in the Corporation," in Tom L. Beauchamp and Norman E. Bowie, eds., *Ethical Theory and Business*, 2nd ed. (Englewood Cliffs, N.J.: Prentice Hall, 1983), 141.

8. Hope Keller, "Can Employees Be Fired over Online Posts? Attorneys Say Yes," *The Daily Record,* February 22, 2023, https://thedailyrecord.com/2023/02/22/little-protection-for-employees-against-being-fired-over-online-posts-attorneys-say/.

9. Business News Daily, "You Won't Believe How Many Bosses Fire Workers Because of Social Media" (April 26, 2023), https://www.businessnewsdaily.com/fired-for-social-media.

10. Ewing, "Civil Liberties," 139–140.

11. *Coppage v. State of Kansas*, 236 U.S. 1 (1915), 1.

12. Kate Andrias and Alexander Hertel-Fernandez, "Ending at Will Employment: A Guide for Just Cause Reform," Roosevelt Institute (January 2021), https://www.niskanencenter.org/forgotten-origins-montanas-just-cause-employment-law/.

13. Stephen Wermiel, "High Court Backs Refusal to Work on Sabbath Day," *Wall Street Journal*, March 30, 1989, B8, and "Faith in the Workplace," *Economist*, April 12, 2014, 66.

14. Abbie VanSickle and Adam Liptak, "Supreme Court Sides with Postal Carrier Who Refused to Work on Sabbath," *New York Times* June 29, 2023, https://www.nytimes.com/2023/06/29/us/politics/supreme-court-religion-sabbath-postal-worker.html.

15. Charles J. Muhl, "The Employment-at-Will Doctrine: Three Major Exceptions," *Monthly Labor Review* 4 (January 2001): 3–11.

16. "Some Whistle-Blowers Lose Free Speech Protections," *New York Times*, May 31, 2006, A14.

17. Ewing, "Civil Liberties," 148.

18. Rasmus Hougaard, Jacqueline Carter, and Kathleen Hogan, "How Microsoft Builds a Sense of Community among 144,000 Employees," *Harvard Business Review* (August 28, 2019), https://hbr.org/2019/08/how-microsoft-builds-a-sense-of-community-among-144000-employees.

19. Alexander J. S. Colvin, "Participation versus Procedures in Non-Union Dispute Resolution," *Industrial Relations* 52 (January 2013), 259–283, https://doi.org/10.1111/irel.12003.

20. Bruce Barry, *Speechless: The Erosion of Free Speech in the American Workplace* (San Francisco: Berrett-Koehler, 2007), 194–195. See also Matthias Seifert, Joel Brockner, Emily C. Bianchi, and Henry Moon "How Workplace Fairness Affects Employee Commitment," *MIT Sloan Management Review* 57 (Winter 2016): 15–17.

21. Richard W. Stevenson, "Do People and Profits Go Hand in Hand?" *New York Times*, May 9, 1996, C1.

22. "The Work Place 100," *USA Weekend*, January 22–24, 1993, 4.

23. See "Trust in Me," *Economist*, December 16, 1995, 61; Sue Shellenbarger, "Workers Leave If Firms Don't Stick to Values," *San Francisco Sunday Examiner and Chronicle*, June 27, 1999, CL31; and Archie B. Carroll, *Business Ethics: Brief Readings on Vital Topics* (New York: Routledge, 2009), 182–183.

24. See Marian M. Extejt and William N. Bockanic, "Issues Surrounding the Theories of Negligent Hiring and Failure to Fire," *Business and Professional Ethics Journal* 8 (Winter 1989).

25. Margaret M. Clark, "How to Address Negligent Hiring Concerns," *HR Magazine,* Spring 2019, https://www.shrm.org/hr-today/news/hr-magazine/spring2019/pages/how-to-address-negligent-hiring-concerns.aspx.

26. "How a Black Mark Can Derail a Job Search," *Wall Street Journal*, February 2, 2010, D4.

27. "Lifting the Curtain on the Hiring Process," *Wall Street Journal*, January 26, 2010, D5.

28. "Short Hours, Big Pay and Other Little Lies," *Wall Street Journal*, October 22, 2003, B1.

29. "The Big Squeeze on Workers," *Business Week*, May 13, 2002, 96–97; "Victims of Misclassification," *New York Times*, December 15, 2013 (online).

30. Associated Press, "Hooters Settles Suit by Men Denied Jobs," *New York Times,* October 1, 1997, https://www.nytimes.com/1997/10/01/us/hooters-settles-suit-by-men-denied-jobs.html.

31. "High Court Issues Narrow Ruling on ADA's Scope," *Wall Street Journal*, December 3, 2003, A3.

32. Eric Matusewitch, "Language Rules Can Violate Title VII," *Personnel Journal* 69 (October 1990): 100. See also "Firms Can Insist on English," *San Jose Mercury News*, July 17, 1993, 9D; and "English Required Near Slots," *Reno Gazette-Journal*, August 11, 2008 (online).

33. "Why Weight-Discrimination Cases Pose Thorny Legal Tests," *Wall Street Journal*, October 2, 2007, B4.

34. "Instructor Wins Weight-Bias Case," *San Jose Mercury News*, May 7, 2002, 1B.

35. "If You Light Up on Sunday, Don't Come in on Monday," *Business Week*, August 26, 1991, 68–70; "Fight over Hiring Bans Reaches Law Makers," *San Jose Mercury News*, April 28, 1994, 1E; "One Whiff of Smoke and You're Out," *San Francisco Chronicle*, January 25, 1997, D2; and "At Risk from Smoking: Your Job," *Business Week*, April 15, 2002, 12.

36. "Smoke? Then You Can't Be a Deputy," *San Francisco Chronicle*, March 5, 2004, A1; "Companies Get Tough with Smokers, Obese to Trim Costs," *Wall Street Journal*, October 14, 2004, B1.

37. "The New Résumé: Dumb and Dumber," *Wall Street Journal*, May 26, 2009, D5.

38. Ibid.

39. "Why Dads Don't Take Paternity Leave," *Wall Street Journal*, June 13, 2013, B1. See also "The Daddy Juggle: Work, Life, Family and Chaos," *Wall Street Journal*, June 13, 2014, B1.

40. Dean Rotbart, "Father Quit His Job for the Family's Sake; Now Hirers Shun Him," *Wall Street Journal*, April 13, 1981, 1.

41. 401 U.S. 424 (1971). For a more recent case on the same point, see "Black Firefighters' Claim Was Timely, Justices Say," *New York Times*, May 25, 2010, A15.

42. "Employers Score New Hires," *USA Today*, July 9, 1997, 1B; "Put Applicants' Skills to the Test," *HR Magazine,* January 2000, 75–80; "Job Applicants' First Screener Is … Screen," *San Francisco Chronicle*, May 31, 2004, D3; "Applicants' Personalities Put to the Test," *Wall Street Journal*, August 26, 2008, D4; and "When Hiring, First Test, and Then Interview," *Harvard Business Review*, November 2013, 34.

43. Kris Maher, "The Jungle," *Wall Street Journal*, September 28, 2004, B10.

44. Roland Wall, "Discovering Prejudice against the Disabled," *ETC* 44 (Fall 1987): 236.

45. Francis Bacon, *The New Organon* (New York: Bobbs-Merrill, 1960), 48.

46. James Surowiecki, "The Financial Page: Valley Boys," *New Yorker*, November 24, 2014, 52.

47. "Improv at the Interview," *Business Week*, February 3, 2003, 63.

48. "Work Week," *Wall Street Journal*, May 21, 1996, A1. See also Adam Bellow, *In Praise of Nepotism* (New York: Doubleday, 2003), 12.

49. "Family Ties," *San Francisco Chronicle*, April 4, 2004, J1.

50. Ibid.

51. John J. McCall, "Just Cause," *Blackwell Encyclopedic Dictionary of Business Ethics*, eds. Patricia Werhane and R. Edward Freeman, (Blackwell: Malden, Mass., 1997), 352.

52. "Workers Are Fired, Celebrated," *Wall Street Journal*, August 20, 2009, A3; "2 Fired from Broomfield Best Buy for Tackling Shoplifter," *Denver Post*, August 18, 2009 (online).

53. Rachel L. Swarns, "Doctor Says No Overtime; Pregnant Worker's Boss Says No Job," *New York Times*, October 30, 2014, A 18.

54. "An Alternative to Cocker Spaniels," *Economist*, August 25, 2001, 49.

55. See, for example, "Termination with Dignity," *Business Horizons* 43 (September–October 2000): 4–10; and Jathan W. Janove, "Don't Add Insult to Injury," *HR Magazine*, May 2002, 113–120.

56. John Challenger, "Downsize with Dignity," *Executive Excellence,* March 2002, 17; "Waging War in the Workplace," *Newsweek*, July 19, 1993.

57. "Special Report: Corporate Governance," *Economist*, June 15, 2002, 70.

58. Dori Meinert, "How to Fire an Employee Safely," Society for Human Resource Management (June 17, 2018), https://www.shrm.org/hr-today/news/hr-news/conference-today/pages/2018/how-to-fire-an-employee-safely.aspx.

59. "Leaving a Job? Better Watch Your Cellphone," *Wall Street Journal*, January 22, 2014, B7.

60. "Employers See Value in Helping Those Laid Off," *Wall Street Journal*, September 24, 2007, B3; "The Three-Minute Manager," *Fortune*, May 26, 2008, 30. See also "You're Fired—But Stay in Touch," *Business Week*, May 4, 2009, 54–55.

61. For example, see "Temporary Employees Sue Wal-Mart," *New York Times*, October 23, 2012, B2, and "McDonald's Workers File Wage Suits in 3 States," *New York Times*, March 14, 2014, B8.

62. John Stuart Mill, *Principles of Political Economy*, ed. Sir William Ashley (Fairfield N.J.: Augustus M. Kelley, 1987), 211–212. Mill does not believe that it will be feasible for employers to pay workers in a way that is perfectly just in this sense until human nature has further improved. This would require paying workers the same, or according to their need, and Mill believes that for the foreseeable future, pay will need to be tied to productivity to incentivize workers to make a good effort. Perfect justice will only be feasible when workers can all be counted on to give their best effort without the external motivation that comes from a higher paycheck.

63. Robert G. Strayton, "A Minimum Wage That Will Work," *Wall Street Journal*, February 10, 2014, A11.

64. See Arindrajit Dube, "The Minimum We Can Do," *New York Times*, November 30, 2013 (online), and Michael Reich and Ken Jacobs, "All Economics Is Local," *New York Times*, March 22, 2014 (online). See also "Crossing Borders and Changing Lives, Lured by Higher State Minimum Wages," *New York Times*, February 16, 2014, A20. On the limits of the empirical evidence, see Megan McArdle, "Everything We Don't Know about Hiking the Minimum Wage," *Chicago Tribune*, December 30, 2014, sec. 1, 13.

65. United States Bureau of Labor Statistics, "Union Members—2022" (January 19, 2023), https://www.bls.gov/news.release/pdf/union2.pdf.

66. "Critics Claim Union Clampdown Is Latest Washington Concession to Big Business," *Financial Times*, April 4, 2005, 1. See also "The Rush to Squash a Promising Union Tactic," *Business Week*, August 2, 2004, 87; "Brothers at Arms," *Economist*, May 14, 2005, 32; and "Unions Fear Rollback of Rights under Republicans," *New York Times*, November 2, 2010, A15.

67. "Can This Man Save Labor?" *Business Week*, September 24, 2004, 84.

68. Simon Head, "Inside the Leviathan," *New York Review of Books*, December 16, 2004, 88, and Anthony Bianco, "No Union, Please, We're Wal-Mart," *Business Week*, February 13, 2006, 78–81. See also "How Wal-Mart Keeps Unions at Bay," *Business Week*, October 28, 2002, 96; Karen Olsson, "Up against Wal-Mart," *Mother Jones*, March–April 2003, 54–59; and the Human Rights Watch report "Discounting Rights: Wal-Mart's Violation of U.S. Workers' Right to Freedom of Association" (May 2007), http://hrw.org.

69. Heidi Shierholz, Margaret Poydock, and Celine McNicholas, "Unionization Increased by 200,000 in 2022," Economic Policy Institute (January 19, 2023), https://www.epi.org/publication/unionization-2022/.

70. "Labor Unions: Context and Crisis," in R. C. Edwards, M. Reich, and T. E. Weisskopf, eds., *The Capitalist System*, 3rd ed. (Englewood Cliffs, N.J.: Prentice Hall, 1986), 165.

71. Justin McCarthy, "U.S. Approval of Labor Unions at Highest Point Since 1965," Gallup (August 20, 2022), https://news.gallup.com/poll/398303/approval-labor-unions-highest-point-1965.aspx.

72. Chris Isidore, "Despite Union Wins at Starbucks, Amazon and Apple, Labor Laws Keep Cards Stacked against Organizers," *CNN Business*, September 5, 2022, https://www.cnn.com/2022/09/05/business/union-organizing-efforts/index.html.

73. Adam Smith, *An Inquiry into the Nature and Causes of the Wealth of Nations* (New York: Modern Library, 1985), 68.

74. Belle Wong, "Average Salary by State In (2023)," *Forbes Advisor*, August 23, 2023, https://www.forbes.com/advisor/business/average-salary-by-state/#:~:text=The%20state%20in%20the%20Northeast,salary%20is%20Maryland%20at%20%2469%2C750.

75. Austin Fagothey and Milton A. Gonsalves, *Right and Reason: Ethics in Theory and Practice* (St. Louis: Mosby, 1981), 428–429.

76. Ibid., 429.

77. See chap. 4 of Mary Gibson, *Workers' Rights* (Totowa, N.J.: Rowman & Allanheld, 1983). The award-winning 1979 film *Norma Rae* portrays the dogged resistance of a company like J. P. Stevens to unionization.

78. Fagothey and Gonsalves, *Right and Reason*, 428–429.

79. "Unions Threaten Huge Bank Withdrawal," *San Jose Mercury News*, April 10, 1996, 1C.

80. This case is based on Willard P. Green, "Pornography at Work," *Business Ethics*, Summer 2003, 19.

81. This case is based on "States Mull Gun-Access Laws," *USA Today*, February 8, 2008, 3A. See also "Do Guns on the Premises Leave Workers More or Less Safe?" NPR: All Things Considered, December 12, 2014, www.npr.org.

82. Reprinted by permission of the National Right to Work Legal Defense Foundation, Inc., 8001 Braddock Road, Suite 600, Springfield, VA 22160.

Chapter 9

1. Darrell M. West, "How Employers Use Technology to Surveil Employees," Brookings Institute (January 5, 2021), https://www.brookings.edu/articles/how-employers-use-technology-to-surveil-employees/.

2. "How Not to Fix a Leak," *San Jose Mercury News*, October 15, 2006, 1A.

3. Quoted in "Privacy," *Newsweek*, March 28, 1988, 61–68.

4. "Snooping E-mail by Software Is Now a Workplace Norm," *Wall Street Journal*, March 9, 2005, B1, and "Watch Your Emails. Your Boss Is," *Wall Street Journal*, May 2, 2010 (online).

5. "Is Office Voice Mail Private?" *Wall Street Journal*, February 28, 1995, B1.

6. "As Abuse of Sick Leave Continues, Crackdown Raises Issues of Privacy," *New York Times*, November 30, 1992, A1. See also "Shirking Working: The War on Hooky," *Business Week*, November 12, 2007, 72.

7. "On the Road Again, but Now the Boss Is Sitting Beside You," *Wall Street Journal*, May 14, 2004, A1.

8. Charles Reich, "The Corporate Control of Big Government," *Business and Society Review* 95 (1996): 61. On office romances, see Sue Shellenbarger, "For Office Romance, the Secret's Out," *Wall Street Journal*, February 10, 2010, D1, and "Navigating Love at the Office," *Bloomberg Businessweek*, March 18–24, 2013, 70.

9. "Firms Find It Tougher to Dismiss Employees for Off-Duty Conduct," *Wall Street Journal*, March 29, 1988, 31.

10. "Up Front," *Business Week*, August 16, 2004, 10.

11. Steve Greenhouse, "Here's a Memo from the Boss: Vote This Way," *New York Times*, October 26, 2012 (online).

12. "Enterprise Takes Idea of Dressed for Success to a New Extreme," *Wall Street Journal*, November 20, 2002, B1. See also "Black Woman Fired from Hooters because of Blonde Highlights," *Huffington Post*, October 22, 2013 (online).

13. "Legal Secretary Fired over Gay Stripper Job," *Santa Cruz Sentinel*, June 7, 1992, A10.

14. Laura P. Hartman, "Technology and Ethics," in Laura P. Hartman, ed., *Perspectives in Business Ethics*, 3rd ed. (New York: McGraw-Hill, 2005), 730–731.

15. Terry L. Leap, "When Can You Fire for Off-Duty Conduct?" *Harvard Business Review* 66 (January–February 1988): 36.

16. Associated Press, "Beer Choice Costs Man Job," *Fox News* (February 14, 2005), https://www.foxnews.com/story/beer-choice-costs-man-job.amp.

17. See Sue Shellenbarger, "Unpaid Overtime: Coping with Pressure to Volunteer for Company Causes," *Wall Street Journal*, November 20, 2003, D1, which is also the source of the next paragraph.

18. Jared Sandberg, "Your Boss's Obsession Too Often Becomes Your Job Obligation," *Wall Street Journal*, December 11, 2007, B1.

19. "Wellness Becomes an Issue in the Workplace," *Santa Cruz Sentinel*, April 28, 2002, D1; "Seeking Savings, Employers Help Smokers Quit," *New York Times*, October 27, 2007, A1; and "Mens Sana in Corporation Sano," *Economist*, July 10, 2010, 65. For some doubts about the benefits of these programs, financial and otherwise, see "Take Your Meds, Exercise—and Spend Billions," *Bloomberg Businessweek*, February 15, 2010, 46–50, and Austin Frakt and Aaron E. Carroll, "Do Workplace Wellness Programs Work? Usually Not," *New York Times*, September 11, 2014 (online).

20. Greg Jaffe, "Weighty Matters," *San Francisco Examiner*, February 22, 1998, J1; "Companies Get Tough with Smokers, Obese to Trim Costs," *Wall Street Journal*, October 12, 2004, B1; and "Wellness Programs May Face Legal Tests," *Wall Street Journal*, January 16, 2008, D9.

21. "Why Wellness Is Making Employees Feel Sick," *Financial Times*, February 17, 2005, 9; "Shape Up—Or Else," *Newsweek*, July 1, 1991, 42; "If You Light Up on Sunday, Don't Come In on Monday," *Business Week*, August 26, 1991, 68–70.

22. Colleen Flaherty, "AARP Says Yale Settled Wellness Program Lawsuit," *Inside Higher Ed* (March 7, 2022), https://www.insidehighered.com/quicktakes/2022/03/08/aarp-says-yale-settled-wellness-program-lawsuit.

23. "Why Wellness Is Making Employees"; "Employees Earn Cash for Exercising More," *Wall Street Journal*, June 2, 2010, D3; "The Big Question," *Money*, June 2010, 124; and "When HR Asks about Your Health," *Money*, October 2009, 33.

24. "Employers Lure Spouses into Wellness Programs to Help Cut Costs," *Wall Street Journal*, August 21, 2009, B4; "Your Boss to Your Kids: Slim Down," *Bloomberg Businessweek*, February 1–8, 2010, 67.

25. Quoted in "Privacy," 68.

26. See David T. Lykken, "Three Big Lies about the Polygraph," *USA Today*, February 17, 1983, 10A. See also William A. Nowlin and Robert Barbato, "The Truth about Lie Detectors," *Business and Society Review* 66 (Summer 1988): 18–21; "Scientists Say Lie Detector Doesn't Always Tell Truth," *Wall Street Journal*, October 9, 2002, B1; and "The Polygraph Paradox," *Wall Street Journal*, March 22–23, 2008, A1.

27. Lynn March, "Lie Detectors Are Accurate and Useful," *USA Today*, February 17, 1983, 10A. See also "Polygraph Paradox," A8; and "Ministry of Truth," *Economist*, April 14, 2007, 34.

28. Lykken, "Three Big Lies."

29. Christopher H. Pyle, "These Tests Are Meant to Scare People," *USA Today*, February 17, 1983, 10A.

30. Heather A. Davis, "Brain Scans Detect Lies More Accurately than the Polygraph," *Penn Today* (December 22, 2016), https://penntoday.upenn.edu/research/brain-scans-detect-lies-more-accurately-than-the-polygraph; Jackie Dunham, "Brain Imaging Lie Detector: Researchers Discover Two Techniques to Beat This Test," *CTV News* (May 2, 2019), https://www.ctvnews.ca/sci-tech/brain-imaging-lie-detector-researchers-discover-two-techniques-to-beat-this-test-1.4405314?cache=yesclipld104062. "Making Windows in Men's Souls," *Economist*, July 10, 2004, 71–72.

31. Vanessa Leikvoll, "80% of Fortune 500 Companies Use Personality Tests, but Are They Ethical?" *Leaders* (September 14, 2022), https://leaders.com/articles/business/personality-tests/#:~:text=Brief%20description%3A%20The%20most%20widely,according%20to%20the%20test's%20website.

32. "Personality Counts," *HR Magazine*, February 2, 2002, 30–31. See also Gladwell, "Personality Plus"; Graham Lawton, "Let's Get Personal," *New Scientist*, September 13, 2003; and Annie Murphy Paul, *The Cult of Personality* (New York: Free Press, 2004).

33. Barbara Ehrenreich, "Two-Tiered Morality," *New York Times*, June 30, 2002, sec. 4, 15.

34. "Trying to Get a Job? Check Yes or No," *New York Times*, November 28, 1997, B1, and "As Personality Tests Multiply."

35. "Trying to Get a Job?"

36. "Study May Spur Job-Applicant Drug Screening," *Wall Street Journal*, November 28, 1990, B1.

37. Kris Maher, "The Jungle," *Wall Street Journal*, April 13, 2004, B4.

38. Danielle Abril and Taylor Telford, "Smoking Weed after Work? A Growing Number of Employers Don't Mind," *Washington Post* (July 17, 2023), https://www.washingtonpost.com/technology/2023/07/17/marijuana-drug-test-weed-work/.

39. "If You Light Up on Sunday," 68.

40. James T. Wrich, "Beyond Testing: Coping with Drugs at Work," *Harvard Business Review* 66 (January–February 1988); "Drug Testing in the Workplace: Report of the Independent Inquiry into Drug Testing at Work," Joseph Roundtree Foundation (June 2004), www.jrf.org.uk.

41. "Privacy," 68. See also Barry A. Friedman and Lisa J. Reed, "Workplace Privacy: Employee Relations and Legal Implications of Monitoring Employee E-mail Use," *Employee Responsibilities and Rights Journal* 19, no. 2 (June 2007): 75–83.

42. "78% of Employers Engage in Remote Work Surveillance, ExpressVPN Survey Finds," ExpressVPN (April 10, 2023). See the 2005 and the 2007 "Electronic Monitoring and Surveillance Survey," https://www.expressvpn.com/blog/expressvpn-survey-surveillance-on-the-remote-workforce/.

43. "US Group Implants Electronic Tags in Workers," *Financial Times*, February 13, 2006, 1.

44. "1 in 3 Remote Employers Are Watching You Work from Home on Camera," ResumeBuilder.com (March 24, 2023), https://www.resumebuilder.com/1-in-3-remote-employers-are-watching-you-work-from-home-on-camera/.

45. Jodi Kantor and Arya Sundaram, "The Rise of the Worker Productivity Score," *New York Times* (August 14, 2022), https://www.nytimes.com/interactive/2022/08/14/business/worker-productivity-tracking.html.

46. "The Boss May Be Listening," *San Jose Mercury News*, February 25, 1996, 1PC (quoting anonymous employee), and Jared Sandberg, "Monitoring of Workers Is Boss's Right but Why Not Include the Top Brass?" *Wall Street Journal*, May 18, 2005, B1 (quoting Nancy Flynn).

47. "What the Boss Knows about You," *Fortune*, August 9, 1993.

48. See the Human Rights Watch Report, "Discounting Rights: Wal-Mart's Violation of U.S. Workers' Right to Freedom of Association" (May 2007), 152, 156–158, available at www.hrw.org.

49. Bureau of Labor Statistics, "Fatal Occupational Injuries Involving Confined Spaces" (July 2020), https://www.bls.gov/iif/factsheets/fatal-occupational-injuries-confined-spaces-2011-19.htm. See "Workplace Health and Safety Topics: Confined Spaces" at the Centers for Disease Control and Prevention website, www.cdc.gov. See also "Silos Loom as Death Traps on American Farms," *New York Times*, October 29, 2012, A1.

50. U.S. Census Bureau, *Statistical Abstract of the United States 2012* (Washington, D.C.: U.S. Government Printing Office, 2011), Tables 657 and 661. This figure excludes homicides and suicides. United States Bureau of Labor Statistics, "Injuries, Illnesses, and Fatalities," https://www.bls.gov/iif/latest-numbers.htm.

51. "Study Finds That U.S. Undercounts Workplace Injuries, Illnesses," *Wall Street Journal*, May 1, 2006, A2, and "Injuries May Be Undercounted," *Wall Street Journal*, June 19, 2008, A4.

52. Quoted in John R. Boatright, *Ethics and the Conduct of Business*, 4th ed. (Upper Saddle River, N.J.: Prentice Hall, 2003), 316.

53. *Whirlpool Corporation v. Marshall*, 445 U.S. 1 (1980).

54. Julia Harte and Peter Eisler, "Left in the Dust: The Dismantling of a U.S. Workplace Safety Rule, and the Political Battle behind It," Reuters Investigates (January 22, 2019), https://www.reuters.com/investigates/special-report/usa-beryllium-rule/.

55. Myron I. Peskin and Francis J. McGrath, "Industrial Safety: Who Is Responsible and Who Benefits?" *Business Horizons* 35 (May–June 1992): 66–70. See also Alan Tidwell, "Ethics, Safety, and Managers," *Business and Professional Ethics Journal* 19 (Fall–Winter 2000): 161–180.

56. "Worker Dies in a Fall at a Construction Site," *New York Times*, March 19, 2009, A25. See also "Fight Erupts over Protecting Rooftop Workers," *Wall Street Journal*, September 29, 2014, B1.

57. Steven Greenhouse, "Workers Assail Night Lock-Ins by Wal-Mart," *New York Times*, January 18, 2004 (online).

58. Beth Rogers, "Creating a Culture of Safety," *HR Magazine* (February 1995): 85. See also James Reason, "Achieving a Safe Culture: Theory and Practice," *Work and Stress* 12 (July–September 1998): 293–306.

59. "Shifting Procedures Upset BP's Rig Team," *Wall Street Journal*, January 29–30, 2011, A3; "BP's Safety Drive Faces Rough Road," *Wall Street Journal*, February 2, 2011, A1; Geoff Colvin, "Who's to Blame at BP?" *Fortune*, July 26, 2010, 60; and Peter Elkin and David Whitford's detailed, investigative report, "An Accident Waiting to Happen," *Fortune*, February 7, 2011, 107.

60. "Deaths at Mine Raising Issues about Safety," *New York Times*, April 7, 2010, A1; "Deadly Mine's Owner Duels with Regulators," *New York Times*, April 28, 2010, A2; "Mine Described as 'Ticking Time Bomb,'" *New York Times*, May 25, 2010, A6; and "The Accountant of Coal," *Bloomberg Businessweek*, April 25, 2010, 48. See also "2 Killed in West Virginia Mine Where Safety Lapses Were Cited," *New York Times*, May 14, 2014, A16; and "Coal Mines Keep Operating Despite Injuries, Violations, and Millions in Fines," *NPR: All Things Considered*, November 12, 2014, www.npr.org.

61. Archie B. Carroll and Ann K. Buchholtz, *Business and Society: Ethics and Stakeholder Management*, 6th ed. (Mason, Ohio: Thomson South-Western, 2006), 552.

62. Susan Podzila, "Safety Starts at the Top," *New York Times*, June 12, 2008, A31.

63. Occupational Safety and Health Administration, "Commonly Used Statistics: Federal OSHA Coverage," https://www.osha .gov/data/commonstats; Debra Berkowitz, "Worker Safety in Crisis," National Employment Law Project (April 28, 2020), https://www.nelp.org/publication/worker-safety-crisis-cost-weakened-osha/.

64. Mark Drajem and Jack Kaskey, "Texas Explosion Seen as Sign of Weak U.S. Oversight," *Bloomberg.com*, April 19, 2013.

65. For a discussion of the Golab case, see James F. Brummer, "Excuses and Vindications: An Analysis of the Film Recovery Systems Case," *Business and Professional Ethics Journal* 18 (Spring 1999): 21–46.

66. David Barstow, "U.S. Rarely Seeks Charges for Deaths in Workplace," *New York Times*, December 22, 2003, A1. See also "Inspectors Adrift in Rig-Safety Push," *New York Times*, December 3, 2010, A1.

67. "U.S. Rarely Seeks Charges."

68. Dana Wilkie, "The Uphill Struggle for Workplace Health," *State Legislatures* 23 (June 2, 1997): 27–32. See also "A Dangerous Business," *Frontline*, January 9, 2003 (interview with Charles Jeffress), available at www.pbs.org; and "OSHA Leaves Worker Safety in Hands of Industry," *New York Times*, April 25, 2007 (online).

69. David Tuller, "The '90s 'Occupational Epidemic,'" *San Francisco Chronicle*, June 12, 1989, C1.

70. "U.S. Acts to Cut Aches on the Job," *New York Times*, February 20, 1999, A1.

71. "Employers Win Ergonomics Duel by Achieving Delay in Guidelines," *Wall Street Journal*, November 3, 2003, A3.

72. See Judith A. Rice et al., "Fatigue in the U.S. Workplace," *Journal of Occupational and Environmental Medicine* 49, no. 1 (2007): 1–10, and the discussion of fatigue in the Society for Human Resource Management's publication, "Workforce Management Trend Survey: Issues in 2010," www.shrm.org. See also "Decoding the Science of Sleep," *Wall Street Journal*, August 4–5, 2012, C1. On pilot fatigue and air safety, see "Some Airlines Fight Proposals on Crew Rest," *Wall Street Journal*, January 5, 2009, B1.

73. American Psychological Association, "2023 Work in America Survey," https://www.apa.org/pubs/reports /work-in-america/2023-workplace-health-well-being.

74. John Schwartz, "Always at Work and Anxious: Employees' Health Is Suffering," *New York Times*, September 5, 2004, sec. 1, 1. Except where noted, this article is the basis also of the next paragraph. For a contrary perspective, see Dan Seligman, "New Crisis—Junk Statistics," *Forbes*, October 18, 2004, 118.

75. Yawen Cheng, I. Kawachi, E. H. Coakley, J. Schwartz, and G. Colditz, "Association between Psychosocial Work Characteristics and Health Functioning in American Women," *British Medical Journal* 30 (May 27, 2000): 1432–1436. For an overview of the physical toll that stress can take on many body systems, see Melinda Beck, "Stress So Bad It Hurts—Really," *Wall Street Journal*, March 17, 2009, D1, and Moises Velasquez-Manoff, "Status and Stress," *New York Times*, July 27, 2013 (online).

76. Thomas Stewart, "Managers Look for the Moral Dimension," *Financial Times*, August 27, 2004, 7; and Timothy Egan, "Checking Out," *New York Times*, June 20, 2013 (online).

77. "Managers Look for the Moral Dimension."

78. Harvey A. Hornstein, *Brutal Bosses and Their Prey* (New York: Putnam, 1996); and Harvey A. Hornstein, *The Haves and the Have Nots: The Abuse of Power and Privilege in the Workplace … and How to Control It* (Upper Saddle River, N.J.: Pearson Education, 2003). See also Jack and Suzy Welch, "An Employee Bill of Rights," *Business Week*, March 16, 2009, 72; and "The Rise of Mediocre Tyrants," *Sunday Morning Post* (Hong Kong), October 9, 2011, 13.

79. Vanessa A. Camilleri, "The Future's Top Workplaces Will Rely on Manager Development" Gallup (November 13, 2020), https://www.gallup.com/workplace/324131/future-top-workplaces-rely-manager-development.aspx.

80. Douglas McGregor, *The Human Side of Enterprise* (New York: McGraw-Hill, 1960).

81. "Bosses Overestimate Their Managing Skills," *Wall Street Journal*, November 1, 2010, B10.

82. "How to Influence Your Boss and Keep Your Friends," *Financial Times*, February 26, 2005, 8. See also Jason Zweig, "What Conflict of Interest? How Power Blinds Us to Our Flaws," *Wall Street Journal*, October 16–17, 2010, B1.

83. Gary Hamel and Michele Zanini, "Excess Management Is Costing the U.S. $3 Trillion per Year" *Harvard Business Review* (September 5, 2016), https://hbr.org/2016/09/excess-management-is-costing-the-us-3-trillion-per-year.

84. "For Ross Perot, GM Ouster Still Rankles," *International Herald Tribune*, November 19, 1987.

85. *Statistical Abstract of the United States 2012*, Table 615. For some related statistics, see Philip N. Cohen, "Jump-Starting the Struggle for Equality," *New York Times*, November 24, 2013, "Sunday Review," 9 United States Bureau of Labor Statistics, "Women in the Labor Force: A Databook," *BLS Reports* (April 2023), https://www.bls.gov/opub/reports/womens-databook/2022/home.htm.

86. United States Bureau of Labor Statistics, "Employment Characteristics of Families—2022" (April 19, 2023), https://www.bls.gov/news.release/pdf/famee.pdf *Statistical Abstract of the United States 2012*, Table 599; see also Lauren Buer and Sarah Yu Wang, "Prime-Age Women Are Going Above and Beyond in the Labor Market Recovery," Brookings Institution Hamilton Project (August 30, 2023), https://www.hamiltonproject.org/publication/post/prime-age-women-are-going-above-and-beyond-in-the-labor-market-recovery/.U.S. Census Bureau, *Statistical Abstract of the United States 2004–5* (Washington, D.C.: U.S. Government Printing Office, 2004), Table 579; and U.S. Bureau of Labor Statistics, *Women in the Labor Force: A Databook*, February 2013 (available online).

87. Claire Cain Miller, "How Other Nations Pay for Child Care. The U.S. Is an Outlier," *New York Times* (October 6, 2021), https://www.nytimes.com/2021/10/06/upshot/child-care-biden.html.

88. For a discussion of the relevant issues, see also Debbie Kaminer, "The Child-Care Crisis and Work-Family Conflict: A Policy Rationale for Federal Legislation," *Berkeley Journal of Employment and Labor Law* 8, no. 2 (2007): 331–373.

89. Vicki Shabo, "Explainer: Paid Leave Benefits and Funding in the United States," *New America* (September 30, 2023), https://www.newamerica.org/better-life-lab/briefs/explainer-paid-leave-benefits-and-funding-in-the-united-states/.

90. Claire Cain Miller, "Mother of a Problem," *New York Times* (June 22, 2023), https://www.nytimes.com/2021/10/25/upshot/paid-leave-democrats.html.

91. Kathryn Meyer, "Parental, Family Leave Programs See Boost in 2023 SHRM Employee Benefits Survey," Society for Human Resource Management (June 12, 2023), https://www.shrm.org/resourcesandtools/hr-topics/benefits/pages/shrm-2023-employee-benefits-survey-paid-parental-family-leave.aspx.

92. Kait Hanson, "How the Pandemic Has Forced a New Generation of Latchkey Kids," *Today* (November 15, 2021), https://www.today.com/parents/how-pandemic-forced-new-generation-latchkey-kids-t238822.

93. Gretchen Livingstone, "The Changing Profile of Unmarried Parents," Pew Research Center (April 25, 2018), https://www.pewresearch.org/social-trends/2018/04/25/the-changing-profile-of-unmarried-parents/. (The number of "solo fathers" has more than doubled since 1968.)

94. See Bonnie Harris, "Child Care Comes to Work," *Los Angeles Times*, November 19, 2000, W1; and Sue Shellenberger, "Rules of Engagement," *Wall Street Journal*, October 1, 2007, R3.

95. "Welcome Campbell Family Center!," Bright Horizons (December 15, 2020), https://www.brighthorizons.com/resources/Blog/campbell-onsite-child-care; Te-Ping Chen, "More Companies Start to Offer Daycare at Work," *Wall Street Journal* (March 9, 2023), https://www.wsj.com/articles/more-companies-start-to-offer-daycare-at-work-95d267bb.

96. Kylie Ora Lobell, "Employers Consider Child Care Subsidies," *Society for Human Resource Management* (September 22, 2020), https://www.shrm.org/resourcesandtools/hr-topics/employee-relations/pages/many-workplaces-consider-child-care-subsidies.aspx.

97. "Kids Go to School at H-P Work Site," *San Jose Mercury News*, February 10, 1993, 1A, and "Companies Providing Schools for Workers' Children," *San Jose Mercury News*, July 28, 1996, 1PC.

98. "Rules of Engagement," R3, and "Special Report: Women and Work," *Economist*, November 26, 2011, 5, 12–13. See also Sue Shellenbarger, "Perking Up: Some Companies Offer Surprising New Benefits," *Wall Street Journal*, March 18, 2009, D1; Lobell, "Employers Consider Child Care Subsidies."

99. "Employers Step Up Efforts to Lure Stay-at-Home Mothers Back to Work," *Wall Street Journal*, February 9, 2006, D1; Lobell, "Employers Consider Child Care Subsidies." See also "Briefing: Women in the Workforce," *Economist*, January 2, 2010, esp. p. 51.

100. "As Demands on Workers Grow, Groups Push for Paid Family and Sick Leave," *New York Times*, March 6, 2005, sec. 1, 15.

101. Sue Shellenbarger, "A Downside of Taking Family Leave: Getting Fired While You're Gone," *Wall Street Journal*, January 23, 2003, D1. See also "Shirking Working: The War on Hooky," *Business Week*, November 12, 2007, 72–73.

102. Sheelah Kolhatkar, "Men Are People Too," *Bloomberg Businessweek*, June 3–9, 2013, 59–63, and "The Daddy Juggle: Work, Life, Family and Chaos," *Wall Street Journal*, June 13, 2014, B1.

103. *Work in America: Report of a Special Task Force to the Secretary of Health, Education, and Welfare* (Cambridge, Mass.: MIT Press, 1972).

104. Juliana Horowitz and Kim Parker, "How Americans View Their Jobs," Pew Research Center (March 30, 2023), https://www.pewresearch.org/social-trends/2023/03/30/how-americans-view-their-jobs/.

105. Selcuk Eren, Allan Schweyer, Malala Lin, and Allen Li, "Job Satisfaction 2023: US Worker Satisfaction Continues to Increase," The Conference Board (2023), https://www.conference-board.org/research/job-satisfaction.

106. Jim Harter, "U.S. Employee Engagement Needs a Rebound in 2023," Gallup (January 25, 2023), https://www.gallup.com/workplace/468233/employee-engagement-needs-rebound-2023.aspx.

107. But for a critical discussion of the original study, see "Light Work," *Economist*, June 6, 2009, 74.

108. For an accessible discussion of Herzberg's ideas, see J. Michael Syptak, David M. Marsland, and Deborah Ulmer, "Job Satisfaction: Putting Theory into Practice," *Family Practice Management*, October 1999, 26.

109. Michael Skapinker, "Money Can't Make You Happy but Being in a Trusted Team Can," *Financial Times*, June 1, 2005, 8.

110. "A Bad Job Can Be Worse Than No Job," *Wall Street Journal*, March 22, 2011, D5.

111. "Bored to Death at Work—Literally," *Business Week*, July 1, 2002, 16.

112. Erdman Palmore, "Predicting Longevity: A Follow-Up Controlling for Age," *Gerontologist* 9 (1960): 247–250; and Erman Palmore, "Predictors of the Longevity Difference: A 25-Year Follow-Up," *Gerontologist* 22 (1982): 513–518.

113. Randy Pennington, "Collaborative Labor Relations: The First Line Is the Bottom Line," *Personnel* (March 1989): 78.

114. "A Top-Flight Employee Strategy," *Financial Times*, April 4, 2005, 8.

115. Sharon Cohen, "Management, Unions Join Forces," *San Francisco Examiner*, December 9, 1990, D3.

116. "A Top-Flight Employee Strategy," 8.

117. Society for Human Resource Management, "How Companies Benefit from Partnering with Unions," *HR Magazine* (Fall 2022), https://www.shrm.org/hr-today/news/hr-magazine/fall2022/pages/companies-partner-with-unions.aspx.

118. John Rosevear, "BMW's First-Quarter Profit Was Okay, but 2020 Will Be a Tough Year," *Motley Fool* (May 7, 2020), https://www.fool.com/investing/2020/05/07/bmws-first-quarter-profit-was-okay-but-2020-will-b.aspx.

119. Alan S. Blinder, "Want to Boost Productivity? Try Giving Workers a Say," *Business Week*, April 17, 1989, 10, and "A Firm of Their Own," *Economist*, June 11, 1994, 59. See also "Workers Who Run the Show," *Financial Times*, August 24, 2005, 7. For academic studies, see Thomas Zwick, "Employee Participation and Productivity," *Labour Economics* 11, no. 6 (December 2004): 715–740; and Tor Eriksson, ed., *Advances in the Economic Analysis of Participatory and Labor-Managed Firms, Vol. 11* (Bingley, England: Emerald Group, 2010).

120. See Roger E. Alcaly, "Reinventing the Corporation," *New York Review of Books*, April 10, 1997; and "Happy Workers Are the Best Workers," *Wall Street Journal*, September 6, 2005, A21.

121. 109 Cal. Rptr. 665 (1973).

122. "This Is a Fine Kettle of . . . Viagra: Salvation Army's Very Odd Catch," *Wall Street Journal*, December 21–22, 2013, A1.

123. Except where noted, this case study is based on "More Employers Attempt to Catch a Thief by Giving Job Applicants 'Honesty' Exams," *Wall Street Journal*, August 3, 1981, 15; "Honest Answers—Postpolygraph," *Personnel*, April 1988, 8; "Job Applicants Would Disappoint Diogenes," *San Francisco Examiner*, December 18, 1988, D15; "Searching for Integrity," *Fortune*, March 8, 1993, 140; "Trying to Get a Job? Check Yes or No," *New York Times*, November 28, 1997, B1; and "Texas Company Settles over Nosy Questions to Employees," *San Francisco Chronicle*, July 8, 2000, A3. On employee theft, see "To Catch a Corporate Thief," *Business Week*, February 16, 2009, 52; "Small Businesses Face More Fraud in Downturn," *Wall Street Journal*, February 19, 2009, B5; and "In-House Fraud Cases Surge," *Financial Times*, May 11, 2009, 1.

124. This case study is based on a case reported in Thomas Garrett et al., *Cases in Business Ethics* (Englewood Cliffs, N.J.: Prentice Hall, 1968), 9–10.

125. Peter T. Kilborn, "Who Decides Who Works at Jobs Imperiling Fetuses?" *New York Times*, September 2, 1990, 1, is the main source for this case study.

126. *New York Times*, March 21, 1991, A1. Excerpts from *Automobile Workers v. Johnson Controls* quoted in the following paragraphs are from page A14.

127. This case study is based on "Briefing: Women in the Workforce," *Economist*, January 2, 2010, 49; and "Paternity Leave Law Helps to Redefine Masculinity in Sweden," *New York Times*, June 15, 2010, A6. See also Joan C. Williams and May J. C. Cuddy, "Will Working Mothers Take Your Company to Court?" *Harvard Business Review*, September 2012, 96, 98; Stephanie Coontz, "Progress at Work, but Mothers Still Pay a Price," *New York Times*, June 9, 2013, "Sunday Review," 5; and "The Daddy Juggle," B1. On the mommy track, see Felice N. Schwartz, "Management Women and the New Facts of Life," *Harvard Business Review* 67 (January–February 1989): 65; and Barbara Ehrenreich and Deirdre English, "Blowing the Whistle on the 'Mommy Track,'" *Ms.*, July–August 1989, 56. See also "Still Lonely at the Top."

128. This paragraph draws on "Why Dads Don't Take Paternity Leave," *Wall Street Journal*, June 13, 2013, B1. See also Claire Cain Miller, "The Motherhood Penalty vs. the Fatherhood Bonus," *New York Times*, September 6, 2014 (online).

Chapter 10

1. See "Nuclear Warriors," *Time*, March 4, 1996, 47–54, from which the details that follow are taken.

2. Jeffrey F. Beatty and Susan S. Samuelson, *Business Law and the Legal Environment*, 5th ed. (Mason, Ohio: South-Western Cengage Learning, 2010), 668, 672.

3. Ronald Duska, "Whistleblowing and Employee Loyalty," in Tom L. Beauchamp, Norman E. Bowie, and Denis G. Arnold, eds., *Ethical Theory and Business*, 8th ed. (Upper Saddle River, N.J.: Prentice Hall, 2009), 158. For a critical assessment of Duska's argument, see John Corvino, "Loyalty in Business?" *Journal of Business Ethics* 41, nos. 1–2 (November–December 2002): 179–185.

4. John H. Fielder, "Organizational Loyalty," *Business and Professional Ethics Journal* 11 (Spring 1992): 80–84.

5. Mahzarin R. Banaji, M. H. Bazerman, and D. Chugh, "How (Un)Ethical Are You?" *Harvard Business Review*, December 2003, 61. See also Jason Zweig, "What Conflict of Interest? How Power Blinds Us to Our Flaws," *Wall Street Journal*, October 16–17, 2010, B1.

6. "A Case of Conflicts at Qwest," *Business Week*, April 22, 2002, 37.

7. "Conflict-of-Interest Disclosures May Not Protect the Unsophisticated," *Wall Street Journal*, January 13, 2005, A2; and "Simply Disclosing Funds behind Studies May Not Erase Bias," *Wall Street Journal*, August 4, 2006, A11.

8. See Daylain M. Cain, George Loewenstein, and Don A. Moore, "Coming Clean but Playing Dirtier: The Shortcomings of Disclosure as a Solution to Conflicts of Interest," in Don A. Moore, Daylain M. Cain, George Loewenstein, and Max H. Bazerman, eds., *Conflicts of Interest: Challenges and Solutions in Business, Law, Medicine, and Public Policy* (New York: Cambridge University Press, 2005), 104–125.

9. Michael Greenstone, "See Red Flags, Hear Red Flags," *New York Times*, December 6, 2013 (online). See also "The Dozy Watchdogs," *Economist*, December 13, 2014, 24.

10. "Tech's Kickback Culture," *Business Week*, February 10, 2003, 76.

11. "Loans to Corporate Officers Unlikely to Cease Soon," *Wall Street Journal*, July 2, 2002, A8.

12. Some business analysts use the term *insider trading* in a broad way to refer to any buying or selling of corporate stock or securities by high-ranking members of the company. If it is not based on material, nonpublic information, such buying or selling does not constitute insider trading as defined in the text and may be perfectly legal.

13. John A. C. Hetherington, "Corporate Social Responsibility, Stockholders, and the Law," *Journal of Contemporary Business* (Winter 1973): 51.

14. "Texas Gulf Ruled to Lack Diligence in Minerals Case," *Wall Street Journal* (Midwest Edition), February 9, 1970, 1.
15. "Supreme Court Upholds S.E.C.'s Theory of Insider Trading," *New York Times*, June 26, 1997, C1.
16. "SEC, Professor Split on Insider Trades," *Wall Street Journal*, March 2, 1984, 8. See also Henry G. Manne, "The Case for Insider Trading," *Wall Street Journal*, March 17, 2003, A14; Manne, "The Welfare of American Investors," *Wall Street Journal*, June 13, 2006, A14 (with replies to Manne on June 21, A13); and Manne, "Busting Insider Trading: As Pointless as Prohibition," *Wall Street Journal*, April 29, 2014, A15.
17. See Jennifer Moore, "What Is Really Unethical about Insider Trading?" *Journal of Business Ethics* 9 (March 1990): 171–182.
18. "Lexar Wins Millions in Damages," *San Francisco Chronicle*, March 23, 2005, C1.
19. See "Cookie Cloak and Dagger," *Time*, September 10, 1984, 44.
20. Sissela Bok, *Secrets* (New York: Vintage, 1983), 136.
21. John R. Boatright, *Ethics and the Conduct of Business*, 6th ed. (Upper Saddle River, N.J.: Prentice Hall, 2009), 111–119. See also "Can You Keep a Secret?" *Economist*, March 16, 2013, 67.
22. "U.S. Probes Hilton over Theft Claims," *Wall Street Journal*, April 22, 2009, B1.
23. "Trade Secret," *Santa Cruz Sentinel*, June 15, 2010, A9.
24. "Mattel Wins Ban on MGA over Rights to Bratz Line," *Wall Street Journal*, December 4, 2008, B1. Although a jury awarded Mattel $100 million in damages, the judgment was later overturned, and Mattel lost when the case was retried. "Mattel Loses to Rival in Bratz Spat," *Wall Street Journal*, April 22, 2011, B1.
25. Rory J. O'Connor, "Trade-Secrets Case Casts Chill," *San Jose Mercury News*, March 7, 1993, 1A.
26. See Michael S. Baram, "Trade Secrets: What Price Loyalty?" *Harvard Business Review* 46 (November–December 1968): 66–74.
27. "Noncompete Clauses Increasingly Pop Up in an Array of Jobs," *New York Times*, June 9, 2014, B1.
28. Karla, Walter, "The Freedom to Leave," Center for American Progress (January 9, 2019), https://www.americanprogress.org/article/the-freedom-to-leave/.
29. "Ties That Bind," *Economist*, December 14, 2013, 76; "Attracting Top Talent," *Wall Street Journal*, January 23, 2014, B5.
30. Kris Mahler, "The Jungle," *Wall Street Journal*, June 8, 2004, B4. See also "Watch for Legal Traps When You Quit a Job to Work for a Rival," *Wall Street Journal*, November 6, 2007, B1.
31. Baram, "Trade Secrets."
32. See Robert Audi, *Business Ethics and Ethical Business* (New York: Oxford University Press, 2009), 113–115.
33. "Bribery Probe Hits Ford," *Wall Street Journal*, December 14, 2010, B4.
34. Kim Murphy, "Accountant for ZZZZ Best Convicted of Fraud," *Los Angeles Times*, December 20, 1988, II-1.
35. "Prosecutors Link Honda Fraud Cases to U.S. Executives," *New York Times*, March 15, 1994, A1.
36. "Botox Allegations Settled with U.S. for $600 Million," *Wall Street Journal*, September 2, 2010.
37. Bill Shaw, "Foreign Corrupt Practices Act: A Legal and Moral Analysis," *Journal of Business Ethics* 7 (October 1988): 789–790.
38. "Johnson & Johnson Settles Bribery Allegations," *Washington Post*, April 9, 2011, A11; "The Bribery Aisle: How Wal-Mart Used Payoffs to Get Its Way in Mexico," *New York Times*, December 18, 2012, A1; "Ralph Lauren Corp. Agrees to Pay Fine in Bribery Case," *Wall Street Journal*, April 23, 2013, B2; "ADM to Pay $36 Million Bribery Fines," *Wall Street Journal*, December 21–22, 2013, B4; "H-P Settles Bribery Investigations," *Wall Street Journal*, April 10, 2014, B1.
39. Robert Anello, "FCPA Cops Back on the Beat: DOJ Touts Reenergized Enforcement Efforts," *Forbes* (December 14, 2022), https://www.forbes.com/sites/insider/2022/12/14/fcpa-cops-back-on-the-beat-doj-touts-reenergized-enforcement-efforts/?sh=19f3fa061280.
40. "Spotlight Lands on Multinationals' Links with Oil-Rich African Nations," *Financial Times*, September 24, 2004, 3.
41. "Decline and Fall of the Freebie," *Financial Times*, April 20, 2005, 8. See also Dan Currell and Tracy Davis Bradley, "Greased Palms, Giant Headaches," *Harvard Business Review*, September 2012, 21–23. On the financial benefits of engaging in bribery overseas, see "You Get Who You Pay For," *Economist*, June 2, 2012, 77.
42. Norman C. Miller, "U.S. Business Overseas: Back to Bribery?" *Wall Street Journal*, April 30, 1981, 22.
43. Bartley A. Brennan, "The Foreign Corrupt Practices Act Amendments of 1988: 'Death' of a Law," *North Carolina Journal of International Law and Commerce Regulation* 15 (1990): 229–247; and Wesley Cragg and William Woof, "The U.S. Foreign Corrupt Practices Act: A Study of Its Effectiveness," *Business and Society Review* 107 (Spring 2002): 99.
44. "Siemens Ruling Suggests Bribery Spanned Globe," *Wall Street Journal*, November 16, 2007, A1. See also "Ungreasing the Wheels," *Economist*, November 21, 2009, 68, and "Squeezing the Sleazy," *Economist*, December 15, 2012, 61.
45. "Bribery Is Losing Its Charm in China," *Bloomberg Businessweek*, July 12–18, 2010, 11.
46. "Schumpeter: The Corruption Eruption," *The Economist* (April 29, 2010), https://www.economist.com/business/2010/04/29/the-corruption-eruption.
47. "A Global War against Bribery," *Economist*, January 16, 1999, 22–23, and "The Worm That Never Dies," *Economist*, March 2, 2002, 12.
48. "Tech's Kickback Culture," 75, 77.
49. J. Dana and G. Loewenstein, "A Social Science Perspective on Gifts to Physicians from Industry," *JAMA* 290, no. 2 (2003): 252–255.
50. "Wal-Mart's Lesson for Wall Street," *Wall Street Journal*, December 6, 2006, A2; "New Kmart Code Bans Gifts, Bribes," *San Jose Mercury News*, April 12, 1996, 6C.
51. "8 Former Fidelity Traders to Pay Fines," *New York Times*, December 12, 2008, B4.
52. "Title Insurers Paid Thousands for Lavish Gifts for Referrals," *New York Times*, October 17, 2006, C3.
53. "Speaking Up Gets Biologist into Big Fight," *Wall Street Journal*, November 26, 1980, sec. 2, 25. For the experiences of another whistle-blower, see "If Only They Had Listened…," *Bloomberg Businessweek*, June 23–29, 2014, 48–53.
54. "A Question of Conscience," *San Francisco Chronicle*, May 14, 2004, C3.
55. "Behind the Vioxx Headlines," *Business Ethics*, Winter 2004, 7.

56. "Question of Conscience," C3.

57. Ronald F. Duska, "Whistleblowing," in R. Edward Freeman and Patricia H. Werhane, eds., *The Blackwell Encyclopedic Dictionary of Business Ethics* (Oxford: Blackwell, 1998), 654.

58. Boatright, *Ethics and the Conduct of Business*, 92.

59. Norman E. Bowie, *Business Ethics* (Englewood Cliffs, N.J.: Prentice Hall, 1982), 142.

60. "The Whistle-Blowers," *Business Week*, January 13, 2003, 90.

61. "The Night Detective," *Time*, December 30, 2002–January 6, 2003, 45–50. See also "How Three Unlikely Sleuths Discovered Fraud at WorldCom," *Wall Street Journal*, October 30, 2002, A1.

62. Jean Chatzky, "Meet the Whistle-Blower," *Money*, February 2004, 156.

63. Bok, *Secrets*, ch. 14.

64. See Dan Seligman, "Blowing Whistles, Blowing Smoke," *Forbes*, September 6, 1999; and "Whistle-Blower Finds a Finger Pointing Back," *New York Times*, October 25, 2007, A1. See also the Scott R. Paeth's discussion of two famous whistle-blowers in "The Responsibility to Lie and the Obligation to Report," *Journal of Business Ethics* 112, no. 4 (January 2013): 559–566.

65. Bowie, *Business Ethics*. I have modified somewhat the statement of Bowie's conditions.

66. "Tobacco Whistle-Blower Acknowledges He's Paid," *New York Times*, May 1, 1996, A12.

67. Steven Davidoff Solomon, "Whistle-Blower Awards Lure Wrongdoers," *New York Times*, December 30, 2014 (online).

68. James Rocha and Edward Song, "Pre-emptive Anonymous Whistle-Blowing," *Public Affairs Quarterly* 26, no.4 (October 2012): 257–271.

69. "Christine Casey: Whistleblower," *Economist*, January 18, 2003, 66.

70. "Peep and Weep," *Economist*, January 12, 2002, 56. See also "Getting More Workers to Whistle," *Business Week*, January 28, 2008, 18.

71. "Peep and Weep," 56. See also Michael Skapinker, "What Would-Be Whistleblowers Should Know," *Financial Times*, February 17, 2009, 13.

72. See "Whistleblowers Score Big," *Wall Street Journal*, December 20–21, 2014, B1, and "Whistle-Blower Awards Lure Wrongdoers."

73. "Learning to Love Whistleblowers," *Inc.*, March 2006, 21–23.

74. On the SEC's battle against insider trading, see "The Federal Dragnet on Wall Street's Inside Game," *Washington Post*, February 13, 2011, G1, and "Hardball Tactics against Insider Trading," *New York Times*, May 12, 2011, B1. For details on the Galleon case, see "Insider-Trade Probe Snares 'Octopussy,'" *Wall Street Journal*, November 6, 2009, A1; "14 Are Charged with Insider Trading as Galleon Case Grows," *New York Times*, November 6, 2009, B1; and "Dangerous Liaisons at IBM," *Fortune*, July 26, 2010, 66. On the Griffiths and Steffes case, see Andrew Ross Sorkin, "So, What Is Insider Trading?" *New York Times*, October 26, 2010, B1.

75. This case study was inspired by one in *Across the Board* 36 (January 1999): 45.

Chapter 11

1. Kevin Seifert, "NFL Says All Teams Must Add Minority Offensive Coach, Expands Rooney Rule to Include Women," ESPN (March 28, 2022), https://www.espn.com/nfl/story/_/id/33617341/nfl-says-all-teams-add-minority-offensive-coach-expands-rooney-rule-include-women.

2. Ken Belson and Jenny Vrentas, "Brian Flores's Discrimination Case against the N.F.L. Can Move to Court," *New York Times* (March 1, 2023), https://www.nytimes.com/2023/03/01/sports/football/brian-flores-discrimination-nfl.html.

3. These figures are from the NCAA demographic database (https://www.ncaa.org/sports/2018/12/13/ncaa-demographics -database.aspx). The following five paragraphs are based on Edward Wong, "The Mystery of the Missing Minority Coaches," *New York Times*, January 6, 2002, sec. 4, 5; Mark Purdy, "Riley Seems Right for Stanford, and That's Just the Problem," *San Jose Mercury News*, January 6, 2002, 1D; Ann Killion, "Willingham Kept Dreams Quiet, Then Played His Hand Wisely," *San Jose Mercury News*, January 3, 2002, 1D; "Notre Dame Fires Willingham," http://msn.foxsports.com (November 30, 2004); Jon Wilner, "Why Does Weis Get a Golden Pass?" *San Jose Mercury News*, January 15, 2007, 1D; and "Diversity Everywhere but the Sidelines," *New York Times*, February 20, 2009, A23.

4. "Barack Obama's Speech on Race" (text of the speech provided by the Obama campaign), *New York Times*, March 18, 2008, https://www.nytimes.com/2008/03/18/us/politics/18text-obama.html. While current practice calls for capitalizing demographic terms such as "Black" and "White," these will be left in their original forms in quotations where inserting updated language using square brackets would be distracting to the reader.

5. Manuel G. Velasquez, *Business Ethics*, 6th ed. (Upper Saddle River, N.J.: Prentice Hall, 2006), 307.

6. "A Texas-Size Case of Discrimination?" *Business Week*, March 18, 2002, 14.

7. "Wal-Mart Facing Possibly Huge Suit," *San Jose Mercury News*, September 24, 2003, 3C.

8. "Karin vs. Kevin," *Atlantic*, May 2013, 16; Don Peck, "They're Watching You at Work," *Atlantic*, December 2013, 77; Ben Waber, "Gender Bias by the Numbers," *Bloomberg Businessweek*, February 3–9, 2013, 9; and Marianne Bertrand and Sendhil Mullainathan, "Are Emily and Greg More Employable Than Lakisha and Jamal? A Field Experiment on Labor Market Discrimination," *American Economic Review* 94 (September 2004), 991–1012, DOI: 10.1257/0002828042002561.

9. "Screening Out Minority Workers," *San Francisco Chronicle*, December 5, 1990, A1.

10. "Restaurant Chain Must Pay $105 Million for Racial Bias," *San Jose Mercury News*, February 5, 1993, 14A.

11. "Lawsuit Claims Race Bias at Wet Seal Retail Chain," *New York Times*, July 12, 2012 (online).

12. Philip Shenon, "Judge Finds F.B.I. Is Discriminatory," *New York Times*, October 1, 1988, 1.

13. Tom L. Beauchamp and Norman E. Bowie, *Ethical Theory and Business*, 4th ed. (Englewood Cliffs, N.J.: Prentice Hall, 1993), 437.

14. Richard Rothstein, "Must Schools Fail?" *New York Review of Books*, December 2, 2004, 29; "Nearer to Overcoming," *Economist*, May 10, 2008, 34; and Tim Hartford, *The Logic of Life: The Rational Economics of an Irrational World* (New York: Random House, 2008), 134–135.

15. "Must Schools Fail?" 29, and "Race and Red Tape," *Economist*, November 15, 2008, 92; Bertrand and Mullainathan, "Are Emily and Greg More Employable Than Lakisha and Jamal?"

16. "Must Schools Fail?" 29. See also Dawn D. Bennett-Alexander, "Such Stuff as Dreams Are Made On," in Laura P. Hartman, ed., *Perspectives in Business Ethics*, 3rd ed. (New York: McGraw-Hill, 2005), 385.

17. Debra Kamin, "Discrimination Seeps into Every Aspect of Home Buying for Black Americans," *New York Times* (November 29, 2022), https://www.nytimes.com/2022/11/29/realestate/black-homeowner-mortgage-racism.html.

18. Claudia Sahm, "Reducing Racial Discrimination in Auto Lending Is an Easy Fix," *Washington Post* (February 24, 2023), https://www.washingtonpost.com/business/reducingracial-discrimination-in-auto-lending-isan-easy-fix/2023/02/24/7892f610-b440-11ed-94a0-512954d75716_story.html.

19. Neil Bhutta, Aurel Hizmo, and Daniel Ringo, "How Much Does Racial Bias Affect Mortgage Lending? Evidence from Human and Algorithmic Credit Decisions," United States Federal Reserve Board (August 2, 2022), https://www.federalreserve.gov/econres/feds/files/2022067pap.pdf.

20. Em Shrider, "Poverty Rate for the Black Population Fell Below Pre-Pandemic Levels," United States Census Bureau (September 12, 2023), https://www.census.gov/library/stories/2023/09/black-poverty-rate.html#:~:text=For%20example%2C%20Black%20individuals%20made,poverty%20(ratio%20of%201.5); Mark Robert Rank, Lawrence M. Eppard, Heather E. Bullock, *Poorly Understood: What America Gets Wrong about Poverty* (New York: Oxford University Press, 2021), 32–8.

21. Neil Bennett, Donald Hays, and Briana Sullivan, "2019 Data Show Baby Boomers Nearly 9 Times Wealthier Than Millennials," United States Census Bureau (August 1, 2022), https://www.census.gov/library/stories/2022/08/wealth-inequality-by-household-type.html.

22. Gloria Guzman and Melissa Kollar, "Income in the United States: 2022," United States Census Bureau (September 12, 2023), https://www.bls.gov/opub/reports/race-and-ethnicity/2021/home.htm; https://www.census.gov/library/publications/2023/demo/p60-279.html.

23. United States Bureau of Labor Statistics, "Labor Force Characteristics by Race and Ethnicity, 2021" (January 2023), https://www.bls.gov/opub/reports/race-and-ethnicity/2021/home.htm.

24. Valerie Wilson, Ethan Miller, and Melat Kassa, "Racial Representation in Professional Occupations," Economic Policy Institute (June 8, 2021), https://www.epi.org/publication/racial-representation-prof-occ/.

25. Nancy DiTomaso, "How Social Networks Drive Black Unemployment," *New York Times*, May 5, 2013, https://archive.nytimes.com/opinionator.blogs.nytimes.com/2013/05/05/how-social-networks-drive-black-unemployment/.

26. Mary Beth Versaci, "HPI: Women Make Up Growing Percentage of Dental Workforce," *ADA News* (March 30, 2021), https://adanews.ada.org/ada-news/2021/march/women-make-up-growing-percentage-of-dental-workforce/; Jeannette Diaz, Linda D. Boyd, Lori Giblin-Scanlon, and Robert D. Smethers, "Work Experiences of Male Dental Hygienists: A Qualitative Study," *Journal of Dental Hygiene* 95 (August 2021), 6–13, https://jdh.adha.org/content/95/4/6.

27. United States Bureau of Labor Statistics, "Median Earnings for Women in 2022 Were 83.0 Percent of the Median for Men," *TED: The Economics Daily* (January 25, 2023), https://www.bls.gov/opub/ted/2023/median-earnings-for-women-in-2022-were-83-0-percent-of-the-median-for-men.htm; Philip N. Cohen, "Jump-Starting the Struggle for Equality," *New York Times*, November 24, 2013, "Sunday Review," 9; "Gender Bias by the Numbers," 9; and Claire Cain Miller, "Pay Gap Is Smaller Than Ever, and Still Stubbornly Large," *New York Times*, September 14, 2014 (online). See also "In Equal-Pay Debate, Disparity Is in the Details," *Wall Street Journal*, April 11, 2014, A5.

28. United States Department of Labor, "Employment and Earnings by Occupation," https://www.dol.gov/agencies/wb/data/occupations. (Data are from 2021.)

29. Christian N. Thoroughgood, Katina Sawyer, and Jennica R. Webster, "Creating a Trans-Inclusive Workplace," *Harvard Business Review* (March–April 2020), https://hbr.org/2020/03/creating-a-trans-inclusive-workplace; Ashley Kirzinger, Audrey Kearney, Alex Montero, Grace Sparks, Lindsey Dawson, and Mollyann Brodie, "KFF/The Washington Post Trans Survey" KFF (March 24, 2023), https://www.kff.org/report-section/kff-the-washington-post-trans-survey-trans-in-america/.

30. Emma Hinchliffe, "Women CEOs Run 10.4% of Fortune 500 Companies. A Quarter of the 52 Leaders Became CEO in the Last Year," Fortune (June 5, 2023), https://fortune.com/2023/06/05/fortune-500-companies-2023-women-10-percent/.

31. Paige McGlauflin, "Black CEOs on the Fortune 500 Reach New Record High in 2023—Meet the 8 Executives," *Yahoo Finance* (June 5, 2023), https://finance.yahoo.com/news/black-ceos-fortune-500-reach-093100572.html.

32. *Wards Cove Packing Co., Inc. v. Atonio*, 109 S. Ct. 2115 (1989).

33. This paragraph and the next are based on Andrew Hacker, "Grand Illusion," *New York Review of Books*, June 11, 1998, 28–29.

34. Tamar Lewin, "Sex Bias Found in Awarding of Partnerships at Law Firm," *New York Times*, November 30, 1990, B14.

35. "Judge Orders Partnership in a Bias Case," *Wall Street Journal*, December 5, 1990, B6; and *Price Waterhouse v. Hopkins*, 109 S. Ct. 1775 (1989).

36. Ellen Goodman, "Women Gain a Better Shot at the Top Rungs," *Los Angeles Times*, May 29, 1984, II, 45.

37. "Science: Still Few Chances for Women," *Los Angeles Times*, March 7, 1984, 1. See also "An Outsider's View of the Corporate World," *San Francisco Chronicle*, October 27, 1997, B2.

38. Deepa Purushothaman, Lisen Stromberg, and Lisa Kaplowitz, "5 Harmful Ways Women Feel They Must Adapt in Corporate America," *Harvard Business Review* (October 31, 2022), https://hbr.org/2022/10/5-harmful-ways-women-feel-they-must-adapt-in-corporate-america.

39. "The Price of Prejudice," *Economist*, January 27, 2009, 77, and Joanne Lipman, "Women at Work: A Guide for Men," *Wall Street Journal*, December 13–14, 2014, C2.

40. "Too Many Women Fall for Stereotypes of Selves, Study Says," *Wall Street Journal*, October 24, 2005, B1.

41. See Charles M. Blow, "A Nation of Cowards?" *New York Times*, February 21, 2009, A17; "The Price of Prejudice," 77–78; and Chris Mooney, "Are You Racist?" *Mother Jones*, January/February 2015, 24. See also Phillip Atiba Goff, Jennifer L. Eberhardt, Melissa J. Williams, and Matthew Christian Jackson, "Not Yet Human: Implicit Knowledge, Historical Dehumanization, and Contemporary Consequences," *Journal of Personality and Social Psychology* 94, no. 2 (2008): 292–306. For a more skeptical view of bias tests, see John Tierney, "In Bias Test, Shades of Gray," *New York Times*, November 18, 2008, D1.

42. "White Men Can't Help It," *Business Week*, May 15, 2006, 54. See also "The War over Unconscious Bias," *Fortune*, October 15, 2007, 90–102, and Mooney, "Are You Racist?" For more on the power of stereotypes, see Dan Ariely, *Predictably Irrational: The Hidden Forces That Shape Our Decisions* (New York: HarperCollins, 2008), 168–172.

43. Edward W. Jones, Jr., "Black Managers: The Dream Deferred," *Harvard Business Review* 64 (May–June 1986): 88.

44. *Ricci v. DeStefano*, 129 S. Ct. 2658 (2009).

45. 590 U.S. ___ (2020).

46. See *Griggs v. Duke Power Co.*, 401 U.S. 424 (1971), and *Wards Cove Packing Co., Inc. v. Atonio*, 109 S. Ct. 2115 (1989) at 2115, in which the Court reiterates that Title VII can be violated by "not only overt discrimination but also practices that are fair in form but discriminatory in practice."

47. United States Department of Labor, "Affirmative Action Frequently Asked Questions," https://www.dol.gov/agencies/ofccp/faqs/AAFAQs.

48. See *United States v. Paradise*, 480 U.S. 149 (1987).

49. Sundiatu Dixon-Fyle, Kevin Dolan, Dame Vivian Hunt, and Sara Prince, "Diversity Wins: How Inclusion Matters," McKinsey & Company (May 2020), https://www.mckinsey.com/featured-insights/diversity-and-inclusion/diversity-wins-how-inclusion-matters#/.

50. 600 U.S. 181.

51. Esther G. Lander and Amanda S. McGinn, "Impact of SCOTUS Affirmative Action Ruling on Employers," American Bar Association (September 6, 2023), https://www.americanbar.org/groups/labor_law/publications/labor_employment_law_news/issue-summer-2023/impact-of-scorus-affirmative-action-ruling-on-ers/.

52. Ronald Dworkin, *Taking Rights Seriously* (Cambridge, Mass.: Harvard, 1978), 223–239.

53. Herman Schwartz, "Affirmative Action," in Gertrude Ezorsky, ed., *Moral Rights in the Workplace* (Albany: State University of New York Press, 1987), 276.

54. Peter Kilborn, "Comparable-Worth Pay Plan Creates Unseen Woe for State," *Denver Post*, June 3, 1990, 3A.

55. "Special Report: Women and Work," 6.

56. Caroline E. Mayer, "The Comparable Pay Debate," *Washington Post National Weekly Edition*, August 6, 1984, 9.

57. Ibid.

58. Nina Totenberg, "Why Women Earn Less," *Parade*, June 10, 1984, 5.

59. Audrey Carlsen, Maya Salam, Claire Cain Miller, Denise Lu, Ash Ngu, Jugal K. Patel, and Zach Wichter, "#MeToo Brought Down 201 Powerful Men. Nearly Half of Their Replacements Are Women," *New York Times* (October 29, 2018), https://www.nytimes.com/interactive/2018/10/23/us/metoo-replacements.html.

60. United States Equal Employment Opportunity Commission, "Sexual Harassment in Our Nation's Workplaces" (April 2022), https://www.eeoc.gov/sites/default/files/2022-04/Sexual%20Harassment%20Awareness%20Month%202022%20Data%20Highlight.pdf.

61. *Oncale v. Sundowner Offshore Service*, 523 U.S. 75 (1998).

62. Rhitu Chatterjee, "A New Survey Finds 81 Percent of Women Have Experienced Sexual Harassment," NPR (February 21, 2018), https://www.npr.org/sections/thetwo-way/2018/02/21/587671849/a-new-survey-finds-eighty-percent-of-women-have-experienced-sexual-harassment. "One-Fifth of Women Are Harassed Sexually," *HR Focus* (April 2002): 2.

63. Mary Jo Shaney, "Perceptions of Harm: The Consent Defense in Sexual Harassment Cases," *Iowa Law Review* 71 (May 1986): 1109.

64. Larry May and John C. Hughes, "Sexual Harassment," in Ezorsky, ed., *Moral Rights*.

65. Terry L. Leap and Larry R. Smeltzer, "Racial Remarks in the Workplace: Humor or Harassment?" *Harvard Business Review* 62 (November–December 1984): 74–78.

66. "Discrimination Has Been Defeated," *Financial Times*, July 25, 2005, 9.

67. United States Equal Employment Opportunity Commission, "Harassment FAQs," https://www.eeoc.gov/youth/harassment-faqs.

68. *City of Richmond v. J. A. Croson Co.*, 109 S. Ct. 706 (1989).

69. Robert E. Suggs, "Rethinking Minority Business Development Strategies," *Harvard Civil Rights–Civil Liberties Law Review* 25 (Winter 1990); Brent Bowers, "Black Owners Fight Obstacles to Get Orders," *Wall Street Journal*, November 16, 1990, B1.

70. This case study is based on Joan Ryan, "Playing Field Is Still Not Level," *San Francisco Chronicle*, June 13, 1999, "Sunday," 1, and Ann Killion, "Belief That Coach Can't Be Pregnant Outdated," *San Jose Mercury News*, September 17, 2002, 1A.

71. "Game, Sex, and Match," *Economist*, September 7, 2013, 61.

72. See Shaney, "Perceptions of Harm," for the relevant legal citations and a presentation of the facts of this case.

73. *Meritor Savings Bank v. Vinson*, 106 S. Ct. 2399 (1986), 61.

74. "Gender Diffs," *Wilson Quarterly*, Summer 2004, 10. The impact of good looks is greater for male instructors than for female.

Index

Faden, Ruth, 153
Fagothey, Austin, 249, 250
Fair Labor Standards Act (1938), 242
Fair price, 176
Fair wage, 242
Fairer competition, affirmative action and, 330
Fairness, 68, 87, 219, 248
False Claims Act (1863), 304
False positives, 264
Family leave, day care and, 272–275
Famine, market entitlements and, 79
Fannie Mae, 96, 148
Fanuchi, Jean, 281–282
Fastow, Andrew, 290
Fatigue, in industrial accidents, 271
Federal Emergency Management Agency
  (FEMA), 219, 220
Federal tax, 157
Federal Trade Commission (FTC)
  advertising, 179, 182–183, 184
  labeling and packaging, 177
Feinberg, Joel, 212
Feiner, Michael, 272
Feinstein, Dianne, 223
Feldbaum, Carl B., 153
Fenton, John, 277
Fertilizer runoff, 196, 199
Fetal protection policies, sex discrimination
  and, 282–284
"Fictitious profits," 34
Fidelity, duties of, 50
Fiduciary duty, 138
Figg, Derek, 29, 30
Financial capitalism, 99
Financial investments, 291
Firing
  for-cause dismissal, 240
  trauma reduction, 241
First Amendment, personal/commercial
  speech protection, 155
Fisher, Don and Doris, 223
Flame-retardant pajamas, 26
Flip This House, 29
Flood insurance necessity, 219
Fluorocarbons, 170
Flynn, Nancy, 267
Foley, Daniel, 230
Food and Drug Administration (FDA), 165–
  166, 292, 304
  caffeinated alcoholic beverages, 194
  food labeling, 177
  silicone implants, 190
Food production, DDT use in, 214
Food security, 93
Foot, Philippa, 35
Football players, scholarship, 125
For-profit corporations, 128–129
Ford, Henry, 261

Ford II, Henry, 167
Ford Motor Company, corporate taxation, 164
Ford Pinto, gas tank hazard (case study),
  60–62, 164
Foreign Corrupt Practices Act (FCPA), 297,
  298, 299
Foreign medical training/students, 120
Formula of humanity, 46, 49
Four Loko, 194–195
Fractional numbers, in pricing, 172
Francis, Karen, 184
Franklin, Brenda, 315
Franklin, David, 304
Freddie Mac, 96
Free competition, 101
Free market, 78
Free-market buying and selling, 187
Free-rider problem, 201
Free speech
  and media, 188
  right of, 228
French, Peter, 132
Friedel, Walter, 166
Friedman, Lawrence M., 133
Friedman, Milton, 140, 204
  on medical licensure, 120–121
  narrow view of corporate responsibility,
    134–135, 146
  perspectives, corporations role in society,
    138
FTC v. Standard Education (1937), 183
Fugger, Hans, 98–99
Fugger, Jacob, 99
Fukushima Daiichi nuclear power plant, 198,
  303
"Future-Gen" project, 208
Future generations, obligation to, 212–213

G

Gaff, Provost Angela, 252–253
Galatis, George, 287–288
Galbraith, John Kenneth, 142, 145, 186–187
Garbage export, 211
Garrett, Angela, 261
Gender discrimination, in workplace, 322
Gender stereotyping, 324
General Electric, 100, 136, 148, 181, 231
General Mills, 148, 177, 181
General Motors, 61, 97, 128, 163
General Services Administration (GSA), 299
General welfare promotion, 50
Genetically modified (GM) food, 176
Gifts
  and entertainment, 299–301
  libertarian view, 79
Gilead Sciences, 153
Gill, Robert, 170
Gini coefficient, 65, 76

Gini, Corrado, 65
Ginsburg, Ruth Bader, 156–157, 293
Glasmeier, Amy K., 243
Glen Canyon Dam, 206
Global fairness, environmental issues,
  211–212
Global supply chains, fragility of, 113
Global warming, 197, 221
Globalization, 100
Globalized capitalism, 100
Gobbell, Lynne, 228
Goffer, Zvi, 312
Goizueta, Roberto C., 140
Golab, Stephen, 270
"Golden Rule," 9, 47
Gonsalves, Milton A., 249, 250
Good Samaritan laws, 7, 44
Good will, 44–45
Goodpaster, Kenneth E., 132
Google/Alphabet, 127, 152
  Chinese censorship compliance, 151
  transfer pricing, 157
Gorsuch, Neil, 325
Goskin, Lawrence O., 154
Gould, Jay, 99
Graham, David, 304
Grand Canyon restoration, 203
"Granting certiorari," 91
Gratitude, duties of, 50
Grease payments, 297
Great Depression of 1930s, 99, 105, 245
Greenberg, Maurice Hank, 149
Greenhouse gas emissions, 204, 206, 209,
  210
Greenman v. Yuba Power Products (1963), 162
Greenpeace, palm oil plantations, 224–225
Greenspan, Alan, 115
Gretzinger, Ralph, 31
Griffiths, Gary, 313
Griggs v. Duke Power Company (1971), 236
Group cohesiveness, 17
Groupthink, 18–19
Grutter v. Bollinger, 328
Guin, Ursula Le, 43
Gullible-consumer standard (FTC), 182
Gun control, 256

H

Habitat Protection Plan, 223
Halperin, Keith M., 280
Hamilton, Alexander, 130
Hand, Learned, 158, 183
Happiness
  maximization of, 40, 71
  as ultimate good, 38
  and unhappiness, 40
Hardin, Garrett, 200
Harmon, Sidney, 232